The
American
Heritage
Dictionary
of
Indo-European
Roots

The
American
Heritage
Dictionary
of Indo-European
Roots

Revised and edited by
Calvert Watkins

Houghton Mifflin Company BOSTON

All correspondence and inquiries should be directed to
Reference Division, Houghton Mifflin Company
One Beacon Street, Boston, MA 01208

Manufactured in the United States of America

Library of Congress Cataloging in Publication Data
Main entry under title:

The American heritage dictionary of Indo-European roots.

    Includes index.
    1. Indo-European languages—Roots—Dictionaries.
2. English language—Etymology—Dictionaries.
I. Watkins, Calvert.
P615.A43   1985   412'.0321   84-27911
ISBN 0-395-37888-5
ISBN 0-395-36070-6 (pbk.)

Contents

Staff

Marion Severynse · *Editor and Etymologist*

Howard Webber · *Publisher*
Margery S. Berube · *Director of Editorial Operations*

Dolores R. Harris · *Senior Editor*
Pamela B. DeVinne · *Editor*
Kaethe Ellis · *Editor*

Christopher Leonesio · *Production Manager*
Patricia McTiernan · *Editorial Production Assistant*
Donna Lee Muise · *Editorial Production Assistant*

Keyboarding Staff

Brenda J. Bregoli   Celester Jackson
Ron Perkins   Caren Raimondi

Design

Geoffrey Hodgkinson

Special Contributors

Elizabeth Collins   Colin Danby
Francine D. Figelman   Susan Innes
Trudy Nelson   Amy Walton

Foreword

The American Heritage Dictionary of Indo-European Roots is a revised and expanded version of the Appendix of Indo-European Roots in *The American Heritage Dictionary of the English Language* published in 1969. This material is presented here for the first time in a separate volume. The present work has been designed as a companion to *The American Heritage Dictionary: Second College Edition* and contains a complete index to all the English words whose antecedents are given in the *Dictionary of Indo-European Roots*. The wealth of information about the Indo-European origins of the English vocabulary has now been made readily accessible to scholars, students, and all those who are interested in the history and development of the English language.

Marion Severynse

Preface

In my article "The Indo-European Origin of English" in the first edition of *The American Heritage Dictionary of the English Language,* I wrote that "a reconstructed grammar and dictionary cannot claim any sort of completeness, to be sure, and the reconstruction may be changed because of new data or better analysis." The present revised edition of *The American Heritage Dictionary of Indo-European Roots* stands as eloquent testimony to the accuracy of that statement. Indo-European studies have not stood still between the 1960's and the 1980's, and both advances in theory and an increase in the database have made a thoroughgoing revision not merely possible but necessary. Many new roots have been added. In part, this is in order to include and extend the etymologies of words new to *The American Heritage Dictionary: Second College Edition*; in part, it is to provide a superior account of the histories of previously existing words. Advances in printing technology have now made it both feasible and economical to present in a work for the general public the sounds and forms of Proto-Indo-European in a manner consistent with current usage in the field. Few entries in the dictionary have escaped revision. Old etymologies have been revised and brought into line with current thinking, and new etymologies have been proposed where it seemed proper to do so. The introductory essay has also been revised and brought up to date.

This dictionary is designed and written for the general English-speaking public and not, needless to say, for specialists in the field of Indo-European. With the indispensable and able assistance of Marion Severynse, the staff etymologist of *The American Heritage Dictionary,* I have tried to put some order into the presentation of a vast amount of linguistic information. I have also tried to introduce only as much technical background explanation as is required without burdening the reader with unnecessary detail. The amount in fact introduced may seem overmuch to some; but human language is not simple, and a part of the fascination of the study of human language lies in the recognition of its complexity.

Calvert Watkins

Indo-European
and the Indo-Europeans

The forms given in **boldface** type are Indo-European roots that are entries in this Dictionary. The words in SMALL CAPITALS are English words whose etymologies in *The American Heritage Dictionary: Second College Edition* relate them to the roots here discussed. For fuller insight into the relationships alluded to, the reader is encouraged to pursue both of these kinds of reference. An asterisk is placed before every reconstructed form (a form that is not attested in documents), except for the boldface root forms.

Speaking to the Asiatick Society in Calcutta on February 2, 1786, the English orientalist and jurist Sir William Jones uttered his famous pronouncement:

> . . . the Sanskrit language, whatever be its antiquity, is of a wonderful structure; more perfect than the Greek, more copious than the Latin, and more exquisitely refined than either, yet bearing to both of them a stronger affinity, both in the roots of verbs and in the forms of grammar, than could possibly have been produced by accident; so strong, indeed, that no philologer could examine them all three, without believing them to have sprung from some common source, which, perhaps, no longer exists.

Jones was content with the assertion of a common original language, without exploring the details. Others took up the cause, notably the German philosopher Friedrich von Schlegel, to whom is principally due the popular diffusion of the long-lived misconception that the European languages were in some sense derived from Sanskrit. But it remained for another German, Franz Bopp, to found the new science of comparative grammar, with the publication in 1816 of his work *On the conjugational system of the Sanskrit language, in comparison with that of the Greek, Latin, Persian, and Germanic languages.* He was twenty-five when it appeared.

It has been rightly said that the comparatist has one fact and one hypothesis. The one fact is that certain languages present similarities among themselves which are so numerous and so precise that they cannot be attributed to chance, and which are such that they cannot be explained as borrowings or as universal features. The one hypothesis is that these languages must then be the result of descent from a common original. Certain similarities may be accidental: the Greek verb "to breathe, blow," has a root *pneu-*, and in the language of the Klamath Indians of Oregon the verb "to blow" is *pniw-*. Other similarities may reflect universal or near-universal features of human language: in the languages of most countries where the bird is known, the *cuckoo* has a name derived from the noise it makes. A vast number of languages around the globe have "baby-talk" words like *mama* and *papa*. Finally, languages commonly borrow words and other features from each other, in a whole gamut of ways ranging from casual or chance contact to learned coinages of the kind that English systematically makes from Latin and Greek. But where all of these possibilities must be excluded, the comparatist assumes genetic filiation: descent from a common ancestor, which, in the case of Indo-European, as Sir William Jones surmised almost two centuries ago, no longer exists.

In the early part of the 19th century, scholars set about exploring systematically the similarities observable among the principal languages spoken now or formerly in the regions from Iceland and Ireland in the west to India in the east, and from Scandinavia in the north to Italy and Greece in the south. They were able to group these languages into a *family* which they called *Indo-European* (the term first occurs in English in 1813, though in a sense slightly different from today's). The similarities among the different Indo-European languages require us to assume that they are the continuation of a single prehistoric language, called *Indo-European* or *Proto-Indo-European*. In the words of the greatest Indo-Europeanist, the

French scholar Antoine Meillet, "we will term *Indo-European language* every language which at any time whatever, in any place whatever, and however altered, is a form taken by this ancestor language, and which thus continues by an uninterrupted tradition the usage of Indo-European."

Those dialects or branches of Indo-European still represented today by one or more languages are Indo-Iranian, Greek, Armenian, Slavic, Baltic, Albanian, Celtic, Italic, and Germanic. The present century has seen the addition of two branches to the family, neither of which has left any living trace: Hittite and other Anatolian languages, the earliest attested in the Indo-European family, spoken in what is now Turkey in the second millennium B.C.; and the two Tocharian languages, the easternmost of Indo-European dialects, spoken in Chinese Turkestan (present-day Xinjiang) in the first millennium A.D.

It should be pointed out that the Indo-European family is only one of many language families that have been identified around the world, comprising several thousand different languages. We have good reason, however, to be especially interested in the history of the Indo-European family. Our own language, English, is the most prevalent member of that family, being spoken as a native language by nearly 350 million people and being the most important second language in the world. The total number of speakers of all Indo-European languages amounts to approximately half the population of the earth.

English is thus one of many direct descendants of Indo-European. One of the dialects of the parent language became prehistoric Common Germanic, which subdivided into dialects of which one was West Germanic; this in turn broke up into further dialects, one of which emerged into documentary attestation as Old English. From Old English we can follow the development of the language directly, in texts, down to the present day. This history is our linguistic heritage; our ancestors, in a real cultural sense, are our linguistic ancestors. Only a small proportion of people in the United States can trace their biological ancestry back more than a century or two; and certainly large segments of the population had languages other than English in their backgrounds only a few generations ago. But every individual is part of a culture, with language its external expression. That language, our language, has an ancestry, a history; indeed, languages have perhaps the longest uninterrupted histories of all the cultural phenomena that we can study.

But it must be stressed that linguistic heritage, while it may well tend to correspond with cultural continuity, does not imply genetic or biological descent. That is, there is no more reason to suppose that we, as speakers of an Indo-European language, are descended biologically from the speakers of Proto-Indo-European, than that the English-speaking population of Nigeria is Anglo-Saxon. The transmission of language by conquest, assimilation, migration, or any other ethnic movement is a complex and enigmatic process which this discussion does not propose to examine, beyond stating the general proposition that in the case of Indo-European no genetic conclusions can or should be drawn.

English, genetically a member of the Germanic branch of Indo-European and retaining much of the basic structure of its origin, has an exceptionally mixed lexicon. During the millennium of its documented history, it has borrowed very extensively from its Germanic and Romance neighbors and from Latin and Greek. At the same time it has lost the great bulk of its original Old English vocabulary. However, the inherited vocabulary, though now numerically a small proportion of the total, remains the genuine core of the language; all of the 100 words shown to be the most frequent in the Brown University *Standard Corpus of Present-Day Edited American English* are native, inherited words; and of the second 100, 83 are native. Precisely because of its propensity to borrow from ancient and modern Indo-European languages, especially those mentioned above but including nearly every other member of the family, English has in a way replaced much of the Indo-European lexicon it lost. Thus, while the distinction between native and borrowed vocabulary remains fundamentally important, more than 50 per cent of the basic roots of Indo-European as represented in Julius Pokorny's *Indogermanisches Etymologisches Wörterbuch* (Bern, 1959) are represented in modern English by one means or the other. Indo-European therefore looms doubly large in the background of our language.

Linguistic History and the Comparative Method

The *comparative method* remains today the most powerful device for elucidating linguistic history. When it is carried to a successful conclusion, the comparative method leads not merely to the assumption of the previous existence of an antecedent common language, but to a reconstruction of all the salient features of that language. In the best circumstances, as with Indo-European, we can reconstruct the sounds, forms, words, even the structure of sentences—in short, both grammar and lexicon—of a language spoken before the human race had invented the art of writing. It is worth reflecting on this accomplishment. A reconstructed grammar and dictionary cannot claim any sort of completeness, to be sure, and the reconstruction may be changed because of new data or better analysis. But it remains true, as one distinguished scholar has put it, that a reconstructed proto-language is "a glorious artifact, one which is far more precious than anything an archaeologist can ever hope to unearth."

An Example of Reconstruction

We may illustrate the comparative method by a concrete case, which will serve at the same time to indicate the high degree of preciseness that the techniques of reconstruction permit.

A number of Indo-European languages show a similar word for the kinship term "daughter-in-law": Sanskrit *snuṣā́,* Old English *snoru,* Old Church Slavonic *snūkha* (Russian *snokhá*), Latin *nurus,* Greek *nuós,* and Armenian *nu.* Albanian has *nuse* in the meaning "bride," a meaning shared by the Armenian form. In a patrilocal and patriarchal society (such as most, if not all, early Indo-European-speaking societies), where the bride went to live in her husband's father's house, "daughter-in-law" and "bride" were equivalents.

All of these forms, spoken of as *cognates,* provide evidence for the phonetic shape of the prehistoric Indo-European word for "daughter-in-law" that is their common ancestor. Sanskrit, Germanic, and Slavic agree in showing an Indo-European word that began with *sn-.* We know that an Indo-European *s* was lost before *n* in other words in Latin, Greek, Armenian, and Albanian, so we can confidently assume that Latin *nurus,* Greek *nuós,* Armenian *nu,* and Albanian *nuse* go back to an Indo-European **sn-.* (Compare Latin *nix* (stem *niv-*), "snow," with English SNOW, which preserves the *s.*) This principle is spoken of as the regularity of sound correspondences; it is basic to the sciences of etymology and comparative linguistics.

Sanskrit, Latin, Greek, Armenian, and Albanian agree in showing the first vowel as *-u-.* We know from other examples that Slavic *ŭ* regularly corresponds to Sanskrit *u* and that Germanic *o* (of Old English *snoru*) in this position has been changed from an earlier *u.* It is thus justifiable to reconstruct an Indo-European word beginning **snu-.*

For the consonant originally following **snu-,* closer analysis is required. The key is furnished first by the Sanskrit form, for we know there is a rule in Sanskrit that *s* always changes to *ṣ* (a *sh*-like sound) after the vowel *u.* Hence a Sanskrit *snuṣ-* must go back to an earlier **snus-.* In the same position, after *u,* an old *s* in Slavic changes to *kh* (like the *ch* in Scottish *loch* or German *ach*); hence the Slavic word, too, reflects **snus-.* In Latin always, and under certain conditions in Germanic, an old *-s-* between vowels became *-r-.* For this reason Latin *nurus* and Old English *snoru* may go back to older **snus-* (followed by a vowel) as well. In Greek and Armenian, on the other hand, an old *-s-* between vowels disappeared entirely, as we know from numerous instances. Greek *nuós* and Armenian *nu* (stem *nuo-*) thus regularly presuppose the same earlier form, **snus-* (followed by a vowel). Finally, that *-s-* between vowels is still preserved—almost accidentally, one might say—in Albanian *nuse.* All the comparative evidence agrees, then, on the Indo-European root form **snus-.*

For the ending, the final vowels of Sanskrit *snuṣā́,* Old English *snoru,* and Slavic *snūkha* all presuppose earlier *-ā* (**snus-ā*), which is the ordinary feminine ending of these languages. On the other hand, Latin *nurus,* Greek *nuós,* and Armenian *nu* (stem *nuo-*) all regularly presuppose the earlier ending **-os* (**snus-os*). Here is an apparent impasse, but the way out is given by the gender of the forms in Greek and Latin. They are feminine, even though most nouns in Latin *-us* and Greek *-os* are masculine.

Feminine nouns in Latin *-us* and Greek *-os,* since they are an abnormal type, cannot have been created afresh; they must have been inherited. This suggests that the original Indo-European form was **snusos,* of feminine gender. On the other hand, the commonplace freely formed ending for feminine nouns was **-ā.* It is reasonable to suggest that the three languages Sanskrit, Germanic, and Slavic replaced the peculiar feminine ending **-os* (because the ending was normally masculine) with the normal ordinary feminine ending **-ā,* and thus that the oldest form of the word was **snusos* (feminine).

One point remains to be ascertained: the accent. Four of the language groups in which the word for "daughter-in-law" is attested reflect the Indo-European accent: Sanskrit, (Balto-)Slavic, Greek, and Germanic. The first three are agreed in showing a form accented on the last syllable: *snuṣā́, snokhá, nuós.* The Germanic form is equally precise, however, since the rule is that old *-s-* became *-r-* (as in Old English *snoru*) only if the accented syllable came after the *-s-*. On this basis we may add the finishing touch to our reconstruction: the complete form of the word for "daughter-in-law" in Indo-European is **snusós.*

It is noteworthy that no single language in the family preserves this word intact. In every language, in every tradition in the Indo-European family, the word has been altered in some way from its original shape. It is the comparative method that permits us to explain the different forms in this variety of languages by the reconstruction of a unitary common prototype, a common ancestor.

Proto-Indo-European

After the initial discovery of a prehistoric language underlying the modern Indo-European family and the foundation of the science of comparative linguistics, the detailed reconstruction of Proto-Indo-European proceeded by stages still fascinating to observe. The main outlines of the reconstructed language were already seen by the end of the 1870's, but it is only in the 20th century that certain of these features have received general acceptance. Though not affecting vocabulary in any serious way, many questions remain open even today, both in reconstruction and in the histories of the individual languages.

Phonology and Morphology

The system of sounds in Proto-Indo-European was rich in stop consonants. There was an unvoiced series, *p, t, k, kʷ* (like the *qu* of *quick*), a voiced series, *b, d, g, gʷ,* and a voiced aspirate series, *bh, dh, gh, gʷh,* pronounced like the voiced series but followed by a puff of breath. Some forms have been taken to suggest also the existence of an unvoiced aspirate series, *ph, th, kh,* as well, at least for the dialect of Indo-European from which Greek, Armenian, and Indo-Iranian came. If the language was rich in stop consonants, it was correspondingly poor in continuants, or fricatives, like English *f, v, th, s, z,* having only *s,* which was voiced to *z* before voiced stop consonants. It had as well three "laryngeals" or *h*-like sounds, all of which are here written as *ə* (equivalent notations are *H* or *h*). The sound *ə* is preserved as such (at least in part) only in Hittite and the other Anatolian languages in cuneiform documents from the second millennium B.C. Compare Hittite *pah(s)-,* "to protect," coming directly from Indo-European **paə(s)-* (PASTOR). In all the other languages of the family, its former presence in a word can only be deduced from indirect evidence such as the contractions discussed immediately below. The elucidation of the details of these laryngeals remains one of the most interesting problems confronting Indo-Europeanists today.

Proto-Indo-European had two nasals, *m* and *n,* two liquids, *r* and *l,* and the glides *w* and *y.* A salient characteristic of Indo-European was that these sounds could function both as consonants and as vowels. Their consonantal value was as in English. As vowels, symbolized *m̥, n̥, l̥, r̥,* the liquids and nasals sounded much like the final syllables of English *bottom, button, bottle, butter.* The vocalic counterparts of *w* and *y* were the vowels *u* and *i.* The laryngeals could function both as consonants and as vowels; their consonantal value was that of *h*-like sounds, while as vowels they were varieties of schwa (*ə*), much like the final syllable of English *sofa*—hence the choice of schwa to represent laryngeals in this Dictionary.

The other vowels of Indo-European were *e, o,* and *a.* These, as well as *i* and *u,* occurred both long and short. Since we can distinguish chronological layers in Proto-Indo-European, it can be said that a number of the long vowels of later Indo-European resulted from

the contraction of early Indo-European short vowels with a following ə. Already in Proto-Indo-European itself, two of the three laryngeals had the property of coloring an adjacent fundamental vowel *e* to *a* and *o*, respectively, before the contractions took place. Thus the root **pā-**, "to protect," is contracted from older **paə-*, with "*a*-coloring"; the root **dō-**, "to give," is contracted from older **doə-*, with "*o*-coloring"; and the root **dhē-**[1], "to set, put," is contracted from older **dheə-*, without coloring. The fundamental vowel in each of these roots, as in most Indo-European roots, was originally *e*. In scholarly usage it is now customary to write the non-coloring laryngeal as $ə_1$, (or h_1), thus **dheə$_1$-*; the *a*-coloring laryngeal as $ə_2$ (or h_2), thus **paə$_2$-*; and the *o*-coloring laryngeal as $ə_3$ (or h_3), thus **doə$_3$-*. This rather cumbersome notation has been simplified in this Dictionary, since the vowel before the schwa is sufficient to distinguish the three in the cases of contraction to a long vowel, and in other positions in most languages other than Greek the three merge to one. No systematic notice has been taken in this Dictionary of word-initial laryngeals before vowels (amply attested in Hittite), since the root forms with initial vowel are readily convertible by the student. Thus **ap-**[2], "water," from **əap-* (Hittite *happ-*, "water"); **op-**[1], "to work, produce in abundance," from **əop-* (Hittite *happ-in-*, "rich"); **ed-**, "to eat," from *əed-* (Hittite *ed-*, "to eat").

A characteristic feature of Indo-European was the system of vocalic alternations termed *apophony* or *ablaut*. This was a set of internal vowel changes expressing different morphological functions. A clear reflex of this feature is preserved in the English strong verbs, where, for example, the vocalic alternations between *write* and *wrote, give* and *gave* express the present and past tenses. Ablaut in Indo-European affected the vowels *e* and *o*. The fundamental form was *e*; this *e* could appear as *o* under certain conditions, and in other conditions both *e* and *o* could disappear entirely. On this basis we speak of given forms in Indo-European as exhibiting, respectively, the *e-grade* (or *full grade*), the *o-grade,* or the *zero grade*. The *e* and the *o* might furthermore occur as long *ē* or *ō*, termed the *lengthened grade*.

To illustrate: the Indo-European root **ped-**[1], "foot," appears in the e-grade in Latin *ped-* (PEDAL) but in the o-grade in Greek *pod-* (PODIATRIST). Germanic **fōtuz* (FOOT) reflects the lengthened o-grade **pōd-*. The zero grade of the same root shows no vowel at all: **pd-*, a form attested in Sanskrit.

When the zero grade involved a root with one of the sounds *m, n, r, l, w, y,* (collectively termed *resonants*), the resonant would regularly appear in its vocalic function, forming a syllable. We have the e-grade root **seng^{w}h-** in English SING, the o-grade form **song^{w}h-* in SANG and SONG, and the zero-grade form **sng^{w}h-* in SUNG.

In the case of roots with long vowels arising from contraction with ə, the ablaut can be most clearly understood by referring to the older, uncontracted forms. Thus **pā-**, "to protect," contracted from **paə-*, has a zero grade **pə-*; **dō-**, "to give," contracted from **doə-*, has a zero grade **də-*; **dhē-**, "to place," contracted from **dheə-*, has a zero grade **dhə-*. The fundamental vowel of the full grade disappears in the zero grade, and only the ə remains. Long *ū* and long *ī* could also arise from contraction: full grade **peuə-**, "to purify," has a zero grade **puə-* contracted to **pū-* (PURE); full grade **k^{w}eiə-**[1], "to value, honor," has a zero grade **k^{w}iə-* contracted to **k^{w}ī-* (TIMOCRACY).

Grammar and Syntax

Proto-Indo-European was a highly inflected language. Grammatical relationships and the syntactic function of words in the sentence were indicated primarily by variations in the endings of the words. Nouns had different endings for different cases, such as the subject and the direct object of the verb, the possessive, and many other functions, and for the different numbers, namely the singular, plural, and a special dual number for objects occurring in pairs. Verbs had different endings for the different persons (first, second, third) and numbers (singular, plural, dual), for the voices active and passive (or middle, a sort of reflexive), as well as special affixes for a rich variety of tenses, moods, and such categories as causative-transitive and stative-intransitive verbs. Practically none of this rich inflection is preserved in Modern English, but it has left its trace in many formations in Germanic and in other languages such as Latin and Greek. These are noted in the Dictionary where they are relevant.

With the exception of the numbers five to ten and a group of particles including certain conjunctions and quasi-adverbial forms, all Indo-European words underwent inflection. The structure of all inflected words, regardless of part of speech, was the same: *root* plus one or more *suffixes* plus *ending.* Thus the word **ker-wo-s,* "a stag," is composed of the root **ker-**¹, "horn," plus the noun suffix *-wo-*, plus the nominative singular ending *-s.* The root contained the basic semantic kernel, the underlying notion, which the suffix could modify in various ways. It was primarily the suffix that determined the part of speech of the word. Thus a single root like **prek-**, "to ask," could, depending on the suffix, form a verb **pr̥k-sko-*, "to ask" (Latin *poscere*), a noun **prek-*, "prayer" (Latin *precēs*), and an adjective **prok-o-*, "asking" (underlying Latin *procus,* "suitor"). Note that **prek-,* **prok-,* and **pr̥k-* have, respectively, *e-, o-,* and zero grade.

The root could undergo certain modifications, spoken of as *extensions* or *enlargements.* These did not affect the basic meaning and simply reflect formal variations between languages.

Suffixes had more specific values. There were verbal suffixes that made nouns into verbs and others that marked different types of action, like transitive and intransitive. There were nominal suffixes that made agent nouns, abstract nouns, verbal nouns and verbal adjectives, and nouns of instrument and other functions.

The root plus the suffix or suffixes constituted the *stem.* The stems represented the basic lexical stock of Indo-European, the separate words of its dictionary. Yet commonly a single root would furnish a large number of derivative stems with different suffixes, both nominal and verbal, much as English *love* is both noun and verb as well as the base of such derivatives as *lovely, lover,* and *beloved.* For this reason it is customary to group such collections of derivatives, in a variety of Indo-European languages, under the root on which they are built. The root entries of this Dictionary are arranged in this way, with derivatives that exhibit similar suffixes forming subgroups consisting of Indo-European stems, or words.

Indo-European made extensive use of suffixation in the formation of words but had very few prefixes. The use of such prefixes ("preverbs") as Latin *ad-, con-, de-, ex-* (AD-VENT, CONVENTION, etc.) or Germanic *be-* (BECALM, BECLOUD) can be shown to be a development of the individual languages after the breakup of the common language. In Indo-European, such "compounds" represented two independent words, a situation still reflected in Hittite and the older Sanskrit of the Vedas (the sacred books of the ancient Hindus) and surviving in isolated remnants in Greek and Latin.

An important technique of word formation in Indo-European was composition, the combining of two separate words or notions into a single word. Such forms were and continue to be built on underlying simple sentences; an example in English would be "he is someone who *cuts wood,*" whence "he is a *woodcutter.*" It is in the area of composition that English has most faithfully preserved the ancient Indo-European patterns of word formation, by continuously forming them anew, recreating them. Thus *housewife* is immediately analyzable into *house + wife,* a so-called descriptive compound in which the first member modifies the second; the same elements compounded in Old English, *hūs + wīf,* have been preserved as an indivisible unit in HUSSY. Modern English has many different types of compound, such as *catfish, housewife, woodcutter, pickpocket,* or *blue-eyed*; exactly similar types may be found in the other Germanic languages and in Sanskrit, Greek, Latin, Celtic, and Slavic.

The comparative study of Indo-European poetics has shown that such compounds were considered particularly apt for elevated, formal styles of discourse; they are a salient characteristic especially of Indo-European poetic language. In addition, it is amply clear that in Indo-European society the names of individual persons—at least in the priestly and ruling (or warrior) classes—were formed by such two-member compounds. Greek names like *Sophocles,* "famed for wisdom," Celtic names like *Vercingetorix,* "warrior-king," Slavic names like *Wenceslas,* "having greater gory," Old Persian names like *Xerxes,* "ruling men," Germanic names like *Bertram,* "bright raven," are all compounds. The type goes as far back as Proto-Indo-European, even if the individual names do not. English family names continue the same tradition with such types as *Cartwright* and *Shakespeare,* as do those of other languages, like Irish *(O')Toole,* "people's valor."

Semantics

A word of caution should be entered about the semantics of the roots. It is perhaps more hazardous to attempt to reconstruct meaning than to reconstruct linguistic form, and the meaning of a root can only be extrapolated from the meanings of its descendants. Often these diverge sharply from one another, and the scholar is reduced in practice to inferring only what seems a reasonable, or even merely possible, semantic common denominator. The result is that reconstructed words and particulary roots are often assigned hazy, vague, or unspecific meanings. This is doubtless quite illusory; no human society from Proto-Indo-European times to the present day would be viable if conversation were limited to vague generalities. The apparent haziness in meaning of a given Indo-European root often simply reflects the fact that with the passage of several millennia the different words in divergent languages derived from this root have undergone semantic changes that are no longer recoverable in detail.

Lexicon and Culture

The reconstruction of a *protolanguage*—the common ancestor of a family of spoken or attested languages—has a further implication. Language is a social fact; languages are not spoken in a vacuum, but by human beings living in a society. When we have reconstructed a protolanguage, we have also necessarily established the existence of a prehistoric society, a speech community that used that protolanguage. The existence of Proto-Indo-European presupposes the existence, in some fashion, of a society of Indo-Europeans.

Language is intimately linked to culture in a complex fashion; it is at once the expression of culture and a part of it. Especially the lexicon of a language—its dictionary—is a face turned toward culture. Though by no means a perfect mirror, the lexicon of a language remains the single most effective way of approaching and understanding the culture of its speakers. As such, the contents of the Indo-European lexicon provide a remarkably clear view of the whole culture of an otherwise unknown prehistoric society.

Archaeology, archaeological evidence, is limited to material remains. But human culture is not confined to material artifacts alone. The reconstruction of vocabulary can offer a fuller, more interesting view of the culture of a prehistoric people than archaeology precisely because it includes nonmaterial culture.

Consider the case of religion. To form an idea of the religion of a people, archaeologists proceed by inference, examining temples, sanctuaries, idols, votive objects, funerary offerings, and other material remains. But these may not be forthcoming; archaeology is, for example, of little or no utility in understanding the religion of the ancient Hebrews. Yet of the Indo-European-speaking society we can reconstruct with certainty the word for "god," *deiw-os,* and the two-word name of the chief deity of the pantheon, *dyeu-pə-ter-* (Latin *Jūpiter,* Greek *Zeus patēr,* Sanskrit *Dyaus pitar,* and Luvian *Tatis Tiwaz*). The forms *dyeu-* and *deiw-os* are both derivatives of a root **deiw-**, meaning "to shine," and appearing in the word for "day" in numerous languages (Latin *diēs*; but English DAY is not related). The notion of deity was therefore linked to the notion of the bright sky.

The second element of the name of the chief god, *dyeu-pəter-,* is the general Indo-European word for FATHER, used not in the sense of father as parent, but with the meaning of the adult male who is head of the household, the sense of Latin *pater familias.* For the Indo-Europeans, the society of the gods was conceived in the image of their own society as patriarchal. The reconstructed words *deiw-os* and *dyeu-pəter-* alone tell us more about the conceptual world of the Indo-Europeans than a roomful of graven images.

The comparative method enables us to construct a basic vocabulary for the society of speakers of Proto-Indo-European that extends to virtually all aspects of their culture. This basic vocabulary is, to be sure, not uniform in its attestation. Most Indo-European words are found only in certain of the attested languages, not in all, which suggests that they may well have been formed only at a period later than the oldest common Indo-European we can reconstruct. There exist certain dialectal words that are limited in the area of their extension, as in the case of such an important sociological term as the word for tribe, **teutā-**, which is confined to the western branches Italic, Celtic, and Germanic. (It is the base of German *Deutsch* and of DUTCH and TEUTONIC.) In cases such as

these, where a word is attested in several traditions, it is still customary to call it Indo-European, even though it may not date from the remotest reconstructible time. It is in this sense, universally accepted by scholars, that the term *Indo-European* has been used in this Dictionary.

We may examine the contents of this Indo-European lexicon, which aside from its inherent interest permits us to ascertain many characteristics of Indo-European society. It is remarkable that by far the greater part of this reconstructed vocabulary is preserved in native or borrowed derivatives in Modern English.

General Terms. It is appropriate to begin with a sampling of basic terms in the lexicon, which have no special cultural value but attest to the richness of the tradition. All are widespread in the family. There are two verbs expressing existence, **es-** and **bheuə-**, found in English IS, Latin *esse,* and English BE, Latin *fu-turus* (FUTURE), respectively. There are verbs "to sit" (**sed-¹**), "to lie" (**legh-, kei-¹**), "to stand" (**stā-**). There are a number of verbs of motion, like **gʷā-**, "to come," **ei-¹**, "to go," **terə-²**, "to cross over," **sekʷ-¹**, "to follow," **kei-³**, "to set in motion," and the variants of rolling or turning motion in **wel-³, wer-³, kʷel-¹**.

Reconstructions are by no means confined to general, imprecise meanings such as these; we have also such specific semantic values as **nes-¹**, "to return safely home" (NOSTALGIA).

The notion of carrying is represented by the widespread root **bher-¹** (BEAR¹), found in every branch except Anatolian. This root is noteworthy in that it formed a phrase **nŏ-men- bher-**, "to bear a name," which is reconstructible from several traditions, including English. This phrase formed a counterpart to **nŏ-men- dhē-**, "to give a name," with the verb **dhē-¹**, "to set, put," in Sanskrit, Greek, and Slavic tradition. The persistence of these expressions attests the importance of the name-giving ritual in Indo-European society.

For the notions of eating and drinking, the roots **ed-** and **pōi-¹** are most widespread. A root **swel-¹** is attested in Avestan and survives in English both in SWALLOW¹ and in as humble a word as SWILL. For drink, a root **srebh-** is found in some dialects (ABSORB). The metaphor in "drunk, intoxicated" seems to have been created independently a number of times in the history of the Indo-European languages; Latin *ēbrius,* "drunk" (INEBRIATED), was without etymology until a cognate turned up in the Hittite verb meaning "to drink"; both are derived from the root **ēgʷh-**.

The verb "to live" was **gʷei-**; it formed an adjective **gʷī-wos,* "alive," which survives in English QUICK, whose original sense is seen in the Biblical phrase *the quick and the dead.* For the notion of begetting there are two roots, **tek-** and the extremely widely represented **genə-**, which appears not only as a verb but also in various nominal forms like **gen-os,* "race," and the prototypes of English KIN and KIND.

A number of qualitative adjectives are attested that go back to the protolanguage. Some come in semantic pairs: **sen-¹**, "old," and **newo-**, "new"; also **sen-¹**, "old," and **yeu-**, "youthful vigor"; **tenu-,* "thin" (under **ten-**), and **tegu-**, "thick"; **gʷerə-²**, "heavy," and **legʷh-**, "light." There are also the two prefixes **su-**, "good, well-," and **dus-**, "bad, ill-," in the Greek forms borrowed as EU- and DYS-. But normally adjectives of value judgments like *good* and *bad* are not widespread in the family and are subject to replacement; English *good,* Latin *bonus,* and Greek *agathos* have nothing to do with each other, and each is confined to its own branch of the family.

The personal pronouns belong to the very earliest layer of Indo-European that can be reached by reconstruction. The forms are unlike those of any other paradigms in the language; they have been called the "Devonian rocks" of Indo-European. The lack of any formal resemblance in English between the subject case (nominative) I and the object case (accusative) ME is a direct and faithful reflex of the same disparity in Proto-Indo-European, respectively **eg** (**egō*) and **me-¹**. The other pronouns are **tu-** (**te-*), "thou," **nes-²**, **we-**, "we," **yu-¹** "you." No pronouns for the third person were in use.

The cognate languages give evidence for demonstrative and interrogative pronouns. Both have also developed into relative pronouns in different languages. The most persistent and widespread pronominal stems are **to-** and **kʷo-**, which are preserved in the English demonstrative and interrogative-relative pronouns and adverbs beginning with *th-* (THIS, THEN) and *wh-* (WHO, WHICH, WHEN).

All the languages of the family show some or all of the Indo-European numerals. The language had a decimal system. There is

complete agreement on the numerals from two to ten: **dwo-** (*duwō*), **trei-** (*treyes*), **kʷetwer-** (*kʷetwores*), **penkʷe**, **s(w)eks**, **septm̥**, **oktō(u)**, **newn̥**, **dekm̥**. For the numeral "one" the dialects vary. We have a root **sem-¹** in some derivatives, while the western Indo-European languages Germanic, Celtic, and Latin share the form **oi-no-**. The word for "hundred," formed from **dekm̥**, "ten," was **(d)km̥tom*. No common form for "thousand" or any other higher number can be reconstructed for the protolanguage.

Man and His Physical Environment. A large number of terms relating to time, weather, seasons, and natural surroundings can be reconstructed from the daughter languages, some of which permit certain inferences about the homeland of the Indo-European-speaking people before the period of migrations took them to the different localities where they historically appear.

There are several words for "year," words that relate to differing conceptions of the passage of time. Such are **yēr-** (YEAR), related to words denoting activity; **wet-²**, the year as a measure of the growth of a domestic animal (WETHER, basically "yearling"); and **at-** in Latin *annus* (ANNUAL), a verb meaning "to go," referring to the year as passage. The seasons were distinguished in Indo-European: **ghei-²**, "winter," **esr-*, "spring," **sem-²**, "summer," and **esen-**, "fall, harvest," the latter plausibly reflected in Germanic *aznōn*, "to earn," referring to harvest labor in an agricultural society.

The lunar month was a unit of time. The word for "month" (**mēns-*) is in some languages identical with the word for "moon," in others a derivative of it, as in Germanic **mēnōth-* from **mēnōn-*. "Moon/month" in Indo-European is a derivative of the verb "to measure," **mē-²**. The adjective **sen-¹** (**seno-*), "old," was also used for the waning of the moon, on the evidence of several languages.

The other celestial bodies recognized were the sun, **sāwel-**, and the stars, **ster-³**. There is evidence from several traditions for similar designations of the constellation Ursa Major, though these may not go back to the earliest Indo-European times. The movement of the sun dictated the names for the points of the compass. EAST is derived from a verbal root **aus-¹**, "to shine," as is the word for "dawn" (Latin *Aurora*), divinized since Indo-European times on the evidence of Greek, Lithuanian, and Sanskrit. The setting sun furnished the word for "evening" and "west":

wes-pero-. The Indo-Europeans oriented themselves by facing east. Therefore the root **deks-**, "right," could also denote "south." "Right" was considered lucky; the terms for "left" vary from language to language (one Indo-European term is **laiwo-**) and were evidently subject to taboo.

The most widespread of the words for "night" was **nekʷ-t-**. Words for "day" include **āmer-** and **agh-²** and such dialectal creations as Latin *diēs*; **ayer-** refers to the morning. The old word for "darkness," **regʷes-**, shows up in Greek as a term for the underworld.

The Indo-Europeans knew snow in their homeland; the word **sneigʷh-** is nearly ubiquitous. Curiously enough the word for "rain," however, varies among the different branches; we have words of differing distribution like **seuə-²**, **ombh-ro-** and **reg-²**.

Conceptions of the sky, heaven, were varied in the different dialects. As we have seen, the root **deiw-** occurs widely as the divinized bright sky. On the other hand, certain languages viewed the heavens as basically cloudy; **nebh-** is "sky" in Balto-Slavic and Iranian, but "cloud" elsewhere. Another divinized natural phenomenon is illustrated by the root **(s)tenə-**, "thunder," and the name of the Germanic god THOR.

A word for the earth can be reconstructed as **dhghem-** (**dheghom*). Other terms of lesser distribution designated forest or uncultivated land, like **kaito-** and **welt-** (WILD). Swampy or boggy terrain was apparently also familiar, from the evidence of the roots **sel-es-**, **pelə-¹**, and **māno-*. But since none of these runs through the whole family, it would not be justifiable to infer anything from them regarding the terrain of a hypothetical original homeland of the Indo-Europeans.

On the other hand, from the absence of a general word for "sea" we may deduce that the Indo-Europeans were originally an inland people. A root **mori-** is attested dialectally (MERE), but it may well have referred to a lake or other smaller body of water. Transportation by or across water was, however, known to the Indo-Europeans, since most of the languages attest an old word for boat or ship, **nāu-²**, probably propelled by oars or a pole (**erə-¹**, "to row").

The names for a number of different trees are widely enough attested to be viewed as Proto-Indo-European in date. The general term for tree and wood was **deru**. The original meaning of the root was doubtless "to be

firm, solid," and from it is derived not only the family of English TREE but also that of English TRUE. Note that the semantic evolution has here been from the general to the particular, from "solid" to "tree" (and even "oak" in some dialects), and not the other way around.

There are very widely represented words for the beech tree, **bhāgo-**, and the birch, **bherəg-**. These formerly played a significant role in attempts to locate the original homeland of the Indo-Europeans, since their distribution is geographically distinct. But their ranges may have changed over several millennia, and, more important, the same word may have been applied to entirely different species of tree. Thus the Greek and Latin cognates of BEECH designate a kind of oak found in the Mediterranean lands.

Of fruit trees in the usual sense, only the apple (**abel-**) and the cherry (**ker-⁶**) were known. Wine was made in the Mediterranean basin before the arrival of the Indo-Europeans, and the pear and the olive, as well as the grape, were cultivated. As immigrants into Greece and Italy the Indo-Europeans adopted the names along with the fruits, and both were later widely diffused.

Indo-European had a generic term for "wild animal," **ghwer-** (FERAL). The wolf was known and evidently feared; its name is subject to taboo deformation (conscious alteration of the form of a tabooed word, as in English *gol-derned, dad-burned*). The variant forms **w̥lkʷo-**, *lupo-*, and **w̥lp-** (also "fox"), are all found. The name of the bear was likewise subject to a hunter's taboo: the animal could not be mentioned by its real name on the hunt. The southern Indo-European languages have the original form, **r̥tko-** (Latin *ursus*, Greek *arktos*), but all the northern languages have a substitute term. In Slavic the bear is the "honey-eater," in Germanic the "brown one" (BEAR, and note also BRUIN).

The BEAVER was evidently known (*bhi-bhru-*, from **bher-³**), at least in Europe, and the MOUSE (**mūs-**) then as now was ubiquitous. The HARE, probably named from its color (**kas-**, "gray"), is also widespread. Domesticated animals are discussed below.

A generic term for "fish" existed, **dhghū-** (also **peisk-** in Europe). The salmon (**laks-**) and the eel (**angʷhi-**) were known, the latter also in the meaning "snake." Several birds were known, including the crane (**gerə-²**), the eagle (**or-**), the THRUSH (**trozdo-**), the STAR-LING (**storo-**), and, at least in some dialects, the SPARROW (**sper-³**), FINCH (**sping-**), and woodpecker (**(s)peik-**). The generic term for "bird" was **awi-** (Latin *avis*), and from this was derived the well-represented word for egg, *ōwyo-*.

The names for a number of insects can be reconstructed in the protolanguage, including the WASP (**wopsā**), the hornet (*krəs-r̥o-*, a derivative of **ker-¹**, "head," from the shape of the insect), and the fly (**mu-²**). The BEE (**bhei-¹**) was particularly important as the producer of honey, for which we have the common Indo-European name **melit-**. Honey was the only source of sugar and sweetness (**swād-**, "sweet," is ancient), and notably was the base of the only certain Indo-European alcoholic beverage, MEAD, **medhu-**, meaning in different dialects both "mead" ("wine" in Greece) and "honey." The Germanic languages have innovated, perhaps from a taboo on speaking the name while gathering wild honey; the common Germanic English word HONEY is from an old color adjective for "yellow," **k(e)nəko-**.

The Indo-Europeans were clearly also troubled by more "personal" insect pests. A root **sker-¹** is the base of a word *kori-*, attested in different languages as either "bedbug" or "moth." English NIT faithfully continues Indo-European **knid-**, "louse, louse egg," attested in many branches of the family. And **lūs-**, "louse," has rhymed with **mūs-**, "mouse," since Indo-European times.

Man and Society. For man himself, a number of terms were employed, with different nuances of meaning. The general terms for "man" and "woman" are **wī-ro-** (VIRILE) and *gʷenā-* from **gʷen-** (GYNECOLOGY). For man as a human being, the oldest word was apparently *manu-* (**man-¹**), as preserved in English MAN and in Slavic and Sanskrit. In other dialects we find interesting metaphorical expressions, which attest a set of religious concepts opposing the gods as immortal and celestial to mankind as mortal and terrestrial. Man is either *mortos*, "mortal" (**mer-²**, "to die"), or *dhghomyo-*, "earthling" (**dhghem-**, "earth").

The parts of the body belong to the basic layer of vocabulary and are for the most part faithfully preserved in Indo-European languages. Such are **ker-¹**, "head" (also **kaput** in dialects, doubtless a more colloquial word), **genu-²**, "chin, jaw," **dent-**, "tooth," **okʷ-**, "to see," whence "eye," **ous-**, "ear," **nas-**, "nose," **leb-²**, "lip," **bhrū-**, "brow," **ōs-**, "mouth,"

dn̥ghū, "tongue," and **mon-**, "neck." The word for "foot" is attested everywhere (**ped-**¹), while that for the hand differs according to dialect.

Internal organs were also named in Indo-European times, including the womb (**gʷelbh-**), gall (**ghel-**²), brain (**mregh-mno-**, confined to Low German and Greek), spleen (**spelgh-**), and liver (**yekʷr̥**). The male sexual organs, **pes-** and **ergh-**, are common patrimony, as is **ors-**, "backside."

A large number of kinship terms have been reconstructed. They are agreed in pointing to a society that was patriarchal, patrilocal (the bride leaving her household to join that of her husband's family), and patrilineal (descent reckoned by the male line). "Father" and "head of the household" are one: **pəter-**, with his spouse, the **māter-**. These terms are ultimately derived from the baby-talk syllables *pa(pa)* and *ma(ma)*, but they had a sociological significance in the Indo-European family over and above this, which is marked by the kinship-term suffix *-ter-*. Related terms are found for the grandfather (**awo-**) and the maternal uncle (**awon-*), and correspondingly the term **nepōt-** (feminine **neptī-*) applied to both grandson (perhaps originally daughter's son) and nephew (sister's son). English SON and DAUGHTER clearly reflect Indo-European **sūnu-* (from **seue-**¹) and **dhughəter-**.

Male blood relations were designated as **bhrāter-** (BROTHER), which doubtless extended beyond those with a common father or mother; the Greek cognate means "fellow member of a clan-like group." The female counterpart was **swesor-** (SISTER), probably literally "the female member of the kin group," with a feminine suffix **-sor-* and the root **s(w)e-**, designating the self, one's own group.

While there exist many special terms for relatives by marriage on the husband's side, like **daiwer-**, "husband's brother," fewer corresponding terms on the wife's side can be reconstructed for the protolanguage. The terms vary from dialect to dialect, providing good evidence for the patrilocal character of marriage.

The root **demə-**¹ denoted both the house (Latin *domus*) and the household as a social unit. The father of the family (Latin *pater familias*) was the "master of the house" (Greek *despotes*) or simply "he of the house" (Latin *dominus*). A larger unit was the village, designated by the word **weik-**¹. The community may have been grouped into divisions by location; this seems to be the basic meaning of the **dā-mo-* (from **dā-**) in Greek *dēmos*, people (DEMOCRACY).

A root designating a human settlement is **sel-**¹. These establishments were frequently built on the top of high places fortified for defense, a practice taken by Indo-European migrants into Central and Western Europe, and Italy and Greece, as confirmed by archaeological finds. Words for such fortified high places vary; there are **pelə-**³, variant **poli-* (ACROPOLIS), **ark-,* **dhūno-** (TOWN), and **bhergh-**² (-*burg* in place names).

Economic Life and Technology. A characteristic of Indo-European and other archaic societies was the principle of exchange and reciprocal gift-giving. The presentation of a gift entailed the obligation of a counter-gift, and the acts of giving and receiving were equivalent. They were simply facets of a single process of generalized exchange, which assured the circulation of wealth throughout the society.

This principle has left clear traces in the Indo-European vocabulary. The root **dō-** of Latin *dōnāre* means "to give" in most dialects but in Hittite means "to take." The root **nem-** is "to distribute" in Greek (NEMESIS), but in German it means "to take," and the cognate of English GIVE (**ghabh-**) has the meaning "to take" in Irish. The notion of exchange predominates in the roots **skamb-** and **gher-**⁵. The root **dap-** means "to apportion in exchange," which may also carry a bad sense; Latin *damnum* is "damage entailing liability." The GUEST (**ghos-ti-**) in Indo-European times was the person with whom one had mutual obligations of hospitality. But he was also the stranger, and the stranger in an uncertain and warring tribal society may well be hostile; the Latin cognate *hostis* means "enemy."

The Indo-Europeans practiced agriculture and the cultivation of cereals. We have several terms of Indo-European antiquity for grain: **gr̥ə-no-** (CORN), **yewo-**, and **pūro-**, which may have designated wheat or spelt. Others of more restricted distribution are **wrughyo-**, "rye," and **bhares-**, "barley." Two roots for grinding are attested, **al-**⁴ and **melə-** (MEAL², MILL). The latter is confined to the European branches of the family. Another European term is **sē-**¹, "to sow," not found in Greek, Armenian, or Indo-Iranian. The verb "to plow" is **arə-**, again a common European term, with the name of the plow, **arə-trom.*

Terms for the furrow are **perk-²** and **selk-**; **wogʷh-ni-** designated the wedge-shaped plowshare. Other related roots are **yeug-**, "to yoke," **serp-¹**, "sickle, hook," and **kerp-**, "to gather, pluck" (HARVEST). The root **gʷerə-²**, "heavy," is the probable base of *gʷerə-nā-*, "hand mill" (QUERN). The term is found throughout the Indo-European-speaking world, including India.

Stockbreeding and animal husbandry were an important part of Indo-European economic life. The names for all the familiar domesticated animals are present throughout the family: **gʷou-**, "cow and bull," **owi-**, "sheep," **agʷh-no-**, "lamb," **aig-** and **ghaido-**, "goat," **sū-**, "swine," and **porko-**, "farrow." The domestic dog was ancient (**kwon-**); its name may underlie the common Indo-European word for horse, **ekwo-**. The expansion and migration of the Indo-European-speaking peoples in the later third and early second millennia B.C. is intimately bound up with the diffusion of the horse. The verbal root **demə-²**, "to force," acquired the special sense of "to tame horses," whence English TAME. Stock was a source and measure of wealth; the original sense of **peku-** was probably "wealth, riches," as in Latin *pecunia,* whence "wealth in cattle" and finally "cattle" proper. The same evolution from the general to the particular may be observed in the root **neud-**, "to make use of," whence English NEAT².

The verbal roots **pā-**, "to protect," and **kʷel-¹**, "to revolve, move around," are widely used for the notion of herding or watching over stock, and it is interesting to note that the metaphor of the god or priest watching over mankind like a shepherd (Latin *pāstor*) over his flock occurs in many Indo-European dialects.

Roots indicating a number of technical operations are attested in most of the languages of the family. One such is **teks-**, which in some dialects means "to fabricate, especially by working with an ax," but in others means "to weave" (TEXTILE). A root **dheigh-**, meaning "to mold, shape," is applied both to bread (DOUGH) and to mud or clay, whence words for both pottery and mud walls (Iranian *pari-daiza,* "walled around," borrowed into Greek as the word that became English PARADISE).

The house (**demə-¹**) included a **dhwer-** (DOOR), which probably referred originally to the gateway into the enclosure of the household. The house would have had a central hearth, denoted in some languages by **aidh-** (properly a verb, "to burn"). Fire itself was known by two words, one of animate gender (**egni-**, Latin *ignis*), and one neuter (**pūr-**, Greek *pur*).

Indo-European had a verb "to cook" (**pekʷ-**, also having the notion "to ripen") and an adjective "raw" (**om-**). Another operation is denoted by **peis-¹**, "to crush." Meat (**mēms-**) was an established item of diet, and some sort of sauce or broth is indicated by the term **yeuə-** (*yū-s-*, JUICE, from Latin). Other household activities included spinning ((**s)nē-¹**), weaving, (**webh-**) and sewing (**syū-**). The verb **wes-⁴** (WEAR) is ancient and everywhere attested. The Indo-European garment was probably belted: **yōs-**, "to gird."

The Indo-Europeans knew metal and metallurgy, to judge from the presence of the word **ayes-** in Sanskrit, Germanic, and Latin. The term designated copper and perhaps bronze. Iron is a latecomer, technologically, and the terms for it vary from dialect to dialect. Latin has *ferrum,* while the Germanic and Celtic term was *isarno-*, properly "holy (metal)," doubtless so called because the first iron was derived from small meteorites. Gold was known from ancient times, though the names for it vary; **ghel-²**, probably "yellow (metal)," and **aurum** (*aus-*, Latin *aurum*), are widespread. Silver was **arg-**, with various suffixes, doubtless meaning "white (metal)."

It was probably not long before the dispersal of the Proto-Indo-European community that the use of the wheel and wheeled transport was adopted. Despite the existence of widespread word families, most terms relating to wheeled vehicles seem to be metaphors formed from already existing words; they are not primitives or primary vocables. So the word for AXLE (**aks-**) may mean simply "a pivotlike juncture"; the NAVE or hub of the wheel (**nobh-**) is the same word as NAVEL. This is clearly the case with WHEEL itself, where the widespread *kʷ(e)-kʷl-o-* is an expressive derivative of a verb (**kʷel-¹**) meaning "to revolve or go around." Other words for "wheel" are dialectal and again derivative, like Latin *rota* from a verbal root **ret-**, "to run." A root **wegh-**, "to go, transport in a vehicle" (WAGON), is attested quite early, though not in Hittite. This evidence for the late appearance of the wheel agrees with archaeological findings that date the distribution of the wheel in Europe to the latter

part of the fifth millennium B.C., the latest possible date for the community of Proto-Indo-European proper.

Ideology. We pointed out earlier that the great advantage of the lexicon as an approach to culture and history is that it is not confined to material remains. Words exist for natural phenomena, objects, and things that can be found in nature or identified from their material remains. But words also exist for ideas, abstractions, and relations. The Indo-European protolanguage is particularly rich in such vocabulary items.

A number of verbs denoting mental activity are found. The most widespread is **men-¹**, preserved in English MIND. Other derivatives refer to remembering, warning (putting in mind), and thinking in general. A root notable for the diversity of its derivatives is **med-**, which may be defined as "to take the appropriate measures." Reflexes of this verb range in meaning from "rule," through "measure" (MODICUM, from Latin), to "physician" (Latin *medicus*).

The notion of government and sovereignty was well represented. The presence of the old word for tribal king, **reg-* (**reg-¹**), only in the extreme east (RAJAH) and the extreme west (Latin *rēx*, Celtic *-rīx*) virtually guarantees its presence in the earliest Indo-European society. (Here is an example of the phenomenon of marginal or peripheral conservation of a form lost in the central innovating area). Roman tradition well attests the sacral character of kingship among the Indo-Europeans. The functions of king and priest were different aspects of a single function of sovereignty. It is this which is symbolized by the divine name **dyeu-pəter-* (**deiw-**), the chief of the gods.

Indo-European is particularly rich in religious vocabulary. An important form, which is also found only in the peripheral languages Sanskrit, Latin, and Celtic, is the two-word metaphoric phrase **kred-dhə-*, literally "to put (**dhē-¹**) heart (**kerd-¹**)." The two words have been joined together in the western languages, as in Latin *crēdō*, "I believe." Here a term of the most ancient pagan religion has been taken over by Christianity. A common word for religious form (**bhlag-men-**) may be preserved in BRAHMIN, a member of the priestly class, from Sanskrit.

Oral prayers, request of the deity, and other ritual utterances must have played a significant role in Indo-European religion. We have the roots **wegʷh-**, "to preach," and **sengʷh-**, "to prophesy, sing, make incantations," now secularized in SING. Another is **gʷerə-³**, "to praise aloud," which in Latin *grātia* (GRACE) has had a considerable fortune in Christianity.

Several words apparently denoted specific ritual actions, like **ghow-ē-**, "to honor, worship," and **sep-el-yo-* (**sep-**), with the specific notion "to venerate the dead," found in the Latin verb *sepelīre*, meaning "to bury." The root **spend-** has the basic meaning of "to make an offering or perform a rite," whence "to engage oneself by a ritual act." Its Latin derivative *spondēre* means "to promise" (SPOUSE).

A hint of Indo-European metaphysics appears in the word **aiw-**, "vital force," whence "long life, the eternal recreation of life, eternity" (EON). It is noteworthy that the idea of "holy" is intimately bound up with that of "whole, healthy" in a number of forms: **kailo-** (WHOLE and HOLY), **swento-** (SOUND²), and **solə-**, whence Latin *salvus* (SALVATION). An ancient root relating solely to religion is **sak-** (SACRED).

Another aspect of the function of sovereignty is the sphere of the law. There is an old word, **yewes-**, probably for "religious law," in Latin *jūs*. Latin *lēx* is also ancient (**leg-¹**), though the details of its etymology are uncertain. In a society that emphasized the principle of exchange and reciprocity, it is scarcely surprising that the notion of contractual obligation should be well represented. Several roots specify the notion of "bond": **bhendh-**, **ned-**, **leig-¹**, all of which have derivatives with technical legal meanings in various languages. The word for "a pledge," **wadh-¹**, exists in western Indo-European, whence the English verb for making a particular kind of contract, WED. An oath then as now was important: the roots **serk-* and **oito-** are found in Celtic and Germanic. The verb **kʷei-¹** meant "to pay compensation for an injury." Its derivative noun, **kʷoinā*, was borrowed from Doric Greek into the most ancient Roman law as Latin *poena, pūnīre*, whence English PUNISH and a host of legal terms. The Greek word for justice, *dikē*, is derived from the notion of "boundary marker" (**deik-**; compare also **ter-**, **termen-*).

In conclusion we may add that poetry and a tradition of poetics are also common patrimony in most of the Indo-European traditions. The hymns of the Rig-Veda are composed in meters related to those used by

the Greek poets, and the earliest verse forms found among the Celts and the Slavs go back to the same Indo-European source. Many, perhaps most, of the stylistic figures and embellishments of poetic language which we associate with "Classical" poetics and rhetoric can be shown, by the comparative method, to have their roots in Indo-European poetics itself.

A number of metaphorical expressions appear to be creations of ancient, even Indo-European date. Thus the verb **dhegʷh-**, "to burn, warm," forms derivatives in Latin and Celtic which mean "to keep warm, cherish," and refer especially to the duties of the pious son toward his aged parent. Latin *terra*, "earth" (TERRAN), is historically a transferred epithet, "dry (land)," from **ters-**, "to dry." One securely reconstructible Indo-European place name rests squarely on a metaphor: *Pīwer-iā* in Greek *Pieria* (PIERIAN SPRING) and *Īwer-ion-*, the prehistoric Celtic name for Ireland (Gaelic *Éire, Érin*), both continue an Indo-European feminine adjective *pīwer-iə*, "fat," metaphorically "fertile," from **peiə-**, the same root which gives English FAT.

Most interesting are the cases where from two or more traditions (usually including Homer and the Rig-Veda) it is possible to reconstruct a poetic phrase or formula consisting of two members. Such are the expressions "imperishable fame," *klewos n̥dhgʷhitom* (**kleu-**[1], **dhgʷhei-**); "holy (mental) force," *isərom menos* (**eis-**[1], **men-**[1]); and the "weaver (or crafter) of words," the Indo-European poet himself, *wekʷōm teks-on* (**wekʷ-**, **teks-**). The immortality of the gods (*n̥-mrto-*, from **mer-**[2]) is emphasized anew by the vivid verb phrase **nek-**[1] **terə-**[2], "to overcome death," appearing in the Greek word *nektar*, the drink of the gods. And at least one three-member formula (in the sense of the word in traditional oral poetry) can be reconstructed for the poetic language of prayer, on the combined evidence of four languages, Latin, Umbrian, Avestan, and Sanskrit: "Protect, keep safe, man and cattle!" (**pā- wī-ro- peku**).

Conclusion

This survey has touched on only a representative sample of the available reconstructed Indo-European lexicon and has made no attempt to cite the mass of evidence in all the languages of the family, ancient and modern, for these reconstructions.

For this essay, we have given only the information about Indo-European culture that could be derived from language and lexicon alone. Other disciplines serve to fill out and complete the picture to be gathered from the study of vocabulary: archaeology, prehistory, comparative religion, and the history of institutions.

Archaeologists have not in fact succeeded in locating the Indo-Europeans. An artifact other than a written record is silent on the language of its user, and prehistoric Eurasia offers an abundant choice of culture areas. Archaeologists are generally agreed that the so-called Kurgan peoples, named after the Russian word for their characteristic "barrow" or "tumulus" grave structure, spoke an Indo-European language. Some time around the middle of the fifth millennium B.C., these people expanded from the steppe zone north of the Black Sea and beyond the Volga into the Balkans and adjacent areas. These Kurgan peoples bore a new mobile and aggressive culture into Neolithic Europe, and it is not unreasonable to associate them with the coming of the Indo-Europeans. But the Kurgan peoples' movement into Europe took place in distinct waves from the fifth to the third millennium B.C. The earliest so far discovered might be compatible with a reasonable date for Proto-Indo-European, that is, a date sufficiently long ago for a single language to develop into forms as divergent as Mycenean Greek and Hittite as they are historically attested by the middle of the second millennium B.C. But the later Kurgan immigrations after 4,000 B.C. are too late to be regarded as incursions of speakers of undifferentiated Proto-Indo-European. The archaeological evidence for the later waves of Kurgan migrations points to their having had an Indo-European culture, but the languages spoken by the later Kurgan peoples must have been already differentiated Indo-European dialects, some of which would doubtless evolve into some of the historical branches of the family tree. We must be content to recognize the Kurgan peoples as speakers of certain Indo-European languages and as sharing a common Indo-European cultural patrimony. The ultimate "cradle" of the Indo-Europeans may well never be known, and language remains the best and fullest evidence for prehistoric Indo-European society.

Guide to the Dictionary

The American Heritage Dictionary of Indo-European Roots carries the etymology of the English language to its logical and natural conclusion, for if the documentary history of words is of interest and value, so is their reconstructed prehistory. The historical component is given in the etymologies in *The American Heritage Dictionary: Second College Edition*. This Dictionary supplies the prehistoric component.

The form given in **boldface** type at the head of each entry is, unless otherwise identified, an Indo-European root in its basic form, which may be followed by one or more variants, also in the boldface type. The basic meaning or meanings of the root are given immediately after the entry form and its variants (but see the caution under "Semantics" in the preceding essay). Meanings that are different parts of speech are separated by a semicolon:

kagh-. To catch, seize; wickerwork, fence.

pelə-². Flat; to spread.

mu-¹. Imitative of inarticulate sounds.

After the basic meaning there may appear further information about the phonological shape or nature of the root:

dhreg-. To draw, glide. Variant form of **dhrag-**.

temp-. To stretch. Extension of **ten-**.

tauro-. Bull. Derivative of **stā-**, but an independent word in Indo-European.

dail-. To divide. Northern Indo-European root.

pipp-. To peep. Imitative root.

pā-. To protect, feed. Contracted from **pəə-*.

kak-². A round object, disk. Germanic root.

mas. Male, Latin adjective of unknown origin.

Most, but not all, of the additional information is self-explanatory. In the first three examples, the boldface forms **dhrag-**, **stā-**, and **ten-** are cross-references to those roots, which are main entries in this Dictionary.

Every boldface form appearing in the text of an entry is such a cross-reference. In the example **pā-** the form **pəə-* represents an older root form; the nature of these contractions is explained in the preceding essay under "Phonology and Morphology." The entries **kak-²** and **mas** are not strictly speaking Indo-European, since they are represented in only one branch of the family. There is a relatively small number of such entries in this Dictionary; they are included because of the number of English words among their descendants. Boldface brackets are placed around these entries, and they are explicitly identified.

The text of each entry describes in detail the development of Modern English words from the root. In some cases no semantic or morphological development needs to be explained, and the *lemma* (the historically attested representative of the root) is immediately given:

kaiko-. One-eyed. Latin *caecus*, blind . . .

Much more commonly, however, intermediate developments require explanation. These intermediate stages are reconstructions representing a word stem in Indo-European that is necessary to explain the lemma following it (see the section "Grammar and Syntax" in the preceding essay). The reconstructed forms are not historically attested; they are preceded by an asterisk (*) to note this fact. Sometimes earlier or later developments of the intermediate forms are given in parentheses, as in the example of **stā-** below. In these cases the symbol < is used to mean "derived from" and the symbol > is used to mean "developed into." The systematic presentation of these reconstructed forms is a feature unique to *The American Heritage Dictionary of Indo-European Roots*. The following terms are used to describe typical morphological processes of Indo-European:

full-grade form. A form with *e*-vocalism (the basic form); so identified for descriptive contrast.

o-grade form. A form with *o*-vocalism.

nekʷ-t-. O-grade form **nokʷ-t-* . . .

zero-grade form. A form with zero-vocalism.

men-¹. I. Zero-grade form **mn̥-* . . .

lengthened-grade form. A form with lengthened vocalism.

ghers-. **2.** Lengthened-grade form **ghēr(s)-* . . .

secondary full-grade form. A new full-grade form created by inserting the fundamental vowel *e* in the zero-grade form of an extended root.

stā-. V. Zero-grade extended root **stū-* (< **stuə*) . . . **VI.** Secondary full-grade form **steuə-* . . .

basic form. The unchanged root; so identified for descriptive contrast.

suffixed form. A form with one or more suffixes, written with an internal hyphen.

mut-. Suffixed form **mut-il-* . . .

āpero. Suffixed form **āper-yo-* . . .

mel-⁴. **1.** Suffixed (comparative) form **mel-yos-* . . .

prefixed form. A form with a prefix, written with an internal hyphen.

op-¹. **6.** Prefixed form **co-op-* . . .

extended form. A form with an extension or enlargement, written solid.

pel-⁶. **II.** Extended form **pelə-* . . .

nasalized form. A form with a nasal infix, written with internal hyphens.

tag-. **1.** Nasalized form **ta-n-g-* . . .

reduplicated form. A form prefixed by its own initial consonant followed by a vowel.

segh-. **5.** Reduplicated form **si-sgh-* . . .

expressive form. A form with "expressive gemination" (doubling of the final consonant), written solid.

gal-². **3.** Expressive form **gall-* . . .

compound form. A form compounded with a form of another root, written with internal hyphens.

demə-¹. **2.** Compound form **dems-pot-* . . .

shortened form. A form with shortened vocalism.

syū-. **5.** Shortened form **syu-* . . .

reduced form. A form with phonological loss of one or more sounds.

konəmo-. Reduced form **kommo-* . . .

oldest root form. A root form showing a laryngeal (ə) in a position, typically at the beginning of a word, where it is preserved in only a few Indo-European languages, such as Greek or Hittite.

ster-³. **3.** Oldest root from **əster-* in Greek *astēr* . . .

variant form. A form altered in any way other than in the above categories.

deru. **2.** Variant form **dreu-* . . .

These terms can be combined freely to describe in as much detail as necessary the development from the root to the lemma. The Modern English words derived from the lemma follow in small capitals. The simple (uncompounded) derivatives are listed first; the compounds follow, separated from the first list by a semicolon.

dhē(i)-. **1.** Suffixed reduced form **dhē-mnā-* in Latin *fēmina,* woman (< "she who suckles"): FEMALE, FEMININE; EFFEMINATE.

peig-². **3.** Suffixed o-grade form **poik-yos* in Germanic **faigjaz* in Old English *fæge,* fated to die: FEY.

petə-. **2.** Suffixed (stative) variant zero-grade form **pat-ē-* in Latin *patēre,* to be open: PATENT, PATULOUS.

stebh-. **2.** Germanic nasalized form **stamp-* in: **a.** Middle English *stampen,* to pound, stamp: STAMP . . .

In order to emphasize the fact that English belongs to the Germanic branch of Indo-European and to give precedence to directly inherited words in contrast to words borrowed from other branches, the intermediate stages in Germanic etymologies are covered in fuller detail. The Common or Proto-Germanic (called simply Germanic) forms

underlying English words are always given. Where no other considerations intervene, Germanic is given first of the Indo-European groups, and Old English is given first within Germanic, although this precedence is not rigidly applied.

The final item in most entries of the *Dictionary of Indo-European Roots* is an abbreviated reference to Julius Pokorny's *Indogermanisches Etymologisches Wörterbuch* (Bern, 1959). This, the standard work of reference and synthesis in the Indo-European field, carries a full range of the actual comparative material on which the roots are reconstructed. This Dictionary presents only those aspects of the material that are directly relevant to English. For example, the English word MANY is found at the root **menegh-**, "copious." This entry describes the transition of the Indo-European form through Germanic *managa-* to Old English *manig, mænig,* "many." It does not cite the evidence on which this assertion is based, but it refers to [Pok. *men(e)gh-* 730]. The entry *men(e)gh-* on page 730 in Pokorny's dictionary cites, in addition to the Old English word, the forms attested in Sanskrit, Celtic, Gothic, Old High German, Old Norse, Slavic, and Lithuanian, from which the reconstruction of the root was made. These references should serve as a reminder that the information given in this Dictionary is assertive rather than expository, and that the evidence and evaluation upon which its assertions are based are not presented here.

The alphabetical listing of roots is followed by a complete index of English derivatives, indicating the root or roots where each English word appears. Every English word in the index is also a main entry in *The American Heritage Dictionary: Second College Edition,* but not every entry in *The American Heritage Dictionary* that is of Indo-European ancestry is included in the *Dictionary of Indo-European Roots.* Many etymologies are cross-referred to the etymologies at other entries, and although some such words are included in the *Dictionary of Indo-European Roots* (appearing in parentheses), in general the words with the fullest etymologies—that is, with etymologies taken back to the earliest historical form—are included. The cross-references between etymologies in *The American Heritage Dictionary* do, however, enable a user of that Dictionary to find the Indo-European root of any English word of Indo-European derivation.

Symbols: * unattested; > developed into; < derived from.

Indo-European Roots

abel-. Apple. Germanic *ap(a)laz* in Old English *æppel*, apple: APPLE. [Pok. *abel-* 1.]

ad-. To, near, at. **1.** Germanic *at* in Old English *æt* (> Middle English *at*), near, by, at: ADO, AT. **2.** Latin *ad*, *ad-*, to, toward: AD-, -AD; (ADJUVANT), AID, AMOUNT, (PARAMOUNT). [Pok. 1. *ad-* 3.]

ag-. To drive. **1.** Latin *agere*, to do, act, drive, conduct, lead: ACT, AGENDUM, AGENT, AGILE, AGITATE; (ALLEGE), AMBAGE, AMBIGUOUS, (ASSAY), (CACHE), COAGULUM, COGENT, ESSAY, EXACT, (EXAMINE), (EXIGENT), FUMIGATE, INTRANSIGENT, LEVIGATE, LITIGATE, NAVIGATE, OBJURGATE, PRODIGAL, RETROACTIVE, SQUAT, TRANSACT. **2.** Greek *agein*, to drive, lead: -AGOGUE, AGONY; ANAGOGE, (ANTAGONIZE), CHORAGUS, DEMAGOGUE, EPACT, GLUCAGON, HYPNAGOGIC, MYSTAGOGUE, PEDAGOGUE, PROTAGONIST, STRATAGEM, SYNAGOGUE. **3.** Suffixed form *ag-to-* in Celtic *amb(i)-ag-to-*, "one sent around" (*ambi*, around; see **ambhi**), in Latin *ambactus*, servant (> Medieval Latin *ambactia*, office): AMBASSADOR, EMBASSAGE, (EMBASSY). **4.** Suffixed form *ag-men-* in Latin *agmen*, a train, a moving forward, a marching column, group: AGMINATE. **5.** Suffixed form *ag-ti-*, "weighing" (Greek *agein*, "to lead," has a sense "to weigh"), whence adjective *ag-ty-o-*, "weighty," in Greek *axios*, worth, worthy, of like value, weighing as much: AXIOM; AXIOLOGY, CHRONAXY. **6.** Possibly suffixed form *ag-ro-*, driving, pursuing, grabbing, in Greek *agra*, a seizing: PELLAGRA, PODAGRA. Derivative **agro-**. [Pok. *aĝ-* 4.]

ag-es-. Fault, guilt. Possibly Old English *acan*, to ache (perhaps < "to cause mental pain"): ACHE. [Pok. *agos-* 8.]

agh-¹. To be depressed, be afraid. **1.** Suffixed form *agh-lo-* in Old English *eglan*, *eglian*, to trouble, afflict: AIL. **2.** Suffixed form *agh-es-* in Old Norse *agi*, frightened: AWE. [Pok. *agh-* 7.]

agh-². A day (considered as a span of time). Germanic *dagaz* (with initial *d-* of obscure origin), day, in: **a.** Old English *dæg*, day: DAY, (DAISY), TODAY; **b.** Old English denominative *dagian*, to dawn: DAWN. [Pok. *agher-* 7.]

agro-. Field. Derivative of **ag-**, "to drive" (< "place to which cattle are driven"). **1.** Germanic *akraz* in Old English *æcer*, field, acre: ACRE. **2.** Latin *ager* (genitive *agrī*), district, property, field: AGRARIAN, AGRESTAL; AGRICULTURE, PEREGRINE, (PILGRIM). **3.** Greek *agros*, field, and *agrios*, wild: AGRIA, AGRO-; AGRIOECOLOGY, AGRIOLOGY, AGROSTOLOGY, ONAGER, STAVESACRE. [In Pok. *ag-* 4.]

agwesī. Ax. Germanic *akwesī*, *akusjō-* in Old English *æx*, ax: AX. [Pok. *agu(e)sī* 9.]

agʷh-no-. Lamb. Germanic *aun-* in verb *aunōn* in Old English *ēanian*, to bring forth young: YEAN. [Pok. *agʷh--no-s* 9.]

ai-¹. To give, allot. **1.** Suffixed form *ai-t-yā* in Greek *aitia*, cause, responsibility: ETIOLOGY. **2.** Suffixed form *ai-tā-* in Greek *diaitan*, to decide, lead one's life: DIET¹. [Pok. 3. *ai-* 10.]

ai-². An utterance. Suffixed form *ai-no-* in Greek *ainos*, tale: ENIGMA. [Pok. 5. *ai-* 11.]

aidh-. To burn. **1.** Suffixed form *aidh-sto-* in: **a.** Germanic *aistaz* in Old English *āst*, kiln: OAST; **b.** Latin *aestās* (stem *aestāt-* for earlier *aestotāt-*), heat, summer: AESTIVAL. **2.** Suffixed form *aidh-lo-* perhaps in Germanic *ail-* in Old English *āl*, fire: ANNEAL. **3.** Suffixed form *aidh-i-* in Latin *aedēs*, *aedis*, building, house (<

"hearth"): AEDILE; EDIFICE, (EDIFY), MAZAEDIUM. **4.** Suffixed form *aidh-stu-* in Latin *aestus*, heat, swell, surge, tide: ESTUARY. **5.** Suffixed form *aidh-er-* in Greek *aithēr*, air: AETHER, ETHER. [Pok. *ai-dh-* 11.]

aig-. Goat. Greek *aigis*, goatskin (shield of Athena): AEGIS. [Pok. 3. *aig-* 13.]

ais-. To wish, desire. Suffixed form *ais-sk-* in Germanic *aiskōn* in Old English *āscian*, *ācsian*, to ask, seek: ASK. [Pok. 1. *ais-* 16.]

aiw-. Vital force, life, long life, eternity; also "endowed with the acme of vital force, young." **1.** Extended form in Germanic *aiwi* in: **a.** Old English *ā*, ever: NO¹; **b.** Germanic *aiwi* + *wihti*, "ever a thing, anything" (*wihti-*, thing; see **wekti-**), in Old English *āwiht*, *āuht*, anything, "ever a creature": AUGHT¹; **c.** Old English *æfre* (second element obscure), ever: EVER; EVERY, NEVER; **d.** Old Norse *ei*, ever: AYE²; NAY. **2.** Suffixed form *ai-wo-* in: **a.** Latin *aevum*, age, eternity: COEVAL, LONGEVITY, MEDIEVAL, PRIMEVAL; **b.** suffixed form *aiwo-tāt-* in Latin *aetās* (stem *aetāt-*), age: AGE; COETANEOUS; **c.** suffixed form *aiwo-terno-* in Latin *aeternus*, eternal: ETERNAL; SEMPITERNAL. **3.** Suffixed form *aiw-en-* in Greek *aiōn*, age, vital force: EON. See also *yuwen-* under **yeu-**. [Pok. *aiu-* 17.]

ak-. Sharp. **1.** Suffixed form *ak-yā-* in: **a.** Germanic *akjō* in Old English *ecg*, sharp side: EDGE; **b.** Germanic *akjan* in Old Norse *eggja*, to incite, goad: EGG². **2.** Suffixed form *ak-u-* in: **a.** Germanic *ahuz* in Old English *ēar*, *ær*, *æhher*, spike, ear of grain: EAR²; ACROSPIRE; **b.** Latin *acus*, needle: ACICULA, (ACUITY), ACUMEN, ACUTE, AGLET, EGLANTINE. **3.** Suffixed form *ak-men-*, stone, sharp stone used as a tool, with metathetic variant *ka-men-*, with variants: **a.** *ka-mer-* in Germanic *hamaraz* in Old English *hamor*, hammer: HAMMER; **b.** *kemen-* (probable variant) in Germanic *himin-*, in dissimilated form *hibin-*, "the stony vault of heaven," in Old English *heofon*, *hefn*, heaven: HEAVEN. **4.** Suffixed form *ak-onā-* in Germanic *aganō* in Old Norse *ögn*, chaff: AWN. **5.** Suffixed lengthened form *āk-ri-* in Latin *ācer*, sharp, bitter: ACERATE, ACRID, ACRIMONY, EAGER¹; CARVACROL, VINEGAR. **6.** Suffixed form *ak-ri-bhwo-* in Latin *acerbus*, bitter, sharp, tart: ACERB; EXACERBATE. **7.** Suffixed (stative) form *ak-ē-* in Latin *acēre*, to be sharp: ACID. **8.** Suffixed form *ak-ēto-* in Latin *acētum*, vinegar: ACETABULUM, (ACETIC), ACETUM; ESTER. **9.** Greek *akantha* (second element of Mediterranean origin), thorn, thorny plant: ACANTHO-, ACANTHUS; COELACANTH, PYRACANTHA, TRAGACANTH. **10.** Suffixed form *ak-mā-* in Greek *akmē*, point: ACME, ACNE. **11.** Suffixed form *ak-ro-* in Greek *akros*, topmost: ACRO-; (ACROBAT), ACROMION. **12.** Variant suffixed form *ok-su-* in Greek *oxus*, sharp, sour: AMPHIOXUS, OXALIS, OXYGEN, OXYURIASIS, PAROXYSM. [Pok. 2. *ak-* 18, 3. *kem-* 556.]

aks-. Axis. **1.** Suffixed form *aks-lo-* in Old Norse *öxull*, axle: AXLE. **2.** Suffixed form *aks-i-* in: **a.** Latin *axis*, axle, pivot: AXIS; **b.** Latin diminutive *axilla*, armpit (< "axis point of the arm and shoulder"): AXILLA. **3.** Suffixed form *aks-lā-* in Latin *āla* (< *axla*), wing, upper arm (see *axilla* in **2. b.** for semantic transition): AISLE, ALA, ALAR, ALARY, ALATE, ALULA; ALIFORM. **4.** Suffixed form *aks-on-* in Greek *axōn*, axis: AXON; MONAXON. [In Pok. *ag-* 4.]

akʷā-. Water. **1.** Germanic *agwjō* becoming *aujō*, "thing on the water," in Old English *īg*, *īeg*, island, and

īgland, īegland (*land,* land; see **lendh-²**), island: ISLAND.
2. Latin *aqua,* water: AQUA, AQUARELLE, AQUARIUM, AQUATIC, AQUI-, EWER, GOUACHE; SEWER¹. [Pok. *akʷā* 23.]

al-¹. Beyond. **1.** Variant **ol-,* "beyond," in: **a.** suffixed forms **ol-se-, *ol-so-* in Old Latin *ollus* in Latin *ille* (feminine *illa*); "yonder," that: ALARM, ALERT, ALLIGATOR; **b.** suffixed forms **ol-s, *ol-tero-* in Latin *uls, *ulter, ultrā;* beyond: OUTRÉ, ULTERIOR, ULTIMATE, ULTRA-, UTTERANCE². **2.** Suffixed form **al-tero-,* "other of two," in: **a.** Latin *alter,* other, other of two: ALTER, ALTERCATE, ALTERNATE, ALTRUISM; SUBALTERN; **b.** Latin *adulter,* "one who approaches another (unlawfully), an adulterer" (*ad-,* to; see **ad-**), hence *adulterāre,* to commit adultery with, pollute: ADULTERATE, ADULTERINE, ADULTERY. **3.** Extended form **alyo-,* "other of more than two," in: **a.** Germanic **aljaz* (with adverbial suffix) in Old English *elles,* else, otherwise: ELSE; **b.** Latin *alius,* other of more than two: ALIAS, ALIEN; ALIBI, ALIQUOT, HIDALGO; **c.** Greek *allos,* other: AGIO, ALLO-; ALLEGORY, ALLELOMORPH, MORPHALLAXIS, PARALLAX, PARALLEL, TROPHALLAXIS. [Pok. 1. *al-* 24.]

al-². To wander. **1.** Latin *ambulāre,* to go about, walk (*ambi-,* around; see **ambhi**): ALLEY¹, AMBULATE; FUNAMBULIST, PREAMBLE. **2.** Latin *exsul, exul,* wanderer, exile (*ex-,* out; see **eghs**): EXILE. [Pok. 3. *al-* 27.]

al-³. To grow, nourish. **I.** Suffixed (participial) form **al-to-,* "grown," in: **1.** Germanic **alda-* in: **a.** Old English *eald, ald,* old: ALDERMAN, OLD; **b.** Old English (comparative) *ieldra, eldra,* older, elder: ELDER¹; **c.** Old English (superlative) *ieldesta, eldesta,* eldest: ELDEST; **d.** Germanic compound **wer-ald-,* "life or age of man" (see **wī-ro-**). **2.** Latin *altus,* high, deep: ALT, ALTIMETER, ALTO, HAUGHTY, HAWSER; ALTITUDE, ALTOCUMULUS, ALTOSTRATUS, ENHANCE, EXALT, HAUTBOY. **II.** Latin *alere,* to nourish: ADOLESCENT, (ADULT), ALIBLE, ALIMENT, ALIMONY, ALTRICIAL, ALUMNUS; COALESCE. **III.** Suffixed (causative) form **ol-eye-* in Latin *abolēre,* to retard the growth of, abolish (*ab-,* from; see **apo-**): ABOLISH. **IV.** Compound form **pro-al-* (*pro-,* forth; see **per¹**) in Latin *prōlēs,* offspring: PROLAN, PROLETARIAN, PROLIFEROUS, PROLIFIC. **V.** Extended form **aldh-* in Greek *althein, althainein,* to get well: ALTHEA. [Pok. 2. *al-* 26.]

al-⁴. To grind, mill. Suffixed form **al-euro-* in Greek *aleuron,* meal, flour: ALEURONE. [Pok. 5. *al-* 28.]

[**al-⁵.** All. Germanic root. Suffixed form **al-na-* in Germanic **allaz* in Old English *all, eall, eal-, al-,* all: ALL; ALSO.]

albho-. White. **1.** Possibly Germanic **albiz, *albaz,* if meaning "white ghostlike apparitions," in: **a.** Old English *ælf,* elf: ELF; **b.** Old Norse *alfr,* elf: OAF; **c.** Old High German *Alberich,* "elf-ruler," akin to the source of Old French *Auberon:* OBERON. **2.** Latin *albus,* white (> Old Spanish *alba,* dawn): ABELE, ALB, ALBEDO, ALBESCENT, ALBINO, ALBITE, ALBUGO, ALBUMEN, ALBURNUM, AUBADE, AUBURN; DAUB. **3.** Greek *alphos,* dull-white leprosy: ALPHOSIS. [Pok. *albho-* 30.]

alek-. To ward off, protect. Earlier form **əlek-.* **1.** Suffixed zero-grade form **alk-ā-* in Greek *alkē,* strength: ANALCIME. **2.** Extended form **aleks-* in Greek *alexein,* to protect: ALEXIPHARMIC. [Pok. *aleq-* 32.]

algʷh-. To earn, be worth. Sanskrit *arhati,* he is worthy: ARHAT. [Pok. *algʷh-* 32.]

alu-. In words related to sorcery, magic, possession, and intoxication. Suffixed form **alu-t-* in Germanic **aluth-* in Old English *(e)alu,* ale: ALE. [Pok. *alu-* 33.]

ambhi. Also **m̥bhi.** Around. Probably derived from **ant-**. **1.** Reduced form **bhi* in Germanic **bi, *bi-* (intensive prefix) in: **a.** Old English *bī, bi, be,* by: BY¹; **b.** Old English *bī-, be-,* on all sides, be-, also intensive prefix: BE-; **c.** Middle Dutch *bie,* by: BILANDER; **d.** Old High German *bi* (> German *bei*), by, at: BIVOUAC. **2.** Germanic **umbi* in: **a.** Old English *ymbe,* around: EMBER DAY;

b. Old Norse *um(b),* about, around: OMBUDSMAN; **c.** Old High German *umbi,* around: UMLAUT. **3.** Latin *ambi-,* around, about: AMBI-. **4.** Greek *amphi,* around, about: AMPHI-. **5.** Celtic **ambi* (see **ag-**). [Pok. *ambhi* 34.]

ambhō. Both. **1.** Reduced form **bhō* in Germanic **bō-, *bā* in Old Norse *bāthir,* both: BOTH. **2.** Latin *ambō,* both: AMBSACE. **3.** Greek *amphō,* both: AMPHOTERIC. [In Pok. *ambhi* 34.]

āmer-. Day. Suffixed form **āmer-ā* in Greek *hēmera,* day: EPHEMERAL, HEMERALOPIA. [Pok. *āmer-* 35.]

ames-. Blackbird. **1.** Suffixed variant form **ams-ol-* in Old English *ōsle,* blackbird: OUZEL. **2.** Suffixed variant forms **mes-olā, *mes-olo-* in Latin *merula, merulus,* merle, blackbird: MERLE, MERLON. [Pok. *ames-* 35.]

[**amma.** Various nursery words. Latin root. **1.** Medieval Latin *amma,* mother: AMAH. **2.** Reduced form **am-* in: **a.** Latin *amāre,* to love: AMATEUR, AMATIVE, AMATORY, AMORETTO, AMOUR; ENAMOR, INAMORATA, PARAMOUR; **b.** Latin *amita,* aunt: AUNT; **c.** Latin *amīcus,* friend: AMICABLE, AMIGO, AMITY; ENEMY, INIMICAL.]

an¹. On. Extended form **ana.* **1.** Germanic **ana, anō* in: **a.** Old English *an, on, a,* on: ON; **b.** Old Norse *ā,* in, on: ALOFT; **c.** Old High German *ana* (> Middle High German *ane*), on: ANLAGE; **d.** Middle Dutch *aan,* on: ONSLAUGHT. **2.** Greek *ana,* on, up, at the rate of: ANA², ANA-. [Pok. 4. *an* 39.]

an². Demonstrative particle. Suffixed form **an-tero-,* "other (of two)" (compare **al-tero-* under **al-¹**) in Germanic **antharaz* in Old English *ōther,* other: OTHER. [Pok. 2. *an* 37.]

an-¹. Old woman, ancestor (nursery word). Latin *anus,* old woman: ANILE. [Pok. 1. *an-* 36.]

an-². To pour, draw water. Suffixed form **an-tlo-* in Greek *antlos,* bilge water, bucket: ANTLIA. [In Pok. 1. *sem-* 901.]

andh-. Bloom. Suffixed form **andh-es-* in Greek *anthos,* flower: ANTHEMION, ANTHER, ANTHESIS, ANTHO-, -ANTHOUS; AGAPANTHUS, CHRYSANTHEMUM, DIANTHUS, EXANTHEMA, HYDRANTH, (MONANTHOUS), STROPHANTHIN. [Pok. *andh-* 40.]

andho-. Blind, dark. Suffixed variant form **ondh-ro-* perhaps in Latin *umbra,* shadow: UMBEL, UMBRA, UMBRELLA; ADUMBRATE. [Pok. *andho-* 41.]

anə-. To breathe. Suffixed form **anə-mo-* in: **a.** Latin *animus,* reason, mind, and *anima,* soul, spirit, life, breath: ANIMA, ANIMADVERT, ANIMAL, ANIMATE, (ANIMATO), ANIMISM, ANIMOSITY, ANIMUS; EQUANIMITY, LONGANIMITY, MAGNANIMOUS, PUSILLANIMOUS, UNANIMOUS; **b.** Greek *anemos,* wind: ANEMO-. [Pok. 3. *an(ə)-* 38.]

anētā. Doorjamb. Latin *antae* (plural), a pair of pillars on the opposite sides of a door: ANTA. [Pok. *anətā-* 42.]

[**angelos.** Messenger. Greek noun, akin to Greek *angaros,* mounted courier, both from an unknown Oriental source. **1.** Greek *angelos,* messenger: ANGEL, (ANGELIC), ANGELICA, (ANGELUS); ARCHANGEL, EVANGEL. **2.** Greek *angaros,* mounted courier: ANGARY.]

angh-. Tight, painfully constricted, painful. **1.** Germanic **ang-,* compressed, hard, painful, in Old English *angnægl,* "painful spike (in the flesh)," corn, excrescence (*nægl,* spike; see **nogh-**): AGNAIL. **2.** Suffixed form **angh-os-* in Germanic **angaz* in Old Norse *angr,* sorrow, grief: ANGER. **3.** Suffixed form **angh-os-ti-* in Germanic **angusti-* in Old High German *angust* (> German *Angst*), anxiety: ANGST. **4.** Latin *angere,* to strangle, draw tight: ANXIOUS. **5.** Suffixed form **angh-os-to-* in Latin *angustus,* narrow: ANGUISH. **6.** Greek *ankhein,* to squeeze, embrace: QUINSY. **7.** Greek *ankhonē,* a strangling: ANGINA. [Pok. *angh-* 42.]

angʷhi-. Snake, eel. **1.** Latin *anguis,* snake: ANGUINE; ANGUILLIFORM. **2.** Taboo deformation or separate root **ogʷhi-* in Greek *ophis,* snake, serpent: OPHIDIAN, OPHITE; OPHIOLOGY, OPHIUCHUS. **3.** Taboo deformation or separate root **eghi-* in Greek *ekhis,* snake, in deriva-

tives: **a.** *ekhinos*, hedgehog (< "snake-eater"): ECHINO-, ECHINUS; **b.** *ekhidna*, snake, viper: ECHIDNA. [Pok. *angʷ(h)i-* 43.]

ank-. Also **ang-**. To bend. **I.** Germanic **ank-* in Old Norse **ankula* and Middle English *ancle*, ankle: ANKLE. **II.** Suffixed form **ank-ulo-*. **1.** Germanic **ang-ul-* in: **a.** Old English *angul*, *angel*, fishhook: ANGLE[1]; **b.** probably Latin *Anglī*, the Angles: ANGLE. **2.** Greek *ankulos*, crooked, bent: ANKYLOSIS; ANCYLOSTOMIASIS. **III.** Greek *ankura*, anchor: ANCHOR. **IV.** Greek *ankōn*, elbow: ANCON. **V.** Sanskrit *anka*, hook, *añcati*, he bends: PALANQUIN. **VI.** Suffixed variant form **onk-o-* in Latin *uncus*, hooked, bent: UNCINARIA, UNCINATE, UNCINUS; UNCUS; UNCIFORM. **VII.** Suffixed form **ang-olo-* in Latin *angulus*, angle, corner: ANGLE[2]. [Pok. 2. *ank-*, *ang-* 45.]

āno-. Ring. **1.** Latin *ānus*, ring, anus: ANUS; ANILINGUS. **2.** Latin diminutive *annulus*, ring, signet ring: ANNULAR, ANNULET, ANNULUS. [Pok. *āno-* 47.]

ans-. Loop, handle. Latin *ānsa*, handle: ANSATE. [Pok. *ansa* 48.]

ansu-. Spirit, demon. **1.** Germanic **ansu-* in Old Norse *āss*, god: AESIR. **2.** Suffixed reduced form **ṇsu-ro-* in Avestan *ahura*, spirit: AHURA MAZDA, ORMAZD. [Pok. *ansu-* 48.]

ant-. Front, forehead. **I.** Inflected form (locative singular) **anti*, "against," with derivatives meaning in front of, before; also end. **1.** Germanic **andi-* in Old English *and-*, indicating opposition: UN-[2]; ALONG. **2.** Germanic **andja-* in Old English *ende*, end: END. **3.** Latin *ante*, before, in front of, against: ANCIENT[1], ANTE, ANTE-, ANTERIOR; ADVANCE. **4.** Greek *anti*, against, in *enantios*, opposite: ANTI-; ENANTIOMER, ENANTIOMORPH. **5.** Compound form **anti-əkʷo-*, "appearing before, having prior aspect" (**əkʷ-*, appearance; see **okʷ-**), in Latin *antīquus*, former, antique: ANTIC, ANTIQUE. **6.** Reduced form **ṇti-* in Germanic **und-* in Old Norse *und* (> Middle English *un-*), until, unto: UNTIL. **7.** Variant form **anto-* in Sanskrit *antaḥ*, end, in *Vedantaḥ*, essence of the Veda: VEDANTA. **II.** Probable inflected form (locative plural) **antbhi*, "on both sides of," whence **ambhi*. See **ambhi**. [Pok. *ant-s* 48.]

ap-¹. To take, reach. **1.** Latin *apere*, to attach, join, tie to: APT, (APTITUDE), ATTITUDE; (INEPT). **2.** Latin *apīscī*, to attain: ADEPT. **3.** Latin *apex*, top, summit (< "something reached"): APEX. **4.** Prefixed form **co-ap-* (*co-*, together; see **kom**) in Latin *cōpula*, bond, tie, link: COPULA, COPULATE, COUPLE. **5.** Perhaps Latin *ammentum*, *āmentum* (< **ap-mentum*, "something tied"), thong, strap: AMENT[1]. [Pok. 1. *ap-* 50.]

ap-². Water, river. Iranian *ap-* in Persian *āb*, water: JULEP. [Pok. 2. *ap-* 51.]

āpero-. Shore. Perhaps a derivative of **ap-²**. Suffixed form **āper-yo-* in Greek *ēpeiros*, land, mainland, continent: EPEIROGENY. [Pok. *āpero-* 53.]

apo-. Also **ap-**. Off, away. **1.** Germanic **af* in: **a.** Old English *of*, *æf* (> Middle English *of*, *of-*), off: OF, OFF, OFFAL; **b.** Old English *ebba*, low tide: EBB; **c.** Old High German *aba*, off, away from: ABLAUT; **d.** Germanic **aftan-* in Old English *æftan*, behind: ABAFT. **2.** Latin *ab*, *ab-*, away from: AB-[1]. **3.** Greek *apo*, away from, from: APO-. **4.** Suffixed (comparative) form **ap(o)-tero-* in Germanic **after-* in Old English *æfter*, after, behind: AFTER. **5.** Suffixed form **ap-t-is-* in Germanic **aftiz* in Old English *eft*, again: EFTSOONS. **6.** Suffixed form **apu-ko-* in Germanic *afug-* in Old Norse *öfugr*, turned backward: AWKWARD. **7.** Possible root **po(s)*, on, in: **a.** Russian *po*, at, by, next to: POGROM; **b.** Latin *post*, behind, back, afterward: POST-, POSTERIOR; POSTMORTEM, PREPOSTEROUS, PUISNE, (PUNY); **c.** Latin *pōnere*, to put, place, from **po-sinere* (*sinere*, to leave, let; of obscure origin): APPOSITE, (APPOSITION), COMPONENT, (COMPOSE), (COMPOSITE), (COMPOSITION), (COMPOUND), DEPONE, DEPOSIT, DISPOSE, EXPOUND, IMPONE, IMPOSE, INTERPOSE, OPPOSE, POSITION, POSITIVE, POST², POST³,

POSTICHE, POSTURE, PREPOSITION, PROPOSE, PROVOST, REPOSIT, SUPPOSE. [Pok. *apo-* 53.]

apsā. Aspen. Germanic *aspōn-* in Old English *æspe*, aspen: ASPEN. [Pok. *apsā* 55.]

ar-. Also **arə-**. To fit together. **I.** Basic form **arə-*. **1.** Suffixed form **ar(ə)-mo-* in: **a.** Germanic *armaz* in Old English *earm*, arm: ARM[1]; **b.** Latin *arma*, tools, arms: ARM², ARMADA, ARMADILLO, ARMATURE, ARMOIRE, ARMY; ALARM, DISARM; **c.** Latin *armus*, upper arm: ARMILLARY SPHERE. **2.** Suffixed form **ar(ə)-smo-* in Greek *harmos*, joint, shoulder: HARMONY. **3.** Suffixed form **ar(ə)-ti-* in: **a.** Latin *ars* (stem *art-*), art, skill, craft: ART[1], ARTEL, ARTISAN, ARTIST; INERT, (INERTIA); **b.** further suffixed form **ar(ə)-ti-o-* in Greek *artios*, fitting, even: ARTIODACTYL. **4.** Suffixed form **ar(ə)-tu-* in Latin *artus*, joint: ARTICLE. **5.** Suffixed form **ar(ə)-to-* in Latin *artus*, tight: COARCTATE. **6.** Suffixed form **ar(ə)-dhro-* in Greek *arthron*, joint: ARTHRO-; ANARTHROUS, DIARTHROSIS, ENARTHROSIS, SYNARTHROSIS. **7.** Suffixed (superlative) form **ar(ə)-isto-* in Greek *aristos*, best: ARISTOCRACY. **II.** Possibly suffixed variant form (or separate root) **ōr-dh-*. **1.** Latin *ōrdō*, order (originally a row of threads in a loom): ORDAIN, ORDER, ORDINAL, ORDINANCE, ORDINARY, ORDINATE, ORDO; COORDINATION, INORDINATE, SUBORDINATE. **2.** Latin *ōrdīrī*, to begin to weave: EXORDIUM, PRIMORDIAL. **3.** Latin *ōrnāre*, to adorn: ORNAMENT, ORNATE; ADORN, SUBORN. **III.** Variant or separate root **rē-* (< **reə-*). **1.** Latin *rērī* (past participle *ratus*), to consider, confirm, ratify: RATE[1], RATIO, REASON; (ARRAIGN). **2.** Suffixed form *rē-dh-* in: **a.** Germanic **rēdan* in *(i)* Old English *rǣdan*, to advise: READ, REDE *(ii)* Old English *rǣden*, condition: HATRED, KINDRED; **b.** Germanic **rēdaz* in *(i)* Old High German *rāt* (> German *Rat*), counsel: BUNDESRAT, RATHSKELLER *(ii)* Old English *rǣdels(e)*, opinion, riddle: RIDDLE². **3.** Zero-grade form **rə-* in Germanic **radam*, number (see **dekm**). **IV.** Variant (or separate root) **rī-*. **1.** Suffixed form **rī-tu-* in Latin *rītus*, rite, custom, usage: RITE. **2.** Suffixed form **(a)rī-dhmo-* in Greek *arithmos*, number, amount: ARITHMETIC, LOGARITHM. [Pok. 1. *ar-* 55.]

arek-. To hold, contain, guard. Variant **ark-*. **1.** Latin *arca*, chest, box: ARCANE, ARK. **2.** Latin *arcēre*, to enclose, confine, contain, ward off: COERCE, EXERCISE. **3.** Greek *arkein*, to ward off, suffice: AUTARKY. [Pok. *areq-* 65.]

arə-. To plow. Latin *arāre*, to plow: ARABLE. [Pok. *ar(ə)-* 62.]

arg-. To shine; white; the shining or white metal, silver. **1.** Suffixed form **arg-ent-* in Latin *argentum*, silver: ARGENT, ARGENTINE. **2.** Suffixed form **arg-i-l(l)-* in Greek *argillos*, white clay: ARGIL. **3.** Suffixed form **argu-ro-* in Greek *arguros*, silver: LITHARGE, PYRARGYRITE. **4.** Suffixed form **arg-i-n-* in Greek *arginoeis*, brilliant, bright-shining: ARGININE. **5.** Extended form **argu-*, brilliance, clarity, in Latin denominative *arguere*, to make clear, demonstrate: ARGUE. **6.** Suffixed form **argro-* in Greek *argos* (< **argros*), white (see **pel-²**). [Pok. *ar(e)g-* 64.]

[arkhein. To begin, rule, command. Greek verb of unknown origin; with derivatives *arkhē*, rule, beginning, and *arkhos*, ruler. (ARCH-), -ARCH, ARCHAEO-, ARCHAIC, ARCHI-, ARCHIVES, ARCHON, (-ARCHY); AUTARCHY, EXARCH, MENARCHE.**]**

arku-. Bow and arrow (uncertain which, perhaps both as a unit). **1.** Germanic **arhwō* in Old English *ar(e)we*, *earh*, and Old Norse **arw-*, arrow: ARROW. **2.** Latin *arcus*, bow: ARC, ARCADE, ARCH[1], ARCHER; ARBALEST, ARCHIVOLT, (ARCIFORM), ARCUATE. [Pok. *arqu-* 67.]

aryo-. Lord, ruler: self-designation of the Indo-Iranians and perhaps of the Indo-Europeans. Lengthened-grade form **āryo-* in Sanskrit *ārya-*, noble, Aryan: ARYAN. [Pok. *ario-* 67.]

as-. To burn, glow. **1.** Extended form **asg-* in Germanic

*askōn- in Old English *æsce, asce,* ash: ASH[1]. **2.** Suffixed form **ās-ā-* in Latin *āra,* altar, hearth: ARA. **3.** Suffixed (stative) form **ās-ē-* in: **a.** Latin *ārēre,* to be dry, hence *āridus,* dry, parched: ARID; **b.** Latin *ardēre,* to burn, be on fire, from *āridus,* parched: ARDENT, ARDOR, ARSON. **4.** Extended form **asd-* in: **a.** Greek *azein,* to dry: ZAMIA; **b.** Greek *azaleos,* dry: AZALEA. [Pok. *as-* 68.]

[**asinus.** Ass. Latin noun, akin to Greek *onos,* probably ultimately from the same source as Sumerian *anše.* **1.** Latin *asinus,* ass: ASININE, EASEL. **2.** Greek *onos,* ass: ONAGER.]

at-. To go; with Germanic and Latin derivatives meaning a year (conceived as "the period gone through, the revolving year"). Suffixed form **at-no-* in Latin *annus,* year: ANNALS, ANNUAL, ANNUITY; ANNIVERSARY, BIENNIUM, DECENNIUM, MILLENNIUM, OCTENNIAL, PERENNIAL, QUADRENNIUM, QUINDECENNIAL, QUINQUENNIUM, SEPTENNIAL, SEXENNIAL, SUPERANNUATED, TRIENNIUM, VICENNIAL. [Pok. *at-* 69.]

āter-. Fire. **1.** Suffixed zero-grade form **ātr-o-* in Latin *āter* (feminine *ātra*), black (< "blackened by fire"): ATRABILIOUS. **2.** Suffixed zero-grade form **ātr-yo-* in Latin *ātrium,* forecourt, hall, atrium (perhaps originally the place where the smoke from the hearth escaped through a hole in the roof): ATRIUM. **3.** Compound shortened zero-grade form **atro-əkʷ-* (**əkʷ-,* "-looking"; see okʷ-) in Latin *ātrōx,* "black-looking," frightful: ATROCIOUS. [Pok. *āt(e)r-* 69.]

[**athal-.** Race, family. Germanic root, possibly related to Greek *atallein,* to foster. **1.** Germanic **athal-* in Old English *ætheling,* prince: ATHELING. **2.** Variant Germanic **ōthel-* in Old High German *edili,* noble: EDELWEISS. [In Pok. *atos* 71.]]

atto-. Father (nursery word). Possibly Latin *atta,* father: ATAVISM. [In Pok. *atos* 71.]

au-¹. To stay the night, dwell. Suffixed form **au-lā-* in Greek *aulē,* court, dwelling: AULIC. [Pok. 2. *au-* 72.]

au-². Pronominal base appearing in particles and adverbs. Suffixed form **au-ge* in Germanic **auke* in Old English *ēac, ēc,* also: EKE². [Pok. 4. *au-* 73.]

au-³. Off, away. **1.** Old Russian *u-,* away, in Russian *ukazat',* to order: UKASE. **2.** Sanskrit *ava,* off, down: AVATAR. [Pok. 3. *au-* 72.]

au-⁴. To weave. Extended form **wedh-* (< **əwedh-*). **1.** Germanic **wēdiz* in Old English *wǣd, wǣde,* garment, cloth: WEED². **2.** Germanic **wadlaz* in Old English *watel, watul,* wattle: WATTLE. [Pok. 5. *aų-* 75.]

au-⁵. To perceive. Compound forms **aw-dh-, *awis-dh-,* "to place perception" (see dhē-¹). **1.** Suffixed form **awisdh-yo-* or **awdh-yo-* in Latin *audīre,* to hear: AUDIBLE, AUDIENCE, AUDIENT, AUDILE, AUDING, AUDIO-, AUDIT, AUDITOR, AUDITORIUM, AUDITORY, OYEZ; OBEY, SUBAUDITION. **2.** Greek *aisthanesthai,* to feel: AESTHETIC; ANESTHESIA. [Pok. 8. *aų-* 78.]

aug-¹. To increase. Variant **(a)weg-* (< **əweg-*). **1.** Germanic **aukan* in: **a.** Old English *ēacan, ēcan,* to increase: EKE¹; **b.** Old English *ēaca,* an addition: NICKNAME. **2.** Variant extended forms **wogs-, *wegs-* in Germanic **wahsan* in Old English *weaxan,* to grow: WAX². **3.** Form **aug-ē-* in: Latin *augēre,* to increase: AUCTION, AUGEND, AUGMENT, AUTHOR, (AUTHORIZE), (OCTROI). **4.** Latin *augur,* diviner (< "he who obtains favorable presage" < "divine favor, increase"): AUGUR; INAUGURATE. **5.** Latin *augustus,* majestic, august: AUGUST. **6.** Suffixed form **aug-s-* in: **a.** Latin *auxilium,* aid, support, assistance: AUXILIARY; **b.** Greek *auxein,* to increase: AUXIN; **c.** Greek *auxanein,* to increase: AUXESIS. [Pok. *aųeg-* 84.]

aug-². To shine. Suffixed form **aug-ā-* in Greek *augē,* light, ray: AUGITE. [Pok. *aug-* 87.]

aukʷ-. Cooking pot. **1.** Germanic suffixed form **uhw-na-* in **ufna-* in Old English *ofen,* furnace, oven: OVEN. **2.** Suffixed form **aukʷ-slā-* in Latin *aulla, aula,* pot, jar: OLLA. [Pok. *auqʷ(h)-* 88.]

aulo-. Hole, cavity. **1.** Metathetic form **alwo-* in Latin *alvus,* the belly, stomach: ALVEOLUS. **2.** Greek *aulos,* pipe, flute, hollow tube: CAROL, HYDRAULIC. [Pok. *aulo-s* 88.]

[**aurum.** Gold. Latin noun with preform **aus-o-* probably from a root **aus-.* Latin *aurum* (> French *or*), gold: AUREATE, AUREOLE, AURIC; AURIFEROUS, DORY², EYRIR, OR³, ÖRE, ORIFLAMME, ORIOLE, ORMOLU, OROIDE, ORPHREY, ORPIMENT.]

aus-¹. To shine. **1.** Germanic **aust-* in: **a.** Old English *ēast,* east (< "the direction of the sunrise"): EAST; **b.** Old High German *ōstan,* east: OSTMARK. **2.** Germanic **austra-* in: **a.** Old English *ēasterne,* eastern: EASTERN; **b.** Late Latin *ostro-,* eastern: OSTROGOTH. **3.** Germanic **austrōn-,* a dawn-goddess whose holiday was celebrated at the vernal equinox, in Old English *ēastre,* Easter: EASTER. **4.** Probably suffixed form **ausōs-,* dawn, also Indo-European goddess of the dawn, in: **a.** Latin *aurōra,* dawn: AURORA; **b.** Greek *ēōs,* dawn: EO-, EOS; EOSIN. [Pok. *aųes-* 86.]

aus-². To draw water. Suffixed form **aus-yo-* in Latin *haurīre,* to draw up: EXHAUST, HAUSTELLUM, HAUSTORIUM. [Pok. *aus-* 90.]

awi-. Bird. **I. 1.** Latin *avis,* bird: AVIAN, AVIARY, AVIATION; AVICULTURE, AVIFAUNA, BUSTARD, OCARINA, OSPREY, OSTRICH. **2.** Compound **awi-spek-,* "observer of birds" (**spek-,* to see; see spek-), in Latin *auspex,* augur: AUSPICE. **II.** Possible derivatives are the Indo-European words for egg, **ōwyo-, *əyo-.* **1.** Germanic **ajja(m)* in: **a.** Old English *æg,* egg: COCKNEY; **b.** Old Norse *egg,* egg: EGG¹. **2.** Latin *ōvum,* egg: OVAL, OVARY, OVATE, OVI-, OVOLO, OVULE, OVUM. **3.** Greek *ōion,* egg: OO-. [Pok. *aųei-* 86.]

awo-. An adult male relative other than one's father. **1.** Latin *avus,* grandfather: ATAVISM. **2.** Latin *avunculus,* maternal uncle: AVUNCULAR, UNCLE. **3.** Latin *avia,* grandmother: AYAH. [Pok. *aųo-s* 89.]

ayer-. Day, morning. **1.** Germanic **airiz* in: **a.** Old English *ǣr,* before: EARLY, ERE; **b.** Old Norse *ār,* before: OR². **2.** Germanic (superlative) **airistaz* in Old English *ǣrest,* earliest: ERST. [Pok. *aįer-* 12.]

ayes-. A metal, copper or bronze. Latin *aes,* bronze, money: AENEOUS, ERA. [Pok. *aįos-* 15.]

baba-. Root imitative of unarticulated or indistinct speech; also a child's nursery word for a baby and for various relatives. **1.** Middle English *babelen,* to babble: BABBLE. **2.** Middle English *babe, babi,* baby: BABE, BABY. **3.** Italian *bambo,* child, simpleton: BAMBINO. **4.** Polish *baba* (diminutive *babka*), old woman: BABA, BABKA. **5.** Russian *baba,* old woman: BABUSHKA. **6.** Russian *balalaika,* balalaika (imitative of the sound): BALALAIKA. **7.** Latin *balbus,* stuttering, stammering: BOOBY. **8.** Greek *barbaros,* non-Greek, foreign, rude (< "one who speaks incomprehensibly"): (BARBARIAN), BARBARISM, BARBAROUS. **9.** Hindi *bābū,* father: BABU. [Pok. *baba-* 91.]

badyo-. Yellow, brown. A Western Indo-European word. Latin *badius,* chestnut brown (used only of horses): BAY³. [Pok. *badįos* 92.]

bak-. Staff used for support. **1.** Probably Middle Dutch *pegge* (> Middle English *pegge*), pin, peg: PEG. **2.** Latin *baculum,* rod, walking stick: BACILLUS, BAGUETTE; BACULIFORM, DEBACLE, IMBECILE. **3.** Greek *baktron,* staff: BACTERIUM; (CORYNEBACTERIUM). [Pok. *bak-* 93.]

bamb-. Word imitative of dull or rumbling sounds. Greek *bombos,* a booming, humming: BOMB, (BOMBARD), BOUND¹. [Pok. *baˣmb-* 93.]

band-. A drop. Possibly Irish *bainne,* milk: BONNYCLABBER. [Pok. *band-* 95.]

[**bassus.** Low. Late Latin adjective (> Medieval Latin *bassus,* Old French *bas,* and Middle English *bas*), possibly from Oscan: BASE², BASS², BASSET¹, BASSO; ABASE, BAS-RELIEF, (DEBASE).]

[**bat-.** Yawning. Latin root of unknown origin; probably imitative. **1.** Latin **batāre* (> Old French *ba(y)er*), to

yawn, gape: BAY², BEVEL; ABASH, ABEYANCE. **2.** Possibly Vulgar Latin *abbaiāre (> Old French (a)baiier), to bay: BAY⁴.]

[**battuere.** To beat. Latin verb of unknown origin. (BATE²), BATTER¹, (BATTER³), (BATTERY), BATTLE; ABATE, COMBAT, DEBATE, (RABBET), (REBATE¹), (REBATO).]

bel-. Strong. **1.** Suffixed o-grade form *bol-iyo- in Russian bol'shoi, large: BOLSHEVIK. **2.** Prefixed form *dē-bel-i- (dē-, privative prefix; see **de-**), "without strength," in Latin dēbilis, weak: DEBILITATE, DEBILITY. [Pok. 2. bel- 96.]

bend-. Protruding point. **1.** Germanic *pannja-, "structure of stakes," in Old English penn, pen for cattle: PEN². **2.** Germanic *pund- possibly in Old English pund- (> Middle English pound), pundfald, enclosure for stray animals: POND, POUND³; IMPOUND, PINFOLD. **3.** Germanic *pin- in Old English pintel, penis: PINTLE. [Pok. bend- 96.]

beu-¹. Also **bheu-**. Appears in words loosely associated with the notion "to swell." **I.** Root form *beu-. **1.** Germanic *puk- in: **a.** Old English pocc, pustule: POCK; **b.** Old French po(u)che and Old North French poke, bag: POACH¹, POCKET, POKE³, POUCH, (PUCKER). **2.** Old English pyffan, to blow out: PUFF. **3.** Old English -pūte, "fish with large head" (in aele-pūte, eelpout): POUT². **II.** Root form *bheu- with various Germanic derivatives. **1.** Old English bōsm, bosom: BOSOM. **2.** Old English būc, belly, pitcher: BUCKBOARD. **3.** Frankish *būk (> Old French buc), trunk of the body: TREBUCHET. **4.** Old English bȳl(e), pustule: BOIL². **5.** German dialectal baustern, to swell, akin to the source of Middle English bost, a bragging: BOAST¹. **III.** Root form *beu-. **1.** Latin bulla, bubble, round object, amulet (> Old French boule and Spanish bola, ball): BILL¹, BILLET¹, BOLA, BOULE², BOWL², (BULL²), BULLA, BULLATE, BULLET, (BULLETIN); BOULEVERSEMENT. **2.** Latin bullīre (> French bouiller), to bubble, boil: BOIL¹, BOUILLON, BUDGE¹, (BULLION), BULLY²; BOUILLABAISSE, EBULLIENCE, GARBOIL, PARBOIL. **3.** Possibly Latin bucca (> Old French bouche, buckle, curl, and Spanish boca, mouth), (inflated) cheek: BOCACCIO, BOUCLE, BUCCAL, BUCKLE¹, BUCKLE²; DEBOUCH, DISEMBOGUE, EMBOUCHURE. **4.** Greek boubōn, groin, swollen gland: BUBO. [Pok. 2. beu- 98.]

beu-². Root imitative of muffled sounds. **1.** Latin būtiō (perhaps > Old French butor), bittern: BITTERN¹. **2.** Latin būteō, a kind of hawk: BUZZARD. [Pok. 1. b(e)u- 97.]

bhā-¹. To shine. Contracted from *bhaə-. **1.** Germanic *baukna-, beacon, signal, in: **a.** Old English bēac(e)n, beacon: BEACON; **b.** Old English denominative bēcnan, bīecnan, to make a sign, beckon: BECKON. **2.** Perhaps Germanic *bazja-, berry (< "bright-colored fruit"), in Old English berie, berige, berry: BERRY. **3.** Germanic *bandwa-, "identifying sign," banner, standard, sash, also "company united under a (particular) banner," in: **a.** Spanish banda, sash: BANDOLEER; **b.** Late Latin bandum, banner, standard: BANNER, (BANNERET). **4.** Suffixed form *bhaw-es- in Greek phōs (stem phōt-), light: PHOS-, PHOT, PHOTO-; PHOSPHORUS. **5.** Extended and suffixed form *bhan-yo- in Greek phainein, "to bring to light," cause to appear, show, and phainesthai (passive), "to be brought to light," appear: FANTASY, (PANT), PHANTASM, (PHANTOM), PHASE, PHENO-, PHENOMENON; DIAPHANOUS, EMPHASIS, EPIPHANY, HIEROPHANT, PHANEROGAM, (PHANTASMAGORIA), PHOSPHENE, SYCOPHANT, THEOPHANY, (TIFFANY). [Pok. 1. bhā- 104.]

bhā-². To speak. Contracted from *bhaə-. **1.** Latin fārī, to speak: FATE; AFFABLE, (FANTOCCINI), INEFFABLE, INFANT, (INFANTRY), PREFACE. **2.** Greek phanai, to speak: -PHASIA; PROPHET. **3.** Suffixed form in Germanic *banwan, *bannan, to speak publicly (used of particular kinds of proclamation in feudal or prefeudal custom; "to proclaim under penalty, summon to the levy, declare

outlaw"), in: **a.** Old English bannan, to summon, proclaim, and Old Norse banna, to prohibit, curse: BAN¹; **b.** Old French ban, feudal jurisdiction, summons to military service, proclamation, Old French bandon, power, and Old English gebann, proclamation: BANAL, BANNS; ABANDON; **c.** Old French banir, to banish: BANISH; **d.** Late Latin bannus, bannum, proclamation: CONTRABAND; **e.** Italian bandire, to muster, band together (< "to have been summoned"): BANDIT. **4.** Suffixed form *bhā-ni in Germanic *bōni- in Old Norse bōn, prayer, request: BOON¹. **5.** Suffixed form *bhā-ma in: **a.** Latin fāma, talk, reputation, fame: FAME, FAMOUS; DEFAME, INFAMOUS; **b.** Greek phēmē, saying, speech: EUPHEMISM. **6.** Suffixed o-grade form *bhō-nā in Greek phōnē, voice, sound, and phōnein, to speak: PHONE¹, -PHONE, PHONEME, PHONETIC, PHONO-, -PHONY; ANTHEM, (ANTIPHON), APHONIA, CACOPHONOUS, EUPHONY, SYMPHONY. **7.** Suffixed zero-grade form *bhə-to- in Latin fatērī, to acknowledge, admit: CONFESS, PROFESS. **8.** Greek blasphēmos, evil-speaking, blasphemous (first element obscure): (BLAME), (BLASPHEME), BLASPHEMOUS. [Pok. 2. bhā- 105.]

bha-bhā-. Broad bean. **1.** Latin faba, broad bean: FAVA BEAN. **2.** Variant form *bha-un- in Germanic *baunō in Old English bēan, broad bean, bean of any kind: BEAN. [Pok. bhabhā 106.]

bhad-. Good. **1.** Germanic (comparative) *batizō in Old English betera, better: BETTER. **2.** Germanic (superlative) *batistaz in Old English bet(e)st, best: BEST. **3.** Germanic noun *bōtō in Old English bōt, remedy, aid: BOOT². **4.** Germanic verb *batnan, to become better, in Old Norse batna, to improve: BATTEN¹. [Pok. bhād- 106.]

bhag-¹. To share out, apportion, also to get a share. **1.** Greek phagein, to eat (< "to have a share of food"): -PHAGE, -PHAGIA, PHAGO-, -PHAGOUS. **2.** Extended form *bhags- in Avestan bakhsh- in Persian bakhshīdan, to give: BAKSHEESH, (BUCKSHEE). [Pok. 1. bhag- 107.]

bhag-². Sharp. Suffixed form *bhag-ro- in Greek phagros, whetstone, also a name for the sea bream: PORGY. [Pok. 2. bhag- 107.]

bhāghu-. Arm. Germanic *bōguz in Old English bōg, bōh, bough: BOUGH. [Pok. bhāghú-s 108.]

bhāgo-. Beech tree. **1.** Germanic *bōkō, beech, also "beech staff for carving runes on" (an early Germanic graphic device), in: **a.** Old English bōc, written document, composition: BOOK; **b.** Middle Dutch boek, beech: BUCKWHEAT. **2.** Germanic *bōkjōn- in Old English bēce, beech: BEECH. [Pok. bhāgo-s 107.]

bhar-. Also **bhor-**. Projection, bristle, point. **1.** Suffixed o-grade form *bhor-so- in Germanic *barsaz in Old English bærs, perch, bass (a fish that has a spiny dorsal fin): BASS¹. **2.** Suffixed zero-grade form *bhr̥-sti- in Germanic *bursti- in Old English byrst (> Middle English bristel), bristle: BRISTLE. **3.** Extended zero-grade form *bhr̥s- in: **a.** Germanic *bur- in Swedish borre, bur, perhaps akin to the Scandinavian source of Middle English burre, bur: BUR¹; **b.** suffixed form *bhr̥s-dh- in Germanic *bruzd-, point, needle, in Old Norse broddr, spike: BRAD; **c.** suffixed form *bhr̥s-ti- in Latin fastīgium, summit, top, extremity: FASTIGIATE, FASTIGIUM; **d.** possibly suffixed form *bhr̥s-tu- in Latin fastus, fastidium, disdain (from the notion of prickliness): FASTIDIOUS; **e.** suffixed form *bhr̥s-tio- in Russian borshch, cow parsley: BORSCHT. [Pok. bhar- 108.]

bhardhā. Beard. Possibly related to **bhar-**. **1.** Germanic *bardaz in Old English beard, beard: BEARD. **2.** Germanic *bardō, beard, also hatchet, broadax (the association of beard and ax is attested elsewhere in the Indo-European family; both were symbols of patriarchal authority), in Old High German barta, beard, ax: HALBERD. **3.** Latin barba, beard: BARB¹, BARBEL, BARBELLATE, BARBER, BARBETTE, BARBICEL, BARBULE; REBARBATIVE. [Pok. bhardhā 110.]

bhares-. Also **bhars-**. Barley. **1.** Germanic *barz- in Old

English *bere, bære, bærlic,* barley: BARLEY; BARN.
2. Latin *far* (stem *farr-*), spelt, grain: FARINA, (FARINA-
CEOUS), FARRAGINOUS, FARRAGO. [Pok. *bhares-* 111.]
bhasko-. Band, bundle. **1.** Latin *fascis,* bundle (as of
rods, twigs, or straw), also crowd of people: FASCES,
FASCICLE, FASCINE, FASCISM. **2.** Latin *fascia,* band, fillet,
bandage: FASCIA, FESS. **3.** Probably Latin *fascinum,
fascinus,* an amulet in the shape of a phallus, hence a
bewitching: FASCINATE. [Pok. *bhasko-* 111.]
bhau-. To strike. **1.** Germanic **bautan* in: **a.** Old English
bēatan, to beat: BEAT; **b.** German *bosseln,* to do odd
jobs: BUSHEL². **2.** Germanic **bautilaz,* hammer, in Old
English *bīetel,* hammer, mallet: BEETLE³. **3.** Germanic
*būtaz in Old English diminutive *buttuc,* end, strip of
land: BUTTOCK. **4.** Germanic **butt-,* name for a flatfish,
in Middle Dutch *butte,* flatfish: HALIBUT. **5.** Germanic
*buttan in Old French *bo(u)ter,* to strike, push (> French
bouton, button): BOUTON, BUTT¹, BUTTON, BUTTRESS;
ABUT, REBUT, SACKBUT. **6.** Variant form **bhūt-* in:
a. Latin *confūtāre,* to check, suppress, restrain (*com-,*
intensive prefix; see **kom**): CONFUTE; **b.** Latin *refūtāre,*
to drive back, rebut (*re-,* back; see **re-**): REFUTE. [Pok. 1.
bhau- 112.]
bhē-. To warm. Contracted from **bheə.* **1.** Suffixed
zero-grade form **bhə-to-* in Germanic **batham* in Old
English *bæth,* a bath, and its denominative *bathian,* to
bathe: BATH¹, BATHE. **2.** Suffixed zero-grade form
*bhə-g- in: **a.** Germanic **bakan* in Old English *bacan,* to
bake: BAKE; **b.** Germanic **bakkan* in German *backen,* to
bake: ZWIEBACK. [Pok. *bhē-* 113.]
bhedh-. To dig. **1.** Germanic **badjam,* garden plot, also
sleeping place, in Old English *bed(d),* bed: BED.
2. O-grade form **bhodh-* in: **a.** Latin *fodere,* to dig:
FOSSA, (FOSSE), FOSSIL, FOSSORIAL; **b.** perhaps Greek
bothros, pit: BOTHRIUM. [Pok. 1. *bhedh-* 113.]
bheg-. To break. Akin to **bhreg-.** Possibly in various
Germanic forms. **1.** Germanic nasalized form **bang-* in:
a. Old Norse *banga,* a hammering, akin to the probable
Scandinavian source of English BANG¹; **b.** Swedish dialectal *bangla,* to work inefficiently, akin to the possible
Scandinavian source of English BUNGLE. **2.** Possibly
Germanic nasalized forms **bankiz* and **bankōn-,* bank of
earth (possibly < "feature where the contour of the
ground is broken," escarpment, riverbank, possibly also
associated with "manmade earthwork"), later also bench,
table, in: **a.** Old English *benc,* bench: BENCH; **b.** Old
Danish *banke,* sandbank, akin to the Scandinavian
source of English BANK¹; **c.** Old High German *banc,* bank,
bench, moneychanger's table (> Italian *banca*): BANK²,
BANT-
LING, BUNCO; BANKRUPT; **d.** Old French *banc,* bench:
BANK³, BANQUET; **e.** Provençal *banca,* bench: BAN-
QUETTE. [Pok. *bheg-* 115.]
bhegʷ-. To run away. **1.** Germanic **bakjaz,* a stream, in
Old Norse *bekkr,* a stream: BECK². **2.** Greek *phebesthai,*
to flee in terror, forming *phobos,* panic, flight, fear:
-PHOBE, -PHOBIA. [Pok. *bhegʷ-* 116.]
bhei-¹. A bee. Germanic suffixed form **bīōn-* in Old
English *bēo,* a bee: BEE¹. [Pok. *bhei-* 116.]
bhei-². To strike. **1.** Germanic suffixed form **bili-* in Old
English *bile,* bird's beak: BILL². **2.** Germanic suffixed
form **bilja-* in Old English *bil(l),* sharp weapon: BILL³.
[Pok. *bhei(ə)-* 117.]
bheid-. To split; with Germanic derivatives referring to
biting (hence also to eating and to hunting) and wood-
working. **1.** Germanic **bītan* in Old English **bītan,* to
bite: BEETLE¹, BITE. **2.** Zero-grade form **bhid-* in: **a.** Germanic **bitiz* in Old English *bite,* a bite, sting: BIT²;
b. Germanic **bitōn-* in Old English *bita,* a piece bitten
off, morsel: BIT¹; **c.** Suffixed form **bhid-ro-* in Old
English *bit(t)er,* "biting," sharp, bitter: BITTER.
3. O-grade form **bhoid-* in Germanic **baitjan* in: **a.** Old
Norse *beita* (verb), to hunt with dogs, and *beita* (noun),
pasture, food: BAIT¹; **b.** Old French *beter,* to harass with
dogs: ABET. **4.** Germanic **bait-,* a boat (< "dugout

canoe" or "split planking"), in Old English *bāt,* boat, and
Old Norse *bātr,* boat: BATEAU, BOAT; (BOATSWAIN).
5. Nasalized zero-grade form **bhi-n-d-* in Latin *findere*
(past participle *fissus*), to split: -FID, FISSI-, (FISSILE),
FISSION, (FISSURE). [Pok. *bheid-* 116.]
bheidh-. To persuade, compel, confide. **1.** Probably Germanic **bīdan,* to await (< "to await trustingly, expect,
trust"), in Old English *bīdan,* to wait, stay: BIDE; ABIDE,
(ABODE). **2.** Latin *fīdere,* to trust, confide, and *fīdus,*
faithful: FIANCÉ, FIDUCIAL, (FIDUCIARY); AFFIANCE,
(AFFIANT), (AFFIDAVIT), (CONFIDANT), CONFIDE, (CONFI-
DENT), (DEFIANCE), DEFY, DIFFIDENT. **3.** Suffixed
o-grade form **bhoidh-es-* in Latin *foedus* (stem *foeder-*),
treaty, league: FEDERAL, FEDERATE, CONFEDERATE.
4. Zero-grade form **bhidh-* in Latin *fidēs,* faith, trust:
FAITH, FEALTY, FIDELITY; INFIDEL, PERFIDY. [Pok.
bheidh- 117.]
bheigʷ-. To shine. An uncertain but plausible root. Greek
phoibos, shining: PHOEBE, PHOEBUS. [Pok. *bheigʷ-* 118.]
bhel-¹. To shine, flash, burn; shining white and various
bright colors. **I. 1.** Russian *byelii,* white: BELUGA.
2. Greek *phalaros,* having a white spot (> *phalaris,*
coot): PHALAROPE. **II. 1.** Suffixed variant form
*bhlē-wo- in Germanic **blēwaz,* blue, in Old French *bleu:*
BLUE. **2.** Suffixed zero-grade form **bhlə-wo-* in Latin
flāvus, golden or reddish yellow: FLAVESCENT, FLAVO-;
(FLAVIN), (FLAVONE), (FLAVOPROTEIN). **III.** Various extended Germanic forms. **1.** **blaikjan,* to make white, in
Old English *blǣcan,* to bleach: BLEACH. **2.** **blaikaz,*
shining, white, in: **a.** Old Norse *bleikr,* shining, white:
BLEAK¹; **b.** Old English *blǣc,* bright: BLEAK². **3.** Germanic **blikkatjan* in Old High German *blecchazzen,* to
flash, lighten (> German *Blitz,* lightning): BLITZKRIEG.
4. **blas-,* shining, white, in: **a.** Old English *blǣse,* torch,
bright fire: BLAZE¹; **b.** Middle Dutch *bles,* white spot:
BLESBOK; **c.** Old French *ble(s)mir,* to make pale: BLEM-
ISH. **5.** **blend-,* **bland-,* to shine, dazzle, blind, confuse,
in: **a.** Old English *blind,* blind: BLIND; (BLINDFOLD),
(PURBLIND); **b.** Old High German *blentan,* to blind,
deceive: BLENDE; **c.** Old English *blandan,* to mingle:
BLEND; **d.** Old French *blond,* blond: BLOND. **6.** **blenk-,*
*blank-, to shine, dazzle, blind, in: **a.** Old English *blen-
can,* to deceive: BLENCH¹; **b.** Old French *blanc,* white:
BLANCH, BLANK, BLANKET, BLANCMANGE. **7.** **blisk-,* to
shine, burn, in Old English *blyscan,* to glow red: BLUSH.
IV. Extended form **bhleg-,* to shine, flash, burn. **1.** Ger-
manic **blakaz,* burned, in Old English *blǣc,* black:
BLACK. **2.** Zero-grade form **bhlg-* in: **a.** Latin *fulgēre,* to
flash, shine: FULGENT, FULGURATE; EFFULGENT, FOU-
DROYANT, REFULGENT; **b.** Latin *fulmen* (< **fulg-men*),
lightning, thunderbolt: FULMINATE. **3. a.** Latin *flagrāre,*
to blaze: FLAGRANT, CONFLAGRANT, CONFLAGRATION,
DEFLAGRATE; **b.** Latin *flamma* (< **flag-ma*), a flame:
FLAMBÉ, FLAMBEAU, FLAMBOYANT, FLAME, FLAMINGO,
FLAMMABLE; INFLAME. **4.** Greek *phlegein,* to burn:
PHLEGM, PHLEGMATIC, PHLEGMON. **5.** Greek *phlox,* a
flame, also a wallflower: PHLOGISTON, PHLOX, PHLOGO-
PITE. [Pok. 1. *bhel-* 118, *bheleg-* 124, *bhleu-(k)-* 159.]
bhel-². To blow, swell; with derivatives referring to
various round objects and to the notion of tumescent
masculinity. **1.** Zero-grade form **bhl-* in Germanic **bul-*
in: **a.** Old English *bolla* (> Middle English *boll*), pot,
bowl: BOLL, BOWL¹; **b.** Old Norse *bolr,* tree trunk: BOLE¹;
c. Old Norse *bulki,* cargo (< "rolled-up load"): BULK¹;
d. Old High German *bolla,* ball: ROCAMBOLE; **e.** Middle
High German *bole,* beam, plank: (BOULEVARD), BUL-
WARK; **f.** Middle Dutch *bolle,* round object: BOLL;
g. Middle Dutch *bille,* buttock: BILTONG; **h.** Swedish
*buller-, "round object," in *bullersten,* "rounded stone,"
boulder, akin to the Scandinavian source of English
BOULDER; **i.** possibly obsolete Swedish *bulde,* a swelling
(see **wer-¹**). **2.** Suffixed zero-grade form **bhl-n-* in:
a. Germanic **bullōn-,* bull, in Old Norse *boli,* bull: BULL¹;
b. Greek *phallos,* phallus: PHALLUS; ITHYPHALLIC.

3. O-grade form *bhol-* in Germanic *ball-* in: **a.** Old English *beallucas,* testicles: BOLLIX; **b.** Old Norse *böllr,* ball: BALL¹; **c.** Danish *bolle,* round roll, akin to the probable Scandinavian source of BILBERRY; **d.** Middle High German *balle* (> Italian *balla, palla*), ball: BALLOON, BALLOT; **e.** French *balle,* ball: BALLOTTEMENT; **f.** Old French *bale,* rolled-up bundle: BALE¹. **4.** Suffixed o-grade form *bhol-to-* possibly in Germanic *balthaz,* bold, in: **a.** Old English *bald, beald,* bold: BOLD; **b.** Old High German *bald,* bold: BAWD. **5.** Suffixed o-grade form *bhol-n-* in Latin *follis,* bellows, inflated ball: FOLLICLE, FOOL¹; (FOLLICULITIS). **6.** Possibly Greek *phal(l)aina,* whale: BALEEN. **7.** Conceivably (but more likely unrelated) Greek *phellos,* cork, cork oak: PHELLEM; PHELLODERM, PHELLOGEN. (The following derivatives of this root are entered separately: **bhel-³, bhelgh-, bhlei-, bhleu-**.) [Pok. 3. *bhel-* 120.]

bhel-³. To thrive, bloom. Possibly from **bhel-²**. **I.** Suffixed o-grade form *bhol-yo-,* leaf. **1.** Latin *folium,* leaf: FOIL², FOLIAGE, FOLIO, FOLIUM; CINQUEFOIL, DEFOLIATE, EXFOLIATE, FEUILLETON, FOLICOLOUS, MILFOIL, PORTFOLIO, TREFOIL. **2.** Greek *phullon,* leaf: (-PHYLL), PHYLLO-, -PHYLLOUS; GILLYFLOWER, PODOPHYLLIN. **II.** Extended form *bhlē-* (< *bhleə-*). **1.** O-grade form *bhlō-* in: **a.** suffixed form *bhlō-w-* in Germanic *blō-w-* in Old English *blōwan,* to flower: BLOW³; **b.** Germanic suffixed form *blō-mōn-* in *(i)* Old Norse *blōm, blōmi,* flower, blossom: BLOOM¹ *(ii)* Old English *blōma,* a hammered ingot of iron (semantic development obscure): BLOOM²; **c.** Germanic suffixed form *blō-s-* in Old English *blōstm, blōstma,* flower, blossom: BLOSSOM; **d.** Latin *flōs* (stem *flōr-*), flower: FERRET², (FLORA), FLORA, (FLORAL), FLORIATED, FLORID, FLORIN, FLORIST, -FLOROUS, FLOSCULUS, FLOUR, FLOURISH, FLOWER; CAULIFLOWER, DEFLOWER, EFFLORESCE, ENFLEURAGE, FLORIGEN. **2.** Germanic suffixed form *blē-do-* in Medieval Latin *bladium,* produce of the land: EMBLEMENTS. **3.** Suffixed zero-grade form *bhlə-to-* in Germanic *bladaz* in Old English *blæd,* leaf, blade: BLADE. [Pok. 4. *bhel-* 122.]

bhel-⁴. To cry out, yell. Germanic *bell-* in: **a.** Old English *bellan,* to bellow, bark, roar: BELL²; **b.** Old English *belle,* a bell: BELL¹; **c.** Old English *belgan, bylgan,* to become enraged: BELLOW; **d.** perhaps Old English *bealcan, *b(i)elcan,* to utter, belch forth: BELCH; **e.** Middle High German *buldern, boldern,* to make noise: POLTERGEIST; **f.** Icelandic *baula,* to low, akin to the Scandinavian source of Middle English *baulen,* to howl: BAWL. [Pok. 6. *bhel-* 123.]

bheld-. To knock, strike. Zero-grade form *bhḷd-* in Germanic *bult-,* missile, in Old English *bolt,* heavy arrow, bolt: BOLT¹. [Pok. *bheld-* 124.]

bhelg-. Also **bhelk-.** A plank, beam. **1.** Germanic *balku-* in Old English *balc(a),* ridge: BALK. **2.** Germanic *balkōn-* in: **a.** Old French *bauch,* beam: DEBAUCH; **b.** Old Italian *balcone,* scaffold: BALCONY. **3.** Suffixed zero-grade form *bhḷk-yo-* in Latin *fulcīre,* to prop up, support: FULCRUM. **4.** Possibly Greek *phalanx,* beam, finger bone, line of battle: PHALANGE, PHALANX. [Pok. 5. *bhel-* 123.]

bhelgh-. To swell. Extension of **bhel-²**. **1.** Germanic *balgiz* in Old English *bel(i)g, bælig,* purse, bellows: BELLOWS, BELLY. **2.** Germanic *bulgjan* in Old Norse *bylgja,* a wave: BILLOW. **3.** Germanic *bolgstraz* in Old English *bolster,* cushion: BOLSTER. **4.** Celtic *bolg-* in Latin *bulga,* leather sack: BUDGET, BULGE. [Pok. *bhelgh-* 125.]

bhelu-. To harm. Germanic *balwaz* in Old English *bealo, b(e)alu,* harm, ruin, bale: BALE². [Pok. *bheleu-* 125.]

bhendh-. To bind. **1.** Germanic *bindan,* to bind: BIND; WOODBINE. **2.** O-grade form *bhondh-* in Germanic *band-* in: **a.** Old English *bend,* band, ribbon, akin to the Germanic source of Old French *bende,* band: BEND²; **b.** Old English *bendan,* to bend: BEND¹; **c.** Old Norse *band,* band, fetter: BAND¹, BOND; **d.** Old French *bande,* bond, tie, link: BAND¹. **3.** Zero-

grade form *bhṇdh-* in Germanic *bund-* in: **a.** Middle High German *bunt,* league: BUND²; **b.** Middle Dutch *bondel,* sheaf of papers, bundle: BUNDLE. **4.** Suffixed form *bhendh-nā-,* "tied structure" (as of wicker), in Celtic *benna,* manger, in Old English *binn(e),* manger: BIN. **5.** Persian *band,* band, bandage, also a river levee: BUND¹; CUMMERBUND. **6.** Sanskrit *badhnāti* (Sanskrit root *bandh-*), he ties: BANDANNA. [Pok. *bhendh-* 127.]

bhengh-. Thick, fat. Extended zero-grade form *bhṇghu-* in Greek *pakhus,* thick, fat: PACHYDERM, PACHYSANDRA. [Pok. *bhengh-* 127.]

bher-¹. To carry; also to bear children. **1. a.** Germanic *beran* in *(i)* Old English *beran,* to carry: BEAR¹ *(ii)* Old English *forberan,* to bear, endure (*for-,* for-; see **per¹**): FORBEAR; **b.** Germanic *bērō* in Old English *bēr, bær,* bier: BIER; **c.** Germanic *bēr-* in Old Norse *bāra,* wave, billow: BORE³. **2. a.** Germanic *barnam* in Old English *bearn,* child: BAIRN; **b.** Germanic *barwōn-* in Old English *bearwe,* basket, wheelbarrow: BARROW¹. **3. a.** Germanic *burthinja* in Old English *byrthen,* burden: BURDEN¹; **b.** Germanic *burthiz* in Old Norse *burdhr,* birth, akin to the source of BIRTH; **c.** Germanic *burja-* perhaps in Old Norse *byrr,* favorable wind: BIRR¹. **4.** Compound root *bhrenk-,* to bring (< *bher-* + *enk-,* to reach; see **nek-²**), in Germanic *brengan* in Old English *bringan,* to bring: BRING. **5.** Latin *ferre,* to carry: -FER, FERTILE; AFFERENT, CONFER, DEFER¹, DEFER², DIFFER, EFFERENT, INFER, OFFER, PREFER, PROFFER, REFER, SUFFER, TRANSFER, VOCIFERATE. **6.** Latin *probrum,* a reproach (< *pro-bhr-o-,* "something brought before one"; *pro-,* before; see **per¹**): OPPROBRIUM. **7.** Lengthened o-grade form *bhōr-* probably in Latin *fūr,* thief: FERRET¹, FURTIVE, FURUNCLE; (FURUNCULOSIS). **8.** Greek *pherein,* to carry: -PHORE, -PHORESIS, -PHOROUS; AMPHORA, ANAPHORA, DIAPHORESIS, EUPHORIA, METAPHOR, PERIPHERY, PHEROMONE, TELPHER, TOCOPHEROL. **9.** Greek *phernē,* dowry ("something brought by a bride"): PARAPHERNALIA. [Pok. 1. *bher-* 128.]

bher-². To cut, pierce, bore. **1.** Germanic *borōn* in Old English *borian,* to bore: BORE¹. **2.** Germanic *baru-ga-,* castrated pig, in Old English *bearg, barg,* castrated pig: BARROW³. **3.** Germanic *bor-,* perhaps in French *burin,* burin: BURIN. **4.** O-grade form *bhor-ā-* in Latin *forāre,* to pierce, bore: FORAMEN, BIFORATE, PERFORATE. **5.** Perhaps Greek *pharunx,* throat (< "a cutting, cleft, passage"): PHARYNX. **6.** Slavic *bor-* in Russian *borot',* to overcome: DUKHOBOR. See extension **bhreu-¹**. [Pok. 3. *bher-* 133.]

bher-³. Bright, brown. **1.** Suffixed variant form *bhrū-no-* in Germanic *brūnaz* in: **a.** Old English *brūn,* brown: BROWN; **b.** Middle Dutch *bruun* (> Dutch *bruin*), brown: BRUIN; **c.** Old French *brun,* shining, brown: BRUNET, BURNET, BURNISH. **2.** Reduplicated form *bhibhru-, *bhebhru-,* "the brown animal," beaver, in Germanic *bebruz* in Old English *be(o)for,* beaver: BEAVER¹. **3.** Germanic *berō,* "the brown animal," bear in Old English *bera,* bear: BEAR². **4.** Germanic *bernuz* in Old Norse *björn* (stem *ber-*), bear: BERSERKER. [Pok. 5. *bher-* 136.]

bher-⁴. To cook, bake. Extended root form *bhrīg-* in Latin *frīgere,* to roast, fry: FRY¹. [Pok. 6. *bher-* 137.]

bherdh-. To cut. **1.** Zero-grade form *bhṛdh-* in Germanic *burd-,* plank, board, table, in: **a.** Old English *bord,* board: BOARD; STARBOARD; **b.** Old Norse *bordh* (> Swedish *bord*), board, table: SMORGASBORD; **c.** Old French *borde,* hut, and *bort,* border: BORDELLO, BORDER. **2.** Possibly Latin *forfex,* a pair of scissors: FORFICATE. [Pok. *bheredh-* 138.]

bherəg-. To shine; bright, white. Compare the by-form **bherek-**. **1.** Germanic *berhtaz,* bright, in Old English *beorht,* bright: BRIGHT. **2.** "The white tree," the birch (also the ash): **a.** Germanic *birkjōn-* in Old English *birc(e),* birch: BIRCH; **b.** suffixed zero-grade form *bhrag-s-* probably in Latin *fraxinus,* ash tree: FRAXINELLA. [Pok. *bherəg-* 139.]

bherək-. To shine, glitter. A by-form of **bherəg-.** Variant form *bhrek-, possible root of various Germanic forms. **1.** Germanic *bregdan, to move jerkily (> "to shimmer"), in Old English bregdan, to move quickly, weave, throw, braid: BRAID; UPBRAID. **2.** Derivative West Germanic *brigdil-, bridle (referring to the movements of a horse's head), in: **a.** Old English brīdel, bridle: BRIDLE; **b.** Middle High German brīdel, bridle, rein: BRIDE². **3.** Germanic *brēhwō, eyelid, eyelash, in Old Norse brā, eyelash: BRAE. **4.** Germanic *breh(w)an, to shine, forming West Germanic *brehsmo, a bream, in Old French bre(s)me, a bream: BREAM¹. [Pok. bherək- 141.]

bherg-. To buzz, growl. Germanic *berk- in Old English beorcan, to bark: BARK¹. [Pok. bhereg- 138.]

bhergh-¹. To hide, protect. **1.** Germanic *bergan in: **a.** compound *h(w)als-berg-, "neck-protector," gorget (*h(w)alsaz, neck; see **kwel-¹**); **b.** compound *skēr-berg-, "sword-protector," scabbard (*skēr-, sword; see **sker-¹**). **2.** Zero-grade form *bhṛgh- in: **a.** Germanic *burgjan in Old English byrgan, to bury: BURY; **b.** Germanic derivative *burgisli- in Old English byrgels, burial: BURIAL. **3. a.** Germanic *borgēn, to borrow (? < "to take care of one's own interests, entrust, pledge, lend, loan"), in Old English borgian, to borrow: BORROW; **b.** Germanic derivative *borganjan in Old French bargaignier, to haggle (> bargaine, haggling): BARGAIN. [Pok. bhergh- 145.]

bhergh-². High; with derivatives referring to hills and hill-forts. **1.** Germanic *bergaz, hill, mountain, in: **a.** Old English beorg, hill: BARROW²; **b.** Old Norse berg (> Danish and Norwegian berg), mountain: ICEBERG. **2.** Compound *harja-bergaz, "army-hill," hill-fort (*harjaz, army; see **koro-**). **3.** Compound *berg-frij-, "high place of safety," tower (*frij-, peace, safety; see **prī-**), in Old French berfrei, tower: BELFRY. **4.** Zero-grade form *bhṛgh- in Germanic *burgs, hill-fort, in: **a.** Old English burg, burh, byrig, (fortified) town: BOROUGH, BURG; **b.** Old High German burg, fortress: BURGHER; **c.** Middle Dutch burch, town: BURGOMASTER; **d.** Late Latin burgus, fortified place (> burgensis, city dweller): BOURG, (BOURGEOIS), BURGESS, BURGLAR, FAUBOURG. **5.** Suffixed zero-grade form *bhṛgh-to- possibly in Latin fortis, strong (but this is also possibly from **dher-²**): FORCE, FORT, FORTALICE, FORTE¹, FORTE², FORTIS, (FORTISSIMO), FORTITUDE, FORTRESS; COMFORT, DEFORCE, EFFORT, ENFORCE, FORTIFY, (PIANOFORTE), REINFORCE. [Pok. bheregh- 140.]

bhers-. Quick. Latin festīnāre (< *fers-tī-), to hasten: FESTINATE. [Pok. bheres- 143.]

bhes-¹. To rub. **1.** Zero-grade form with unclear suffix *(bh)s-amadho-, sand (in Greek psamathos), in Germanic *sam(a)dam, *sandam in Old English sand, sand: SAND. **2.** Suffixed form *(bh)s-abh- in the further suffixed form *sabh-lo- in Latin sabulum, coarse sand: SABULOUS. **3.** Suffixed form *bhs-ā- in (i) Greek psēn, to rub, scrape: PALIMPSEST (ii) Greek psēphos, ballot, pebble: PSEPHOLOGY. **4.** Perhaps suffixed form *bhs-īlo- in Greek psīlos, smooth, simple: EPSILON, PSILOMELANE, UPSILON. [Pok. bhes- 145.]

bhes-². To breathe. Probably imitative. Zero-grade form *bhs- in Greek psukhein (< *bhs-ū-kh-), to breathe, hence psukhē, spirit, soul: PSYCHE, PSYCHIC, PSYCHO-; METEMPSYCHOSIS. [Pok. 2. bhes- 146.]

bheudh-. To be aware, to make aware. **1.** Germanic *(for)beudan (*for, before; see **per¹**) in: **a.** Old English bēodan, to proclaim: BID; **b.** Old English forbēodan, to forbid: FORBID; **c.** Old High German farbiotan, to forbid: VERBOTEN. **2.** Germanic *budōn- in Old English boda, messenger, hence bodian, to announce: BODE¹. **3.** Germanic *budilaz, herald, in Old English bydel, herald, messenger: BEADLE. **4.** Germanic *budam in Old Norse bodh, command: OMBUDSMAN. **5.** Sanskrit bodhati, he awakes, is enlightened, becomes aware, and bodhih, perfect knowledge: BUDDHA; BODHISATTVA, BO TREE. [Pok. bheudh- 150.]

bheuə-. Also **bheu-.** To be, exist, grow. **I.** Extended forms *bhwiy(o)-, *bhwī-. **1.** Germanic *biju in Old English bēon, to be: BE. **2.** Latin fierī, to become (third person singular present subjunctive fiat): FIAT. **3.** Possibly suffixed form *bhwī-lyo- in Latin fīlius, son; but this is possibly from **dhē(i)-**. **II.** Lengthened o-grade form *bhōw- in Germanic *bōwan in: **a.** Old Norse būa, to live, prepare (present participle bondi): BONDAGE, BOUND⁴; HUSBAND; **b.** Middle Dutch bouwen, to cultivate: BOWERY; **c.** Old Danish bōth, dwelling, stall, akin to the Scandinavian source of Middle English bothe, market stall: BOOTH. **III.** Zero-grade form *bhu-. **1.** Germanic *buthla- in: **a.** Old English bold, dwelling, house, hence byldan, to build: BUILD; **b.** alternate Germanic form *bōthla in Middle Dutch bōdel, riches, property: BOODLE. **2.** Greek phuein, to bring forth, make grow, phutos, a plant, and phusis, growth, nature: PHYSIC, PHYSIO-, PHYSIQUE, -PHYTE, PHYTO-, PHYTON; DIAPHYSIS, DIPHYODONT, EPIPHYSIS, HYPOPHYSIS, IMP, MONOPHYSITE, NEOPHYTE, PERIPHYTON, SYMPHYSIS, TRACHEOPHYTE. **3.** Suffixed form *bhu-tā- in Welsh bod, to be: EISTEDDFOD. **4.** Suffixed form *bhu-tu- in Latin futūrus, "that is to be," future: FUTURE. **IV.** Zero-grade form *bhū- (< *bhuə-). **1.** Germanic *būram, dweller, especially farmer, in: **a.** Old English būr, "dwelling space," bower, room: BOWER¹; **b.** Old English gebūr, dweller (ge-, collective prefix; see **kom**): NEIGHBOR; **c.** Middle Dutch gheboer, ghebuer, peasant: BOER, BOOR. **2.** Germanic *būrjam, dwelling, in Old English bȳre, stall, hut: BYRE. **3.** Suffixed form *bhū-lo- in Greek phulon, tribe, class, race, and phulē, tribe, clan: PHYLE, PHYLETIC, PHYLUM; PHYLOGENY. **V.** Suffixal forms in Latin. **1.** *du-bhw-io-, "being two," in Latin dubius, doubtful, and dubitāre, to doubt (see **dwo-**). **2.** *pro-bhw-o-, "growing well or straightforward" (see **per¹**). **3.** *super-bhw-o-, "being above," in Latin superbus, superior, proud (see **uper**). **VI.** Possibly Germanic *baumaz (and *bagmaz), tree (? < "growing thing"), in: **a.** Old English bēam, tree, beam: BEAM; **b.** Middle Dutch boom, tree: BOOM². [Pok. bheu- 146.]

bheug-¹. To flee. **1.** Zero-grade form *bhug- in Latin fugere, to flee: FUGACIOUS, FUGITIVE; CENTRIFUGAL, FEVERFEW, REFUGE, SUBTERFUGE. **2.** Extended form *bhugā in: **a.** Latin fuga, flight (> fugāre, to drive away): -FUGE, FUGUE; FEBRIFUGE; **b.** Greek phugē, flight: APOPHYGE. [Pok. 1. bheug- 152.]

bheug-². To enjoy. Nasalized zero-grade form *bhu-n-g- in Latin fungī, to discharge, perform: FUNCTION, FUNGIBLE; DEFUNCT, PERFUNCTORY. [Pok. 4. bheug- 153.]

bheug-³. To bend; with derivatives referring to bent, pliable, or curved objects. **1.** Germanic *baugaz in: **a.** Old English bēag, a ring: BEE²; **b.** Old High German boug, a ring: BAGEL. **2.** Germanic *bugōn- in: **a.** Old English boga, a bow, arch: BOW³; **b.** compound *alino-bugōn-, "bend of the forearm," elbow (*alino-, forearm; see **el-¹**). **3.** Germanic būgan in Old English būgan, to bend: BOW², BUXOM. **4.** Germanic causative form *baugjan in Old Norse beyla, a swelling, akin to the probable Scandinavian source of Middle English baile, baill, a handle: BAIL³. **5.** Germanic *buhtiz in Old English byht, a bend, angle: BIGHT. **6.** Celtic *buggo-, "flexible, malleable," in Scottish and Irish Gaelic bog, soft: BOG. [Pok. 3. bheug- 152.]

bhilo-. Dear, familiar. Possible source of Greek philos, dear, loving (> philein, to love): -PHILE, -PHILIA, PHILO-, -PHILOUS, PHILTER; PAM. [Pok. bhili- 153.]

bhlād-. To worship. Suffixed form *bhlād-(s)men- in Latin flāmen, priest (of a particular deity): FLAMEN. [In Pok. bhlag-men- 154.]

bhlag-. To strike. **1.** Germanic *blak-, perhaps in the probable Scandinavian source of Middle English bakke, bat: BAT². **2.** Latin flagrum, a whip (> flagellum, little whip): FLAGELLATE, FLAGELLUM, FLAIL, FLOG. **3.** Latin

flāgitāre, to demand importunately: FLAGITIOUS. [Pok. *bhlag-* 154.]

bhlagh-men-. Form, ritual form. Sanskrit *brahmā, brahmán-*, priest, and *brahma, bráhman-*, prayer: BRAHMA[1], BRAHMAN, (BRAHMIN). [Pok. *bhlagh-men-* 154.]

bhlē-[1]. To howl. Probably imitative. **1.** Germanic suffixed form **blē-t-* in Old English *blǣtan*, to bleat: BLEAT. **2.** Germanic suffixed form **blē-r-* in Middle English *bleren*, to roar: BLARE. **3.** Latin *flēre*, to weep: FEEBLE. [Pok. *bhlē-* 154.]

bhlē-[2]. Also **bhlā-**. To blow. **1.** Germanic suffixed form **blē-w-* in Old English *blāwan*, to blow: BLOW[1]. **2.** Germanic suffixed form **blē-dram*, "something blown up," in: **a.** Old English *blǣdre*, blister, bladder: BLADDER; **b.** Old Norse *bladhra* (noun), bladder, and *bladhra* (verb), to prattle: BLATHER. **3.** Germanic extended form **blēs-* in: **a.** Old English *blǣst*, a blowing, blast: BLAST; **b.** Middle Dutch *blas(e)*, a bladder: ISINGLASS. **4.** Variant form **bhlā-* in Latin *flāre*, to blow (> *flabellum*, fan): FLABELLUM, FLATUS, FLAVOR; AFFLATUS, CONFLATE, (DEFLATE), INFLATE, SOUFFLÉ. [In Pok. 3. *bhel-* 120.]

bhlei-. To blow, swell. Extension of **bhel-[2]**. **1.** Germanic **blajjinōn-*, a swelling, in Old English *blegen*, a boil, blister: BLAIN. **2.** Perhaps in the Germanic source of Old French *blestre*, a blister: BLISTER. [Pok. 2. *bhlei-* 156.]

bhleu-. To swell, well up, overflow. Extension of **bhel-[2]**. **1.** Possibly Germanic **blaut-* in Old Norse *blautr*, soft, wet: BLOAT. **2.** Extended form *bhleugʷ-* in Latin *fluere*, to flow, and *-fluus*, flowing: FLUCTUATE, FLUENT, FLUERIC, FLUID, FLUME, FLUOR, (FLUORO-), (FLUSH[2]), FLUVIAL, FLUX; AFFLUENT, CONFLUENT, EFFLUENT, (EFFLUVIUM), (EFFLUX), (FLUORIDE), FLUVIOMARINE, INFLUENCE, (IN-FLUENZA), MELLIFLUOUS, REFLUX, SUPERFLUOUS. **3.** Zero-grade form **bhlu-* in Greek *phluein, phluzein*, to boil over: PHLYCTENA. **4.** Possibly Greek *phloos, phloios*, tree bark (< "swelling with growth"): PHLOEM. [Pok. *bhleu-* 158.]

bhlīg-. To strike. Latin *flīgere*, to strike: AFFLICT, CONFLICT, INFLICT, PROFLIGATE. [Pok. *bhlīg-* 160.]

bhoso-. Naked. Germanic **bazaz* in: **a.** Old English *bær*, bare: BARE[1]; **b.** Old Swedish and Old Danish *bar*, bare: BALLAST. [Pok. *bhoso-s* 163.]

bhrag-. To smell. **1.** Germanic **brak-* in Old High German *bracc(h)o*, dog that hunts game by scent: BRACH. **2.** Suffixed form **bhrag-ro-* in Latin *fragrāre*, to smell: FLAIR, FRAGRANT. [Pok. *bhrag-* 163.]

bhrāter-. Brother, male agnate. **1.** Germanic **brōthar-* in Old English *brōthor*, brother: BROTHER. **2.** Latin *frāter*, brother: FRA, FRATERNAL, FRIAR; CONFRERE, FRATRICIDE. **3.** Greek *phratēr*, fellow member of a clan: PHRATRY. **4.** Sanskrit *bhratā, bhrātar-*, brother: PAL. [Pok. *bhrāter-* 163.]

bhreg-. To break. **1.** Germanic **brekan* in: **a.** Old English *brecan*, to break: BREAK; **b.** Old English *brēc*, a breaking: BREACH; **c.** Old High German *brehhan*, to break, akin to the Germanic source of Italian *breccia*, breccia: BRECCIA; **d.** Old French *breier*, to break: BRAY[2]; **e.** Old French *brier* (dialectal) and *broyer*, to knead: BRIOCHE. **2.** Germanic **brak-*, bushes (< "that which impedes motion"), in Old Norse **brakni*, undergrowth, akin to the probable Scandinavian source of Middle English *brake(n)*, bracken: BRACKEN, BRAKE[3], BRAKE[4]. **3.** Nasalized zero-grade form **bhr-n-g-* in Latin *frangere*, to break: (FRACTED), FRACTION, (FRACTIOUS), FRACTURE, FRAGILE, FRAGMENT, FRAIL[1], FRANGIBLE; ANFRACTUOUS, CHAMFER, DIFFRACTION, (INFRACT), INFRANGIBLE, INFRINGE, OSSIFRAGE, REFRACT, (REFRAIN[2]), (REFRINGENT), SAXIFRAGE, SEPTIFRAGAL. **4.** Latin *suffrāgārī*, to vote for (? < "to use a broken piece of tile as a ballot"), hence *suffrāgium*, the right to vote: SUFFRAGAN, SUFFRAGE. [Pok. 1. *bhreg-* 165.]

bhrēi-. Also **bhrī-**. To cut, break. **1.** Possibly Latin *fricāre* (> French *frotter*), to rub: FRAY[2], FRICATIVE, FRICTION, FROTTAGE; AFFRICATE, DENTIFRICE. **2.** Possibly Latin *friāre*, to crumble: FRIABLE. **3.** In the Celtic source of Vulgar Latin **brīsāre*, the source of Old French *brisier* and French *briser*, to break: BRISANCE; DEBRIS. [Pok. *bhrēi-* 166.]

bhrekʷ-. To cram together. **1.** Probably Latin *frequens*, frequent, crowded: FREQUENT. **2.** Suffixed zero-grade form **bhr̥kʷ-yo-* in: **a.** Latin *farcīre*, to cram, stuff: FARCE, FARCI, FARCY; INFARCT; **b.** Greek *phrassein*, to fence in, enclose, block up: DIAPHRAGM. [Pok. *bharekᵘ-* 110.]

bhrem-[1]. To growl. **1.** Latin *fremere*, to growl, roar: FREMITUS. **2.** Perhaps variant **brem-* in Greek *brontē*, thunder: BRONTOSAUR. [Pok. 2. *bherem-* 142.]

bhrem-[2]. To project; a point, spike; an edge. **1.** Germanic **brēma-*, name of prickly shrubs, in: **a.** Old English *brōm*, broom: BROOM; **b.** Old English diminutive *bremel, brǣmbel*, bramble: BRAMBLE. **2.** Germanic **berm-, *brem-*, in: **a.** Middle English *brimme*, edge: BRIM; **b.** Middle Dutch *berme, barm*, edge of a dike: BERM. [Pok. 1. *bherem-* 142.]

bhres-. To burst. Germanic **brestan* in Old English *berstan*, to burst: BURST. [Pok. *bhres-* 169.]

bhreu-[1]. To cut, break up. Extension of **bher-[2]**. **1.** Suffixed form **bhreu-d-* in Germanic **breutan*, to break up, in Middle English *britel*, brittle: BRITTLE. **2.** Suffixed form **bhreu-t-* in Germanic **breuthan*, to be broken up, in Old English *brēothan*, to deteriorate: BROTHEL. [Pok. 1. *bhreu-* 169.]

bhreu-[2]. To boil, bubble, effervesce, burn; with derivatives referring to cooking and brewing. **I. 1.** Germanic **breuwan*, to brew, in Old English *brēowan*, to brew: BREW. **2.** Germanic **braudam*, (cooked) food, (leavened) bread, in Old English *brēad*, piece of food, bread: BREAD. **3.** Germanic **brudam*, broth, in: **a.** Old English *broth*, broth: BROTH; **b.** Old French *breu*, broth (diminutive *brouet*): BREWIS; IMBRUE. **II.** Variant form **bhrē-* in Germanic **brēdan*, to warm, with derivatives. **1.** **brōd-ō*, "a warming," hatching, rearing of young, in: **a.** Old English *brōd*, offspring, brood: BROOD; **b.** denominative **brōdjan*, to rear young, in Old English *brēdan*, to beget or cherish offspring, breed: BREED. **2.** Germanic **brēdōn-*, roast flesh, in: **a.** Old High German *brāt, brāto* (> German *Braten*), roast meat: BRATWURST, SAUERBRATEN; **b.** Old French *braon*, meat: BRAWN. **3.** Perhaps distantly related is the Germanic source of Old French *brese*, burning coal, ember (> French *braise*): BRAISE, BRAZE[2], BRAZIER[2], BREEZE[2]. **III.** Reduced form **bher-*, especially in derivatives referring to fermentation. **1.** Suffixed form **bher-men-*, yeast, in: **a.** Germanic **bermōn-* in Old English *beorma*, yeast: BARM, (BARMY); **b.** further suffixed form **bhermen-to-* in Latin *fermentum*, yeast: FERMENT. **2.** Extended form **bherw-* in Latin *fervēre*, to be boiling or fermenting: FERVENT, FERVID, (FERVOR); DEFERVESCENCE, EFFERVESCE. **IV.** As a very archaic word for a spring. **1.** Suffixed zero-grade form **bhrun(e)n-* in Germanic **brunnōn-* in Old English *burn, burna*, spring, stream: BOURN[1], BURN[2]. **2.** Suffixed form **bhrēw-r̥* in Greek *phrear*, spring: PHREATIC. [Pok. *bh(e)reu-* 143, 2. *bher-* 132.]

bhreus-[1]. To swell. **1.** Suffixed form **bhreus-t-* in Germanic **breustam*, "swelling," breast, in Old English *brēost*, breast: BREAST. **2.** Suffixed zero-grade form **bhrus-t-* in Germanic **brust-*, bud, shoot, in Old French *broust, brost*, shoot, twig: BROWSE. [Pok. 1. *bhreu-s-* 170.]

bhreus-[2]. To break. **1.** Germanic **brūsjan*, to crush, in Old English *brȳsan*, to crush, pound: BRUISE. **2.** Suffixed zero-grade form **bhrus-to-*, fragment, in Latin *frustum*, piece: FRUSTULE, FRUSTUM. [Pok. 2. *bhreu-s-* 171.]

bhrū-. Eyebrow. Contracted from **bhruⱳ-*. **1.** Germanic **brūs* in Old English *brū*, eyebrow, eyelid, eyelash: BROW. **2.** Possibly in the sense of a beam of wood, and perhaps a log bridge, found in Germanic **brugjō* (with cognates in Celtic and Slavic) in Old English *brycg(e)*, bridge: BRIDGE[1]. [Pok. 1. *bhrū-* 172, 2. *bhrū-* 173.]

bhrūg-. Agricultural produce; also to enjoy (results,

produce). **1.** Germanic *brūkan* in Old English *brūcan*, to enjoy, use: BROOK². **2.** Latin *frūx* (stem *frūg*-), fruit: FRUGAL; FRUGIVOROUS. **3.** Suffixed form *bhrūg-wo-* in Latin *fruī*, to enjoy, and *frūctus*, enjoyment, produce, results: FRUIT, FRUITION, FRUMENTACEOUS, FRUMENTY; FRUCTIFY. [Pok. *bhrūg-* 173.]

bhudh-. Bottom, base. (The precise preforms of the words listed below are obscure.) **1.** Old English *botm*, bottom: BOTTOM. **2.** Dutch *bodem*, (ship's) bottom: BOTTOMRY. **3.** Latin *fundus*, bottom, base: FOND², FOUND¹, FOUNDER, FUND, FUNDAMENT, FUNDUS; LATIFUNDIUM, PROFOUND. [Pok. *bhudh-* 174.]

bhugo-. Male animal of various kinds; stag, ram, he-goat. **1.** Germanic *bukkaz* (possibly borrowed from the Celtic form in **2.** below) in: **a.** Old English *buc, bucca*, stag, he-goat: BUCK¹; **b.** Middle Dutch *boc, bok*, buck: BLESBOK, BONTEBOK, SPRINGBOK, STEENBOK; **c.** Old High German *boc*, buck: GEMSBOK. **2.** Celtic *bukkos*, he-goat, in Old French *boc*, buck: BUTCHER. [Pok. *bhūgo-s* 174.]

[brāk-. Trousers. A northern European word, only in Celtic and Germanic. **1.** Germanic *brōks* in Old English *brōc* (plural *brēc*), breeches: BREECH, (BREEKS). **2.** Gaulish *brāka* in Latin *brāca*, trousers (plural *brācae*): BRACKET, BRAIL.]

[bursa. Hide, wineskin. Greek noun of unknown origin. (BOURSE), BURSA, (BURSAR), BURSE, PURSE; DISBURSE, REIMBURSE, SPORRAN.]

[busk-. A bush. Germanic root, possibly connected with the root **bheuə-**. **1.** Old French *bosc*, forest: BOSCAGE, BOUQUET. **2.** Old French *bois*, wood: HAUTBOY, (OBOE). **3.** Italian *busco*, splinter: BUSK¹. **4.** Latin *buscus*, forest: (AMBUSCADE), AMBUSH.]

[carcer. Enclosure, prison, barrier. Latin noun, probably borrowed from an unidentified source. **1.** Latin *carcer* (representing reduplicated form *kar-kr-o-*): INCARCERATE. **2.** Latin *cancer* (representing a dissimilated form *kankro-*), lattice: CANCEL, CHANCEL, (CHANCELLOR).]

[caupō. Small trader. Latin noun of unknown origin. CHEAP; (CHAP²), CHAPMAN.]

[cūra. Care. Latin noun of unknown origin (earliest form Old Latin *coisa-*). Derived verb *cūrāre*, to care for. CURATE, CURATOR, CURE, CURETTE, (CURIO), CURIOUS; ACCURATE, (ASSURE), (ENSURE), (INSURE), MANICURE, PEDICURE, POCOCURANTE, (PROCTOR), PROCURATOR, PROCURE, (PROXY), SCOUR¹, SECURE, SINECURE, SURE.]

dā-. To divide. Contracted from *daə-*. Variant *dai-* from extended root *daəi-*. **1.** Root form *dai-* in Greek *daiesthai*, to divide: GEODESY. **2.** Suffixed variant form *dī-ti-* in Germanic *tīdiz*, division of time, in: **a.** Old English *tīd*, time, season: TIDE¹; EVENTIDE; **b.** Old English denominative *tīdan*, to happen (< "to occur in time"): TIDE²; **c.** Old Norse *tidhr*, occurring: TIDINGS. **3.** Suffixed variant form *dī-mon-* in Germanic *tīmōn-* in Old English *tīma*, time, period: TIME. **4.** Suffixed form *dā-mo-*, perhaps "division of society," in Greek *dēmos*, people, land: DEME, DEMOS, DEMOTIC; DEMAGOGUE, DEMIURGE, DEMOCRACY, DEMOPHOBIA, EPIDEMIC, PANDEMIC. **5.** Suffixed form *dai-mon-*, divider, provider, in Greek *daimōn*, divinity: DEMON. [Pok. *dā-* 175.]

dail-. To divide. Northern Indo-European root. **1.** Germanic *dailjan* in Old English *dǣlan*, to share: DEAL¹. **2.** Germanic *dailaz* in Old English *dāl*, portion, lot: DOLE¹. **3.** Germanic prefixed form *uz-dailjam*, "a portioning out," judgment (*uz-*, out; see **ud-**), in Old English *ordāl*, lot, apportionment: ORDEAL. [In Pok. *dā-* 175.]

daiwer-. Husband's brother. Latin *lēvir*, husband's brother: LEVIRATE. [Pok. *dāiu̯r* 179.]

dakru-. Tear. **1.** Germanic *tahr-*, *tagr-* in: **a.** Old English *tēar, tehher*, tear: TEAR²; **b.** Middle Low German *trān*, tear, drop: TRAIN OIL. **2.** Suffixed form *dakru-mā* in Latin *lacrima* (Old Latin *dacruma*), tear: LACHRYMAL. [Pok. *dakru-* 179.]

[dan-. Low ground. Germanic root. Suffixed form *dan-jam* in: **a.** Old English *denn*, lair of a wild beast: DEN; **b.** possibly Old English *Dene* (genitive plural *Dena*), the Danes, and Old Norse *Danr*, Dane: DANE, DANISH; DANELAW. [In Pok. **2.** *dhen-* 249.]]

dap-. To apportion (in exchange). Suffixed form *dap-no-* in Latin *damnum*, damage entailing liability (for reparation), harm: DAMAGE, DAMN; CONDEMN, DAMNIFY, INDEMNIFY, (INDEMNITY). [In Pok. *dā-* 175.]

de-. Demonstrative stem, base of prepositions and adverbs. **1.** Germanic *tō* in Old English *tō*, to: TO, TOO. **2.** Perhaps Latin *dē, dē-*, from: DE-. **3.** Latin *dēterior*, worse: DETERIORATE. **4.** Latin *dēbilis*, weak (see **bel-**). [Pok. *de-, do-* 181.]

dē-. To bind. Contracted from *deə-*. Greek *dein*, to bind: DESMID; ANADEM, ASYNDETON, PLASMODESMA, (SYNDESMOSIS), SYNDETIC. [Pok. *dē-* 183.]

deigh-. Insect. Possibly in Germanic *tīk-ō, tikk-ō* in Middle English *teke*, tick: TICK². [Pok. *deigh-* 187.]

deik-. To show, pronounce solemnly; also in derivatives referring to the directing of words or objects. **I.** Variant *deig-*. **1.** O-grade form *doig-* in: **a.** Germanic *taikjan*, to show, in Old English *tǣcan*, to show, instruct: TEACH; **b.** Germanic *taiknam (i)* Old English *tācen, tācn*, sign, mark: TOKEN *(ii)* Old English *tācnian*, to signify: BETOKEN *(iii)* Gothic *taikns*, sign: TETCHY *(iv)* Old French *tache, teche*, mark, stain: TACHISM. **2.** Latin *digitus*, finger (< "pointer," "indicator"): DIGIT. **II.** Basic form *deik-*. **1.** O-grade form *doik-* possibly in Germanic *taihwō* in Old English *tā, tahe*, toe: TOE. **2.** Basic form *deik-* in Latin *dīcere*, to say, tell: DICTATE, DICTION, DICTUM, DITTO, DITTY; ADDICT, BENEDICTION, CONDITION, CONTRADICT, EDICT, FATIDIC, (INDICT), INDITE, INTERDICT, JURIDICAL, JURISDICTION, MALEDICT, PREDICT, VALEDICTION, VERDICT, VERIDICAL. **3.** Zero-grade form *dik-ā-* in Latin *dicāre*, to proclaim: ABDICATE, DEDICATE, PREACH, PREDICATE. **4.** Agential suffix *-dik-* in: **a.** Latin *index*, indicator, forefinger (*in-*, toward; see **en**): INDEX, INDICATE; **b.** Latin *jūdex* (< *yewes-dik-*), judge, "one who shows or pronounces the law" (*jūs*, law; see **yewes-**): JUDGE, JUDICIAL; PREJUDICE; **c.** Latin *vindex* (first element obscure), claimant, avenger: (VENDETTA), VINDICATE, (AVENGE) REVENGE. **5.** Greek *deiknunai*, to show: DEICTIC; APODICTIC, PARADIGM, POLICY². **6.** Zero-grade form *dik-* in Greek *dikein*, to throw (< "to direct an object"): DISK. **7.** Form *dikā* in Greek *dikē*, justice, right, court case: DICAST; EURYDICE, SYNDIC, THEODICY. [Pok. *deik-* 188.]

deiw-. To shine (and in many derivatives, "sky, heaven, god"). **I.** Noun *deiwos*, god. **1.** Germanic *Tīwaz* in: **a.** Old English *Tīw* (genitive *Tīwes*), god of war and sky: TIU, (TUESDAY); **b.** Old Norse *Tȳr*, sky god: TYR. **2.** Latin *deus*, god: DEISM, DEITY, JOSS; ADIEU, DEICIDE, DEIFIC. **3.** Latin *dīvus*, divine, god: DIVA, DIVINE¹, (DIVINE²). **4.** Latin *dīves*, rich (< "fortunate, blessed, divine"): DIVES. **5.** Suffixed zero-grade form *diw-yo-*, heavenly, in Latin *Diāna*, moon goddess: DIANA. **6.** Sanskrit *devaḥ*, god, and *deva-*, divine: DEVI; DEODAR, DEVANAGARI. **II.** Variant *dyeu-*, Jove, the name of the god of the bright sky, head of the Indo-European pantheon. **1.** Latin *Jovis*, Jupiter (> Italian *Giove*): JOVE, JOVIAL. **2.** Derivative *jou-il-* in Latin *Jūlius*, "descended from Jupiter" (name of a Roman gens): JULY. **3.** Vocative compound *dyeu-pəter-* (*pəter-*, father; see **pəter-**), "O father Jove," in Latin *Juppiter, Jūpiter*, head of the Roman pantheon: JUPITER. **4.** Greek *Zeus*, Zeus: ZEUS; (DIOSCURI). **III.** Variant *dyē-* (< *dyeə-*) in Latin *diēs*, day (> Late Latin *diurnum*, day): DIAL, DIARY, DIET²; DISMAL, DIURNAL; ADJOURN, CIRCADIAN, (JOURNAL), (JOURNEY), MERIDIAN, QUOTIDIAN, (POSTMERIDIAN), SOJOURN. **IV.** Variant *deiə-* in Greek *dēlos* (< *deyalos*), clear: PSYCHEDELIC. [Pok. **1.** *dei-* 183.]

dek-¹. To take, accept. **1.** Suffixed (stative) form *dek-ē-* in Latin *decēre*, to be fitting (< "to be acceptable"):

DECENT. **2.** Suffixed (causative) o-grade form **dok-eye-in:* **a.** Latin *docēre*, to teach (< "to cause to accept"): DOCENT, DOCILE, DOCTOR, DOCTRINE, DOCUMENT; **b.** Greek *dokein*, to appear, seem, think (< "to cause to accept or be accepted"): DOGMA, (DOGMATIC); DOCETISM, DOXOLOGY, HETERODOX, ORTHODOX, PARADOX. **3.** Suffixed form **dek-es-* in: **a.** Latin *decus*, grace, ornament: (DÉCOR), DECORATE; **b.** Latin *decor*, seemliness, elegance, beauty: DECOROUS. **4.** Suffixed form **dek-no-* in Latin *dignus*, worthy, deserving, fitting: DAINTY, DEIGN, DIGNITY; CONDIGN, DIGNIFY, DISDAIN, INDIGN, INDIGNANT, INDIGNATION. **5.** Reduplicated form **di-dk-ske-* in Latin *discere*, to learn: DISCIPLE, (DISCIPLINE). **6.** Greek *dekhesthai*, to accept: PANDECT, SYNECDOCHE. **7.** Greek *dokos*, beam, support: DIPLODOCUS. [Pok. 1. *dek-* 189.]

dek-². Referring to such things as a fringe, lock of hair, horsetail. **1.** Suffixed o-grade form **dok-lo-* in Germanic **taglaz* in Old English *tæg(e)l*, tail: TAIL¹. **2.** Perhaps Germanic **tag-* in: **a.** Swedish *tagg*, prickle, akin to the Scandinavian source of Middle English *tagge*, pendent piece: TAG¹; **b.** Middle High German *zacke*, nail (> German *Zacken*, point): SHAKO; **c.** Old French *tache*, fastening, nail: TACHE, TACK¹. [Pok. 2. *dek-* 191.]

dekm. Ten. **I.** Basic form **dekm̥.* **1.** Germanic **tehun* in: **a.** Old English *tīen*, ten: TEN; **b.** Old Norse *tjan*, ten (see **oktō(u)**). **2.** Latin *decem*, ten: DECEMBER, DECEMVIR, DECI-, DECIMAL, DECIMATE, DECUPLE, DICKER, DIME; (DECENARY), DECENNIUM, DECUSSATE, DOZEN, DUODECIMAL, OCTODECIMO, SEXTODECIMO. **3.** Irregular Latin distributive *dēnī*, by tens, ten each (formed by analogy with *nōnī*, nine each): (DENARIUS), DENARY, (DENIER²). **4.** Greek *deka*, ten: DEAN, DECA-, DECADE, (DECANAL), (DOYEN); DECAGON, DODECAGON. **II.** Extended form **dekm̥t-* in Germanic **-tig* in Old English *-tig*, ten (see **dwo-**). **III.** Ordinal number **dekm̥to-* in Germanic **teguntha-* in Old English *teogotha, tēotha*, tenth: TENTH, (TITHE). **IV.** Suffixed zero-grade form **-dkm̥-tā*, reduced to *-km̥tā*, and lengthened o-grade form **-dkōm-tā*, reduced to **-kontā*. **1.** Latin *-gintā*, ten times: NONAGENARIAN, OCTOGENARIAN, SEPTUAGINT, SEXAGENARY. **2.** Greek **-konta*, ten times: PENTECOST. **V.** Suffixed zero-grade form **dkm̥-tom*, hundred, reduced to *km̥tom.* **1.** Germanic **hundam*, hundred, in Old English *hundred* (*-red*, from Germanic **radam*, number; see **ar-**): HUNDRED. **2.** Germanic **thūs-hundi*, "swollen hundred," thousand (see **teuə-**). **3.** Latin *centum*, hundred: CENT, CENTAL, CENTAVO, (CENTENARIAN) CENTENARY, CENTESIMAL, CENTI-, CENTIME, (CENTNER), CENTUM, CENTURY; CENTENNIAL, PER CENT, QUATROCENTO, SEICENTO, (SEN¹), (SEN²), (SENITI), SEXCENTENARY, TRECENTO. **4.** Greek *hekaton*, a hundred (? dissimilated from **hem-katon*, one hundred; see **sem-¹**): HECATOMB, HECTO-. **5.** Avestan *satəm*, hundred: SATEM. See also compound root **wīkm̥tī.** [Pok. *dekm̥* 191.]

deks-. Right (opposite left); hence, with an eastward orientation, south. Suffixed form **deks(i)-tero-* in Latin *dexter*, right, on the right side: DESTRIER, DEXTER, DEXTERITY, DEXTRO-; AMBIDEXTROUS. Compare **ner-¹.** [In Pok. 1. *dek-* 189.]

del-¹. Long. Probably extended and suffixed zero-grade form **dlon-gho-.* **1.** Germanic **langaz*, long, in: **a.** Old English *lang, long*, long (comparative *lengra*): LINGER, LONG¹; **b.** Old High German *lang* (> German *lang*), long: LANGLAUF; **c.** Old English denominative *langian*, to grow longer, yearn for: LONG²; **d.** Latin compound *Longobardus, Langobardus* (with Germanic ethnic name **Bardi*): LOMBARD. **2.** Germanic abstract noun **langithō* in: **a.** Old English *lengthu*, length: LENGTH; **b.** West Germanic **langitinaz*, lengthening of day, in Old English *lengten, lencten*, spring, Lent: LENT; **c.** Dutch *lenghe, linghe*, "long one," akin to the Low German source of Middle English *lenge, ling*, ling: LING¹. **3.** Latin *longus* (> French *long*), long: LONGERON, LONGITUDE; ELOIGN, ELONGATE, LONGEVITY, LUNGE, OBLONG, PROLONG, PUR-

LOIN. **4.** Possibly suffixed variant **dlə-gho-* in Greek *dolikhos*, long: DOLICHOCEPHALIC, DOLICHOCRANIAL. [Pok. 5. *del-* 196.]

del-². To recount, count. **1.** Germanic **taljan* in Old English *tellan*, to count, recount: TELL. **2.** Germanic **talō* in: **a.** Old English *talu*, story: TALE; **b.** Middle Dutch *tāle*, speech, language: TAAL. **3.** Old English denominative *talian*, to tell, relate, probably akin to the source of Middle English *talken*, to talk: TALK. **4.** Perhaps Greek *dolos*, ruse, snare: DOLERITE. [Pok. 1. *del-* 193.]

del-³. To split, carve, cut. **1.** Suffixed form **del-to-* in Germanic **teldam*, "thing spread out," in Old English *teld*, awning, tent: TILT². **2.** Germanic extended form **telg-* in Old English *telgor, telgra*, twig, branch: TILLER³. **3.** Perhaps o-grade form **dol-ē-* in Latin *dolēre*, to suffer (? < "to be beaten"): DOLE², DOLOR; CONDOLE, INDOLENT. **4.** Suffixed o-grade form **dolā-dhrā* in Latin *dolābra*, a heavy chopping tool (< *dolāre*, to chisel, hew): DOLABRIFORM. [Pok. 3. *del-* 194.]

del-⁴. To drip. Perhaps suffixed (stative) o-grade form **dol-* in Germanic **talgaz* in Middle Low German *talg, talch*, tallow (< "dripping fat"), perhaps akin to the source of Middle English *talow*, tallow: TALLOW. [Pok. 4. *del-* 196.]

demə-¹. Also **dem-.** House, household. **1.** Suffixed reduced o-grade form **dom-o-, dom-u-*, house, in: **a.** Latin *domus*, house: DOME, DOMESTIC, DOMICILE; MAJOR-DOMO; **b.** suffixed form **dom-o-no-* in Latin *dominus*, master of a household (feminine *domina* > Old French *dame*, lady): DAME, DAN², DANGER, DOM, DOMAIN, DOMINATE, DOMINICAL, DOMINIE, DOMINION, DOMINO¹, (DOMINO²), DUENNA, DUNGEON; (MADAM), MADAME, MADEMOISELLE, MADONNA, PREDOMINATE. **2.** Compound **dems-pot-*, "house-master" (**-pot-*, powerful; see **poti-**), in Greek *despotēs*, master, lord: DESPOT. **3.** Root form **dem(ə)-*, to build (possibly a separate root), in: **a.** Germanic **timram* in Old English *timber*, building material, lumber: TIMBER; **b.** Germanic **tumftō* in Old Norse *topt*, homestead: TOFT. [Pok. *dem-* 198.]

demə-². To constrain, force, especially to break in (horses). **1.** Suffixed o-grade form **dom-o-* in Germanic **tamaz* in Old English *tam*, domesticated: TAME. **2.** O-grade form **domə-* in Latin *domāre*, to tame, subdue: DAUNT; INDOMITABLE. **3.** Zero-grade form **dmə-* in Greek *daman*, to tame (> *adamas*, unconquerable): ADAMANT, DIAMOND. [Pok. *(demə-), domə-* 199.]

denk-. To bite. **1.** Germanic **tanhuz* in Old English *tōh*, tenacious, sticky (< "holding fast"): TOUGH. **2.** Germanic **tanguz* in Old English *tang(e), tong(e)*, pincers, tongs: TONGS. **3.** Germanic **tang-* in Old Norse *tangi*, a point, sting, akin to the Scandinavian source of Middle English *tonge, tange*, point, tang: TANG¹. **4.** Germanic **teng-* in Old High German *zinko*, spike, prong: ZINC. [Pok. *denk-* 201.]

dens-¹. To use mental force. Reduplicated and suffixed zero-grade form **di-dn̥s-sko-* in Greek *didaskein*, to teach: DIDACTIC. [Pok. 1. *dens-* 201.]

dens-². Dense, thick. **1.** Suffixed form **dens-o-* or **dn̥s-o-* in Latin *dēnsus*, thick: DENSE; CONDENSE. **2.** Suffixed zero-grade form **dn̥s-u-* in Greek *dasus*, hairy, shaggy: DASYURE. [Pok. 2. *dens-* 202.]

dent-. Tooth. (Originally participle of **ed-** in the earlier meaning "to bite.") **1.** O-grade form **dont-* in Germanic **tanthuz* in Old English *tōth*, tooth: TOOTH. **2.** Zero-grade form **dn̥t-* perhaps in Germanic **tunth-sk-* in Old English *tūsc, tūx*, canine tooth: TUSK. **3.** Full-grade form **dent-* in Latin *dēns* (stem *dent-*), tooth: DENTAL, DENTATE, DENTI-, DENTICLE; (BIDENTATE), DANDELION, EDENTATE, INDENT¹, (INDENTURE), TRIDENT. **4.** O-grade variant form **(o)dont-* in Greek *odōn, odous*, tooth: -ODON, -ODONT, ODONTO-; CERATODUS. [In Pok. *ed-* 287.]

deph-. To stamp. **1.** Suffixed form **deph-s-ter-* in Greek

diphthera, prepared hide, leather (used to write on): DIPHTHERIA. **2.** Latin *littera,* letter (possibly borrowed from Greek *diphthera* in the sense of "tablet" via Etruscan): LETTER, LITERAL, LITERARY, LITERATE, LITERATIM; (ALLITERATE), ALLITERATION, (ILLITERATE), OBLITERATE, TRANSLITERATE. [Pok. *deph-* 203.]

der-¹. Assumed base of roots meaning "to run, walk, step." **1.** Zero-grade form **dr-* in extended Germanic form **tred-* in: **a.** Old English *tredan,* to step: TREAD, TREADLE; **b.** Middle Low German *trade,* course, track: TRADE. **2.** Extended form **dreb-* in Germanic **trep-,* "something on or into which one steps," in: **a.** Old English *træppe, treppe,* snare: TRAP¹; **b.** Middle Low German *trappe,* stair: TRAP³. **c.** Middle Dutch *trappe,* stair: WENTLETRAP; **d.** Old French *trap(p)e,* snare: ENTRAP; **e.** Middle Dutch *trippen,* to stamp, trample: TRIP. **3.** Nasalized Germanic root **tremp-* in: **a.** Middle Low German *trampen,* to stamp, tread: TRAMP; **b.** Italian *trampoli,* stilts: TRAMPOLINE. **4.** Germanic **trott-* (expressive derivative of **tred-*) in Old French *troter,* to trot: TROT. **5.** Root form **drā-* possibly in reduplicated Germanic form **ti-trā-* in Old Norse *titra,* to tremble: TEETER. **6.** Root form **drem-* in suffixed o-grade form **drom-o-* in: **a.** Greek *dromos,* a running, race, racecourse: -DROME, DROMOND, -DROMOUS; ANADROMOUS, LOXODROMIC, PALINDROME, PRODROME; **b.** Greek *dromas,* running: DROMEDARY. [Pok. 3. *(der-)* 204.]

der-². To split, peel, flay; with derivatives referring to skin and leather. **1.** Germanic **teran* in Old English *teran,* to tear: TEAR¹. **2.** Germanic **ter-t-* in Old English *teart,* sharp, severe: TART¹. **3.** Suffixed zero-grade form **dr̥-tom,* "something separated or discarded," in Germanic **turdam,* turd, in Old English *tord,* turd: TURD. **4.** Reduplicated form **de-dr-u-* in Old English *tet(e)r,* eruption, skin disease: TETTER. **5.** Greek *derris,* leather covering: DERRIS. **6.** Suffixed form **der-mn̥* in Greek *derma,* skin: -DERM, DERMA¹, -DERMA, DERMATO-; EPIDERMIS. **7.** Perhaps extended root **drep-* in the Celtic source (itself borrowed) of Late Latin *drappus,* cloth (> Old French *drap*): (DRAB¹), DRAPE, TRAP². [Pok. 4. *der-* 206.]

derbh-. To wind, compress. Zero-grade form **dr̥bh-* in Germanic **turb-* in: **a.** Old English *turf,* slab of sod or peat: TURF; **b.** Medieval Latin *turba,* turf: TURBARY. [Pok. *derbh-* 211.]

dere-. To work. Variant form **drā-* (< **drəa-*) in Greek *dran,* to do: DRAMA, DRASTIC. [Pok. *derə-* 212.]

dergh-. To grasp. **1.** Perhaps Germanic **targ-* in Old French *targe,* shield: (TARGE), TARGET. **2.** Perhaps zero-grade form **dr̥gh-* in Greek *drassesthai,* to grab (> *drakhmē,* "handful," drachma): DRACHMA. [Pok. *dergh-* 212.]

derk-. To see. Suffixed zero-grade form **dr̥k-on(t)-* in Greek *drakōn* (> Latin *dracō*), serpent, dragon (< "monster with the evil eye"): DRAGON, (DRAGOON), (DRAKE²), RANKLE. [Pok. *derk-* 213.]

deru. Also **dreu-.** To be firm, solid, steadfast; hence specialized senses "wood," "tree," and derivatives referring to objects made of wood. **1.** Suffixed variant form **drew-o-* in: **a.** Germanic **trewam* in Old English *trēow,* tree: TREE; **b.** Germanic **treuwō* in Old English *trēow,* pledge: TRUCE. **2.** Variant form **dreu-* in Germanic **treuwaz* in: **a.** Old English *trēowe,* firm, true: TRUE; **b.** Old English *trēowian, trūwian,* to trust: TROW; **c.** Old Norse *tryggr,* firm, true: TRIG¹; **d.** Germanic abstract noun **treuwithō* in Old English *trēowth* (> Middle English *tro(u)the*), faith, loyalty, truth: TROTH, TRUTH; BETROTH; **e.** Germanic abstract noun **traustam* in Old Norse *traust,* confidence, firmness: TRUST; **f.** Old Norse denominative *treysta,* to trust, make firm, akin to the probable source of Old French *triste,* waiting place (< "place where one waits trustingly"): TRYST. **3.** Variant form **drou-* in Germanic **traujam* in Old English *trēg, trīg,* wooden board: TRAY. **4.** Suffixed zero-grade form

*dru-ko- in Germanic **trugaz* in Old English *trog,* wooden vessel, tray: TROUGH. **5.** Suffixed zero-grade form **dru-mo-* in Germanic **trum-* in Old English *trum,* firm, strong (> *trymman,* to strengthen, arrange): TRIM. **6.** Variant form **derw-* in Germanic **terw-* in Old English *te(o)ru,* resin, pitch (obtained from the pine tree): TAR¹. **7.** Suffixed variant form **drū-ro-* in Latin *dūrus,* hard (of whose English derivatives many represent a semantic cross with Latin *dūrāre,* to last long; see **deuə-**): DOUR, DURAMEN, DURESS, DURUM; (DURA MATER), ENDURE, INDURATE, OBDURATE. **8.** Lengthened zero-grade form **drū-* in Greek *drus,* oak: DRUPE, DRYAD; GERMANDER, HAMADRYAD. **9.** Reduplicated form **der-drew-,* dissimilated with suffix in **den-drewon* in Greek *dendron,* tree: DENDRO-, DENDRON; PHILODENDRON, RHODODENDRON. **10.** Celtic compound **dru-wid-,* "knower of trees" (**wid-,* to know; see **weid-**), the Celtic priestly caste, associated with a tree-cult, probable source of Latin *druides,* druids: DRUID. **11.** O-grade form **doru-* in Sanskrit *dāru,* wood, timber: DEODAR. [Pok. *deru-* 214.]

deu-¹. To lack, be wanting. **1.** Possibly suffixed form **deu-s-* in: **a.** Germanic **teuzōn* in Old English *tēorian, tyrian,* to fail, tire (< "to fall behind"): TIRE¹; **b.** Greek *dein,* to lack, want: DEONTOLOGY. **2.** Suffixed form **deu-tero-* in Greek *deuteros,* "missing," next, second: DEUTERO-; DEUTERAGONIST, (DEUTERIUM), DEUTERONOMY. (For suffixed zero-grade form **du-s-,* combining form of **dew-es-,* a lack, see **dus-**.) [Pok. 3. *deu-* 219.]

deu-². To do, perform, show favor, revere. **1.** Suffixed form **dw-enos* in Latin *bonus* (> Old French *bon,* feminine *bonne*), good (< "useful, efficient, working"): BONANZA, BONBON, BONITO, BONNE, BONUS, BOON²; BOUNTY; BONHOMIE, DEBONAIR. **2.** Adverbial form **dw-enē* in Latin *bene,* well: BENEFACTION, (BENEFACTOR), BENEFIC, (BENEFICENCE), BENEFIT, BENEVOLENT, BENIGN, (HERB BENNET). **3.** Diminutive **dw-ene-lo-* in Latin *bellus* (> Italian *bello,* feminine *bella*), handsome, pretty, fine: BEAU, BEAUTY, BELLE; BELDAM, BELLADONNA, BELVEDERE, EMBELLISH. **4.** Possibly suffixed zero-grade form **dw-eye-* in Latin *beāre,* to make blessed: BEATITUDE; BEATIFIC, BEATIFY. **5.** Possible (but unlikely for formal and semantic reasons) suffixed zero-grade form **du-nə-* in Greek *dunasthai,* to be able: DYNAMIC, DYNAMITE, DYNAST, (DYNASTY); AERODYNE. [Pok. 2. *deu-* 218.]

deu-³. To burn, hurt. Germanic suffixed form **teu-nō* in Old English *tēona,* injury: TEEN². [Pok. *dāu-* 179.]

deuə-. Also **dwaə-.** Long (in duration). Suffixed zero-grade form **dū-ro-* (< **duə-ro-*) in Latin *dūrāre,* to last: DURABLE, DURANCE, DURATION, DURING; PERDURABLE, THERMODURIC. [In Pok. 3. *deu-* 219.]

deuk-. To lead. **1.** Germanic **teuhan* in Old English *tēon* (> Middle English *tuggen*), to pull, draw, lead: TUG; WANTON. **2.** Suffixed zero-grade form **duk-ā-* in Germanic **tugōn* in Old English *togian,* to draw, drag: TOW¹. **3.** Suffixed o-grade form **douk-eyo-* in Old English *tīegan, tīgan,* to bind: TIE. **4.** Suffixed o-grade form **douk-mo-* in Germanic **tau(h)maz* in Old English *tēam,* descendant, family, race, brood: TEAM. **5.** Germanic denominative **tau(h)mjan* in Old English *tēman, tīeman,* to beget: TEEM¹. **6.** Basic form **deuk-* in Latin *dūcere,* to lead: DOCK¹, DOGE, DOUCHE, (DUCAL), (DUCAT), (DUCHESS), (DUCHY), DUCT, DUCTILE, DUKE; (ABDUCENS), ABDUCT, ADDUCE, CIRCUMDUCTION, CON³, (CONDOTTIERE), CONDUCE, CONDUCT, DEDUCE, (DEDUCT), EDUCE, (ENDUE), INDUCE, INTRODUCE, PRODUCE, REDOUBT, REDUCE, SEDUCE, SUBDUCTION, SUBDUE, TRADUCE, TRANSDUCER. **7.** Suffixed zero-grade form **duk-ā-* in Latin *ēducāre,* to lead out, bring up (*ē-* < *ex-,* out; see **eghs**): EDUCATE. [Pok. *deuk-* 220.]

dhabh-. To fit together. **1.** Germanic **dab-,* to be fitting, in participial adjective **gadaftaz,* fitting, becoming (**ga-,* collective prefix; see **kom**), in Old English *gedæfte,*

mild, gentle: DAFT. **2.** Probably suffixed form *dhabh-ro- in Latin *faber*, artisan (< "he who fits together"): FABRIC, (FABRICATE), FORGE[1]. [Pok. 2. *dhabh-* 233.]

dhal-. To bloom. Suffixed form *dhal-yo- in Greek *thallein*, to flourish, bloom, sprout (> *thallos*, a shoot): THALIA, THALLUS; PROTHALLUS. [Pok. *dhāl-* 234.]

dhē-[1]. To set, put. Contracted from *dheə-. **1.** O-grade form *dhō- in Germanic *dōn in Old English *dōn*, to do: DO[1]; FORDO. **2.** Suffixed form *dhē-ti-, "thing laid down or done, law, deed," in Germanic *dēdiz in Old English *dǣd*, doing, deed: DEED. **3.** Suffixed o-grade form *dhō-mo- in Germanic *dōmaz in: **a.** Old English *dōm*, judgment (< "thing set or put down"): DOOM; **b.** Old English *-dōm*, abstract suffix indicating state, condition, or power: -DOM; **c.** Old Norse *-dōmr*, condition (see **kā-**); **d.** Gothic *dōms*, judgment, akin to the Germanic source of Russian *Duma*, Duma: DUMA; **e.** Germanic denominative *dōmjan in Old English *dēman*, to judge: DEEM. **4.** Suffixed o-grade form *dhō-t- in Latin agential suffix *-dōs* in Latin *sacerdōs*, priest, "performer of sacred rites" (see **sak-**). **5.** Zero-grade form *dhə- in: **a.** prefixed form *kom-dhə- in Latin *condere*, to put together, establish, preserve (*kom, together; see **kom**): CONDIMENT; ABSCOND, INCONDITE, RECONDITE, SCONCE[2]; **b.** compound *kred-dhə- (see **kerd-**[1]). **6.** Suffixed zero-grade form *dhə-k- in: **a.** Latin *facere* (< *fak-yo-), to do, make (> French *faire*, to do), and Latin combining form *-fex* (< *-fak-s), "maker": -FACIENT, FACT, FACTION, FACTITIOUS, FACTOR, FASHION, FEASIBLE, FEAT[1], FEATURE, (FETISH), -FIC, (-FY); AFFAIR, AFFECT[1], (AFFECT[2]), (AFFECTION), AMPLIFY, ARTIFACT, ARTIFICE, BEATIFIC, BENEFACTION, BENEFIC, (BENEFICE), (BENEFICENCE), BENEFIT, CHAFE, COMFIT, CONFECT, (CONFETTI), COUNTERFEIT, (DEFEASANCE), DEFEAT, DEFECT, (DEFICIENT), (DISCOMFIT), EDIFICE, (EDIFY), EFFECT, (EFFICACIOUS), (EFFICIENT), FACSIMILE, FACTOTUM, FORFEIT, HACIENDA, INFECT, JUSTIFY, MALEFACTOR, MALFEASANCE, MANUFACTURE, MISFEASANCE, MODIFY, MOLLIFY, NIDIFY, NOTIFY, NULLIFY, OFFICINAL, PERFECT, PETRIFY, (PLUPERFECT), PONTIFEX, PREFECT, (PROFICIENT), PROFIT, PUTREFY, QUALIFY, RAREFY, RECTIFY, REFECT, (REFECTORY), RUBEFACIENT, SACRIFICE, SCIRE FACIAS, SPINIFEX, SUFFICE, (SUFFICIENT), SURFEIT, TUBIFEX, TUMEFACIENT, VIVIFY; **b.** Latin derivative *faciēs*, shape, face (< "form imposed on something"): FAÇADE, FACE, (FACET), (FACIAL), FACIES; (DEFACE), EFFACE, PRIMA FACIE, (SURFACE); **c.** Latin compound *officium* (< *opi-fici-om), service, duty, business, performance of work (*opi-, work; see **op-**[1]): OFFICE; **d.** further suffixed form *dhə-k-li- in Latin *facilis* (< Old Latin *facul*), feasible, easy: FACILE, (FACILITY), FACULTY; DIFFICULTY. **7.** Suffixed zero-grade form *dhə-s- in Latin *fās*, divine law, right: NEFARIOUS. **8.** Possibly Latin *-fārius*, -doing: MULTIFARIOUS, OMNIFARIOUS. **9.** Reduplicated form *dhi-dhē- in Greek *tithenai*, to put: THESIS, THETIC; ANATHEMA, ANTITHESIS, APOTHECARY, (APOTHECIUM), BODEGA, BOUTIQUE, DIATHESIS, EPENTHESIS, EPITHET, HYPOTHESIS, METATHESIS, PARENTHESIS, PROSTHESIS, PROTHESIS. **10.** Suffixed form *dhē-k- in Greek *thēkē*, receptacle: THECA, TICK[3]; AMPHITHECIUM, BIBLIOTHECA, CLEISTOTHECIUM, ENDOTHECIUM, PERITHECIUM. **11.** Suffixed zero-grade form *dhə-mn in Greek *thema*, "thing placed," proposition: (THEMATIC), THEME. **12.** Reduplicated form *dhe-dhē- in Sanskrit *dadhāti*, he places: SANDHI. **13.** Reduced form *dh- (see **aw-**). [Pok. 2. *dhē-* 235.]

dhē-[2]. To vanish. Contracted from *dheə-. **1.** Possibly Old Norse *dǣsa, to languish, decay: DASTARD. **2.** Possibly Old Norse *dasa, to tire out (attested only in reflexive form *dasask*, to become exhausted), akin to the Scandinavian source of Middle English *dasen*, to stun: DAZE. [Pok. 3. *dhē-* 239.]

dheb-. Dense, firm, compressed. Germanic suffixed form *dap-ra- in Middle Dutch and Middle Low German

dapper, heavy, strong; later quick, nimble: DAPPER. [Pok. *dheb-* 239.]

dheg^wh-. To burn, warm. Suffixed o-grade form *dhog^wh-eye- in Latin *fovēre*, to warm, cherish, foment (> *fomentāre*, to foment, and *fōmes*, tinder): FOMENT, FOMITE. [Pok. *dheg^wh-* 240.]

dhē(i)-. To suck. Contracted from *dheə(i)-. **1.** Suffixed reduced form *dhē-mnā- in Latin *fēmina*, woman (< "she who suckles"): FEMALE, FEMININE, EFFEMINATE. **2.** Suffixed reduced form *dhē-to- in Latin *fētus*, pregnancy, childbearing, offspring: FAWN[2], (FETAL), FETUS; EFFETE, (FETICIDE), SUPERFETATE. **3.** Suffixed reduced form *dhē-kundo- in Latin *fēcundus*, fruitful: FECUND. **4.** Suffixed reduced form *dhē-no- in Latin *fēnum, faenum*, hay (< "produce"): FENNEL, FINOCHIO, (FENUGREEK), SAINFOIN. **5.** Perhaps suffixed zero-grade form *dhī-lyo- (< *dhiə-lyo-) in Latin *fīlius*, son, and *fīlia*, daughter (but these are equally possibly from the root **bheuə-**): FILIAL, FILIATE; AFFILIATE, HIDALGO. **6.** Suffixed reduced form *dhē-lo- in Latin *fēl(l)āre*, to suck: FELLATIO. **7.** Suffixed reduced form *dhē-l-īk- in Latin *fēlix*, fruitful, fertile, lucky, happy: FELICITATE, FELICITY, FELICIFIC, INFELICITY. **8.** Suffixed reduced form *dhē-lā- in Greek *thēlē*, nipple: ENDOTHELIUM, EPITHELIUM, (MESOTHELIUM). **9.** Suffixed reduced form *dhē-l-u- in Greek *thēlus*, female: THEELIN. [Pok. *dhē(i)-* 241.]

dheiə-. To see, look. Variant form *dhyā- (< *dhyaə-) in: **a.** suffixed form *dhyā-mn in Greek *sēmeion* and *sēma* (stem *sēmat-*), sign: SEMANTIC, SEMATIC; SEMAPHORE, SEMASIOLOGY, SEMEME, SEMIOLOGY, SEMIOTIC; **b.** Sanskrit *dhyāti*, he meditates (< "he observes mentally"): ZEN BUDDHISM. [Pok. *dheiə-* 243.]

dheigh-. To form, build. **1.** Germanic *daigjōn in Old English *dǣge*, bread kneader: DAIRY. **2.** Germanic *-dīg in Old English compound *hlǣfdige*, mistress of a household (< "bread kneader"; *hlǣf*, bread, loaf): LADY. **3.** Extended o-grade form *dhoigho- in Germanic *daigaz in: **a.** Old English *dāg*, dough: DOUGH; **b.** Old High German *teic*, dough: TEIGLACH. **4.** Suffixed zero-grade form *dhigh-ūrā, in Latin *figūra*, form, shape (< "result of kneading"): FIGURE; CONFIGURATION, DISFIGURE, PREFIGURE, TRANSFIGURE. **5.** Nasalized zero-grade form *dhi-n-gh- in Latin *fingere*, to shape: (FAINT), FEIGN, (FEINT), FICTILE, FICTION, FIGMENT, EFFIGY. **6.** Nasalized zero-grade form *dhi-n-g(h)- in Greek *thinganein*, to touch: THIGMOTAXIS, THIXOTROPY. **7.** Suffixed o-grade form *dhoigh-o- in Avestan *daēza-, wall (originally made of clay or mud bricks): PARADISE. [Pok. *dheigh-* 244.]

dhel-. A hollow. **1.** Germanic *daljō in Old English *dell*, valley: DELL. **2.** Germanic *dalam in Old English *dæl*, valley: DALE. **3.** Germanic *del- in Old Norse *dæla*, wooden gutter on a ship: DALLES. [Pok. 1. *dhel-* 245.]

dhelbh-. To dig, excavate. Germanic *delban in Old English *delfan*, to dig: DELVE. [Pok. *dhelbh-* 246.]

dhembh-. To bury. Suffixed zero-grade form *dhm̥bh-o- in Greek *taphos* (< *thaphos), tomb: CENOTAPH, EPITAPH. [Pok. (dhembh-), dhm̥bh- 248.]

dhen-[1]. To run, flow. Suffixed o-grade form *dhon-ti- in Latin *fons* (stem *font-*), spring, fountain: FONT[1], FOUNTAIN. [Pok. 1. *dhen-* 249.]

dhen-[2]. Palm of the hand. Suffixed form *dhen-r in Greek *thenar*, palm of the hand: THENAR. [Pok. 2. *dhen-* 249.]

dher-[1]. To make muddy; darkness. **1.** Suffixed form *dher-g- in Germanic *derk- in Old English *deorc*, dark: DARK. **2.** Suffixed zero-grade form *dhr-egh- in: **a.** Germanic suffixed form *drah-sta- in Old English *drōs*, dregs: DROSS; **b.** Germanic *dragjō in Old Norse *dregg*, dregs: DREGS. **3.** Suffixed extended zero-grade form *dhrə-bh- in Germanic *drab- in: **a.** Old English *dreflian*, to drivel: DRIVEL; **b.** probably Low German *drabbelen*, to paddle in water or mire, draggle, akin to the Low German source of Middle English *drabelen*, to draggle: DRABBLE; **c.** Middle Irish *drab*, dregs, probably akin to the Celtic source of DRAB[2]. **4.** Suffixed extended

zero-grade form *dhrə-gh- in: **a.** Greek *tarassein* (Attic *tarattein*), to confuse, disturb: ATARACTIC; **b.** Greek *trakhus*, rough: TRACHEA, TRACHOMA, TRACHYTE. [Pok. 1. *dher-* 251.]

dher-². To hold firmly, support. **1.** Suffixed form *dher-mo-* in Latin *firmus*, firm, strong: FARM, FERMATA, FIRM, FIRMAMENT; AFFIRM, CONFIRM, INFIRM, (INFIRMARY). **2.** Extended form *dhergh-* possibly in Latin *fortis*, strong (but this is also possibly from **bhergh-²**). **3.** Suffixed zero-grade form *dhr-ono-* in Greek *thronos*, seat, throne (< "support"): THRONE. **4.** Suffixed form *dher-mṇ* in Sanskrit *dharma*, statute, law (< "that which is established firmly"): DHARMA. **5.** Old Persian *dar-*, to hold (whence Persian -*dār*, "-holder"): SIRDAR, TAHSILDAR, ZAMINDAR. [Pok. 2. *dher-* 252.]

dher-³. To drone, murmur, buzz. Extended zero-grade form *dhrēn-* in: **a.** Germanic *dren-* in Old English *drān*, *drǣn*, male honeybee: DRONE¹; **b.** Greek *thrēnos*, dirge, lament: THRENODY. [Pok. 3. *dher-* 255.]

dhers-. To venture, be bold. **1.** O-grade form *dhors-* and zero-grade form *dhṛs-* respectively in Germanic *ders-* and *durs-* in Old English *dearr* and *durst*, first and third person singular present and past indicative of *durran*, to venture: DARE, (DURST). **2.** Possibly Latin -*festus* in: **a.** *infestus*, hostile (? < "directed against"; *in-*, into, against; see **en**): INFEST; **b.** *manifestus*, palpable, evident (< "caught red-handed, grasped by the hand"; *manus*, hand; see **man-²**): MANIFEST. [Pok. *dhers-* 259.]

dhēs-. Root of words in religious concepts. Possibly an extension of **dhē-¹**. **1.** Suffixed form *dhēs-yā* in Latin *fēriae* (Old Latin *fēsiae*), holidays: FAIR², FERIA. **2.** Suffixed form *dhēs-to-* in Latin *fēstus*, festive (> German *Fest*, festival): FEAST, (-FEST), (FESTAL), FESTIVAL, FESTIVE, FESTOON, (FETE), FIESTA; (GABFEST), OKTOBERFEST. **3.** Suffixed zero-grade form *dhəs-no-* in Latin *fānum*, temple: FANATIC; PROFANE. **4.** Possibly suffixed zero-grade form *dhəs-o-* becoming *dhes-o-* in Greek *theos* (< *thes-os*), god: THEO-; APOTHEOSIS, ATHEISM, ENTHUSIASM, PANTHEON, POLYTHEISM. [Pok. *dhēs-* 259.]

dheu-¹. Also **dheuə-**. The base of a wide variety of derivatives meaning "to rise in a cloud," as dust, vapor, or smoke, and related to semantic notions of breath, various color adjectives, and forms denoting defective perception or wits. **1.** Suffixed extended zero-grade form *dhū-mo-* (<*dhuə-mo-*), smoke, in: **a.** Latin *fūmus*, smoke: FUMAROLE, FUMATORIUM, FUMATORY, FUME; FUMARIC ACID, FUMIGATE, FUMITORY, PERFUME; **b.** Greek *thumos*, soul, spirit: -THYMIA; ENTHYMEME; **c.** Greek *thumon*, *thumos*, thyme (< "plant having a strong smell"): THYME. **2.** Suffixed lengthened zero-grade form *dhū-li-* in Latin *fūlīgō*, soot: FULIGINOUS. **3.** Extended form *dheus-* possibly in Germanic *dus-* in: **a.** Old English *dysig*, foolish (< "stupefied," "confused"): DIZZY; **b.** Danish *døse*, to make drowsy, akin to the probable Scandinavian source of DOZE. **4.** Suffixed extended form *dheus-o-* in Germanic *deuzam*, breathing creature, animal, in: **a.** Old English *dēor*, animal: DEER; **b.** Old Norse *dȳr*, animal, deer: REINDEER. **5.** Suffixed o-grade form *dhous-o* in Slavic *dukh-* in Russian *dukh*, breath, spirit: DUKHOBOR. **6.** Variant extended form *dhwes-* in nasalized form *dhwens-* in Germanic *duns-*, dust, meal, in: **a.** Germanic suffixed form *duns-to-* in Old English *dūst*, dust: DUST; **b.** Old Norse *dūnn*, bird's down (< "fine like dust"): DOWN², DUVETYN; (EIDERDOWN). **7.** Extended zero-grade form *dhus-* in Greek *thuos*, burnt sacrifice, incense (> Latin *thus*, incense), and *thuia*, cedar: THUJA, THURIBLE; (THURIFER). **8.** Suffixed extended zero-grade form *dhus-ko-* in: **a.** Germanic *duskaz* in Old English *dox*, twilight: DUSK; **b.** Latin *fuscus*, dark, dusky: OBFUSCATE. **9.** Suffixed extended zero-grade form *dhus-no-* in Welsh *dwn*, dull brown color, whence Old English *dun(n)*, dark-brown: DUN². **10.** Zero-grade extended form *dhubh-* in Greek *tuphein* (< *thuphein*), to make smoke, and *tuphlos*,

blind: TYPHUS; TYPHLOSOLE. **11.** Extended form *dheubh-*, "beclouded in the senses," in suffixed o-grade form *dhoubh-o-* in: **a.** Germanic *daubaz* in Old English *dēaf*, deaf: DEAF; **b.** nasalized form *dhu-m-bho-* in Germanic *dumbaz* in Old English *dumb*, dumb: DUMB; **c.** Germanic *dūbōn-* in Old English *dūfe*, dove (< "dark-colored bird"): DOVE¹. **12.** Extended zero-grade form *dhwel-* in: **a.** Germanic *dwelan*, to go or lead astray, in Old English *dwellan*, to deceive (but influenced in sense by cognate Old Norse *dvelja*, to tarry): DWELL; **b.** Germanic *dulaz* in *(i)* Old English *dol*, dull: DOLDRUMS *(ii)* Middle Low German *dul*, dull: (DOLT), DULL. **13.** Extended zero-grade form *dhwes-* in Greek suffixed form *th(w)es-es-*, smoke, whence Greek *th(w)es-es-yon*, becoming *theion*, brimstone, sulfur: THIO-, THION-. **14.** Perhaps Old English *docce*, dock (< "dark-colored plant"): DOCK⁴. **15.** Perhaps Irish *dūd*, pipe: DUDEEN. [Pok. 4. *dheu-* 261.]

dheu-². To flow. Germanic *dauwaz*, dew, in: **a.** Old English *dēaw*, dew: DEW; **b.** compound *melith-dauwaz*, "honeydew" (see **melit-**). [Pok. 1. *dheu-* 259.]

dheu-³. To become exhausted, die. **1.** Suffixed o-grade form *dhou-to-* in Germanic *daudaz* in Old English *dēad*, dead: DEAD. **2.** Suffixed o-grade form *dhou-tu-* in Germanic *dauthuz* in Old English *dēath*, death: DEATH. **3.** Suffixed o-grade form *dhow-yo-* in Old Norse *deyja*, to die: DIE¹. **4.** Suffixed extended zero-grade form *dhwī-no-* in Germanic *dwīnan* in Old English *dwīnan*, to diminish, languish: DWINDLE. [Pok. 2. *dheu-* 260.]

dheub-. Deep, hollow. **1.** Germanic *deupaz* in Old English *dēop*, deep: DEEP, DEPTH. **2.** Germanic expressive denominative *duppjan* in Old English *dyppan*, to immerse, dip: DIP. **3.** Parallel root form *dheubh-* in Germanic *deub-*, *dub-* in verb *dūbjan* in Old English *dȳfan*, to dip, and *dūfan*, to sink, dive: DIVE. [Pok. *dheu-b-* 267.]

dheubh-. Wedge, peg, plug. Germanic *dub-* in: **a.** Old English *dubbian*, to tap, strike (with a sword): DUB¹; **b.** Low German *dubben*, to hit: DUB²; **c.** Germanic diminutive *dub-ila-* in Middle Low German *dövel*, peg: DOWEL. [Pok. *dheubh-* 268.]

dheugh-. To produce something of utility. **1.** Germanic extended form *duht-* in Old English *dyhtig*, *dohtig*, strong (< "useful"): DOUGHTY. **2.** Suffixed form *dheugh-os-* in Greek *teukhos* (< *theukhos*), gear, anything produced, tool: HEPTATEUCH, HEXATEUCH, PENTATEUCH. [Pok. *dheugh-* 271.]

dhghem-. Earth. **1.** Suffixed zero-grade form *(dh)ghm-on-*, "earthling," in Germanic *gumōn-* in Old English *guma*, man: BRIDEGROOM. **2.** O-grade form *dhghōm-* in Greek *khthōn*, earth: CHTHONIC; AUTOCHTHON. **3.** Zero-grade form *dhghṃ-* in Greek *khamai*, on the ground: CHAMAEPHYTE, CHAMELEON, CHAMOMILE, GERMANDER. **4.** Suffixed o-grade form *(dh)ghom-o-* in Latin *humus*, earth: HUMBLE, (HUMILIATE), (HUMILITY), HUMUS; EXHUME, INHUME, TRANSHUMANCE. **5.** Suffixed o-grade form *(dh)ghom-on-*, "earthling," in: **a.** Latin *homō*, human being, man: HOMAGE, HOMBRE¹, HOMINID, HOMO¹, HOMUNCULUS, OMBRE; BONHOMIE, HOMICIDE; **b.** (in part) Latin *hūmānus*, human, kind, humane: HUMAN, (HUMANE). **6.** Suffixed form *(dh)ghem-ya* in Russian *zemlya*, land, earth: SIEROZEM, ZEMSTVO. **7.** Full-grade form *(dh)ghem-* in Persian *zamīn*, earth, land: ZAMINDAR. [Pok. *ghdhem-* 414.]

dhghū-. Fish. Greek *ikhthus*, fish: ICHTHYO-. [Pok. *ghdhū-* 416.]

dhgh(y)es-. Yesterday. Suffixed (comparative) form *(dh)ghes-ter-* in Germanic *ges-ter-* in Old English *geostran*, *giestran*, "yester-": YESTER-, (YESTERDAY). [Pok. *ghdhi̯es* 416.]

dhgʷhei-. To perish, die away. Zero-grade form *dhgʷhi-* in Greek *phthinein*, to die away: PHTHISIS. [Pok. *gʷhdhei(ə)-* 487.]

dhgʷher-. To run. Perhaps Greek *phtheir,* louse: (ICH), PHTHIRIASIS. [Pok. *gⁿhdher-* 487.]

dhīgʷ-. To stick, fix. **1.** Germanic **dīk-* in: **a.** Old English *dīc,* trench, moat: DIKE, DITCH; **b.** Old French *digue,* trench, perhaps akin to the source of Middle English *diggen,* to dig: DIG. **2.** Latin *fīgere,* to fasten, fix: FIBULA, FICHU, FIX, (FIXATE), (FIXITY), (FIXTURE); AFFIX, ANTE-FIX, CRUCIFY, INFIX, MICROFICHE, PREFIX, SUFFIX, TRANSFIX. [Pok. *dhēigʷ-* 243.]

dhragh-. To draw, drag on the ground. Rhyming variant **tragh-.** **1.** Germanic **dragan* in: **a.** Old English *dragan,* to draw, pull: DRAW; **b.** Old English *draga,* to draw, pull (or Old English *dragan*): DRAG; **c.** Old English *dræge,* dragnet: DRAY; **d.** Old Norse **drāhtr, drāttr,* act of drawing, akin to the source of Middle English *draught,* a pull: DRAFT. **2.** Russian *drogi,* a wagon: DROSHKY. See also variant form **dhreg-.** [Pok. *dheragh-* 257.]

dhreg-. To draw, glide. Variant form of **dhragh-.** **1.** Nasalized Germanic form **drinkan,* to draw into the mouth, drink, in Old English *drincan* to drink: DRINK. **2.** Nasalized Germanic form **drankjan,* "to cause to drink," in: **a.** Old English *drencan,* to soak: DRENCH; **b.** Scandinavian **drunkna, drugna,* to drown, akin to the Scandinavian source of Middle English *drounen,* to drown: DROWN. [Pok. *dhreg-* 273.]

dhregh-. To run. **1.** Greek *trekhein* (< **threkhein*), to run (> *trokhos,* wheel): TROCHAL, TROCHANTER, TROCHE, TROCHEE; TROCHOPHORE. **2.** O-grade form **dhrogh-* in Greek *trokhileia, trokhilia,* system of pulleys, roller of a windlass: TROCHLEA, TRUCK¹, (TRUCKLE). [Pok. 1. *dhregh-* 273.]

dhreibh-. To drive, push; snow. **1.** Germanic **drīban* in Old English *drīfan,* to drive, rush: DRIVE, DROVE². **2.** Germanic noun form **driftiz* in Old Norse *drift,* snowdrift, and Middle Dutch *drift,* herd, both akin to Middle English *drift,* drove, herd: DRIFT. [Pok. *dhreibh-* 274.]

dhreu-. To fall, flow, drip, droop. **1.** Extended form **dhreus-* in Germanic **dreusan* in Old English *drēosan,* to fall: DRIZZLE. **2.** Extended o-grade form **dhrous-* in: **a.** Germanic **drauzaz* in Old English *drēor,* flowing blood: DREARY; **b.** Germanic **drūsjan* in Old English *drūsian,* to be sluggish: DROWSE. **3.** Extended zero-grade form **dhrub-* in: **a.** Germanic **drupan* in Old English *dropa,* drop: DROP; **b.** Germanic **drūpjan,* to let fall, in Old Norse *drūpa,* to hang down: DROOP; **c.** Germanic **drupjan* in Old English *dryppan,* to drip: DRIP. **4.** Suffixed zero-grade form **dhrubh-yo-* in Greek *thruptein,* to crumble: LITHOTRITY. [Pok. *dhreu-* 274.]

dhreugh-. To deceive. Germanic suffixed form **drau(g)ma-* in Old English *drēam,* vision, illusion, dream (but attested only in the senses of "joy," "music"): DREAM. [Pok. 2. *dhreugh-* 276.]

dhughəter-. Daughter. Germanic **dohtēr* in Old English *dohtor,* daughter: DAUGHTER. [Pok. *dhug(h)ətēr* 277.]

dhūno-. Fortified, enclosed place. (Only in Celtic and Germanic.) **1.** Possibly Germanic **dūnaz,* hill, in: **a.** Old English *dūn,* hill: DOWN¹, DOWN³; **b.** Middle Dutch *dūne,* sandy hill: DUNE. **2.** Celtic **dūn-o-,* hill, stronghold, borrowed into Germanic as **tūnaz,* fortified place, in Old English *tūn,* enclosed place, homestead, village: TOWN. [In Pok. 4. *dheu-* 261.]

dhwen-. To make noise. Germanic **duniz* in Old English *dyne,* noise: DIN. [Pok. *dhu̯en-* 277.]

dhwenə-. To disappear, die. Suffixed zero-grade form *dhwnə-tos* in Greek *thanatos,* death: THANATOS; EUTHANASIA, TANSY. [In Pok. 4. *dheu-* 261.]

dhwer-. Door, doorway (usually in plural). Originally an apophonic noun **dhwor-, *dhur-,* in the plural, designating the entrance to the enclosure (**dhwor-o-*) surrounding the house proper. **1.** Zero-grade form **dhur-* in suffixed forms **dhur-n̥s* (accusative plural) and **dhur-o-* (neuter) respectively in Germanic **durunz* and **duram* in Old English *duru,* door (feminine, originally plural), and *dor,* door (neuter): DOOR. **2.** Suffixed o-grade form

*dhwor-āns (accusative plural) in Latin *forās,* (toward) out of doors, outside: FOREIGN. **3.** Suffixed o-grade form **dhwor-ois* (locative plural) in Latin *forīs,* (being) out of doors: FOREST; (AFFOREST), FAUBOURG, FORECLOSE, FORFEIT. **4.** Suffixed o-grade form **dhwor-o-* in Latin *forum,* marketplace (originally the enclosed space around a home): FORENSIC, FORUM. **5.** Zero-grade form **dhur-* in Greek *thura,* door (> *thureos,* shield): THYROID. **6.** Persian *dar,* door, gate: DURBAR. [Pok. *dhu̯ēr-* 278.]

digh-. She-goat. Germanic **tigon* (with expressive consonantism) in Old Norse *tík,* bitch: TYKE. [Pok. *digh-* 222.]

dḷk-u-. Sweet. **1.** Suffixed form **dḷkw-i-* in Latin *dulcis* (> French *doux*), sweet: DOLCE, DOUCEUR, DULCET; BILLET-DOUX, DULCIFY. **2.** Basic form **dḷku-* (with **dl-* dissimilated to **gl-* in Greek because of the following *k*) in: **a.** Greek *glukus,* sweet: LICORICE; **b.** Greek *glukeros* (with suffix **-ero-*), sweet: GLYCERIN; **c.** Greek *gleukos* (with suffix *-es-*), must, sweet wine: GLUCOSE. [Pok. *dḷkú-* 222.]

dn̥ghū. Tongue. **1.** Germanic **tungōn-* in: **a.** Old English *tunge,* tongue: TONGUE; **b.** Middle Dutch *tonghe,* tongue: BILTONG. **2.** Latin *lingua* (< Old Latin *dingua*), tongue, language: LANGUAGE, LANGUET, LIGULE, LINGO, LINGUA, LINGUIST; (BILINGUAL). [Pok. *dn̥ghū* 223.]

dō-. To give. Contracted from **doə-.* **1.** Zero-grade form **də-* in Latin *dare,* to give: DADO, DATE, DATIVE, DATUM, DIE²; ADD, BETRAY, EDITION, PERDITION, RENDER, (RENT¹), (SURRENDER), TRADITION, (TRAITOR), (TREASON), VEND. **2.** Suffixed form **dō-no-* in Latin *dōnum,* gift (> *dōnāre,* to present, forgive): DONATION, DONATIVE, DONOR; CONDONE, PARDON. **3.** Suffixed form **dō-t(i)-* in: **a.** Latin *dōs* (genitive *dōtis*), dowry: DOT², DOWAGER, DOWER, (DOWRY); ENDOW; **b.** Slavic **datja* in Russian *dacha,* gift: DACHA; **c.** Russian *dat',* to give, in *izdat',* to publish: SAMIZDAT. **4.** Reduplicated form **di-dō-* in Greek *didonai,* to give: DOSE; ANECDOTE, ANTIDOTE, APODOSIS, EPIDOTE. [Pok. *dō-* 223.]

[dorsum. The back. Latin noun of unknown origin. DORSAL, DORSO-, DORSUM, DOSS, (DOSSAL), DOSSIER; ENDORSE, INTRADOS, REREDOS.]

drem-. To sleep. Suffixed zero-grade form **dr̥m-yo-* in Latin *dormīre,* to sleep: DORMANT, DORMER, DORMITORY. [Pok. *drē-* 226.]

[dreug-. Dry. Germanic root. **1.** Old English *drūgoth, drūgath,* dryness, drought: DROUGHT. **2.** Suffixed form **drūg-iz* in Old English *drȳge,* dry: DRY. **3.** Suffixed variant form **draug-n-* in Old English *drēahnian,* to strain, drain: DRAIN.]

[dub-. Also **dup-.** To drop, dip. Germanic imitative root. **1.** Old English *-doppa,* a kind of bird (< "one that dips"): DIDAPPER. **2.** Dutch *doopen,* to dip: DOPE. **3.** Old English **dympel* (diminutive with nasal infix), pool, dimple (> Middle English *dimpel*): DIMPLE. **4.** Norwegian *dumpa,* to fall suddenly, akin to the Scandinavian source of Middle English *dumpen,* to dump: DUMP. [In Pok. *dheu-b-* 267.]]

[dud-. To shake, deceive. Germanic root. **1.** Norwegian *dudra,* to quiver, akin to: **a.** Middle English *daderen,* to tremble: DODDER¹; **b.** Middle English *doder,* vine (< "that which quivers in the wind"): DODDER². **2.** Middle English *doten,* to be foolish: DOTE. [In Pok. 4. *dheu-* 261.]]

[duellum. War. Latin noun (later form *bellum*) of unknown origin. BELLICOSE, BELLONA, DUEL; ANTEBELLUM, BELLIGERENT, POSTBELLUM, REBEL, (REVEL).]

dus-. Bad, evil; mis- (used as a prefix). Derivative of **deu-¹.** Greek *dus-,* bad: DYS-. [Pok. *dus-* 227.]

dwei-. To fear. **1.** Suffixed form **dwei-ro-* in Latin *dīrus,* fearful, horrible (originally a dialectal form): DIRE. **2.** Suffixed form **dwey-eno-* in Greek *deinos,* fearful, monstrous: DINOSAUR, DINOTHERE. (This root originally meant "to be in doubt, be of two minds," and is related to **dwo-.**) [Pok. *du̯ei-* 227.]

dwo-. Two. **I.** Variant form *duwo.* **1.** Germanic **twa,* two,

in: **a.** Old English *twā*, two (nominative feminine and neuter): TWO; **b.** Old English *twēgen*, two (nominative and accusative masculine): TWAIN. **2.** Germanic compound *twa-lif-*, "two left (over from ten)," twelve (*-lif-*, left; see **leikw-**), in Old English *twelf*, twelve, and *twelfta*, twelfth: TWELFTH, TWELVE. **II.** Adverbial form *dwis* and combining form *dwi-*. **1.** Germanic *twi-* in: **a.** Old English *twi-* (> Middle English *twi-*), two: TWIBIL, TWILIGHT; **b.** Old High German *zwi-* (> German *zwie-*), twice: ZWIEBACK, ZWITTERION. **2.** Latin *bis* (combining form *bi-*), twice: BI-, BIS; BAROUCHE, BISCUIT. **3.** Greek *dis* (combining form *di-*), twice: DI-¹. **4.** Germanic *twisten* in Middle English *twisten*, to twist: TWIST. **5.** Germanic *twiyes* in Old English *twige*, *twiga*, twice: TWICE. **6.** Germanic compound *twēgentig*, "twice ten" (*-tig*, ten; see **dekm̥**) in Old English *twēntig*, twenty: TWENTY. **7.** Germanic *twīhna*, double thread, twisted thread, in Old English *twīn*, double thread: TWINE. **8.** Germanic compounds *bi-twīhna* and *bi-twisk*, "at the middle point of two" (*bi*, at, by; see **ambhi**), in Old English *betwēonum* and *betweohs*, *betwix*, between: BETWEEN, BETWIXT, (TWIXT). **9.** Germanic compound *twilic-*, "two-threaded fabric" in Old English *twilic*, woven of double thread: TWILL. **10.** Suffixed form *dwis-no-* in: **a.** Germanic *twisnaz*, double, in Old English *twinn*, *getwinn*, two by two, twin: TWIN; **b.** Latin *bīnī*, two by two, two each: BINAL, BINARY; COMBINE. **11.** Suffixed form *dwi-ko-* in Germanic *twig(g)a*, a fork, in Old English *twigge*, a branch: TWIG¹. **12.** Compound *dwi-plo-*, twofold (*-plo-*, -fold; see **pel-³**), in Greek *diploos*, *diplous*, twofold: DIPLO-, DIPLOE, DIPLOMA; ANADIPLOSIS. **13.** Suffixed reduplicated form *dwi-du-mo-* in Greek *didumos*, double, the testicles: (DIDYMIUM), DIDYMOUS; EPIDIDYMIS, TETRADYMITE. **14.** Suffixed form *dwi-kha* in Greek *dikha*, in two: DICHASIUM, DICHO-. **III.** Inflected form *duwō*. **1.** Latin *duo*, two: DEUCE¹, DOZEN, DUAL, DUET, DUO-; DUODECIMAL. **2.** Greek *duo*, *duō*, two: DUAD, DYAD; DODECAGON, HENDIADYS. **IV.** Variant form *du-*. **1.** Compound *du-plo-*, twofold (*-plo-*, -fold; see **pel-³**), in Latin *duplus*, double: DOUBLE, (DOUBLET), (DOUBLOON), (DOUBLURE), DUPLE. **2.** Compound *du-plek-* (*-plek-*, -fold; see **plek-**), twofold, in Latin *duplex*, double: DUPLEX, DUPLICATE, (DUPLICITY); CONDUPLICATE. **3.** Suffixed form *du-bhw-io-* in Latin *dubius*, doubtful (< "hesitating between two alternatives"), and *dubitāre*, to be in doubt: DOUBT, DUBIOUS, (REDOUBTABLE). [Pok. *duō(u)* 228.]

ē. Adverbial particle. Germanic *ē* in Old English *ā-*, *ǣ-*, away, off: OAKUM. [Pok. *ē* 280.]

ed-. To eat; original meaning "to bite." See **dent-**. **1.** Germanic *etan* in: **a.** Old English *etan*, to eat: EAT; **b.** Old High German *ezzen*, to feed on, eat: ETCH; **c.** Middle Dutch *eten*, to eat: ORT; **d.** Germanic compound *fra-etan*, to eat up (*fra-*, completely; see **per¹**) in Old English *fretan*, to devour: FRET¹. **2.** Latin *edere*, to eat: EDACIOUS, EDIBLE, ESCAROLE, ESCULENT, ESURIENT; COMEDO, COMESTIBLE, OBESE. **3.** Zero-grade form *d-* in Latin compound *prandium* (< *pram-d-ium*), "first meal," lunch (*pram-*, first; see **per¹**): PRANDIAL. **4.** Suffixed form *ed-un-ā* in Greek *odunē*, pain (< "gnawing care"): ANODYNE. [Pok. *ed-* 287.]

eg. **I.** Nominative form of the personal pronoun of the first person singular. For oblique forms see **me-¹**. **1.** Germanic *ek* in Old English *ic*, I: I. **2.** Extended form *egō* in Latin *ego*, I: EGO, EGOIST, (EGOTISM). [Pok. *eg̑* 291.]

eg-. To lack. Suffixed (stative) form *eg-ē-* in Latin *egēre*, to lack, be in want: INDIGENT. [Pok. *eg-* 290.]

ēg-. To speak. Suffixed zero-grade form *ǝg-yo-* in: **a.** Latin *adagium*, saying, proverb, "a speaking to" (*ad-*, to; see **ad-**): ADAGE; **b.** Latin *prōdigium*, a portent, "a foretelling" (*prōd-*, variant of *prō-*, before; see **per¹**): PRODIGY. [Pok. *ēg̑-* 290.]

eghero-. Lake. Possibly a suffixed variant form *agher-*

ont- in Greek *Akherōn*, a river in Hades: ACHERON. [Pok. *eg̑hero-* 291.]

eghs. Out. **1.** Variant *eks* in: **a.** Latin *ex*, *ex-*, out of, away from: EX¹, EX-; **b.** Greek *ex*, *ek*, out of, from: ECTO-, EXO-, EXOTERIC, EXOTIC; SYNECDOCHE. **2.** Suffixed (comparative) variant form *eks-tero-* in Latin *exterus*, outward (feminine ablative *extera*, *extrā*, on the outside): EXTERIOR, EXTERNAL, EXTRA-, STRANGE. **3.** Suffixed (superlative) form in Latin *extrēmus*, outermost (*-mo-*, superlative suffix): EXTREME. **4.** Suffixed form *eghs-ko-* in Greek *eskhatos*, outermost, last: ESCHATOLOGY. [Pok. *eghs* 292.]

egni-. Also **ogni-**. Fire. **1.** Latin *ignis*, fire: IGNEOUS, IGNITE; GELIGNITE, IGNITRON. **2.** Sanskrit *agniḥ*, fire: AGNI. [Pok. *egnis* 293.]

ēgwh-. To drink. Suffixed form *ēgwh-r-yo-* in: **a.** Latin *ēbrius*, drunk: INEBRIATE; **b.** Latin compound *sōbrius* (*sē-*, without; see **s(w)e-**).

ei-¹. To go. **1.** Full-grade form *ei-* in: **a.** Latin *īre*, to go: ADIT, AMBIENT, (AMBITION); CIRCUIT, COITUS, COMITIA, EXIT¹, EXIT², INTROIT, ISSUE, OBITUARY, PERISH, PRAETOR, PRETERIT, SEDITION, SUBITO, SUDDEN, (TRANCE), TRANSIENT, (TRANSIT), (TRANSITIVE); **b.** Greek *ienai*, to go: ION; ANION, COITION, DYSPROSIUM. **2.** Suffixed zero-grade form *i-t-* in: **a.** further suffixed form *i-t-yo-* in Latin *initium*, entrance, beginning (*in-*, in; see **en**): COMMENCE, INITIAL, (INITIATE); **b.** Latin *comes* (stem *comit-*), companion (< "one who goes with another"; *com-*, with; see **kom**): COUNT²; CONCOMITANT, CONSTABLE, (VISCOUNT). **3.** Suffixed form *i-ter* in Latin *iter*, journey (> Late Latin *itinerāre*, to travel): (ERRANT), EYRE, ITINERANT, ITINERARY. **4.** Extended form *yā-* (< *yǝ₂-*) in suffixed forms *yā-no-*, *yā-nu-* in: **a.** Latin *jānus*, archway, and *Jānus*, god of doors and of the beginning of a year: JANITOR, JANUARY, JANUS; **b.** Sanskrit *yānam*, way (in Buddhism, "mode of knowledge," "vehicle"): HINAYANA, MAHAYANA. [Pok. 1. *ei-* 293.]

ei-². Reddish, motley; yew. Suffixed form *ei-wo-* in Germanic *īwaz*, yew, in Old English *īw*, yew: YEW. [Pok. 3. *ei-* 297.]

ēik-. To be master of, possess. **1.** Germanic *aigan*, to possess, in Old English *āgan*, to possess: OUGHT¹, OWE. **2.** Germanic participial form *aiganaz*, possessed, owned, in Old English *āgen*, one's own: OWN. **3.** Germanic prefixed form *fra-aihtiz*, absolute possession, property (*fra-*, intensive prefix; see **per¹**), in Middle Low German and Middle Dutch *vrecht*, *vracht*, "earnings," hire for a ship, freight: FRAUGHT, FREIGHT. [Pok. *ēik-* 289.]

eis-¹. In words denoting passion. **1.** Suffixed form *eis-ā-* in Latin *īra*, anger: IRASCIBLE, IRATE, IRE. **2.** Suffixed zero-grade form *is-(ǝ)ro-*, powerful, holy, in Greek *hieros*, "filled with the divine," holy: HIERATIC, HIERO-; HIERARCH, (HIERARCHY), HIEROGLYPHIC, HIEROPHANT. **3.** Germanic *isarno-*, "holy metal" (possibly from Celtic), in Old English *īse(r)n*, *īren*, iron: IRON. **4.** Suffixed o-grade form *ois-tro-*, madness, in Greek *oistros*, gadfly, goad, anything causing madness: ESTRUS; (ESTRONE). [Pok. 1. *eis-* 299.]

eis-². Ice, frost. Germanic *īs-* in Old English *īs*, ice: ICE; ICICLE. [Pok. 2. *ei-s-* 301.]

ekwo-. Horse. Possibly originally derived from **kwon-**. **1.** Latin *equus*, horse: EQUESTRIAN, EQUINE, EQUITANT, (EQUITATION); EQUISETUM. **2.** Greek *hippos*, horse: EOHIPPUS, HIPPOCAMPUS, HIPPOGRIFF, HIPPOPOTAMUS. [Pok. *eku̯o-s* 301.]

el-¹. Elbow, forearm. Extended o-grade form *olinā*, elbow, in: **a.** Germanic *alinō* in Old English *eln*, forearm, cubit: ELL²; **b.** Germanic compound *alino-bugōn*, "bend of the forearm," elbow (*bugōn-*, bend, bow; see **bheug-³**), in Old English *elnboga*, elbow: ELBOW; **c.** Latin *ulna*, forearm: ULNA; **d.** lengthened variant form *ōlenā* in Greek *ōlenē*, elbow: OLECRANON. [Pok. 8. *el-* 307.]

el-². Red, brown (forming animal and tree names). **1.** Ex-

tended form *elmo- in Germanic *elmo-, *almo- in Old English elm, elm: ELM. **2.** Germanic extended form *aliza, alder, in Old English alor, alder: ALDER. **3.** Possibly Old English ellen, ellærn, the elder: ELDER². **4.** Extended o-grade form *olki- in Germanic *alkiz, elk, in Old Norse elgr, elk, akin to Old English eolh, elk: ELK. **5.** Perhaps Germanic extended form *alk- in Old Norse alka, auk: AUK. **6.** Extended form *elno- in Greek ellos, hellos, fawn: HELLEBORE. **7.** Extended form *eləni- in Lithuanian élnis, stag: ELAND. [Pok. 1. el- 302.]

el-³. To go. Suffixed extended form *ela-un-yo- in Greek elaunein, to drive (< "to cause to go"): ELASTIC, ELATER, ELATERITE; ELASMOBRANCH. [Pok. 6. el- 306.]

[elaia. Olive. Greek noun (earlier form elaiwā) of Mediterranean origin. OIL, (-OLE), OLEAGINOUS, OLEASTER, OLEO-, OLIVE; (AIOLI), (ANELE), (PETROLEUM).]

elk-es-. Wound. Latin ulcus (stem ulcer-), a sore: ULCER. [Pok. elkos- 310.]

em-. To take, distribute. **1.** Latin emere, to obtain, buy (> demere, to take away): ADEMPTION, EXAMPLE, (EXEMPLARY), (EXEMPLIFY), EXEMPLUM, (EXEMPT), (IMPROMPTU), PEREMPTORY, PREEMPTION, PREMIUM, PROMPT, (RANSOM), REDEEM, (REDEMPTION), (SAMPLE), VINTAGE. **2.** Latin sūmere (< *sus(e)m-), to take, obtain, buy (sus-, variant of sub-, up from under; see **upo**): SUMPTUARY, (SUMPTUOUS), ASSUME, CONSUME, PRESUME, RESUME, SUBSUME. [Pok. em- 310.]

en. In. **1.** Germanic *in in: **a.** Old English in, in: IN; **b.** Germanic (comparative) *inn(e)ra in Old English innera, farther in, inner: INNER; **c.** Germanic *innan in Old English binnan, within (be, by; see **ambhi** + innan, in, within): BEN¹. **2.** Latin in, in-, in, into: EN-¹, IN-². **3.** Greek en, en-, in: EN-²; ENKEPHALIN, PARENCHYMA, PARENTHESIS. **4.** Suffixed form *en-t(e)ro- in: **a.** Latin intrō, inward, within: INTRO-; INTRODUCE, INTROIT, INTROMIT, INTRORSE, INTROSPECT; **b.** Latin intrā, inside, within: ENTER, INTRA-; INTRADOS, INTRINSIC. **5.** Suffixed form *en-ter in Latin inter, inter-, between, among: ENTRAILS, INTER-, INTERIM, INTERIOR, INTERNAL. **6.** Latin (superlative) intimus (*-mo-, superlative suffix), innermost: INTIMA, INTIMATE². **7.** Old Latin endo, Latin indu-, within, in industria, diligence, activity (*stru-, to construct; see **ster-²**): INDUSTRY. **8.** Suffixed form *en-tos in: **a.** Latin intus, within, inside: DEDANS, INTESTINE, INTINE, INTUSSUSCEPTION; **b.** Greek entos, within: ENTO-. **9.** Suffixed form *en-tero- in Greek enteron, entrails: ENTERIC, ENTERO-, ENTERON; DYSENTERY, MESENTERY. **10.** Extended form *ens in: **a.** Greek eis, into: EPISODE; **b.** suffixed form *ens-ō in Greek esō, within: ESOTERIC. **11.** Suffixed zero-grade form *n̥-dha possibly in Germanic *anda, *unda in Old English and, and: AND. [Pok. 1. en 311.]

en-. Year. Zero-grade form *n- in compound *per-n-yo-, of last year (see **per¹**). [Pok. 2. en- 314.]

en-es-. Burden. Latin onus (stem oner-), burden: ONEROUS, ONUS; EXONERATE. [Pok. enos- 321.]

engʷ-. Groin, internal organ. Suffixed zero-grade form *n̥gʷ-en- in: **a.** Latin inguen, groin: INGUINAL; **b.** Greek adēn, gland, gut: ADENO-; LYMPHADENITIS, SIALADENITIS. [Pok. engʷ- 319.]

epi. Also **opi.** Near, at, against. **1.** Latin ob, ob-, before, to, against: OB-. **2.** Greek epi, on, over, at: EPI-. **3.** Greek opisthen, behind, at the back: OPISTHOBRANCH, OPISTHOGNATHOUS. **4.** Zero-grade *pi-, on, in Greek piezein, to press tight (see **sed-¹**). **5.** Old Church Slavonic ob, on, in Russian oblast', oblast: OBLAST. **6.** Prefix *op- in *op-wer-yo-, to cover over (see **wer-⁵**). [Pok. epi 323.]

er-¹. To move, set in motion. **1.** Probably Germanic *ar-, *or-, *art(a), to be, exist, in Old English eart and aron, second person singular and plural present of bēon, to be: ARE¹, ART². **2.** Perhaps in Germanic suffixed form *er-n-os-ti- in Old English eornoste, zealous, serious: EARNEST¹. **3.** Suffixed form *or-yo- in Latin orīrī, to arise,

appear, be born: ORIENT, ORIGIN, ORIGINAL; ABORT. [Pok. 3. er- 326; ergh- 339.]

er-². Earth, ground. Extended form *ert- in Germanic *erthō in: **a.** Old English eorthe, earth: EARTH; **b.** Middle Dutch aerde, eerde, earth (> Afrikaans aarde): AARDVARK, AARDWOLF. [Pok. 4. er- 332.]

er-³. Base of designations of various domestic horned animals. Extended form *eri- in Latin ariēs, ram: ARIES. [Pok. 2. er- 326.]

erə-¹. To row. **1.** Variant form *rē- (< *reə-) in: **a.** Germanic *rō- in Old English rōwan, to row: ROW²; **b.** suffixed form *rō-thra- in Germanic *rōthra, rudder, in Old English rōther, steering oar: RUDDER; **c.** suffixed form *rē-smo- in Latin rēmus, oar: BIREME, REMEX, TRIREME. **2.** Oldest variant form *ərea- becoming *erē- in Greek triērēs, trireme: TRIERARCH. [Pok. 1. erə- 338.]

erə-². To separate. Variant *rē-, contracted from *reə-. **1.** Suffixed variant form *rā-ro- in Latin rārus, "having intervals between," "full of empty spaces," rare: RARE¹. **2.** Suffixed zero-grade form *rə-ti- in Latin ratis, raft (< "grating," "latticework"): RATITE. **3.** Suffixed lengthened-grade form *rē-ti- in Latin rēte, rētis, a net: RÉSEAU, RETE, RETIARY, RETICLE, RETICULE, RETINA; RETIFORM. **4.** Suffixed form *erē-mo- in Greek erēmos, empty, desolate, bereft: EREMITE, HERMIT; EREMURUS. [Pok. 5. er- 332.]

erəd-. High. Suffixed zero-grade form *rəd-wo- in Latin arduus, high, steep: ARDUOUS. [Pok. er(ə)d- 339.]

ergh-. To mount. **1.** Suffixed o-grade form *orgh-i- in Greek orkhus, testicle: ORCHID. **2.** Suffixed o-grade form *orgh-eyo- in Greek orkheisthai, to dance: ORCHESTRA. [Pok. orghi- 782, ergh- 339.]

erkʷ-. To radiate, beam, praise. Sanskrit r̥c, r̥k, "brightness," praise, poem: RIG-VEDA. [Pok. erkʷ- 340.]

ers-¹. To be in motion. **1.** Variant form *rēs- in Germanic *rēs- in Old Norse rās, rushing: RACE². **2.** Form ers-ā- in Latin errāre, to wander: ERR, ERRATIC, ERRATUM, ERRONEOUS, ERROR; ABERRATION. [Pok. 2. ere-s- 336.]

ers-². To be wet. Variant form *ros- in Latin rōs, dew: ROSEMARY. [Pok. 2. ere-s- 336.]

es-. To be. **1.** Athematic first person singular form *es-mi in Germanic *izm(i) in Old English eam, eom, am: AM. **2.** Athematic third person singular form *es-ti in: **a.** Germanic *ist(i) in Old English is, is: IS; **b.** Sanskrit asti, is: SWASTIKA. **3.** Optative stem *sī- in Germanic *sijai- in Old English sīe, may it be (so) in gēse (gēa, yea; see **i-** + sīe), yes: YES. **4.** Participial form *sont-, being, existing, hence real, true, in: **a.** Germanic *santhaz in Old English sōth, true: SOOTH, SOOTHE; **b.** suffixed (collective) zero-grade form *sn̥t-yā, "that which is," in Germanic *sun(d)jō, sin (< "it is true," "the sin is real"), in Old English synn, sin: SIN¹; **c.** Sanskrit sat-, sant-, existing, true, virtuous: SUTTEE; BODHISATTVA, SATYAGRAHA. **5.** Basic form *es- in Latin esse, to be: ENTITY, ESSENCE; ABSENT, (IMPROVE), INTEREST, PRESENT¹, (PRESENT²), PROUD, (QUINTESSENCE), (REPRESENT). **6.** Basic form *es- in Greek einai (present participle ont-), being, to be (in pareinai, to be present): -ONT, ONTO-; (BIONT), HOMOIOUSIAN, PAROUSIA, (SCHIZONT). See extension **esu-**. [Pok. es- 340.]

esen-. Harvest, fall. O-grade form *osn- in Germanic *aznōn, to do harvest work, serve, in Old English earnian, to serve, gain as wages: EARN¹. [Pok. es-en- 343.]

esu-. Good. Extension of **es-**. Greek esus, good, combining form eu-, well: EU-. [Pok. esu-s 342.]

eti. Above, beyond. **1.** Germanic *ith- in Old Norse idha, whirlpool: EDDY. **2.** Latin et, and (< "furthermore"): ET CETERA. [Pok. eti 344.]

ētī-. Eider duck. A probable root. Germanic *ēthī in North Germanic *āthī in Old Norse æðhr, eider: EIDER. [Pok. ētī- 345.]

ētmen-. Breath. Sanskrit ātman, breath, soul: ATMAN; MAHATMA. [Pok. ēt-men- 345.]

eu-¹. To dress. **1.** Latin induere, to don (ind-, variant of

in-, in, on; see **en**): ENDUE. **2.** Latin *exuere*, to doff (*ex-*, off; see **eghs**): EXUVIAE. **3.** Latin *reduvia*, fragment (*red-*, back, in reverse; see **re-**): REDUVIID. See extension **wes-⁴**. [Pok. 2. *eu-* 346.]

eu-². Lacking, empty. Extended forms **euǝ-*, **wā-*, **wǝ-*. **1.** Suffixed form **wǝ-no-* in: **a.** Germanic **wanēn* in Old English *wanian*, to lessen, and *wana*, lack: WANE; **b.** North Germanic **wanatōn* in Old Norse *vanta*, to lack: WANT. **2.** Suffixed form **wā-no-* in Latin *vānus*, empty: VAIN, VANITY, VAUNT; EVANESCE, VANISH. **3.** Extended form **wak-* in Latin *vacāre* (variant *vocāre*), to be empty: VACANT, VACATE, VACATION, (VACUITY), VACUUM, VOID, (AVOID), (DEVOID), EVACUATE. **4.** Extended and suffixed form **wās-to-* in Latin *vāstus*, empty, waste (> *vāstāre*, to make desolate): WASTE; DEVASTATE. [Pok. 1. *eu-* 345.]

euǝdh-. Udder. **1.** Suffixed zero-grade form **ūdh-r̥* in Germanic **ūdr-* in Old English *ūder*, udder: UDDER. **2.** Suffixed o-grade form **oudh-r̥* in Latin *ūber*, "breast," with derivative adjective *ūber*, fertile: (EXUBERANT), EXUBERATE. [Pok. *ēudh-* 347.]

euk-. To become accustomed. Zero-grade form **uk-* in: **a.** suffixed (feminine) form **uk-sor-* in Latin *uxor*, wife (< "she who gets accustomed to the new household" after patrilocal marriage): UXORIAL, UXORIOUS, UXORICIDE; **b.** nasalized form **u-n-k-* in Old Irish *to-ucc*, to understand, "get accustomed to" (> Irish Gaelic *tuigim*, I understand): TWIG². [Pok. *euk-* 347.]

eus-. To burn. **1.** Latin *ūrere*, to burn: UREDO; ADUST, COMBUSTION. **2.** Zero-grade form **us-* in: Germanic **uzjōn*, to burn, in compound **aim-uzjōn-*, ashes (**aim-*, ashes, ember), in Old English *ǣmerge*, ember: EMBER. **3.** Possibly in the non-Greek source of Greek *Euros*, the east wind: EURUS. [Pok. *eus-* 347.]

[ferrum. Iron. Latin noun, possibly borrowed (via Etruscan) from the same obscure source as Old English *bræs*, brass. **1.** Latin *ferrum*: FARRIER, FERRI-, FERRO-, (FERROUS), FERRUGINOUS; FER-DE-LANCE. **2.** Old English *bræs*: BRASS, BRAZEN, (BRAZIER¹).]

[Frankon-. Frank (member of a Germanic tribe), "javelin." Germanic root. **1.** Frankish **Frank-*, Frank, borrowed into Late Latin as *Francus*, Frank: (FRANK¹), FRANK. **2.** Derivative adjective **frankiskaz*, of the Franks, in Old English *frencisc*, French: FRENCH.]

[gagina. Also **gagana**. Against. Germanic root. **1.** Old English *gegn-*, against: GAINSAY. **2.** Germanic **ana-ga-gina* (**ana*, toward; see **an¹**), in the opposite direction, in Old English *ongeagn*, *ongēan*, against, back, again: AGAIN, AGAINST. **3.** Old Norse *gegn*, straight, direct, helpful: GAINLY; (UNGAINLY). **4.** Old High German *gegin*, *gagan*, against: GEGENSCHEIN.]

gal-¹. Bald, naked. Suffixed form **gal-wo-* in Germanic **kalwaz* in Old English *calu*, bare, bald: CALLOW. [Pok. 1. *gal-* 349.]

gal-². To call, shout. **1.** Germanic expressive form **kall-* in Old Norse *kalla*, to call: CALL. **2.** Germanic **klat-* in Old English **clatrian* (> Middle English *clateren*), to clatter: CLATTER. **3.** Expressive form **gall-* in Latin *gallus*, cock (< "the calling bird"; but probably also associated with *Gallus*, Gallic, as if to mean "the bird of Gaul," the cock being archaeologically attested as an important symbol in the iconography of Roman and pre-Roman Gaul): GALLINACEOUS, (GALLINULE). [Pok. 2. *gal-* 350.]

gal-³. To be able, to have power. Gallo-Roman **galia*, strength, power, in Old French *galliart*, lively: GALLIARD. [Pok. 3. *gal-* 351.]

gar-. To call, cry. Expressive root. **1.** Germanic **karō*, lament, hence grief, care, in: **a.** Old English *cearu*, care: CARE; **b.** adjective **karagaz*, sorrowful, in Old English *cearig*, sorrowful: CHARY. **2.** Celtic suffixed form **gar-(s)mn̥* in Gaelic *gairm*, shout, cry, call: SLOGAN. **3.** Suffixed form (with expressive gemination) **garr-iyo-* in Latin *garrīre*, to chatter: GARRULOUS. [Pok. *gar-* 352.]

[garwian. To make, prepare, equip. Germanic verb. **1.** Old Norse *gera*, to make, do: GAR². **2.** Form **garwi-*, equipment, adornment, in Italian *garbo*, grace, elegance of dress: GARB. **3.** Form **garwa-*, prepared, in Old English *gearu*, *gearo*, ready: YARE. **4.** Form **garwīn-* in Old Norse *gervi*, equipment, gear: GEAR.]

gāu-. To rejoice; also to have religious fear or awe. Contracted from **gaǝu-*. **1.** Suffixed form **gau-d-ē-* in Latin *gaudēre*, to rejoice: GAUD, (GAUDY¹), GAUDY², JOY; ENJOY, REJOICE. **2.** Form (with nasal infix) **gǝ-n-u-* in Greek *ganusthai*, to rejoice (> *ganos*, brightness, gladness): GANOID. [Pok. *gāu-* 353.]

[gē. Also **gaia**. The earth. Greek noun of unknown origin. GAEA, GEO-; APOGEE, EPIGEAL, (GEANTICLINE), GEODE, (GEORGIC), HYPOGEAL, NEOGAEA, PERIGEE.]

gēi-¹. To sprout, split open. Contracted from **geǝi-*. Zero-grade form **gī-* (< **giǝ-*) in: **a.** Germanic **kī-nan* in Old English *cine*, *cinu*, cleft, ravine cut by a stream: CHINK¹; **b.** Germanic **ki-dōn-* in Frankish **kid-*, sprout, young shoot, in Old French *cion*, shoot: SCION. [Pok. *gēi-* 355.]

gēi-². To sing. Contracted from **geǝi-*. Zero-grade form **gī-* (< **giǝ-*) in Sanskrit *gītā*, song: BHAGAVAD-GITA. [Pok. *gē(i)-* 355.]

gel-¹. To form into a ball; conventional base of loosely connected derivatives referring to a compact mass or coagulated lump, and to the qualities of viscosity and adhesiveness. **I.** Words meaning a mass or lump. **1.** Germanic **klamp-* in Middle Low German *klumpe*, compact group of trees: CLUMP. **2.** Germanic **klub(b)-* in Old Norse *klubba*, a lump of wood, club: CLUB¹. **3.** Germanic **kliw-* in Old English *cliewan*, a ball, ball of wool: CLEW¹, (CLUE). **4.** Germanic **klūd-* in: **a.** Old English *clūd*, hill, rock: CLOUD; **b.** Old English *clott*, lump: CLOD, CLOT, (CLUTTER); **c.** Middle High German *kloz*, block, lump: KLUTZ. **5.** Germanic **klūt-* in Old English *clūt*, patch (< "lump, piece of stuff, piece of cloth"): CLOUT. **6.** Germanic **klaut-* in Old English *clēat*, lump, wedge: CLEAT. **7.** Extended form **glob-* perhaps in Latin *globus*, ball, globe: GLOBE, (GLOBULE); CONGLOBATE. **8.** Extended form **glom-* in Latin *glomus* (stem *glomer-*), ball: GLOMERATE, GLOMERULE; AGGLOMERATE, CONGLOMERATE. **9.** Extended form **glēb-* in Latin *glēba*, lump, clod of earth, soil, land: GLEBE. **10.** Extended form **gleu-* in Greek *gloutos*, buttock: GLUTEUS. **11.** Reduplicated form **gal-gl-* dissimilated in Greek *ganglion*, cystlike tumor, hence nerve-bundle: GANGLION. **II.** Words meaning to stick, cling. **1.** Germanic **klupjan* (< **gleb-*) in Old English *clyppan*, to embrace, fasten: CLIP². **2.** Germanic **klimban* (< **gle-m-bh-*), to hold fast, hold on in climbing, in Old English *climban*, to climb: CLIMB. **3.** Germanic **klam-* in: **a.** Old English *clamm*, bond, fetter: (CLAM¹), CLAM²; **b.** Middle Low German *klam*, stickiness: CLAMMY. **4.** Germanic **klamp-* in Middle Dutch *klampe*, metal clasp: CLAMP. **5.** Germanic **kleb-* (< **glebh-*) in: **a.** Old English *cleofian*, to stick, cleave: CLEAVE²; **b.** Old English *clīfe*, goosegrass (a plant with hooked prickles on the stem): CLEAVERS. **6.** Germanic **kling-* in: **a.** Old English *clingan*, to cling: CLING; **b.** Old English *beclencan*, to hold fast (*be-*, on all sides; see **ambhi**): CLENCH, (CLINCH). **7.** Germanic **kluk-* in Old English *clyccan*, to clutch: CLUTCH¹. **8.** Germanic *klēwō*, remade to **klawō*, in Old English *clawu*, a claw: CLAW. **III.** Words meaning "sticky material." **1.** Extended form **glei-* in: **a.** Germanic **klajjō-*, clay, in Old English *clǣg*, clay: CLAY; **b.** probably Medieval Greek *glia*, *gloia*, glue: GLIADIN; MESOGLEA, NEUROGLIA, ZOOGLOEA; **c.** Russian *gleĭ*, clay: GLEY. **2.** Germanic **kleg-* in Danish *klagge*, mud, akin to the Scandinavian source of English dialectal *clag*, to daub with mud: CLAG. **3.** Extended form **gleu-* in Latin *glūten*, glue: GLUE, GLUTEN, GLUTINOUS; AGGLUTINATE, CONGLUTINATE, DEGLUTINATE. **4.** Extended form **glit-* possibly in Latin *glittus*, sticky: GLEET. [Pok. 1. *gel-* 357.]

gel-². Bright. **1.** Extended form **glei-* in Germanic

klai-ni-, bright, pure, in: **a.** Old English *clǣne*, pure, clean: CLEAN; **b.** Old English *clǣnsian*, to purify, cleanse: CLEANSE. **2.** Extended and suffixed zero-grade form *glə-nā* in Greek *glēnē*, eyeball: EUGLENA. [Pok. *gel-* 366.]
gel-³. Cold; to freeze. **1.** Germanic *kaliz*, coldness, in Old English *c(i)ele*, chill: CHILL. **2.** Germanic *kaldaz*, cold, in Old English *ceald*, cold: COLD. **3.** Germanic *kōl-*, cool, in: **a.** Old English *cōl*, cold, cool: COOL; **b.** Germanic *kōljan*, to cool, in Old English *cēlan*, to cool: KEEL³. **4.** Suffixed form *gel-ā-* in Latin *gelāre*, to freeze: GELATIN, GELATION, JELLY; CONGEAL. **5.** Suffixed form *gel-u-* in Latin *gelu*, frost, cold: GELID. **6.** Probably suffixed zero-grade form *gl̥-k-* in Latin *glaciēs*, ice: GLACE, GLACIAL, GLACIATE, GLACIER, GLACIS. [Pok. 3. *gel(ə)-* 365.]
gembh-. Tooth, nail. **I.** Suffixed o-grade form *gombh-o-*. **1.** Germanic *kambaz*, comb, in: **a.** Old English *camb*, comb: COMB, KAME; **b.** Old High German *kamb*, comb: CAM; **c.** Germanic denominative *kambjan*, to comb, in Old English *cemban*, to comb: OAKUM, UNKEMPT. **2.** Greek *gomphos*, tooth, peg, bolt: GOMPHOSIS. **II.** Perhaps Germanic *kimb-* in Old English *cim-, cimb-*, rim (only in compounds): CHIME². **III.** Possibly suffixed form *gembh-mā* in Latin *gemma*, bud, hence gem: GEM, GEMMA, GEMMATE, GEMMULE. [Pok. *gembh-* 369.]
geme-. To marry. Suffixed zero-grade form *gmə-o-* in Greek *gamos*, marriage: GAMETE, GAMO-, -GAMOUS, -GAMY; GAMOSEPALOUS. [Pok. *gem(e)-* 369.]
gen-. To compress into a ball. Hypothetical Indo-European base of a range of Germanic words referring to compact, knobby bodies and projections, sharp blows. **1.** Germanic *kn-a-pp-* in: **a.** Old English *cnæpp*, hilltop: KNAP²; **b.** Middle Dutch *cnoppen*, to snap, and Low German *knappen*, to snap, hence "to have a bite," akin to Middle English *knappen*, to strike sharply, snap: KNAP¹; KNAPSACK; **c.** Old English *cnop*, knob: KNOP. **2.** Germanic *kn-a-k-* in Middle High German *knacken*, to crack: KNACKWURST. **3.** Germanic *kn-a-r-* in: **a.** Norwegian *knart*, knot in wood, akin to the source of Middle English *knarre*, knob: KNAR; **b.** Middle English *knor*, a swelling: KNUR. **4.** Germanic *kn-u-b-* in Middle Low German *knobbe, knubbe*, knot in wood, knob: KNOB, NUB. **5.** Germanic *kn-u-k-* in: **a.** Old English *cnocian*, to knock: KNOCK; **b.** Italian *gnocco, nocchio*, knot in wood: GNOCCHI; **c.** Middle Low German *knökel*, knuckle, akin to Middle English *knakel*, knuckle: KNUCKLE. **6.** Germanic *kn-u-l-* in: **a.** Old English *cnyllan*, to strike: KNELL, KNOLL²; **b.** Old English *cnoll*, a knoll: KNOLL¹. **7.** Germanic *kn-u-p-* in Middle Dutch *cnoppe*, knob, bud: KNOBKERRIE. **8.** Germanic *kn-u-t-* in: **a.** Old English *cnyttan*, to tie in a knot, knit: KNIT; **b.** Old English *cnotta*, knot in cord: KNOT¹; **c.** Old Norse *knūtr*, knot in cord: KNOUT. **9.** Germanic *kn-u-th-* in Old High German *knodo*, knob, knot (> French *quenelle):* QUENELLE **10.** Germanic *kn-ī-b-* in Old English *cnīf*, knife: KNIFE. **11.** Germanic *kn-e-th-* in Old English *cnedan*, to knead: KNEAD. [Pok. *gen-* 370.]
genə-. Also **gen-.** To give birth, beget; with derivatives referring to aspects and results of procreation and to familial and tribal groups. **1.** Suffixed zero-grade form *gn-yo-* in Germanic *kunjam*, family, in: **a.** Old English *cyn(n)*, race, family, kin: KIN, KINDRED; **b.** *kuningaz*, king (< "son of the royal kin"), in Old English *cyning*, king: KING. **2.** Suffixed zero-grade form *gn-ti-* in: **a.** Germanic *kundjaz*, family, race, in Old English *cynd, gecynd(e)*, origin, birth, race, family, kind: KIND¹; **b.** Germanic *kundiz*, natural, native, in Old English *gecynde* (*ge-*, collective prefix; see **kom**), natural, native, fitting: KIND²; **c.** Germanic variant *kinth-* in Old High German *kind*, child: KINDERGARTEN, KRISS KRINGLE; **d.** Latin *gēns* (stem *gent-*), race, clan (> French *gens*, men): GENS, GENTEEL, GENTILE, GENTLE; GENDARME. **3.** Suffixed full-grade form *gen-es-* in: **a.** Latin *genus* (stem *gener-*), race, kind: GENDER, GENERAL, GENERATE, (GENERA-TION), GENERIC, GENEROUS, GENRE, GENUS; CONGENER, (CONGENIAL), DEGENERATE, (ENGENDER), MISCEGENA-TION; **b.** Greek *genos* and *genea*, race, family: GENEALOGY, GENOCIDE, GENOTYPE, HETEROGENEOUS; **c.** Greek suffix *-genēs*, "-born": -GEN, -GENY. **4.** Suffixed full-grade form *gen-yo-* in: **a.** Latin *genius*, procreative divinity, inborn tutelary spirit, innate quality: GENIAL¹, GENIUS; **b.** Latin *ingenium* (*in-*, in; see **en**), inborn character: ENGINE, INGENIOUS. **5.** Suffixed full-grade form *gen-ā-* in Latin *indigena* (*indu-*, within; see **en**), born in (a place), indigenous: INDIGEN, (INDIGENOUS). **6.** Suffixed full-grade form *genə-wo-* in Latin *ingenuus* (*in-*, in; see **en**), born in (a place), native, natural, freeborn: INGENUOUS. **7.** Suffixed full-grade form *genmen-* dissimilated in Latin *germen*, shoot, bud, embryo, germ: GERM, GERMAN², (GERMANE), GERMINAL, GERMINATE. **8.** Suffixed full-grade form *genə-ti-* in Greek *genesis*, birth, beginning: GENESIS, -GENESIS. **9.** Reduplicated form *gi-gn-* in: **a.** Latin *gignere* (past participle *genitus*), to beget: GENITAL, GENITIVE, GENITOR, GENT¹, (GINGERLY); CONGENITAL, PRIMOGENITURE, PROGENITOR, (PROGENY); **b.** Greek *gignesthai*, to be born: EPIGENE. **10.** Suffixed zero-grade form *-gn-o-* in Latin *benignus* (*bene*, well; see **deu-²**), good-natured, kindly, and *malignus* (*male*, ill; see **mel-⁵**), evil-natured, malevolent: BENIGN, MALIGN. **11.** Zero-grade form *gnə-* becoming *gnā-* in Latin *praegnās* (*prae-*, before; see **per¹**), pregnant: PREGNANT¹. **12.** Suffixed zero-grade form *gnə-sko-* becoming *gnā-sko-* in Latin *gnāscī, nāscī* (present participle *nāscēns*, past participle *gnātus, nātus*), to be born: NAIVE, NASCENT, NATAL, NATION, NATIVE, NATURE, NÉE, NOËL, (ADNATE), AGNATE, COGNATE, CONNATE, ENATE, INNATE, NEONATE, PUISNE, (PUNY) RENAISSANCE. **13.** Suffixed zero-grade form *gon-o-* in Greek *gonos* (combining form *-gonos*), child, procreation, seed: GONAD, GONO-; ARCHEGONIUM, EPIGONE. **14.** Zero-grade form *gn̥-* in Sanskrit *ja-* in *kr̥mi-ja-*, "produced by worms" (see **kʷr̥mi-**). [Pok. 1. *gen-* 373.]
genu-¹. Knee; also angle. **1.** Variant form *gneu-* in: **a.** Germanic *knewam* in Old English *cnēo*, knee: KNEE; **b.** Germanic *knewljan* in Old English *cnēowlian*, to kneel: KNEEL. **2.** Basic form *genu-* in Latin *genū*, knee: GENICULATE, GENUFLECT. **3.** Suffixed variant form *gōn-ya-* in Greek *gōnia*, angle, corner: -GON, GONION; AMBLYGONITE, DIAGONAL, GONIOMETER, GONIOMETRY, ORTHOGONAL. [Pok. 1. *genu-* 380.]
genu-². Jawbone, chin. **1.** Form *genw-* in Germanic *kinnuz* in Old English *cin(n)*, chin: CHIN. **2.** Basic form *genu-* in Greek *genus*, chin: GENIAL². **3.** Suffixed variant form *genə-dho-* in Greek *gnathos*, jaw: GNATHIC, -GNATHOUS; CHAETOGNATH **4.** Variant form *g(h)enu-* in Sanskrit *hanu*, jaw: HANUMAN. [Pok. 2. *genu-* 381.]
gep(h)-. Also **gebh-.** Jaw, mouth. **1.** Probably Germanic *kaf-*, to gnaw, chew, in Old English *ceaf*, husks, chaff: CHAFF¹. **2.** Germanic *kabraz*, "gnawer," in Old English *ceafor, ceafer*, beetle: CHAFER, (COCKCHAFER). **3.** Germanic *kēfalaz* in Old English *cēafl*, jaw, cheek: JOWL¹. [Pok. *geph-, gebh-* 382.]
ger-¹. To gather. **1.** Extended form *grem-* in Germanic *kram-* in Old English *crammian*, to stuff, cram: CRAM. **2.** Reduplicated form *gre-g-* in Latin *grex* (stem *greg-*), herd, flock: GREGARIOUS; AGGREGATE, CONGREGATE, EGREGIOUS, SEGREGATE. **3.** Earliest forms *əger-, əgor-ā-*, in Greek *ageirein*, to assemble, and *aguris, agora*, marketplace (> *agoreuein*, to speak): AGORA¹; (AGORAPHOBIA), ALLEGORY, CATEGORY, PANEGYRIC. [Pok. 1. *ger-* 382.]
ger-². Curving, crooked; hypothetical Indo-European base for a variety of Germanic words with initial *kr-*. **I.** Words meaning to bend, curl; bent, crooked, hooked; something bent or hooked. **1.** Germanic *krāppōn-*, a hook, especially one used in harvesting grapes, in: **a.** Old High German *krāpfo*, a hook: AGRAFFE; **b.** Old French *graper*, to harvest grapes, hence (back-formation) *grape*,

vine, grape: GRAPE; **c.** Old French *grapon*, grapnel: GRAPNEL; **d.** Old French *grape*, a hook: GRAPPLE; **e.** Italian dialectal *grappa*, vine stem, brandy: GRAPPA. **2.** Old English *crump*, *crumb*, crooked, bent, stooping: CRUMMIE, CRUMPET, (CRUMPLE). **3.** Low German *krimpen*, to wrinkle: CRIMP[1]. **4.** Middle Dutch *crampe*, hook, and Frankish **kramp*, hook: CRAMP[2]. **5.** Old High German *krampfo*, a cramp, akin to the Germanic source of Old French *crampe*, cramp: CRAMP[1]. **6.** Old English *crypel*, a cripple: CRIPPLE. **7.** Germanic **kreupan* in Old English *crēopan*, to creep: CREEP. **8.** Middle Low German *krink*, a ring: CRINGLE. **9.** Germanic **krengan* in Old English *cringan*, to yield: CRINGE. **10.** Middle Dutch *crinkelen*, akin to Middle English *crinkelen*, to make kinks in: CRINKLE. **11.** Old Norse *kriki*, a bend, nook: CREEK. **12.** Old Norse *krōkr*, a hook: CROOK. **13.** Frankish **krōk-* (> Old French *croc*), a hook: CROCHET, (CROCKET), (CROQUET), (CROUCH); ENCROACH. **14.** Old English *crycc*, (bent) staff, crutch: CRUTCH. **15.** Old French *crosse*, crook: CROSIER, LACROSSE. **16.** Middle Dutch *crulle*, curly: CRULLER, CURL. **17.** Old English *cranc-(stæf)*, a weaving implement: CRANK[1]. **18.** Norwegian *krake*, a sickly beast, akin to the source of Middle English *crok*, an old ewe: CROCK[3]. **19.** Old Norse *karpa*, to boast: CARP[1]. **20.** Middle Dutch *kroes*, curled, akin to the source of Old French *grosele*, gooseberry: GROSSULARITE. **II.** Words meaning "a rounded mass, collection; a round object, vessel, container." **1.** Old English *cruma*, a fragment: CRUMB. **2.** Frankish **kruppa*, rump, akin to the Germanic source of Old French *croup*, rump: CROUP[2], (CROUPIER), CRUPPER. **3.** Old English *cropp*, cluster, bunch, ear of corn: CROP. **4.** Italian *gruppo*, an assemblage: GROUP. **5.** Old English *crocc*, pot: CROCK[1]. **6.** Middle Dutch *cruyse*, pot: CRUSE. **7.** Old English *cribb*, manger: CRIB. **8.** Old English *cradel*, cradle: CRADLE. **9.** Frankish **kripja*, cradle, akin to the Germanic source of Old French *cre(s)che*, crib: CRÈCHE. **10.** Old English *cræt* and Old Norse *kartr*, wagon: CART. **11.** Old English *croft*, small enclosed field: CROFT. [Pok. 3. *ger-* 385.]

gerbh-. To scratch. **1.** Germanic **kerban* in Old English *ceorfan*, to cut: CARVE. **2.** Zero-grade Germanic form **kurbiz* in Old English *cyrf*, a cutting (off): KERF. **3.** Variant form **grebh-* in: **a.** Germanic **krab(b)-* in Old English *crabba*, a crab: CRAB[1]; **b.** Germanic **krabiz-* in Old French *crevise*, crayfish: CRAYFISH; **c.** perhaps Germanic **krab-* in Old Norse *krafla*, to crawl: CRAWL[1]. **4.** Zero-grade form **gr̥bh-* in Greek *graphein*, to scratch, draw, write, and *gramma* (< **gr̥bh-mn̥*), a picture, written letter, piece of writing, and *grammē*, a line: GRAFFITO, GRAM[1], -GRAM, GRAMMAR, GRAPH, -GRAPH, -GRAPHER, GRAPHIC, -GRAPHY; AGRAPHA, AGRAPHIA, DIAGRAM, EPIGRAM, (EPIGRAPH), GRAPHITE, ICONOGRAPHY, PARAGRAPH, PROGRAM, PSEUDEPIGRAPHA, TETRAGRAMMATON, TOPOGRAPHY. [Pok. *gerebh-* 392.]

[gerere. To carry, carry on, act, do. Latin verb of unknown origin. Oldest form *ges-*, past participle *gestus*. GERENT, GERUND, (GEST), GESTATION, (GESTICULATE), GESTURE, JEST; ARMIGER, BELLIGERENT, (CONGERIES), CONGEST, DIGEST, EGEST, INGEST, REGISTER, SUGGEST, VELIGER.]

gere-[1]. To grow old. **1.** Suffixed lengthened-grade form **gērǝ-s-* in Greek *gēras*, old age: AGERATUM, CALOYER, GERIATRICS. **2.** Suffixed form **gerǝ-ont-* in Greek *gerōn* (stem *geront-*), old man: GERONTO-. [Pok. *ger-* 390.]

gere-[2]. To cry hoarsely; also the name of the crane. **I.** Words meaning "to cry hoarsely"; also words denoting the crow. **1.** Germanic **krē-* in: **a.** Old English *crāwe*, a crow: CROW[1]; **b.** Old English *crāwan*, to crow: CROW[2]; **c.** Old English *cracian*, to resound: CRACK; **d.** Middle Dutch *krāken*, to crack: CRACKNEL; **e.** Old Norse *krāka*, a crow: CRAKE. **f.** Middle Dutch *krōnen*, to groan, lament: CROON. **2.** Possibly (but more likely imitative) Germanic **kur(r)-* in Old Norse *kurra*, to growl, akin to Middle English *curre*, cur: CUR. **II.** Words denoting a

crane. **1.** Germanic **kran-*, crane, in: **a.** Old English *cran*, crane: CRANE; **b.** Middle Low German *kran*, crane: CRANBERRY. **2.** Extended form **grū-* in Latin *grūs*, crane: GRUS; PEDIGREE. **3.** Suffixed variant form **grā-k-* in Latin *grāculus*, jackdaw: GRACKLE. **4.** Suffixed extended form **gerǝ-no-* in Greek *geranos*, crane: GERANIUM. [Pok. 2. *ger-* 383.]

gēu-. To bend. Proposed by some as the root of Greek *guros*, ring (which is more likely of unknown origin): GYRE, GYRO[2], GYRO-; AUTOGIRO. [Pok. *gēu-* 393.]

geue-. To hasten. Possibly the base of Germanic **kaurjan* in Old Norse *keyra*, to drive: SKIJORING. [Pok. *geu-* 399.]

g(e)u-lo-. A glowing coal. Germanic **kulam*, **kolam* in: **a.** Old English *col*, a glowing coal: COAL, (COLLIE), (COLLIER); **b.** probably dialectal Old French *cholle*, round lump, head: CHOLLA. [Pok. *g(e)u-lo-* 399.]

geus-. To taste, choose. **1.** Germanic **keusan* in: **a.** Old English *cēosan*, *ceōsan*, to choose: CHOOSE. **b.** Gothic **kausjan*, to choose: CHOICE. **2.** Zero-grade **gus-* in Germanic **kuz-*, becoming **kur-* in Old Norse *Valkyrja*, "chooser of the slain," Valkyrie (*valr*, the slain; see **wel-ǝ-[2]**). **3.** Suffixed zero-grade form **gus-tu-* in: **a.** Latin *gustus*, taste: (GUST[2]), GUSTO; DISGUST, RAGOUT; **b.** Latin *gustāre*, to taste: DEGUST. [Pok. *geus-* 399.]

ghabh-. Also **ghebh-.** To give or receive. **1.** Form **ghebh-* in Germanic **geban* in: **a.** Old English *giefan*, to give: GIVE; **b.** compound **far-geban* (**far-*, away; see **per[1]**), to give away, in Old English *forgi(e)fan*, to give, give up, leave off (anger), remit, forgive: FORGIVE. **2.** Suffixed form **ghebh-ti-*, something given (or received), in Germanic **giftiz* in Old Norse *gipt*, *gift*, a gift: GIFT. **3.** O-grade form **ghobh-* in Germanic **gab-ulam*, something paid (or received), in Old English *gafol*, tribute, tax, debt: GAVEL[2]. **4.** Form **ghabh-ē-* in: **a.** Latin *habēre*, to hold, possess, have, handle (> *habitāre*, to dwell): ABLE, BINNACLE, HABILE, HABIT, HABITABLE, (HABITANT), (HABITAT); (COHABIT), EXHIBIT, INHABIT, INHIBIT, PREBEND, PROHIBIT, (PROVENDER); **b.** Latin *dēbēre* (*dē-*, away from; see **de-**; third person plural present passive *debentur*), to owe: DEBENTURE, (DEBIT), DEBT, DEVOIR, DUE, (DUTY); (ENDEAVOR). Compare **kap-.** [Pok. *ghebh-* 407.]

ghabholo-. A fork, branch of a tree. Celtic **gablakko-* probably in Old French *javelot*, a throwing spear: JAVELIN. [Pok. *ghabolo-* 409.]

ghāi-. To yawn, gape. Contracted from **ghǝi-*. **1.** Variant form **ghyā-* (< **ghyǝǝ-*) in: **a.** nasalized form **ghi-n-ā-* in Germanic **ginōn* in Old English *ginan*, *ginian*, *geonian*, to yawn: YAWN; **b.** Latin *hiāre*, to gape, be open: HIATUS; DEHISCE. **2.** Suffixed variant form **ghǝ-smn̥* in Greek *khasma*, yawning gulf, chasm: CHASM. **3.** Suffixed variant form **ghǝ-n-yo-* in Greek *khainein*, to gape: ACHENE. **4.** Labial extensions: **a.** Old Norse *gap*, chasm: GAP; **b.** Old Norse *gapa*, to open the mouth: GAPE; **c.** Old Norse *geispa*, to yawn: GASP. **5.** Germanic **gil-* in Old Norse *gil*, ravine, chasm: GILL[3]. **6.** Germanic **gīr-*, vulture (< "voracious or yawning bird"), in Old High German *gīr*, vulture (> German *Geier*): LAMMERGEIER. [Pok. 2. *ghē-* 419.]

ghaido-. A goat. Germanic **gaitaz* in Old English *gāt*, goat: GOAT. [Pok. *ghaido-* 409.]

ghais-. To adhere, hesitate. Form **ghais-ē-* in Latin *haerēre*, to stick, cling: HESITATE; ADHERE, COHERE, INHERE. [Pok. *ghais-* 410.]

ghaiso-. A stick, spear. **1.** Germanic **gaizaz* in: **a.** Old English *gār*, spear: GORE[1]; (GARFISH), GARLIC; **b.** compound **nabō-gaizaz*, tool for piercing wheel hubs (**nabō*, hub; see **nobh-**); **c.** Old Norse *geirr*, spear (in *geirfalki*, gyrfalcon, akin to the source of Old French *girfaut*): GYRFALCON. **2.** Germanic **gaizō* in Old English *gāra*, corner, point of land: GORE[2]. [Pok. *ghaiso-* 410.]

ghait-. Curly or wavy hair. Possible root. Suffixed form

*ghait-ā in Greek khaitē, long hair: CHAETA; (CHAETOG-NATH). [Pok. ghait-ā- 410.]

ghalgh-. Branch, rod. Germanic *galgōn- in: **a.** Old English g(e)alga, cross, gallows: GALLOWS; **b.** Old North French gauge, gauge: GAUGE. [Pok. ghalgh- 411.]

ghans-. Goose. **1.** Germanic *gans- (nominative plural *gansiz) in: **a.** Old English gōs (nominative plural gēs), goose: GOOSE[1]; (GOSHAWK); **b.** Old Norse gās, goose, diminutive gæslingr, gosling: GOSLING. **2.** Germanic *ganr- in Old English ganra, gandra, gander: GANDER. **3.** Germanic *ganōtōn- in Old English ganot, gannet: GANNET. **4.** Suffixed form *ghans-er- in Latin ānser (< *hanser), goose: ANSERINE; MERGANSER. **5.** Basic form *ghans- in Greek khēn, goose: CHENOPOD. [Pok. ghans- 412.]

ghasto-. Rod, staff. **1.** Variant form *ghazdh- in Germanic *gazdaz in: **a.** Old English gierd, gerd, staff, twig, measuring rod: YARD[1]; **b.** Old Norse gaddr, rod, goad, spike: GAD[2]. **2.** Form *ghast-ā- in Latin hasta, spear: HASLET, HASTATE. [Pok. 1. ghasto- 412.]

ghē-. To release, let go; (in the middle voice) to be released, go. Contracted from *gheə-. **1.** Germanic variant form *gaian in Old English gān, to go: GO; AGO, FOREGO[1], FORGO. **2.** Suffixed form *ghē-ro- in Latin hērēs, heir (? < "orphan" < "bereft"): HEIR, HEREDITA-MENT, HEREDITY, HERITAGE; INHERIT. **3.** Suffixed o-grade form *ghō-ro-, "empty space," possibly in: **a.** Greek khōros, place, country, particular spot: CHO-ROGRAPHY; **b.** Greek denominative khōrein, to move, go, spread about, make room for: -CHORE; ANCHORITE. **4.** Perhaps suffixed zero-grade form *ghə-l- in Greek khalan, to slacken, let down (but this is more likely of unknown origin): CALANDO, CHALONE; ACHALASIA. **5.** Suffixed zero-grade form *ghə-t(w)ā- in Germanic *gatwōn-, a going, in Old Norse gata, path, street: GAIT. [Pok. ghē- 418.]

ghebh-el-. Head. **1.** Germanic *gablaz, top of a pitched roof, in Old Norse gafl, gable: GABLE. **2.** Dissimilated form *khephel- in Greek kephalē, head: CEPHALIC, CEPH-ALO-, -CEPHALOUS; ENCEPHALO-, ENKEPHALIN, HYDRO-CEPHALUS. [Pok. ghebh-el- 423.]

ghedh-. To unite, join, fit. **1.** Lengthened o-grade form *ghōdh- in Germanic *gōdaz, "fitting, suitable," in Old English gōd, good: GOOD. **2.** Germanic *gadurī, "in a body," in Old English tōgædere (tō, to; see de-), together: TOGETHER. **3.** Germanic *gadurōn, "to come or bring together," in Old English gad(e)rian, to gather: GATHER. [Pok. ghedh- 423.]

ghei-[1]. To propel, prick. **1.** Suffixed and extended o-grade form *ghoidh-ā in Germanic *gaidō, goad, spear, in Old English gād, goad: GOAD. **2.** Suffixed form *ghei-s- perhaps in nasalized zero-grade form *ghi-n-s- in Sanskrit himsati, he injures: AHIMSA. [Pok. 1. ghei- 424.]

ghei-[2]. Theoretical base of *ghyem-, *ghiem-, winter. **1.** Form *ghiem- in Latin hiems, winter: HIEMAL. **2.** Suffixed variant form *gheim-ri-no- in Latin hībernus, pertaining to winter: HIBERNACULUM, HIBERNATE. **3.** Suffixed zero-grade form *ghim-ar-ya, "female animal one year (winter) old," in Greek khimaira, she-goat: CHIMERA. [Pok. 2. ghei- 425.]

gheis-. Used of the emotion of fear or amazement (original part of speech uncertain). Suffixed o-grade form *ghois-do- in Germanic *gaistaz, a ghost, in: **a.** Old English gāst, ghost: GHOST; AGHAST; **b.** Old High German geist, ghost: POLTERGEIST; **c.** Germanic denominative *gaistjan in Old English gæstan, to scare: GAST. [Pok. gheis- 427.]

ghel-[1]. To call. **1.** Germanic *gel-, *gal-, in: **a.** Old English gellan, giellan, to sound, shout: YELL; **b.** Old English gielpan, to boast, exult: YELP; **c.** Old English galan, to sing: NIGHTINGALE. **2.** Reduplicated form *ghi-ghl- in Greek kikhlē, thrush, later also the name for a kind of wrasse (a sea fish that has bright colors and jagged waving fins, reminiscent of the plumage of a bird):

CICHLID. **3.** Greek khelidwōn, khelidōn, the swallow: CELANDINE. [Pok. ghel- 428.]

ghel-[2]. To shine; with derivatives referring to colors, bright materials (probably "yellow metal"), and bile or gall. **I.** Words denoting colors. **1.** Suffixed form *ghel-wo- in Germanic *gelwaz in Old English gealu, yellow: YELLOW. **2.** Suffixed variant form *ghlō-ro- in Greek khlōros, green, greenish yellow: CHLORO-; CHLORITE[1]. **3.** Suffixed variant form *ghlo-wo- in Greek khloos (< *khlo-wo-s), green color: CHLOASMA. **4.** O-grade form *ghol- in Russian zola, ashes (from their color): PODZOL. **II.** Words denoting gold. **1.** Suffixed zero-grade form *ghḷ-to- in Germanic *gultham, gold, in: **a.** Old English gold, gold: GOLD; **b.** denominative verb *gulthjan in Old English gyldan, to gild: GILD[1]; **c.** Middle Dutch gulden, golden: GUILDER, GULDEN; **d.** Old Norse gulinn, golden, akin to the possible source of Middle English gollan, yellow flower: GOWAN. **2.** Suffixed o-grade form *ghol-to- in Polish złoto, gold: ZLOTY. **3.** Suffixed full-grade form *ghel-i- in the unknown Iranian source of Syriac zarnīkā, orpiment: ARSENIC. **III.** Words denoting bile. **1.** Suffixed o-grade form *ghol-no- in Germanic *gallōn-, bile, in Old English gealla, gall: GALL[1]. **2.** Suffixed o-grade form *ghol-ā in Greek kholē, bile: CHOLE-, CHOLER, (CHOL-ERA); ACHOLIA, MELANCHOLY. **3.** Suffixed full-grade form *ghel-n- in Latin fel, bile: FELON[2]. **IV.** A range of Germanic words (where no preforms are given, the words are late creations). **1.** Germanic *glaimiz in Old English glǣm, bright light, gleam: GLEAM. **2.** Middle High German glimsen, to gleam, akin to the source of Middle English glimsen, to glimpse: GLIMPSE. **3.** Swedish dialectal glinta, to shine, akin to the source of Middle English glent, a glint: GLINT. **4.** Swedish glimra, akin to the source of Middle English glimeren, to glimmer: GLIM-MER. **5.** Old Norse glitra, to shine: GLITTER. **6.** Old English glisnian, to shine: GLISTEN. **7.** Middle Dutch glisteren, to shine: GLISTER. **8.** Germanic *glasam, glass, in Old English glæs, glass: GLASS, GLAZE. **9.** Germanic *glaz- in Middle Low German glaren, to glisten, akin to the source of Middle English glaren, to glitter, stare: GLARE[1]. **10.** Icelandic glossi, a spark, perhaps akin to the source of GLOSS[1]. **11.** Old High German glanz, bright: GLANCE[2]. **12.** Old Norse glöggr, clear-sighted: GLEG. **13.** Germanic *gladaz in Old English glæd, shining, joyful: GLAD. **14.** Germanic *gleujam in Old English glēo, sport, merriment: GLEE. **15.** Old English glēd, ember: GLEED. **16.** Germanic *glō- in: **a.** Old English glōwan, to glow: GLOW; **b.** Norwegian dialectal glora, to gleam, stare, akin to the probable source of Middle English gloren, to gleam, stare: GLOWER; **c.** Old Norse glotta, to smile (scornfully), perhaps akin to the source of GLOAT. **17.** Germanic *glō-m- in Old English glōm, twilight: GLOAMING. **18.** Possibly distantly related is Germanic *glīdan, to glide, in: **a.** Old English glīdan, to slip, glide: GLIDE; **b.** Old French glier, to glide: GLISSADE; **c.** Old High German glītan, to glide: GLITCH; **d.** derivative Germanic *glidōn- in Old English glida, kite (< "gliding, hovering bird"): GLEDE. **19.** Middle Low German glibberich, slippery, possibly akin to the source of GLIB. [Pok. 1. ĝhel- 429.]

ghel-[3]. To cut. **1.** Germanic *galdjan, to castrate, in Old Norse gelda, to castrate, and geldingr, a castrated animal: GELD[1], (GELDING). **2.** Germanic *gulti- in Old Norse gyltr, a sow (< "castrated pig"): GILT[2]. [Pok. 2. ĝhel- 434.]

gheldh-. To pay. Only in Germanic and Slavic. **1.** Germanic *geldam, payment, in: **a.** Old English geld, gield, payment, service: GELD[2]; DANEGELD, WERGELD; **b.** Old High German gelt, payment, reward: GELT[1]. **2.** Germanic *geldan, to pay, in Old English gieldan, to pay, yield: YIELD. **3.** Germanic *geldjam, payment, contribution, hence an association founded on contributions, a craftsmen's guild, in Old Norse gildi, guild: GUILD. [Pok. ghel-tō 436.]

ghelegh-. A metal. Possible root of Greek khalkos,

copper; which, however, is more likely borrowed from an unknown source: CHALCID, CHALCOCITE; CHALCOPYRITE, CHALCOSIS. [Pok. *ghelegh-* 435.]

gheləd-. Hail. Zero-grade form **ghl̥əd-* in Greek *khalaza* (< **khalad-ya*), a hailstone, hard lump, also a small cyst: CHALAZA, CHALAZION. [Pok. *gheləd-* 435.]

ghelū-. Tortoise. Suffixed form **ghel-ōnā* in Greek *khelōnē*, tortoise: CHELONIAN. [Pok. *ghel-ōu-* 435.]

ghel-unā. Jaw. 1. Germanic **geliz* in Old Norse **gil*, gill of a fish, akin to the Scandinavian source of Middle English *gile*, gill: GILL[1]. 2. Suffixed variant form **ghel-wo-* in Greek *kheilos*, lip: CHEILOSIS, CHILOPOD. [Pok. *ghelunā* 436.]

ghen-. To gnaw. Hypothetical base of various Germanic forms. 1. Germanic **gnagan* in: **a.** Old English *gnagan*, to gnaw: GNAW; **b.** Old Norse *gnaga*, to bite, akin to the probable Scandinavian source of NAG[1]. 2. Suffixed Germanic form **gnag-sk-* in **(g)naskōn* in Old High German *nascon*, to nibble: NOSH. 3. Perhaps related is Germanic **gnatt-*, "biting insect," in Old English *gnæt*, gnat: GNAT. [Pok. *ghen-* 436.]

ghend-. Also **ghed-.** To seize, take. 1. Germanic **getan* in: **a.** Old Norse *geta*, to get: GET; **b.** compound **bigetan* (**bi-*, intensive prefix; see **ambhi**), to acquire, in Old English *begietan*, to get, beget: BEGET; **c.** compound **fer-getan* (**fer-*, prefix denoting rejection; see **per**[1]), "to lose one's hold," forget, in Old English *forg(i)etan*, to forget: FORGET. 2. Germanic **getisōn*, "to try to get," aim at, in Old Swedish *gissa*, to guess, akin to the Scandinavian source of Middle English *gessen*, to guess: GUESS. 3. Basic form **ghend-* in Latin *prendere, prehendere* (*pre-, prae-*, before; see **per**[1]), to get hold of, seize, grasp: PREHENSILE, PREHENSION, PRISON, PRIZE[2], (PRIZE[3]), (PRY[2]); APPREHEND, (APPRENTICE), (APPRISE), COMPREHEND, COMPRISE, EMPRISE, ENTERPRISE, (ENTREPRENEUR), MISPRISION, PREGNABLE, REPREHEND, (REPRISAL), (REPRISE), SURPRISE. 4. Form **ghed-* in Latin *praeda*, booty (< **prai-heda*, "something seized before"; *prai-, prae-*, before; see **per**[1]): PREDATORY, PREY, SPREE; DEPREDATE, OSPREY. [Pok. *ghend-* 437.]

ghendh-. Abscess, boil. Zero-grade form **ghn̥dh-* in Germanic **gund-* in Old English *gund*, pus: GROUNDSEL[1]. [Pok. *ghendh-* 438.]

ghengh-. To go, walk. 1. Germanic **gang-*, a going, in: **a.** Old English *gang*, a going: GANG[1]; **b.** Old High German *gang*, a going: GANGUE. 2. Germanic **gangan*, to go, walk, in Old English *gangan*, to go: GANGLING. [Pok. *ghengh-* 438.]

gher-[1]. To grasp, enclose; with derivatives meaning "enclosure." 1. Suffixed zero-grade form **ghr̥-dh-* in: **a.** Germanic **gurdjan* in Old English *gyrdan*, to gird: GIRD; **b.** Old English *gyrdel*, girdle: GIRDLE; **c.** Old Norse *gjördh*, girdle, girth: GIRTH. 2. Suffixed o-grade form **ghor-dho-* (in Germanic) or **ghor-to-*, an enclosure, in: **a.** Germanic **gardaz* in (i) Old English *geard*, enclosure, garden, yard: YARD[2]; ORCHARD (ii) Old Norse *gardhr*, garden, yard: GARTH (iii) Old High German *garto*, garden: KINDERGARTEN (iv) Old North French *gardin*, garden: GARDEN (v) compound **midja-gardaz*, "middle zone," earth (see **medhyo-**); **b.** Latin *hortus*, garden: HORTICULTURE, ORCHARD, ORTOLAN. 3. Prefixed and suffixed zero-grade form **ko(m)-ghr̥-ti-* (**ko(m)-*, collective prefix; "together"; see **kom**) in Latin *cohors* (stem *cohort-*), enclosed yard, company of soldiers, multitude: COHORT, CORTEGE, COURT, COURTEOUS, COURTESAN, (COURTESY), COURTIER, (CURTILAGE), (CURTSY). 4. Perhaps suffixed o-grade form **ghor-o-* in Greek *khoros*, dancing ground (? perhaps originally a special enclosure for dancing), dance, dramatic chorus: (CHOIR), (CHORAL), (CHORALE), CHORIC, (CHORISTER), CHORUS; CHORAGUS, TERPSICHORE. [Pok. 4. *gher-* 442, *gherd-* 444.]

gher-[2]. To call out. Extended root **ghrēd-*. Germanic **grōtjan* in Old English *grētan*, to speak to, greet: GREET. [Pok. 1. *gher-* 439.]

gher-[3]. To shine, glow; gray. Hypothetical base of various Germanic forms. 1. Germanic **grēwaz*, gray, in: **a.** Old English *græg*, gray: GRAY; **b.** probably Old English *grīghund*, greyhound: GREYHOUND. 2. Germanic **grīsjaz*, gray, in: **a.** Old French *gris* (> French *gris*), gray: GRISAILLE, (GRISETTE), (GRISON), GRIZZLE; AMBERGRIS; **b.** Medieval Latin *griseus*, gray, grayish: GRISEOUS. [Pok. 3. *ĝher-* 441.]

gher-[4]. To scrape, scratch. 1. Extended zero-grade form **ghr(ə)-k-* in: **a.** Greek *kharax*, a pointed stake, also a kind of sea bream: CHARACIN; **b.** Greek *kharassein*, to sharpen, notch, carve, cut: CHARACTER, GASH. 2. Extended form **ghers-* in suffixed zero-grade form **ghr̥s-to-* perhaps (but unlikely) in Sanskrit *ghaṭṭaḥ*, ghat: GHAT. See also extensions **ghrēi-** and **ghrēu-**. [Pok. 2. *ĝher-* 439.]

gher-[5]. To like, want. 1. Suffixed form **gher-n-* in Germanic **gernjan* in Old English *giernan, gyrnan*, to strive, desire, yearn: YEARN. 2. Extended form **ghrē-* possibly in: **a.** Germanic **grēduz*, hunger, forming **grēdagaz*, hungry, in Old English *grǣdig*, hungry, covetous, greedy: GREEDY; **b.** Greek *khrē*, it is necessary, whence *krēsthai*, to lack, want, use: CATACHRESIS, CHRESARD, CHRESTOMATHY. 3. Suffixed zero-grade form **ghr̥-tā-* in Latin *hortārī*, to urge on, encourage (< "to cause to strive or desire"): HORTATIVE; EXHORT. 4. Suffixed zero-grade form **ghr̥-i-* in Greek *kharis*, grace, favor: CHARISMA; EUCHARIST. [Pok. 1. *ĝher-* 440.]

gherə-. Gut, entrail. 1. Suffixed form **gherə-no-* in Germanic **garnō*, string, in Old English *gearn*, yarn: YARN. 2. Suffixed form **gherə-n-* in Latin *hernia*, "protruded viscus," rupture, hernia: HERNIA. 3. Suffixed o-grade form **ghorə-d-* in Greek *khordē*, gut, string: (CHORD[2]), CORD, (CORDON); HARPSICHORD, TETRACHORD. 4. O-grade form **ghorə-* in Greek *khorion*, intestinal membrane, afterbirth: CHORION. 5. Possible suffixed zero-grade form **ghr̥-u-* in Latin *haruspex* (*-spex*, "he who sees" < **spek-*, "to see"; see **spek-**), "he who inspects entrails," diviner (but perhaps borrowed from Etruscan): HARUSPEX. [Pok. 5. *ĝher-* 443.]

ghers-. To bristle. 1. Extended zero-grade form **ghr̥zd-*, prickly plant, in: **a.** Germanic **gorst-* in Old English *gorst*, furze, gorse: GORSE; **b.** Latin *hordeum*, barley: ORGEAT. 2. Lengthened-grade form **ghēr(s)-* in Latin *hēr, ēr*, hedgehog: URCHIN. 3. Suffixed lengthened-grade form **ghēr(s)-ūkā* in Latin *ērūca*, caterpillar: ROCKET[2]. 4. Suffixed full-grade form **gher-tu-*, remade to **hirsu-* in Latin *hirsūtus*, bristly, shaggy, hairy: HIRSUTE. 5. Suffixed full-grade form **ghers-kʷo-* in Latin *hispidus* (probably a dialectal borrowing), bristly, shaggy, prickly: HISPID. 6. Suffixed o-grade form **ghors-eyo-* in Latin *horrēre*, to bristle, shudder, be terrified, look frightful: HORROR; ABHOR, ORDURE. 7. Suffixed full-grade form **ghers-o-* in Greek *khersos*, dry land: CHERSONESE. [Pok. *ĝhers-* 445.]

gheslo-. Seen by some as a base for words meaning "thousand." 1. Suffixed form **ghesl-yo-* in Greek *khilioi*, thousand: CHILIAD, KILO-. 2. Latin *mīlle*, thousand, which has been analyzed as **smī-*, "one" + a form **ghslī-*, is of obscure origin: MIL[1], MIL[2], MILE, MILLENARY, MILLESIMAL, MILLI-, MILLIEME, MILLION; MILFOIL, MILLENNIUM, MILLEPORE, MILLIARY, MILLIPEDE. [Pok. *ĝhéslo-* 446.]

ghesor-. Hand. Reduced form **ghesr-* in Greek *kheir*, hand: CHIRO-; (CHIRURGEON), ENCHIRIDION, (SURGEON), SURGERY. [Pok. 1. *ĝhesor-* 447.]

gheu-. To pour, pour a libation. I. Extended form **gheud-*. 1. Zero-grade form **ghud-* in Germanic **gut-* in Old English *guttas*, intestines: GUT. 2. Nasalized zero-grade form **ghu-n-d-* in Latin *fundere*, to pour: FOISON, FONDANT, FONDUE, FONT[2], FOUND[2], FUNNEL, FUSE[2], FUSILE, FUSION; AFFUSION, CIRCUMFUSE, CONFOUND, CONFUSE, DIFFUSE, EFFUSE, INFUSE, PERFUSE, PROFUSE, REFUND[1], (REFUSE[1]), (REFUSE[2]), SUFFUSE,

TRANSFUSE. **II.** Extended form *gheus-. **1.** Germanic zero-grade form *gus- in: **a.** suffixed form *gustiz in Old Norse gustr, a cold blast of wind: GUST[1]; **b.** Icelandic gusa, to gush, perhaps akin to Middle English gushen, to gush: GUSH. **2.** Germanic suffixed o-grade form *gausjan in Old Norse geysa, to gush: GEYSER. **III.** Suffixed form *gheu-ti- in Latin fūtilis, "(of a vessel) easily emptied, leaky," hence untrustworthy, useless: FUTILE. **IV.** Basic form *gheu- in Greek khein, to pour: CHOANA, CHYLE, (CHYME); CHOANOCYTE, ECCHYMOSIS, PARENCHYMA. [Pok. gheu- 447.]

ghēu-. To yawn, gape. Compare **ghāi-.** **1.** Germanic suffixed form gō-ma- in Old English gōma, palate, jaw: GUM[2]. **2.** Variant form *ghau- in Greek khaos, chasm, empty space, chaos: CHAOS, GAS. [Pok. ghēu- 449.]

gheu(e)-. To call, invoke. Suffixed zero-grade form *ghu-to-, "the invoked," god, in Germanic *gudam, god, in: **a.** Old English god, god: GOD; **b.** Germanic *gud-igaz, possessed by a god, in Old English gydig, gidig, possessed, insane: GIDDY. [Pok. ghau- 413.]

ghō. Behind, after. Slavic *za in Russian za, by, to: SASTRUGA. [Pok. ĝhō 451.]

ghos-ti-. Stranger, guest, host; properly "someone with whom one has reciprocal duties of hospitality." **1.** Basic form *ghos-ti- in: **a.** Germanic *gastiz in Old Norse gestr, guest: GUEST; **b.** Latin hostis, enemy (< stranger): HOST[2], (HOSTILE). **2.** Compound *ghos-pot-, *ghos-po(d)-, "guest-master," one who symbolizes the relationship of reciprocal obligation (*pot-, master; see **poti-**), in Latin hospes (stem hospit-), host, guest, stranger: (HOSPICE), (HOSPITAL), (HOSPITALITY), HOST[1], (HOSTAGE), (HOSTEL), (HOSTLER). See also **xenos.** [Pok. ghosti-s 453.]

ghow-ē-. To honor, revere, worship. **1.** Germanic *gawōn in Old Norse gā, to heed: GAWK. **2.** Basic form *ghow-ē- in Latin favēre, to favor, be favorable: FAVOR, (FAVORITE). [Pok. ghou̯(ē)- 453.]

ghrē-. To grow, become green. Contracted from *ghreə-. **1.** O-grade form *ghrō- in Germanic *grō(w)an in Old English grōwan, to grow: GROW. **2.** Suffixed o-grade form *ghrō-nyo- in Germanic *grōnjaz, green, in Old English grēne, green: GREEN. **3.** Suffixed zero-grade form *ghrə-so- in Germanic *grasam, grass, in Old English græs, grass: GRASS. [Pok. ghrē- 454.]

ghrebh-[1]. To seize, reach. **1.** Zero-grade form *ghr̥bh- in Sanskrit gr̥bhnāti, gr̥hnāti, he seizes: SATYAGRAHA. **2.** Parallel (imitative) Germanic creations with base *grab-, *grap- in: **a.** Middle English graspen, to grasp: GRASP; **b.** Middle Dutch and Middle Low German grabben, to seize: GRAB[1]. [Pok. 1. ghrebh- 455.]

ghrebh-[2]. To dig, bury, scratch. **1.** O-grade form *ghrobh- in: **a.** Germanic *graban in (i) Old English grafan, to dig, engrave, scratch, carve: GRAVE[3]; (ENGRAVE) (ii) Old High German graban, to dig: GRABEN (iii) Old French graver, to engrave: GRAVURE; **b.** Germanic *grabam in Old English græf, trench, grave: GRAVE[1]. **2.** Germanic *grub(b)jan (with secondary ablaut) in Old English *grybban (> Middle English grubben), to dig: GRUB. **3.** Germanic *grōbō in Middle Dutch groeve, ditch: GROOVE. **4.** Perhaps Germanic *greub- in Low German greven, fibrous refuse of tallow: GREAVES. [Pok. 2. ghrebh- 455.]

ghredh-. To walk, go. Suffixed zero-grade form ghr̥dh-yo- in: **a.** Latin gradī (past participle gressus), to walk, go: GRESSORIAL; AGGRESS, CONGRESS, DEGRESSION, DIGRESS, EGRESS, INGRESS, PLANTIGRADE, PROGRESS, REGRESS, RETROGRESS, TRANSGRESS; **b.** Latin gradus (< deverbative *grad-u-), step, stage, degree, rank: GRADE; CENTIGRADE, DEGRADE, DEGREE, RETROGRADE. [Pok. ghredh- 456.]

ghrēi-. To rub. A derivative of **gher-[4].** **1.** Germanic *gris-, to frighten (< "to grate on the mind"), in Old English grislic, terrifying: GRISLY. **2.** Germanic *grīm-, smear, in Middle Dutch grīme, grime, akin to the source of Middle English grime, grime: GRIME. **3.** Extended form *ghrīs-

in Greek khrein, to anoint: CHRISM, CHRIST, CHRISTEN, (CHRISTIAN); (CHRISTMAS). [Pok. ghrēi- 457.]

ghreib-. To grip. **1.** Germanic *grip- in Old English gripe, grasp, and gripa, handful: GRIP[1]. **2.** Germanic *grīpan in: **a.** Old English grīpan, to grasp: GRIPE; **b.** Old French gripper, to seize: GRIPPE. **3.** Suffixed o-grade form *ghroib-eyo- in Germanic *graipjan in Old English grāpian, to feel for, grope: GROPE. [Pok. ghreib- 457.]

ghrem-. Angry. **1.** Germanic *grimmaz in: **a.** Old English grim(m), fierce, severe: GRIM; **b.** Old French grimace, a grimace: GRIMACE. **2.** Germanic *grum- in Middle Dutch grommen, to mutter angrily, probably akin to Middle English grummen, to grumble: GRUMBLE. **3.** Suffixed o-grade form *ghrom-o- in Russian grom, thunder: POGROM. [Pok. 2. ghrem- 458.]

ghrendh-. To grind. **1.** Germanic *grindan in Old English grindan, to grind: GRIND. **2.** Germanic *grinst-, a grinding, in Old English grīst, the action of grinding: GRIST. **3.** Latin frēnum (< frendere, to grind), horse's bit (on which its teeth grind), bridle: FRENULUM, FRENUM; REFRAIN[1]. **4.** Variant form *ghrend- is sometimes but improbably regarded as the root of Greek khondros, granule, groats, hence cartilage: CHONDRO-; HYPOCHONDRIA, MITOCHONDRION. [Pok. ghren- 459.]

ghrēu-. To rub, grind. Extension of **gher-[4].** **1.** Germanic *greut- in Old English grēot, sand, gravel: GRIT. **2.** Germanic *grut- in Old English grotan, pieces of hulled grain, groats: GROATS. **3.** Germanic *grūt- in: **a.** Old English grūt, coarse meal: GROUT; **b.** Old French gruel, porridge: GRUEL. **4.** Germanic *grautaz, coarse, thick (< "coarsely ground"), in: **a.** Old English grēat, coarse, thick, bulky, large: GREAT; **b.** Middle Dutch groot, thick: GROAT. **5.** Germanic *grūw-, to recoil from (< "to be offended, be grated on by"), in Middle Dutch grūwen, to abhor, akin to Middle English grue, horrible: GRUESOME. **6.** Variant form *ghrow- in Greek khrōs, skin (< "rough surface" ?), hence flesh, complexion, color: RHODOCHROSITE. **7.** Suffixed variant form *ghrō-mn̥ in Greek khrōma, skin, complexion, color (semantic development as in **6.** above): CHROMA, CHROMATIC, CHROMATO-, CHROME, -CHROME, (CHROMIUM), CHROMO-; ACHROMATIC. **8.** Probably Celtic *graw- in Old French grave, greve, coarse sand, gravel: GRAVEL. **9.** Probably Latin *grau-, to touch, graze, in con-gruere, to agree (com-, together; see **kom**): CONGRUENT. [Pok. 2. ghrēu- 460.]

ghwer-. Wild beast. **1.** Suffixed form *ghwer-o- in Latin ferus, wild: FERAL, FIERCE. **2.** Compound *ghwero-əkw-, "of wild aspect" (*-əkw-, "-looking"; see **okw-**), in Latin ferōx (stem ferōc-), fierce: FEROCIOUS. **3.** Lengthened-grade form *ghwēr- in Greek thēr, wild beast: TREACLE; THEROPOD. [Pok. ghu̯ēr- 493.]

gladh-. Smooth. Suffixed form *gladh-ro- in Latin glaber, smooth, bald: GABRO, (GLABELLA), GLABROUS.

gleubh-. To cut, cleave. **1.** Germanic *kleuban in Old English clēofan, to split, cleave: CLEAVE[1]. **2.** Germanic *klub-, a splitting, in: **a.** Old English clufu, clove (of garlic): CLOVE[2]; **b.** Middle Dutch clove, a cleft: KLOOF. **3.** Germanic *klaubri- in: **a.** Old Norse kleyfr, easy to split, perhaps akin to Middle English cliver, "expert in seizing," skillful: CLEVER; **b.** Old Norse klofi, a cleft, akin to English clevi, "cleft instrument," clevis: CLEVIS. **4.** Zero-grade form *glubh- in Greek gluphein, to carve: GLYPH, GLYPTIC; ANAGLYPH, HIEROGLYPHIC. **5.** Suffixed zero-grade form *glubh-mā- in Latin glūma, husk of grain: GLUME. [Pok. gleubh- 401.]

glōgh-. Thorn, point. **1.** Suffixed form *glōgh-i- in Greek glōkhis, barb of an arrow: GLOCHIDIUM. **2.** Suffixed form *glōgh-ya in Greek glōssa, glōtta, tongue, hence also language: GLOSS[2], (GLOSSARY), GLOTTIS; BUGLOSS, GLOSSOLALIA, ISOGLOSS, POLYGLOT, PROGLOTTID. [Pok. glōgh- 402.]

gnō-. To know. Contracted from *gnoə-. **1.** Variant form *gnē- in Germanic *knē(w)- in Old English cnāwan, to know: KNOW. **2.** Zero-grade form *gnə- in: **a.** Germanic

kunnan in Old English *cunnan,* to know, know how to, be able to (Old English first and third singular *can* from Germanic **kann* from o-grade **gonə-*): CAN¹, CON², CUNNING; **b.** Germanic causative verb **kannjan,* to make known, in Old English *cennan,* to declare, and Old Norse *kenna,* to name (in a formal poetic metaphor): KEN, KENNING; **c.** Germanic **kunthaz* in Old English *cūth,* known, well-known, usual, excellent, familiar: (COUTH); UNCOUTH; **d.** Germanic **kunthithō* in Old English *cȳth(the), cȳthhthu,* knowledge, acquaintance, friendship, kinfolk: KITH. **3.** Suffixed form **gnō-sko-* in Latin *(g)nōscere, cognōscere,* to get to know, get acquainted with: NOTICE, NOTIFY, NOTION, NOTORIOUS; (ACQUAINT), COGNITION, (COGNIZANCE), (CONNOISSEUR), (QUAINT), RECOGNIZE. **4.** Suffixed form **gnō-ro-* in Latin *ignōrāre,* not to know, to disregard (*i-* for *in-,* not; see **ne**): IGNORANT, IGNORE. **5.** Suffixed form **gnō-dhli-* in Latin *nōbilis,* knowable, known, famous, noble: NOBLE. **6.** Reduplicated and suffixed form **gi-gnō-sko-* in Greek *gignōskein,* to know, think, judge (and **gnō-* in *gnōmōn,* a judge, interpreter): GNOME², GNOMON, GNOSIS; AGNOSIA, DIAGNOSIS, PATHOGNOMIC, PHYSIOGNOMY, PROGNOSIS. **7.** Suffixed zero-grade form **gnə-ro-* in Latin *gnārus,* knowing, expert, whence *narrāre* (< **gnarrāre*), to tell, relate: NARRATE. (**8.** Traditionally but improbably referred here are: **a.** Latin *nota,* a mark, note, sign, cipher, shorthand character: NOTE; ANNOTATE, CONNOTE, PROTHONOTARY; **b.** Latin *norma,* carpenter's square, rule, pattern, precept: NORM, NORMA, NORMAL; ABNORMAL, ENORMOUS.) [Pok. 2. *gen-* 376.]

gras-. To devour. **1.** Germanic **krasjōn-,* fodder, in Old English *cresse, cærse,* cress: CRESS. **2.** Suffixed form **gras-men* in Latin *grāmen,* "fodder," grass: GRAMA, GRAMINEOUS. **3.** Suffixed form **gras-ter-,* "the devourer," dissimilated in Greek *gastēr,* stomach, belly: (GASTRIC), GASTRO-, GASTRULA; EPIGASTRIUM. **4.** Reduplicated form **gar-gr-* dissimilated in Greek *gangraina,* gangrene: GANGRENE. [Pok. *gras-* 404.]

[grat-. Also **krat-**. To scratch. Germanic root. **1.** Germanic **krattōn* in Middle Dutch *cratsen,* to scrape: SCRATCH. **2.** Germanic **grat-* in Old French *grater,* to scrape: GRATE¹; REGRATE. [Pok. *gred-* 405.]]

[gravo-. Also **grāfo-**. A designation of rank, later corresponding with the feudal title of count. West Germanic noun. Middle Dutch *grave,* count: MARGRAVE, PALSGRAVE.]

greut-. To compress, push. **1.** Germanic **krūdan* in Old English *crūdan,* to press, hasten: CROWD¹. **2.** Germanic **krudam* in Old English *crod,* a squeezing (> Middle English *crud, crudde*): CRUD, CURD. [Pok. *greut-* 406.]

grə-no-. Grain. **1.** Germanic **kornam* in: **a.** Old English *corn,* grain: CORN¹; **b.** Old English derivative noun *cyrnel,* seed, pip: KERNEL; **c.** Old High German *korn,* grain: EINKORN. **2.** Latin *grānum,* grain: GARNER, GRAIN, GRAM², GRANADILLA, GRANARY, GRANGE, GRANITE, GRANULE, GRENADE; FILIGREE. [In Pok. *ĝer-* 390.]

gru-. To grunt. Imitative. **1.** Germanic **grun-* in Old English *grunnian,* to grunt, probably akin to Old English *grunettan,* to grunt: GRUNT. **2.** Germanic intensive form **grunnatjan* in Old High German *grunnizōn,* to grunt: GRUDGE. **3.** Latin *grunnīre, grundīre,* to grunt: GRUNION. [Pok. *gru-* 406.]

gʷā-. Also **gʷem-**. To go, come. **1.** Germanic **kuman* in: **a.** Old English *cuman,* to come: COME; **b.** Germanic **kumōn-,* he who comes, a guest, in compound **wil-ku-mōn-,* a desirable guest (**wil-,* desirable; see **wel-²**), in Old English *wilcuma,* a welcome guest, and *wilcume,* the greeting of welcome: WELCOME; **c.** compound **bi-kuman,* to arrive, come to be (**bi-,* intensive prefix; see **ambhi**), in Old English *becuman,* to become: BECOME. **2.** Suffixed form **gʷ(e)m-yo-* in Latin *venīre,* to come: VENIRE, VENUE; ADVENT, (ADVENTITIOUS), (ADVENTURE), (AVENUE), CIRCUMVENT, CONTRAVENE, CONVENE, (CONVENIENT), (CONVENT), (CONVENTICLE), (CONVENTION),

(COVEN), (COVENANT), EVENT, INTERVENE, INVENT, MISADVENTURE, PARVENU, PREVENIENT, PREVENT, PROVENANCE, (PROVENIENCE), REVENANT, REVENUE, SOUVENIR, SUBVENTION, SUPERVENE. **3.** Suffixed zero-grade form **gʷm̥-yo-* in Greek *bainein,* to go, walk, step, with *basis* (< **gʷm̥-ti-*), a stepping, tread, base, and *-batēs* (< **gʷə-to-,* zero-grade of *gʷā-,* contraction of **gʷaə-*), agential suffix, "one that goes or treads, one that is based": BASE¹, BASIS; ABASIA, ACROBAT, ADIABATIC, AMPHISBAENA, ANABAENA, DIABASE, DIABETES, STEREOBATE, STYLOBATE. **4.** Suffixed zero-grade form **gʷ(ə)-u-* in compound form **pres-gʷu-,* "going before" (see **per¹**). **5.** Basic form **gʷā-* in Greek *bēma,* step, seat, raised platform: BEMA. **6.** Sanskrit *jigāti,* he goes: JUGGERNAUT. [Pok. *gʷā-* 463.]

gʷadh-. To sink. Possible root. **1.** Suffixed form **gʷadh-u-* in Greek *bathus,* deep (> *bathos,* depth): BATHOS, BATHY-. **2.** Greek *benthos,* depth, may be formed on *bathus* by analogy with *penthos,* grief, and *pathos,* passion, suffering (or it may be from an unrelated root **gʷ(e)ndh-*): BENTHOS. **3.** Suffixed variant form **gudh-yo-* in Greek *bussos,* bottom of the sea: ABYSS. [Pok. *gʷādh-* 465.]

gʷēbh-¹. To dip, sink. Suffixed zero-grade form **gʷəbh-yo-* in Greek *baptein,* to dip: (BAPTIST), BAPTIZE; ANABAPTIST. [Pok. *gʷēbh-* 465.]

gʷēbh-². Hypothetical base of some Germanic words associated with the notion of sliminess. **1.** Middle Dutch *quac-,* unguent, liquid, in obsolete Dutch *quacksalver,* quacksalver: QUACKSALVER. **2.** Low German *quabbeln,* to shake like jelly, tremble, akin to Middle English *quaven,* to tremble: QUAVER. [Pok. 2. *gʷēbh-* 466.]

gʷei-. Also **gʷeiə-**. To live. **I.** Suffixed zero-grade form **gʷi-wo-, *gʷī-wo-* (< **gʷiə-wo-*), living. **1.** Germanic **kwi(k)waz* in: **a.** Old English *cwic, cwicu,* living, alive: QUICK, QUICKSILVER; **b.** as a name for couch grass (from its rapid growth), in Old English *cwice,* couch grass: (COUCH GRASS), QUITCH GRASS. **2. a.** Latin *vīvus,* living, alive: VIVIFY, VIVIPAROUS; **b.** Latin denominative *vīvere,* to live: VIAND, VICTUAL, VIVA, VIVACIOUS, VIVID; CONVIVIAL, REVIVE, SURVIVE. **3.** Further suffixed form **gʷī-wo-tā* in Latin *vīta,* life: VIABLE, VITAL; LIGNUM VITAE, VITAMIN. **II.** Suffixed zero-grade form **gʷiə-o-* in Greek *bios,* life (> *biotē,* way of life): BIO-, BIOTA, BIOTIC; AEROBE, AMPHIBIOUS, ANABIOSIS, CENOBITE, MICROBE, RHIZOBIUM, SAPROBE, SYMBIOSIS. **III.** Variant form **gʷyō-* (< **gʷyoə-*). **1.** Greek *zoē,* life: AZO-, (DIAZO). **2.** Suffixed form **gʷyō-on* in Greek *zōion, zōion,* living being, animal: (-ZOA), -ZOIC, ZOO-, ZOON, -ZOON. **IV.** Prefixed and suffixed form **su-gʷiə-es-* (**su-,* well; see **su-**), "living in good condition," in Greek *hugiēs,* healthy: HYGEIA, HYGIENE. [Pok. 3. *gʷei-* 467.]

gʷeiə-. To press down, conquer. Sanskrit *jayati,* he conquers: JAIN. [Pok. *gʷeiə-* 469.]

gʷel-¹. To pierce. **1.** Suffixed o-grade form **gʷol-eyo-* in Germanic **kwaljan* in Old English *cwellan,* to kill, destroy: QUELL. **2.** Suffixed zero-grade form **gʷl̥-yo-* in Germanic **kuljan* in Old English **cyllan,* to kill, perhaps the source of Middle English *killen,* to kill: KILL¹. **3.** Full-grade form **gʷel-* in Greek *belonē,* needle: BELONEPHOBIA. [Pok. 1. *gʷel-* 470.]

gʷel-². To fly; a wing. Possibly in Latin *volāre,* to fly: VOLANT, VOLATILE, VOLE², VOLITANT, VOLLEY.

gʷel-³. To swallow. Dissimilated to **gel-.* **1.** Germanic **kel-* in Old English *ceolu,* throat, dewlap, perhaps akin to Middle English *cholle,* throat: JOWL². **2.** Germanic **keluz* in Old Norse *kjölr,* keel: KEEL¹. **3.** Suffixed zero-grade form **gul-ā* in Latin *gula,* gullet, throat, palate: GOLIARD, GULAR, GULES, GULLET. **4.** Extended (expressive) form **glutt-* in: **a.** Latin *gluttīre, glūtīre,* to swallow: GLUT; DEGLUTITION; **b.** Latin *gluttō,* a glutton: GLUTTON. [In Pok. 2. *gel-* 365.]

gʷelbh-. Womb. **1.** Suffixed form **gʷelbh-u-* in Greek *delphus,* womb, whence *delphis,* dolphin (referring to its

shape): DELPHINIUM, DOLPHIN. **2.** Prefixed and suffixed form *sm̥-gʷelbh-o-, "born of one womb" (*sm̥-, one; see **sem-¹**), in Greek *adelphos*, brother: -ADELPHOUS. [Pok. gʷelbh- 473.]

gʷelə-¹. To throw, reach. Variant *gʷlē-, contracted from *gʷleə-. **1.** Suffixed zero-grade form *gʷl̥-n-ə- in: **a.** Greek *ballein*, to throw (with o-grade *bol- and variant *blē-): BALLISTA; AMPHIBOLE, ASTROBLEME, CATABOLISM, DEVIL, (DIABOLIC), (EBLIS), ECBOLIC, EMBLEM, EPIBOLY, (HYPERBOLA), HYPERBOLE, METABOLISM, (PALAVER), PARABLE, (PARABOLA), (PARLEY), (PARLIAMENT), (PARLOR), (PAROL), (PAROLE), PROBLEM, SYMBOL; **b.** Greek *ballizein*, to dance: BALL², (BALLAD), (BALLET), BAYADERE. **2.** Suffixed o-grade form *gʷolə-ā in Greek *bolē*, beam, ray: BOLOMETER. **3.** Suffixed o-grade form *gʷolə-sā in Greek *boulē*, determination, will (< "throwing forward of the mind"), council: BOULE¹; ABULIA. **4.** Suffixed variant zero-grade form *gʷele-mno- in Greek *belemnos*, dart, javelin: BELEMNITE. [Pok. 2. gʷel- 471.]

gʷelə-². An acorn. **1.** Suffixed zero-grade form *gʷl̥ə-nd- in Latin *glāns* (stem *gland-*), an acorn: GLAND, GLANDERS, (GLANDULAR), GLANS. **2.** Suffixed zero-grade form *gʷl̥ə-no- in Greek *balanos*, acorn, date: VALONIA; MYROBALAN. [Pok. 3. gʷel- 472.]

gʷen-. Woman. **1.** Suffixed form *gʷen-ā- in: **a.** Germanic *kwenōn- in Old English *cwene*, woman, prostitute, wife: QUEAN; **b.** Old Irish *ben* (> Irish Gaelic *bean*), woman: BANSHEE; **c.** Persian *zan*, woman: ZENANA. **2.** Suffixed lengthened-grade form *gʷēn-i- in Germanic *kwēniz, woman, wife, queen, in Old English *cwēn*, woman, wife, queen: QUEEN. **3.** Suffixed zero-grade form *gʷn-ā- in Greek *gunē*, woman: GYNO-, -GYNOUS, -GYNY; GYNAECEUM, GYNECOCRACY, (GYNECOLOGY), POLYGYNY. [Pok. gʷenā 473.]

gʷerə-¹. Mountain. Possibly o-grade form *gʷorə- in: **a.** Greek *boreios*, "coming from the north" (? < "coming from the mountains of Thrace, north of Greece"), whence *Boreas*, the north wind: BOREAS; **b.** Greek *Huperboreioi*, *Huperboreoi*, name of a people living in the far north, variously explained as "they who live beyond the north wind" and "they who live beyond the mountains" (*huper-*, beyond; see **uper**): HYPERBOREAN. [Pok. 3. gʷer- 477.]

gʷerə-². Heavy. **I.** Zero-grade form *gʷr̥ə-. **1.** Suffixed form *gʷr̥ə-u-i- in Latin *gravis*, heavy, weighty: GRAVE², GRAVID, (GRIEF), GRIEVE; AGGRAVATE, AGGRIEVE. **2.** Suffixed form *gʷr̥ə-u- in: **a.** Greek *barus*, heavy: BARITE, BARITONE, (BARIUM), BARYON, (BARYSPHERE), BARYTA; **b.** Sanskrit *guru-*, heavy, venerable: GURU. **3.** Suffixed form *gʷr̥ə-es- in Greek *baros*, weight: BAR², BARO-; CENTROBARIC, ISALLOBAR, ISOBAR. **4.** Possibly *gʷrī- in Greek *bri-* in compound *u(d)-bri-* (see **ud-**). **II.** Suffixed extended form *gʷrū-to- in Latin *brūtus*, heavy, unwieldy, dull, stupid, brutish: BRUT, BRUTE. **III.** Suffixed extended form *gʷrī-g- in: **a.** Celtic *brīg-o-, strength, in Italian *brio*, vigor: BRIO; **b.** Germanic *krīg- in Old High German *krēg*, *chrēg*, stubbornness (> German *Krieg*, war): BLITZKRIEG, SITZKRIEG. **IV.** Suffixed full-grade form *gʷerə-nā-, millstone, in Old English *cweorn*, quern: QUERN. [Pok. 2. gʷer- 476.]

gʷerə-³. To praise (aloud). **1.** Suffixed zero-grade form *gʷr̥ə-to- in Latin *grātus*, pleasing, beloved, agreeable, favorable, thankful: GRACE, GRATEFUL, GRATIFY, GRATIS, GRATITUDE, GRATUITY; AGREE, CONGRATULATE, INGRATE, INGRATIATE. **2.** Suffixed zero-grade form *gʷr̥ə-do-, "he who praises," in Celtic *bardo-*, bard, in Welsh *bardd* and Scottish and Irish Gaelic *bard*, bard: BARD¹. [Pok. 4. gʷer(ə)- 478.]

gʷerə-⁴. To swallow. **1.** Possibly suffixed extended form *gʷ(u)ro-gh- in Germanic *krag-, throat, in: **a.** Old English *craga*, throat, possible source of Middle English *crawe*, craw: CRAW; **b.** Middle Dutch *crāghe*, throat: SCRAG. **2.** Suffixed o-grade form *gʷor-ā- in Latin *vorāre*, to swallow up: VORACIOUS, -VOROUS; DEVOUR. **3.** Expres-

sive reduplicated form *gʷr̥-g- in Latin *gurges*, throat, also gulf, whirlpool: GARGET, GORGE, GORGET, GURGITATION; INGURGITATE, REGURGITATE. **4.** Extended form *gʷrō- (< *gʷroə-) in Greek *brō-* in: **a.** suffixed reduplicated form *bi-brō-sko- in Greek *bibrōskein*, to eat: HELLEBORE; **b.** nasalized variant form *bro-n-kh- in Greek *bronkhos*, windpipe, throat: BRONCHO-, BRONCHUS; **c.** suffixed form *gʷrō-mn̥ in Greek *brōma*, food: THEOBROMINE; **d.** suffixed form *gʷrō-ti- in Greek *brōsis*, eating: ABROSIA. [Pok. 1. gʷer- 474.]

gʷes-. To extinguish. Suffixed variant form *sgʷes-nu- in Greek *sbennunai*, to extinguish: ASBESTOS. [Pok. gʷes- 479.]

gʷet-¹. Resin (?). Only in Germanic and Celtic. Suffixed form *gʷet-u- in: **a.** Germanic *kwithu- in Old English *cwudu*, *cwidu*, *cudu*, resin, mastic gum, "that which is chewed," cud: CUD, QUID¹; **b.** Celtic *betu-*, birch, birch resin, in Latin *bitumen*, resin (Gaulish loanword): BITUMEN. [Pok. 1. gʷet- 480.]

gʷet-². To say, speak. Germanic *kwithan in Old English *cwethan*, *becwethan*, to say, speak: BEQUEATH, BEQUEST, QUOTH. [Pok. 2. gʷet- 480.]

gʷet-³. Intestine. Suffixed o-grade form *gʷot-olo- in Latin *botulus*, intestine, sausage: BOTULINUM, BOTULISM, BOWEL; (BOTULIN). [Pok. gʷet- 481.]

gʷhedh-. To ask, pray. **1.** Germanic *bidjan, to entreat, in Old English *biddan*, to ask, pray: BID. **2.** Germanic *bidam, entreaty in Old English *gebed* (*ge-*, intensive and collective prefix; see **kom**), prayer: BEAD. [Pok. gʷhedh- 488, 2. bhedh- 114.]

gʷhen-¹. To strike, kill. **1.** O-grade *gʷhon- in Germanic suffixed form *ban-ōn- in: **a.** Old English *bana*, slayer, cause of ruin or destruction: BANE; **b.** Middle High German *ban*, *bane* (> German *Bahn*), way, road (? < "path hewn through woods"): AUTOBAHN. **2.** Suffixed zero-grade form *gʷhn̥-tyā- in Germanic *gundjō, war, battle, in: **a.** Old Norse *gunnr*, war: GUN; **b.** compound *gund-fanōn-, "battle flag" (*fanōn-*, flag; see **pan-**), in Italian *gonfalone*, standard: GONFALON. **3.** Suffixed form *gʷhen-do- in: **a.** Latin *dēfendere*, to ward off (*dē-*, away; see **de-**): DEFEND, (DEFENSE), (FENCE); **b.** Latin *offendere*, to strike against, be offensive, offend (*ob-*, against; see **epi**): OFFEND, (OFFENSE). **4.** Suffixed zero-grade form *gʷhn̥-tro- in Persian *zahr*, poison: BEZOAR. [Pok. 2. gʷhen-(ə)- 491, bhen- 126.]

gʷhen-². To swell, abound. Suffixed form *gʷhen-eyo- in Greek *euthenein* (*eu-*, well; see **esu-**), to flourish: EUTHENICS. [Pok. 1. gʷhen- 491.]

gʷher-. To heat, warm. **1.** Zero-grade *gʷhr- with nasal suffix and analogical vocalism in Germanic *brenw-, to burn, forming *brennan (intransitive) and *brannjan (transitive) in: **a.** Old English *beornan*, *byrnan* (intransitive) and *bærnan* (transitive), to burn: BURN¹; **b.** late Old English *brynstān*, "burning mineral," sulfur (*stān*, stone; see **stei**): BRIMSTONE. **2.** Germanic *brandaz, a burning, a flaming torch, hence also a sword, in: **a.** Old English *brand*, piece of burning wood, sword: BRAND; **b.** Old Norse *brandr*, piece of burning wood, akin (in the sense "blackened by fire," dark-colored) to the possible Scandinavian source of Middle English *brende*, brindled: BRINDLED; **c.** Dutch *branden*, to burn, distill: BRANDY; **d.** Old French *brand*, sword: BRANDISH. **3.** Suffixed form *gʷher-mo- in Greek *thermos*, warm, hot (> *thermē*, heat): THERM, -THERM, THERMO-, -THERMY; HYPOTHERMIA. **4.** O-grade form *gʷhor- in Latin *forceps*, pincers, fire tongs (< "that which holds hot things"; -*ceps*, agential suffix, "-taker"; see **kap-**): FORCEPS, FORCIPATE. **5.** Suffixed o-grade form *gʷhor-no- in: **a.** Latin *fornus*, *fornāx*, oven: FORNAX, FURNACE, HORNITO; **b.** probably Latin *fornix*, arch, vault (< "vaulted brick oven"): FORNICATE. [Pok. gʷher- 493, bhereu- 143.]

gʷhī-. Thread, tendon. Suffixed form *gʷhī-slo- in Latin *fīlum*, thread: FILAMENT, FILAR, FILARIA, FILE¹, FILLET,

FILOSE, FILUM; DEFILE², ENFILADE, FILIFORM, FILIGREE, FILOPLUME, PROFILE, PURFLE. [Pok. gʷheiə- 489.]

gʷhrē-. To smell, breathe. Contracted from *gʷhreə-. Germanic suffixed form *brē-thaz in Old English brǣth, odor, exhalation: BREATH, (BREATHE).

gʷhren-. To think. **1.** Greek phrēn, the mind, also heart, midriff, diaphragm: (FRANTIC), FRENETIC, FRENZY, -PHRENIA, PHRENO-; EUPHROSYNE, (PHRENITIS). **2.** Extended zero-grade root form *gʷhr̥n-d- in Greek phrazein, to point out, show: PHRASE; HOLOPHRASTIC, METAPHRASE, PARAPHRASE, PERIPHRASIS. [Pok. gʷhren- 496.]

gʷl̥tur-. Vulture. Possible root. Latin vultur, vulture: VULTURE. [Pok. gʷl̥tur(os) 482.]

gʷō-. To feed. Contracted from *gʷoə-. Suffixed zero-grade *gʷə-sko-, Greek *gʷo-sko-, in Greek boskein, to feed: PROBOSCIS. [In Pok. gʷou- 482.]

gʷou-. Ox, bull, cow. Nominative singular form *gʷōu-s. **1.** Germanic *kōuz (> *kūz) in Old English cū, cȳ, cȳe, cow: COW¹, (KINE); COWSLIP. **2.** Latin bōs (stem bov-), ox, bull, cow: BEEF, BOVINE, BUGLE¹; OVIBOS. **3.** Greek bous, ox, bull, cow: BOUSTROPHEDON, BUCEPHALUS, BUCOLIC, BULIMIA, BUPRESTID, BUTTER, (BUTYRIC). **4.** Sanskrit go-, gauḥ, cow: GAYAL. **5.** Suffixed form *gʷōu-ro- in Sanskrit gauraḥ, wild ox: GAUR. **6.** Zero-grade form *gʷw-ā- in Greek hekatombē, "sacrifice of a hundred oxen" (hekaton, hundred; see dekm̥): HECATOMB. [Pok. gʷou- 482.]

gʷres-. Thick, fat. Perhaps Latin grossus (from an uncertain preform), thick: GROCER, GROSCHEN, GROSS, GROSZ; ENGROSS. [Pok. gʷretso- 485.]

gyeu-. Also **geu-.** To chew. Germanic *kewwan in Old English cēowan, to chew: CHEW. [Pok. g(i)eu- 400.]

[hulē. Forest, timber, hence stuff, matter. Greek noun of unknown origin. -YL, YLEM; HYLOZOISM, METHYLENE.]

i-. Pronominal stem. **1.** Germanic *is-līk-, same (*līk-, like; see līk-), in Old English ilca, same: ILK. **2.** Germanic *jaino-, *jeno-, in Old English geon, that: YON. **3.** Germanic *jend- in Old English geond, as far as, yonder: YOND, (YONDER). **4.** Extended forms *yām, *yāi, in Germanic *jā, *jai, in Old English gēa, affirmative particle, and gēse, yes (see es-): YEA, YES. **5.** Old English gīet, gīeta (preform uncertain), still: YET. **6.** Old English gif (preform uncertain), if: IF. **7.** Basic form *i-, with neuter *id-em, in Latin is, he (neuter id), and īdem, same: ID, IDEM, (IDENTICAL), IDENTITY; (IDENTIFY). **8.** Suffixed form *i-tero- in Latin iterum, again: ITERATE; (REITERATE). **9.** Suffixed and extended form *it(ə)-em in Latin item, thus, also: ITEM. **10.** Suffixed variant form *e-tero- (see ko-). [Pok. 3. e- 281.]

kā-. To like, desire. Contracted from *kaə-. **1.** Suffixed form *kā-ro- in: **a.** Germanic *hōraz (feminine *hōrōn-), "one who desires," adulterer, in (i) Old English hōre, whore: WHORE (ii) Old Norse compound hōrdōmr, whoredom (-dōmr, "condition"; see dhē-¹): WHOREDOM; **b.** Latin cārus, dear: CARESS, CHARITY, CHERISH. **2.** Suffixed form *kā-mo- in Sanskrit kāmaḥ, love, desire: KAMA; KAMASUTRA. [Pok. kā- 515.]

kad-. To fall. Latin cadere, to fall, die: CADAVER, CADENCE, CADENT, CADUCOUS, CASCADE, CASE¹, CHANCE, CHUTE; ACCIDENT, CADUCICORN, DECAY, DECIDUOUS, ESCHEAT, INCIDENT, OCCASION, RECIDIVISM. [Pok. 1. kad- 516.]

kād-. Sorrow, hatred. Suffixed zero-grade form *kəd-i- in: **a.** Germanic *hatiz in Old English hete, hate, envy (> Middle English hate): HATRED. **b.** Germanic *hatōn in Old English hatian, to hate: HATE; **c.** Germanic *hatjan in Old French hair, to hate: HEINOUS. [Pok. kād- 517.]

kādh-. To shelter, cover. **1.** Suffixed zero-grade form *kəd-u- in Germanic *haduz in expressive form *hattuz in Old English hæt(t), hat: HAT. **2.** Basic form *kādh- in: **a.** Germanic *hōda in Old English hōd, hood: HOOD¹;

b. Germanic *hōdjan in Old English hēdan, to heed, care for, protect: HEED. [Pok. kadh- 516.]

kae-id-. To strike. **1.** Latin caedere, to cut, strike: CAESURA, CEMENT, CESTUS², CHISEL, -CIDE, SCISSORS; ABSCISE, CIRCUMCISE, CONCISE, DECIDE, EXCISE², INCISE, PRECISE, RECISION. **2.** Latin caelum (? < *caedum), sculptor's chisel: CAELUM. [Pok. (s)k(h)ai- 917.]

kagh-. To catch, seize; wickerwork, fence. **1.** Germanic *hag- in: **a.** Old French hagard, wild, wild hawk (< "raptor"): HAGGARD; **b.** Germanic *hagōn- in Old English haga, hedge, hawthorn: HAW²; **c.** Germanic *hagjō in Old English hecg, hedge: HEDGE. **2.** Suffixed unaspirated form *kag-yon- in Gaulish caio, rampart, retaining wall (> Old French quai, quay): (CAY), KEY², QUAY. **3.** Possible variant *kogh- in: **a.** Latin cohum, strap from yoke to harness: INCHOATE; **b.** possibly Latin cōlum, sieve (< wickerwork), and its derivative cōlāre, to filter: COLANDER, COULEE, (COULOIR), CULLIS; PERCOLATE. [Pok. kagh- 518.]

kaghlo-. Pebble, hail. Germanic *haglaz in Old English hagol, hægel, hail: HAIL¹. [Pok. kaghlo- 518.]

kai-. Heat. Extended form *kaid- in: **a.** Germanic *haitaz in Old English hāt, hot: HOT; **b.** Germanic *haitī- in Old English hǣtu, heat: HEAT. [Pok. kāi- 519.]

kaiko-. One-eyed. Latin caecus, blind: CAECILIAN, CAECUM. [Pok. kai-ko- 519.]

kailo-. Whole, uninjured, of good omen. **1.** Germanic *hailaz in: **a.** Old English hāl, hale, whole: HALE¹, WHOLE; **b.** Old English hālsum, wholesome (> Middle English holsom): WHOLESOME; **c.** Old Norse heill, healthy: (HAIL²); WASSAIL. **2.** Germanic *hailithō in Old English hǣlth, health: HEALTH. **3.** Germanic *hailjan in Old English hǣlan, to heal: HEAL. **4.** Germanic *hailagaz in: **a.** Old English hālig, holy, sacred: HOLY; **b.** Germanic derivative verb *hailagōn in Old English hālgian, to consecrate, bless: HALLOW. [Pok. kailo- 622.]

kaito-. Forest, uncultivated land. **1.** Germanic *haithiz in Old English hǣth, heath, untilled land: HEATH. **2.** Germanic *haithinaz in: **a.** Old English hǣthen, heathen, "savage" (< "one inhabiting uncultivated land"): HEATHEN; **b.** Middle Dutch heiden, heathen: HOYDEN. [Pok. kaito- 521.]

kak-¹. To enable, help. Sanskrit śaknoti, he is able, he is strong: SHAKTI, SIKH. [Pok. kak- 522.]

[kak-². A round object, disk. Germanic root. **1.** Old Norse kaka, cake: CAKE. **2.** Middle Dutch koeke, a cake: COOKY. **3.** Middle Low German kōke, cake: COCKAIGNE. **4.** Old High German kuocho, cake: KUCHEN, QUICHE. [In Pok. gag- 349.]]

kakka-. Also **kaka-.** To defecate. Imitative root. **1.** Old Norse *kūka, to defecate, akin to the source of Middle English cukken, to defecate: CUCKING STOOL. **2.** Latin cacāre, to defecate: POPPYCOCK. **3.** Greek kakos, bad: CACO-; CACODYL, CACOËTHES, CACOPHONOUS, CACOPHONY. [Pok. kakka- 521.]

kal-¹. Cup. **1.** Suffixed zero-grade form *kl̥-ik- in: **a.** Latin calix, cup, goblet: CALIX, CHALICE; **b.** Greek kulix, cup: KYLIX. **2.** Suffixed zero-grade form *kl̥-uk- in Greek kalux, seed-vessel, cup: CALYX. [Pok. 7. kel- 550.]

kal-². Beautiful. **1.** Suffixed form *kal-wo- in Greek kalos, beautiful: CALLISTO; CALOMEL, CALOYER, KALEIDOSCOPE. **2.** Suffixed form *kal-yo- in Greek kallos, beauty: CALLIGRAPHY, CALLIOPE, CALLIPYGIAN. [Pok. 2. kal- 524.]

kal-³. Hard. **1.** Latin callum, hard skin: (CALLOSE), CALLOUS, CALLUS. **2.** Celtic *kal-eto- in Welsh caled, hard, in Caledvwlch, Excalibur: EXCALIBUR. [Pok. 1. kal- 523.]

kamer-. To bend; a vault. **1.** Greek kamara, a vault: (CABARET), CAMARILLA, (CAMERA), CHAMBER, (COMRADE); (BICAMERAL). **2.** Persian kamar, waist, girdle, loins, something arched: CUMMERBUND. [Pok. kam-er- 524.]

kamp-. To bend. **1.** Suffixed form *kamp-ā in Greek kampē, a bending, a winding: (GAM²), (GAMBADO²), (GAM-

BIT), GAMBOL, (GAMBREL), (GAMMON³), (JAMB). **2.** Suffixed form *kamp-ulo- in Greek kampulos, bent: CAMPYLOTROPOUS. [Pok. kam-p- 525.]

kan-. To sing. **1.** Germanic *han(e)nī in Old English hen(n), hen: HEN. **2.** Latin canere, to sing (> cantāre, to sing): CANOROUS, CANT², CANTABILE, CANTICLE, CANTILLATE, (CANTO), CANTOR, CANZONE, CHANT; ACCENT, DESCANT, ENCHANT, (INCANTATION), INCENTIVE, PRECENTOR, RECANT. **3.** Latin oscen, a singing bird used in divination (< *obs-cen, "one that sings before the augurs"; ob-, before; see **epi**): OSCINE. **4.** Suffixed form *kan-men- in Latin carmen, song, poem: CHARM¹. [Pok. kan- 525.]

kand-. To shine. **1.** Suffixed (stative) form *kand-ē- in Latin candēre, to shine: CANDENT, CANDID, (CANDIDA), (CANDIDATE), CANDLE, CANDOR; INCANDESCE. **2.** Latin transitive *candere, to kindle, in compound incendere, to set fire to, kindle (in-, in; see **en**): (INCENDIARY), INCENSE. [Pok. kand- 526.]

kannabis. Hemp. Late Indo-European word borrowed from an unknown source. **1.** Germanic *hanipiz in Old English henep, hænep, hemp: HEMP. **2.** Greek kannabis, hemp: CANNABIS, (CANVAS).

kanto-. A corner, a bending. Celtic *cantos, rim, border, in Latin cantus, canthus, iron ring around a carriage wheel, a wheel, rim (> Italian canto, corner): CANTEEN, CANTON; DECANT. [Pok. kan-tho- 526.]

kap-. To grasp. **I.** Basic form *kap-. **1.** Germanic *haf- in Old English hefeld, thread used for weaving, heddle (a device which grasps the thread): HEDDLE. **2.** Germanic *haftjam in Old English hæft, handle: HAFT. **3.** Form *kap-o- in Germanic *habai-, *habēn in Old English habban, to have, hold: HAVE. **4.** Germanic hafigaz, "containing something," having weight, in Old English hefig, heavy: HEAVY. **5.** Germanic *hafnō-, perhaps "place that holds ships," in Old English hæfen, a haven: HAVEN. **6.** Germanic habukaz in Old English h(e)afoc, hawk: HAWK¹. **7.** Latin combining form -ceps (< *kap-s), "taker." **II.** Suffixed form *kap-yo-. **1.** Germanic *hafjan in Old English hebban, to lift: HEAVE. **2.** Latin capere, to take, seize, catch: CABLE, CAPABLE, CAPACIOUS, CAPIAS, CAPSTAN, CAPTION, CAPTIOUS, CAPTIVATE, CAPTIVE, CAPTOR, CAPTURE, CATCH, (CHASE¹); ACCEPT, ANTICIPATE, CONCEIVE, DECEIVE, EXCEPT, INCEPTION, (INCIPIENT), INTERCEPT, INTUSSUSCEPTION, MUNICIPAL, NUNCUPATIVE, OCCUPY, PARTICIPATE, PERCEIVE, PRECEPT, RECEIVE, (RECOVER), RECUPERATE, (Rx), SUSCEPTIBLE. **III.** Suffixed form *kap-s- in Latin capsa, repository, case: CAISSON, CAPSICUM, CAPSID, CAPSULE, CASE², CHASE², CHASE³, CHASSIS, CHESS³; ENCHASE. **IV.** Lengthened-grade variant form *kōp-. **1.** Germanic *hōf- in compound *bi-hōf, "that which binds," requirement, obligation (*bi-, intensive prefix; see **ambhi**), in: **a.** Old English behōf, use, profit, need: BEHOOF; **b.** Old English behōfian, to have need of: BEHOOVE. **2.** Greek kōpē, oar, handle: COPEPOD. Compare **ghabh-**. [Pok. kap- 527.]

kap(h)o-. Hoof. Lengthened-grade form kāp(h)-o- in Germanic *hōfaz in Old English hōf, hoof: HOOF. [Pok. kapho- 530.]

kapro-. He-goat, buck. Latin caper, he-goat (> capra, she-goat): CABRILLA, CABRIOLET, CAPELLA, CAPRIOLE, CHEVRON; CAPRIC ACID, CAPRICORN, CAPRIFIG, CAPROIC ACID. [Pok. kapro- 529.]

kaput. Head. **1.** Germanic *haubidam, *haubudam, in Old English hēafod, head: HEAD. **2.** Latin caput, head (> Italian capo, head): CABEZON, CADET, CAPE², CAPITAL¹, CAPITAL², CAPITATE, CAPITATION, CAPITELLUM, CAPITULATE, CAPITULUM, CAPO¹, CAPRICE, CAPTAIN, CATTLE, CAUDILLO, CHAPITER, CHAPTER, CHIEF, CHIEFTAIN; BICEPS, CHAMFRON, DECAPITATE, KERCHIEF, MISCHIEF, OCCIPUT, PRECIPITATE, RECAPITULATE, SINCIPUT, TRICEPS. [Pok. kap-ut- 529.]

kar-¹. Hard. **I.** Variant form ker-. **1.** Suffixed o-grade form *kor-tu- in Germanic *harduz in: **a.** Old English hard,

heard, hard: HARD; **b.** Frankish *hard, hard, perhaps the source of Old French estandard, rallying place: STANDARD; **c.** Old French hardir, to make hard: HARDY¹. **2.** Extended zero-grade form *kṛt-es- in Greek kratos, strength, might, power: -CRACY. **II.** Basic form *kar- in derivatives referring to things with hard shells. **1.** Possibly Latin carīna, keel of a ship, nutshell: CAREEN, CARINA. **2.** Possibly Greek karuon, nut: KARYO-; EUCARYOTE, GILLYFLOWER, SYNKARYON. **3.** Reduplicated form *kar-kr-o dissimilated to Latin cancer, crab: CANCER, CANKER, CHANCRE. **4.** Suffixed form *kar-k-ino- in Greek karkinos, cancer, crab: CARCINO-, CARCINOMA; (CARCINOGEN). [Pok. 3. kar- 531.]

kar-². To praise loudly, extol. Hypothetical base form. **1.** Perhaps Germanic *hrōm- in Dutch roemen, to praise: RUMMER. **2.** Lengthened-grade form *kāru- in Greek (Doric) karux, (Attic) kērux, herald: CADUCEUS. [Pok. 2. kar- 530.]

[karlaz. Man. Germanic root. **1.** Old English ceorl, man, churl: CHURL. **2.** Old Norse karl, man, freeman: CARL, CARLING. [In Pok. ĝer- 390.]]

kars-. To card. **1.** Latin cārere, carrere, to card wool (> carmen, a card for wool): CARMINATIVE. **2.** Perhaps Latin carduus, thistle, artichoke: CARD², CARDOON, (CHARD). [Pok. kars- 532.]

kas-. Gray. **1.** Germanic *hasōn-, *hazōn- in Old English hara, hare: HARE. **2.** Suffixed form *kas-no- in Latin cānus, white, gray, grayed hair: CANESCENT. [Pok. kas- 533.]

kat-¹. Something thrown down; offspring. **1.** Possibly Greek kata, down: CATA-; CATHEPSIN. **2.** Suffixed form *kat-olo- in Latin catulus, young puppy, young of animals: CADELLE. [Pok. 2. kat- 534.]

kat-². To fight. Suffixed form *kat-u- in Old Irish cath, battle: KERN¹. [Pok. kat- 534.]

kau-¹. To howl (imitative). **1.** Reduplicated suffixed form *ka-kau-ro- in Sanskrit cakorah, partridge: CHUKAR. **2.** Reduplicated form *kō-kū-o- in Greek kōkuein, to wail, lament: COCYTUS. [Pok. kau- 535.]

kau-². To hew, strike. **1.** Germanic *hawwan in: **a.** Old English hēawan, to hew: HEW; **b.** Old Norse höggva, to cut: HAGGLE; **c.** Old French hove, a hoe: HOE. **2.** Germanic *hawwō in Old Norse högg, a gap, a cutting blow, akin to the source of HAG². **3.** Germanic *haujam in Old English hīeg, hay, cut grass: HAY. **4.** Suffixed form *kau-do- in Latin cūdere (< *caudere), to strike, beat: INCUS. [Pok. kāu-, 535.]

kaul-. Stalk, stem. Latin caulis, stalk, stem, cabbage-stalk, cabbage: CAULICLE, CAULINE, COLE, KALE; AMPLEXICAUL, CAULESCENT, CAULIFLOWER, COLCANNON, COLESLAW, KAILYARD SCHOOL, KOHLRABI. [Pok. kau-l- 537.]

ked-. To go, yield. **1.** Lengthened-grade form *kēd- in Latin cēdere, to go, withdraw, yield: CEASE, CEDE, CESSION; ABSCESS, ACCEDE, ACCESS, ANCESTOR, ANTECEDE, CONCEDE, CONCESSION, DECEASE, EXCEED, INTERCEDE, PRECEDE, PREDECESSOR, PROCEED, RECEDE, RETROCEDE, SECEDE, SUCCEED. **2.** Prefixed and suffixed form *ne-ked-ti-, "from which one cannot draw back" (*ne-, not; see **ne**), in Latin necesse, inevitable, unavoidable: NECESSARY. [In Pok. sed- 884.]

keg-. Hook, tooth. **1.** Germanic *hakan- in: **a.** Old Norse haki, hook, akin to Old English haca, hook: HAKE; **b.** Middle Low German hake, hook: HARQUEBUS. **2.** Germanic lengthened form *hōka- in: **a.** Old English hōc, hook: HOOK; **b.** Middle Dutch hōk, hoec, hook: HOOKER¹. **3.** Germanic *hakila- in Middle Dutch hekel, hatchel, a flax comb with long metal hooklike teeth: HECKLE. **4.** Germanic *hakkijan in Old English -haccian, to hack to pieces as with a hooked instrument: HACK¹. [Pok. keg- 537.]

kei-¹. To lie; bed, couch; beloved, dear. **I.** Basic form *kei-. **1.** Suffixed form *kei-wo- in: **a.** Germanic *hīwa- in Old English hīwan, members of a household: HIND³;

b. suffixed Germanic form *hīwidō in Old English hīgid, hīd, a measure of land (< 'household"): HIDE³. **2.** Suffixed form *kei-wi- in Latin cīvis, citizen (< "member of a household"): CITY, CIVIC, CIVIL. **II.** O-grade form *koi-. **1.** Suffixed form *koi-nā- in Latin cūnae, a cradle: INCUNABULUM. **2.** Suffixed form *koi-m-ā- in Greek koiman, to put to sleep: CEMETERY. **III.** Suffixed zero-grade form *ki-wo- in Sanskrit śiva, auspicious, dear: SHIVA. [Pok. 1. kei- 539.]

kei-². Referring to various adjectives of color. **1.** Suffixed o-grade form *koi-ro- in German *hairaz, "gray-haired," old, venerable, hence master, in: **a.** Old English hār, gray, hoary: HOAR; **b.** Old High German hēr, worthy, exalted: JUNKER; **c.** Middle Dutch here, master, lord: YOUNKER. **2.** Suffixed zero-grade form *ki-wo- in Germanic *hiwam in Old English hīw, hēo, color, appearance, form: HUE¹. [Pok. 2. ḱei- 540.]

kei-³. To set in motion. **I.** Possibly extended o-grade form *koid- with suffixed form *koi-d-ti- in Germanic *haissiz in: **a.** Old English hǣs, a command, a bidding: HEST; **b.** Old English compound behǣs, a vow, promise, command (be-, intensive prefix; see **ambhi**): BEHEST (but perhaps to be referred to a separate root *kaid-). **II.** Zero-grade form *ki-. **1.** Form *ki-eyo- in Latin ciēre (past participle citus), with its frequentative citāre, to set in motion, summon: CITE; EXCITE, INCITE, OSCITANCY, RESUSCITATE, SOLICITOUS. **2.** Suffixed form *ki-neu- in Greek kinein, to move (> kinēsis, motion): KINEMATICS, -KINESIS, KINETIC; CINEMATOGRAPH, CINEMATORADIOGRAPHY, HYPERKINESIA, KINESIOLOGY, KINESTHESIA, KININ, (TELEKINESIS). [Pok. kei- 538.]

kekʷ-. To excrete. Suffixed o-grade form *kokʷ-ro- in Greek kopros, dung: COPRO-. [Pok. kekʷ- 544.]

kel-¹. To strike, cut. Hypothetical base of derivatives referring to something broken or cut off; twig, piece of wood. **I.** Basic form *kel- in suffixed o-grade form *kol-o- in Greek kolos, docked, kolobos, maimed: COLOBOMA. **II.** Extended form *keld-. **1.** Germanic *helt- in Old English hilt: HILT. **2.** Zero-grade extended form *kḷd- in **a.** Germanic *hulta- in Old English holt, wood: HOLT; **b.** Greek klados, branch, shoot: CLADOCERAN, CLADODE, CLADOGENESIS, CLADOPHYLL, PHYLLOCLADE. **3.** Variant Celtic zero-grade extended form *klad- in: **a.** suffixed form *klad-yo-, Celtic source of Latin gladius, sword: GLADIATE, GLADIATOR, GLAIVE; **b.** suffixed form *klad-ibo- in Gaelic claidheamh, sword: CLAYMORE. **4.** O-grade extended form *kold- in: **a.** Germanic *haltaz, "with a broken leg," in Old English compound lemphealt, limping, halting (lemp-, hanging loosely; see **leb-¹**), probable source of obsolete limphalt, lame: LIMP; **b.** Germanic derivative verb *haltōn in Old English healtian, to limp: HALT². **III.** Extended form *kelə-. **1.** Zero-grade form *kḷə- in: **a.** Greek kla- in (i) Greek klan, to break: CLAST, CLASTIC, CLASMATOCYTE, OSTEOCLAST, PLAGIOCLASE (ii) Greek klōn (< *kla-ōn), twig: CLONE; **b.** suffixed form *kḷə-ro- in Greek klēros, lot, allotment (< "that which is cut off"): CLERK; **c.** suffixed form *kḷə-mn̥ in Greek klēma, twig: CLEMATIS; **d.** suffixed form *kḷə-mo- in Latin calamitās, injury, damage, loss: CALAMITY. **2.** O-grade form *kolə- in suffixed form *kolə-bho- in Greek kolaphos, a blow: COPE¹, COUP. See extension **kleg-**. [Pok. 3 kel- 545.]

kel-². To cover, conceal, save. **I.** O-grade form *kol-. **1.** Germanic *haljō, the underworld (< "concealed place"), in: **a.** Old English hell, hell: HELL; **b.** Old Norse Hel, the underworld, goddess of death: HEL. **2.** Germanic *hallō, covered place, hall, in: **a.** Old English heall, hall: HALL; **b.** Old Norse höll, hall: VALHALLA. **3.** Suffixed form *kol-eyo- in Greek koleon, koleos, sheath: COLEUS; COLEOPTERA, COLEOPTERAN, COLEOPTILE, COLEORHIZA. **II.** Zero-grade form *kḷ-. **1.** Germanic *hul- in: **a.** Old English hulu, husk, pod (< "that which covers"): HULL; **b.** Old English hol, a hollow: HOLE; **c.** Old English holh, hole, hollow: HOLLOW; **d.** Old English healh, secret place,

small hollow: HAUGH; **e.** Dutch holster, holster, (< "that which covers"): HOLSTER. **2.** Suffixed Germanic form *hulftī- in Medieval Latin hultia, protective covering: HOUSING². **3.** Suffixed form *kl̥-to- in Latin occultus (see **III. 5.** below). **4.** Extended form *klā (< *kḷə-) in Latin clam, in secret: CLANDESTINE. **5.** Suffixed variant form *kal-up-yo- in Greek kaluptein, to cover, conceal: CALYPSO, CALYPTRA; APOCALYPSE, EUCALYPTUS. **III.** Full-grade form *kel-. **1.** Germanic *helmaz, "protective covering," in: **a.** Old English helm, protection, covering: HELM²; **b.** Frankish *helm, helmet, akin to the source of Middle English helmet, helmet: HELMET. **2.** Latin occulere (part participle occultus; see **II. 4.** above), to cover over (ob-, over; see **epi**): OCCULT. **3.** Suffixed form *kel-os- in Latin color, color, hue (< "that which covers"): COLOR. **4.** Suffixed form *kel-nā in Latin cella, storeroom, chamber: CELL, CELLA, CELLAR, CELLARER; (RATHSKELLER). **5.** Suffixed form *kel-yo- in Latin cilium, lower eyelid: CILIUM, SEEL; SUPERCILIOUS, (SUPERCILIUM). **IV.** Lengthened-grade form *kēl-ā- in Latin cēlāre, to hide: CONCEAL. See extension **klep-**. [Pok. 4. kel- 553.]

kel-³. To drive, set in swift motion. Hypothetical base of various loosely connected derivatives. **1.** Extended form *kelt- or *keldh- possibly in Germanic *haldan, to drive flocks, keep or pasture cattle, in: **a.** Old English healdan, to hold, retain: HOLD¹; **b.** Old High German haltan, to stop, hold back: HALT¹; **c.** Middle Dutch houden, to hold: AVAST. **2.** Suffixed form *kel-es- in: **a.** Latin celer, swift: CELERITY; ACCELERATE; **b.** possibly further suffixed form *keles-ri- in Latin celeber, (of a place) much frequented, hence famous: CELEBRATE, CELEBRITY. **3.** Suffixed zero-grade form *kl-on- in Greek klonos, turmoil, agitation: CLONUS. [Pok. 5. kel- 548.]

kel-⁴. To lean, tilt. Germanic *halthjan in Old English hieldan, to tilt: HEEL². [Pok. 2. ḱel- 552.]

kel-⁵. Gray, black, dark. Suffixed form *kel-omb(h)- in Latin columba, dove, pigeon: COLUMBA, COLUMBARIUM, COLUMBINE, CULVER. [Pok. 4. ḱel- 547.]

kel-⁶. To be prominent; hill. **1.** Zero-grade form *kl̥- in: **a.** suffixed Germanic form *hul-ni- in Old English hyll, hill: HILL; **b.** suffixed Germanic form *hul-ma- in Old Norse holmr, islet in a bay, meadow: HOLM. **2.** Suffixed form *kel-d- in Latin excellere, to raise up, elevate, also to be eminent (ex-, up out of; see **eghs**): EXCEL. **3.** O-grade form *kol- in: **a.** Greek kolophōn, summit: COLOPHON; **b.** suffixed form *kol(u)men- in Latin culmen, top, summit: CULMINATE; **c.** extended and suffixed form *kolumnā in Latin columna, a projecting object, column: COLONEL, COLONNADE, COLUMN. [Pok. 1. kel- 544.]

kel-⁷. To prick. Germanic *hulin- in Old English holen, holly (from its spiny leaves): HOLLY. [Pok. 2. ḱel- 545.]

kel-⁸. To deceive, trick. Extended form *kelu-, variant *kalu-, in: **a.** Latin calvī, to deceive, trick: CALUMNY, CHALLENGE; **b.** Latin cavilla (< *calvilla), a jeering: CAVIL. [Pok. ḱēl- 551.]

kelb-. To help. Germanic *helpan in Old English helpan, to help: HELP. [Pok. kelb- 554.]

kelə-¹. Warm. Variant *klē-, contracted from *kleə-. **1.** Suffixed variant form *klē-wo- in Germanic *hlēwaz in Old English hlēo, hlēow, covering, protection (as from cold): LEE. **2.** Suffixed zero-grade form *kḷə-ē- in: **a.** Latin calēre, to be warm: CALENTURE, CHAFE; DECALESCENCE, NONCHALANT, RECALESCENCE; **b.** Latin derivative adjective calidus, warm (> French chaud, warm): CALDRON, CAUDLE, (CHOWDER); CHAUDFROID, SCALD¹. **3.** Suffixed zero-grade form *kḷ-os- in Latin calor, heat: CALORIC, CALORIE; CALORECEPTOR, CALORIFIC, CALORIMETER, CALORIMETRY. [Pok. 1. kel- 551.]

kelə-². To shout. **I.** Variant form *klā- (< *klaə-). **1.** Germanic *hlō- in Old English hlōwan, to roar, low: LOW². **2.** Suffixed form *klā-mā- in Latin clāmāre, to call, cry out: CLAIM, CLAMANT, CLAMOR; ACCLAIM, DECLAIM, EXCLAIM, PROCLAIM, RECLAIM. **II.** O-grade form *kolə-.

Germanic *halōn, to call, in: **a.** Dutch halen, to haul, pull (? < "to call together, summon"): KEELHAUL; **b.** Old French haler, to haul: HALE², HAUL. **III.** Zero-grade form *klə- (> *kal-). **1.** Suffixed form *kal-yo- in Latin concilium, a meeting, gathering (< "a calling together"; con-, together; see **kom**): CONCILIATE, COUNCIL. **2.** Suffixed form *kal-ēnd- in Latin kalendae, the calends, the first day of the month, when it was publicly announced on which days the nones and ides of that month would fall: CALENDAR, CALENDS. **3.** Suffixed form *kal-e- in Greek kalein (variant klē-), to call: ECCLESIA, PARACLETE. **4.** Suffixed form *kal-ā- in Latin calāre, to call, call out: INTERCALATE, NOMENCLATOR. **5.** Suffixed form *klə-ro- or suffixed variant form *klaə-ro- contracted to *klā-ro- in Latin clārus, bright, clear: CLEAR, GLAIR; CHIAROSCURO, CLAIRVOYANCE, DECLARE, ÉCLAIR, ÉCLAIRISSEMENT. **IV.** Possibly extended zero-grade form *kld-, becoming *klad- in suffixed form *klad-ti- in Latin classis, summons, division of citizens for military draft, hence army, fleet, also class in general: CLASS. [Pok. 6. kel- 548.]

kelp-. To hold, grasp. O-grade form *kolp- in Germanic *halb- in: **a.** Old English hielfe, handle: HELVE; **b.** suffixed form *halb-ma- in (i) Old English helma, rudder, tiller: HELM¹ (ii) Middle High German helm, handle: HALBERD; **c.** suffixed form *half-tra- in Old English hælftre, halter: HALTER¹. [In Pok. 1. (s)kel- 923.]

kem-¹. Hornless. **1.** Germanic *skamm- in Old Norse skammr, "hornless," short: SCANT. **2.** Suffixed form *kem-tyā in Germanic *hinthjō in Old English hind, doe: HIND². [Pok. 2. kem- 556.]

kem-². To compress. Germanic *hamjam, a compressing, hence a doubling, in Old English hem(m), a doubling over, a hem: HEM¹. [Pok. 1. kem- 555.]

kem-³. To hum. Germanic *hum- in Middle English hummen, to hum: HUM. [Pok. 2. kem- 556.]

kemə-. To be tired, to tire. Suffixed lengthened o-grade form *kōm-n̥ proposed by some as the preform of Greek kōma, deep sleep, which is more likely of obscure origin: COMA¹. [Pok. 4. kem(ə)- 557.]

ken-¹. To be active. **1.** Suffixed o-grade form *kon-o- in Greek diakonos, servant, attendant (dia-, thoroughly): DEACON. **2.** Lengthened o-grade form *kōn-ā- in Latin cōnārī, to endeavor: CONATION. [Pok. 4. ken- 564.]

ken-². Hypothetical base of a number of loosely related Germanic words referring to pinching, closing the eyes, and other obscurely associated notions. **1.** Old English hnappian, to doze, nap: NAP¹. **2.** Old English nēpflōd, neap tide (flōd, tide; see **pleu-**): NEAP TIDE. **3.** Middle Dutch nipen, to bite: NIP¹. **4.** Old Norse hnöggr, miserly, akin to the Scandinavian source of Middle English nigard, miser: NIGGARD. **5.** Middle Dutch noppe, pile: NAP². **6.** Low German nibbeln, to nibble: NIBBLE. **7.** Middle High German notten, to nod, perhaps akin to Middle English nodden, to nod: NOD. [Pok. 2. ken- 559.]

ken-³. Fresh, new, young. **1.** Suffixed form *ken-t- in Latin recens, young, fresh, new (re-, again; see **re-**): RECENT. **2.** Suffixed zero-grade form kn̥-yo- in Greek kainos, new, fresh (> kainotēs, newness): -CENE; CAINOTOPHOBIA, CENOGENESIS, CENOZOIC, KAINITE. [Pok. 3. ken- 563.]

ken-⁴. Empty. Suffixed form *ken-wo- in Greek kenos (< *kenwos), empty: KENOSIS; CENOTAPH. [Pok. ken- 564.]

ken-⁵. Hypothetical base of several roots associated with the notions "to compress," "something compressed." **1.** Germanic root *hnekk-, "neck" (a narrow or compressed part), in: **a.** Old English hnecca, neck: NECK; **b.** Old Norse hnakkur, saddle, and Old Norse hnakki, back of the neck, perhaps akin to the source of KNACKER. **2.** Root *knu-, nut (< "small hard object"), in: **a.** extended form *knud- in Old English hnutu, nut: NUT; **b.** extended form *knuk- in Latin nux, nut: NEWEL, NOUGAT, NUCELLUS, NUCLEUS. **3.** Germanic root *hnukk-, sharp projection, tip, in: **a.** Middle Dutch nocke, tip of a bow,

perhaps akin to the source of Middle English nokke, nock: NOCK; **b.** Norwegian (dialectal) nok, projection, hook, akin to the Scandinavian source of Middle English nok, corner, nook: NOOK. [Pok. 1. ken- 558.]

k(e)nəko-. Yellow, golden. Germanic *hunagam in Old English hunig, honey: HONEY. [Pok. k(e)nəko- 564.]

keni-. Dust, ashes. **1.** Latin cinis, ashes: CINERARIUM, CINEREOUS; INCINERATE. **2.** O-grade form *koni- in Greek konis, konia, dust: CONIOSIS; CONIDIUM. [Pok. 2. ken- 559.]

kenk-¹. To gird, bind. Variant form *keng- in Latin cingere, to gird: CINCH, CINCTURE, CINGULUM; ENCEINTE², PRECINCT, SHINGLES, SUCCINCT. [Pok. 1. kenk- 565.]

kenk-². To suffer from hunger or thirst. Suffixed zero-grade form *kn̥k-ru- in Germanic *hungruz in Old English hungor, hungur, hunger: HUNGER. [Pok. 2. kenk- 565.]

kenk-³. Heel, bend of the knee. **1.** Germanic *hanhaz in Old English hōh, heel: HOCK¹. **2.** Germanic *hanhilōn- in Old English hēla, heel: HEEL¹. [Pok. 3. kenk- 566.]

kens-. To proclaim, speak solemnly. Form *kens-ē- in Latin cēnsēre, to judge, assess, estimate, tax: CENSOR, CENSUS; RECENSION. [Pok. kens- 566.]

kent-. To prick, jab. **1.** Greek kentein, to prick (> kentron, point): CENTER, CENTESIS; AMNIOCENTESIS, DICENTRA, ECCENTRIC. **2.** Suffixed form *kent-to- in Greek kestos, belt, girdle: CESTUS¹. [Pok. kent- 567.]

kentho-. Also **kento-.** Cloth, rag. Latin centō, cento, patchwork: CENTO. [Pok. kenth(o)- 567.]

ker-¹. Horn, head; with derivatives referring to horned animals, horn-shaped objects, and projecting parts. **I.** Zero-grade form *kr̥-. **1.** Suffixed form *kr̥-n- in: **a.** Germanic *hurnaz in (i) Old English horn, horn: HORN, (HORNBEAM) (ii) German Horn, horn: ALPENHORN, ALTHORN, FLÜGELHORN, HORNBLENDE; **b.** Latin cornū, horn: CORN², CORNEA, CORNEOUS, CORNER, CORNET, CORNICULATE, CORNU; BICORN, CADUCICORN, CAPRICORN, CLAVICORN, CORNIFICATION, LAMELLICORN, LONGICORN, TRICORN, UNICORN. **2.** Suffixed and extended form *krs-n- in Germanic *hurznuta in Old English hyrnet, hornet: HORNET. **3.** Suffixed form *kr-ei- in: **a.** Germanic *hraina- in Old Norse hreinn, reindeer: REINDEER; **b.** Germanic *hrinda- in Old High German hrind, ox (> German Rinder, cattle): RINDERPEST. **4.** Suffixed extended form *krs-no- in Greek kranion, skull, upper part of the head: CRANIUM, MIGRAINE, OLECRANON. **5.** Suffixed form *kr̥-ə- in: **a.** Greek karē, kara, head: CHARIVARI; CHEER; **b.** Greek karoun, to stupefy, be stupefied (< "to feel heavy-headed"): CAROTID; CARROT. **6.** Possibly extended form *krī- in Greek krios, ram: CRIOSPHINX. **II.** Suffixed form *ker-wo-. **1.** Latin cervus, deer: CERVINE, SERVAL. **2.** Latin cervix, neck: CERVIX. **III.** Extended and suffixed form *keru-do- in Germanic *herutaz in: **a.** Old English heorot, hart, stag: HART; **b.** Dutch hart, deer, hart: HARTEBEEST. **IV.** Extended form *kerəs-. **1.** Greek keras, horn: CARAT, CERASTES, KERATO-; CERATODUS, (CERATOID), CHELICERA, CLADOCERAN, KERATIN, RHINOCEROS, TRICERATOPS. **2.** Persian sar, head: SIRDAR. **3.** Suffixed form *kerəs-ro- in Latin cerebrum, brain: CEREBELLUM, CEREBRUM, SAVELOY. **V.** Extended o-grade form *koru-. **1.** Greek korumbos, uppermost point (< "head"): CORYMB. **2.** Greek koruphē, head: CORYPHAEUS. **3.** Suffixed form *koru-do- in Greek korudos, crested lark: CORYDALIS. **4.** Suffixed form *koru-nā in Greek korunē, club, mace: CORYNEBACTERIUM. [Pok. 1. ker- 574.]

ker-². Echoic root, base of various derivatives indicating loud noises or birds. **I.** Zero-grade form *kr-, becoming Germanic *hr-. **1.** Germanic *hring- in Old English hringan, to resound, clink: RING². **2.** Germanic *hraik- in Old English hrǣcan, to clear the throat: RETCH. **3.** Germanic *hrōkaz, "croaking bird," crow, in Old English

hrōc, rook: ROOK¹. **4.** Germanic **hraban, *hrabnaz,* raven, in Old English *hræfn,* raven: RAVEN¹. **5.** Extended form **krep-* in Latin *crepāre,* to crack, burst, creak: CREPITATE, CREVICE; DECREPIT, DECREPITATE, QUEBRACHO. **6.** Extended form **krik-* in Germanic **krik-* in Old French *criquer,* to creak, click: CRICKET¹. **II.** Variant form **skr-.* **1.** Germanic **skrīk-* in Old English *scrīc,* thrush: SHRIKE. **2.** Germanic **skrēkjan-* in Old Norse *skrækja,* to shriek: SCREAK, SCREECH. **3.** Germanic **skrainjan,* to shout, shriek, in Old Norse *scræma,* to scream, perhaps akin to the possible Scandinavian source of Middle English *scremen,* to scream: SCREAM. **III.** O-grade form **kor-.* **1.** Latin *corvus,* raven: CORBEL, CORBINA, CORMORANT, CORVINE, CORVUS. **2.** Greek *korax,* raven (> *korakias,* chough): CORACIIFORM, CORACOID. [Pok. 1. *ker-* 567.]

ker-³. To grow. **1.** Suffixed form **ker-es-* in Latin *Cerēs,* goddess of agriculture, especially the growth of grain: CEREAL, CERES. **2.** Extended form **krē-* (< **krea-*) in: **a.** suffixed form **krē-yā-* in Latin *creāre,* to bring forth, create, produce (< "to cause to grow"): CREATE, CREOLE; PROCREATE; **b.** suffixed form **krē-sko-* in Latin *crēscere,* to grow, increase: CRESCENDO, CRESCENT, CREW¹; ACCRUE, CONCRESCENCE, CONCRETE, DECREASE, EXCRESCENCE, INCREASE, RECRUIT. **3.** Suffixed o-grade form **kor-wo-,* "growing," adolescent, in Greek *kouros, koros,* boy, son: DIOSCURI, HYPOCORISM. **4.** Compound **sm̥-kēro-,* "of one growth" (**sm̥,* same, one; see **sem-¹**), in Latin *sincērus,* pure, clean: SINCERE. [Pok. 2. *ker-* 577.]

ker-⁴. Heat, fire. **1.** Suffixed form **ker-tā* in Germanic **herthō* in Old English *heorth,* hearth: HEARTH. **2.** Zero-grade form **kr̥-* in: **a.** Latin *carbō,* charcoal, ember: CARBON, CARBUNCLE; **b.** extended form **krem-* in Latin *cremāre,* to burn: CREMATE. **3.** Possibly suffixed and extended form **kera-mo-* in Greek *keramos,* potter's clay, earthenware: CERAMIC. **4.** Possibly variant extended form **krās-* in Russian *krasa,* beauty (< "brilliance of fire"): CRASH². [Pok. 3. *ker(ə)-* 571.]

ker-⁵. Also **kerə-.** To injure. Suffixed zero-grade form **krə-yē-* in Latin *cariēs,* decay, caries: CARIES. [Pok. 4. *ker-* 578.]

ker-⁶. A kind of cherry. **1.** Suffixed zero-grade form **kr̥-no-* in Latin *cornus,* cornel tree: CORNEL. **2.** Fullgrade form **ker-* probably in Greek *kerasos,* cherry: CHERRY. [Pok. 4. *ker-* 572.]

kerd-¹. Heart. **1.** Suffixed form **kerd-en-* in Germanic **hertōn-* in Old English *heorte,* heart: HEART. **2.** Zero-grade form **kr̥d-* in: **a.** Latin *cor* (stem *cord-*), heart: CORDATE, CORDIAL, COURAGE, QUARRY¹; ACCORD, CONCORD, CORDIFORM, DISCORD, MISERICORD, RECORD; **b.** suffixed form **kr̥d-yā-* in Greek *kardia,* heart, stomach, orifice: CARDIA, CARDIAC, CARDIO-; DIPLOCARDIAC, ENDOCARDIUM, EPICARDIUM, MEGALOCARDIA, MYOCARDIUM, PERICARDIUM. **3.** Possibly **kred-dhə-,* "to place trust" (an old religious term; **dhə-,* to do, place; see **dhē-¹**), in Latin *crēdere,* to believe: CREDENCE, CREDIBLE, CREDIT, CREDO, CREDULOUS, GRANT; MISCREANT, RECREANT. [Pok. *kered-* 579.]

kerd-². Craft. Suffixed form **kerd-ā* in Old Irish *cerd,* art, artist: CAIRD. [Pok. 2. *kerd-* 579.]

kerdh-. Row, herd. Suffixed form **kerdh-ā* in Germanic **herdō* in Old English *heord,* herd: HERD. [Pok. *kerdho-* 579.]

kerə-. To mix, confuse, cook. **1.** Variant form **krā-* (< **kraə-*) in Germanic **hrōr-* in: **a.** possibly Old English *hrēr,* lightly boiled, half-cooked: RARE²; **b.** Middle Dutch *roer,* motion: UPROAR. **2.** Zero-grade form **krə-* in: **a.** suffixed form **krə-ti-* in Greek *krasis,* a mixing: IDIOSYNCRASY; **b.** suffixed form **krə-ter-* in Greek *kratēr,* mixing vessel: CRATER. [Pok. *ker(ə)-* 582.]

kerp-. To gather, pluck, harvest. Variant *karp-.* **1.** Germanic **harbistaz* in Old English *hærfest,* harvest: HARVEST. **2.** Latin *carpere,* to pluck: CARPET; EXCERPT,

(SCARCE). **3.** Greek *karpos,* fruit: -CARP, CARPEL, CARPO-, -CARPOUS. [In Pok. 4. *sker-* 938.]

kers-¹. Dark, dirty. **1.** Suffixed form **ker(s)-no-* in Russian *chërnyi* (feminine *chërnaya*), black: CHERNOZEM. **2.** Suffixed zero-grade form **kr̥s-no-* in Sanskrit *kr̥ṣṇā-*), black, dark: KRISHNA. [Pok. *kers-* 583.]

kers-². To run. Zero-grade form **kr̥s-.* **1.** Latin *currere* (past participle *cursus*), to run: CORRIDOR, (CORSAIR), COURANTE, COURIER, COURSE, CURRENT, CURSIVE, CURSOR, CURULE; CONCOURSE, CONCUR, DECURRENT, DISCOURSE, EXCURSION, HUSSAR, INCUR, INTERCOURSE, OCCUR, PERCURRENT, PRECURSOR, RECOURSE, RECUR, SUCCOR. **2.** Suffixed form **kr̥s-o-* in Gaulish *carros,* a wagon, cart, in: **a.** Latin *carrus,* a two-wheeled wagon: CAR, CAREER, CARGO, CARICATURE, CARIOLE, CAROCHE, (CARRY), CHARGE, CHARIOT; **b.** Latin *carpentum,* a two-wheeled carriage: CARPENTER. [Pok. 2. *kers-* 583.]

kert-. To turn, entwine. **I.** Zero-grade form **kr̥t-.* **1.** Suffixed form **kr̥t-i-* in Germanic **hurdiz,* wickerwork frame, hurdle, in: **a.** Old English *hyrdel,* hurdle, frame: HURDLE; **b.** Old French *hourd,* fence, hurdle, scaffold: HOARDING. **2.** Suffixed form **kr̥t-sti-* in Germanic **hursti-* in Old High German *hurst,* thicket: HORST. **II.** Perhaps suffixed variant form **krət-i-* in Latin *crātis,* wickerwork hurdle: CRATE, GRATE², (GRID), GRIDDLE; (GRIDIRON). [Pok. *kert-* 584.]

kes-¹. To scratch. **1.** Germanic **hezdō* in Old English *heordan,* coarse parts of flax: HARDS. **2.** Extended form **kseu-* in Greek *xuein,* to scrape: XYSTER. **3.** Nasalized form **ks-n-eu-* in: **a.** Germanic **snaww-* in Old Norse *snöggr,* "close-cropped," perhaps akin to the source of SNUG¹; **b.** Latin *novācula,* razor: NOVACULITE. [Pok. *kes-* 585.]

kes-². To cut. Variant *kas-.* **1.** Suffixed form **kas-tro-* in: **a.** Latin *castrāre,* to castrate: CASTRATE; **b.** Latin *castrum,* fortified place, camp (perhaps "separated place"): CASTLE. **2.** Suffixed form **kas-to-* in Latin *castus,* chaste, pure (< "cut off from, free of, faults"): CASTE, CHASTE; CASTIGATE, INCEST. **3.** Suffixed (stative) form **kas-ē-* in Latin *carēre,* "to be cut off from," lack: CARET. **4.** Extended geminated form **kasso-* in Latin *cassus,* empty, void: (CASHIER), QUASH. [Pok. *kes-* 586.]

kes-³. To order. Suffixed o-grade form **kos-mo-* in Greek *kosmos,* order: COSMOS; MACROCOSM, MICROCOSM.

keu-¹ Also **əkeu-.** To perceive, see, hear. O-grade form **əkou-.* **1.** Extended form **kous-* in: **a.** Germanic **hausjan* in (i) Old English *hīeran,* to hear: HEAR (ii) Old English *he(o)rcnian,* to harken: HEARKEN; **b.** suffixed form **ə-kous-yo-* in Greek *akouein,* to hear: ACOUSTIC. **2.** Variant **skou-* in: **a.** Germanic **skauwon* in (i) Old English *scēawian,* to look at: SHOW (ii) Flemish *scauwen,* to look at: SCAVENGER; **b.** Germanic **skaunjaz* in Middle Dutch *schoon,* beautiful, bright (< "conspicuous, attractive"): SCONE; **c.** Germanic **skauniz* in Old English *scīene,* bright, sheen: SHEEN. [Pok. 1. *keu-* 587.]

keu-². Base of various loosely related derivatives with assumed basic meaning "to bend," whence "a round or hollow object." **I.** Extended forms **keub-, *keup-.* **1.** Germanic **haup-* in: **a.** Old English *hēap,* heap: HEAP; **b.** Dutch *hoop,* heap, troop: FORLORN HOPE. **2.** Germanic **hupp-,* to leap (by first bending the legs), in Old English *hoppian,* to hop: HOP¹. **3.** Germanic **hupiz* in Old English *hype,* hip: HIP¹. **4.** Zero-grade form **kup-,* vessel, in: **a.** suffixed form **kup-s-* in Greek *kupselē,* chest, hollow vessel: CYPSELA; **b.** long-vowel form **kūp-* in (i) Germanic **hūfi-* in Old English *hȳf,* hive: HIVE (ii) suffixed form **kūp-a* in Latin *cūpa,* tub, vat: CUPOLA, CUPULE; **c.** expressive form **kupp-* in Late Latin *cuppa,* drinking vessel: CUP. **5.** Zero-grade form **kub-* in: **a.** Greek *kubos,* cube: CUBE; **b.** suffixed form **kub-ā-* in (i) Latin *cubāre,* to lie down on (< "to bend down, prostrate"): COUVADE, COVEY, CUBICLE; CONCUBINE, INCUBATE, SUCCUBUS (ii) Latin *cubitum,* elbow: CUBIT; **c.** nasalized form **ku-m-b-* in (i) Latin *-cumbere,* to lie down, recline: ACCUMBENT,

DECUMBENT, INCUMBENT, PROCUMBENT, RECUMBENT, SUCCUMB *(ii)* Greek *kumbē*, boat, bowl: (CEMBALO), (CHIME[1]), CYMBAL, CYMBIDIUM; **d.** aspirated long-vowel form **kūbh-* in Greek *kuphos*, bent: KYPHOSIS. **II.** Extended o-grade form **kouk-*. **1.** Suffixed form **kouk-o-* in: **a.** Germanic **hauhaz*, "arched," high, in Old English *hēah*, high: HIGH; **b.** Germanic **hauhithō* in Old English *hēhthu*, *hēahthu*, height: HEIGHT. **2.** Germanic **huk-* in: **a.** Middle Low German *hōken*, to bend, squat, bear on the back, peddle: HAWKER; **b.** Old Norse *hokra*, to crouch, akin to the Scandinavian source of HUNKER; **c.** Middle Dutch *hokester*, "one who squats," peddler, perhaps akin to the source of Middle English *hukster*, peddler: HUCKSTER. **III.** Reduplicated form **ka-ku-bh-* in Latin *cacūmen*, summit, point (< "arch, vault"): CACUMINAL. [Pok. 2. *keu-* 588.]

kēu-. To burn. Zero-grade form **kəu-* becoming **kaw-* in suffixed form **kaw-yo-* in Greek *kaiein*, to burn: CALM, CAUSTIC, CAUTERY; ENCAUSTIC, HOLOCAUST, (INK). [Pok. 2. *kēu-* 595.]

keub-. Thorn. Germanic **heup-* in Old English *hēope*, brier, seed vessel of the wild rose: HIP[3]. [Pok. *keub-* 595.]

keuə-[1]. To pay attention, perceive (preternaturally). **1.** Suffixed o-grade form **kowə-o-* becoming **kaw-* in denominative (stative) Latin *cavēre*, to beware, watch, guard against: CAUTION, CAVEAT; PRECAUTION. **2.** Suffixed zero-grade form **kū-dos* (< **kuə-dos*) in Greek *kudos*, magical glory: KUDOS. [In Pok. 1. *keu-* 587.]

keuə-[2]. To swell; vault, hole. **I.** O-grade form **kowə-*. **1.** Basic form **kowə-* becoming **kaw-* in Latin *cavus*, hollow, and *cavea*, a hollow: CAGE, CAVE, CAVERN, CAVETTO, GABION, JAIL; CONCAVE, DECOY, EXCAVATE. **2.** Suffixed form **kow-ilo-* in Greek *koilos*, hollow: (-CELE[2]), -CELIAC, -COEL, COELOM. **3.** Suffixed lengthened-grade form **kōw-o-* in Greek *kōos*, hollow place, cavity (> *kōdeia*, poppy head): CODEINE. **II.** Zero-grade form **kū-* (< **kuə-*). **1.** Suffixed shortened form **ku-m-olo-* in Latin *cumulus*, heap, mass: CUMULATE, CUMULUS; ACCUMULATE. **2.** Basic form **kū-* in: **a.** suffixed form **kū-ro-*, "swollen," strong, powerful, in Greek *kurios* (vocative *kurie*), master, lord: CHURCH, (KIRK), KYRIE; **b.** suffixed form **kuw-eyo-* in Greek *kuein*, to swell, and derivative *kūma* (< **kū-mn*), "a swelling," wave: CYMA. [Pok. 1. *keu-* 592.]

keuk-. To be white, be bright, shine. Suffixed zero-grade form **kuk-no-* in Greek *kuknos*, swan: CYGNET, CYGNUS. [Pok. *keuk-* 597.]

kēwero-. North, north wind. **1.** Germanic **skūra-* in Old English *scūr*, shower, storm: SHOWER[1]. **2.** Germanic **skūrō* in Old Norse *skūr*, a shower, akin to the probable Scandinavian source of Middle English *scouren*, to range over: SCOUR[2]. [Pok. *kēuero-* 597.]

kīgh-. Fast, violent. Germanic **hīg-* in Old English *hīgian*, to strive, exert oneself: HIE. [Pok. *kei-gh-* 542.]

kistā. Basket. Greek *kistē*, basket (> Old English *cest*, box): CHEST, CIST[1], CISTERN. [Pok. *kistā* 599.]

klā-. To spread out flat. Extended shortened form **klat-*. **1.** Germanic **hlathan* in Old English *hladan*, to lade, lay on, load: LADE. **2.** Suffixed form **klat-sto-* in Germanic **hlasta-* in: **a.** Old English *hlæst*, burden, load: LAST[4]; **b.** Old Swedish and Old Danish *last*, burden: BALLAST. [Pok. *klā-* 599.]

kleg-. To cry, sound. Extension of **kel-[1].** Variant form **klag-*. **1.** Variant form **klak-* in: **a.** Germanic **hlahjan* in Old English *hlieh(h)an*, to laugh: LAUGH; **b.** Germanic **hlahtraz* in Old English *hleahtor*, laughter: LAUGHTER. **2.** Nasalized form **kla-n-g-* in Latin *clangere*, to sound: CLANG. [Pok. *kleg-* 599.]

klei-. To lean. **I.** Full-grade form **klei-*. **1.** Suffixed form **klei-n-* in Latin *-clīnāre*, to lean, bend: DECLINE, INCLINE, RECLINE. **2.** Suffixed form **klei-tro-* in **clītra*, litter, with diminutive *clītellae*, packsaddle: CLITELLUM. **3.** Suffixed form **klei-wo-* in Latin *clīvus*, a slope: ACCLIVITY, DECLIVITY, PROCLIVITY. **II.** Zero-grade

form **kli-*. **1.** Germanic **hlid-*, "that which bends over," cover, in Old English *hlid*, cover: LID. **2.** Suffixed form **kli-n-* in Germanic **hlinēn*, in Old English *hlinian* and *hleonian*, to lean: LEAN[1]. **3.** Suffixed form **kli-ent-* in Latin *cliēns*, dependent, follower: CLIENT. **4.** Suffixed form **kli-to-* in Latin **aus-klit-ā-* in *auscultāre*, "to hold one's ear inclined," to listen to (see **ous-**). **5.** Suffixed form **kli-n-yo-* in Greek *klinein*, to lean: CLINAL, CLINE, -CLINIC, CLINO-; (ACLINIC LINE), CLINANDRIUM, ENCLITIC, (ISOCLINE), MATRICLINOUS, (MONOCLINIC), PATRICLINOUS, PERICLINE, PROCLITIC, SYNCLINAL. **6.** Greek lengthened form **klī-* in: **a.** suffixed form **klī-n-ā* in Greek *klīnē*, bed: CLINIC; DICLINOUS, MONOCLINOUS, TRICLINIUM; **b.** suffixed form **klī-m-* in Greek *klimax*, ladder: CLIMAX; **c.** suffixed form **klī-mn* in Greek *klīma*, sloping surface of the earth: CLIMATE. **III.** Suffixed o-grade form **kloi-tr-* in Germanic **hlaidr-* in Old English *hlǣd(d)er*, ladder: LADDER. [Pok. *klei-* 600.]

kleng-. To bend, turn. **1.** Germanic **hlink-* in: **a.** Old English *hlinc*, ridge: LINKS; **b.** Old Norse **hlenkr*, loop of a chain, akin to the Scandinavian source of Middle English *linke*, loop of a chain: LINK[1]; **c.** Old French *flenchir*, to turn aside, flich: FLINCH. **2.** Germanic **hlank-* in: **a.** Old English *hlanc*, lean, thin (< "flexible"): LANK; **b.** Old French *flanc*, hip, side (where the body curves): FLANK. [Pok. *kleng-* 603.]

klep-. To steal. Extension of **kel-[2].** Suffixed form **klep-yo-* in Greek *kleptein*, to steal: CLEPSYDRA, KLEPTOMANIA. [Pok. *klep-* 604.]

kleu-[1]. To hear. **I.** Extended form **kleus-* in Germanic **hleuza-* in Old English *hlēor*, cheek (< "side of the face" < "ear"): LEER. **II.** Zero-grade form **klu-*. **1.** Germanic **hlustjan* in Old English *hlystan*, to listen: LIST[4]. **2.** Germanic **hlusinōn* in Old English *hlysnan*, to listen: LISTEN. **3.** Suffixed lengthened form **klū-to-* in Germanic **hlūdaz*, "heard," loud, in: **a.** Old English *hlūd*, loud: LOUD; **b.** Old High German *hlūti*, sound: ABLAUT, UMLAUT. **III.** Suffixed form **klew-yo-* in Greek *kleiein*, to praise, tell: CLIO. [Pok. 1. *kleu-* 605.]

kleu-[2]. To wash, clean. **1.** Latin *cloāca*, sewer, canal: CLOACA. **2.** Zero-grade form **klu-* in Greek *kluzein*, to wash out: CLYSTER; CATACLYSM. [Pok. 2. *kleu-* 607.]

kleu-[3]. Possibly hook, peg. **I.** Extended zero-grade form **klud-* possibly in Germanic **hluta-*, lot, portion (semantic development obscure). **1.** Old English *hlot*: LOT. **2.** Dutch *lot*, lot: LOTTERY. **3.** Old French *lot* (> French *lot*), lot, portion: LOTTO; ALLOT. **II.** Suffixed variant form **klau-do-* in Latin *claudere*, to close (< "to lock with a hook, bolt"): CLAUSE, CLOISONNÉ, CLOISTER, CLOSE, (CLOSURE), (CLOZE); CONCLUDE, ECLOSION, EXCLUDE, INCLUDE, OCCLUDE, PRECLUDE, RECLUSE, SECLUDE. **III.** Variant form **klāw-*. **1.** Suffixed form **klāw-i-* in Latin *clāvis*, key: CEMBALO, CLAVICLE, CLAVIER, CLEF, KEVEL; CLAVICHORD, CONCLAVE, ENCLAVE. **2.** Suffixed form **klāw-o-* in: **a.** Latin *clāvus*, nail: CLOVE[1], CLOY; **b.** Latin *clāva*, club: CLAVATE; CLAVICORN, CLAVIFORM. **3.** Suffixed form **klāw-yo-* in: **a.** Greek *kleiein*, to close: CLATHRATE; **b.** Greek verbal adjective *kleistos*, closed: CLEISTOGAMOUS, CLEISTOTHECIUM. [Pok. *kleu-* 604.]

klewo-. Bald. Variant **kal(a)wo-* in Latin *calvus*, bald: CALVARIUM. [Pok. *kₑləuo-* 554.]

klou-. To bend. Proposed by some as the root of Germanic **hlaupan*, to leap, which is more likely of unknown origin. Germanic **hlaupan* in: **a.** Old English *hlēapan*, to leap: LEAP; **b.** Old English *hlēapwince*, lapwing (-*wince*, perhaps "move sideways," akin to Old English *wincian*, to wink; see **weng-**): LAPWING; **c.** Old Norse *hlaupa*, to leap: LOPE; **d.** Middle Dutch *loopen*, to leap, run: INTERLOPE, ORLOP; **e.** Middle Low German *lōp*, course, running (> Swedish *lopp*, course): GAUNTLET[2]; **f.** Old High German *hlouf(f)an*, to leap (> German *Lauf*, race): LANGLAUF; **g.** Old French *galoper* and Old North French *waloper*, to gallop: GALLOP, WALLOP;

h. Anglo-Norman *aloper,* to run away from one's husband with a lover: ELOPE.

kneig*h-. To lean on. **1.** Latin *cōnīvēre* (< *con-nīguēre; com-,* together; see **kom**), "to lean together" (said of eyelids), to close the eyes, be indulgent: CONNIVE. **2.** Suffixed zero-grade form *knig***h-to- in Latin *nictāre,* to move the eyelids, wink: NICTITATE. **3.** Uncertain preform in Latin *nītī,* to lean forward, strive: NISUS; RENITENT. [Pok. *knei-g*h-* 608.]

knid-. Egg of a louse. Suffixed form *knid-ā* in Germanic *hnitō* in Old English *hnitu,* egg of a louse: NIT. [Pok. *knid-* 608.]

ko-. Stem of demonstrative pronoun meaning "this." **I.** Variant form *ki-. **1.** Germanic *hi- in: **a.** Old English *he,* he: HE¹; **b.** Old English *him,* him: HIM; **c.** Old English *his,* his: HIS; **d.** Old English *hire,* her: HER; **e.** Old English *hit,* it: IT. **f.** Old English *hēr,* here: HERE; **g.** Old English *heonane, heonon,* from here: HENCE. **2.** Suffixed form *ki-tro- in Germanic *hi-thra- in Old English *hider,* hither: HITHER. **3.** Suffixed form *ki-s in Latin *cis,* on this side of: CIS-. **II.** Variant form *ke-. **1.** Preposed in *ke-etero- (*e-tero-, a second time, again; see **i-**) in Latin *cēterus* (neuter plural *cētera*), the other part, that which remains: ET CETERA. **2.** Latin *-ce* (see **nu-**). **III.** Attributed by some to this root (but more likely of obscure origin) is Germanic root *hind-, behind. **1.** Old English *bihindan,* in the rear, behind (*bi,* at; see **ambhi**): BEHIND, HIND¹. **2.** Old High German *hintar* (> German *hinter-*), behind: HINTERLAND. **3.** Germanic derivative verb *hindrōn, to keep back, in Old English *hindrian,* to check, hinder: HINDER¹. [Pok. *ko-* 609.]

kō-. To sharpen, whet. Contracted from *koə-. **1.** Suffixed extended form *koəi-no- in Germanic *hainō in Old English *hān,* stone: HONE¹. **2.** Perhaps Greek *kōnos,* cone, conical object (< "a sharp-pointed object"): CONE. [Pok. *k̂ēi-* 541.]

kob-. To suit, fit, succeed. Germanic *hap- in Old Norse *happ,* chance, good luck: HAP, (HAPPEN), (HAPPY); (HAPLESS), (MISHAP). [Pok. *kob-* 610.]

[kokkos. Kermes berry, pit, grain. Greek noun of unknown origin: COCCID, COCCUS, COCHINEAL; MONOCOQUE.]

koksā. Body part. Latin *coxa,* hip: COXA, CUISSE, CUSHION. [Pok. *koksā* 611.]

koləm-. Grass, reed. Suffixed form *koləm-o-. **1.** Germanic *halmaz in Old English *healm, halm,* straw: HAULM. **2.** Latin *culmus,* stalk: CULM¹. **3.** Zero-grade form *kl̥m-o- in Greek *kalamos,* a reed, straw: CALAMITE, CALAMUS, CALUMET, CARAMEL, SHAWM. [Pok. *koləmo-s* 612.]

koli-. Glue. Suffixed variant form *koly-a in Greek *kolla,* glue: COLLAGE, COLLO-, COLLODION; PROTOCOL. [Pok. *kol(e)i-* 612.]

kom. Beside, near, by, with. **1.** Germanic *ga-, together, with (collective and intensive prefix and marker of the past participle), in Old English *ge-,* with, also participial, collective, and intensive prefix: ENOUGH, HANDIWORK, YCLEPT. **2.** Latin *cum,* co-, with: CUM; CONQUIAN. **3.** Old Latin *com,* with (collective and intensive prefix): CO-, COM-. **4.** Suffixed form *kom-trā in Latin *contrā,* against, opposite: (CON¹), CONTRA-, CONTRARY, (COUNTER¹), COUNTER-, COUNTRY; ENCOUNTER. **5.** Suffixed form *kom-yo- in Greek *koinos,* common, shared: COENO-; CENOBITE, EPICENE, KOINE. **6.** Reduced form *ko- (see **gher-¹, mei-¹, smei-**). [Pok. *kom* 612.]

konəm-. Shinbone, bone. Reduced form *kommo- perhaps in Germanic *hamma in Old English *hamm,* ham, thigh: HAM. [Pok. *konəmo-* 613.]

konk-. To hang. **1.** Germanic *hanhan in: **a.** Old English *hon,* to hang: HANG; **b.** Dutch (dialectal) *hankeren,* to long for: HANKER; **c.** possibly Middle English *he(e)ng, hinge,* hinge (ultimately from the base of Old English *hangian,* to hang): HINGE. **2.** Suffixed form *konk-t-ā- in

Latin *cūnctārī,* to delay: CUNCTATION. [Pok. *k̂enk-* 566, *k̂onk-* 614.]

konk(h)o-. Mussel, shellfish. **1.** Greek *konkhē, konkhos,* mussel, conch: COCKLE¹, CONCH, CONCHA, CONCHO-. **2.** Greek *kokhlos,* land snail: COCHLEA. [Pok. *k̂onkho-* 614.]

kormo-. Pain. Germanic *harmaz in Old English *hearm,* harm: HARM. [Pok. *k̂ormo-* 615.]

koro-. War; also war-band, host, army. **I.** Germanic *harjaz, army. **1.** Old English *here,* army: HERIOT. **2.** Old French *herban,* a summoning to military service: ARRIÈRE-BAN. **3.** Compound *harja-bergaz, "army hill," hillfort, later shelter, lodging, army quarters (*bergaz, hill; see **bhergh-²**), in: **a.** Old English *hereberg* (> Middle English *herberwe*), lodging: HARBOR; **b.** Old French *herberge,* lodging: HARBINGER. **4.** Compound *harjawaldaz, "army commander" (*wald-, rule, power; see **wal-**), in Anglo-Norman *herald,* herald: HERALD. **II.** Germanic denominative *harjōn in Old English *hergian,* to ravage, plunder, raid: HARRY. **III.** Germanic compound *harihring, assembly, "host-ring" (*hringaz, ring; see **sker-³**), in Medieval Latin *harenga,* harangue: HARANGUE. [Pok. *koro-s* 615.]

koselo-. Hazel. Germanic *haselaz in Old English *hæsel,* hazel: HAZEL. [Pok. *kos(e)lo-* 616.]

kost-. Bone. Probably related to **ost-.** Latin *costa,* rib, side: COAST, COSTA, COSTARD, COSTREL, CUESTA, CUTLET; ACCOST, INTERCOSTAL, STERNOCOSTAL. [Pok. *kost-* 616.]

krāu-. Also **krŭ-.** To conceal, hide. Suffixed extended form *krup-yo- in Greek *kruptein,* to hide: CRYPT, CRYPTIC, CRYPTO-, KRYPTON; APOCRYPHA. [Pok. *krā(u)-* 616.]

kred-. Framework, timberwork. Possible root. Germanic *hrō(d)-st- in Old English *hrōst,* roost: ROOST. [Pok. *kred-* 617.]

krei-. To sieve, discriminate, distinguish. **1.** Basic form with variant instrumental suffixes in: **a.** suffixed form *krei-tro- in Germanic *hridra-, a sieve, in Old English *hridder, hriddel,* sieve: RIDDLE¹; **b.** suffixed form *krei-dhro- in Latin *crībrum,* a sieve: CRIBRIFORM, GARBLE. **2.** Suffixed form *krei-men- in (i) Latin *crīmen,* judgment, crime: CRIME; RECRIMINATE (ii) Latin *discrīmen,* distinction (*dis-*, apart): DISCRIMINATE. **3.** Suffixed zero-grade form *kri-no- (participial form *kri-to-) in Latin *cernere* (past participle *certus*), to sift, separate, decide: CERTAIN; CONCERN, DECREE, DISCERN, EXCREMENT, INCERTITUDE, RECREMENT, SECERN, SECRET. **4.** Suffixed zero-grade form *kri-n-yo- in Greek *krinein,* to separate, decide, judge (> *krinesthai,* to explain): CRISIS, CRITIC, CRITERION; APOCRINE, DIACRITICAL, ECCRINE, ENDOCRINE, EPICRITIC, EXOCRINE, HEMATOCRIT, HYPROCRISY. [Pok. 4. *sker-,* Section II. 945.]

krek-¹. To weave, beat. **1.** Germanic *hreh-ulaz in Old English *hrēol,* reel, spool for winding cord: REEL¹. **2.** Suffixed o-grade form *krok-u- in Greek *krokus,* nap of cloth: CROCIDOLITE. [Pok. 1. *krek-* 618.]

krek-². Frog spawn, fish eggs. Germanic *hrog- in Middle English *row,* roe: ROE¹. [Pok. 2. *krek-* 619.]

krem-. Wild garlic, onion. O-grade form *krom- in Germanic *hram- in Old English *hramsan,* onion, garlic: RAMSON. [Pok. *kerem-* 580.]

kret-¹. To shake. O-grade form *krot- in Germanic *hrathaz, swift, nimble, in Old English *hræth(e),* nimble, quick, prompt, ready: RATHE, (RATHER). [Pok. 1. *kret-* 620.]

kret-². To beat. O-grade form *krot- in Greek *krotein,* to strike, beat: DICROTISM, TRICROTIC. [Pok. 2. *kret-* 621.]

kreuə-¹. Raw flesh. **1.** Lengthened-grade form *krēw- in Germanic *hrēwaz in Old English *hrēaw,* raw: RAW. **2.** Suffixed form *krewə-s- in Greek *kreas,* flesh: CREATINE, CREODONT, CREOSOTE, PANCREAS. **3.** Suffixed zero-grade form *krū-do- (< *kruə-do-) in: **a.** Latin *crūdus,* bloody, raw: CRUDE; ECRU, RECRUDESCE; **b.** Latin *crūdēlis,* cruel: CRUEL. [Pok. 1. A. *kreu-* 621.]

kreuə-². To push, strike. **1.** Germanic *hrewwan in Old

English *hrēowan*, to distress, grieve: RUE¹, RUTH. 2. Extended o-grade form **krous-* in Greek *krouein*, to strike: ANACRUSIS. [Pok. 3. *kreu-* 622.]

kreup-. Scab; to become encrusted. 1. Germanic **hrub-in:* **a.** Middle Low German *ruffelen*, to crumple, akin to the Germanic source of Middle English *ruffelen*, to ruffle, roughen: RUFFLE¹; **b.** Germanic compound **ga-hrub-* (**ga-*, intensive prefix; see **kom**) in Middle Dutch *grof*, harsh: GRUFF. 2. Suffixed o-grade form **kroup-ā* in Serbo-Croatian *krupa*, groats (perhaps > German *Graupe*, barley): GRAUPEL. [Pok. *kreup-* 623.]

kreus-. To begin to freeze, form a crust. 1. Suffixed zero-grade form **krus-to-* in: **a.** Latin *crusta*, crust: CROUTON, CRUST, CRUSTACEAN, CRUSTACEOUS, CRUSTOSE; **b.** Greek *krustallos*, ice: CRYSTAL, CRYSTALLINE, CRYSTALLO-. 2. Suffixed zero-grade form **krus-es-* in Greek *kruos*, icy cold, frost: CRYO-. [Pok. 1. B. *kreu-* 621.]

kreut-. Also **kreudh-.** Reed. Germanic **hreuda-* in Old English *hrēod*, reed: REED. [Pok. *kreut-* 623.]

krŏpo-. Roof. Germanic **hrōfam* in Old English *hrōf*, roof: ROOF. [Pok. *krā̆po-* 616.]

krut-. Musical instrument. 1. Germanic **hrut-* in Old French *rote*, a stringed instrument: ROTE³. 2. Geminated form **kruttā* in Welsh *crwth*, an ancient Celtic instrument: CROWD². [Pok. *krut-* 624.]

ksero-. Dry. 1. Lengthened-grade form **ksēro-* in Greek *xēros*, dry: XERO-; ELIXIR, PHYLLOXERA, XEROPHTHALMIA. 2. Perhaps suffixed variant form **kseres-no-* in Latin *serēnus*, serene, bright, clear: SERENE. [Pok. *ksero-* 625.]

ksun. Preposition and preverb meaning "with." 1. Greek *sun*, *xun*, together, with: SYN-. 2. Russian *so-*, *s-*, with, in *sputnik*, fellow traveler (see **pent-**): SPUTNIK. [In Pok. 2. *sem-* 902.]

ku-. Hypothetical base of a variety of conceivably related Germanic words meaning "a hollow space or place, enclosing object, round object, lump," and some other derivative denotations. 1. Germanic **kubōn-*, hut, shed, room, in: **a.** Old English *cofa*, bedchamber, closet: COVE¹; **b.** Middle Dutch *cubbe*, "pen, stall," fish basket, akin to the probable source of CUBBY; **c.** Germanic compound **kubawald-*, probably "house ruler," household god (*wald-*, power; see **wal-**), in Middle High German *kobolt*, an underground goblin: COBALT, KOBOLD. 2. Germanic **kutam* in Old English *cot*, cottage: COT², (COTTAGE). 3. Germanic **kutōn-* in Old English *cote*, shelter: COTE¹. 4. Germanic **k(e)ud-* in: **a.** Old English *codd*, bag, husk: COD²; **b.** Old English *cudele*, cuttlefish (from its ink bag): CUTTLE. 5. Germanic *k(e)ut-* in Old English **cieter*, intestines (probably > Middle English *chiterling*): CHITTERLINGS. 6. Germanic **kukk-* in Middle English *cok*, haycock, pile of straw: COCK². 7. Germanic **kuk-* in Old English *cīcen*, chicken: CHICKEN. 8. Germanic **kugg-* in Swedish *kugge*, cog, akin to the possible Scandinavian source of Middle English *cogge*, cog: COG¹. 9. Germanic **kuggila* in Old English *cycgel*, rod, cudgel: CUDGEL. 10. Germanic **keulaz* in: **a.** Low German *kielswin*, keelson: KEELSON; **b.** Middle Dutch *kiel*, ship, keel of a ship: KEEL². 11. Germanic **kūp-* in Middle Dutch *kūpe*, cask, tub, basket: COOPER. 12. Germanic **kunt-* in Middle Low German *kunte*, vulva, akin to the Low German source of Middle English *cunte*, vulva: CUNT. 13. Germanic *kūrā-* in Icelandic *kūrā*, to crouch, lie in wait, akin to the Scandinavian source of Middle English *couren*, to cower: COWER. 14. Possibly Old Norse *kūga*, to oppress, akin to the probable source of COW². [In Pok. *gēu-* 393.]

kus-. A kiss. Germanic **kussaz*, a kiss, with denominative **kussjan* in Old English *cyssan*, to kiss: KISS. [Pok. *ku-, kus-* 626.]

kwat-. To ferment, be sour. Possible root. Suffixed variant form **kwāt-so-* in Common Slavic **kvasŭ* in Russian *kvas*, kvass: KVASS. [Pok. *ku̯āt(h)-* 627.]

kʷe. And (enclitic). Latin *-que*, and: SESQUI-, UBIQUITY. [Pok. *kʷe* 635.]

kʷed-. To sharpen. Germanic **hwatjan* in Old English *hwettan*, to whet: WHET. [Pok. *kʷed-* 636.]

kwei-. To hiss, whistle. Imitative root. Germanic **hwī-n-* and **hwis-* in: **a.** Old English *hwīnan*, to whine: WHINE; **b.** Old English *hwisprian*, to whisper: WHISPER; **c.** Old English *hwistlian*, to whistle: WHISTLE. [Pok. 2. *ku̯ei-* 628.]

kʷei-¹. To pay, atone, compensate. Suffixed o-grade form **kʷoi-nā* in Greek *poinē*, fine, penalty, borrowed into Latin as *poena*, penalty: PAIN, PENAL, (PENALTY), PINE², PUNISH; IMPUNITY, PENOLOGY, (PUNITORY), (REPINE), SUBPOENA. [Pok. *kʷei-t-* 636.]

kʷei-². To pile up, build, make. O-grade form **kʷoi-* in: **a.** Sanskrit *kayah*, body: CHEETAH; **b.** suffixed form **kʷoi-wo-*, making, in denominative verb **kʷoiw-eyo-* in Greek *poiein*, to make, create: POEM, POESY, POET, POETIC, -POIESIS, -POIETIC; MYTHOPOEIC, ONOMATOPOEIA, PHARMACOPOEIA, PROSOPOPEIA. [Pok. 2. *ku̯ei-* 637.]

kʷeiə-¹. To value, honor. Suffixed zero-grade form **kʷī-mā* (< **kʷiə-mā*) in Greek *timē*, honor, worth: TIMOCRACY. [In Pok. *ku̯ei-(t-)* 636.]

kʷeiə-². To rest, be quiet. **I.** Suffixed zero-grade variant form **kʷī-lo-* (< **kʷiə-lo-*). 1. Germanic **hwīlō* in: **a.** Old English *hwīl*, while: WHILE; **b.** Old English *hwīlum*, sometimes: WHILOM. 2. Possibly Latin *tranquillus*, tranquil (*trāns-*, across, beyond; see **terə-²**): TRANQUIL. **II.** Variant form **kʷyē-* (< **kʷyeə-*) in Latin *quiēs*, quiet (> *quiētus*, calm, retiring), and in *requiēs*, rest, and *requiescere*, to rest: COY, QUIET, ACQUIESCE, REQUIEM, REQUIESCAT. [Pok. *ku̯eiə-* 638.]

kweit-. White; to shine. Suffixed form **kweit-o-*. 1. Germanic **hwītaz* in: **a.** Old English *hwīt*, white: WHITE; **b.** Middle Dutch *wijting*, whiting: WHITING²; **c.** Old High German *hwīz*, *wīz*, white: EDELWEISS. 2. Germanic **hwaitjaz* in Old English *hwǣte*, wheat (from the fine white flour it yields): WHEAT. [Pok. 3. *ku̯ei-* 628.]

kʷek-. To appear, see, show. Variant form **kʷeg-* in Slavic **kaz-* in Russian *ukazat'*, to order: UKASE. [Pok. *ku̯ek-* 638.]

kʷel-¹. To revolve, move around, sojourn, dwell. **I.** Basic form **kʷel-* in Latin *colere*, to till, cultivate, inhabit: COLONY, CULT, CULTIVATE, (CULTURE); INCULT, INQUILINE, SILVICOLOUS. **II.** Suffixed form **kʷel-es-* in Greek *telos*, "completion of a cycle," consummation, perfection, end, result (> *teleos*, perfect, complete): TELIC, TELIUM, TELO-; ENTELECHY, TALISMAN, (TELEOLOGY), TELEOST, TELEUTOSPORE. **III.** Suffixed reduplicated form **kʷ(e)-kʷl-o-*, circle. 1. Germanic **hwewlaz* in Old English *hwēol*, *hweogol*, wheel: WHEEL. 2. Greek *kuklos*, circle, wheel: CYCLE, CYCLO-, CYCLOID, CYCLONE, CYCLOSIS; BICYCLE, ENCYCLICAL. 3. Sanskrit *cakram*, circle: CHUKKER. **IV.** O-grade form **kʷol-*. 1. Suffixed form **kʷol-so-*, "that on which the head turns," neck, in: **a.** Germanic **h(w)alsaz* in (*i*) Old Norse *hals*, neck, ship's bow: HAWSE (*ii*) Middle Dutch *hals*, neck: RINGHALS (*iii*) Germanic compound **h(w)als-berg-*, "neck-protector," gorget (**bergan*, to protect; see **bhergh-¹**), in Old French *hauberc*, hauberk: HAUBERK; **b.** Latin *collum*, neck: COL, COLLAR, COLLET, CULLET; ACCOLADE, DECOLLATE¹, DÉCOLLETÉ, MACHICOLATE, (MACHICOLATION), TORTICOLLIS. 2. Suffixed form **kʷol-ā* in Latin *-cola* and *incola*, inhabitant (*in-*, in; see **en**): -COLOUS; PRATINCOLE. 3. Suffixed form **kʷol-o-* in: **a.** Latin *anculus*, "he who bustles about," servant (*an-*, short for *ambi-*, around, about; see **ambhi**): ANCILLARY; **b.** Greek *polos*, axis of a sphere: POLE¹, PULLEY; **c.** Greek *-kolos*, herdsman, in *boukolos*, cowherd: BUCOLIC. 4. Suffixed zero-grade form **kʷḷ-i-* in Greek *palin*, again (< "revolving"): PALIMPSEST, PALINDROME, PALINGENESIS, PALINODE. [Pok. 1. *ku̯el-* 639.]

kʷel-². Far (in space and time). 1. Lengthened-grade form **kʷēl-* in Greek *tēle*, far off: TELE-. 2. Suffixed zero-grade form **kʷḷ-ai* in Greek *palai*, long ago: PALEO-. [Pok. 2. *ku̯el-* 640.]

kwelək-. Bundle. Proposed by some as the root of Latin *culcita,* mattress, sack, which is more likely of unknown origin: QUILT. [Pok. *k̯u̯elək-* 630.]

kwelp-. To arch. **1.** Germanic **hwalbjan* in Old English **hwelfan, hwylfan,* with parallel form **hwelman* (> Middle English *whelman*), to turn over: WHELM. **2.** Suffixed o-grade form **kwolp-o-* in Greek *kolpos,* bosom, womb, vagina: GULF; COLPITIS, COLPOSCOPE, COLPOSCOPY. [Pok. 2. *k̯u̯elp-* 630.]

kwen-. Holy. Suffixed zero-grade form **kwn̥-s-lo-* in Germanic **hunslam* in Old English *hūsl, hūsel,* Eucharist: HOUSEL. [Pok. *k̯u̯en-* 630.]

kwenth(h)-. To suffer. **1.** Suffixed form **kwenth-es-* in Greek *penthos,* grief: NEPENTHE. **2.** Zero-grade form **kwn̥th-* in: **a.** Greek *pathos,* suffering, passion, emotion, feelings: PATHETIC, PATHO-, PATHOS, -PATHY; PATHOGNOMONIC, SYMPATHY; **b.** suffixed form **kwn̥th-sko-* in Greek *paskhein,* to feel, suffer: PROTOPATHIC. [Pok. *k̯u̯enth-* 641.]

kwēp-. To smoke, cook, move violently, be agitated emotionally. Hypothetical base of possibly related words. **1.** Suffixed variant form **kup-yo-* in Latin *cupere,* to desire: COVET, CUPID, CUPIDITY; CONCUPISCENCE. **2.** Zero-grade form **kwəp-,* becoming **kwap-* possibly in: **a.** Latin *vapor,* steam, vapor: VAPOR; EVAPORATE; **b.** Latin *vapidus,* that has emitted steam or lost its vapor, flat, poor: VAPID; **c.** Greek *kapnos,* smoke: ACAPNIA. [Pok. *k̯u̯ēp-* 596.]

kwer-¹. To make. **1.** Sanskrit *karoti,* he makes: SANSKRIT. **2.** Suffixed form **kwer-ōr* with dissimilated form **kwel-ōr* in Greek *pelōr,* monster (perhaps "that which does harm"): PELORIA. **3.** Suffixed form **kwer-əs-* in Greek *teras,* monster: TERATOCARCINOMA, TERATOGEN, TERATOID, TERATOMA. **4.** Suffixed form **kwer-mn̥* in Sanskrit *karma,* act, deed: KARMA. [Pok. 1. *k̯u̯er-* 641.]

kwer-². Something shaped like a dish or shell. Suffixed variant form **kwar-yo-* in Scottish Gaelic *coire,* cauldron, hollow, whirlpool: CORRIE. [Pok. 2. *k̯u̯er-* 642.]

kwerp-. To turn oneself. **1.** Germanic **hwarb-* in Old English *hwearf,* wharf (< "place where people move about"): WHARF. **2.** Germanic **hwerban* in: **a.** Old Norse *hverfa,* to turn: VARVE; **b.** Old Norse **hvirfa,* to whirl, perhaps assimilated to Danish *hvirre,* to whir, akin to the Scandinavian source of Middle English *whirren,* to whir: WHIR; **c.** Old Norse *hvirfla,* to whirl: WHIRL; **d.** Old North French *werble,* a warbling: WARBLE¹. **3.** Possibly suffixed zero-grade form **kwr̥p-o-* in Greek *karpos,* wrist: CARPAL, CARPUS. [Pok. *k̯u̯erp-* 631.]

kwes-. To pant, wheeze. **1.** Germanic **hwēsjan* in Old Norse *hvæsa,* to hiss: WHEEZE. **2.** Latin *querī,* to complain: QUARREL¹, QUERULOUS. **3.** Suffixed zero-grade form **kus-ti-* in Latin *kustis,* bladder, bag (< "bellows"): CYST, CYSTO-. [Pok. *k̯u̯es-* 631.]

kwēt-. To shake. Zero-grade form **kwət-,* becoming **kwat-* in Latin *quatere* (past participle *quassus,* in composition *-cussus*), to shake, strike: CASCARA, KVETCH, SCUTCH, SQUASH²; CONCUSS, DISCUSS, PERCUSS, RESCUE, SUCCUSSION. [Pok. *k̯u̯ēt-* 632.]

kwetwer-. Four. **I.** O-grade form **kwetwor-.* **1.** Probably Germanic **fe(d)wor-* in: **a.** Old English *fēower,* four: FOUR; **b.** Old English *fēowertig,* forty: FORTY; **c.** Old English *fēowertēne,* fourteen: FOURTEEN. **2.** Latin *quattuor* (> Italian *quattro*), four: CAHIER, CARNET, QUATRAIN; CATER-CORNERED, QUATTROCENTO. **II.** Multiplicatives **kweturs, kwetrus,* and combining forms **kwetur-, kwetru-.* **1.** Latin *quater,* four times: (CARILLON), QUATERNARY, QUATERNION, QUIRE¹. **2.** Latin *quadrus,* four-sided thing, square: CADRE, QUADRATE, QUARREL², QUARRY²; SQUAD, SQUARE, TROCAR. **3.** Latin *quadri-,* four: QUADRI-. **4.** Latin *quadra,* square: QUADRILLE¹. **5.** Latin *quadrāns,* a fourth part: QUADRANT. **6.** Latin *quadrāgintā,* forty (*-gintā,* ten times; see **dekm̥**): QUARANTINE. **7.** Variant form **kwet(w)r̥-* in: **a.** Greek *tetra-,* four: TETRA-; **b.** Greek *tessares, tettares,*

four (genitive *tessarōn*): TESSERA; DIATESSARON. **c.** Greek *tetras,* group of four: TETRAD; **d.** zero-grade form **kwt(w)r̥-* in Greek *tra-,* four: TRAPEZIUM. **III.** Ordinal adjective **kwetur-to-.* **1.** Germanic **fe(d)worthōn-* in: **a.** Old English *fēortha, fēowertha,* fourth: FOURTH; **b.** Middle Dutch *veerdel,* one-fourth: FIRKIN; **c.** Old English *fēorthing, fēorthung,* fourth part of a penny: FARTHING. **2.** Latin *quārtus,* fourth, quarter: QUADRILLE², QUADROON, QUART, QUARTAN, QUARTER, QUARTO. [Pok. *k̯u̯etu̯er-* 642.]

kwo-. Also **kwi-.** Stem of relative and interrogative pronouns. **1.** Germanic **hwa-, hwi-* in: **a.** personal pronouns **hwas, *hwasa, *hwam* in Old English *hwā, hwæs, hwæm,* who, whose, whom: WHO, WHOSE, WHOM; **b.** pronoun **hwat* in Old English *hwæt,* what: WHAT; **c.** adverb **hwī* in Old English *hwȳ,* why: WHY; **d.** relative pronoun **hwa-līk-* (**līk-,* body, form; see **līk-**) in Old English *hwilc, hwelc,* which: WHICH; **e.** adverb **hwō* in Old English *hū,* how: HOW¹; **f.** adverb **hwan-* in *(i)* Old English *hwenne, hwanne,* when: WHEN *(ii)* Old English *hwanon,* whence: WHENCE; **g.** adverb **hwithrē* in Old English *hwider,* whither: WHITHER; **h.** adverb **hwar-* in Old English *hwǣr,* where: WHERE. **2.** Germanic **hwatharaz* in: **a.** Old English *hwæther, hwether,* which of two, whether: WHETHER; NEITHER; **b.** Germanic phrase **aiwo gihwatharaz,* "ever each of two" (**aiwo, *aiwi,* ever; see **aiw-**; **gi-* from **ga-,* collective prefix; see **kom**), in Old English *ǣghwæther, ǣther,* either: EITHER. **3.** Latin *quī,* who (genitive plural *quōrum*): QUA, QUIBBLE, QUORUM. **4.** Latin *quid,* what, something: HIDALGO, QUIDDITY, QUIDNUNC, QUIP. **5.** Latin *quam,* as, than, how, in *quasi* (*quam + si,* if; see **swo-**), as if: QUASI. **6.** Latin *quod,* what: QUODLIBET. **7.** Latin *quot,* how many: QUOTE, QUOTIDIAN, QUOTIENT; ALIQUOT. **8.** Latin *quom,* when: QUONDAM. **9.** Latin *quem,* whom: CONQUIAN. **10.** Latin *quantus,* how great: QUANTITY. **11.** Latin *quālis,* of what kind: QUALITY. **12.** Latin *ut,* that: (UT). **13.** Latin *uter,* either of two: NEUTER. **14.** Latin *ubi,* where, and *ibi,* there: ALIBI, UBIQUITY. **15.** Persian *chīz,* thing: CHEESE³. [Pok. *k̯u̯o-* 644.]

kwon-. Dog. **1.** Germanic *kuōn,* dog: CYNIC; CYNOSURE, PROCYON, QUINSY. **2.** Suffixed zero-grade form **kwn̥-to-* in Germanic **hundaz* in: **a.** Old English *hund,* dog: HOUND; **b.** Old High German *hunt* (> German *Hund*), dog: DACHSHUND; **c.** Dutch *hond,* dog: KEESHOND. **3.** Nominative form **kwō* in Welsh *ci,* dog: CORGI. **4.** Variant **kan-i-* in Latin *canis,* dog: CANAILLE, CANARY, CANICULA, CANINE, CHENILLE, KENNEL¹. [Pok. *k̯u̯on-* 632.]

kwrep-. Body. **1.** Suffixed form **kwrep-es-* in Germanic **hrifiz* in Old English *hrif,* belly: MIDRIFF. **2.** Suffixed zero-grade form **kwr̥p-es-* in Latin *corpus,* body, substance: CORPORAL¹, CORPORAL³, CORPORATE, CORPOREAL, CORPOSANT, CORPS, CORPSE, CORPULENCE, CORPUS, CORPUSCLE, CORSAGE, CORSE, CORSET; LEPRECHAUN. [Pok. 1. *krep-* 620.]

kwrmi-. Mite, worm. Rhyme word to **wr̥mi-,* worm (see **wer-³**). Sanskrit *kr̥mi-,* worm, in compound *kr̥mi-ja-,* "(red dye) produced by worms" (*ja-,* produced; see **genə-**), borrowed into Arabic as *qirmiz,* kermes: (CRIMSON), KERMES. [Pok. *k̯r̥mi-* 649.]

lā-. Echoic root. **1.** Middle Dutch *lollen,* to mutter, akin to the Low German source of Middle English *lollen,* to loll: LOLL. **2.** Middle Low German *lollen,* to lull, akin to the Low German source of Middle English *lullen,* to lull: LULL. **3.** Old Norse *lōmr,* loon: LOON¹. **4.** Latin *lāmentum,* expression of sorrow: LAMENT. **5.** Greek *lalos,* talkative: ECHOLALIA. **6.** Greek *lalein,* to talk: GLOSSOLALIA. [Pok. 1. *lā-* 650.]

lab-. Lapping, smacking the lips; to lick. Variant of **leb-².** **1.** Germanic **lapjan* in Old English *lapian,* to lap up: LAP³. **2.** Nasalized form **la-m-b-* in: **a.** Germanic **lampin* French *lamper,* to gulp down: LAMPOON; **b.** Latin *lambere,* to lick: LAMBENT. [Pok. *lab-* 651.]

lādh-. To be hidden. **1**. Greek *lēthē*, forgetfulness: LETH-ARGY, LETHE. **2**. Zero-grade form **ladh-* (< **lədh-*), with nasalized form **landh-*, in Greek *lanthanein* (aorist *lathein*), to escape the notice of, with middle *lanthanesthai*, to forget: LANTHANUM; ALASTOR. **3**. Suffixed (stative) variant form **lat-ē-* in Latin *latēre*, to lie hidden: LATENT. [In Pok. 2. *lā-* 651.]

laiwo-. Left. Latin *laevus*, left: LEVO-; (LEVOROTATION), (LEVOROTATORY). [Pok. *laiu̯o-* 652.]

laks-. Salmon. Suffixed form **laks-o-* in Germanic **lahsaz* in Old High German *lahs,* salmon: LOX¹. [Pok. *lak-* 653.]

laku-. Body of water, lake, sea. **1**. Latin *lacus,* lake, pond, basin: LAKE¹. **2**. Greek *lakkos,* cistern: LACCOLITH. **3**. O-grade form **loku-* in Old Irish and Scottish Gaelic *loch,* lake: LOCH, LOUGH. [Pok. *laku-* 653.]

lāp-. To light, burn. Nasalized shortened form **la-m-p-* in Greek *lampein,* to shine: LAMP, LANTERN; ECLAMPSIA. [Pok. *lā(i)p-* 652.]

las-. To be eager, wanton, or unruly. **1**. Suffixed Germanic zero-grade form **lustuz* in: **a**. Old English *lust,* lust: LUST; **b**. Old High German *lust* (> German *Lust*), desire: WANDERLUST; **c**. Germanic denominative verb **lustjan* in Old English *lystan,* to please, satisfy a desire: LIST⁵. **2**. Suffixed form **las-ko-* in Latin *lascīvus,* wanton, lustful: LASCIVIOUS. [Pok. *las-* 654.]

lat-. Wet, moist. Latin *latex,* liquid: LATEX. [Pok. *lat-* 654.]

lau-. Gain, profit. **1**. Suffixed form **lau-no-* in Germanic **launam* in Old High German *lōn,* reward: GUERDON. **2**. Suffixed zero-grade form **lu-tlo-* in Latin *lucrum,* gain, profit: LUCRATIVE, LUCRE. **3**. Suffixed variant form **low-ero-* in Irish Gaelic *leór,* sufficiency, enough: GALORE. [Pok. *lāu-* 655.]

lē-¹. To get. Contracted from **leə-*. Suffixed zero-grade form **lə-tr-* in: **a**. Greek *latreia,* service (for pay), duties, worship: -LATRY; **b**. Greek *latron,* pay, akin to the Greek source of Latin *latrō,* robber: LARCENY; **c**. Greek *-latrēs,* worshiper: IDOLATER. [Pok. 2. *lē(i)-* 665.]

lē-². To let go, slacken. Contracted from **leə-*. **1**. Extended form **lēd-* in: **a**. Germanic **lētan* in Old English *lǣtan,* to allow, leave undone: LET¹; **b**. Germanic derivative **lēthigaz,* freed, in Medieval Latin *lētus,* serf (< "free man"): LIEGE. **2**. Extended zero-grade form **ləd-* in: **a**. Germanic **lataz* in Old English *læt,* late, with its comparative *lætra,* latter, and its superlative *latost,* last: LATE, LATTER, LAST¹; **b**. Germanic **latjan* in Old English *lettan,* to hinder, impede (< "to make late"): LET²; **c**. suffixed form **ləd-to-* in Latin *lassus,* tired, weary: LASSITUDE; ALAS. **3**. Suffixed reduced form **lē-ni-* in Latin *lēnis,* soft, gentle: LENIENT, LENIS, LENITIVE, LENITY. [Pok. 3. *lē(i)-* 666.]

leb-¹. Base of loosely related derivatives meaning "hanging loosely." **I**. Variant form **lep-* in Germanic **lap-* in Old English *læppa, lappa,* flap of a garment: LAP¹. **II**. Nasalized form **lemb(h)-,* with variant form **slemb(h)-*. **1**. Germanic **lemp-* probably in obsolete English *limphalt,* lame (*halt,* lame; see **kel-¹**): LIMP. **2**. Germanic **lump-* in: **a**. Dutch *lomp,* rag, akin to the Low German source of Middle English *lump,* lump: LUMP¹; **b**. possibly obsolete English *lump,* lumpfish: LUMPFISH; **c**. German *Lumpen,* rags: LUMPEN. **3**. Germanic **slimp-* in Middle Dutch *slim(p),* slanting, bad: SLIM. **4**. Middle High German *slam,* mud: SLUMGULLION. **5**. Old Norse *slambra,* to strike at, akin to the Scandinavian source of SLAM¹. **6**. Norwegian *slumpa,* to slump, akin to the Scandinavian source of SLUMP. **III**. Variant **(s)lab-* in Germanic **slab-*. **1**. Danish *slab,* mud, akin to the Scandinavian source of SLAB². **2**. Swedish *slabb,* slime, mud, akin to the Scandinavian source of Irish *slab,* mud: SLOB. **IV**. Variants **slap-, *slep-*. Germanic **slap-* in: **a**. Low German *slapp,* slap: SLAP; **b**. Old Norse *slafra,* to slaver: SLAVER¹. **V**. Variant **lab-*. **1**. Germanic **lab-* in Old French *label,* ribbon, strip: LABEL. **2**. Latin

lābī (past participle *lapsus*), to fall, slip: LABILE, LAPSE; COLLAPSE, ELAPSE, PRELAPSARIAN, PROLAPSE, RELAPSE, SUPRALAPSARIAN. **3**. Suffixed form **lab-os-* perhaps in Latin *labor,* labor, toil, exertion: LABOR; COLLABORATE, ELABORATE. (But both Latin *lābī* and *labor* may belong to a root **slēb-*.) **VI**. O-grade form **lob-* in Greek *lobos,* lobe: LOBE. [Pok. *lēb-* 655.]

leb-². Lip. **1**. Germanic **lep-* in Old English *lippa,* lip: LIP. **2**. Variant form *lab-* in: **a**. suffixed form **lab-yo-* in Latin *labium,* lip: LABIAL, LABIUM; **b**. suffixed form **lab-ro-* in Latin *labrum,* lip: LABELLUM, LABRET, LABRUM. Compare **lab-**. [Pok. *lēb-* 655.]

leg-¹. To collect; with derivatives meaning "to speak." **1**. Perhaps Germanic **lēkjaz,* enchanter, one who speaks magic words, in Old English *lǣce,* physician: LEECH¹. **2**. Latin *legere,* to gather, choose, pluck, read: LECTERN, LECTION, LECTURE, LEGEND, LEGIBLE, LEGION, (LESSON); (COIL¹), COLLECT¹, DILIGENT, ELECT, INTELLIGENT, NEGLECT, PRELECT, SACRILEGE, SELECT, SORTILEGE. **3**. Greek *legein,* to gather, speak: LEXICON; ALEXIA, ANALECTS, BRADYLEXIA, CATALOGUE, DIALECT, (DIALOGUE), DYSLEXIA, ECLECTIC, EPILOGUE, PROLEGOMENON. **4**. Suffixed form **leg-no-* in Latin *lignum,* wood, firewood (< "that which is gathered"): LIGNEOUS, LIGNI-. **5**. Lengthened-grade form **lēg-* possibly in: **a**. Latin *lēx,* law (? < "collection of rules"): LEGAL, LEGIST, LEGITIMATE, LEX, LOYAL; LEGISLATOR, PRIVILEGE; **b**. Latin denominative *lēgāre,* to depute, commission, charge (< "to engage by contract"; but possibly from **legh-**): LEGACY, LEGATE; ALLEGE, COLLEAGUE, (COLLEGIALITY), DELEGATE, RELEGATE. **6**. Suffixed o-grade form **log-o-* in Greek *logos,* speech, word, reason: LOGIC, LOGISTIC, LOGO-, LOGOS, -LOGY; ANALOGOUS, APOLOGUE, APOLOGY, DECALOGUE, HOMOLOGOUS, LOGARITHM, PARALOGISM, PROLOGUE, SYLLOGISM. [Pok. *leĝ-* 658.]

leg-². To dribble, trickle. Germanic **lek-* in: **a**. Middle English *leke,* a leak: LEAK; **b**. Middle English *lack,* deficiency: LACK. [Pok. 1. *leg-* 657.]

legh-. To lie. **1**. Suffixed form **leg-yo-* in: **a**. Germanic **ligjan* in Old English *licgan,* to lie: LIE¹; **b**. Germanic **lagjan* in (*i*) Old English *lecgan,* to lay: LAY¹, LEDGE, (LEDGER) (*ii*) Old English *belecgan,* to cover, surround (*be-,* over; see **ambhi**): BELAY. **2**. Suffixed form **leg-ro-* in Germanic **legraz* in: **a**. Old English *leger,* lair: LAIR; **b**. Dutch *leger,* lair, camp: LEAGUER¹; BELEAGUER; **c**. Old High German *legar,* bed, lair (> German *Lager,* store, and Afrikaans *lager,* laager): LAAGER, LAGER; (STALAG). **3**. Celtic **leg-yā-* in Medieval Latin *lia,* sediment: LEES. **4**. Lengthened-grade form **lēgh-* in Germanic **lēgaz,* "lying flat," low, in Old Norse *lāgr,* low: LOW¹. **5**. Suffixed form **legh-to-* in Latin *lectus,* bed: LITTER; WAGON-LIT. **6**. Suffixed o-grade form **logh-o-* in Germanic **lagam* in: **a**. Old Norse **lagu, lag-,* law, "that which is set down" (> Old English *lagu,* law): LAW; DANELAW; **b**. Old Norse *lag,* a laying down: FELLOW; **c**. Old Norse *lög,* law: OUTLAW; **d**. Old High German *lāga* (> Middle High German *lāge* > German *Lage*), act of laying: ANLAGE, VORLAGE. **7**. Suffixed o-grade form **logh-o-* in Greek *lokhos,* childbirth, place for lying in wait: LOCHIA. [Pok. *legh-* 658, 2. *lēĝh-* 660.]

legʷh-. Light, having little weight. **1**. Suffixed form **legʷh-t-* in Germanic **līht(j)az* in: **a**. Old English *līht, lēoht,* light: LIGHT²; **b**. Old English *līhtan,* to lighten: LIGHTER². **2**. Suffixed form **legʷh-u-i-* in Latin *levis* (> Old French *leger*), light, with its derivative *levāre,* to lighten, raise: LEAVEN, LEVER, LEVITY; ALLEVIATE, CARNIVAL, ELEVATE, LEGERDEMAIN, LEVIGATE, (MEZZO-RELIEVO), RELIEVE. **3**. Variant form **lagʷh-* in Old Irish *lū-,* small: LEPRECHAUN. **4**. Nasalized form **l(e)ngʷh-* in Germanic **lung-* in Old English *lungen,* lungs (from their lightness): LUNG. **5**. Attributed by some to this root is Latin *oblīvīscī,* to forget, which is more likely from **lei-**. [Pok. *legʷh-* 660.]

lei-. Also **slei-**. Slimy. **1**. Germanic **slī-* with various

extensions in: **a.** Old English *slīm*, slime: SLIME; **b.** Old English *slipor*, slippery: SLIPPERY; **c.** Old English *slice*, smooth (> Middle English *slike*, smooth): SLICK; **d.** Old English *līm*, cement, birdlime: LIME³; **e.** Old English *lām*, loam: LOAM; **f.** Old Norse *slēttr*, smooth, sleek, akin to the probable Scandinavian source of Middle English *slight*, slender: SLIGHT; **g.** Middle Dutch and Middle Low German *slippen*, to slip, slip away, akin to the probable source of Middle English *slippen*, to slip: SLIP¹; **h.** Middle Low German *slēpen*, to drag: SCHLEP. **2.** Suffixed form *lei-mo-* in Latin *līmus*, slime: LIMACINE, LIMICOLINE. **3.** Suffixed form *lei-w-* in Latin *oblīvīscī* (*ob-*, away; see **epi**), to forget (< "to wipe, let slip from the mind"): OBLIVION, OUBLIETTE. **4.** Extended form *(s)leia-* in: **a.** nasalized zero-grade form *li-n-ə-* in Latin *linere*, to anoint: LINIMENT; **b.** Suffixed zero-grade form *lī-* (< *liə-*) in Greek *litos*, plain, simple: LITOTES. [Pok. 3. *lei-* 662.]

lēi-. Also **lei-**. To flow. **1.** Extended form *leib-* in Latin *lībāre*, to pour out, taste: LIBATION; PRELIBATION. **2.** Possibly suffixed extended form *leit-os-* in Latin *lītus*, shore: LITTORAL. [Pok. 4. *lēi-* 664.]

leid-. To play, jest. Suffixed o-grade form *loid-o-* in Latin *lūdus*, game, play, with its derivative *lūdere*, to play (but both words may possibly be from Etruscan): LUDICROUS; ALLUDE, COLLUDE, DELUDE, ELUDE, ILLUSION, INTERLUDE, PRELUDE, PROLUSION. [Pok. *leid-* 666.]

leiə-. To waste away. Zero-grade form *lī-* (< *liə-*) in Greek *limos*, hunger, famine: BULIMIA. [In Pok. 2. *lei-* 661.]

leig-¹. To bind. **1.** Germanic *līk-* in Middle Low German *līk*, leech line: LEECH². **2.** O-grade form *lig-ā-* in Latin *ligāre*, to bind: LEAGUE¹, LEGATO, LIABLE, LIEN, LIGASE, LIGATE; ALLOY, (ALLY), COLLIGATE, COLLIGATIVE, FURL, OBLIGE, (RALLY), RELY. [Pok. 4. *leig-* 668.]

leig-². Poor. Perhaps Greek *oligos*, few, little: OLIGO-. [Pok. 1. *leig-* 667.]

leig-³. To leap, tremble. O-grade form *loig-* in Germanic *laik-* in: **a.** Old English *-lac*, suffix denoting activity: WEDLOCK; **b.** Old Norse *leika*, tó play: LARK². [Pok. 3. *leig-* 667.]

leigh-. To lick. **1.** Greek *leikhein*, to lick: ELECTUARY. **2.** Zero-grade form *lig-* in Germanic *likkōn* in: **a.** Old English *liccian*, to lick: LICK; **b.** Old French *lechier*, to live in debauchery: LECHER. **3.** Nasalized zero-grade form *ling-* in Latin *lingere*, to lick: ANILINGUS, CUNNILINGUS. [Pok. *leigh-* 668.]

leikʷ-. To leave. **1.** Basic form *leikʷ-* in Greek *leipein*, to leave: ECLIPSE, ELLIPSIS. **2.** O-grade form *loikʷ-* in: **a.** Germanic *laihwnjan* in Old English *lǣnan*, to lend, give (< "to leave to"): LEND; **b.** suffixed form *loikʷ-nes-* in Germanic *laihwniz* in Old Norse *lān*, loan: LOAN. **3.** Zero-grade form *likʷ-* in Germanic *-lif-*, left, in: **a.** Germanic *ain-lif-*, "one (beyond ten)," in Old English *endleofan*, eleven (see **oi-no-**); **b.** Germanic *twa-lif-*, "two left (beyond ten)," in Old English *twelf*, twelve (see **dwo-**). **4.** Nasalized zero-grade form *li-n-kʷ-* in Latin *linquere*, to leave: DELINQUENT, DERELICT, RELINQUISH. [Pok. *leikʷ-* 669.]

leip-. To stick, adhere; fat. **1.** Germanic *lībam* in Old English *līf*, life (< "continuance"): LIFE, LIVELY. **2.** Germanic *lībēn* in Old English *lifian, libban*, to live: LIVE¹. **3.** Germanic *laibjan* in Old English *lǣfan*, to leave, have remaining: LEAVE¹. **4.** Germanic *librō* in Old English *lifer*, liver (formerly believed to be the blood-producing organ): LIVER¹. **5.** Zero-grade form *lip-* in Greek *lipos*, fat: LIPO-. **6.** Variant form *aleibh-* in Greek *aleiphein*, to anoint with oil (> *aleiphar*, unguent): ALIPHATIC; SYNALEPHA. [Pok. *leip-* 670.]

leis-¹. Track, furrow. **1.** O-grade form *lois-* in: **a.** Germanic *laist-* in Old English *lāst, lǣst*, sole, footprint: LAST³; **b.** Germanic *laistjan*, "to follow a track," in Old English *lǣstan*, to continue: LAST²; **c.** suffixed form *lois-ā-* in Germanic *laizō* in Old English *lār*, learning:

LORE¹. **2.** Germanic zero-grade form *liznōn*, "to follow a course (of study)," in Old English *leornian*, to learn: LEARN. **3.** Suffixed full-grade form *leis-ā* in Latin *līra*, a furrow: DELIRIUM. [Pok. *leis-* 671.]

leis-². Small. Germanic comparative *lais-iz(a)* and superlative *lais-ista-* in Old English comparative *lǣs, lǣssa* and superlative *lǣst, lǣrest*: LEAST, LESS.

leit-¹. To detest. **1.** Germanic *laithaz* in Old English *lāth*, loathsome: LOATH. **2.** Germanic *laithōn* in Old English *lāthian*, to loathe: LOATHE. [Pok. 1. *leit-* 672.]

leit-². To go forth, die. **1.** Suffixed o-grade form *loit-eyo-* in Germanic *laidjan* in: **a.** Old English *lǣdan*, to lead: LEAD¹; **b.** Old High German *leiten*, to lead: LEITMOTIF. **2.** Suffixed variant o-grade form *loit-ā* in Germanic *laidō* in Old English *lād*, course, way: LOAD, LODE; LIVELIHOOD. [Pok. *leit(h)-* 672.]

leizd-. Border, band. Germanic *līstōn-* in: **a.** Old English *līste*, border, edge, strip: LIST²; **b.** Old Italian *lista*, border, strip of paper, list: LIST¹. [Pok. *leizd-* 672.]

lek-. To leap, fly. Possibly suffixed o-grade form *lok-ost-* in Latin *locusta, lōcusta*, a marine shellfish, lobster: LOBSTER, LOCUST. [Pok. 2. *lek-* 673.]

lēk-. To tear. Zero-grade form *lək-* becoming *lak-*. **1.** Latin *lacīnia*, flap of a garment: LACINIATE. **2.** Suffixed form *lak-ero-* in Latin *lacer*, torn: LACERATE. [Pok. 2. *lēk-* 674.]

lem-¹. To break in pieces; broken, soft, with derivatives meaning "crippled." **1.** Germanic *lamōn-* in Old English *lama*, lame: LAME¹. **2.** Germanic *lamjan* in Old Norse *lemja*, to flog, cripple by beating, akin to the Scandinavian source of LAM¹. **3.** Perhaps Swedish dialectal *loma*, to move heavily, akin to the Scandinavian source of Middle English *lomeren*, to lumber: LUMBER². [Pok. 1. *lem-* 674.]

lem-². Nocturnal spirits. **1.** Suffixed form *lem-or-* in Latin *lemurēs*, ghosts: LEMURES. **2.** Suffixed variant form *lam-ya-* in Greek *lamia*, monster: LAMIA. [Pok. 2. *lem-* 675.]

lendh-¹. Loin. Suffixed o-grade form *londh-wo-* in Latin *lumbus*, loin: LOIN, LUMBAGO, LUMBAR; SIRLOIN. [Pok. 2. *lendh-* 675.]

lendh-². Open land. Germanic *landam* in: **a.** Old English *land*, land: LAND; **b.** Middle Dutch *land*, land: BILANDER, LANDSCAPE, UITLANDER; **c.** Old High German *lant* (> German *Land*), land: AUSLANDER, GELÄNDESPRUNG, HINTERLAND, LANDSMAN²; **d.** Old French *launde*, heath, pasture: LAWN¹. [Pok. 3. *lendh-* 675.]

lenk-. To bend. Germanic *lengwa-* in Old Norse *lyng*, heather: LING². [Pok. *lenk-* 676.]

lento-. Flexible. **1.** Suffixed form *lent-yo-* in Germanic *linthjaz* in: **a.** Old English *līthe*, flexible, mild: LITHE; **b.** Old English *lind(e)*, linden tree (from its pliant bast): LINDEN. **2.** Suffixed form *lent-o-* in Latin *lentus*, flexible, tenacious, sluggish, slow: LENTO; RALLENTANDO, RELENT. [Pok. *lento-* 677.]

lep-¹. To peel. **1.** Greek *lepein*, to peel (> *lemma*, husk): LEMMA², LEPTO-, LEPTON¹; SARCOLEMMA. **2.** Suffixed form *lep-i-* in Greek *lepis, lepos*, a scale: LEPER, LEPIDO-, LEPIDOTE. **3.** Suffixed variant form *lap-aro-* in Greek *laparos*, soft: LAPAROTOMY. **4.** O-grade form *lop-* in Greek *elops, ellops*, a fish (< *en-lopos*, having scales; *en-*, in; see **en**): ELAPID. [Pok. 2. *lep-* 678.]

lep-². To be flat; palm, sole, shoulder blade. Lengthened o-grade form *lōp-* in Germanic *lōfō* in: **a.** Germanic *galōfō* (*ga-*, collective prefix; see **kom**), "covering for the hand," in Old English *glōf*, glove: GLOVE; **b.** Middle Dutch *loef*, windward side of a ship, akin to the probable Germanic source of Old French *lof*, spar: LUFF. [Pok. 2. *lēp-* 679.]

lerd-. Bent, curved. Suffixed o-grade form *lord-o-* in Greek *lordos*, bent backward: LORDOSIS. [Pok. *lerd-* 679.]

letro-. Leather. Germanic *lethram* in Old English *lether-*, leather: LEATHER. [Pok. *letro-* 681.]

leu-¹. To loosen, divide, cut apart. **1.** Germanic *leusan*

in: **a.** Old English *-lēosan*, to lose: LORN, (LOSEL); **b.** Germanic **fer-leusan*, **far-leusan* (**fer-*, **far-*, prefix denoting rejection or exclusion; see **per¹**) in *(i)* Old English *forlēosan*, to forfeit, lose: FORLORN *(ii)* Dutch *verliezen*, to lose (past participle *verloren*): FORLORN HOPE. **2.** Germanic **lawwō* in Swedish *lagg*, barrel stave (< "split piece of wood"), akin to the probable source of LAG². **3.** Germanic **lausaz* in: **a.** Old English *lēas*, "loose," free from, without, untrue, lacking: LEASING, -LESS; **b.** Old English *los*, loss: LOSE, (LOSS); **c.** Old Norse *lauss*, *louss*, loose: LOOSE; **d.** Swiss German *lösch*, loose: LOESS. **4.** Zero-grade form **lu-* in: **a.** Greek *luein*, to loosen, release, untie: LYSIS, LYSO-, -LYTE, -LYTIC, ANALYSIS, CATALYSIS, DIALYSIS, LYASE, PARALYSIS, TACHYLYTE; **b.** Latin *luēs*, plague, pestilence (< "dissolution, putrefaction"): LUES; **c.** prefixed form **se-lu-* (*se-*, apart; see **s(w)e-**) in Latin *solvere*, to loosen, untie: SOLUBLE, SOLUTE, SOLVE; ABSOLUTE, (ABSOLVE), ASSOIL, CONSOLUTE, DISSOLVE, RESOLVE. [Pok. 2. *leu-* 681.]

leu-². Dirt; to make dirty. **1.** Latin *polluere*, to pollute (< **por-luere*; *por-* for *prō-*, forth, forward; see **per¹**): POLLUTE. **2.** Suffixed zero-grade form **lu-to-* in Latin *lutum*, mud, mire, clay: LUTE². [Pok. 1. *leu-* 681.]

lēu-¹. Stone. Welsh *llech*, flat stone (from an uncertain preform): CROMLECH. [Pok. 2. *lēu-* 683.]

lēu-². Echoic root. **1.** Extended form **leut-* in Germanic **leuth-* in Old High German *liod* (> German *Lied*), song: LIED; VOLKSLIED. **2.** Extended variant form **laud-* in Latin *laus*, praise, glory, fame: LAUD. [Pok. 3. *lēu-* 683.]

leubh-. To care, desire; love. **I.** Suffixed form **leubh-o-* in Germanic **leubaz* in Old English *lēof*, dear, beloved: LIEF; LEMAN, LIVELONG. **II.** O-grade form **loubh-*. **1.** Germanic **laubō* in: **a.** Old English *lēaf*, permission (< "pleasure, approval"): LEAVE²; **b.** Middle Dutch *verlof*, leave, permission (*ver-*, intensive prefix, from Germanic **fer-*; see **per¹**): FURLOUGH; **c.** Germanic **galaubō* (**ga-*, intensive prefix; see **kom**) in Old English *gelēafa*, *bilēafa* (*bi-*, about; see **ambhi**), belief, faith: BELIEF. **2.** Germanic **galaubjan* (**ga-*, intensive prefix; see **kom**), "to hold dear," esteem, trust, in Old English *gelēfan*, *belēfan* (*be-*, about; see **ambhi**), to believe, trust: BELIEVE. **III.** Zero-grade form **lubh-*. **1.** Suffixed form **lubh-ā-* in Germanic **lubō* in Old English *lufu*, love: LOVE. **2.** Suffixed (stative) form **lubh-ē-* in Latin *libēre*, to be dear, be pleasing: QUODLIBET. **3.** Latin *libīdō*, pleasure, desire: LIBIDO. [Pok. *leubh-* 683.]

leud-. Small. Germanic **lūt-* in: **a.** West Germanic **luttilaz* in Old English *lȳtel*, little: LITTLE; **b.** Old English *lūtan*, to bend down: LOUT²; **c.** Old Norse *lūta*, to bend down (< "to make small"): (LOUT¹); **d.** perhaps Middle Dutch *loteren*, to shake, totter (< "to make smaller"), perhaps akin to the source of Middle English *loitren*, to idle away time: LOITER. [Pok. *leud-* 684.]

leudh-¹. To go. Zero-grade form **(e)ludh-* in suffixed unextended form **elu-to-* in Greek *prosēlutos*, "one who comes to a place," stranger (*pros-*, to; see **per¹**): PROSELYTE. [In Pok. 6. *el-* 306.]

leudh-². To mount up, grow. Suffixed form **leudh-ero-* in Latin *līber*, free (the precise semantic development is obscure): LIBERAL, LIBERATE, LIBERTINE, LIBERTY, LIVERY; DELIVER. [Pok. 1. *leudh-* 684.]

leu(ə)-. To wash. **1.** Suffixed form **lou-kā-* in Germanic **laugō* in Old English *lēag*, lye: LYE. **2.** Suffixed form **lou-tro-* in Old English *lēathor*, washing soda: LATHER. **3.** Variant form **law-* in: **a.** Latin *lavere*, to wash, with its derivative *-luere*, to wash: LOTION; ABLUTION, ALLUVION, COLLUVIUM, DELUGE, DILUTE, (ELUANT), ELUTE, ELUVIUM; **b.** form **law-ā-* in Latin *lavāre*, to wash: LAVE, LOMENT; **c.** Latin *lavātrīna*, *lātrīna*, a bath, privy: LATRINE. [Pok. *lou-* 692.]

leug-¹. To bend, turn, wind. **1.** Germanic **lauk-*, leek (semantic transition obscure), in Old English *lēac*, leek: LEEK; GARLIC. **2.** Zero-grade form **lug-* in Germanic **luk-* in: **a.** Old English *loc*, lock (perhaps < "a bending

together, shutting"): LOCK¹, LOCKET; **b.** Old English *locc*, strand of hair: LOCK²; **c.** possibly Old French *lucane*, dormer: LUCARNE. **3.** Suffixed zero-grade form **lug-so-* in Latin *luxus*, dislocated, and *luxus*, excess, extravagance (originally of plants, "growing obliquely or to excess"): LUXATE, LUXURY. **4.** Suffixed zero-grade form **lug-to-* in Latin *luctārī*, to wring, wrestle, struggle: INELUCTABLE, RELUCT. [Pok. 1. *leug-* 685.]

leug-². To break. Suffixed form **leug-ē-* in Latin *lūgēre*, to mourn (? < "to break down mentally"): LUGUBRIOUS. [Pok. *leug̑-* 686.]

leugh-. To tell a lie. **1.** Germanic **leugan* in: **a.** Old English *lēogan*, to lie: WARLOCK; **b.** Old English *belēogan*, to tell lies about (*be-*, about; see **ambhi**): BELIE. **2.** Germanic **lugiz* in Old English *lyge*, a lie, falsehood: LIE². [Pok. *leugh-* 686.]

leuk-. Light, brightness. **I.** Basic form **leuk-*. **1.** Suffixed form **leuk-to-* in Germanic **leuhtam* in Old English *lēoht*, *līht*, light: LIGHT¹. **2.** Latin *lūx*, light: LUCINA, LUCULENT, LUX; LUCIFER, LUCIFERIN. **3.** Suffixed form **leuk-smen-* in Latin *lūmen*, light, opening: LIMN, LUMEN, LUMINARY, LUMINOUS; ILLUMINATE, PHILLUMENIST. **4.** Suffixed form **leuk-snā-* in Latin *lūna*, moon: LUNA, LUNAR, LUNATE, LUNATIC, LUNE, LUNULA; DEMILUNE, SUBLUNARY. **5.** Suffixed form **leuk-stro-* in: **a.** Latin *lūstrum*, purification: LUSTER, (LUSTRUM); **b.** Latin *lūstrāre*, to purify, illuminate: ILLUSTRATE. **6.** Suffixed form **leuko-dhro-* in Latin *lūcubrāre*, to work by lamplight: LUCUBRATE. **II.** O-grade form **louk-*. **1.** Suffixed form **louk-o-* in Germanic **lauhaz* in Old English *lēah*, meadow (< "place where light shines"): LEA. **2.** Suffixed (iterative) form **louk-eyo-* in Latin *lūcēre*, to shine (> *lūcidus*, shining): LUCENT, LUCID; ELUCIDATE, NOCTILUCA, PELLUCID, RELUCENT, TRANSLUCENT. **III.** Zero-grade form **luk-*. **1.** Suffixed form **luk-sno-* in Greek *lukhnos*, lamp: LINK², LYCHNIS. **2.** Attributed by some to this root (but more likely of obscure origin) is Greek *lunx*, lynx (as if from its shining eyes): LYNX, OUNCE². [Pok. *leuk-* 687.]

leup-. To peel off, break off. **1.** Germanic **laubaz* in Old English *lēaf*, leaf: LEAF. **2.** Germanic **laubja*, "roof made from bark," shelter, in: **a.** Old French *loge*, lodge: LODGE, (LOGE); **b.** Medieval Latin *lobium*, *lobia*, *laubia*, monastic cloister: LOBBY. **3.** Attributed by some to this root is Germanic **luftuz*, sky (traditionally explained as < "roof of the world," vault of heaven), but probably a separate Germanic root, in: **a.** Old Norse *lopt*, air, attic, sky: LOFT; ALOFT; **b.** Germanic **luftjan*, to hold up in the air, in Old Norse *lypta*, to lift: LIFT. [Pok. *leup-* 690.]

[līk-. Body, form; like, same. Germanic root. **1.** Old English *līc*, form, body: LICH GATE. **2.** Old English *-līc*, having the form of: -LY¹, -LY². **3. a.** Germanic **galīkaz* in Old English *gelīc*, similar: ALIKE, LIKE²; **b.** Germanic phrase **aiwo galīkaz*, "ever alike" (**aiwo*, **aiwi*, ever; see **aiw-**), in Old English *ǣlc*, each: EACH. **4.** Germanic **is-līk* in Old English *ilca*, the same (see *i-*). **5.** Old Norse *līkr*, like: LIKELY. **6.** Middle Dutch *-lijc*, -ly: FROLIC. **7.** Germanic **līkjan* in Old English *līcian*, to please: LIKE¹. **8.** Germanic **hwa-līk-*, which (see **kʷo-**). [In Pok. 2. *leig-* 667.]]**

līno-. Flax. **1.** Form **lino-* in Greek *linon*, flax: LINOLEIC ACID. **2.** Form **līno-* in Latin *līnum*, flax, linen: LINE¹, LINE², LINEN, LINGERIE, LININ, LINNET, LINT; CRINOLINE, LINSEED. [Pok. *lī-no-* 691.]

[līthrā. A scale. Mediterranean word. **1.** Probably Latin *lībra*, a pound, balance: LEVEL, LIBRA, LIRA, LIVRE; DELIBERATE, EQUILIBRIUM. **2.** Probably Greek *litra*, unit of weight, pound: LITER.]

lūs-. Louse. Germanic **lūs-* in Old English *lūs*, louse: LOUSE. [Pok. *lŭs-* 692.]

mā-¹. Good; with derivatives meaning "occurring at a good moment, timely, seasonable, early." **1.** Suffixed form **mā-tu-* in: **a.** further suffixed form **mā-tu-ro-* in Latin *mātūrus*, seasonable, ripe, mature: MADURO, MA-

TURE; IMMATURE, PREMATURE; **b.** further suffixed form *mā-tu-to- in Latin *Mātūta*, name of the goddess of dawn: (MATINEE), MATINS, (MATUTINAL). **2.** Suffixed form *mā-ni- in: **a.** Latin *māne*, (in) the morning (> Spanish *mañana*, morning, tomorrow): MAÑANA; **b.** Latin *mānis*, *mānus*, good: MANES. [Pok. 2. *mā*- 693.]

mā-². Mother. An imitative root derived from the child's cry for the breast (a linguistic near-universal found in many of the world's languages, often in reduplicated form). **1.** Latin *mamma*, breast: MAMMA², MAMMALIA, MAMMILLA. **2.** Probably Greek *Maia*, "good mother" (respectful form of address to old women), also nurse: MAIA, MAIEUTIC. (**3.** More recently formed in the same way is English MAMA.) [Pok. 3. *mā*- 694.]

mā-³. Damp. **1.** Suffixed form *mā-ro- in Germanic *mōra- in Old English *mōr*, marsh, wilderness: MOOR². **2.** Suffixed form *mā-no- in Latin *mānāre*, to flow, trickle: EMANATE. [Pok. *mā-no-* 699.]

[macula. A spot, blemish; also a hole in a net, mesh. Latin noun of unknown origin. MACKLE, MACLE, MACULA, MACULATE, MACULE, MAIL², MAILLOT, MAQUIS; IMMACULATE, TRAMMEL.]

mad-. Moist, wet; also refers to various qualities of food. **1.** Sanskrit *madati*, "it gladdens, it bubbles," hence *madana-*, delightful, joyful, hence *madanaḥ*, a myna bird: MYNA. **2.** Suffixed form *mad-i- in Germanic *mati- in: **a.** Old English *mete*, food: MEAT; **b.** Middle Low German (ge)*mate* (ge-, together, from Germanic *ga-; see **kom**), "he with whom one shares one's food," companion: MATE¹. **3.** Suffixed form *mad-sto-, becoming *mazdo-, in Germanic *masta- in Old English *mæst*, fodder: MAST². [Pok. *mad-* 694.]

mag-. Also **mak-.** To knead, fashion, fit. **1.** Germanic *mak- in: **a.** Germanic verb *makōn, to fashion, fit, in (i) Old English *macian*, to make: MAKE (ii) Old French *mason*, mason: MASON; **b.** Germanic compound noun *ga-mak-(j)ōn (*ga-, with, together; see **kom**), "he who is fitted with (another)," in Old English *gemæcca*, mate, spouse: MATCH¹. **2.** Germanic nasalized form *mangjan, to knead together, in: **a.** Old English *mengan*, to mix: MINGLE; **b.** Old English *gemang* (ge-, together; see **kom**), mixture, crowd: AMONG, MONGREL. **3.** Suffixed form *mak-yo- in Greek *massein* (aorist stem *mag-*), to knead, hence *magma*, unguent: MAGMA. **4.** Suffixed lengthened-grade form *māg-ya- in Greek *maza*, a (kneaded) lump, barley cake: MASS; (AMASS), MAZAEDIUM. **5.** Suffixed lengthened-grade form *māk-ero- in Latin *mācerāre*, to tenderize, to soften (food) by steeping: MACERATE. [Pok. *mag-* 696, 2. *māk-* 698, *men(ə)k-* 730.]

magh-¹. To be able, have power. **1.** Germanic *mag- in: **a.** Old English *magan*, to be able: MAY; **b.** Old French *esmaier*, to frighten: DISMAY. **2.** Germanic suffixed form *mah-ti-, power, in Old English *miht*, power: MIGHT¹. **3.** Germanic suffixed form *mag-inam, power, in Old English *mægen*, power: MAIN¹. **4.** Suffixed lengthened-grade form *māgh-anā-, "that which enables," in Greek (Attic) *mēkhanē*, (Doric) *mākhanā*, device: MACHINE, MECHANIC, (MECHANISM), (MECHANO-). **5.** Possibly suffixed form *magh-u- in Old Persian *maguš*, member of a priestly caste (< "mighty one"): (MAGI), (MAGIC), MAGUS; ARCHIMAGE. [Pok. *magh-* 695.]

magh-². To fight. Hypothetical Old Iranian *ha-maz-an-, "warrior" (*ha-, with < *sm̥-; see **sem-¹**), possibly borrowed into Greek as *Amazōn*, Amazon: AMAZON. [Pok. *magh-* 697.]

maghu-. Young person of either sex. Suffixed form *magho-ti- in Germanic *magadi-, with diminutive *magadin-, in Old English *mægden*, virgin: MAID, MAIDEN. [Pok. *maghos* 696.]

mai-¹. To cut. **1.** Suffixed form *mai-d- in Germanic *mait- in: **a.** Germanic *ē-mait-jōn, "the biter" (prefix *ē-, meaning uncertain from Indo-European *ē*, *ō*; see Pok. *ē*, *ō* 280), a small biting insect, in Old English *æmette*, ant: ANT, EMMET; **b.** Germanic *mītōn-, "the

biter," a small biting insect, in (i) Old English *mīte*, mite: MITE (ii) Middle Dutch *mīte*, insect, small object, small coin: MITE²; **c.** possibly Old French *mahaigner*, to maim (> Anglo-Norman *mangler*, to hack): MAIM, MANGLE¹, MAYHEM. **2.** Suffixed form *mai-lo- in Old Irish *máel*, shorn, bald, hornless, akin to the source of MULEY. [Pok. 1. *mai-* 697.]

mai-². To soil, defile. Possible root. **1.** Suffixed form *mai-lo- in Germanic *mail- in Old English *māl*, spot, blemish: MOLE¹. **2.** Suffixed variant form *mi-an-yo- in Greek *miainein*, to pollute: MIASMA; AMIANTHUS. [Pok. 2. *mai-* 697.]

mak-¹. Poppy. Probably borrowed into Indo-European, as the plant is of Mediterranean origin. Lengthened-grade form *māk- in Greek *mēkōn*, poppy: MECONIUM. [Pok. *māk(en)-* 698.]

mak-². (Leather) bag. Germanic form *magōn-, bag, stomach, in Old English *maga*, stomach: MAW. [Pok. *mak-* 698.]

māk-. Long, thin. **1.** Zero-grade form *mək- becoming *mak- in suffixed form *mak-ro- in: **a.** Latin *macer*, thin: MAIGRE, MEAGER; EMACIATE; **b.** Greek *makros*, long, large: MACRO-, MACRON; AMPHIMACER. **2.** Suffixed form *māk-es- in Greek *mēkos*, length: MECOPTERAN, PARAMECIUM. [Pok. *māk-* 699.]

[malakhē. Mallow. Greek noun, akin to Latin *malva*, mallow, both probably borrowed from a pre-Indo-European Mediterranean language. **1.** Greek *malakhē*, *molokhē*, mallow: MALACHITE. **2.** Latin *malva*, mallow: MALLOW, MAUVE.]

man-¹. Also **mon-.** Man. **1.** Extended forms *manu-, *manw- in Germanic *manna- (plural *manniz), in: **a.** Old English *man(n)* (plural *menn*), man: MAN; NORMAN; **b.** Old High German *man* (> Middle High German *man* > German *Mann*), man: FUGLEMAN, LANDSMAN²; **c.** Middle Dutch *man*, man: MANIKIN, (MANNEQUIN); **d.** Old Norse *madhr*, *mannr*, man: NORMAN, OMBUDSMAN. **2.** Germanic adjective *manniska-, human, in Old High German *mennisco*, human: MENSCH. **3.** Slavic suffixed form *mon-gyo- in Russian *muzh*, man: MUZHIK. [Pok. *manu-s* 700.]

man-². Hand. **1.** Latin *manus*, hand: MANACLE, MANAGE, (MANEGE), MANNER, MANUAL, MANUBRIUM, MANUS; AMANUENSIS, MAINTAIN, MANEUVER, MANICOTTI, MANICURE, MANIFEST, MANIPLE, MANIPULATION, MANSUETUDE, MANUFACTURE, MANUMIT, MANURE, MANUSCRIPT, MASTIFF, MORTMAIN, QUADRUMANOUS. **2.** Suffixed form *man-ko-, maimed in the hand, in Latin *mancus*, maimed, defective: MANQUÉ. **3.** Latin compound *manceps*, "he who takes by the hand" (-ceps, agential suffix, "taker"; see **kap-**), purchaser: EMANCIPATE. **4.** Latin compound *mandāre*, "to give into someone's hand" (*dare*, to give; see **dō-**), entrust, order: MANDAMUS, MANDATE; COMMAND, (COMMANDO), COMMEND, COUNTERMAND, DEMAND, RECOMMEND, REMAND. [Pok. *mə-r* 740.]

[mappa. Napkin, towel, cloth. Latin noun, said by Quintilian to be of Carthaginian origin. APRON, MAP, MOP, NAPERY, NAPKIN, NAPPE.]

[margaritēs. Pearl. Greek noun of Oriental origin (probably immediately from Iranian). Greek *margaritēs*, *margaron*, pearl: MARGARIC, MARGARIC ACID, (MARGARINE), MARGARITE¹, MARGARITE².]

mari-. Young woman. Suffixed form *mari-to-, "provided with a bride," in Latin *marītus*, married, a husband: MARITAL, MARRY¹. [Pok. *merǐo-* 738.]

marko-. Horse. **1.** Germanic *marhaz in Old High German *marahscalc*, "horse-servant" (Germanic *skalkaz, slave; see **skalkaz**), hence groom, later a title for a cavalry leader, akin to the Germanic source of Old French *mareschal*, cavalry officer: MARSHAL. **2.** Germanic feminine *marhjōn- in Old English *mere*, *miere*, mare: MARE¹. [Pok. *marko-* 700.]

[mas. Male. Latin adjective of unknown origin. Deriva-

tive *masculus,* male, manly: MACHO, MALE, MASCULINE; EMASCULATE.]

mat-. A kind of tool. Old English *mattuc,* mattock (probably borrowed from Vulgar Latin **mattea*): MATTOCK. [Pok. 2. *mat-* 700.]

māter-. Mother. Based ultimately on the baby-talk form **mā-²,** with the kinship term suffix *-ter-.* 1. Germanic **mōthar-* in Old English *mōdor,* mother: MOTHER¹. 2. Latin *māter,* mother: MATER, MATERNAL, MATERNITY, (MATRICULATE), MATRIX, MATRON; MADREPORE, MATRIMONY. 3. Greek *mētēr,* mother: METRO-; METROPOLIS. 4. Latin *māteriēs, māteria,* tree trunk (< "matrix," the tree's source of growth), hence hard timber used in carpentry, hence (by a calque on Greek *hulē,* wood, matter) substance, stuff, matter: MATERIAL, MATTER. 5. Greek compound *Dēmētēr,* name of the goddess of produce, especially cereal crops (*dē-,* possibly meaning "earth"): DEMETER. [Pok. *māter-* 700.]

math-. Worm. With uncertain preform, but clearly related, is Old English *moththe,* moth: MOTH. [Pok. 1. *math-* 700.]

[**Māwort-.** Name of an Italic deity who became the god of war at Rome (and also had agricultural attributes), hence also the name of the planet Mars (doubtless from its red color, the color of blood). Latin *Mārs* (stem *Mārt-*), Mars: MARCH, MARS, MARTIAL, MARTIAN.]

mazdo-. Pole, rod, mast. Germanic **mastaz* in Old English *mæst,* mast: MAST¹. [Pok. *mazdo-s* 701.]

me-¹. Oblique form of the personal pronoun of the first person singular. For the nominative see **eg.** 1. Germanic **mĕ-* in Old English *mē* (dative and accusative): ME, MYSELF. 2. Possessive adjective **mei-no-* in: **a.** Old English *mīn-* in: **a.** Old English *mīn,* my: MINE², MY; **b.** Middle Dutch *mijn,* my: MYNHEER. [Pok. 1. *me-* 702.]

me-². In the middle of. 1. Suffixed form **me-dhi* in Germanic **mid-* in Old English *mid,* among, with: MIDWIFE. 2. Suffixed form **me-ta* in Greek *meta,* between, with, beside, after: META-. See also **medhyo-.** [Pok. 2. *me-* 702.]

mē-¹. Expressing certain qualities of mind. Contracted from **meə-.* 1. Suffixed o-grade form **mō-to-* in Germanic **mōthaz* in (*i*) Old English *mōd,* mind, disposition: MOOD¹ (*ii*) Old High German *muot,* mind, spirit, in German *Gemüt,* spirit, feelings, temperament: GEMÜTLICH, GEMÜTLICHKEIT. 2. Perhaps Latin *mōs* (< **mō-s-*), wont, humor, manner, custom: MORAL, (MORALE), MORES, MOROSE. [Pok. 5. *mē-* 704.]

mē-². To measure. Contracted from **meə-.* **I.** Basic form *mē-.* 1. Suffixed form **mē-lo-* in Germanic **mēlaz* in Old English *mǣl,* "measure, mark, appointed time, time for eating, meal": MEAL²; PIECEMEAL. 2. Suffixed form **mē-ti-* in Latin *mētīrī,* to measure: MEASURE, (MENSURAL); (COMMENSURATE); DIMENSION, IMMENSE. 3. Possibly Greek *metron,* measure, rule, length, proportion, poetic meter (but this is referred by some to **med-**): METER¹, METER², (METER³), -METER, METRICAL, -METRY; DIAMETER, GEOMETRY, ISOMETRIC, METROLOGY, METRONOME. 4. Suffixed form **mē-trā-* in Sanskrit *mātrā,* a measure: MAHOUT. **II.** Extended and suffixed forms **mēn-, *mēn-en-, *mēn-s-, *mēn-ōt-,* moon, month (an ancient and universal unit of time measured by the moon). 1. Germanic **mēnōn-* in Old English *mōna,* moon: MOON, (MONDAY). 2. Germanic **mēnōth-* in Old English *mōnath,* month: MONTH. 3. Greek *mēn, mēnē,* month: AMENORRHEA, CATAMENIA, DYSMENORRHEA, (MENARCHE), MENISCUS, MENOPAUSE. 4. Latin *mēnsis,* month: MENSES, MENSTRUAL, (MENSTRUATE); BIMESTRIAL, SEMESTER, TRIMESTER. [Pok. 3. *mē-* 703, *mēnōt-* 731.]

mē-³. Big. Contracted from **meə-.* 1. Suffixed (comparative) form **mē-is-* in Germanic **maizōn-* in Old English *māra,* greater, and *māre* (adverb): MORE. 2. Suffixed (superlative) form **mē-isto-* in Germanic **maista-* in Old English *mǣst,* most: MOST. 3. Suffixed o-grade

form **mō-ro-* in Gaelic *mōr,* big, great: CLAYMORE. [Pok. 4. *mē-* 704.]

mē-⁴. To cut down grass or grain with a sickle or scythe. Contracted from **meə-.* 1. Germanic **mē-* in Old English *māwan,* to mow: MOW². 2. Suffixed form **mē-ti-* in Germanic **mēdiz* in Old English *mæth,* a mowing, a mown crop: AFTERMATH. 3. Suffixed form **mē-twā-,* a mown field, in Germanic **mēdwō* in Old English *mǣd* (oblique case *mǣdwe*), meadow: MEAD², MEADOW. [Pok. 2. *mē-* 703.]

med-. To take appropriate measures. 1. **a.** Germanic **metan* in Old English *metan,* to measure (out): METE¹; **b.** Germanic derivative **mētō,* measure, in Old English *gemǣte* (*ge-,* with; see **kom**), "commensurate," fit: MEET². 2. **a.** Latin *medērī,* to look after, heal, cure: MEDICAL, MEDICATE, (MEDICINE), (MEDICO); METHEGLIN, REMEDY; **b.** Latin *meditārī,* to think about, consider, reflect: MEDITATE. 3. Suffixed form **med-es-,* replaced in Latin by **modes-* by influence of *modus* (see 4. below), in: **a.** Latin *modestus,* "keeping to the appropriate measure," moderate: MODEST; IMMODEST. **b.** Latin *moderāre,* "to keep within measure," to moderate, control: MODERATE; IMMODERATE. 4. Suffixed o-grade form **mod-o-* in Latin *modus,* measure, size, limit, manner, harmony, melody: MODAL, MODE, MODEL, MODERN, MODICUM, MODIFY, MODULATE, MODULE, MODULUS, MOLD¹, (MOOD²), (MOULAGE); (ACCOMMODATE), (COMMODE), COMMODIOUS, (COMMODITY). 5. Suffixed o-grade form **mod-yo-* in Latin *modius,* a measure of grain: MODIOLUS, MUTCHKIN. 6. Possibly lengthened o-grade form **mōd-* in Germanic **mōt-,* ability, leisure, in: **a.** Old English *mōtan,* to have occasion, to be permitted or obliged: MOTE², MUST¹; **b.** Germanic compound **ē-mōt-ja-* (prefix **ē-,* meaning uncertain, from Indo-European *ē, ō;* see Pok. *ē̆, ō̆* 280) in Old English *ǣmetta,* rest, leisure: EMPTY. [Pok. 1. *med-* 705.]

medhu-. Honey; also mead. 1. Germanic **medu* in Old English *meodu,* mead: MEAD¹. 2. Greek *methu,* wine (> *methuein,* to be intoxicated): AMETHYST, METHYLENE. [Pok. *médhu* 707.]

medhyo-. Middle. 1. Germanic **midja-* in: **a.** Old English *midd(e),* middle: MID¹; AMID; **b.** West Germanic diminutive form **middila-* in Old English *middel,* middle: MIDDLE; **c.** Germanic compound **midja-gardaz,* "middle zone" (**gardaz,* enclosure, yard; see **gher-¹**), name of the earth conceived as an intermediate zone lying between heaven and hell, in Old Norse *Midhgardhr,* Midgard: MIDGARD. 2. Latin *medius,* middle, half: MEAN³, MEDIAL, MEDIAN, MEDIASTINUM, MEDIATE, MEDIUM, MITTEN, MIZZEN, MOIETY, MULLION; INTERMEDIATE, MEDIEVAL, MEDIOCRE, MEDITERRANEAN, MERIDIAN, MILIEU. 3. Greek *mesos,* middle: MESO-. See also **me-².** [Pok. *medhi-* 706.]

meg-. Great. 1. Germanic suffixed form **mik-ila-* in: **a.** Old English *micel, mycel,* great: MUCH; **b.** Old Norse *mikill,* great: MICKLE. 2. Suffixed form **mag-no-* in Latin *magnus,* great: MAGNATE, MAGNITUDE, MAGNUM; MAGNANIMOUS, MAGNIFIC, (MAGNIFICENT), (MAGNIFICO), (MAGNIFY), MAGNILOQUENT. 3. Suffixed (comparative) form **mag-yos-* in: **a.** Latin *mājor,* greater: MAJOR, MAJOR-DOMO, MAJORITY, MAJUSCULE, MAYOR; **b.** Latin *mājestās,* greatness, authority: MAESTOSO, MAJESTY; **c.** Latin *magister,* master, high official (< "he who is greater"): MAESTRO, MAGISTERIAL, MAGISTRAL, MAGISTRATE, MASTER, (MISTER), MISTRAL, (MISTRESS). 4. Suffixed (superlative) form **mag-samo-* in Latin *maximus,* greatest: MAXIM, MAXIMUM. 5. Suffixed form **mag-to-,* "made great," in Latin *mactus,* worshiped, blessed, sacred: MATADOR. 6. Suffixed (feminine) form **mag-ya-,* "she who is great," in Latin *Maia,* name of a goddess: MAY. 7. Suffixed form **meg-ə-l-* in Greek *megas* (stem *megal-*), great: MEGA-, MEGALO-; ACROMEGALY, ALMAGEST, OMEGA. 8. Variant form **megh-* in Sanskrit *mahā-,*

mahat-, great: MAHARAJAH, MAHARANI, MAHARISHI, MAHATMA, MAHAYANA, MAHOUT. [Pok. *meg(h)-* 708.]

mei-¹. To change, go, move; with derivatives referring to the exchange of goods and services within a society as regulated by custom or law. **1.** Latin *meāre*, to go, pass: MEATUS, CONGÉ, IRREMEABLE, PERMEATE. **2.** Suffixed o-grade form *moi-t-* in: **a.** Germanic *ga-maid-az* (*ga-*, intensive prefix; see **kom**), "changed (for the worse)," abnormal, in Old English *gemād*, insane: MAD; **b.** Latin *mūtāre*, to change: MEW¹, MOLT, MUTATE; COMMUTE, PERMUTE, REMUDA, TRANSMUTE; **c.** Latin *mūtuus*, "done in exchange," borrowed, reciprocal, mutual: MUTUAL. **3.** Suffixed extended zero-grade form *mit-to-* in Germanic *missa-*, "in a changed manner," abnormally, wrongly, in: **a.** Old English *mis-*, mis-: MIS-¹; **b.** Old Norse *mis(s)*, *mis(s)-*, miss, mis-: AMISS, MISTAKE; **c.** Germanic *missjan*, to go wrong, in Old English *missan*, to miss: MISS¹. **4.** Suffixed o-grade form *moi-n-* in compound adjective *ko-moin-i-*, "held in common" (*ko-*, together; see **kom**), in: **a.** Germanic *gamainiz* in Old English *gemǣne*, common, public, general: MEAN²; (DE-MEAN²); **b.** Latin *commūnis*, common, public, general: COMMON, COMMUNE, COMMUNICATE, (COMMUNISM). **5.** Suffixed o-grade form *moi-nes-* in: **a.** Latin *mūnus*, "service performed for the community," duty, work, "public spectacle paid for by a magistrate," gift: MUNICIPAL, MUNIFICENT, REMUNERATE; **b.** Latin *immūnis* (*in-*, negative prefix; see **ne**), exempt from public service: IMMUNE. **6.** Extended form *(ə)meigw-* in: **a.** Greek *ameibein*, to change: AMOEBA; **b.** Latin *migrāre*, to change one's place of living: MIGRATE; EMIGRATE. [Pok. 2. *mei-*, 3. *mei-* 710, *meigu-* 713, 2. *meit(h)-* 715.]

mei-². Small. **1.** Greek *meiōn*, less, lesser: MEIOSIS; MIOCENE. **2.** Latin *nimis*, too much, very (< *ne-mi-s*, "not little"; *ne-*, negative prefix; see **ne**). **3.** Suffixed zero-grade form *mi-nu-* in: **a.** Latin *minuere*, to reduce, diminish: MENU, (MINCE), MINUEND, MINUTE²; COMMINUTE, DIMINISH; **b.** Latin *minor* (influenced by the comparative suffix *-or*), less, lesser, smaller: MINOR, MINUS, MIS-¹; MINUSCULE; **c.** further suffixed (superlative) form *minu-mo-* in Latin *minimus*, least: MINIMUM; **d.** Latin *minister*, an inferior, servant (formed after *magister*, master; see **meg-**): MINESTRONE, MINISTER, MINISTRY, MYSTERY²; PREMUNITION. **3.** Russian *men'she*, less: MENSHEVIK. [Pok. 5. *mei-* 711.]

mei-³. To fix; to build fences or fortifications. **1.** Suffixed o-grade form *moi-ro-* in: **a.** Germanic *mair-ja-* in Old English *mǣre*, boundary, border, landmark: MERE³; **b.** Latin *mūrus*, wall: MURAL, MURAMIC ACID, MURE; IMMURE. **2.** Suffixed o-grade form *moi-ni-* in Latin *mūnīre*, to fortify, protect, strengthen: MUNITION; (AMMUNITION), PRAEMUNIRE, PREMUNITION. **3.** Possibly suffixed lengthened-grade form *mēi-t-* in Latin *mēta*, boundary stone, limit: METE². [Pok. 1. *mei-* 709.]

mei-⁴. To tie. **1.** Suffixed zero-grade form *mi-tro-*, "contract, that which binds," in: **a.** Greek *mitra*, headband, earilier a piece of armor worn around the waist: MITER; **b.** Old Persian *Mithra-*, name of a god (< "contract" < "bond"): MITHRAS; **c.** Russian *mir*, commune, joy, peace (possibly borrowed from Iranian): MIR. **2.** Possibly a suffixed zero-grade form *mi-to-* in Greek *mitos*, a warp thread: MITOSIS; DIMITY, MITOCHONDRION, SAMITE. [Pok. 4. *mei-* 710.]

mēi-. Mild. Contracted from *meəi-*. Suffixed zero-grade form *mī-ti-* (< *miə-ti-*) in Latin *mītis*, soft: MITIGATE. [Pok. 7. *mei-* 711.]

meigh-. To urinate. **1.** Germanic suffixed form *mih-stu-*, urine, hence mist, fine rain, in: **a.** Old English *mist*, mist: MIST; **b.** Middle Dutch *mieselen*, to drizzle, perhaps akin to the source of Middle English *misellen*, to drizzle: MIZZLE; **c.** Germanic diminutive form *mihst-ila-*, mistletoe (which is propagated through the droppings of the missel thrush), in Old English *mistel*, mistletoe: (MISSEL THRUSH), MISTLETOE. **2.** Suffixed form *migh-tu-* in

Latin *micturīre*, to want to urinate (desiderative of *meiere*, to urinate): MICTURATE. [Pok. *meigh-* 713.]

meik-. To mix. **1.** Variant form *meig-* in Greek *mignunai*, to mix: AMPHIMIXIS, APOMIXIS, PANMICTIC, PANMIXIS. **2.** Suffixed zero-grade form *mik-sk-* in Latin *miscēre* (past participle *mixtus*), to mix: MEDDLE, (MEDLEY), (MELANGE), MESTIZO, MISCELLANEOUS, MISCIBLE, MIX, MIXTURE; ADMIX, COMMIX, IMMIX, MISCEGENATION, (PELL-MELL), PROMISCUOUS. **3.** Possibly a Germanic form *maisk-* in Old English *māsc, mācs, māx*, mashed malt: MASH. [Pok. *meik-* 714.]

mei-no-. Opinion, intention. **1.** Germanic *main-* in Old English *mān*, opinion, complaint (> Middle English *mone*, complaint): MOAN; (BEMOAN). **2.** Germanic *mainjan* in Old English *mǣnan*, to signify, tell, complain of, moan: MEAN¹. [Pok. *mei-no-* 714.]

mel-¹. Soft; with derivatives referring to soft or softened materials of various kinds. **I.** Extended form *meld-*. **1.** Germanic *meltan* in Old English *meltan*, to melt: MELT. **2.** Possibly Germanic *miltja-* in Old English *milte*, spleen, and Middle Dutch *milte*, milt: MILT. **3.** Possibly Germanic *malta* in Old English *mealt*, malt: MALT. **4.** Suffixed variant form *mled-sno-* in Greek *blennos*, slime, also a name for the blenny: BLENNY. **5.** Suffixed zero-grade form *mḷd-wi-* in Latin *mollis*, soft: MOIL, MOLLIFY, MOLLUSK, MOUILLÉ; EMOLLIENT; **6.** Possibly nasalized variant form *mlad-* in Latin *blandus*, smooth, caressing, flattering, soft-spoken: BLAND, BLANDISH. **II.** Variant form *smeld-*. Germanic *smelt-* in: **a.** Middle Dutch and Middle Low German *smelten*, to smelt: SMELT¹; **b.** Old High German *smalz*, animal fat: SCHMALTZ; **c.** Italian *smalto*, melted glass: SMALT; **d.** Old French *esmail*, enamel: ENAMEL; **e.** perhaps Old English *smelt, smylt*, a marine fish, smelt: SMELT². **III.** Extended form *meldh-*. **1.** Germanic *mildja-* in Old English *milde*, mild: MILD. **2.** Possibly Greek *maltha*, a mixture of wax and pitch: MALTHA. **IV.** Suffixed form *mel-sko-* in Germanic *mil-sk-* in Old English *mel(i)sc, mylsc*, mild, mellow (> Middle English *melsche*, friable): MULCH. **V.** Extended form *mḷək-* in Greek *malakos*, soft: CHONDROMALACIA, MALACOLOGY, OSTEOMALACIA. **VI.** Possibly Celtic *molto-*, sheep, in Old French *moton*, sheep: MUTTON. **VII.** Suffixed zero-grade form *(ə)ml-u-* in Greek *amblus*, blunt, dull, dim: AMBLYGONITE, AMBLYOPIA. [Pok. 1. *mel-* 716.]

mel-². Of a darkish color. **1.** Greek *melas*, black: MELANO-; MELANCHOLY, PSILOMELANE. **2.** Greek *mullos*, a marine fish: MULLET; (SURMULLET). **3.** Latin *mulleus*, reddish purple (used only to designate a ceremonial shoe worn by Roman magistrates): MULE². **4.** Perhaps Germanic *mal-* in Middle Dutch *malen*, to paint: MAULSTICK. [Pok. 6. *mel-* 720.]

mel-³. A limb. Greek *melos*, limb, hence a musical member or phrase, hence music, song, melody: MELISMA; ACROMELIC, MELODRAMA, MELODY. [Pok. 5. *mel-* 720.]

mel-⁴. Strong, great. **1.** Suffixed (comparative) form *mel-yos-* in Latin *melior*, better: (AMELIORATE), MELIORATE, MELIORISM. **2.** Suffixed zero-grade form *mḷ-to-* in Latin *multus* (neuter *multum*), much, many: MOLTO, MULTI-, MULTITUDE. [Pok. 4. *mel-* 720.]

mel-⁵. Bad. Latin *malus*, bad, and *male*, ill (> *malignus*, harmful): MAL-, MALICE, MALIGN; DISMAL, MALADY, MALEDICT, MALEFACTOR, MALEVOLENT, MALVERSATION. [Pok. *mēlo-* 724.]

mel-⁶. Wool. Possibly suffixed zero-grade form *mḷ-no-* in Greek *mallos*, wool. [Pok. 2. *mel-* 719.]

mel-⁷. To miss, deceive. Germanic *mal-* in Middle Dutch *mal*, foolish, silly: MALLEMUCK. [Pok. 2. *mel-* 719.]

meldh-. To pray, speak words to a deity. Germanic *meld-* in Old High German *meldōn*, to proclaim, reveal: MELD¹. [Pok. 1. *meldh-* 722.]

melə-. Also **mel-**. To crush, grind; with derivatives referring to various ground or crumbling substances (such as flour) and to instruments for grinding or crush-

ing (such as millstones). **1.** O-grade form **mol-* in Germanic **mal-* in: **a.** obsolete Dutch *malen*, to whirl: MAELSTROM; **b.** Germanic suffixed form **mal-mōn-* in Old English *mealm-*, perhaps "crumbling, friable" (only in compounds, as *mealmstān*, sandstone): MALM. **2.** Full-grade form **mel-* in Germanic suffixed form **mel-wa-* in Old English *melu*, flour, meal: MEAL¹. **3.** Zero-grade form **ml̥-* in Germanic **mul-* in: **a.** suffixed form **mul-dō* in *(i)* Old English *molde*, soil: MOLD³ *(ii)* Old Norse **muldhra*, to crumble, akin to the probable Scandinavian source of MOLDER; **b.** Middle Dutch *mul*, dust: MULL². **4.** Full-grade form **mel-* in: **a.** Latin *molere*, to grind (grain), and its derivative *mola*, a millstone, mill, coarse meal customarily sprinkled on sacrificial animals: MILL¹, MOLAR², MOLE⁴, (MOULIN); IMMOLATE, ORMOLU; **b.** suffixed form **mel-iyo-* in Latin *milium*, millet: MEALIE, MILIUM, MILLET. **5.** Suffixed variant form **mal-ni-* in Latin *malleus*, hammer, mallet: MALLEABLE, (MALLET), MALLEUS, MAUL; PALL-MALL. **6.** Zero-grade form **ml̥-* in Greek *mulē, mulos*, millstone, mill: AMYLUM, MYLONITE. **7.** Possibly extended form **mlī-* in: **a.** possibly Greek *bliton*, blite (a plant that in some varieties has dusty leaves): BLITE; **b.** Russian *blin*, pancake: BLINI, BLINTZ. [Pok. 1. *mel-* 716.]

melg-. To rub off; also to milk. **I. 1.** Zero-grade form **mlg-* in Latin *mulgēre*, to milk: EMULSION. **2.** Full-grade form **melg-* in Germanic **melkan*, to milk, was contaminated with an unrelated noun for milk, cognate with the Greek and Latin forms given in II. below, to form the blend **meluk-* in: **a.** Old English *meolc, milc*, milk: MILK; **b.** suffixed form **meluk-ja-*, giving milk, in Old English *-milce*, milch: MILCH **c.** Old High German *miluh*, milk: MILCHIG. **II.** Included here to mark the unexplained fact that no common Indo-European noun for milk can be reconstructed is another root **g(a)lag-, *g(a)lakt-*, milk, found only in: **a.** Greek *gala* (stem *galakt-*): (GALACTIC), GALACTO-, GALAXY, AGALACTIA, POLYGALA; **b.** Latin *lac* (stem *lact-*), milk: (LACTATE), LACTEAL, LACTESCENT, LACTO-, LETTUCE; **c.** the blended Germanic form cited in I. 2. above. [Pok. *melg-* 722, *glag-* 400.]

melit-. Honey. **1.** Greek *meli*, honey: HYDROMEL, MARMALADE, MELILOT, OENOMEL. **2.** Latin *mel* (stem *mell-*), honey: MELLIFEROUS, MELLIFLUOUS, MOLASSES. **3.** Germanic **melith-* in compound **melith-dauwaz* (**dauwaz*, dew; see **dheu-²**), honeydew (a substance secreted by aphids on leaves; it was formerly imagined to be distilled from the air like dew), in Old English *mildēaw*, honeydew, nectar, later also mildew: MILDEW. [Pok. *melit-* 723.]

mēlo-. Also **smēlo-.** Small animal. Zero-grade form **smǝlo-* in Germanic **smal-*, small animal, hence also "small," in Old English *smæl*, small: SMALL. [Pok. *mēlo-* 724.]

[**mēlon.** An apple, or any seed- or pit-bearing fruit. Attic Greek noun (Doric *mālon*), possibly borrowed from a Mediterranean language. Earliest form **maǝlo-*, attested in Hittite *mahla*, grapevine. MELINITE, MELON; CHAMOMILE, MALIC ACID, MARMALADE.]

melst-. To burgeon. Zero-grade form **ml̥st-* in Greek *blastanein*, to burgeon, and *blastos*, shoot, bud, hence embryo, germ: -BLAST, BLASTEMA, BLASTO-, BLASTULA. [Pok. *melōdh-* 725.]

mēms-. Flesh, meat. **1.** Suffixed form **mēms-ro-* in Latin *membrum*, limb, member: MEMBER, MEMBRANE. **2.** Suffixed form **mēms-no-* in Greek *mēninx*, membrane: MENINX. [Pok. *mēmso-* 725.]

men-¹. To think; with derivatives referring to various qualities and states of mind and thought. **I.** Zero-grade form **mn̥-*. **1.** Suffixed form **mn̥-ti-* in: **a.** Germanic **ga-mundi-* (**ga-*, intensive prefix; see **kom**), in Old English *gemynd*, memory, mind: MIND; **b.** Latin *mēns* (stem *ment-*), mind: MENTAL; AMENT², DEMENT; **c.** Latin *mentiō*, remembrance, mention: MENTION. **2.** Suffixed form **mn̥-to-* in Greek *-matos*, "willing": AUTOMATIC. **3.** Suffixed form **mn̥-yo-* in: **a.** Greek *mainesthai*, to be

mad: MAENAD; **b.** Avestan *mainyu*, spirit: AHRIMAN. **II.** Full-grade form **men-*. **1.** Suffixed form **men-ti-* in Germanic **minthjō* in: **a.** Old High German *minna*, love: MINNESINGER; **b.** Middle Dutch *minne*, love: MINIKIN. **2. a.** Reduplicated form in Latin *meminisse*, to remember: MEMENTO; **b.** Latin *comminīscī* (*com-*, intensive prefix; see **kom**), to contrive by thought: COMMENT; **c.** Latin *reminīscī* (*re-*, again, back; see **re-**), to recall, recollect: REMINISCENT; **d.** possibly Latin *Minerva*, name of the goddess of wisdom: MINERVA. **3. a.** Greek *menos*, spirit: EUMENIDES; **b.** Greek *Mentōr*, man's name (probably meaning "adviser"): MENTOR; **c.** Greek *mania*, madness: MANIA, MANIAC; **d.** Greek *mantis*, seer (< "he who is mad"): -MANCY, MANTIC, MANTIS. **4.** Sanskrit *mantrah*, counsel, prayer, hymn: MANDARIN, MANTRA. **III.** O-grade form **mon-*. **1.** Suffixed (causative) form **mon-eyo-* in Latin *monēre*, to remind, warn, advise (with probable derivative *monēta*, an epithet of Juno): (MINT¹), MONEY, MONISH, MONITION, MONITOR, MONSTER, MONUMENT, MUSTER; ADMONISH, DEMONSTRATE, PREMONITION, SUMMON. **2.** Suffixed o-grade form **montwa* in Greek *mousa*, a muse: MOSAIC, MUSE, MUSEUM, MUSIC. **IV.** Extended form *mnā-*. **1.** Reduplicated form in Greek *mimnēskein*, to remember (> *amnēsia*, forgetfulness, and *amnēstos*, forgotten): MNEMOSYNE; AMNESIA, AMNESTY, ANAMNESIS. **2.** Greek *mnēmōn*, mindful: MNEMONIC. **V.** Indo-European verb phrase **mens dhē-*, "to set mind" (see **dhē-¹**), underlying compound **mns-dhē* in Avestan *mazdā-*, wise: AHURA MAZDA, ORMAZD. [Pok. 3. *men-* 726, *mendh-* 730.]

men-². To project. **1.** Suffixed zero-grade form **mn̥-to-* in a western Indo-European word for a projecting body part, variously "chin, jaw, mouth," in Germanic **munthaz* in Old English *mūth* mouth: MOUTH. **2.** Latin *minae*, projecting points, threats (> *minārī*, to threaten): MENACE, MINACIOUS; AMENABLE, DEMEAN¹, PROMENADE. **3.** Latin *-minēre*, to project, jut, threaten: EMINENT, IMMINENT, PROMINENT. **4.** Suffixed o-grade form **mon-ti-* in Latin *mōns* (stem *mont-*), mountain: MONS, (MONTAGNARD), MONTANE, MONTE, MONTICULE, MOUNT¹, MOUNT², MOUNTAIN; AMOUNT, ULTRAMONTANE. [Pok. 1. *men-* 726, 2. *menth-* 732.]

men-³. To remain. Variant suffixed (stative) form **man-ē-* in Latin *manēre*, to remain: MANOR, MANSE, MANSION, (MÉNAGE); IMMANENT, PERMANENT, REMAIN. [Pok. 5. *men-* 729.]

men-⁴. Small, isolated. **1.** Greek *manos*, rare, sparse: MANOMETER. **2.** Suffixed o-grade form **mon-wo-* in Greek *monos*, alone, only, single, sole: MONAD, MONASTERY, MONK, MONO-; PSEUDOMONAD. **3.** Possibly also suffixed form **men-i-*, a small fish, in Old English *myne, mynwe*, minnow, perhaps the source of Middle English *meneu*, a small fish: MINNOW. [Pok. 4. *men-* 728, *meni-* 731.]

mend-. Physical defect, fault. **1.** Latin *mendum, menda*, defect, fault: MENDICANT; AMEND, EMEND, (MEND). **2.** Latin *mendāx*, lying, liar: MENDACIOUS. [Pok. *mend(ā)* 729.]

mendh-¹. To learn. Zero-grade form **mn̥dh-* in Greek *manthanein* (aorist stem *math-*), to learn: MATHEMATICAL, (MATHEMATICS); CHRESTOMATHY, POLYMATH. [Pok. *mendh-* 730.]

mendh-². To chew. **1.** Latin *mandere*, to chew: MANDIBLE, (MANGE), MANGER. **2.** Zero-grade form **mn̥dh-* in: **a.** Greek *masasthai* (< **math-ya-*), to chew: MASSETER; **b.** Greek *mastax*, the model for expressive Greek (Doric) *mustax*, upper lip, mustache: (MOSTACCIOLI), MUSTACHE; **c.** Greek *mastikhan*, to grind the teeth: MASTICATE. [Pok. 2. *menth-* 732.]

menegh-. Copious. Germanic **managa-* in Old English *manig, mænig*, many: MANY. [Pok. *men(e)gh-* 730.]

meng-. To furbish. **1.** Latin *mangō*, furbisher, gem polisher, swindler: MONGER. **2.** Greek *manganon*, magic

charm, contrivance, engine of war: MANGONEL. [Pok. *meng-* 731.]

mer-¹. To flicker; with derivatives referring to dim states of illumination. **1.** Suffixed form **mer-o-* in Latin *merus*, pure, unadulterated (< "unmixed wine" < "clear liquid"): MERE¹. **2.** Extended form **merk-* in Germanic **murgana-* in: **a.** Old English *morgen*, morning: MORN, MORNING, MORROW; **b.** Middle Dutch *morghen*, morning: MORGEN; **c.** Old High German *morgan*, morning: MORGANATIC. **3.** Possibly extended root **mergʷ-* in Germanic **merkwia-*, twilight, in Old English *mirce*, darkness: MURK. [Pok. 2. *mer-* 733.]

mer-². To rub away, harm. **I. 1.** Germanic **marōn-*, goblin, in Old English *mare*, *mære*, goblin, incubus: NIGHTMARE. **2.** Greek *marainein*, to waste away, wither: MARASMUS; AMARANTH. **3.** Probably suffixed zero-grade form **mr̥-to-*, "ground down," in Latin *mortārium*, mortar: MORTAR. **4.** Possibly extended root **merd-* in Latin *mordēre* (past participle *morsus*), to bite: MORDACIOUS, MORDANT, MORDENT, MORSEL; PREMORSE, REMORSE. **5.** Possibly suffixed form **mor-bho-*, "undying, immortal" disease (but more likely of unknown origin): MORBID. **II.** Possibly the same root, but more likely distinct, is **mer-*, "to die," with derivatives referring to death and to human beings as subject to death. **1.** Zero-grade form **mr̥-* in: **a.** suffixed form **mr̥-tro-* in Germanic suffixed form **mur-thra-* in Old English *morthor*, murder: MURDER; **b.** suffixed form **mr̥-ti-* in Latin *mors* (stem *mort-*), death: MORT¹, MORTAL, MORTUARY; AMORTIZE, (IMMORTAL), MORTGAGE, MORTIFY, MORTMAIN, POSTMORTEM; **c.** suffixed form **mr̥-yo-* in Latin *morī*, to die: MORIBUND, MURRAIN; **d.** prefixed and suffixed form **n̥-mr̥-to-*, "undying, immortal" (**n̥-*, negative prefix; see **ne**), in *(i)* Greek *ambrotos*, immortal, divine (*a-* + *mbrotos*, *brotos*, mortal): AMBROSIA *(ii)* Sanskrit *amṛta*, immortal (*a-* + *mṛta*, death): AMRITA. **2.** Suffixed o-grade form **mor-t-yo-* in Old Persian *martiya-*, a mortal man, in Iranian compound **martiya-khvāra-* (attested in Persian *mard-khvār*), "man-eater" (**khvāra-*, to eat; see **swel-¹**), probable source of Greek *mantikhōras* (corrupted from *martiokhōras*), manticore: MANTICORE. See extended root **smerd-**. [Pok. 4. *mer-*, 5. *mer-* 735.]

mer-³. To tie. Possibly in: **a.** Middle Dutch *marren*, to tie: MARLINE; **b.** Middle Low German *mōren*, to tie: MOOR¹. [Pok. 1. *mer-* 733.]

mere-. To hinder, delay. Latin *mora*, a delay: MORA, (MORATORIUM), MORATORY; DEMUR, REMORA. [In Pok. *(s)mer-* 969.]

merg-. Boundary, border. **1.** Germanic **mark-*, boundary, border territory; also to mark out a boundary by walking around it (ceremonially "beating the bounds"); also a landmark, boundary marker, and a mark in general (and in particular a mark on a metal currency bar, hence a unit of currency); these various meanings are widely represented in Germanic descendants and in Romance borrowings: **a.** Old English *mearc*, boundary, landmark, sign, trace: MARK¹; **b.** Middle Dutch *mark*, border: MARGRAVE; **c.** Old French *marc*, *marche*, border country: MARCH², (MARQUEE), MARQUIS, (MARQUISE); **d.** Late and Medieval Latin *marca*, boundary, border: MARCHIONESS; **e.** Old Italian *marcare*, to mark out: DEMARCATION; **f.** Old English *marc* and Middle High German *marke*, a mark of weight or money: MARK²; **g.** Swedish *mark*, a mark of money: MARKKA. **2.** Germanic **markja-*, mark, border, in Old Norse *merki*, a mark, possible source of Old French *marque*, a mark: MARQUETRY; REMARK. **3.** Germanic denominative verb **markōn* in Frankish **markōn*, to mark out (> Old French *march(i)er*, to trample): MARC, MARCH¹. **4.** Latin *margō*, border, edge: MARGIN. [Pok. *mereg-* 738.]

mergh-. To wet, sprinkle, rain. Variant form **mregh-* in Greek *brekhein*, to wet: EMBROCATE. [Pok. *meregh-* 738.]

merk-¹. To decay. Latin *marcēre*, to decay, wither: MARCESCENT. [Pok. 1. *merk-* 739.]

[merk-². Italic root, possibly from Etruscan, referring to aspects of commerce. **1.** Latin *merx* (stem *merc-*), merchandise (> *mercārī*, to trade): MARKET, (MART), MERCER, MERCHANT; COMMERCE. **2.** Latin *merces*, pay, reward, price: MERCENARY, MERCY. **3.** Probably Latin *Mercurius*, the god of (inter alia) commerce: MERCURY. [In Pok. *merk-* 739.]]

[merph-. Form. Greek root of unknown origin. **1.** Suffixed o-grade form **morph-ā-* in Greek *morphē*, form, beauty, outward appearance: -MORPH, MORPHEME, MORPHO-, MORPHOSIS. **2.** Possibly borrowed from Greek *morphē*, via Etruscan, is Latin *forma*, form, shape, contour, appearance, beauty: FORM, FORMAL, FORMULA; CONFORM, CORACIIFORM, DEFORM. [In Pok. 2. *mer-* 733.]]

mers-. To trouble. Suffixed o-grade form **mors-eyo-* in Germanic **marzjan* in Old English *merran*, *mierran*, to impede: MAR. [Pok. 6. *mer-* 737.]

meu-. Damp; with derivatives referring to swampy ground and vegetation and to figurative qualities of wetness. **1.** Extended form **meus-* in Germanic **meus-*, **mus-* in: **a.** Old English *mos*, bog: MOSS; **b.** Old Norse *mosi*, bog, moss, akin to the Scandinavian source of LITMUS. **2.** Germanic suffixed form **meuz-i-* in Old Norse *mȳrr*, bog: MIRE; (QUAGMIRE). **3.** Suffixed zero-grade form **mus-to-* in Latin *mustus*, new, newborn (< "wet"): MUST³, MUSTARD. **4.** Possibly suffixed extended zero-grade form **mū-ro-* in Greek *murios*, countless (< "flowing, endless"): MYRIAD. **5.** Possibly suffixed extended zero-grade form **mud-so-* in Greek *musos*, uncleanness: MYSOPHILIA, MYSOPHOBIA. [Pok. 1. *meu-* 741.]

meue-. To push away. Latin *movēre*, to move (> *mobilis*, neuter *mobile*, fickle, changeable): MOB, MOBILE, MOMENT, (MOMENTOUS), MOMENTUM, MOSSO, (MOTIF), MOTION, MOTIVE, MOTOR, MOVE, MOVEMENT; COMMOTION, EMOTION, PROMOTE, (REMOTE), (REMOVE). [Pok. 2. *meu-* 743.]

meug-¹. To act surreptitiously. Germanic **muk-* or Celtic **mug-* in Old French *muchier*, to skulk: MOOCH. [Pok. 1. *meug-* 743.]

meug-². Slimy, slippery; with derivatives referring to various wet or slimy substances and conditions. Enlarged form of **meu-**. **1.** Nasalized form **mu-n-g-* in Latin *mungere*, to blow the nose: EMUNCTORY. **2.** Possibly Germanic **(s)mug-*, referring to wetness and also to figurative slipperiness: **a.** Old English *smoc*, shirt: SMOCK; **b.** Middle High German *smuck*, "clothing," adornment, jewel: SCHMUCK; **c.** Old Norse *mugga*, drizzle, akin to the source of Middle English *muggen*, to drizzle: MUGGY; **d.** Low German *smukkelen*, *smuggeln*, to smuggle (< "to slip contraband through"): SMUGGLE; **e.** Middle Low German *smucken*, to adorn (< "to make sleek"): SMUG; **f.** Old Norse *mygla*, mold, mildew, akin to the source of Middle English *molde*, mold: MOLD². **3.** Germanic **meuk-* in Old Norse *mjūkr*, soft: MEEK. **4.** Variant form **meuk-* in Latin *mūcus*, mucus: MOIST, MUCILAGE, MUCO-, MUCUS, (MUSTY). **5.** Zero-grade variant form **muk-* in Greek *mukēs*, fungus, mushroom: -MYCETE, MYCO-; STREPTOMYCES, (STREPTOMYCIN); **b.** suffixed form **muk-so-* in Greek *muxa*, mucus, lamp wick (< "nozzle of a lamp" < "nostril"): MATCH², MYXO-. [Pok. 2. *meug-* 744.]

mezg-¹. To dip, plunge. **1.** Latin *mergere*, to dip, dive: MERGE; EMERGE, IMMERSE, SUBMERGE. **2.** Latin *mergus*, diver (water bird): MERGANSER. [Pok. 1. *mezg-* 745.]

mezg-². To knit. Germanic **mēsk-* in Middle Dutch *masche*, *maesche*, knitted fabric: MESH. [Pok. 2. *mezg-* 746.]

[mimos. A mime. Greek noun of unknown origin. MIME, MIMESIS, MIMIC.]

[miser. Wretched, unfortunate. Latin adjective of unknown origin. MISER, MISERABLE, MISERY; COMMISERATE.]

mizdho-. Reward. West Germanic *mēdō- in Old English mēd, reward, compensation, meed: MEED. [Pok. mizdho- 746.]

mō-. To exert oneself. Suffixed form *mō-l- in: **a.** Latin mōlēs, heavy bulk, mass, massive structure: MOLE[3], MOLECULE; DEMOLISH; **b.** Latin molestus (irregularly from mōlēs), labored, difficult, troublesome: MOLEST. [Pok. mō- 746.]

mōd-. To meet, assemble. **1.** Germanic *mōtjan in Old English mētan, to meet: MEET[1]. **2.** Germanic *mōta- in Old English mōt, gemōt (ge-, together; see kom), meeting, moot, assembly, council: MOOT; FOLKMOTE, GEMOT, WITENAGEMOT. **3.** Perhaps suffixed zero-grade form *mədʰ-tlo- in Germanic *mathla- in Old Norse māl, speech, agreement (> Norwegian mål, speech): MAIL[3]; (BLACKMAIL), RIKSMAL. [Pok. mōd- 746.]

modhro-. A color. Germanic *madraz in Old English mædere, madder: MADDER[1]. [Pok. modhro- 747.]

molko-. Skin bag. Germanic *malhō- in Old High German malha, pouch, bag, akin to the Germanic source of Old French male, bag: MAIL[1]. [Pok. molko- 747.]

mon-. Neck, nape of the neck. **1.** Germanic *manō in Old English manu, mane: MANE. **2.** Latin monīle, necklace: MONILIFORM. [Pok. mono- 747.]

mori-. Body of water; lake (?), sea (?). **1.** Germanic *mari- in: **a.** Old English mere (> Middle English mere), sea, lake, pond: MERE[2]; (MERMAID); **b.** Old Norse marr, sea, akin to the Scandinavian source of MARRAM; **c.** Old High German mari (> German Meer), sea: MEERSCHAUM. **2.** Germanic *mariska-, water-logged land, in: **a.** Old English mersc, merisc, marsh: MARSH; **b.** Old French marasc, maresc, marsh: MORASS. **3.** Latin mare (> French mer), sea: MARE[2], (MARINARA), MARINE, MARITIME; BÊCHE-DE-MER, MARICOLOUS, MARICULTURE, ORMER, ULTRAMARINE. [Pok. mori 748.]

mormor-. Also **murmur-.** Murmur. Imitative root. Latin murmur, a murmur: MURMUR. [Pok. mormor- 748.]

moro-. Blackberry, mulberry. **1.** Greek moron, mulberry, in sukomoros, an African fig tree: SYCAMORE. **2.** Latin mōrum, mulberry (probably from Greek): MORULA, MURREY; MULBERRY. [Pok. moro- 749.]

morwi-. Ant. **1.** Germanic variant form *meur- in Danish myre, ant, akin to the Scandinavian source of Middle English mire, ant: PISMIRE. **2.** Variant form *morm- in: **a.** Greek murmēx, ant: MYRMECO-; **b.** (with dissimilation) Latin formīca, ant: FORMIC, FORMICARY; FORMICIVOROUS. [Pok. moru̯i- 749.]

mō(u)lo-. Name of a plant. Greek mōlu, moly: MOLY. [Pok. mō(u)-lo- 750.]

mō(u)ro-. Foolish. Greek mōros, foolish: MORON; OXYMORON. [Pok. mō(u)ro- 750.]

mozgo-. Marrow. Germanic *mazgō- in Old English mærg, mærh, marrow: MARROW. [Pok. moz-g-o- 750.]

mregh-m(n)o-. Brain. **1.** Germanic *bragna- in Old English brægen, brain: BRAIN. **2.** Greek bregma, the front part of the head: BREGMA. [Pok. mregh-m(n)o- 750.]

mregh-u-. Short. **I.** Suffixed form *mregh-w-i- in Latin brevis, short (> brūma, the shortest day, winter): BRIEF, BRUMAL; ABBREVIATE, (ABRIDGE). **II.** Zero-grade form *mr̥ghu-. **1.** Germanic *murgja-, short, also pleasant, joyful, in: **a.** Old English myrge, mirige, pleasant: MERRY; **b.** Germanic *murgithō, pleasantness, in Old English myrgth, pleasure, joy: MIRTH. **2.** Greek brakhus, short: BRACHY-; AMPHIBRACH, TRIBRACH. **3.** Greek comparative brakhiōn, shorter, hence also "upper arm" (as opposed to the longer forearm): BRACE, BRACERO, BRACHIUM, BRASSARD, BRASSIERE, PRETZEL; EMBRACE. [Pok. mreghu- 750.]

mu[1]-. Imitative of inarticulate sounds. **1.** Reduplicated form in Germanic *mum- in: **a.** Middle Low German mummen, to be silent, akin to Middle English mum, silent: MUM[1]; **b.** Icelandic mumpa, to eat greedily, akin to the probable Scandinavian source of dialectal English mump, to mumble, grimace: MUMPS; **c.** Low German

mops, fool, also pug dog (> German Mops, pug dog): ROLLMOPS; **d.** Old French momer, to act (in dumb show): MUM[2]. **2.** Germanic *mut- in Old Norse mudhla, akin to the source of Middle English muteren, muttren, to mutter: MUTTER. **3.** Latin muttīre, to mutter: MOT, MOTTO. **4.** Lengthened-grade form *mū- in Latin mūtus, silent, dumb: MUTE. **5.** Greek muein, to close the eyes (< "to close the lips"): MIOSIS, MYOPIA, MYSTERY[1], (MYSTIC). [Pok. 1. mū- 751.]

mu-[2]. Gnat, fly. Imitative root. **1.** Germanic *mukjō- in Old English mycg, midge: MIDGE. **2.** Suffixed form *mus-kā in Latin musca, a fly: MOSQUITO, MUSCA, MUSCARINE, MUSH[2], MUSKET. **3.** Suffixed form *mus-ya in Greek muia, mua, a fly: MYIASIS. [Pok. 2. mū- 752.]

mūk-. A heap. Germanic *mūgōn-, *mūhōn- in: **a.** Old English mūga, mūha, mūwa, heap of grain: MOW[1]; **b.** Old Norse mūgi, heap, akin to the probable Scandinavian source of MOGUL[1]. [Pok. mŭk- 752.]

[mundus. Women's cosmetics, also world (probably by a calque on Greek kosmos, order, feminine adornment, world-order, universe). Latin noun of unknown origin; possibly from Etruscan. MUNDANE; ULTRAMUNDANE.]

mūs-. A mouse; also a muscle (from the resemblance of a flexing muscle to the movements of a mouse). **1.** Germanic *mūs- (plural *mūsiz) in Old English mūs (plural mȳs), mouse: MOUSE. **2.** Latin mūs, mouse: MURINE, MUSCLE, MUSTELINE. **3.** Greek mus, mouse, muscle: MYELO-, MYO-; EPIMYSIUM, MYOSOTIS, MYSTICETE, PERIMYSIUM, SYRINGOMYELIA. [Pok. mūs 752.]

[mūsum. Snout. Medieval Latin noun of unknown origin. MUSE, MUZZLE.]

mut-. Cut short. Suffixed form *mut-il- in Latin mutilus, maimed: MUTILATE. [Pok. mut-o-s 753.]

[nabja-. Bird's beak. Germanic root. Old English neb(b), beak: NEB, (NIB), (NIPPLE).]

nana. Child's word for a nurse or female adult other than its mother. **1.** Greek nanna, aunt, whence nannas, uncle, whence nan(n)os, "little old man," dwarf: NANO-. **2.** Late and Medieval Latin nonna, aunt, old woman, nun: NUN[1]. **3.** English (directly from baby talk) NANA, NANNY. [Pok. nana 754.]

nas-. Nose. **1.** Germanic zero-grade form *nusō in Old English nosu, nose: NOSE, (NUZZLE); NOSTRIL. **2.** Germanic nasja- in Old English næss, headland: NESS. **3.** Lengthened-grade form *nās-, in: **a.** Latin nāris, nostril: NARES; **b.** expressive form *nāss- in Latin nāsus, nose: NASAL, NASO-; NASTURTIUM, PINCE-NEZ. **4.** Expressive Indo-Aryan form *nakka- in Romany nāk, nose: NARK[2]. [Pok. nas- 755, neu-ks 768.]

nāu-[1]. Death; to be exhausted. Contracted from *naəu-. **1.** Suffixed zero-grade form *nəu-ti- in Germanic *naudi- in Old English nēod, nēd, distress, necessity: NEED. **2.** Suffixed form *nāw-i-, corpse, in Germanic *nawi- in Old Norse nār, corpse: NARWHAL. **3.** Slavic suffixed extended form *naud-ā in: **a.** Polish nuda, boredom: NUDNIK; **b.** Russian nudnyi, tedious: NUDGE[2]. [Pok. 2. nāu- 756.]

nāu-[2]. Boat. Contracted from *naəu-. **1.** Latin nāvis, ship: NACELLE, NAVAL, NAVICULAR, NAVIGATE, NAVY. **2.** Greek naus, ship, and nautēs, sailor: NAUSEA, NAUTICAL, NAUTILUS, (NOISE); AERONAUT, AQUANAUT, ARGONAUT, ASTRONAUT, COSMONAUT. [Pok. 1. nāu- 755.]

n̥dher-. Under. **1.** Germanic *under- in Old English under, under: UNDER. **2.** Latin īnferus, lower: INFERIOR. **3.** Latin īnfernus, lower: INFERNAL, (INFERNO). **4.** Latin īnfrā, below: INFRA-. [Pok. n̥dhos 771.]

ne. Not. **1.** Germanic *ne-, *na- in: **a.** Old English ne (> Middle English ne), not, and nā, no: NAUGHT, (NAUGHTY), NEITHER, NEVER, NILL, NO[1], NO[2], NONE, (NOR[1]), NOT, NOTHING; **b.** Old Norse ne, not: NAY; **c.** Old High German ne, ni, not: NIX[2]. **2.** Latin ne-, not, and nullus, none (ne- + ūllus, any; see oi-no-): ANNUL, NEFARIOUS, NESCIENCE, NEUTER, (NICE), NISI, NULL, NULLIFY, NULLIPARA. **3.** Latin nimis, too much, exces-

sively, very (< *ne-mi-s, "not little"; *mi-, little; see **mei-²**): NIMIETY. **4.** Latin *nihilum*, nothing (< *nehīlum, "not a whit, nothing at all"; *hīlum*, a thing, trifle; origin unknown), contracted to *nihil*, *nīl*, nothing: NIHILISM, (NIHILITY), NIL; ANNIHILATE. **5.** Latin *nōn*, not (< *ne-oinom, "not one thing"; *oino-, one; see **oi-no-**): NON-. **6.** Italic *nek, not, in: **a.** Latin prefix *neg-*, not: NEGLECT, (NEGLIGEE), NEGOTIATE; **b.** Latin *negāre*, to deny: NEGATE; ABNEGATE, DENY, RENEGADE, (RENEGE). **7.** Greek *nē-*, not: NEPENTHE. **8.** Zero-grade combining form *n̥- in: **a.** Germanic *un- in Old English *un-*, not: UN-¹; **b.** Latin *in-*, not: IN-¹; **c.** Greek *a-, an-*, not: A-¹, (AN-); **d.** Sanskrit *a-, an-*, not: AHIMSA, AMRITA. [Pok. *ne* 756.]

nebh-. Cloud. **1.** Suffixed form *nebh-lo- in Germanic *nibla- probably in Old Norse *nifl-*, "mist" or "dark": NIFLHEIM. **2.** Suffixed form *nebh-elā- in: **a.** Latin *nebula*, cloud: NEBULA, NEBULOUS; **b.** Greek *nephelē*, cloud: NEPHELINE; NEPHELOMETER. **3.** Suffixed form *nebh-es- in Greek *nephos*, cloud: NEPHOLOGY. **4.** Nasalized form *ne-m-bh- in Latin *nimbus*, rain, cloud, aura: NIMBUS. See **ombhro-**. [Pok. *(enebh-)* 315.]

ned-. To bind, tie. **1.** O-grade form *nod- in: **a.** Germanic *nati- in Old English *net(t)*, a net: NET¹; **b.** Germanic *nat-ilo*, a nettle (nettles or plants of closely related genera such as hemp were used as a source of fiber), in Old English *netel(e)*, *netle*, nettle: NETTLE; **c.** Germanic *nat-sk- in Anglo-Norman *nouch*, brooch: OUCH². **2.** Lengthened o-grade form *nōdo- in Latin *nōdus*, a knot: NODE, NODULE, NODUS; DÉNOUEMENT. **3.** Re-formation of the root in Latin *nectere* (past participle *nexus*), to tie, bind, connect: NEXUS; (ADNEXA), ANNEX, CONNECT [Pok. 1. *ned-* 758.]

negʷh-ro-. Kidney. Greek *nephros*, kidney: NEPHRO-; MESONEPHROS, METANEPHROS, PERINEPHRIUM, PRONEPHROS. [In Pok. *engʷ-* 319.]

negʷr-o-. Adjective denoting various colors; with derivatives like Greek *nebros*, "fawn." Latin *niger*, black: NEGRO, NIELLO, NIGRESCENCE, NIGRITUDE; DENIGRATE, NECROMANCY, NIGROSINE.

[**nēhw-iz**. Near. Germanic root. Old English *nēah*, near: NEAR, NEIGHBOR, NEXT, NIGH.]

nei-. To be excited, shine. **1.** Suffixed form *nei-to- in Germanic *nītha-*, animosity, in Old Norse *nīdh*, scorn (> *nīdhingr*, villain): NIDDERING. **2.** Suffixed zero-grade form *ni-to- in Latin *nitēre*, to shine: NEAT¹, (NET²). **3.** Possibly Persian *nīl*, indigo: ANIL, LILAC. [Pok. 2. *nei-* 760.]

neiə-. To lead. Sanskrit *nayati*, he leads: NAINSOOK. [Pok. 1. *nei-* 760.]

neigʷ-. To wash. Germanic *nikwiz, *nikuz in Old High German *nihhus*, river monster, water spirit: NIX¹. [Pok. *neigʷ-* 761.]

nek-¹. Death. **1.** Latin *nex* (stem *nec-*), death: PERNICIOUS. **2.** Latin *necāre*, to kill: INTERNECINE. **3.** Suffixed (causative) o-grade form *nok-eyo- in Latin *nocēre*, to injure, harm: NOCENT, NOCUOUS, NUISANCE; INNOCENT, INNOCUOUS. **4.** Suffixed o-grade form *nok-s- in Latin *noxa*, injury, hurt, damage: NOXIOUS; OBNOXIOUS. **5.** Suffixed full-grade form *nek-ro- in Greek *nekros*, corpse: NECRO-, NECROSIS; NECROMANCY. **6.** Greek *nektar*, the drink of the gods, "overcoming death" (*tar-, overcoming; see **terə-²**): NECTAR, (NECTARINE). [Pok. *nek-* 762.]

nek-². To reach, attain. **I.** O-grade form *nok- in Germanic *ga-nah- (*ga-, intensive prefix; see **kom**), "satisfies," forming *ganōga-*, sufficient, in Old English *genōg*, enough: ENOUGH. **II.** Variant form *enk-. **1.** Reduplicated in Greek *enenkein*, to carry, whence *onkos*, a burden, mass, hence a tumor: ONCOGENESIS, ONCOLOGY. **2.** Compound root *bhrenk- (see **bher-¹**). [Pok. *enek-* 316.]

nek-t-. Night. O-grade form *nokʷ-t-. **1.** Germanic *naht- in Old English *niht*, *neaht*, night: NIGHT. **2.** Latin

nox (stem *noct-*), night: NOCTI-, NOCTURN, NOCTURNAL, NOTTURNO; EQUINOX. **3.** Latin *noctua*, night owl: NOCTUID, NOCTULE. **4.** Greek *nux* (stem *nukt-*), night: NYCTALOPIA, NYCTITROPISM. **5.** Possibly suffixed zero-grade form *n̥kt-i- in Greek *aktis*, ray of light: ACTINO-. [Pok. *nekʷ(t)- 762.]

nem-. To assign, allot; also to take. **1.** Germanic *nem- in: **a.** Old English *niman*, to take, seize: NIM, NUMB; (BENUMB); **b.** Old English *næmel*, quick to seize, and *numol*, quick at learning, seizing: NIMBLE. **2.** Greek *nemein*, to allot: NEMESIS. **3.** O-grade form *nom- in: **a.** Greek *nomos*, portion, usage, custom, law, division, district: NOME, -NOMY; ANOMIE, ANTINOMIAN, ANTINOMY, (ASTRONOMER), (ASTRONOMY), AUTONOMOUS, BINOMIAL, DEUTERONOMY, METRONOME, NOMOGRAM, NOMOGRAPH, NUMISMATICS; **b.** Greek *nomē*, pasturage, grazing, hence a spreading, a spreading ulcer: NOMA; **c.** Greek *nomas*, wandering in search of pasture: NOMAD; **d.** Greek *nomimos*, legal, probably borrowed in Latin *nummus*, coin: NUMMULAR, NUMMULATE. **4.** Perhaps suffixed o-grade form *nom-eso- in Latin *numerus*, number, division: NUMBER; ENUMERATE, SUPERNUMERARY. [Pok. 1. *nem-* 763.]

nepōt-. Grandson, nephew. Feminine *neptī-. Latin *nepōs*, grandson, nephew, and *neptis*, granddaughter, niece: NEPHEW, NEPOTISM, NIECE. [Pok. *nepōt-* 764.]

ner-¹. Under, also on the left; hence, with an eastward orientation, north. Suffixed zero-grade form *n̥r-t(r)o- in Germanic *north-*, north, in: **a.** Old English *north*, north: NORDIC, NORTH; NORMAN; **b.** Old English *northerne*, northern: NORTHERN; **c.** Middle Dutch *nort*, north: NORSE. Compare **deks-**. [Pok. 2. *ner-* 765.]

ner-². Also **əner-**. Man; basic sense "vigorous, vital, strong." **1.** Oldest root form *əner- (with prothetic vowel) in Greek *anēr* (stem *andr-*, from zero-grade *ənr-*), man: ANDRO-, -ANDROUS, -ANDRY; PHILANDER. **2.** Extended zero-grade form *(ə)nr̥t- in Sanskrit *nr̥tyati*, he dances ("moves vigorously"): NAUTCH. **3.** Referred by some to this root (as if "having human eyes"; *ōps, eye; see **okʷ-**) but more likely of unknown origin is Greek *anthrōpos*, man (earliest Greek form *anthrōkʷos*): ANTHROPIC, ANTHROPO-; LYCANTHROPE, MISANTHROPE, PHILANTHROPY, THEANTHROPIC. [Pok. 1. *ner-(t)- 765.]

nerə-. To dive, swim. Possibly in Greek *Nēreus*, name of a sea god: NEREID, (NEREIS), NEREUS, NERITIC. [Pok. 3. *ner-* 766.]

nes-¹. To return safely home. **1.** Germanic *nes-tam in Old English, Old High German (in composition), and Old Norse *nest*, food for a journey, akin to the possible Germanic source of Old French *harnes*, harness: HARNESS. **2.** Suffixed o-grade form *nos-to- in Greek *nostos*, a return home: NOSTALGIA. [Pok. *nes-* 766.]

nes-². Oblique cases of the personal pronoun of the first person plural. For the nominative see **we-**. **1.** Zero-grade form *n̥s- in Germanic *uns in Old English *ūs*, us (accusative): US. **2.** Suffixed (possessive) zero-grade form *n̥s-ero- in Germanic *unsara- in Old English *ūser*, *ūre*, our: OUR, OURS. **3.** O-grade form *nos-, with suffixed (possessive) form *nos-t(e)ro-, in Latin *nos*, we, and *noster*, our: NOSTRUM; PATERNOSTER. [Pok. 3. *ne-* 758.]

nētr-. Snake. Germanic *nēthrō- in Old English *nædre*, snake: ADDER. [Pok. *nē-tr-* 767.]

neu-¹. To shout. Suffixed (participial) o-grade form *now-ent-(yo-), "shouting," in Latin *nūntius*, "announcing," hence a messenger, also a message, and *nūntium*, message: NUNCIO; ANNOUNCE, DENOUNCE, ENUNCIATE, PRONOUNCE, RENOUNCE. [Pok. 1. *neu-* 767.]

neu-². To nod. **1.** Latin *nuere, to nod (attested only in compounds), frequentative *nutāre*, to nod: NUTATION; INNUENDO. **2.** Suffixed form *neu-men- in Latin *nūmen*, "a nod," hence "command," divine power, deity: NUMEN. [Pok. 2. *neu-* 767.]

neud-. To make use of, enjoy. Germanic *nautam, "thing of value, possession," in: **a.** Old English *nēat*, bovine

animal: NEAT[2]; **b.** compound form *ga-nauta- (*ga-, with, together; see **kom**), "he with whom one shares possessions," companion, fellow, in *(i)* Middle Dutch *ghenōt, noot*, fellow: MATELOTE *(ii)* Old High German *ginōz*, companion, in German *Eidgenosse*, confederate: HUGUENOT. [Pok. *neu-d-* 768.]

newn̥. Nine. **1.** Germanic *niwun, with variant *nigun, in Old English *nigon*, nine: NINE, NINETEEN, NINETY, NINTH. **2.** Latin *novem*, nine (< *noven, with *m* for *n* by analogy with the *m* of *septem*, seven, and *decem*, ten): NOVEMBER, NOVENA; NONAGENARIAN. **3.** Ordinal form *neweno- in Latin *nōnus*, ninth: NONA, NONES, NOON; (NONAGON), (NONANOIC ACID). **4.** Prothetic forms *enewn̥, *enwn̥ in Greek *ennea*, nine (> *ennewa, *enwa-): ENNEAD. [Pok. *e-neuen* 318.]

newo-. New. Related to **nu-**. **1.** Suffixed form *new-yo- in Germanic *neuja- in: **a.** Old English *nēowe, nīwe*, new: NEW; **b.** Old Norse *nȳr*, new: SPAN-NEW. **2.** Basic form *newo- in Greek *newos, neos*, new: NEO-, NEON, NEOTERIC; MISONEISM. **3.** Suffixed form *new-aro- in Greek *nearos*, young, fresh, contracted into *nēros*, fresh (used of fish and of water), hence *nēron*, water: ANEROID. **4.** Basic form *newo- in Latin *novus*, new: NOVA, NOVATION, NOVEL[1], NOVEL[2], (NOVELTY), NOVICE, INNOVATE, RENOVATE. **5.** Suffixed form *new-er-ko- in Latin *noverca*, stepmother (< "she who is new"): NOVERCAL. [Pok. *neu̯os* 709.]

ni. Down. **1.** Suffixed form *ni-t- in Germanic *nith- in Old English *nithan, neothan*, below: BENEATH, UNDERNEATH. **2.** Suffixed (comparative) form *ni-tero-, lower, in Germanic *nitheraz in Old English *nither*, lower: NETHER. See compound root **nizdo-**. [In Pok. 1. *en* 311.]

[nikē. Victory. Greek noun of unknown origin. NIKE.]

nizdo-. Bird's nest. Compound root formed from **ni** + *sd-, zd-, zero-grade form of **sed-**[1]; literally, "place where the bird sits down." **1.** Germanic *nist- in: **a.** Old English *nest*, nest: NEST; **b.** Germanic *nistilōn in Old English *nestlian*, to make a nest: NESTLE. **2.** Latin *nīdus*, nest: NICHE, NIDE, NIDUS; EYAS, NIDIFY. [In Pok. *sed-* 887.]

nobh-. Also **ombh-**. Navel; later also "central knob," boss of a shield, hub of a wheel. **1.** Germanic *nabō in: **a.** Old English *nafu, nafa*, hub of a wheel: NAVE[2]; **b.** compound *nabō-gaisaz, tool for piercing wheel hubs (*gaizaz, spear, piercing tool; see **ghaiso-**), in Old English *nafogār*, auger: AUGER. **2.** Variant form *ombh- in Latin *umbō*, boss of a shield: UMBO. **3.** Suffixed form *nobh-alo- in Germanic *nabalō in Old English *nafela*, navel: NAVEL. **4.** Suffixed variant form *ombh-alo- in: **a.** Latin *umbilīcus*, navel: UMBILICUS; NOMBRIL; **b.** Greek *omphalos*, navel: OMPHALOS. [Pok. 1. *(enebh-)* 314.]

nogh-. Also **ənogh-, ongh-**. Nail, claw. **1.** Suffixed (diminutive) form *nogh-ela- in Germanic *nagla- in Old English *nægl*, nail: NAIL. **2.** Form *ənogh- in Greek *onux* (stem *onukh-*), nail: ONYX; PARONYCHIA, PERIONYCHIUM, SARDONYX. **3.** Variant form *ongh- in Latin *unguis*, nail, claw, hoof, with diminutive *ungula*, hoof, claw, talon (< *ongh-elā-): UNGUIS. [Pok. *onogh-* 780.]

nogʷ-. Naked. **1.** Suffixed form *nogʷ-eto-, *nogʷ-oto- in Germanic *nakweda-, *nakwada- in Old English *nacod*, naked: NAKED. **2.** Suffixed form *nogʷ-edo- in Latin *nūdus*, naked: NUDE, NUDI-; DENUDE. **3.** Suffixed form *nogʷ-mo- differentiated or developed into Greek *gumnos*, naked: GYMNASIUM, GYMNAST, GYMNOSOPHIST, GYMNOSPERM. [Pok. *nogʷ-* 769.]

nō-men. Name. Earlier form *(ə)noə-mn̥, zero-grade form *(ə)nə-men-. **1.** Germanic *namōn- in Old English *nama*, name: NAME. **2.** Latin *nōmen*, name, reputation: NOMINAL, NOMINATE, NOUN; AGNOMEN, COGNOMEN, DENOMINATE, IGNOMINY, MISNOMER, NOMENCLATOR, NUNCUPATIVE, PRAENOMEN, (PRONOUN), RENOWN. **3.** Greek *onoma, onuma*, name: ONOMASTIC, -ONYM, -ONYMY; ANONYMOUS, ANTONOMASIA, EPONYM, (EPONYMOUS), EUONYMUS, HETERONYMOUS, HOMONYMOUS,

METONYMY, METRONYMIC, ONOMATOPOEIA, PARONOMASIA, PARONYMOUS, PATRONYMIC, PSEUDONYM, SYNONYMOUS. [Pok. *en(o)mn̥-* 321.]

nōt-. Buttock, back. **1.** Greek *nōton, nōtos*, back: NOTOCHORD. **2.** Zero-grade form *nət- in Latin *natis*, buttock: NATES; AITCHBONE. [Pok. *nōt-* 770.]

[nous. Mind, sense, reason, intellect. Greek noun (earliest form *noos*) of unknown origin. NOESIS, NOUMENON, NOUS; PARANOIA.]

n̥si-. Sword. Latin *ēnsis*, sword: ENSIFORM. [Pok. *n̥si-s* 771.]

nu-. Now. Related to **newo-**. **1.** Old English *nū*, now: NOW. **2.** Latin *nunc* (< *nun-ce; -ce, a particle meaning "this," "here"; see **ko-**), now: QUIDNUNC. [Pok. *nu-* 770.]

ō-. To believe, hold as true. Suffixed form *ō-men- in Latin *ōmen*, a prognostic sign, omen: OMEN.

obhel-. Also **əbhel-**. To augment, increase. Greek *ophelos*, advantage: ANOPHELES. [Pok. *obhel-* 772.]

od-[1]. To smell. **1.** Suffixed form *od-os- in Latin *odor*, smell: ODOR. **2.** Suffixed form *od-ē- in Latin *olēre*, to smell (with *l* for *d* representing a Sabine borrowing): OLFACTORY, REDOLENT. **3.** Suffixed form *od-yo- in Greek *ozein*, to smell: OZONE. **4.** Suffixed form *od-mā- in Greek *osmē*, smell: OSMATIC, OSMIUM; ANOSMIA. [Pok. 1. *od-* 772.]

od-[2]. To hate. Latin *ōdī*, I hate, and *odium*, hatred: ANNOY, ENNUI, (NOISOME); ODIUM. [Pok. 2. *od-* 773.]

ōg-. Fruit, berry. **1.** Zero-grade form *əg- in Germanic *ak-ran- in Old English *æcern*, acorn: ACORN. **2.** Latin *ūva* (preform uncertain), grape: UVEA, UVULA; PYRUVIC ACID. [Pok. *ōg-* 773.]

oid-. To swell. **1.** Possibly Old English *āte*, oat: OAT. **2.** Greek *oidein*, to swell: EDEMA. [Pok. *oid-* 774.]

oi-no-. One, unique. **I.** Basic form *oi-no-. **1.** Germanic *ainaz in: **a.** Old English *ān*, one: A[1], AN[1], ONCE, ONE; (ALONE), ANON, (ATONE), (LONE), (LONELY), NONE; **b.** compound *ain-lif-, "one left (beyond ten)," eleven (*lif-, left over; see **leikʷ-**), in Old English *endleofan*, eleven: ELEVEN; **c.** Old High German *ein*, one, in German *vereinen*, to unite: EINKORN, TURNVEREIN. **2.** Latin *ūnus*, one: INCH[1], OUNCE[1], UNCIAL, UNI-, UNION, UNITE; UNITY; COADUNATE, QUINCUNX, TRIUNE, UNANIMOUS, UNICORN, UNIVERSE. **3.** Latin *nōn* (< *ne-oinom, "not one thing"; *ne, not; see **ne**). **II.** Suffixed form *oino-ko- in: **a.** Germanic *ainigaz in Old English *ǣnig*, one, anyone: ANY; **b.** Latin *ūnicus*, sole, single: UNIQUE. **III.** Suffixed form *oino-lo- in Latin *ūllus*, any (see **ne**). [In Pok. *e-* 281.]

oito-. An oath. Probably derived from **ei-**[1]. Germanic *aithaz in: **a.** Old English *āth*, oath: OATH; **b.** Old High German *eid*, oath, in German *Eidgenosse*, confederate: HUGUENOT. [In Pok. 1. *ei-* 293.]

oktō(u). Eight. **1.** Germanic *ahtō in: **a.** Old English *eahta*, eight: EIGHT; **b.** Old Norse *āttjan (tjan*, ten; see **dekm̥**), eighteen: ATTO-. **2.** Latin *octō*, eight: OCTANS, OCTANT, OCTAVE, OCTAVO, OCTET, OCTO-, OCTOBER, OCTONARY; OCTODECIMO, OCTOGENARIAN. **3.** Greek *oktō*, eight: OCTAD; OCTOPUS. [Pok. *oktō-* 775.]

ōku-. Swift. Zero-grade form *əku- in compound *əku-petro-, "swift-flying," in Latin *accipiter*, hawk (*pet-ro-, flying; see **pet-**): ACCIPITER. [Pok. *ōku-s* 775.]

okʷ-. To see. **1.** Germanic *augōn- (with taboo deformation) in: **a.** Old English *ēage*, eye: EYE; DAISY; **b.** Old Norse *auge*, eye: WALLEYED, WINDOW; **c.** Low German *oog*, eye: OGLE. **2.** Suffixed form *okʷ-olo- in: **a.** Latin *oculus*, eye: EYELET, OCELLUS, OCULAR, OCULIST, ULLAGE; INOCULATE, MONOCLE, OCULOMETER, OCULOMOTOR; **b.** Gallo-Latin compound *ab-oculus, blind, modeled on Gaulish *ex-ops*, blind, in French *aveugle*, blind: INVEIGLE. **3.** Form *okʷ-s in Greek *ōps*, eye (and stem *op-*, to see): METOPIC, MYOPIA, NYCTALOPIA, PELOPS, PHLOGOPITE, PYROPE. **4.** Suffixed form *okʷ-ti- in Greek *opsis*, sight, appearance: OPSIN, -OPSIS, -OPSY; AUTOPSY, (IODOPSIN), (RHODOPSIN), SYNOPSIS. **5.** Suf-

fixed form *ok^w-to- in Greek optos, seen, visible: OPTIC; CATOPTRIC, DIOPTER, OPTOMETRY, PANOPTIC. **6.** Suffixed form *ok^w-ā in Greek opē, opening: METOPE. **7.** Suffixed form *ok^w-mn̥ in Greek omma (< *opma), eye: OMMATIDIUM, OMMATOPHORE. **8.** Greek ophthalmos, eye (with taboo deformation): OPHTHALMO-; EXOPHTHALMOS. **9.** Zero-grade form *$ək^w$- (of oldest full-grade form *$ɔok^w$-) in: **a.** Latin antīquus, "appearing before, having prior aspect," former (*anti-, before; see **ant-**); **b.** Latin ătrōx, "black-looking," frightful (*atro- black; see **āter-**); **c.** Latin ferōx, "wild-looking," fierce (*ghwero-, wild; see **ghwer-**). [Pok. ok^u- 775.]

ol-. To destroy. Possibly suffixed zero-grade form *l-ē-to- in Latin lētum, lēthum, death: LETHAL. [Pok. ol-(e)- 777.]

om-. Raw. Possibly (but doubtful both in form and meaning) Latin amārus, bitter-tasting (> Italian marasca, bitter, bitter cherry): AMARELLE, AMARETTO, MARASCA, (MARASCHINO), MORELLO. [Pok. om- 777.]

ombh-ro-. Rain. **1.** Zero-grade form *m̥bh-ro- in Latin imber, rain: IMBRICATE. **2.** Possibly zero-grade suffixed form *m̥bh-u- in Latin imbuere, to moisten, stain: IMBUE. See **nebh-**. [In Pok. 2. (enebh-) 315.]

omeso-. Also **omso-.** Shoulder. **1.** Form *omso- in Germanic *amsa- in Old Norse āss, a (mountain) ridge: OS³. **2.** Form *omeso- in Latin humerus, shoulder: HUMERUS. **3.** Lengthened-grade form *ōmso- in Greek ōmos, shoulder: ACROMION. [Pok. om(e)so-s 778.]

oner-. Dream. Suffixed form *oner-yo- in Greek oneiros, dream: ONEIROMANCY. [Pok. oner- 779.]

ong^w-. To salve, anoint. Latin unguere, to smear, anoint: OINTMENT, UNCTION, UNCTUOUS, UNGUENT; ANOINT, INUNCTION. [Pok. ong^u- 779.]

op-¹. To work, produce in abundance. **1.** Suffixed form *op-es- in Latin opus (stem oper-), work, with its denominative verb operari, to work, and secondary noun opera, work: OPERA¹, OPERATE, OPEROSE, OPUS; COOPERATE, INURE, MANEUVER, MANURE, OFFICINAL. **2.** Latin officium, service, duty, business (< *opi-fici-om, "performance of work"; -fici-, doing; see **dhē-¹**). **3.** Suffixed form *op-en-ent- dissimilated in Latin opulentus, rich, wealthy: OPULENT. **4.** Suffixed form *op-ni- in Latin omnis, all (< "abundant"): OMNI-, OMNIBUS, OMNIUM-GATHERUM. **5.** Suffixed (superlative) form *op-tamo- in Latin optimus, best (< "wealthiest"): OPTIMUM. **6.** Prefixed Latin form *co-op- (co-, collective and intensive prefix; see **kom**) in Latin cōpia, profusion, plenty: COPIOUS, COPY; CORNUCOPIA. [Pok. 1. op- 780.]

op-². To choose. **1.** Latin optiō, choice (from *opere, to choose): OPTION. **2.** Latin optāre (frequentative of *opere), to choose: OPT, OPTATIVE; ADOPT, CO-OPT. **3.** Possibly suffixed form *op-yen- in Latin opīnārī, to be of an opinion: OPINE, OPINION. [Pok. 2. op- 781.]

or-. Large bird. **1.** Suffixed form *or-n- in Germanic *arnuz, eagle, in Old English earn, eagle: ERNE. **2.** Suffixed form *or-n-īth- in Greek ornis (stem ornith-), bird: ORNITHO-; AEPYORNIS, ICHTHYORNIS, NOTORNIS. [Pok. 1. er- 325.]

ōr-. To pronounce a ritual formula. Latin ōrāre, to speak, plead, pray: ORACLE, ORATION, ORATOR, ORATORY¹, ORATORY²; ADORE, INEXORABLE, PERORATE. [Pok. ōr- 781.]

orbh-. To put asunder, separate. Suffixed form *orbh-o-, "bereft of father," also "deprived of free status," in: **a.** Greek orphanos, orphaned: ORPHAN; **b.** Old Slavic *orbŭ in Old Church Slavonic rabŭ, slave > rabota, servitude, in Czech robota, compulsory labor, drudgery: ROBOT. [Pok. orbho- 781.]

ors-. Buttocks, backside. **1.** Suffixed form *ors-o- in Germanic *arsaz in Old English ærs, ears, backside: ASS². **2.** Suffixed form *ors-ā- in: **a.** Greek oura, tail: URO-², -UROUS; ANTHURIUM, ANURAN, CYNOSURE, EREMURUS, OXYURIASIS, SQUIRREL, TRICHURIASIS; **b.** probably Greek silouros, sheatfish (< obscure first element + oura): SILURID. [Pok. ers- 340.]

os-. Ash tree. Germanic *aski- in Old English æsc, ash: ASH². [Pok. ōs- 782.]

ōs-. Mouth. **1.** Latin ōs (stem ōr-), mouth, face, orifice, and derivative ōstium (< suffixed form *ōs-to-), door: ORAL, OS¹, OSCULATE, OSCULUM, OSTIARY, OSTIUM, USHER; INOSCULATE, ORIFICE, ORINASAL, OROTUND, OSCITANCY, PERORAL. **2.** Possibly Latin aurīga, charioteer (< *ōr-ig-, "he who manages the (horse's) bit"; -ig-, driving, from *ag-; see **ag-**): AURIGA. [Pok. 1. ōus- 784.]

ost-. Bone. **1.** Latin os (stem oss-), bone: OS², OSSEOUS, OSSICLE, OSSUARY, OSSIFRAGE, OSSIFY. **2.** Greek osteon, bone: OSTEO-; ENDOSTEUM, EXOSTOSIS, PERIOSTEM, SYNOSTOSIS, TELEOST. **3.** Suffixed form *ost-r- in: **a.** Greek ostrakon, shell, potsherd: OSTRACIZE, OSTRACOD; **b.** Greek ostreon, oyster: OYSTER; **c.** variant form in Greek astragalos, vertebra, ball of the ankle joint, knucklebone, Ionic molding: ASTRAGAL, ASTRAGALUS. [Pok. ost(h)- 783.]

ous-. Also **aus-.** Ear. **1.** Suffixed form *ous-en- in Germanic *auzan- in Old English ēare, ear: EAR¹. **2.** Suffixed form *aus-i- in Latin auris, ear: AURAL, AURICLE, AURIFORM, ORMER. **3.** Latin auscultāre, to listen to (*aus- + *kli-to-, inclined; see **klei-**): AUSCULTATION, SCOUT¹. **4.** Suffixed basic form *ous-os- in: **a.** Greek ous (stem ōt-), ear: OTIC, OTO-; MYOSOTIS, PAROTID GLAND; **b.** Greek lagōs, hare (< *lag-ous-, "with drooping ears"; *lag-, to droop; see **slēg-**). [Pok. ōus- 785.]

owi-. Sheep. **1.** Germanic *awi in Old English ewe, eowu, ewe: EWE. **2.** Latin ovis, sheep: OVINE; OVIBOS. [Pok. oui-s 784.]

pā-. To protect, feed. Contracted from *paə-. **1.** Suffixed form *pā-trom in Germanic *fōdram in: **a.** Old English fōdor, fodder: FODDER; **b.** Old French feurre, fodder: FORAGE; **c.** Old French forreure, trimming made from animal skin, fur (< "sheath, case, lining"): FUR. **2.** Suffixed form *pā-dhlom (doublet of *pā-trom) in Latin pābulum, food, fodder: PABULUM. **3.** Extended form *pāt- in: **a.** Germanic *fōd-, food, in Old English fōda, food: FOOD; **b.** Germanic denominative *fōdjan, to give food to, in Old English fēdan, to feed: FEED; **c.** suffixed form *pāt-tro- in Germanic *fōstra- in Old English fōstor, food, nourishment: FOSTER. **4.** Extended form *pās- in: **a.** suffixed form *pās-sko- in Latin pāscere, to feed: PASTURE; ANTIPASTO, PESTER, REPAST; **b.** Latin pāstor, shepherd: PASTOR; **c.** suffixed form *pās-t-ni- in Latin pānis, bread (diminutive pastillus, medicine tablet): PANADA, PANATELA, PANNIER, PANOCHA, PANTRY, PASTILLE, (PENUCHE); APPANAGE, COMPANION, (COMPANY). **5.** Suffixed form *pā-ti- in Iranian *pāti- in Persian pād, protecting against: BEZOAR. **6.** Suffixed form *pā-won-, protector, in Old Persian khshathra-pāvā, protector of the province: SATRAP. [Pok. pā- 787, 1. pō(i)- 839.]

pag-. Also **pak-.** To fasten. **1.** Lengthened-grade form *pāk- in Germanic *fōgjan, to join, fit, in Old English fēgan, to fit closely: FAY¹. **2.** Nasalized form *pa-n-g- in: **a.** Germanic *fangiz, seizure, in (i) Old English fang, feng, plunder, booty: FANG (ii) Dutch vangen, to catch: VANG; **b.** Latin pangere, to fasten: COMPACT¹, IMPINGE. **3.** Root form *pāk- in: **a.** Latin pāx, peace (< "a binding together by treaty or agreement"): PACE², PAY¹, PEACE; APPEASE, PACIFIC, PACIFY; **b.** Latin pacīscī, to agree: PACT. **4.** Suffixed form *pak-slo- in: **a.** Latin pālus, stake (fixed in the ground): PALE¹, PALISADE, PEEL³, POLE²; IMPALE, TRAVAIL, (TRAVEL); **b.** probably Latin pāla, spade: PALETTE, PEEL². **5.** Lengthened-grade form *pāg- in: **a.** Latin pāgus, "boundary staked out on the ground," district, village, country: PAGAN, PEASANT; **b.** Latin pāgina, "trellis to which a row of vines is fixed," hence (by metaphor) column of writing, page: PAGE², PAGEANT; **c.** Latin prōpāgēs (prō-, before, in front; see **per¹**), layer of vine, offspring (< "a fixing before"): PROPAGATE; **d.** Greek pēgnunai, to fasten, coagulate: PECTIN, PEGMATITE. [Pok. pǎk- 787.]

pan-. Fabric. **1.** Germanic *fanōn- in: **a.** Old English

fana, flag, banner, weathercock: VANE; **b.** compound *gund-fanōn-*, "battle-flag" (see **gʷhen-¹**). **2.** Extended form *panno-* in Latin *pannus*, piece of cloth, rag: PANE, PANEL. **3.** Possibly Greek *pēnos*, web (> Latin *pānus*, a swelling): PANICLE. [Pok. *pan-* 788.]

[**pandoura.** Three-stringed lute. Greek noun of obscure origin. BANDORE, MANDOLIN, PANDORE.]

pant-. All. Attested only in Tocharian and Greek. Greek *pas* (neuter *pan*, stem *pant-*), all: PAN-, PAN; DIAPASON, PANCRATIUM, PANCREAS. [In Pok. 1. *k̑eu-* 592.]

pap-¹. Teat (sound symbolism). Probably the same word as **pap-².** **1.** Middle English *pap(p)e*, nipple: PAP¹. **2.** Latin diminutive *papula*, pimple (diminutive *papilla*, nipple): PAPILLA, PAPULE. **3.** Variant form *pup(p)-* in Latin *pūpus*, boy, and *pūpa*, girl: PUPA, PUPIL¹. [In Pok. *baˣb-* 91.]

pap-². Food (baby-talk root). Reduplication of **pā-.** **1.** Germanic nasalized form *pamp-* in Flemish frequentative *pamperen*, to cram with food, akin to the source of Middle English *pamperen*, to pamper: PAMPER. **2.** Latin *pappa*, food (> Middle English *pap*, soft food): PAP², POPPYCOCK. [Pok. *pap(p)a* 789, *baˣmb-* 94.]

papa. A child's word for "father," a linguistic near-universal found in many languages. **1.** French *papa*, father: PAPA. **2.** Greek *pappas*, father, and *pappos*, grandfather: PAPPUS, POPE. [Pok. *pap(p)a* 789.]

pāso-. Kinsman by marriage. Latin *parri-* (for *pāri-*) in compound *parri-cīda* (oldest form *paricidas*), murderer of a near relation: PARRICIDE. [Pok. *pāso-s* 787.]

past-. Solid, firm. **1.** Germanic *fastuz*, firm, fast, in: **a.** Old English *fæst*, fixed, firm: FAST¹; STEADFAST; **b.** Middle Dutch *vast*, firm, fast: AVAST. **2.** Germanic *fastinōn*, to make firm or fast, in Old English *fæstnian*, to fasten, establish: FASTEN. **3.** Germanic *fastēn*, to hold fast, observe abstinence, in: **a.** Old English *fæstan*, to abstain from food: FAST²; **b.** Old Norse *fasta*, to abstain from food: BREAKFAST. [Pok. *pasto-* 789.]

pau-. Few, little. **I.** Adjectival form *pau-*, few, little. **1.** Germanic *fawaz* in Old English *fēawe*, few: FEW. **2.** Suffixed form *pau-ko-* in Latin *paucus*, little, few: PAUCITY, POCO. **3.** Suffixed form *pau-ro-* in metathetical form *par-wo-* in Latin *parvus*, little, small, neuter *parvum*, becoming *parum*, little, rarely: PARAFFIN, PARVOVIRUS. **4.** Compound *pau-paros*, producing little, poor (*par-os*, producing; see **pere-¹**), in Latin *pauper*, poor: PAUPER, POOR, POVERTY. **II.** Suffixed reduced variant form *pu-lo-*, young of an animal. **1.** Germanic *fulōn-* in Old English *fola*, young horse, colt: FOAL. **2.** Germanic derivative *fuljō* in Old Norse *fylja*, female colt: FILLY. **3.** Latin *pullus* (probably with expressive gemination), young of an animal, chicken: POLTROON, PONY, POOL², POULARD, PULLET; CATCHPOLE. **III.** Basic form *pau-* and variant form *pū-*, boy, child. **1.** Suffixed form *pu-ero-* in Latin *puer*, child: PUERILE, PUERPERAL. **2.** Suffixed form *pū-sso-* in Latin *pūsus*, boy: PUSILLANIMOUS. **3.** Suffixed form *paw-id-* in Greek *pais* (stem *paid-*), child (> *paideia*, education): PEDO-²; ENCYCLOPEDIA, ORTHOPEDICS. [Pok. *pōu-* 842.]

paus-. To leave, desert, cease, stop. Greek *pauein*, to stop (> Latin *pausa*, a stopping): PAUSE, (PESADE), (POSE¹); COMPOSE, DIAPAUSE, (REPOSE¹). [Pok. *paus-* 79.]

ped-¹. Foot. **I.** Nominal root. **1.** Lengthened o-grade form *pōd-* in Germanic *fōt-* in Old English *fōt*, foot: FOOT. **2.** Suffixed form *ped-ero-* in Germanic *feterō* in Old English *fetor, feter*, leg iron, fetter: FETTER. **3.** Suffixed form *ped-el-* in Germanic *fetel-* in Old High German *vizzelach*, fetlock, akin to the Germanic source of Middle English *fitlock, fetlock*, fetlock: FETLOCK. **4.** Basic form *ped-* in Latin *pēs* (stem *ped-*), foot: PAWN², -PED, PEDAL, PEDATE, PEDESTRIAN, PEDI-, PEDICEL, PEDUNCLE, (PEON), PES, PIONEER; MILLIPEDE, SESQUIPEDALIAN, TRIPEDAL, TRIVET, VAMP¹. **5.** Form *ped-yo-* in: **a.** Latin *expedīre*, to free from a snare (*ex-*, out of; see **eghs**): EXPEDITE; **b.** Latin *impedīre*, "to put in fetters, hobble,"

shackle," entangle, hinder (*in-*, in; see **en**): IMPEDE. **6.** Suffixed form *ped-ikā-* in Latin *pedica*, fetter, snare: DISPATCH, IMPEACH. **7.** O-grade form *pod-* in: **a.** Greek *pous* (stem *pod-*), foot: PEW, -POD, PODITE, PODIUM; ANTIPODES, APODAL, APPOGGIATURA, APUS, CALIBER, LYCOPODIUM, MONOPODIUM, OCTOPUS, PELECYPOD, PHALAROPE, PLATYPUS, PODAGRA, PODIATRY, PODOPHYLLIN, POLYP, POLYPOD, SYMPODIUM; **b.** Russian *pod*, under: PODZOL. **8.** Suffixed form *ped-ya* in Greek *peza*, foot: TRAPEZIUM. **9.** Suffixed form *ped-o-* in: **a.** Greek *pedon*, ground, soil: PEDO-¹; PARALLELEPIPED; **b.** Sanskrit *padam*, footstep, foot, and *pāt* (> Hindi *paisā*), foot: PAISA, PICE, PIE³, PUG³; **c.** Middle Persian *pāī*, leg, foot: PAJAMAS, TEAPOY; **d.** lengthened-grade form *pēdo-* in *(i)* Greek *pēdon*, rudder, steering oar: PILOT *(ii)* Greek *pēdan*, to leap: DIAPEDESIS. **10.** Suffixed form *ped-ī-* in Greek *pedilon*, sandal: CYPRIPEDIUM. **II.** Verbal root *ped-*, to stumble, fall. **1.** Germanic *fetēn* in Old English *fetian, feccean*, to bring back: FETCH¹. **2.** Latin *ped-* in: **a.** suffixed (comparative) form *ped-yos* in Latin *pējor*, worse (< "stumbling"): PEJORATION; IMPAIR; **b.** suffixed (superlative) form *ped-samo-* in Latin *pessimus*, worst: PESSIMISM; **c.** suffixed form *ped-ko-* in Latin *peccāre*, to stumble, sin: PECCABLE, PECCADILLO, PECCANT; IMPECCABLE. [Pok. 2. *pĕd-* 790.]

ped-². Container. **1.** Suffixed o-grade form *pod-om* in Germanic *fatam* in Old English *fæt*, cask: VAT. **2.** Suffixed o-grade form *pod-ilo-* in Germanic *fatilaz* in Old English *fetel*, girdle: FETTLE. **3.** Probably full-grade form *ped-* in Germanic *fet-* in Middle High German *vetze*, "clothes," rags, probably akin to the source of obsolete English *fritter*, fragment: FRITTER¹. [Pok. 1. *pĕd-* 790.]

peg-. Breast. **1.** Suffixed variant form *pek-tos-* in Latin *pectus*, breast: PECTORAL; EXPECTORATE, PARAPET. **2.** Possibly suffixed variant form *pek-so-* in Sanskrit *pakṣaḥ*, wing: PUNKA. [Pok. *(peg-), pŏg-* 792.]

pē(i)-. Also **pē-, pī-.** To hurt. Possible root; contracted from *peə(i)-*. **1.** Suffixed (participial) form *pī-ont-* (< *piə-ont-*) in Germanic *fījand-*, hating, hostile, in Old English *fēond, fīond*, enemy, devil: FIEND. **2.** Possibly *pē-* in suffixed zero-grade form *pə-to-* in Latin *patī*, to suffer: PASSIBLE, PASSION, PASSIVE, PATIENT; COMPASSION. [Pok. *pē(i)-* 792.]

peiə-. Also **pei-.** To be fat, swell. **1.** Extended o-grade form *poid-* in Germanic *faitaz*, plump, fat, in derivative Germanic verb *faitjan*, to fatten, whence Germanic past participle *faitidaz*, fattened, in Old English *fǣt(t)*, fat: FAT. **2.** Possibly suffixed zero-grade form *pī-tu-* in Latin *pītuīta*, moisture exuded from trees, gum, phlegm: PIP⁵, PITUITARY, PITUITOUS. **3.** Possibly suffixed zero-grade form *pī-nu-* in Latin *pīnus*, pine tree (yielding a resin): PINE¹, PINEAL, PIÑON, PINNACE; PIÑA CLOTH. **4.** Suffixed zero-grade form *pī-won-* in Greek *piōn*, fat: PROPIONIC ACID. **5.** Suffixed zero-grade form *pī-wer-*, "fat, fertile," in: **a.** *Īwer-iū*, the prehistoric Celtic name for Ireland, in Old English *Īras*, the Irish: (ERSE), IRISH; **b.** *Pīwer-iā* in Greek *Pieria*, a region of Macedonia: PIERIAN SPRING. [Pok. *pei(ə)-* 793.]

peig-¹. Also **peik-.** To cut, mark (by incision). **1.** Alternate form *peik-* in Germanic *fīhala*, cutting tool, in Old English *fīl*, file: FILE². **2.** Nasalized zero-grade form *pi-n-g-* in Latin *pingere*, to embroider, tattoo, paint, picture: PAINT, PICTOR, PICTURE, PICTURESQUE, PIGMENT, PIMENTO, PINTO; DEPICT, PICTOGRAPH. **3.** Suffixed zero-grade form *pik-ro-* in Greek *pikros*, sharp, bitter: PICRO-. **4.** O-grade form *poik-* in Greek *poikilos*, spotted, pied, various: POIKILOTHERM. [Pok. 1. *peig-* 794.]

peig-². Also **peik-.** Evil-minded, hostile. **1.** Suffixed zero-grade form *pig-olo-* in Germanic *fikala-* in Old English *ficol*, treacherous, false: FICKLE. **2.** Suffixed o-grade form *poik-os* in Germanic *gafaihaz* (*ga-*, collective prefix; see **kom**), in Old English *gefāh*, enemy: FOE. **3.** Suffixed o-grade form *poik-yos* in Germanic *faigjaz* in Old English *fǣge*, fated to die: FEY. **4.** Suf-

fixed o-grade form *poik-itā in Germanic *faihithō in Old French faida, hostility, feud: FEUD¹. [Pok. 2. peiĝ-795.]

peis-¹. To crush. **1.** Suffixed zero-grade form *pis-to- in Latin pistillum, pestle: PESTLE, PISTIL. **2.** Nasalized zero-grade form *pi-n-s- in Latin pinsāre, to pound: PISTON. **3.** Possibly suffixed form *pis-lo- in Latin pīlum, javelin, pestle: PILE². **4.** Perhaps Greek ptissein (pt- for p-), to crush, peel: PTISAN, (TISANE). [Pok. 1. (peis-?), pis-796.]

peis-². To blow. Germanic *fīs- in Old Norse fīsa, to fart, akin to the Scandinavian source of Middle English fise, fart: FIZGIG. [Pok. 2. peis- 796.]

peisk-. Fish. Zero-grade form *pisk-. **1.** Suffixed Germanic form *fisk-a- in: **a.** Old English fisc, fish: FISH; **b.** Middle Dutch vische, vis, fish: WEAKFISH. **2.** Suffixed form *pisk-i- in Latin piscis, fish: PISCARY, PISCATORIAL, PISCES, PISCI-, PISCINA, PISCINE; GRAMPUS, PORPOISE. [Pok. peisk- 796.]

pek-¹. To make pretty. **1.** Possibly Germanic *fagra- in Old English fæger, beautiful: FAIR¹. **2.** Possibly Germanic *fagin-, *fagan-, to enjoy, in Old English fægen, joyful, glad (> fagnian, to rejoice): FAIN, FAWN¹. [Pok. 1. pek- 796.]

pek-². To pluck the hair, fleece, comb. **1.** Extended form *pekt- in Germanic *fehtan, to fight, in Old English feohtan, to fight: FIGHT. **2.** Suffixed extended form *pekt-en- in: **a.** Latin pecten, a comb: PECTEN; **b.** zero-grade form *pkt-en- in Greek kteis (genitive ktenos < *pktenos), a comb: CTENIDIUM; CTENOID, CTENOPHORE. [Pok. 2. pek- 797.]

peku-. Wealth, movable property. **1.** Germanic *fehu- in: **a.** Old Norse fē, property, cattle: FELLOW; **b.** Old French fie, fief: FEE; **c.** Medieval Latin feudum, feudal estate: FEUD²; INFEUDATION. **2.** Suffixed form *peku-n- in Latin pecūnia, property, wealth: PECUNIARY; IMPECUNIOUS. **3.** Suffixed form *peku-l- in Latin pecūlium, riches in cattle, private property: PECULATE, PECULIAR. [In Pok. 2. pek- 797.]

pekʷ-. To cook, ripen. **1.** Assimilated form (in Italic and Celtic) *kʷekʷ- in Latin coquere, to cook: COOK, CUISINE, (CULINARY), KILN, KITCHEN, QUITTOR; APRICOT, BISCUIT, CONCOCT, DECOCT, PRECOCIOUS, RICOTTA. **2.** Greek pepōn, ripe: PEPO. **3.** Greek peptein, to cook, ripen, digest (> peptos, cooked): PEPTIC, DRUPE, EUPEPTIC, PEPSIN, PEPTONE, PUMPKIN. **4.** Greek -pepsia, digestion: DYSPEPSIA. **5.** Sanskrit pakva-, ripe: PUKKA. [Pok. pekʷ- 798.]

pel-¹. Dust, flour. **1.** Latin pollen, fine flour, dust: POLLEN. **2.** Latin pulvis, dust: POWDER, PULVERIZE. **3.** Latin palea, chaff: PAILLASSE, PALEA. **4.** Greek palunein, to sprinkle flour: PALYNOLOGY. **5.** Greek poltos, porridge (made from flour), probably borrowed via Etruscan into Latin as puls, pottage: POULTICE, PULSE². [Pok. 2 b. pel-802.]

pel-². Pale. **1.** Suffixed variant form *pal-wo- in: **a.** Germanic *falwaz in Old English fealu, fealo, reddish yellow: FALLOW DEER; **b.** Latin pallēre, to be pale: PALE², PALLID, PALLOR; APPALL; **c.** Latin palumbēs (influenced in form by Latin columbus, dove), ringdove, "gray bird": PALOMINO. **2.** Suffixed form *pel-ko- probably in Germanic *falkōn-, falcon (< "gray bird"), in: **a.** Old French girfaut, gyrfalcon: GYRFALCON; **b.** Late Latin falcō, falcon (but Germanic *falkōn- is also possibly from the Late Latin): FALCON. **3.** Suffixed extended form *peli-wo- in: **a.** Greek pelios, dark: PELOPS; **b.** o-grade form *poli-wo- in Greek polios, gray: POLIOMYELITIS. **4.** Perhaps Greek pelargos (< *pelawo-argos), stork (< "black-white bird"; argos, white; see **arg-**): PELARGONIUM. [Pok. 6. pel- 804.]

pel-³. To fold. **1.** Extended o-grade form *polt- in Germanic *falthan, *faldan in: **a.** Old English fealdan, faldan, to fold: FOLD¹; **b.** Old High German faldan, to fold: FALTBOAT; **c.** Germanic compound *faldistōlaz, "folding stool" (*stōlaz, stool; see **stā-**), in Medieval Latin compound faldistolium, folding chair: FALDSTOOL;

d. Germanic combining form *-falthaz, *-faldaz in Old English -feald, -fald, -fold: -FOLD. **2.** Combining form *-plo- in: **a.** Latin -plus, -fold (as in triplus, threefold): DECUPLE, MULTIPLE, OCTUPLE, QUADRUPLE, SEPTUPLE, (SEXTUPLE), TRIPLE; TRIPLOBLASTIC; **b.** Greek -plos, -ploos, -fold (as in haploos, haplous, single): -PLOID; (DIPLOID), HAPLOID. [Pok. 3. a. pel- 802.]

pel-⁴. Skin, hide. **1.** Suffixed form *pel-no- in Germanic *felnam in Old English fell, skin, hide: FELL³. **2.** Germanic suffixed form *fel-men- in Old English filmen, membrane: FILM. **3.** Suffixed form *pel-ni- in Latin pellis, skin: PELISSE, PELLICLE, (PELT¹), PELTRY, PILLION; PELLAGRA, SURPLICE. **4.** Greek -pelas, skin in: ERYSIPELAS. **5.** Suffixed form *pel-to- in Greek peltē, a shield (made of hide): PELTATE. [Pok 3 b. pel- 803.]

pel-⁵. To sell. Lengthened o-grade form *pōl- in Greek pōlein, to sell: BIBLIOPOLE, MONOPOLY. [Pok. 5. pel- 804.]

pel-⁶. To thrust, strike, drive. **I.** Suffixed form *pel-de-. **1.** Germanic *felt-, *falt-, to beat, in: **a.** Old English anfilt(e), anfealt, anvil ("something beaten on"): ANVIL; **b.** Germanic *feltaz, *filtiz, compressed wool, in (i) Old English felt, felt: FELT¹ (ii) Medieval Latin filtrum, filter, piece of felt: FILTER. **2.** Latin pellere (past participle pulsus), to push, drive, strike: POUSETTE, PULSATE, PULSE¹, PUSH; COMPEL, DISPEL, EXPEL, IMPEL, PROPEL, REPEL. **3.** Suffixed o-grade form *pol-o-, fuller of cloth, in Latin polīre, to make smooth, polish (< "to full cloth"): POLISH. **II.** Extended form *pelə-. **1.** Present stem *pelnā- in: **a.** Latin appellāre, "to drive to," address, entreat, appeal, call (ad-, to; see **ad-**): APPEAL; **b.** Latin compellāre, to accost, address (com-, intensive prefix; see **kom**): COMPELLATION; **c.** Latin interpellāre, "to thrust between," interrupt (inter-, between; see **en**): INTERPELLATE. **2.** Suffixed zero-grade extended adverbial form *plə-ti, in pre-Greek *plāti in Greek plēsios, near (< "pushed toward"): PLESIOSAURUS. [Pok. 2. a. pel- 801.]

pel-⁷. Dish. Suffixed lengthened-grade form *pēl-owi- in Latin pēlvis, basin: PELVIS. [Pok. 4. pel- 804.]

pelə-¹. **1.** To fill; with derivatives referring to abundance and multitude. Variant *plē-, contracted from *pleə-. **I.** Suffixed zero-grade form *plə-no-. **1.** Germanic *fulnaz, *fullaz, full, in Old English full, full: FULL¹. **2.** Derivative Germanic verb *fulljan, to fill, in Old English fyllan, to fill: FILL. **3.** Latin root *plāno- (influenced by Latin verb plēre, to fill; see **III. 1.** below) in Latin plēnus, full: PLENARY, PLENITUDE, PLENTY, PLENUM; PLENIPOTENTIARY, REPLENISH, TERREPLEIN. **II.** Suffixed form *p(e)lə-u- **1.** Possibly Latin palūs, marsh (? < "inundated"; but possibly rather from **pel-²**): PALUDAL, PALUDISM. **2.** Obscure comparative form (Old Latin plous) in Latin plūs, more: PIÙ, PLURAL, PLUS; NONPLUS, PLUPERFECT, SURPLUS. **3.** O-grade form *pol(ə)-u- in Greek polus, much, many: POLY-; HOI POLLOI. **III.** Variant form *plē-. **1.** Latin plēre, to fill: (ACCOMPLISH), COMPLETE, COMPLIMENT, COMPLY, EXPLETIVE, IMPLEMENT, REPLETE, SUPPLY. **2.** Possibly suffixed form *plē-dhw- in Latin plēbs, plēbēs, the people, multitude: PLEBE, PLEBEIAN, PLEBS; PLEBISCITE. **3.** Suffixed form *plē-dhwo- in: **a.** Greek plēthos (Ionic plēthus), great number: ISOPLETH; **b.** Greek derivative verb plēthein, to be full: PLETHORA; PLETHYSMOGRAPH. **4.** Suffixed (comparative) form *plē-i(s)on- in Greek pleōn, pleiōn, more: PLEO-, PLEONASM; PLEIOTAXY, PLEIOTROPISM, PLIOCENE. **5.** Suffixed (superlative) form *plē-isto- in Greek pleistos, most: PLEISTOCENE. **IV.** Possibly Sanskrit pūraḥ, cake (< "that which fills or satisfies"): POORI. [Pok. 1. pel- 798.]

pelə-². Flat; to spread. Variant *plā-, contracted from *pleə-. **1.** Suffixed form *pel(ə)-tu- in Germanic *felthuz, flat land, in Old English feld, open field: FIELD. **2.** Suffixed form *pel(ə)-tu-es- (by-form of *pel(ə)-tu-) in Germanic *feltha-, flat land, in: **a.** Old High German feld, field: FELDSPAR; **b.** Middle Dutch veld, velt, field: VELDT. **3.** Variant form *plā- in: **a.** suffixed form

*plā-ru- in Germanic *flōruz, floor, in Old English flōr, floor: FLOOR; **b.** suffixed form *plā-no- in Latin plānus, flat, level, even, plain, clear: LLANO, PIANO², PLAIN, PLANARIAN, PLANE¹, PLANE², PLANE³, PLANISH, PLANO-, PLANULA; AIRPLANE, EXPLAIN. **4.** Suffixed zero-grade form *plə-mā in Latin palma (< *palama), palm of the hand: PALM¹, PALM². **5.** Possibly extended variant form *plan- in: **a.** Greek planasthai, to wander (< "to spread out"): PLANET; APLANATIC; **b.** possibly Germanic *flan- in Old Norse flana, to wander aimlessly, akin to the Germanic source of French flâner, to walk the streets idly: FLÂNEUR. **6.** Suffixed zero-grade form *plə-dh- in Greek plassein (< *plath-yein), to mold, "spread out": -PLASIA, PLASMA, -PLAST, PLASTER, PLASTIC, PLASTID, -PLASTY; DYSPLASIA, METAPLASM, (TOXOPLASMA). **7.** O-grade form *polə- in: **a.** Russian polyĭ, open: POLYNYA; **b.** Slavic polje, broad flat land, field, in Polish Polak, Pole: POLACK, POLKA. See also extensions **plāk-**¹ and **plat-**. [Pok. pelə- 805.]

pelə-³. Citadel, fortified high place. Greek polis, city: POLICE, (POLICY¹), POLIS, POLITIC, (POLITY); ACROPOLIS, COSMOPOLIS, MEGALOPOLIS, METROPOLIS, NECROPOLIS, POLICLINIC, PROPOLIS. [In Pok. 1. pel- 798.]

pelis-. Also **pels-.** Rock, cliff. Germanic *felzam, rock, in Old Norse fjall, fell, rock, barren plateau: FJELD. [Pok. peli-s- 807.]

pen-. Swamp. Suffixed o-grade form *pon-yo- in Germanic *fanjam, swamp, marsh, in Old English fenn, marsh: FEN. [Pok. 2. pen- 807.]

penkʷe. Five. **I.** Basic form *penkʷe. **1.** Assimilated form *pempe in Germanic *fimf in: **a.** Old English fīf, five: FIVE; **b.** Old High German finf, funf, five: FIN². **2.** Germanic compound *fimftehun, fifteen (*tehun, ten; see **dekm̥**), in: **a.** Old English fīftēne, fifteen: FIFTEEN; **b.** Old Norse fimmtān, fifteen: FEMTO-. **3.** Assimilated form *kʷenkʷe in: **a.** Latin quīnque, five: CINQUAIN, CINQUE, QUINQUE-; CINQUEFOIL, QUINCUNX; **b.** Latin distributive quīnī, five each: KENO, QUINATE; **c.** Latin compound quīndecim, fifteen (decem, ten; see **dekm̥**): QUINDECENNIAL. **4.** Greek pente, five: PENTA-, PENTAD; PENTACLE, PENTADACTYL, PENTAGON, PENTAMETER, PENTARCHY, PENTASTICH, PENTATEUCH, PENTATHLON. **5.** Sanskrit pañca, five: PUNCH³; PACHISI. **II.** Compound *penkʷe-(d)konta, "five tens," fifty (*-(d)konta, group of ten; see **dekm̥**). **1.** Latin quīnquāginta, fifty: QUINQUAGENARIAN, QUINQUAGESIMA. **2.** Greek pentēkonta, fifty: PENTECOST. **III.** Ordinal adjective *penkʷ-to-. **1.** Germanic *fimftōn- in Old English fīfta, fifth: FIFTH. **2.** Latin quīntus (< *quinc-tos), feminine quīnta, fifth: QUINT¹, QUINTAIN, QUINTET, QUINTILE; QUINTESSENCE, QUINTILLION, QUINTUPLE. **IV.** Suffixed form *penkʷ-ro- in Germanic *fingwraz, finger (< "one of five"), in Old English finger, finger: FINGER. **V.** Suffixed reduced zero-grade form *pn̥k-sti- in Germanic *fū(nh)stiz in: **a.** Old English fŷst, fist: FIST; **b.** Dutch vuist, fist: FOIST. [Pok. penkʷe 808, pn̥ksti- 839.]

pent-. To tread, go. **1.** Germanic *finthan, to come upon, discover, in Old English findan, to find: FIND. **2.** Suffixed o-grade form *pont-i- in: **a.** Latin pōns (stem pont-), bridge (earliest meaning, "way, passage," preserved in the priestly title pontifex, "he who prepares the way"; -fex, maker; see **dhē-**¹): PONS, PONTIFEX, PONTIFF, PONTINE, PONTOON, PUNT¹ (TRANSPONTINE); **b.** Russian put', path, way, in sputnik, fellow traveler: SPUTNIK. **3.** Zero-grade form *pn̥t- in Greek patein, to tread, walk: PERIPATETIC. **4.** Suffixed zero-grade form *pn̥t-ə- in Iranian *path-, probably borrowed (? via Scythian) into Germanic as *patha-, way, path, in: **a.** Old English pæth, path: PATH; **b.** Middle Dutch pad, way, path: FOOTPAD. [Pok. pent- 808.]

per¹. Base of prepositions and preverbs with the basic meanings of "forward," "through," and a wide range of extended senses such as "in front of," "before," "early," "first," "chief," "toward," "against," "near," "at,"

"around." **I.** Basic form *per and extended form *peri. **1.** Germanic *fer-, *far-, used chiefly as an intensive prefix denoting destruction, reversal, or completion, in: **a.** Old High German far-, in German vereinen, to unite: TURNVEREIN; **b.** Middle Dutch vieren, to let out, slacken: VEER²; **c.** compound *fer-getan, "to lose one's hold," forget (see **ghend-**). **2.** Suffixed (comparative) form *per-ero-, farther away, in Germanic *fer(e)ra in Old English feor(r), far: FAR. **3.** Compound *per-n-yo-, of last year (*-n-, year; see **en-**), in Germanic *fernja- in Old High German firni, old: FIRN. **4.** Latin per, through, for, by: PER, PER-; PARAMOUNT, PARAMOUR, PARGET, PARVENU. **5.** Greek peri, around, near, beyond: PERI-; PERISSODACTYL, PERIOSTEUM. **6.** Sanskrit pari, through, around: PALANQUIN. **7.** Avestan pairi, around: PARADISE. **II.** Zero-grade form *pr̥-. **1.** Germanic *fur, before, in: **a.** Old English for, before, instead of, on account of: FOR; **b.** Old English for-, prefix denoting destruction, pejoration, exclusion, or completion: FOR-. **2.** Extended form *pr̥t- in Germanic *furth-, forward, in Old English forth, forth: FORTH; AFFORD. **3.** Suffixed (comparative) form *pr̥-tero- in Germanic *furthera- in Old English furthra, furthor, farther away: FURTHER. **4.** Compound *pr̥-st-i- (or *por-st-i-, with o-grade form *por-), "that which stands before," stake, post (see **stā-**). **III.** Extended zero-grade form *prə-. **1.** Suffixed (superlative) form *prə-mo- in: **a.** Germanic *fruma-, *furma- in Old English forma, first, foremost: FOREMOST, FORMER²; **b.** Latin compound prandium, "first meal," late breakfast, lunch (probably < *prām-d-ium < *prəm-(e)d-yo-; second element *-(e)d-, to eat; see **ed-**). **2.** Suffixed (superlative) form *prə-isto- in Germanic *furista-, foremost, in Old English fyrst, fyrest, first: FIRST. **3.** Suffixed form *prə-wo- in Greek *prōwo-, first, foremost, in: **a.** analogically suffixed Greek form *prōw-arya in Greek prōira, forward part of a ship: PROW; **b.** suffixed (superlative) Greek form *prōw-ato- in Greek prōtos, first, foremost: PROTEIN, PROTIST, PROTO-, PROTON. **4.** Suffixed form *prə-i in Celtic *(p)ari, *are in Gaulish ari (combining form are-), before, in Latin arepennis, half-acre (second element obscure): ARPENT. **IV.** Extended form *prəā. **1.** Germanic *fura, before, in: **a.** Old English fore, for (> Middle English fore-), before: FORE, FORE-; FOREFATHER; **b.** Old High German fora (> German vor), before: VORLAGE; **c.** Germanic prefixed and suffixed form *bi-fora-na, in the front (*bi-, at, by; see **ambhi**), in Old English beforan, before: BEFORE. **2.** Greek para, beside, alongside of, beyond: PARA-¹; PALFREY. **V.** Extended form *prō. **1. a.** Germanic *fra, forward, away from, in Old Norse frā (> Middle English fro), from: FRO; FROWARD; **b.** Germanic *fra-, completely (see **ed-, ēik-**). **2.** Suffixed form *pro-mo- in: **a.** Germanic *fram, from, in Old English from, from: FROM; **b.** Germanic *frum, forward, hence derivative verb *frumjan, to further, in Old French f(o)urnir, to supply, provide: FURNISH, VENEER; **c.** Czech prám, raft: PRAAM. **3.** Suffixed form *prō-wo- in Germanic *frōwō-, lady, in: **a.** Old High German frouwa, lady: FRAU, (FRÄULEIN); **b.** Middle Dutch vrouwe, woman: VROUW. **4.** Latin prō, prō-, before, for, instead of: PRO¹, PRO-¹; PURCHASE. **5.** Suffixed form *prō-no- in Latin prōnus, leaning forward: PRONE. **6.** Possible suffixed form *pro-ko- in Latin compound reciprocus, alternating, "backward and forward" (*re-ko-, backward; see **re-**): RECIPROCAL. **7.** Suffixed adverb *pro-kʷe in: **a.** Latin prope, near: APPROACH, RAPPROCHEMENT, REPROACH; **b.** suffixed form *prokʷ-inkʷo- in Latin propinquus, near: PROPINQUITY; **c.** suffixed (superlative) form *prokʷ-samo- in Latin proximus, nearest: PROXIMATE; APPROXIMATE. **8.** Compound *pro-bhw-o-, growing well or straightforward (*bhw-o-, to grow; see **bheuə-**), in Latin probus, upright, good, virtuous (PROBABLE), PROBE, PROBITY, (PROOF), PROVE; APPROVE, IMPROBITY, (IMPROVE), (REPROVE). **9.** Greek pro, before, in front, forward: PRO-². **10.** Suffixed (com-

parative) form *pro-tero- in Greek *proteros*, before, former: HYSTERON PROTERON, PROTEROZOIC. **VI.** Extended forms *prai-, *prei-. **1.** Latin *prae*, before: PRE-; PRETERIT. **2.** Suffixed (comparative) form *prei-yos- in Latin *prior*, former, higher, superior: PRIOR². **3.** Suffixed form *prei-wo- in: **a.** Latin *prīvus*, single, alone (< "standing in front," "isolated from others"): PRIVATE, PRIVILEGE, PRIVITY, PRIVY; DEPRIVE; **b.** Latin *proprius*, one's own, particular (< *prō prīvō*, in particular, from the ablative of *prīvus*, single): PROPER, PROPERTY; APPROPRIATE, PROPRIOCEPTION, PROPRIOCEPTOR. **4.** Extended form *preis- in: **a.** suffixed (superlative) form *preis-mo- in *(i)* Latin *prīmus* (< *prīsmus*; ablative plural *prīmīs*), first, foremost: PREMIER, PRIMAL, PRIMARY, PRIMATE, PRIME, PRIMITIVE, PRIMO, PRIMUS; IMPRIMIS, PRIMA FACIE, PRIMAVERA, PRIMEVAL, PRIMIPARA, PRIMOGENITOR, PRIMOGENITURE, PRIMORDIAL *(ii)* Latin compound *prīnceps*, "he who takes first place" (*-ceps*, "-taker"; see **kap-**), leader, chief, emperor: PRINCE, PRINCIPAL, PRINCIPLE; **b.** suffixed form *preis-tano- in Latin *prīstinus*, former, earlier, original: PRISTINE. **VII.** Extended form *pres- in compound *pres-gʷu-, "going before" (*gʷu-, to go; see **gʷā-**), in Greek *presbus*, old, old man, elder: PRESBYTER, (PRIEST); PRESBYOPIA. **VIII.** Extended form *proti in Greek *pros*, against, toward, near, at: PROS-; PROSOPOPEIA. Other possibly related forms are grouped under **per-²**, **per-³**, **per-⁴**, **per-⁵**, and **per-⁷**. [Pok. 2. A. *per* 810.]

per-². To lead, pass over. A verbal root belonging to the group of **per¹. I.** Full-grade form *per-. **1.** Suffixed form *per-tu-s in Germanic *ferthuz, place for crossing over, ford, in Old Norse *fjördhr*, an inlet, estuary: FIRTH, FJORD. **2.** Suffixed form *per-onā in Greek *peronē*, pin of a brooch, buckle (< "that which pierces through"): PERONEAL. **II.** O-grade form *por-. **1.** Germanic *faran, to go, in: **a.** Old English *faran* (> Middle English *faren*), to go on a journey, get along: FARE; WAYFARER, WAYFARING, (WELFARE); **b.** Old High German *faran*, to go, travel: GABERDINE. **2.** Suffixed form *por-o-, passage, journey, in Greek *poros*, journey, passage: PORE²; EMPORIUM, POROMERIC. **3.** Suffixed (causative) form *por-eyo-, to cause to go, lead, conduct, in Germanic *farjan, to ferry, in Old English *ferian*, to transport: FERRY. **4.** Lengthened-grade form *pōr- in: **a.** Germanic suffixed form *fōr-ja- in Old English *(ge)fēra*, "fellow-traveler," companion (*ge-*, together, with; see **kom**): FERE; **b.** Germanic suffixed (causative) form *fōr-jan in Old High German *fuoren*, to lead: FÜHRER. **5.** Possibly suffixed form *por-no-, feather, wing (< "that which carries a bird in flight"), in: **a.** Germanic *farnō, feather, leaf, in Old English *fearn*, fern (having feathery fronds): FERN; **b.** Sanskrit *parṇam*, leaf, feather: PAN². **III.** Zero-grade form *pṛ-. **1.** Suffixed form *pṛ-tu-, passage, in: **a.** Germanic *furdu- in Old English *ford*, shallow place where one may cross a river: FORD; **b.** Latin *portus*, harbor (< "passage"): PORT¹; IMPORTUNE, OPPORTUNE. **2.** Suffixed form *pṛ-tā in Latin *porta*, gate (> Old French *porte*, door): PORCH, PORT³, PORTAL, PORTCULLIS, PORTE-COCHÈRE, PORTER², PORTICO, PORTIÈRE, PORTULACA. **3.** Suffixed (denominative) form *pṛ-to- in Latin *portāre*, to carry: PORT⁵, PORTABLE, PORTAGE, PORTAMENTO, PORTATIVE, PORTER¹; COMPORT, DEPORT, EXPORT, IMPORT, (IMPORTANT), PORTFOLIO, PURPORT, RAPPORT, REPORT, (SPORT), SUPPORT, TRANSPORT. [Pok. 2. B. *per* 816.]

per-³. The young of an animal (< "a bringing forth," "offspring"). Derivative root belonging to the group of **per¹. 1.** Suffixed o-grade form *por-sī- in Germanic *farzī-, young cow, in Old English *fearr*, calf, and compound *heahfore*, calf (first element obscure): HEIFER. [In Pok. 2. D. *per* 818.]

per-⁴. To try, risk (< "to lead over," "press forward"). A verbal root belonging to the group of **per¹. 1.** Lengthened grade *pēr- in Germanic *fēraz, danger, in Old English

fǣr, danger, sudden calamity: FEAR. **2.** Suffixed form *perī-tlo- in Latin *perīclum, perīculum*, trial, danger: (PARLOUS), PERIL. **3.** Suffixed form *per-yo- in Latin *experīrī*, to try, learn by trying (*ex-*, from; see **eghs**): EXPERIENCE, EXPERIMENT, EXPERT. **4.** Suffixed form *per-ya in Greek *peira*, trial, attempt (> *peiran*, to attempt): PIRATE; EMPIRIC. [Pok. 2. E. *per* 818.]

per-⁵. To strike. Extended forms *prem-, pres- in Latin *premere* (past participle *pressus*), to press: PREGNANT², PRESS¹, PRESSURE, PRINT; APPRESSED, COMPRESS, DEPRESS, EXPRESS, IMPRESS¹, (IMPRINT), OPPRESS, REPRESS, (REPRIMAND), SUPPRESS. [Pok. 3. *per* 818.]

per-⁶. To traffic in, sell (< "to hand over," "distribute"). A verbal root belonging to the group of **per¹**. Base of two distinct extended roots. **I.** Root form *pret-. **1.** Latin compound *inter-pres* (stem *inter-pret-*), go-between, negotiator (*inter-*, between; see **en**): INTERPRET. **2.** Suffixed form *pret-yo- in Latin *pretium*, price: PRAISE, PRECIOUS, PRICE; APPRAISE, (APPRECIATE), DEPRECIATE. **II.** Root form *perǝ-. Suffixed form *p(e)r-n-ǝ- in Greek *pernanai*, to sell, whence o-grade *por(ǝ)-nā in Greek *pornē*, prostitute: PORNOGRAPHY. [In Pok. 2. C. *per* 817.]

perd-. To fart. **1.** Germanic *fertan, *fartōn in Old English *feortan* (> Middle English *farten*), to fart: FART. **2.** Greek *perdix*, partridge (which makes a sharp whirring sound when suddenly flushed): PARTRIDGE. See also **pezd-**. [Pok. *perd-* 819.]

perǝ-¹. To produce, procure. Perhaps an extension of **per-³**, a verbal root belonging to the group of **per¹**. Possibly the same root as **perǝ-²**. Zero-grade form *prǝ- (becoming *par- in Latin) in: **a.** root form *par-ā- in Latin *parāre*, to try to get, prepare, equip: PARADE, PARE, PARRY, (PARURE); APPARATUS, (APPAREL), COMPRADOR, DISPARATE, EMPEROR, (IMPERATIVE), (IMPERIAL), (PARACHUTE), PARASOL, PREPARE, RAMPART, REPAIR¹, SEPARATE, (SEVER), (SEVERAL); **b.** suffixed form *par-yo- in Latin *parere, parīre*, to get, beget, give birth (> *partus*, accusative *partum*, birth): -PARA, PARENT, -PAROUS, PARTURIENT, POSTPARTUM, REPERTORY; **c.** suffixed form *par-os, producing, in compound *pau-paros, producing little, poor (see **pau-**); **d.** suffixed form *par-ikā in Latin *Parcae*, the Fates (who assign one's destiny): PARCAE. [Pok. 2. D. *per* 818.]

perǝ-². To grant, allot (reciprocally, to get in return). Possibly the same root as **perǝ-¹**. Zero-grade form *prǝ- (becoming *par- in Latin) in: **a.** suffixed form *par-ti- in Latin *pars* (stem *part-*), a share, part: PARCEL, (PARCENER), PARSE, PART; BIPARTITE, COMPART, IMPART, IMPARTEE; **b.** possibly suffixed form *par-tiō in Latin *portiō*, a part (first attested in the phrase *prō portiōne* in proportion, according to each part, perhaps assimilated from *prō partiōne*): PORTION, PROPORTION; **c.** perhaps Latin *pār*, equal (> French *pari*, wager): PAIR, PAR, PARITY², PARLAY, PEER²; COMPARE, IMPARITY, NONPAREIL, PARI-MUTUEL. [Pok. 2. *per*, Section C. 817.]

perg-. Pole, stem. Possibly Latin *pergula*, a projection, balcony, outhouse: PERGOLA. [Pok. 1. *perg-* 819.]

perk-¹. Speckled. Often used in names of spotted or pied animals. Greek *perkē*, the perch: PERCH². [Pok. 2. *perk-* 820.]

perk-². To dig out, tear out. Zero-grade form *pṛk- in Germanic *furh- in Old English *furh*, trench: FURROW. [Pok. 3. *perk-* 821.]

perkʷu-. Oak. **1.** Zero-grade form *pṛkʷ- in Germanic *furhu- in Old English *furh, fyrh*, fir: FIR. **2.** Assimilated form *kʷerkʷu- in Latin *quercus*, oak: QUERCETIN, QUERCITRON. [Pok. *perkʷu-s* 822.]

persnā. Heel. Latin *perna*, ham, leg, sea mussel: PEARL¹. [Pok. *persnā* 823.]

pes-. Penis. Suffixed form *pes-ni- in Latin *pēnis* (< *pesnis*), penis, tail: PENCIL, (PENICILLIUM), PENIS. [Pok. 3. *pes-* 824.]

pet- Also **petǝ-**. To rush, fly. Variant *ptē-, contracted from *pteǝ-. **1.** Suffixed form *pet-rā in Germanic *feth-

rō, feather, in Old English *fether*, feather: FEATHER.
2. Latin *petere*, to go toward, seek: -PETAL, PETITION,
PETULANT; APPETITE, COMPETE, IMPETUS, PERPETUAL,
REPEAT. **3.** Suffixed form **pet-nā* in Latin *penna, pinna*,
feather, wing: PANACHE, PEN[1], PENNA, PENNATE, PEN-
NON, PINNA, PINNACLE, PINNATE, PINNATI-, PINNULE.
4. Suffixed form **pet-ro-* (see **ōku-**). **5.** Suffixed form
*pet-yo- in Latin *propitius*, favorable, gracious, originally
a religious term meaning "falling or rushing forward,"
hence "eager," "well-disposed" (said of the gods; *prō-*,
forward; see **per¹**): PROPITIOUS. **6.** Suffixed zero-grade
form **pt-ero-* in Greek *pteron*, feather, wing, and *pterux*,
wing: -PTER; ACANTHOPTERYGIAN, APTERYX, ARCHAEOP-
TERYX, COLEOPTERA, MECOPTERAN, PERIPTERAL, PLE-
COPTERAN, PTERIDOLOGY, PTEROCERCOID, PTERYGOID.
7. Suffixed zero-grade form **pt-ilo-* in Greek *ptilon*, soft
feathers, down, plume: COLEOPTILE. **8.** Suffixed variant
form **ptē-no-* in Greek *ptēnos*, winged, flying: STEAROP-
TENE. **9.** Reduplicated form **pi-pt-* in Greek *piptein*, to
fall: PTOMAINE, PTOSIS; PERIPETEIA, PROPTOSIS, SYMP-
TOM. **10.** O-grade form **pot-* in Greek *potamos* (*-amo-*,
Greek suffix), "rushing water," river: HIPPOPOTAMUS.
[Pok. 2. *pet-* 826.]
pete-. To spread. **1.** Suffixed o-grade form **pot(ə)-mo-* in
Germanic **fathmaz*, "length of two arms stretched out,"
in Old English *fæthm*, fathom: FATHOM. **2.** Suffixed
(stative) variant zero-grade form **pat-ē-* in Latin *patēre*,
to be open: PATENT, PATULOUS. **3.** Variant zero-grade
form in nasalized form **pat-no-* probably in Latin *pan-
dere* (past participle *passus* < **pat-to-*), to spread out:
PACE¹, (PAS), (PASS), PASSIM; EXPAND, REPAND. **4.** Suffixed form **pet-alo-* in Greek *petalon*, leaf: PETAL. **5.** Suffixed form **pet-ano-* in Greek *patanē* (? < **petanā*),
platter, "thing spread out": (PAELLA), PAN¹, PATEN,
(PATINA¹), (PATINA²). [Pok. 1. *pet-* 824.]
[petra. Cliff. Greek noun. Collective formation from
petros, rock, stone (of unknown origin). PETRO-, PET-
ROUS; PARSLEY, PETRIFY, SALTPETER.]
peu-. To cut, strike, stamp. **1.** Suffixed (participial)
zero-grade form **pu-to-*, cut, struck, in: **a.** Latin *putāre*,
to prune, clean, settle an account, think over, reflect,
consider: PUTAMEN, PUTATIVE; (ACCOUNT), AMPUTATE,
COMPUTE, COUNT¹, DEPUTE, DISPUTE, IMPUTE, REPUTE;
b. possibly Latin *puteus*, well (> Old English *pytt*): PIT¹.
2. Variant form **pau-* in: **a.** suffixed form **pau-yo-* in
Latin *pavīre*, to beat: PAVE, (PAVÉ); **b.** suffixed (stative)
form **paw-ē-* in Latin *pavēre*, to fear (< "to be struck"):
PAVID; **c.** perhaps Greek *paiein*, to beat: ANAPEST. [Pok.
3. *pēu-* 827.]
peue-. To purify, cleanse. Suffixed zero-grade form
*pū-ro- (< **puə-ro-*) in Latin *pūrus*, pure, and *pūrgāre*, to
purify (< **pūr-igāre;* second element *agere*, to drive; see
ag-): PURE, PURGE, PURITAN; COMPURGATION, DEPU-
RATE, EXPURGATE, (SPURGE). [Pok. 1. *peu-* 827.]
peuk-. Also **peug-**. To prick. Zero-grade form **pug-*.
1. Suffixed form **pug-no-* in Latin *pugil*, pugilist, and
pugnus, fist, with denominative *pugnāre*, to fight with
the fist: PONIARD, PUGILISM, PUGIL STICK, PUGNACIOUS;
IMPUGN, OPPUGN, REPUGN. **2.** Nasalized zero-grade form
*pu-n-g- in Latin *pungere*, to prick: BUNG, POIGNANT,
POINT, POINTILLISM, PONTIL, (POUNCE¹), (POUNCE³);
PUNCHEON¹, PUNCTUATE, PUNCTURE, PUNGENT; COM-
PUNCTION, EXPUNGE, SPONTOON, TRAPUNTO. **3.** Greek
pugmē, fist: PYGMAEAN, PYGMY. [Pok. *peuk-* 828.]
pezd-. To fart. **1.** Suffixed form **pezd-i-* in Germanic
*fistiz, a fart, in Middle English *fisten*, to fart: FEIST,
FIZZLE. **2.** Latin *pēdere*, to fart: PETARD. **3.** Possibly
Latin *pēdis*, louse (? < "foul-smelling insect"): PEDICU-
LAR. See also **perd-**. [Pok. *pezd-* 829, 2. *peis-* 796.]
peter-. Father. **1.** Germanic **fadar* in Old English *fæder*
(> Middle English *fader*), father: FATHER; FOREFATHER.
2. Latin *pater*, father (> *patrāre*, to bring about): PADRE,
PATER, PATERNAL, PATRI-, PATRICIAN, PATRIMONY, PA-
TRON; EXPATRIATE, IMPETRATE, PERPETRATE. **3.** Greek

patēr, father: PATRIOT; ALLOPATRIC, EUPATRID, PATRI-
ARCH, SYMPATRIC. [Pok. *potě(r)* 829.]
p(h)ol-. To fall. Suffixed form **phol-no-* in Germanic
*fallan in: **a.** Old English *feallan*, to fall: FALL; **b.** Germanic causative **falljan*, "to cause to fall," strike down,
in Old English *fellan, fyllan*, to cut down: FELL¹; **c.** Germanic compound **bi-fallan*, to fall, happen (**bi-*, by, at;
see **ambhi**), in Old English *befeallan*, to fall: BEFALL.
[Pok. *phōl-* 851.]
[phulax. Watcher, guard. Greek noun of unknown origin,
related to *phulassein* (Attic *phulattein*), to guard, protect. PHYLACTERY, PHYLAXIS; PROPHYLACTIC.]
pik-. Pitch. Latin *pix* (stem *pic-*), pitch: PAY²; PICEOUS,
PITCH¹; PICOLINE, PITCHBLENDE. [In Pok. *pei(ə)-* 793.]
pilo-. Hair. A possible root. **1.** Latin *pilus*, hair: PELAGE,
PILAR, PILE³, PILOSE, PILUS, PLUCK, PLUSH, POILU; CAT-
ERPILLAR, DEPILATE. **2.** Suffixed reduced form **pil-so-*
possibly in: **a.** Latin *pilleus, pīleus*, felt cap: PILEUS,
PILLAGE; **b.** Greek *pilos*, felt: PILOCARPINE. [Pok. *pi-lo-*
830.]
pipp-. To peep. Imitative root. **1.** Latin *pīpāre*, to chirp
(> Old High German *pfīffa*, pipe): FIFE, PIPE. **2.** Latin
pīpīre, to chirp: PIGEON. **3.** Gaelic *pīob*, a pipe, in Scottish Gaelic *piobaireachd*, pipe music: PIBROCH. [Pok.
pīp(p)- 830.]
[pippalī. Pepper. Sanskrit noun of unknown origin.
Possibly related to *pippala*, the bo tree. **1.** Sanskrit
pippalī: PEPPER, (PIMPERNEL). **2.** Sanskrit *pippalam*:
PEEPUL.]
[pius. Dutiful, devoted, pious. Latin word having cognates in other Italic languages. PIACULAR, (PIETÀ), PI-
ETY, PIOUS, PITTANCE, PITY; EXPIATE, IMPIOUS.]
plab-. To flap. Imitative root. Middle English *flappen*, to
flap: FLAP [Pok. *plab-* 831.]
plāk-¹. Also **plak-**. To be flat. Extension of **pele-²**.
1. Germanic **flōhō* in Old Norse *flō*, layer, coating: FLOE.
2. Variant form **plāg-* in: **a.** Germanic **flōk-* in Old
English *flōc*, flatfish: FLUKE¹; **b.** Germanic **flakaz* in
Norwegian *flak*, flat piece, flake, probably akin to the
Scandinavian source of Middle English *flake*, flake:
FLAKE¹; **c.** Germanic **flak-* in Old Norse *flaki, fleki*,
hurdle: FLAKE². **3.** Extended form **plakā* in Germanic
*flagō in Old Norse *flaga*, layer of stone: FLAG⁴, FLAW¹.
4. Possibly suffixed (stative) form **plak-ē-*, to be calm
(as of the flat sea), in Latin *placēre*, to please, be
agreeable: PLACEBO, PLACID, PLEA, (PLEAD), PLEASANT,
PLEASE; COMPLACENT. **5.** Lengthened suffixed form
*plāk-ā- in Latin *plācāre*, to calm (causative of *placēre*):
PLACABLE, PLACATE. **6.** Nasalized form **pla-n-k-* in
Latin *plancus*, flat, flat-footed, whence *planca*, board:
PLANCHET, PLANK, PLANK-SHEER. **7.** Variant form **plag-*
in: **a.** perhaps Latin *plaga*, net (? < "something extended"): PLAGIARY; **b.** Greek *plagos*, side: PLAGAL,
PLAGIO-, PLAYA. **8.** Root form **plak-* in Greek *plax*, flat,
flat land, surface: PLACENTA, PLACOID. **9.** Variant form
*pelag- in Greek *pelagos*, sea: PELAGIC; ARCHIPELAGO.
[Pok. 1. *plā-k-* 831.]
plāk-². To strike. **1.** Nasalized variant forms **pla-n-k-*,
*pla-n-g- in: **a.** Germanic **flang-* in Old Norse *flengja*, to
flog, whip, akin to the Scandinavian source of Middle
English *flingen*, to fling: FLING; **b.** Latin *plangere*, to
strike (one's own breast), lament: PLAINT, PLANGENT;
COMPLAIN. **c.** suffixed form **plag-yo-* in Greek *plazein*,
to drive away, turn aside: PLANKTON. **2.** Variant form
*plāg- in Latin *plāga*, a blow, stroke: PLAGUE. **3.** Suffixed form **plāk-yo-* in Greek *plēssein*, to beat, strike:
PLECTRUM, -PLEGIA, PLEXOR; APOPLEXY, CATAPLEXY,
PARAPLEGIA. [Pok. 2. *plāk-* 832.]
plat-. To spread. Extension of **pele-²**. **1.** Variant form
*plad- in Germanic **flataz*, flat, in: **a.** Old Norse *flatr*,
flat: FLAT¹; **b.** Old French *flater*, to flatter: FLATTER¹.
2. Suffixed variant form **plad-yo-* in Germanic **flatjam*
in Old English *flet(t)*, floor, dwelling: FLAT². **3.** Basic form
*plat- in Germanic **flathō(n)*, flat cake, in Late Latin

fladō, flat cake, pancake: FLAN. **4.** Germanic nasalized suffixed form **flu-n-th-r-jō-* in Old Swedish *flundra*, flatfish, flounder, probably akin to the Scandinavian source of Middle English *flounder*, flounder: FLOUNDER². **5.** Nasalized form **pla-n-t-* in Latin *planta*, sole of the foot, and denominative *plantāre*, to drive in with the sole of the foot, plant, whence *planta*, a plant: CLAN, PLAN, PLANT, PLANTAIN¹, PLANTAR; PLANTIGRADE, SUPPLANT. **6.** Suffixed form **plat-u-* in Greek *platus* (feminine *plateia*), flat, broad: PIAZZA, PLACE, PLAICE, PLANE⁴, (PLANE TREE), PLATE, (PLATEAU), (PLATITUDE), (PLATY²), PLATY-, (PLAZA). [Pok. *plat-* 833.]

[plegan. To pledge for, stake, risk, exercise oneself. West Germanic verb. **1.** Old English *plegian*, to exercise oneself, play: PLAY. **2.** Late Latin *plevium* (> Old French *plevir*, to pledge), pledge, guarantee: PLEDGE; REPLEVIN. **3.** Germanic derivative noun **plehti-* in Old English *pliht*, danger, peril: PLIGHT².]

plek-. To plait. Extension of **pel-³.** **1.** Suffixed o-grade form **plok-so-* in Germanic **flahsam*, flax, in Old English *fleax*, flax: FLAX. **2.** Full-grade form **plek-* in Latin *-plex*, -fold (in compounds such as *duplex*, twofold; and *supplex*, "with legs folded under one," kneeling, entreating; see **dwo-, upo-**): MULTIPLEX, QUINTUPLE, SUPPLE. **3.** Latin *plicāre*, to fold (also in compounds used as denominatives of words in *-plex*, genitive *-plicis*): PLAIT, PLIANT, PLICA, PLICATE, PLIGHT¹, PLISSÉ, PLY¹; APPLY, COMPLICATE, COMPLICE, DEPLOY, DISPLAY, EMPLOY, EXPLICATE, IMPLICATE, REPLICATE, SUPPLICATE. **4.** Suffixed forms **plek-to-* and **plek-t-to-* in Latin *plectere* (past participle *plexus*), to weave, plait, entwine: PLEACH, PLEXUS; AMPLEXICAUL, COMPLECT, (COMPLEX), PERPLEX. **5.** Greek *plekein*, to plait, twine, and *plektos*, twisted: PLECOPTERAN, PLECTOGNATH. [Pok. *plek-* 834.]

plēk-. Also **pleik-.** To tear. **1.** Zero-grade form **plǝk-* becoming **plak-* in Germanic **flahan* in Old English *flēan*, to strip the skin from: FLAY. **2.** Suffixed o-grade form **ploik-sk-* perhaps in Germanic **flaiskjan*, piece of flesh torn off, in Old English *flǣsc*, flesh: FLESH. **3.** Zero-grade form **plik-* in Germanic **flikkja* in: **a.** Old English *flicce*, side of a hog: FLITCH; **b.** Germanic ablaut form **flekkja* in Old Norse *flekkr*, piece of skin or flesh, spot, stain: FLECK. [Pok. *plēk-* 835.]

pleu-. To flow. **I.** Basic form **pleu-*. **1.** Latin *pluere*, to rain: (PLOVER), (PLUVIAL), PLUVIOUS. **2.** Greek *pleusis*, sailing: PLEUSTON. **3.** Suffixed zero-grade form **plu-elos* dissimilated into Greek *puelos*, trough, basin: PYELITIS. **4.** Suffixed form **pl(e)u-mon-*, "floater," lung(s), in: **a.** Latin *pulmō* (< **plumonēs*), lung(s): PULMONARY; **b.** Greek *pleumōn*, *pneumōn*, lung: PNEUMONIA, PNEUMONIC. **5.** Suffixed o-grade form **plou-to-* in Greek *ploutos*, wealth, riches (< "overflowing"): PLUTO; PLUTOCRACY. **6.** Lengthened o-grade form **plō(u)-* in: **a.** Germanic **flōwan*, to flow, in (i) Old English *flōwan*, to flow: FLOW (ii) perhaps Middle Dutch *vluwe*, fishnet: FLUE²; **b.** suffixed form **plō-tu-* in Old English *flōd*, flowing water, deluge, flood: FLOOD. **II.** Extended form **pleuk-*. **1.** Germanic **fleugan*, to fly, in Old English *flēogan*, to fly: FLY¹. **2.** Germanic **fleugōn-*, flying insect, fly, in Old English *flēoge*, a fly: FLY². **3.** Probably Germanic **fleuhan*, to run away, in Old English *flēon*, to flee: FLEE. **4.** Germanic causative **flauhjan* in Old English *flȳgan*, *flēgan*, to put to flight: FLEY. **5.** Germanic suffixed form **fleug-ika* in Old French *fleche*, arrow: FLÈCHE, FLETCHER. **6.** Zero-grade form **pluk-* in: **a.** Germanic **flugja-*, feather, in Old English *-flycge*, with feathers (only in *unfligge*, featherless): FLEDGE; **b.** suffixed form **flug-ti-* in Old English *flyht*, act of flying, and **flyht*, act of fleeing, escape: FLIGHT¹, FLIGHT²; **c.** possibly (but unlikely) suffixed form **fluglaz*, dissimilated into **fuglaz*, bird, in Old English *fugol*, bird: FOWL; **d.** Germanic suffixed form **flug-ila* in Middle High German *vlügel* (> Germanic *Flügel*), wing: FLÜGELHORN, FUGLEMAN. **III.** Extended form **pleud-*.

1. Germanic **fleutan* in Old English *flēotan*, to float, swim: FLEET¹, FLEET². **2.** Zero-grade form **plud-* in Germanic **flut-*, **flot-* in: **a.** Germanic derivative **flotōn*, to float, in (i) Old English *flotian*, to float: FLOAT (ii) Old French *floter*, to float: FLOTSAM; **b.** Old Norse *floti*, raft, fleet: FLOTILLA; **c.** Old English *floterian*, *flotorian*, to float back and forth (*-erian*, iterative and frequentative suffix): FLUTTER; **d.** Germanic **flutjan*, to float, in Old Norse *flytja*, to further, convey: FLIT. **3.** Probably Germanic suffixed form **flaut-stā-*, contracted into **flausta-* in Icelandic *flaustr*, hurry, and *flaustra*, to bustle, akin to the probable Scandinavian source of FLUSTER. [Pok. *pleu-* 835, pl(e)u-mon- 837.]

pleus-. To pluck; a feather, fleece. **1.** Germanic **fleusaz*, fleece, in Old English *flēos*, fleece: FLEECE. **2.** Suffixed zero-grade form **plus-mā* in Latin *plūma*, a feather: PLUMATE, PLUME, PLUMOSE, PLUMULE; DEPLUME. [Pok. *pleus-* 838.]

plou-. Flea. **1.** Extended form **plouk-* in Germanic **flauhaz* in Old English *flēa(h)*, flea: FLEA. **2.** Extended zero-grade form **plus-* metathesized into **pusl-* in: **a.** Latin *pūlex* (< **puslex*), flea: PUCE; PULICIDE; **b.** Greek *psulla*, flea: PSYLLA. [Pok. *blou-* 102.]

[plumbum. Lead. Latin noun, probably borrowed from the same unidentified source as Greek *molubdos*, lead. **1.** Latin *plumbum*: PLUMB, PLUMBAGO, PLUMBER, PLUMBISM, PLUMMET, PLUNGE; APLOMB, PLUMBIFEROUS. **2.** Greek *molubdos*: MOLYBDENUM.]

pneu-. To breathe. Imitative root. **1.** Germanic **fneu-* in Old English *fnēosan*, to sneeze: SNEEZE. **2.** Greek *pnein*, to breathe (> *pnoia*, breathing): APNEA, DIPNOAN, DYSPNEA, EUPNEA, HYPERPNEA, HYPOPNEA, POLYPNEA, TACHYPNEA. **3.** Suffixed form **pneu-mn̥* in Greek *pneuma*, breath, wind, spirit: PNEUMA, PNEUMATIC, PNEUMATO-, PNEUMO-. [Pok. *pneu-* 838.]

pō(i)-. To drink. Contracted from **poǝ(i)-*. **I.** Basic form **pō(i)-*. **1.** Suffixed reduced form **pō-to-* in Latin *pōtus*, drunk (> *pōtāre*, to drink): POISON, POTABLE, POTATION, POTATORY, POTION. **2.** Reduplicated form **pi-pǝ-o-*, whence **pi-bo-*, assimilated to **bi-bo-* in Latin *bibere*, to drink: BEVERAGE, BIB, BIBULOUS; IMBIBE. **3.** Suffixed zero-grade form **pǝ-ti-*, **po-ti-* in Greek *posis*, drink, drinking: SYMPOSIUM. **II.** Zero-grade form **pī-* (< **piǝ-*). **1.** Suffixed form **pī-ro-* in Old Church Slavonic *pirŭ*, feast (> Russian *pir*, feast): PIROG. **2.** Suffixed (nasal present) form **pī-no-* in Greek *pinein*, to drink: PINOCYTOSIS. [Pok. 2. *pō(i)-* 839.]

pol-. Finger. Possibly the same root as **pōl-.** Latin *pollex*, thumb: POLLEX. [Pok. *polo-* 840.]

pōl-. To touch, feel, shake. **1.** Germanic **fōljan*, to feel, in Old English *fēlan*, to examine by touch, feel: FEEL. **2.** Reduplicated zero-grade form **pal-p-* in: **a.** Latin *palpus*, a touching: PALP; **b.** Latin *palpārī*, *palpāre*, to stroke gently, touch: PALPABLE, PALPATE¹, PALPITATE; **c.** Latin *palpebra*, eyelid (< "that which shakes or moves quickly"): PALPEBRAL. **3.** Perhaps suffixed zero-grade form **pal-yo-* in Greek *pallein*, to sway, brandish: CATAPULT. **4.** Perhaps suffixed form **psal-yo-* in Greek *psallein*, to pluck, play the harp (but more likely of imitative origin): PSALM, PSALTERY. [Pok. 1. G. *pel-* 801.]

[pōmum. Apple. Latin noun of unknown origin. POMACE, POMADE, POME.]

[populus. People. Latin noun of Etruscan origin. PEOPLE, POPULACE, POPULAR, POPULATE, PUBLIC, PUEBLO; DEPOPULATE.]

porko-. Young pig. **1.** Germanic **farhaz* in: **a.** Old English *fearh*, little pig: FARROW¹; **b.** diminutive form in Middle Dutch *varken*, small pig: AARDVARK. **2.** Latin *porcus* (> Old French *porc*), pig: PORCELAIN, PORCINE, PORK; PORCUPINE, PORPOISE, (PURSLANE). [Pok. *porko-s* 841.]

poti-. Powerful; lord. **1.** Latin *potis*, powerful, able (> *potestas*, power): PODESTA, POSSESS, POWER. **2.** Latin compound *posse*, to be able (contracted from *potis*, able

+ *esse,* to be; see **es-**): POSSIBLE, POTENT; (IMPOTENT), PREPOTENT. **3.** Form **pot-* in: **a.** compound **ghos-pot-*, "guest-master," host (see **ghos-ti-**); **b.** compound **dems-pot-*, "house-master," ruler (see **dem∂-¹**). **4.** Old Persian *pati-,* master: PADISHAH. [Pok. *poti-s* 842.]

[prāk-. To make, do. Greek root. Greek *prassein* (Attic *prattein*), to effect, do: PRACTICAL, (PRACTICE), PRAGMATIC, PRAXIS. [In Pok. 1. *per* 811.]]

prek-. To ask, entreat. **1.** Basic form **prek-* in Latin **prex,* prayer (attested only in the plural *precēs*), with denominative *precārī,* to entreat, pray: PRAY, PRAYER², PRECARIOUS; DEPRECATE, IMPRECATE. **2.** Suffixed zero-grade form **prk̑-sk-* becoming **pork-sk-*, contracted into **posk-* in suffixed form **posk-to-*, contracted into **posto-*, which appears in Latin *postulāre,* to ask, request: POSTULATE; EXPOSTULATE. [Pok. 4. *perk̑-* 821.]

prep-. To appear. Suffixed zero-grade form **prp-yo-* in Germanic **furbjan,* to cause to have a (good) appearance, polish, in Old French *fo(u)rbir,* to polish, burnish: FURBISH. [Pok. *prep-* 845.]

preu-. To hop. **1.** Zero-grade form **pru-* in Germanic **fru-* in Old English *frogga* (with obscure expressive suffix *-gga*), frog: FROG. **2.** Extended o-grade form **prowo-* in Germanic **frawaz* in: **a.** Middle Dutch *vro,* "leaping with joy," happy: FROLIC; **b.** Old High German *frō,* happy, in *frewida,* joy (> German *Freude*): SCHADENFREUDE. [Pok. *preu-* 845.]

preus-. To freeze, burn. **1.** Germanic **freusan,* to freeze, in Old English *frēosan,* to freeze: FREEZE. **2.** Suffixed zero-grade form **prus-to-* in Germanic **frustaz,* frost, in Old English *forst, frost,* frost: FROST. **3.** Suffixed form **preus-i-* in Latin **preusis, *preuris,* act of burning, whence denominative *prūrīre,* to burn, itch, yearn for: PRURIENT, PRURIGO, PRURITUS. **4.** Suffixed zero-grade form **prus-īna* in Latin *pruīna,* hoarfrost: PRUINOSE. [Pok. *preus-* 846.]

prī-. To love. Contracted from **priǝ-*. **1.** Suffixed form **priy-o-* in Germanic **frijaz,* beloved, belonging to the loved ones, not in bondage, free, in: **a.** Old English *frēo,* free; FREE; **b.** Dutch *vrij,* free: FILIBUSTER. **2.** Suffixed (participial) form **priy-ont-,* loving, in Germanic **frijand-,* lover, friend, in Old English *frīond, frēond,* friend: FRIEND. **3.** Suffixed shortened form **pri-tu-* in Germanic **frithuz,* peace, in: **a.** Old High German *fridu,* peace: SIEGFRIED; **b.** Old French *esfreer,* to disturb: AFFRAY; **c.** Germanic **frij-,* peace, safety, in compound **berg-frij-,* "high place of safety" (see **bhergh-²**). **4.** Suffixed feminine form **priy-ā,* beloved, in Germanic **frijjō,* beloved, wife, in: **a.** Old Norse *Frigg,* goddess of the heavens, wife of Odin: FRIGG; **b.** Germanic compound **frije-dagaz,* "day of Frigg" (translation of Latin *Veneris diēs,* "Venus's day"), in Old English *frīgedæg,* Friday: FRIDAY. [Pok. *prāi-* 844.]

prōkto-. Anus. Greek *prōktos,* anus: PROCTITIS, PROCTOLOGY, PROCTOSCOPE. [Pok. *prōkto-* 846.]

pster-. Also **ster-.** To sneeze. Imitative root. **1.** Suffixed form **ster-nu-* in Latin *sternuere,* to sneeze: STERNUTATION. **2.** Suffixed form **ster-t-* in Latin *stertere,* to snore: STERTOR. [Pok. *pster-* 846.]

pŭ-¹. Also **phŭ-.** To blow, swell. Imitative root. **1.** Extended form **pus-* in Latin *pustula,* a bubble, blister: PUSTULE. **2.** Perhaps extended form **pūt-,* penis, in Latin *praepūtium,* foreskin (*prae-,* before, in front; see **per¹**): PREPUCE. **3.** Variant form **phū-* in Greek *phusa* (> *phusan,* to blow), bellows, bladder: EMPHYSEMA, PHYSOSTIGMINE, PHYSOSTOMOUS. [Pok. 1. *pu-* 847.]

pŭ-². To rot, decay. **1.** Suffixed form **pū-lo-* in Germanic **fūlaz,* rotten, filthy, in: **a.** Old English *fūl,* unclean, rotten: FOUL; **b.** Old Norse *fūll,* foul, akin to the Scandinavian source of FULMAR; **c.** Germanic abstract noun **fūlithō* in Old English *fylth,* foulness: FILTH; **d.** Germanic denominative **fūljan,* to soil, dirty, in Old English *fȳlan,* to sully: FILE³; DEFILE¹. **2.** Extended form **pug-* in Germanic **fuk-* in Icelandic *fūki,* rotten sea grass, and

Norwegian *fogg,* rank grass, probably akin to the Scandinavian source of Middle English *fog, fogge,* aftermath grass: FOG². **3.** Extended variant form **pous-* in Germanic **fausa-* in Low German *fussig,* spongy: FUZZY. **4.** Suffixed form **pu-tri-* in Latin *puter* (stem *putri-*), rotten: PUTRESCENT, PUTRID; OLLA PODRIDA, (POTPOURRI), PUTREFY. **5.** Suffixed form **puw-os-* in: **a.** Latin *pus,* pus: PURULENT, PUS; SUPPURATE; **b.** Greek *puon, puos,* pus: PYO-. **6.** Greek compound *empuein,* to suppurate (*en-,* in; see **en**): EMPYEMA. [Pok. 2. *pū-* 848.]

[pūbēs. Pubic hair. Latin noun of obscure origin. Related to Latin *pūber, pūbēs,* adult, grown-up. **1.** Latin *pūbēs,* pubic hair: PUBES, PUBIC, PUBIS. **2.** Latin *pūber, pūbēs,* adult: PUBERTY, PUBERULENT, PUBESCENT.]

puk-¹. To make fast. Suffixed form **puk-ino-* in Greek *pukinos,* later *puknos,* strong, fast, thick: PYKNIC; PYCNIDIUM, PYCNOMTER. [Pok. 2. *puk̑-* 849.]

puk-². Bushy-haired. Suffixed form **puk-so-* in: **a.** Germanic **fuhsaz,* fox, in Old English *fox,* fox: FOX; **b.** Germanic feminine **fuhsōn-* in Old English *fyxe* (> Middle English *fixen*), she-fox: VIXEN. This root is in part a taboo deformation of **wlk̑ʷo-** and **wlp-ē-**. [Pok. *puk̑-* 849.]

[pulē. Gate. Greek noun of obscure origin. PYLON, PYLORUS; AEOLIPILE, MICROPYLE, PROPYLAEUM, PROPYLON.]

pūr-. Fire. Contracted from **puǝr-,* zero-grade form of **paǝwr̥.* **1.** Germanic suffixed form **fūr-i-* in Old English *fȳr,* fire: FIRE. **2.** Greek *pur,* fire: PYRE, PYRETIC, PYRITES, PYRO-, PYRRHOTITE, PYROSIS; EMPYREAL. [Pok. *peuǝr* 828.]

pūro-. Grain. **1.** Suggested by some, but unlikely for semantic reasons, is a suffixed form (with suffix *-iso-*) in Old English *fyrs,* furze: FURZE. **2.** Suffixed form **pūr-ēn-* in Greek *purēn,* stone of fruit: PYRENE. [Pok. *pū-ro-* 850.]

[puxos. Box tree. Greek noun borrowed from an unknown source. **1.** Greek *puxos,* box tree: BOX³. **2.** Derivative adjective *puxis,* (box) made of boxwood: BOX¹.]

p(y)el-. Tree name. Possible root. Possibly broken reduplicated form **pō-pel-* in Latin *pōpulus,* poplar: POPLAR, POPPLE². [Pok. *ptel(e)i̯ā* 847.]

[quaerere. To seek. Earliest form *quais-*. Latin verb of unknown origin. QUAESTOR, QUERIST, QUERY, QUEST, QUESTION; ACQUIRE, CONQUER, DISQUISITION, EXQUISITE, INQUIRE, PERQUISITE, REQUIRE.]

rāp-. Tuber. Late Indo-European root borrowed from an unknown source. Latin *rāpa, rāpum,* turnip: RAMPION, RAPE², RAVIOLI; KOHLRABI. [Pok. *rāp-* 852.]

[re-. Also **red-.** Backward. Latin combining form conceivably from Indo-European **wret-,* metathetical variant of **wert-,* to turn (< "turned back"), an extended form of **wer-³**. **1.** Latin *re-, red-,* backward, again: RE-. **2.** Suffixed form **re(d)-tro-* in Latin *retrō,* backward, back, behind, with its derivative Old French *rere,* backward: RETRAL, RETRO-; ARREARS, REAR GUARD, REARWARD², REREDOS. **3.** Suffixed form **re-ko-* in Latin *reciprocus,* "backward and forward" (see **per¹**).]

rē-. To bestow, endow. Contracted from **reǝ-*. Suffixed form **reǝ-i-* goods, wealth, property, in Latin *rēs,* thing: RE², REAL¹, REBUS, REIFY, REPUBLIC. [Pok. 4 *rei-* 850.]

rebh-¹. Violent, impetuous. Suffixed zero-grade form **rabh-yo-* in Latin *rabere,* to rave, be mad: RABID, RABIES, RAGE. [Pok. *rabh-* 852.]

rebh-². To roof over. Germanic **rebja-, *rebjō,* "covering of the chest cavity," in: **a.** Old English *ribb,* rib: RIB; **b.** Old Norse *rif,* rib, ridge: REEF¹, REEF²; **c.** Middle Low German *ribbe,* rib: SPARERIBS. [Pok. 2. *rebh-* 853.]

rēd-. To scrape, scratch, gnaw. **1.** O-grade form **rōd-* in: **a.** Latin *rōdere,* to gnaw: RODENT; CORRODE, ERODE; **b.** suffixed (instrumental) form **rōd-tro-* in Latin *rōstrum,* beak, ship's bow: ROSTRUM. **2.** Possibly variant form **rād-* in: **a.** Latin *rādere,* to scrape: RADULA, RASH², RASORIAL; ABRADE, CORRADE, ERASE; **b.** suffixed (instrumental) form **rād-tro-* in Latin *rāstrum,* a rake, with diminutive **rāsculum,* whence denominative verb **ras-*

culāre, to rake, in Provençal *rasclar* (> French *racler*), to rake, scrape: RACLETTE. [Pok. 2. *rēd-* 854.]

reg-¹. To move in a straight line, with derivatives meaning "to direct in a straight line, lead, rule." **I.** Basic form **reg-.* **1.** Suffixed form **reg-to-* in Germanic **rehtaz* in Old English *riht,* right, just, correct, straight: RIGHT. **2.** Latin *regere,* to lead straight, guide, rule (past participle *rēctus,* hence adjective *rēctus,* right, straight): REALM, RECTITUDE, RECTO, RECTOR, RECTUM, REGENT, REGIME, REGIMENT, REGION; CORRECT, DIRECT, ERECT, RECTANGLE, RECTIFY, RECTILINEAR, RISORGIMENTO, SURGE. **3.** Greek *oregein* (with prothetic vowel from oldest root form **ɔreg-),* to stretch out, reach out for: ANORECTIC, ANOREXIA. **II.** Lengthened-grade form **rēg-,* Indo-European word for a tribal king. **1.** Celtic suffixed form **rīg-yo-* in Germanic **rīkja-* in: **a.** Old English *rīce,* realm: BISHOPRIC; **b.** Old Norse *rīki* (> Norwegian *rik*), realm: RIKSMAL; **c.** Old English *rīce,* strong, powerful: RICH. **2.** Latin *rēx,* king (royal and priestly title): REAL², REGAL, REGULUS, REIGN, ROYAL; INTERREX, REGICIDE, REGIUS PROFESSOR, VICEREINE, VICEROY. **3.** Suffixed form **rēg-en-* in Sanskrit *rājā, rājan-,* king, rajah (feminine *rājñī,* queen, rani), and *rājati,* he rules: RAJ, RAJAH, (RANI), (RYE²); MAHARAJAH, MAHARANI. **III.** Suffixed lengthened-grade form **rēg-olā* in Latin *rēgula,* straight piece of wood, rod: RAIL¹, REGLET, REGULAR, REGULATE, RULE. **IV.** O-grade form **rog-.* **1.** Germanic **rakō* in Old English *raca, racu,* rake (implement with straight pieces of wood): RAKE¹. **2.** Germanic **rak-* in Middle Dutch *rakke,* framework: RACK¹. **3.** Possibly Germanic **rankaz* (with nasal infix) in Old English *ranc,* straight, strong, hence haughty, overbearing: RANK². **4.** Germanic **rak-inaz,* ready, straightforward, in Old English *gerecenian,* to arrange in order, recount (*ge-,* collective prefix; see **kom**): RECKON. **5.** Suffixed form **rog-ā-* in Latin *rogāre,* to ask (< "stretch out the hand"): ROGATION, ROGATORY; ABROGATE, ARROGATE, CORVÉE, DEROGATE, INTERROGATE, PREROGATIVE, PROROGUE, SUBROGATE, SUPEREROGATE. **6.** Suffixed form **rog-o-* in a possible Latin noun **rogus,* "extension, direction," perhaps in a Latin phrase **ē rogō,* "from the direction of" (*ē* < *ex,* out of; see **eghs**), contracted into *ergō,* therefore, in consequence of: ARGAL², ERGO. **V.** Lengthened o-grade form **rōg-.* **1.** Germanic **rōkjan* in Old English *rec(c)an,* to pay attention to, take care (formally influenced by Old English *reccan,* to extend, stretch out, from Germanic **rakjan*): RECK. **2.** Germanic **rōkja-* in Old English *receleas,* careless (*-lēas,* lacking; see **leu-¹**): RECKLESS. [Pok. 1. *reg-* 854.]

reg-². Moist. **1.** Suffixed variant form **rek-no-* in Germanic **regnaz,* rain, in Old English *reg(e)n, rēn,* rain: RAIN; RAINBOW. **2.** Possibly Latin *rigāre,* to wet, water: IRRIGATE. [Pok. 2. *reg-* 857.]

reg-³. To dye. Lengthened-grade form **rēg-.* **1.** Suffixed form **rēg-ēs-* in Greek *rhēgos,* blanket, rug: REGOLITH. **2.** Sanskrit *rāgaḥ,* color, red: RAGA. **3.** Perhaps Sanskrit *rākshā,* earlier form of *lākshā,* red dye: LAC¹. [Pok. 1. *reg-* 854.]

regʷ-es-. Darkness. Oldest root form **ɔregʷ-es-.* Greek *Erebos* (with prothetic vowel), Erebus, a place of darkness under the earth: EREBUS. [Pok. *regʷ-os-* 857.]

rei-¹. To scratch, tear, cut. **I.** Extended form **reik-.* **1.** Germanic **rīgōn-* in Italian *riga,* line (< "something cut out"): RIGATONI. **2.** Suffixed form **rei-mā* or **reig-smā* in Latin *rīma,* crack, cleft, fissure: RIMOSE. **3.** Suffixed o-grade form **roik-wo-* in Germanic **rai(h)-wa-* in Old English *rāw, rēw,* a line, row: ROW¹. **II.** Possible extended form **reipp-.* Germanic **raipaz,* rope, in: **a.** Old English *rāp,* rope: ROPE; **b.** compound **stig-raipaz,* "mount-rope," in Old English *stīgrāp,* stirrup (see **steigh-**). **III.** Extended form **reip-.* **1.** Germanic **rīfan,* in Old Norse *rīfa,* to tear: RIVE. **2.** Zero-grade form **rip-* in: **a.** Germanic **rifti-* in Danish *rift,* breach, akin to the Scandinavian source of Middle English *rift,* rift: RIFT¹; **b.** Germanic **rif-* in Old English

rȳfe, abundant: RIFE. **3.** Suffixed form **reip-ā-* in Latin *rīpa,* bank (< "that which is cut out by a river"): RIPARIAN, RIVAGE, RIVER; ARRIVE. **IV.** Extended form **reib-* in Germanic **rīp-.* **1.** Germanic **rīpja-* in Old English *rīpe,* ripe, ready for reaping: RIPE. **2.** Germanic **rīpan* in Old English *rīpan,* to reap: REAP. **3.** Middle Low German *repelen,* to remove seeds, akin to the source of Middle English *ripelen,* to remove seeds: RIPPLE². [Pok. 1. *rei-* 857.]

rei-². Striped in various colors, flecked. Suffixed o-grade form **roi-ko-* in Germanic **raihaz* in Old English *rā, rāha,* deer: ROE². [Pok. 2. *rei-* 859.]

rei-³. To flow, run. **1.** Suffixed zero-grade form **ri-nu-* in: **a.** Germanic **ri-nw-an,* whence **rinnan,* to run, in Old English *rinnan,* to run, and Old Norse *rinna,* to run: RUN, RUNNEL; **b.** secondary Germanic derivative **runiz* in Old English *ryne,* a running: EMBER DAY. **2.** Suffixed zero-grade form **ri-l-* in Germanic **ril-* in Dutch *ril* and Low German *rille,* running stream: RILL. **3.** Suffixed form **rei-wo-* in Latin *rīvus,* stream: RIVAL, RIVULET; DERIVE. [Pok. 3. *er-* 326.]

reidh-. To ride. **I.** Basic form **reidh-.* **1.** Germanic **rīdan* in: **a.** Old English *rīdan,* to ride: RIDE; **b.** Middle Dutch *rīden,* to ride (> *ridder,* rider, knight): RITTER. **2.** Celtic **vo-rēd-* in Latin *verēdus,* post horse (**vo-,* under; see **upo**): PALFREY. **II.** O-grade form **roidh-.* **1.** Germanic **raid-* in: **a.** Old English *rād,* a riding, road: RAID, ROAD; **b.** possibly Middle High German *reidel,* rod between upright stakes (< "wooden horse"): RADDLE¹. **2.** Probably Germanic **raid-ja-* in Old English *rǣde, gerǣde,* ready (< "prepared for a journey"): READY. **3.** Germanic **raidjan* in Vulgar Latin **arrēdāre,* to arrange: ARRAY. [Pok. *reidh-* 861.]

reig-¹. To bind. **1.** Germanic **rigg-* (the *-gg-* is anomalous) in Norwegian *rigga,* to bind, akin to the Scandinavian source of Middle English *riggen,* to rig: RIG. **2.** Zero-grade form **rig-* in Latin *corrigia* (probably borrowed from Gaulish), thong, shoelace (*cor-,* from *com-,* together; see **kom**): SCOURGE. [Pok. *reig-* 861.]

reig-². To reach, stretch out. **1.** O-grade form **roig-* in Germanic **raikjan* in Old English *rǣcan,* to stretch out, reach: REACH. **2.** Possibly suffixed (stative) zero-grade form **rig-ē-* in Latin *rigēre,* to be stiff (? < "be stretched out"): RIGID, RIGOR. [Pok. (*reiĝ-*) 862.]

rendh-. To tear up. **1.** Germanic **randjan* in Old English *rendan,* to tear: REND. **2.** Germanic **rind-* in Old English *rind(e),* rind (< "thing torn off"): RIND. [Pok. *rendh-* 865.]

rep-. To snatch. Suffixed zero-grade form **rap-yo-* in Latin *rapere,* to seize: RAPACIOUS, RAPE¹, RAPID, RAPT, RAVEN², RAVIN, RAVISH; EREPSIN, SURREPTITIOUS. [Pok. *rep-* 865.]

rēp-¹. To creep, slink. Latin *rēpere,* to creep: REPENT², REPTILE; SUBREPTION. [Pok. 1. *rēp-* 865.]

rēp-². Stake, beam. Suffixed variant form **rap-tro-* in Germanic **raf-tra-* in: **a.** Old English *ræfter,* rafter: RAFTER; **b.** Old Norse *raptr,* beam: RAFT¹. [Pok. 2. *rēp-* 866.]

ret-. To run, roll. **1.** Prefixed form **to-vo-ret-,* "a running up to" (*to-,* to; *vo,* under, up, up from under; see **upo**), in Old Irish *tóir,* pursuit: TORY. **2.** Suffixed o-grade form **rot-ā-* in Latin *rota,* wheel: RODEO, ROLL, ROTA, ROTARY, ROTATE, ROTUND, (ROTUNDA), ROULETTE, ROUND¹, ROWEL; BAROUCHE, CONTROL, PRUNE², ROTIFORM, ROTOGRAVURE. [Pok. *ret(h)-* 866.]

rēt-. Post. O-grade form **rōt-* in Germanic **rōd-* in Old English *rōd,* rod, cross: ROOD. [Pok. *rēt-* 866.]

reu-¹. To bellow. **1.** Extended form **reud-* in Germanic **rautōn* in Old Norse *rauta,* to roar (akin to the Scandinavian source of ROTE²): ROUT³. **2.** Suffixed extended form **reum-os-* in Latin *rūmor,* rumor, "common talk": RUMOR. **3.** Extended form **reug-* in Latin *rūgīre,* to roar: RIOT, RUT². **4.** Variant **rau-ko-* in Latin *raucus,* hoarse: RAUCOUS. [Pok. 1. *reu-* 867.]

reu-². Also **reuə-**. To smash, knock down, tear out, dig up, uproot. **1.** Suffixed o-grade form *rouə-o- in Germanic *rawwa- in: **a.** Old Norse rögg, röggr, woven tuft of wool: RAG¹; **b.** Norwegian rugga, rogga, coarse coverlet, akin to the Scandinavian source of RUG. **2.** Basic form *reu- in Latin ruere, to collapse, cause to collapse: RABBLE², RUIN. [Pok. 2. reu- 868.]

reudh-¹. Red, ruddy. **I.** O-grade form *roudh-. **1.** Germanic *raudaz in: **a.** Old English rēad, red: RED; **b.** Old Norse rauthr, red (> reythr, rorqual): RORQUAL. **2.** Germanic *raudnia- in Old Norse reynir, mountain ash, rowan (from its red berries), akin to the source of ROWAN. **3.** Latin rūfus (of dialectal Italic origin), reddish: RUFESCENT, RUFOUS. **4.** Latin rōbus, red, in rōbīgō, rūbīgō, rust: RUBIGINOUS. **II.** Zero-grade form *rudh-. **1.** Form *rudh-ā- in Germanic *rudō in: **a.** Old English rudu, red color: RUDDLE, RUDDY; **b.** Old English rudduc, robin: RUDDOCK. **2.** Suffixed form *rudh-sto- in Germanic *rūst- in Old English rūst, rust: RUST. **3.** Latin rubeus, red: ROUGE, RUBEOLA, RUBY; RUBEFACIENT **4.** Latin rubicundus, red, ruddy: RUBICUND. **5.** Latin rubidus, red: RUBIDIUM. **6.** Suffixed (stative) form *rudh-ē- in Latin rubēre, to be red: RUBESCENT; ERUBESCENCE. **7.** Suffixed form *rudh-ro- in: **a.** Latin ruber, red: RUBELLA, RUBRIC; BILIRUBIN; **b.** Latin rutilus, reddish: RUTILANT; **c.** Greek eruthros, red (with prothetic vowel, from oldest root form * əreudh-): ERYTHEMA, ERYTHRO-; **d.** possibly remade Greek erusi-, red, reddening: ERYSIPELAS. **8.** Suffixed form *rudh-to- in Latin russus, red: RISSOLE, ROUX, RUSSET. [Pok. reudh- 872.]

reudh-². To clear land. **1.** Suffixed zero-grade form *rudh-yo- in Germanic *rudjan in Old Norse rydhja, to clear land: RID. **2.** Possibly Germanic expressive variant *rudd- stick, club, in Old English rodd, stick: ROD. [In Pok. 2. reu- 868.]

reuə-. To open; space. **1.** Suffixed variant form *rū-mo- (< *ruə-mo-) in Germanic *rūmaz in: **a.** Old English rūm, space: ROOM; **b.** Old French run, ship's hold, space: RUMMAGE. **2.** Suffixed form *reu(ə)-es- in Latin rūs, "open land," the country: RURAL, RUSTIC. [Pok. reuə-, rū- 874.]

reug-. To vomit, belch, smoke, cloud. **1.** Germanic *reukan in Old English rēocan, to smoke, reek: REEK. **2.** Suffixed zero-grade form *rug-to- in Latin ructāre, to belch: ERUCT. [Pok. 4. reu- 871.]

reugh-men-. Cream. O-grade form *roughmen- in Germanic *rau(g)ma- in Middle Low German rōm(e), cream: RAMEKIN. [Pok. reugh-m(e)n- 873.]

reup-. Also **reub-**. To snatch. **I.** Basic form *reub- in Germanic *rupja in Flemish rippen, to rip: RIP¹. **II.** O-grade form *roup-. **1.** Germanic *raufian in: **a.** Old English rēafian, to plunder: REAVE¹; **b.** Old English berēafian, to take away (be-, bi-, intensive prefix; see ambhi): BEREAVE. **2.** Germanic *raubōn, to rob, in: **a.** Middle Dutch and Middle Low German rōven, to rob: ROVER; **b.** Old French rober, to rob: ROB; **c.** Italian rubare, to rob: RUBATO. **3.** Germanic *raubō, booty, in Old French robe, robe (> "clothes taken as booty"): ROBE. **4.** Suffixed form *roup-tro- in Sanskrit loptram, booty, from lumpati, he breaks, removes: LOOT. **III.** Zero-grade form *rup-. **1.** Latin ūsūrpāre (< *ūsu-rup-; ūsus, use, usage, from ūtī, to use), originally "to interrupt the orderly aquisition of something by the act of using," whence to take into use, usurp: USURP. **2.** Nasalized form *ru-m-p- in Latin rumpere, to break (> rūpēs, rock): ROUT¹, RUPTURE; ABRUPT, BANKRUPT, CORRUPT, DISRUPT, ERUPT, INTERRUPT, IRRUPT, RUPICOLOUS. [Pok. 2. reu- 868.]

rezg-. To plait, weave, wind. Germanic *ruski- in Old English risc, rysc, rush: RUSH². [Pok. rezg- 874.]

[rīsan. To rise. Germanic word. **1.** Germanic *rīsan in:

a. Old English rīsan, to rise: RISE; **b.** Old English ārīsan, to arise (ā-, up, out): ARISE. **2.** Germanic causative *raizjan in: **a.** Old English rēran, to rear, raise, lift up: REAR²; **b.** Old Norse reisa, to raise: RAISE.]

ṛtko-. Bear. **1.** Latin ursus, bear (< *orcsos): URSINE. **2.** Greek arktos, bear: ARCTIC, ARCTURUS. **3.** Celtic *arto- in Welsh arth, bear, in the name Arthur (> Medieval Latin Artorius, Arthur): ARTHUR. [Pok. ṛktho-s 875.]

ruk-¹. Fabric, spun yarn. Celtic and Germanic root. **1.** Germanic *rukkōn- in: **a.** Italian rocca, distaff: ROCKET¹; **b.** Old High German rocko, distaff: ROCAMBOLE; **c.** Old French rocquet, head of a lance: RATCHET. **2.** Germanic *rukka- in Old French rochet, rochet: ROCHET. [Pok. ruk(k)- 874.]

ruk-². Rough. Extension of reu-². **1.** Lengthened-grade form *rūk- in Germanic *rūhwaz in Old English rūh, rough, coarse: ROUGH. **2.** Lengthened variant form *rūg- in Latin rūga, wrinkle: RUGA, RUGOSE; CORRUGATE. [In Pok. 2. reu- 868.]

rūno-. Mystery, secret. Germanic and Celtic technical term of magic. Germanic *rūnaz in: **a.** Old English rūnian, to whisper: ROUND²; **b.** Old Norse rūn, secret writing (akin to the Germanic source of Finnish runo, song, poem): RUNE¹, RUNE². [In Pok. 1. reu- 867.]

sā-. To satisfy. Contracted from *saə-. **1.** Suffixed zero-grade form *sə-to- in: **a.** Germanic *sadaz, sated, in Old English sæd, sated, weary: SAD; **b.** derivative Germanic verb *sadōn, to satisfy, sate, in Old English sadian, to sate: SATE¹. **2.** Suffixed zero-grade form *sə-ti- in Latin satis, enough, sufficient: SATIATE, SATIETY; (ASSAI²), ASSET, SATISFY. **3.** Suffixed zero-grade form *sə-tu-ro- in Latin satur, full (of food), sated: SATIRE, SATURATE. **4.** Suffixed zero-grade form *sə-d-ro- in Greek hadros, thick: HADRON. [Pok. sā- 876.]

sab-. Juice, fluid. **1.** Germanic *sapam, juice of a plant, in Old English sæp, sap: SAP¹. **2.** Illyrian sabaium, beer, probably akin to the source of Italian zabaglione, zabaione, a frothy dessert: ZABAGLIONE. [In Pok. sap- 880.]

sāg-. To seek out. **1.** Suffixed form *sāg-yo- in Germanic *sōkjan in Old English sæcan, sēcan, to seek: SEEK. **2.** Suffixed form *sāg-ni- in Germanic *sōkniz in Old English sōcn, attack, inquiry, right of local jurisdiction: SOKE. **3.** Zero-grade form *səg- in Germanic *sak- in: **a.** derivative noun *sakō, "a seeking," accusation, strife, in Old English sacu, lawsuit, case: SAKE¹; **b.** Germanic *sakjan, to lay claim to (denominative of *sakō), in Old French seisir, to take possession of, seize: (SEISIN), SEIZE; **c.** Germanic *sakan, to seek, accuse, quarrel, in (i) Old English forsacan, to renounce, refuse (for-, prefix denoting exclusion or rejection; see per¹): FORSAKE (ii) Old Norse saka, to seek: RANSACK. **4.** Independent suffixed form *sāg-yo- in Latin sāgīre, to perceive, "seek to know": PRESAGE. **5.** Zero-grade form *səg- in Latin sagāx, of keen perception: SAGACIOUS. **6.** Suffixed form *sāg-eyo- in Greek hēgeisthai, to lead (< "to track down"): EXEGESIS, HEGEMONY. [Pok. sāg- 876.]

sai-. Suffering. **1.** Germanic *sairaz, suffering, sick, ill, in Old English sār, painful: SORE. **2.** Derivative Germanic adjective *sairigaz, painful, in Old English sārig, suffering mentally, sad: SORRY. [Pok. sāi-, 877.]

sak-. To sanctify. **1.** Suffixed form *sak-ro- in: **a.** Latin sacer, holy, sacred, dedicated: SACRED; CONSECRATE, EXECRATE; **b.** compound *sakro-dhōt-, "performer of sacred rites" (*-dhōt-, doer; see dhē-¹), in Latin sacerdōs, priest: SACERDOTAL. **2.** Nasalized form *sa-n-k- in Latin sancīre (past participle sanctus), to make sacred, consecrate: SAINT, SANCTUM; CORPOSANT, SACROSANCT, SANCTIFY. [Pok. sak- 878.]

sal-¹. Salt. Extended form *sald- in: **a.** suffixed form *sald-o- in Germanic *saltam in Old English sealt, salt: SALT; **b.** Germanic zero-grade suffixed extended form *sult-jō in (i) Old French sous, pickled meat: SOUSE (ii)

Danish and Norwegian *sylt*, salt marsh, probably akin to the source of Middle English *cylte*, fine sand: SILT; **c.** Latin *sallere* (past participle *salsus*), to salt: (SALSA), SAUCE. **2.** Latin *sāl* (genitive *salis*), salt: SAL, SALAD, SALAMI, SALARY, SALI-, SALINE; SALTCELLAR, SALTPETER. **3.** Greek *hals*, salt, sea: HALO-. [Pok. 1. *sal-* 878.]

sal-². Dirty gray. Suffixed form **sal-wo-* in Germanic **salwaz* in Old English *salu, salo*, dusky, dark: SALLOW¹. [Pok. 2. *sal-* 879.]

sal(i)k-. Willow. A derivative of **sal-²**. **1.** Variant form **salk-* in Germanic suffixed form **salh-jōn-* in Old English *sealh*, willow: SALLOW². **2.** Latin *salix*, willow: SALICIN. [In Pok. 2. *sal-* 879.]

sāno-. Healthy. Italic root. Latin *sānus*, healthy: SANE, (SANITARY); SAINFOIN. [Pok. *sāno-s* 880.]

saus-. Dry. **1.** Extended form **sauso-* in Germanic **sausaz* in: **a.** Old English *sēar*, withered: SEAR¹, SERE¹; **b.** Frankish **saur*, dry, whence Old French *saur, sor*, red-brown: SORREL²; SURMULLET. **2.** Suffixed form **saus-t-* in Greek *austeros*, harsh: AUSTERE. [Pok. *saus-* 880.]

sāwel-. Also **s(u)wel-, su(ə)el-, su(ə)en-, sun-**. The sun. Contracted from **saəwel-*. **1.** Variant forms **swen-, *sun-* in: **a.** Germanic **sunnōn-* in Old English *sunne*, sun: SUN; **b.** Germanic compound **sunnōn-dagaz*, "day of the sun" (translation of Latin *diēs sōlis*), in Old English *sunnandæg*, Sunday: SUNDAY; **c.** Germanic derivative **sunthaz*, "sun-side," south, in Old English *sūth*, south, and *sūtherne*, southern: SOUTH, SOUTHERN. **2.** Variant form **s(ə)wōl-* in: **a.** Latin *sōl*, the sun: SOL³, SOL, SOLAR, SOLARIUM; GIRASOL, INSOLATE, PARASOL, SOLANINE, TURNSOLE; **b.** Latin compound *sōlstitium*, "a standing of the sun," solstice (-*stitium*, a standing; see **stā-**): SOLSTICE. **3.** Suffixed form **sāwel-yo-* in Greek *hēlios*, sun: HELIACAL, HELIO-, HELIOS, HELIUM; ANTHELION, APHELION, ISOHEL, PARHELION, PERIHELION. [Pok. *sāwel-* 881.]

sē-¹. To sow. Contracted from **seə-*. **1.** Germanic **sēan* in Old English *sāwan*, to sow: SOW¹. **2.** Suffixed form **sē-ti-*, sowing, in Germanic **sēdiz*, seed, in: **a.** Old English *sǣd*, seed: SEED; **b.** Middle Dutch *saet* and Middle Low German *sāt*, seed: COLZA. **3.** Reduplicated zero-grade form **si-s(ə)-* in Latin *serere*, to sow: SEASON; INSERT. **4.** Suffixed form **sē-men-*, seed, in Latin *sēmen*, seed: SEME, SEMEN, SEMINARY, SEMINATION; DISSEMINATE. [In Pok. 2. *sē(i)-* 889.]

sē-². Long, late. Contracted from **seə-*. Variant **seəi-*, zero-grade form **siə-*, contracted to **sī-*. **1.** Suffixed form **sē-ro-* in: **a.** Latin *sērus*, late: SEROTINOUS, SOIREE; **b.** Middle Breton *hir*, long: MENHIR. **2.** Possibly Germanic **sī-* in: **a.** Germanic **sīdō*, "long surface or part," in Old English *sīde*, side: SIDE; **b.** Germanic **sīth*, "later," after, in Old English *siththon, siththan*, after that, since: SINCE, SITH. [In Pok. 2. *sē(i)-* 891.]

sē-³. To sift. Contracted from **seə-*. Suffixed form **sē-dho-* in Greek *ēthein*, to sift: ETHMOID. [Pok. 1. *sē(i)-* 889.]

sē-⁴. To bind, tie. Contracted from **seə-*. Variant **seəi-*, zero-grade form **si-*. Suffixed form **si-nw-* in Germanic **sinwō-* in Old English *sinu, seonu*, tendon: SINEW. [Pok. 3. *sē(i)-* 891.]

sed-¹. To sit. **1.** Suffixed form **sed-yo-* in Germanic **sitjan* in: **a.** Old English *sittan*, to sit: SIT; **b.** Old High German *sizzen*, to sit (> German *Sitz*, act of sitting): SITZ BATH, SITZKRIEG, SITZMARK. **2.** Suffixed (causative) o-grade form **sod-eyo-* in Germanic **satjan*, to cause to sit, set, in: **a.** Old English *settan*, to place: SET¹; **b.** Old High German *sezzan*, to set, in *irsezzan*, to replace: ERSATZ. **3.** Suffixed form **sed-lo-*, seat, in Germanic **setlaz* in Old English *setl*, seat: SETTLE. **4.** O-grade form **sod-* in Germanic **sadulaz*, seat, saddle, in Old English *sadol*, saddle: SADDLE. **5.** Suffixed lengthened o-grade form **sōd-o-* in Germanic **sōtam* in Old English *sōt*, soot (< "that which settles"): SOOT. **6.** Suffixed lengthened-

grade form **sēd-yo-* in Germanic **(ge)sētjam*, seat (**ge-, *ga-*, collective prefix; see **kom**), in Old Norse *sæti*, seat: SEAT. **7.** Form **sed-ē-* in Latin *sedēre*, (third person plural perfect indicative *sēdērunt*), to sit: SÉANCE, SEDENTARY, SEDERUNT, SEDILIA, SEDIMENT, SESSILE, SESSION, SEWER², SIEGE; ASSESS, ASSIDUOUS, DISSIDENT, HOSTAGE, (INESSORIAL), OBSESS, POSSESS, PRESIDE, RESIDE, (SUBSIDY), SUPERSEDE. **8.** Reduplicated form **si-zd-* in: **a.** Latin *sīdere*, to sit down, settle: SUBSIDE; **b.** Greek *hizein*, to sit down, settle down: SYNIZESIS. **9.** Lengthened-grade form *sēd-* in Latin *sēdēs*, seat, residence: SEE². **10.** Lengthened-grade form **sēd-ā-* in Latin *sēdāre*, to settle, calm down: SEDATE¹. **11.** Suffixed o-grade form **sod-yo-* in Latin *solium*, throne, seat: SOIL¹. **12.** Suffixed form **sed-rā-* in Greek *hedra*, seat, chair, face of a geometric solid: -HEDRON; CATHEDRA, (CHAIR), EPHEDRINE, EXEDRA, SANHEDRIN, TETRAHEDRON. **13.** Prefixed and suffixed form **pi-sed-yo-*, to sit upon (**pi-*, on; see **epi**), in Greek *piezein*, to press tight: PIEZO-; ISOPIESTIC. **14.** Basic form **sed-* in: **a.** Greek *edaphos*, ground, foundation (with Greek suffix *-aphos*): EDAPHIC; **b.** Sanskrit *sad-* in *upaniṣad*, Upanishad: UPANISHAD. **15.** Suffixed form **sed-ā-*, seat, in Welsh *sedd*, seat: EISTEDDFOD. See also compound root **nizdo-**. [Pok. *sed-* 884.]

sed-². To go. Suffixed o-grade form **sod-o-* in Greek *hodos*, way, journey: -ODE; ANODE, CATHODE, EPISODE, EXODUS, HYATHODE, METHOD, ODOGRAPH, ODOMETER, PERIOD, STOMODEUM, SYNOD. [Pok. *sed-* 887.]

segh-. To hold. **1.** Suffixed form **segh-es-* in Germanic **sigiz*, victory (< "a holding or conquest in battle"), in Old High German *sigu, sigo*, victory: SIEGFRIED. **2.** Greek *ekhein*, to hold, possess, be in a certain condition (> *hexis*, habit): HECTIC; CACHEXIA, ECHARD, ENTELECHY, EUNUCH, OPHIUCHUS. **3.** O-grade form **sogh-* in Greek *epokhē*, "a holding back," pause, cessation, position in time (*epi-*, on, at; see **epi**): EPOCH. **4.** Zero-grade form **sgh-* in: **a.** Greek *skhēma*, "a holding," form, figure: SCHEME; **b.** Greek *skholē*, "a holding back," stop, rest, leisure, employment of leisure in disputation, school: (SCHOLAR), SCHOLASTIC, SCHOLIUM, SCHOOL¹. **5.** Reduplicated form **si-sgh-* in Greek *iskhein*, to keep back: ISCHEMIA. [Pok. *seĝh-* 888.]

seib-. To pour out, sieve, drip, trickle. **1.** Basic form in Germanic **sīpon* in Old English *sīpian, sypian*, to drip, seep: SEEP. **2.** Suffixed o-grade form **soib-on-* in Germanic **saipōn-*, "dripping thing," resin, in: **a.** Old English *sāpe*, soap (originally a reddish hair dye used by Germanic warriors to give a frightening appearance): SOAP; **b.** Latin *sāpō*, soap: SAPONATE, SAPONIFY, SAPONIN, SAPONITE; SAPONACEOUS. **3.** Variant Germanic form **sib-* in: **a.** Old English *sife*, a filter, sieve: SIEVE. **b.** Old English *sīftan*, to sieve, drain: SIFT. [Pok. *seip-* 894.]

seikʷ-. To flow. Extended expressive zero-grade form **sikko-* in Latin *siccus*, dry (probably < "flowed out"): SACK³, SECCO, SICCATIVE; DESICCATE, EXSICCATE. [Pok. *seiku-* 893.]

sek-. To cut. **1.** Germanic **segithō*, sickle, in Old English *sithe, sigthe*, sickle: SCYTHE. **2.** Suffixed o-grade form **sok-ā-* in Germanic **sagō*, a cutting tool, saw, in Old English *sagu, sage*, saw: SAW¹. **3.** Suffixed o-grade form **sok-yo-* in Germanic **sagjaz*, "sword," plant with a cutting edge, in Old English *secg*, sedge: SEDGE. **4.** Suffixed o-grade form **sok-so-* in Germanic **sahsam*, knife, sword, traditionally (but quite doubtfully) regarded as the source of West Germanic tribal name **Saxon-*, Saxon (as if "warrior with knives"), in Late Latin *Saxō* (plural *Saxonēs*), a Saxon: SAXON. **5.** Extended root **skend-*, to peel off, flay, in Germanic **skinth-* in Old Norse *skinn*, skin: SKIN. **6.** Basic form **sek-* in Latin *secāre*, to cut: SECANT, -SECT, SECTILE, SECTION, SECTOR, SEGMENT; DISSECT, EXSECT, INSECT, INTERSECT, NOTCH, RESECT, (TRANSECT). **7.** Lengthened-grade form **sēk-* in Latin

sĕcula, sickle: SICKLE. **8.** Suffixed variant form **sak-so-** in Latin *saxum*, stone (< "broken-off piece"): SAXATILE; SAXICOLOUS, SAXIFRAGE. See also extended roots **sked-**, **skei-**, **sker-¹**, **sker-⁴**. [Pok. 2. *sĕk-* 895, *sken-(d)-* 929.]

sĕk-. Slack, calm: relax. Greek *(h)ēka*, slowly, a little (> *hēssōn*, inferior): ESSONITE. [Pok. 3. *sēk-* 896.]

sekʷ-¹. To follow. **1.** Latin *sequī*, to follow: SECT, SEGUE, SEGUIDILLA, SEQUACIOUS, SEQUEL, SEQUENCE, SUE, SUITOR; CONSEQUENT, ENSUE, EXECUTE, OBSEQUIOUS, PERSECUTE, PROSECUTE, (PURSUE), SUBSEQUENT. **2.** Latin *sequester*, "follower," mediator, depositary: SEQUESTER, SEQUESTRUM. **3.** Suffixed (participial) form **sekʷ-ondo-** in Latin *secundus*, following, coming next, second: SECOND², SECONDO, SECUND, SECUNDINES. **4.** Suffixed form **sekʷ-os**, following, in Latin *secus*, along, alongside of: INTRINSIC. **5.** Suffixed form **sekʷ-no-** in Latin *signum*, identifying mark, sign (< "standard that one follows"): SEAL¹, SEGNO, SIGN; ASSIGN, CONSIGN, DESIGNATE, INSIGNIA, RESIGN. **6.** Suffixed o-grade form **sokʷ-yo-** in Latin *socius*, ally, companion (< "follower"): SOCIABLE, SOCIAL, SOCIETY, SOCIO-; ASSOCIATE, CONSOCIATE, DISSOCIATE. [Pok. 1. *sekʷ-* 896.]

sekʷ-². To perceive, see. **1.** Germanic *sehwan*, to see, in Old English *sēon*, to see: SEE¹. **2.** Germanic abstract noun **sih-tiz** in Old English *sihth, gesiht*, vision, spectacle: SIGHT. [Pok. 2. *sekʷ-* 872.]

sekʷ-³. To say, utter. **1.** O-grade form **sokʷ-** in: **a.** suffixed form **sokʷ-yo-** in Germanic *sagjan* in Old English *secgan*, to say: SAY; **b.** suffixed form **sokʷ-ā-** in Germanic *sagō*, a saying, in *(i)* Old English *sagu*, a saying, speech: SAW² *(ii)* Old Norse *saga*, narrative: SAGA. **2.** Suffixed zero-grade form **skʷ-e-tlo-**, narration, perhaps in North Germanic *skathla* in Old Norse *skāld*, poet, "narrator," perhaps akin to the probable Scandinavian source of Middle English *scolde*, an abusive person: SCOLD, SKALD. [In Pok. 3. *sekʷ-* 897.]

sel-¹. Human settlement. **1.** O-grade form **sol-** in Germanic *sal-*, room, in Italian *sala*, hall, room: SALON, (SALOON). **2.** Suffixed form **sel-o-** in Latin *solum*, bottom, foundation, hence sole of the foot: SOLE¹, SOLUM, ENTRESOL. [Pok. 1. *sel-* 898, 3. *(s̑uel-)* 1046.]

sel-². Also **selə-.** Of good mood; to favor. **1.** Germanic lengthened form **sēl-** in Old English *gesǣlig*, happy (*ge-*, completely; see **kom**): SILLY. **2.** Suffixed lengthened o-grade form **sōl-ā-** in Latin *sōlārī*, to comfort, console: SOLACE; CONSOLE¹. **3.** Possibly suffixed form **selə-ro-** in Greek *hilaros* (< *helaros*), gay: HILARITY; EXHILARATE. [Pok. 6. *sel-* 900.]

sel-³. To take, grasp. **1.** Suffixed o-grade (causative) form **sol-eyo-** in Germanic *saljan*, to offer up, deliver, whence West and North Germanic "to sell," in Old English *sellan*, to sell, betray: SELL. **2.** Germanic *sal-*, giving, sale, in: **a.** Old Norse *sala*, sale: SALE; **b.** Old Norse compound *handsal*, giving of the hand (in closing a bargain): HANDSEL. [Pok. 3. *sel-* 899.]

sel-⁴. To jump. **1.** Suffixed zero-grade form **sal-yo-** in: **a.** Latin *salīre*, to leap: SALACIOUS, SALIENT, SALLY, (SAUTÉ); ASSAIL, DESULTORY, DISSILIENT, EXULT, INSULT, RESILE, RESULT, SOMERSAULT; **b.** Greek *hallesthai*, to leap, jump: HALTER². **2.** Perhaps Latin *salmō* (borrowed from Gaulish), salmon (< "the leaping fish"): SALMON. [Pok. 4. *sel-* 899.]

sel-es-. Swamp, marsh, sea. Greek *helos*, marsh: ELODEA. [Pok. *selos* 901.]

selk-. To pull, draw. **1.** Perhaps Germanic *selhaz*, seal (the animal), "that which drags its body along with difficulty" (but more likely an early Germanic borrowing from Finnic), in Old English *seolh*, seal: SEAL². **2.** Suffixed o-grade form **solk-o-** in Latin *sulcus*, furrow, groove (< "result of drawing or plowing"): (SULCATE), SULCUS. [Pok. *selk-* 901.]

selp-. Fat, butter. **1.** Germanic *salb-* in Old English *sealf*, healing ointment: SALVE¹. **2.** Germanic denomina-

tive verb *salbōn* in Middle Dutch *salven*, to anoint, salve, in obsolete Dutch *quacksalver*, a quack: QUACKSALVER. [Pok. *selp-* 901.]

sem-¹. One; also adverbially "as one," together with. **I.** Full-grade form **sem-**. **1.** Greek *hem-* in: **a.** Greek *heis* (< nominative singular masculine *hen-s* < *hem-s*), one: HENDECASYLLABIC, HENDIADYS, HENOTHEISM; **b.** Greek *he-* in *hekaton*, one hundred (? dissimilated from *hem-katon*; see **dekm̥**). **2.** Suffixed form **sem-el-** in Latin *simul*, at the same time: SIMULTANEOUS; ASSEMBLE, ENSEMBLE. **3.** Suffixed form **sem-golo-** in Latin *singulus*, alone, single: SINGLE. **4.** Compound **sem-per-** (*per*, during, for; see **per¹**) in Latin *semper*, always, ever (< "once for all"): SEMPRE; SEMPITERNAL. **II.** O-grade form **som-**. **1.** Sanskrit *sam*, together: SAMSARA, SANDHI, SANSKRIT. **2.** Suffixed form **som-o-** in: **a.** Germanic *samaz*, same, in Old Norse *samr*, same: SAME; **b.** Greek *homos*, same: HOMEO-, HOMO-; ANOMALOUS; **c.** Greek *homilos*, crowd: HOMILY. **3.** Suffixed form **som-alo-** in Greek *homalos*, like, even, level: HOMOLOGRAPHIC, HOMOLOSINE PROJECTION. **III.** Lengthened o-grade form **sōm-**. **1.** Suffixed form **sōm-i-** in Germanic *sōmiz* in Old Norse *sœmr*, fitting, agreeable (< "making one," "reconciling"): SEEM, SEEMLY. **2.** Suffixed lengthened o-grade form **sōm-o-** in Russian *sam, samo-*, self: SAMIZDAT, SAMOVAR. **IV.** Zero-grade form **sm̥-**. **1.** Greek *ha-, a-*, together, in compound *a-kolouthos*, accompanying (*a-* + *keleuthos*, way, path): ANACOLUTHON. **2.** Greek compound *haplous*, simple (*-plous, -ploos*, -fold; see **pel-³**): HAPLOID. **3.** Suffixed form **smm-o-** in Germanic *sumaz* in: **a.** Old English *sum*, one, a certain one: SOME; **b.** Old English *-sum*, like: -SOME¹. **4.** Suffixed form **smm-alo-** in Latin *similis*, of the same kind, like: SIMILAR; ASSIMILATE, RESEMBLE. **5.** Compound **sm̥-kĕro-**, of one growing (see **ker-³**). **6.** Suffixed form **sm̥-tero-** in Greek *heteros* (earlier *hateros*), one of two, other: HETERO-. **7.** Compound **sm̥-plek-**, "one-fold," simple (*plek-*, -fold; see **plek-**), in Latin *simplex*, simple: SEMPLICE, SIMPLEX, SIMPLICITY. **8.** Compound **sm̥-plo-**, "one-fold," simple (*-plo-*, -fold; see **pel-³**) in Latin *simplus*, simple: SIMPLE. **9.** Extended form **smma** in Greek *hama*, together with, at the same time: HAMADRYAD. **10.** Basic form **sm-** in Old Russian *sŭ-*, together, in compound *sŭvĕtŭ* (> Russian *sovet*), assembly (*vĕtŭ*, council; see **weitə-**): SOVIET. [Pok. 2. *sem-* 902.]

sem-². Also **semə-.** Summer. Suffixed zero-grade form **smə-aro-** in Germanic *sumaraz* in Old English *sumor*, summer: SUMMER¹. [Pok. 3. *sem-* 905.]

sēmi-. Half. **1.** Germanic *sēmi-* in Old English *sām-*, half: SAND-BLIND. **2.** Latin *sēmi-*, half: SEMI-. **3.** Latin *sēmis*, half: SESQUI-, SESTERCE. **4.** Greek *hēmi-*, half: HEMI-. [Pok. *sēmi-* 905.]

sen-¹. Old. **1.** Latin *senex*, old, an elder: SEIGNIOR, SENATE, SENECTITUDE, SENESCENT, SENILE, SENIOR, SENOPIA, (SIGNORY), (SIR), SIRE, (SURLY). **2.** Suffixed form **sen-o-** in Germanic *senaz* in compound *sini-skalkaz*, old servant (Germanic *skalkaz*, servant, slave; see **skalkaz**), in Medieval Latin *siniscalcus*, seneschal: SENESCHAL. [Pok. *sen(o)-* 907.]

sen-². Also **seni-.** Apart, separated. **1.** Suffixed zero-grade form **sn̥-ter-** in: **a.** Germanic *sundrō* in Old English *sundor, sunder*, apart: ASUNDER; **b.** Germanic denominative *sundrōn* in Old English *syndrian, sundrian*, to put apart: SUNDER; **c.** Germanic derivative adjective *sundriga-* in Old English *syndrig*, apart, separated: SUNDRY. **2.** Zero-grade form **sn̥ni-** in Latin *sine*, without (< "outside," "out of"): SANS; SINECURE. [Pok. *seni-* 907.]

sendhro-. Crystalline deposit. Germanic *sendra-*, slag, in: **a.** Old English *sinder*, iron slag, dross: CINDER; **b.** Old High German *sintar* (> German *Sinter*), slag: SINTER. [Pok. *sendhro-* 906.]

sengʷ-. To sink. Germanic *sinkwan* in: **a.** Old English *sincan*, to sink: SINK; **b.** Scandinavian intensive form

*sakk- in Swedish *sacka*, to sink, akin to the Scandinavian source of Middle English *saggen*, to subside: SAG. [Pok. *seng^u-* 906.]

seng^wh-. To sing, make an incantation. **1.** Germanic **singan* in: **a.** Old English *singan*, to sing: SING; **b.** Old High German *singan* (> German *singen*), to sing: MEISTERSINGER, MINNESINGER, SINGSPIEL. **2.** Suffixed o-grade form **song^wh-o-*, singing, song, in Germanic **sangwaz* in Old English *sang, song*, song: SONG. [Pok. *seng^uh-* 906.]

senk-. To burn. Suffixed (causative) o-grade form **sonk-eyo-* in Germanic **sangjan*, to cause to burn, in Old English *sengan*, to singe: SINGE. [Pok. *senk-* 907.]

sent-. To head for, go. **1.** Germanic suffixed form **sinth-nan* in Old High German *sinnan*, to go: WITHERSHINS. **2.** Suffixed (causative) o-grade form **sont-eyo-* in Germanic **sandjan*, to cause to go, in Old English *sendan*, to send: SEND[1]. **3.** Suffixed o-grade form **sont-o-* in Germanic **sandaz*, that which is sent, in Old English *sand*, message, messenger: GODSEND. **4.** Perhaps suffixed form **sent-yo-* in Latin *sentīre*, to feel (< "to go mentally"): SCENT, SENSE, (SENSILLUM), SENTENCE, SENTIENT, SENTIMENT, SENTINEL; ASSENT, CONSENT, DISSENT, PRESENTIMENT, RESENT. [Pok. *sent-* 908.]

sep-[1]. To taste, perceive. Suffixed zero-grade form **sap-yo-* in Latin *sapere*, to taste, have taste, be wise: SAGE[1], SAPID, SAPIENT, SAPOR, SAVANT, SAVOR, SAVVY. [Pok. *sap-* 880.]

sep-[2]. To foster, serve, venerate (the dead). Suffixed form **sep-el-yo-* in Latin *sepelīre*, to bury: SEPULCHER, SEPULTURE. [Pok. *sep-* 909.]

septm̥. Seven. **1.** Germanic **sebum* in Old English *seofon*, seven: SEVEN. **2.** Latin *septem*, seven: SEPTEMBER, SEPTENNIAL, SEPTET, SEPTI-, SEPTUAGINT, SEPTUPLE; SEPTENTRION. **3.** Greek *hepta*, seven: HEBDOMAD, HEPTA-, HEPTAD. [Pok. *septm̥* 909.]

ser-[1]. To protect. **1.** Extended form **serw-* in Latin *servāre*, to keep, preserve: CONSERVE, OBSERVE, PRESERVE, RESERVE, (RESERVOIR). **2.** Suffixed lengthened-grade form **sēr-ōs-* perhaps in Greek *hērōs*, "protector," hero: HERO. [Pok. 2. *ser-* 910.]

ser-[2]. To flow. **1.** Suffixed form **ser-o-* in Latin *serum*, whey: SERAC, SERUM. **2.** Basic form **ser-* in Sanskrit *sarati, sasarti*, it flows, it runs: SAMSARA. **3.** Extended roots **sr-edh-, *sr-et-*, to whirl, bubble, in Germanic **stred-* in Old High German *stredan*, to whirl, swirl, whence ablaut formation in Middle High German *strudel*, whirlpool: STRUDEL. [Pok. 1. *ser-* 909; *sr-edh-* 1001.]

ser-[3]. To line up. **1.** Latin *serere*, to arrange, attach, join (in speech), discuss: SERIES, SERTULARIAN; ASSERT, DESERT[3], DISSERTATE, EXERT, INSERT. **2.** Suffixed form **ser-mon-* in Latin *sermō* (stem *sermōn-*), speech, discourse: SERMON. **3.** Suffixed form **ser-ā-* perhaps in Latin *sera*, a lock, bolt, bar (? < "that which aligns"): SEAR[2], (SERRIED). **4.** Suffixed zero-grade form **sr̥-ti-* in Latin *sors* (stem *sort-*), lot, fortune (probably from the lining up of lots before drawing): SORCERER, SORT; ASSORT, CONSORT, SORTILEGE. [Pok. 4. *ser-* 911.]

serk-. To make whole. Latin *sarcīre*, to mend, repair: SARTORIUS. [Pok. *serk-* 912.]

serp-[1]. Sickle, hook. **1.** Latin *sarpere*, to cut off, prune (> *sarmentum*, twigs): SARMENTOSE. **2.** Greek *harpē*, sickle (> Old French *harper*, to seize): HARPOON. [Pok. 5. *ser-* 911.]

serp-[2]. To crawl, creep. **1.** Latin *serpere*, to crawl: SERPENT, SERPIGO. **2.** Greek *herpein*, to crawl, creep: HERPES, HERPETOLOGY. [Pok. *serp-* 912.]

[servus. Slave. Latin noun of unknown origin. SERF, SERGEANT, SERVE, SERVICE, SERVILE, SERVITUDE, SIRVENTE; CONCIERGE, DESERVE.**]**

seuə-[1]. To give birth. Suffixed zero-grade form in derivative noun **su(ə)-nu-*, son, in Germanic **sunuz* in Old English *sunu*, son: SON. See also **sū-**. [Pok. 2. *seu-* 913.]

seuə-[2]. To take liquid. **I.** Suffixed zero-grade form

*suə-yo-, contracted to **sū-yo-* in Greek *huein*, to rain, and *huetos*, rain: ISOHYET. **II.** Possible extended zero-grade form **sūb-*. **1.** Germanic **sūp-* in: **a.** Old English *sūpan, sūpian*, to drink, sip: SUP[1]; **b.** Old French *soup(e)*, soup: SOUP, (SUP[2]). **2.** Germanic **supp-* in: **a.** Old English *sopp*, bread dipped in liquid: SOP; **b.** possibly Low German *sippen*, to sip, probably akin to the source of Middle English *sippen*, to sip: SIP. **III.** Possible extended zero-grade form **sūg-*. **1.** Germanic **sūk-* in Old English *sūcan*, to suck: SUCK. **2.** Germanic shortened form **sukōn* in Old English *socian*, to steep: SOAK. **3.** Latin *sūgere*, to suck: SUCTION, SUCTORIAL. **4.** Variant form **sūk-* in Latin *sūcus, succus*, juice: SUCCULENT. [Pok. 1. *seu-* 912.]

seut-. To seethe, boil. **1.** Germanic **seuthan* in Old English *sēothan*, to boil: SEETHE, (SODDEN). **2.** Germanic **suth-* in: **a.** Middle Dutch *sudde, sudse*, marsh, swamp: SUDS; **b.** suffixed form **suth-l-* in Middle High German *sudelen*, to soil, do sloppy work, akin to Middle Dutch *soetler*, sutler: SUTLER. [Pok. 4. *seu-* 914.]

si-lo-. Silent. Suffixed (stative) form **sil-ē-* in Latin *silēre*, to be silent: SILENT. [In Pok. 2. *sē(i)-* 889.]

skabh-. To prop up, support. Suffixed form **skabh-no-* in Latin *scamnum*, a bench (> Old English *sceamel*, table, stool): SHAMBLES. [Pok. *skabh-* 916.]

skai-. Also **kai-.** Bright, shining. **1.** Extended form **kaid-* in Germanic **haiduz*, "bright appearance," manner, quality, in Old English *-hād*, quality, condition: -HOOD. **2.** Suffixed form **ki-t-ro-* in Sanskrit *citra-*, variegated, many-colored: CHEETAH, CHINTZ. [Pok. *(s)kāi-* 916.]

[skalkaz. Servant, slave. Germanic noun of unknown origin. **1.** Old High German compound *marahscalc*, "horse-servant" (see **marko-**). **2.** Germanic compound **sini-skalkaz*, "old servant" (see **sen-[1]**). [In Pok. *(s)kel-* 929.]**]**

skamb-. Also **kamb-.** To curve, bend. Suffixed form **kamb-o-* in Celtic **kambo-*, crooked, and denominative verb **k(a)mb-yo-*, to turn, exchange, whence Gallo-Latin *cambiāre*, to exchange: CAMBIST, CAMBIUM, CHANGE. [Pok. *(s)kamb-* 918.]

skand-. Also **skend-.** To leap, climb. **1.** Latin *scandere*, to climb: SCAN, SCANDENT, SCANSION, SCANSORIAL; ASCEND, (CONDESCEND), DESCEND, TRANSCEND. **2.** Suffixed form **skand-alo-* in Greek *skandalon*, a snare, trap, stumbling block: SCANDAL. **3.** Suffixed form **skand-slā-* in Latin *scālae*, steps, ladder: ECHELON, ESCALADE, SCALE[2].

sked-. To split, scatter. Extension of **sek-**. **1.** O-grade form **skod-* in Germanic **skat-* in Old English *sc(e)ater-ian*, to scatter: SHATTER. **2.** Variant nasalized form **ska-n-d-* in Latin *scandula*, a shingle for roofing (< "split piece"): SHINGLE[1]. [Pok. *(s)k(h)ed-* 918.]

skeəi-. To gleam. **1.** Suffixed form **ske(ə)i-no-* in Germanic **skīnan*, to gleam, shine, in: **a.** Old English *scīnan*, to shine: SHINE; **b.** Old High German *scīnan*, to shine: GEGENSCHEIN. **2.** Germanic extended form **ski-m-* in Old English *scimerian, scymrian*, to shine brightly: SHIMMER. **3.** Possibly suffixed form **ski-nto-*, shining, in Latin *scintilla*, a spark: SCINTILLA, SCINTILLATE, STENCIL, (TINSEL). **4.** Suffixed zero-grade form **skiə-ā-*, **skiy-ā-* in Greek *skia*, shadow: SKIAGRAM, SKIASCOPE, SQUIRREL. [Pok. *skai-* 917.]

skei-. To cut, split. Extension of **sek-**. **1.** Germanic suffixed form **ski-nō-* in: **a.** Old English *scinu*, shin, shinbone (< "piece cut off"): SHIN[1-]; **b.** Old French *eschine*, backbone, piece of meat with part of the backbone: CHINE. **2.** Latin *scīre*, to know (< "to separate one thing from another," "discern"): SCIENCE, SCILICET, SCIOLISM, SCIRE FACIAS; ADSCITITIOUS, CONSCIENCE, CONSCIOUS, NESCIENCE, (NICE), OMNISCIENT, PLEBISCITE, PRESCIENT. **3.** Suffixed zero-grade form **skiy-enā* in Old Irish *scīan*, knife: SKEAN. **4.** Extended root **skeid-* in: **a.** Germanic **skītan*, to separate, defecate, in Old English *scītan*, to defecate: SHIT; **b.** suffixed zero-grade

form *sk(h)id-yo- in Greek skhizein, to split: SCHISM, SCHIST, SCHIZO-; **c.** nasalized zero-grade form *ski-n-d- in Latin scindere, to split: SCISSION; EXSCIND, PRESCIND, RESCIND. **5.** Extended root *skeit- in: **a.** Germanic *skaith-, *skaidan in (i) Old English scēadan, to separate: SHED¹ (ii) perhaps Old English scēath, sheath (< "split stick"): SHEATH; **b.** Germanic *skīdam in Old Norse skīdh, log, stick, snowshoe: SKI; **c.** o-grade form *skoit- in Latin scūtum, shield (< "board"): ÉCU, ESCUDO, ESCUTCHEON, ESQUIRE, SCUDO, SCUTUM, (SQUIRE). **6.** Extended root *skeip- in Germanic *skif- in: **a.** Middle English sheve, pulley (< "piece of wood with grooves"): SHEAVE²; **b.** Old Norse skīfa, to slice, split, akin to the Scandinavian source of SKIVE; **c.** Middle Low German schever, splinter, akin to the possible Low German source of Middle English schivere, scivre, splinter: SHIVER². [Pok. skei- 919.]

skel-¹. Also **kel-**. To cut. **1.** Germanic *skaljō, piece cut off, shell, scale, in: **a.** Old English scell, sciel, shell: SHELL; **b.** Italian scaglia, chip: SCAGLIOLA. **2.** Germanic *skalō in: **a.** Old English sc(e)alu, husk, shell: SHALE; **b.** Old French escale, husk: SCALE¹. **3.** Germanic *skal- in: **a.** Old Norse skalli, bald head (< "closely shaved skull"): SCALL; **b.** Old Norse skalpr, sheath, shell, akin to the source of Middle English scalp, scalp: SCALP. **4.** Germanic *skēlō in Old Norse skāl, bowl, drinking vessel (made from a shell): SCALE³, SKOAL. **5.** Germanic *skelduz in Old English scield, shield (< "board"): SHIELD. **6.** Germanic *skeli- in: **a.** Old Norse skil, reason, discernment, knowledge (< "incisiveness"): SKILL; **b.** Middle Dutch schillen, to diversify, with past participle schillede, separated, variegated, akin to the Low German source of Middle English scheld, variegated: SHELDRAKE. **7.** Germanic skulō, a division, in Middle Low German schōle, troop: SCHOOL², SHOAL². **8.** Suffixed variant form *kel-tro- in Latin culter, knife: COLTER, CULTRATE, CUTLASS. **9.** Suffixed zero-grade form *skl̥-yo- in Greek skallein, to stir up, hoe (> skalenos, uneven): SCALENE. **10.** Extended root *skelp- in: **a.** Germanic *skelf- in Middle Low German schelf, shelf (< "split piece of wood"): SHELF; **b.** possibly Germanic *halbaz (< variant root *kelp-), divided, in Old English healf, half: HALF; **c.** perhaps variant *skalp- in Latin scalpere, to cut, scrape, with derivative sculpere (originally as the combining form of scalpere), to carve: SCALPEL, SCULPTURE. [Pok. 1. (s)kel- 923.]

skel-². To be under an obligation. O-grade (perfect) form *skol- in Germanic *skal-, I owe, hence I ought, in Old English sceal (used with the first and third person singular pronouns), shall: SHALL. [Pok. 2. (s)kel- 927.]

skel-³. Also **kel-**. Crooked. With derivatives referring to a bent or curved part of the body, such as a leg, heel, knee, or hip. **1.** Suffixed form *skel-ko- in Germanic *skelha- in Old High German scilihen, to wink, blink (> German Schiller, iridescence): SCHILLER. **2.** Suffixed form *skel-es- in Greek skelos, leg: ISOSCELES, TRISKELION. **3.** Suffixed o-grade form *skol-yo- in Greek skolios, crooked: SCOLIOSIS. **4.** Lengthened o-grade form *skōl- in Greek skōlēx, earthworm, grub (< "that which twists and turns"): SCOLEX. **5.** Suffixed lengthened-grade form *kōl-o- in Greek kōlon, limb, member: COLON¹. **6.** Attributed (quite doubtfully) by some to this root is Greek kulindein, to roll: CALENDER, CYLINDER. [Pok. 4. skel- 928.]

skelə-. To parch, wither. Variant *sklē-, contracted from *skleə-. **1.** Greek skellesthai, to dry, whence skeletos (< suffixed form *skelə-to-), dried up (body), mummy: SKELETON. **2.** Suffixed variant form *sklē-ro- in Greek sklēros, hard: SCLERA, SCLERO-, SCLEROMA, (SCLEROSIS), (SCLEROTIC), SCLEROTIUM, SCLEROUS; SCLEROTIZATION. [Pok. 3. (s)kel- 927.]

skeng-. Crooked. Germanic *skankōn-, "that which bends," leg, in Old English sc(e)anca, shinbone: SHANK. [Pok. (s)keng- 930.]

skep-. Also **kep-**. Base of words with various technical meanings such as "to cut," "to scrape," "to hack." **1.** Germanic *skap- in: **a.** Old English gesceap (ge-, collective prefix; see **kom**), form, creation (< "cutting"): SHAPE; **b.** Old English -scipe, state, condition (collective suffix): -SHIP; **c.** Dutch -schap, "-ship," condition (collective suffix): LANDSCAPE. **2.** Germanic ablaut variant *skōpō-, "thing cut out," container, in Middle Dutch and Middle Low German schōpe, bucket for bailing water: SCOOP. **3.** Germanic *skaftaz in Old English sceaft, rod of a spear: SHAFT¹. **4.** Germanic expressive form *skabb- in: **a.** Old English sceabb, a scab, scratch: SHABBY; **b.** Old Norse skabb, a scab: SCAB. **5.** Variant form *skabh- in: **a.** Germanic *skaban in (i) Old English sceafan, to scrape, pare away: SHAVE (ii) Old High German skaban, to scrape: SAPSAGO; **b.** Latin scabere, to scrape: SCABIES; **c.** suffixed form *skabh-ro- in Latin scaber, rough (< "scratched"): SCABROUS; **d.** Greek skaphē, boat (< "thing cut out"): SCAPHOID; BATHYSCAPH. **6.** Variant form *skap- in Latin scapula, shoulder blade (used as a tool for scraping): SCAPULA. **7.** Variant form *kap- in: **a.** Latin capō, castrated cock: CAPON; **b.** Late Latin capulāre, to cut: SCABBLE. **8.** O-grade form *kop- in: **a.** suffixed form *kop-yā- in Germanic *hapjō, a cutting tool, ax, sickle, in (i) Old High German hāppa, happa, sickle, akin to the Germanic source of Old Provençal apcha, small ax: PIOLET (ii) Medieval Latin hapia, ax, and Old French hache, small ax: HASH¹, HATCHET; NUTHATCH, QUEBRACHO; **b.** suffixed form *kop-yo- in Greek koptein, to strike, cut: COMMA; APOCOPE, SARCOPTIC MANGE, SYNCOPE; **c.** Russian kopat', to hack, with derivative kop'e, lance, in kopeĭka, kopeck: KOPECK. **9.** Possibly zero-grade variant form *skup(h)- in Greek skuphos, a cup (but more likely of obscure origin): SCYPHISTOMA, SCYPHOZOAN. [Pok. 2. (s)kep- 931.]

sker-¹. Also **ker-**. To cut. **I.** Basic forms *sker-, *ker-. **1.** Germanic *skeran in Old English scieran, sceran, to cut: SHEAR. **2.** Germanic *skeraz in: **a.** Old English scēar, plowshare: SHARE²; **b.** Old English scearu, scaru, portion, division (but recorded only in the senses of "fork of the body," "tonsure"): SHARE¹. **3.** Germanic *skēr- in: **a.** *skēr-ō- and *sker-ez- in Old English scēar, scissors: SHEARS; **b.** compound *skēr-berg-, "sword protector," scabbard (see **bhergh-**¹) in Old High German scarberc, scabbard, akin to the possible Germanic source of Anglo-Norman escaubers, scabbard: SCABBARD. **4.** Germanic *skur- in Old Norse skor, notch, tally, twenty: SCORE. **5.** Germanic suffixed form *skar-jam in Old Norse sker, low reef (< "something cut off"): SCAR². **6.** Suffixed o-grade extended form *skord-o- in Germanic *skardaz in Old English sceard, a cut, notch: SHARD. **7.** Extended form *skerd- in suffixed zero-grade form *skr̥d-o- in Germanic *skurtaz in: **a.** Old English scort, sceort, "cut," short: SHORT; **b.** Old English scyrte, undergarment (< "cut piece"): SHIRT; **c.** Old Norse skyrta, shirt: SKIRT. **8.** Germanic extended form *skerm- in: **a.** Old High German skirmen, to protect, akin to the source of Old French eskermir, to fight with a sword, fence: SKIRMISH; **b.** Middle Dutch scherm, shield: SCREEN. **9.** Variant form *kar- in Latin carō (stem carn-), flesh: CARNAGE, CARNAL, CARNASSIAL, CARNATION, CARNIVAL, CARRION, CARUNCLE, CHARNEL, CRONE; CARNIVOROUS, INCARNATE. **10.** Suffixed o-grade form *kor-yo- in Latin corium, leather (originally "piece of hide"): CORIACEOUS, CORIUM, CUIRASS, CURRIER; EXCORIATE. **11.** Suffixed zero-grade form *kr̥-to- in Latin curtus, short: CURT, CURTAL, KIRTLE. **12.** Suffixed o-grade form *kor-mo- in Greek kormos, a trimmed tree trunk: CORM. **13.** Suffixed o-grade form *kor-i- in Greek koris, bedbug (< "cutter"): COREOPSIS. **II.** Extended roots *skert-, *kert-. **1.** Zero-grade form *kr̥t- or o-grade form *kort- in Latin cortex, bark (< "that which can be cut off"): CORTEX; DECORTICATE. **2.** Suffixed form *kert-snā- in Latin cēna, meal (< "portion of food"): CENACLE. **III.** Extended root

*skerb(h)-, *skreb(h)-. **1.** Germanic *skarpaz, cutting, sharp, in: **a.** Old English scearp, sharp: SHARP; **b.** Gothic skarpō, pointed object, akin to the possible Germanic source of Italian scarpa, embankment: SCARP. **2.** Germanic *skrap- in: **a.** Old Norse skrap, "pieces," remains: SCRAP¹; **b.** Old Norse skrapa, to scratch: SCRAPE. **3.** Germanic skrab- in: **a.** Middle Dutch schrabben, to scrape: SCRABBLE; **b.** Middle Dutch schrobben, to scrape: SCRUB¹. **4.** Germanic *skrub- in Old English scrybb, shrub (< "rough plant"): SHRUB¹. **5.** Latin scrobis, trench, ditch: SCROBICULATE. **6.** Latin scrōfa, a sow (< "rooter, digger"): SCREW, SCROFULA. [Pok. 4. sker-, Section I. 938.]

sker-². To leap, jump about. Perhaps same root as **sker-³.** **1.** Extended form *skerd- in Germanic *skert- in Middle High German scherzen, to leap with joy: SCHERZO. **2.** O-grade variant form *kor- in Latin coruscāre, to vibrate, glisten, glitter: CORUSCATE. [Pok. 2. (s)ker- 933.]

sker-³. Also **ker-.** To turn, bend. Presumed base of a number of distantly related derivatives. **1.** Extended form *(s)kreg- in nasalized form *(s)kre-n-g- in: **a.** Germanic *skrink- in Old English scrincan, to wither, shrivel up: SHRINK; **b.** variant *kre-n-g- in Germanic *hrunk- in (i) Old Norse hrukka, a crease, fold: RUCK² (ii) Frankish *hrunkjan, to wrinkle (> Old French fronce, pleat): FLOUNCE¹. **2.** Extended form *(s)kregh- in nasalized form *skre-n-gh- in Germanic *hringaz, something curved, circle, in: **a.** Old English hring, a ring: RING¹; **b.** Old French renc, reng, line, row: RANCH, RANGE, RANK¹, RINK; ARRANGE, DERANGE; **c.** Middle Dutch rinc (combining form ring-), a ring: RINGHALS. **3.** Extended form *kreuk- in Germanic *hrugjaz in: **a.** Old English hrycg, spine, ridge: RIDGE; **b.** Old High German hrukki, back: RUCKSACK. **4.** Suffixed variant form *kur-wo- in Latin curvus, bent, curved: CURB, CURVATURE, CURVE, CURVET. **5.** Suffixed extended form kris-ni- in Latin crīnis (< *crisnis), hair: CRINITE, CRINOLINE. **6.** Suffixed extended form *kris-tā- in Latin crista, tuft, crest: CREST, CRISTA, CRISTATE. **7.** Suffixed extended form *krip-so- in Latin crispus (metathesized from *cripsus), curly: CREPE, CRISP, CRISPATE. **8.** Extended expressive form *krīss- in Latin crīsāre, (of women) to wiggle the hips during copulation: CRISSUM. **9.** Perhaps reduplicated form *ki-kr-o- metathesized into Greek krikos, a ring (> Latin circus, ring, circle): CIRCA, CIRCLE, CIRCUM-, SEARCH; CRICOID. **10.** Suffixed o-grade form *kor-ōno- in Greek korōnos, curved: (CORONA), CROWN; CORONOID. **11.** Suffixed variant form *kur-to- in Greek kurtos, bent: KURTOSIS. [Pok. 3. (s)ker- 935.]

sker-⁴. Excrement, dung. Extension of **sek-**, "to cut, separate," hence "to void excrement." **1.** Form *sk-ōr- in Greek skōr (genitive skatos < *sk-ṇt-), dung: SCATO-, SCORIA, SKATOLE. **2.** Extended form *skert- in base metathesis *sterk-os- in: **a.** Latin stercus, dung: STERCORACEOUS; **b.** variant forms *(s)terg-, *(s)treg- in Germanic *threkka- in Middle High German drëc, dung: DRECK. [Pok. sker-d- 947; 8. (s)ter- 1031.]

skerbh-. Also **skerb-.** To turn, bend. Extension of **sker-³.** **1.** Variant form *skreb- in Germanic *skrip- in Old Norse skreppa, to slip, and derivative Old Norse skorpna, to shrink, be shriveled, akin to the probable Scandinavian source of Middle English scorchen, to scorch: SCORCH. **2.** Nasalized variant form *(s)kre-m-b- in: **a.** Germanic *hrimp-, *hrump- in (i) Old English hrympel, wrinkle, fold: RIMPLE (ii) Middle Dutch rompelen, to wrinkle: RUMPLE (iii) Old French ramper, to climb, rear up: RAMP²; **b.** Germanic *skrimp- in (i) Middle Low German schrempen, to shrink, wrinkle, perhaps akin to the possible Low German source of Middle English shrimp, pygmy, shrimp: SHRIMP (ii) Swedish skrympa, to shrink, perhaps akin to the possible Scandinavian source of SCRIMP. **3.** Variant form *kramb- in Greek krambē, cabbage (having wrinkled, shrunken

leaves): CRAMBO. **4.** Perhaps Celtic *krumb-i- in Welsh crwn, crooked, arched: CROMLECH. [Pok. (s)kerb(h)- 948.]

skēt(ə)-. To injure. Suffixed zero-grade form *skət-on- in Germanic *skathōn- in: **a.** Old Norse skadha, to harm: SCATHE; **b.** Old High German scado (> German Schaden), harm, injury, damage: SCHADENFREUDE. [Pok. skēth- 950.]

(s)keu-. To cover, conceal. Zero-grade form *(s)ku-. Variant *(s)keuə-, zero-grade form *(s)kuə-, contracted to *(s)kū-. **1.** Suffixed basic form in Germanic *skeu-jam, cloud ("cloud cover"), in Old Norse skȳ, cloud: SKY. **2.** Zero-grade form *skū- in: **a.** suffixed form *skū-mo- in Germanic *skūmaz, foam, scum (< "that which covers the water"), in (i) Old High German scūm, scum (> German Schaum, foam): MEERSCHAUM (ii) Middle Dutch schūm, scum: SCUM; **b.** suffixed form *skū-ro- in Latin obscūrus, "covered," dark (ob-, away from; see **epi-**): OBSCURE; CHIAROSCURO. **3.** Zero-grade form *kū- in: **a.** suffixed form *kū-ti- in Germanic *hūdiz in Old English hȳd, skin, hide: HIDE²; **b.** suffixed form *ku-ti- in Latin cutis, skin: CUTANEOUS, CUTICLE, CUTIS; CUTIN; **c.** possibly suffixed form *kū-lo- in Latin cūlus (> French cul), the rump, backside: CULET, CULOTTES; BASCULE, RECOIL; **d.** suffixed form *ku-to- in Greek kutos, a hollow, vessel: -CYTE, CYTO-. **4.** Extended zero-grade form *kus- in: **a.** Germanic *husōn- in Old English hosa, hose, covering for the leg: HOSE; **b.** suffixed form *kus-dho- (or suffixed extended form *kudh-to-) in Germanic *huzdam in Old English hord, stock, store, treasure (< "thing hidden away"): HOARD; **c.** Russian kishka, gut (< "sheath"), akin to the Slavic source of Yiddish kishke, kishke: KISHKE. **5.** Suffixed zero-grade form *kut-no- in Latin cunnus, vulva (< "sheath"): CUNNILINGUS. **6.** Extended root *keudh- in: **a.** Germanic suffixed lengthened zero-grade form *hūdjan in Old English hȳdan, to hide, cover up: HIDE¹; **b.** Germanic suffixed zero-grade form *hūd-jōn- in French hutte, hut: HUT. [Pok. 2. (s)keu- 951.]

skeubh-. To shove. **1.** Germanic *skeuban and derivative lengthened zero-grade form *skūban in: **a.** Old English scūfan, to shove: SHOVE; **b.** Old Norse skūfa, to push, perhaps akin to the probable Scandinavian scource of SCUFF, SCUFFLE¹. **2.** Germanic suffixed form *skub-ilō- in: **a.** Old English scofl, a shovel: SHOVEL; **b.** Middle Dutch schoffel, schuffel, a shovel, hoe: SCUFFLE². **3.** Germanic *skub-, *skuf-, *skup- in: **a.** Danish skof, jest, teasing, probably akin to the Scandinavian source of Middle English scof, mocking: SCOFF; **b.** possibly (but quite doubtfully) Old English scop, poet (< "jester"): SCOP; **c.** Low German schüffeln, to walk clumsily, shuffle cards, probably akin to the source of SHUFFLE. [Pok. skeub- 955.]

skeud-. To shoot, chase, throw. **1.** Germanic *skeutan, to shoot, in: **a.** Old English scēotan, to shoot: SHOOT; **b.** Old Norse skjōta, to shoot: SKEET. **2.** Germanic *skutaz, shooting, shot, in: **a.** Old English sceot, scot, shooting, a shot: SHOT¹; **b.** Old High German scuz, shooting, a shot: SCHUSS; **c.** Old Norse skot and Old French escot, contribution, tax (< "money thrown down"): SCOT, (SCOT AND LOT). **3.** Germanic *skutjan probably in Old English scyttan, to shut (by pushing a crossbar): SHUT. **4.** Germanic *skutilaz in Old English scytel, a dart, missile: SHUTTLE. **5.** Germanic *skautjōn- in: **a.** Old English scēata, corner of a sail: SHEET²; **b.** Old English scēte, piece of cloth: SHEET¹. **6.** Germanic *skut- in Old Norse skūta, mockery (< "shooting of words"), akin to the Scandinavian source of SCOUT². **7.** Germanic *skaut-, perhaps in Old French escoutille, hatchway: SCUTTLE¹. [Pok. 2. (s)keud- 956.]

skeup-. Cluster, tuft, hair of the head. **1.** Germanic *skauf- in Old English scēaf, bundle, sheaf: SHEAF. **2.** Possibly Germanic *hupp- in Middle Dutch hoppe, the hop plant (having tuftlike inflorescence): HOP². [Pok. (s)keup- 956.]

[skipam. Ship. Germanic noun of obscure origin. **1.** Old English *scip*, ship: SHIP. **2.** Middle Dutch *schip*, ship: (SCHIPPERKE), SKIPPER[1]. **3.** Italian *schifo*, ship, skiff: SKIFF. **4.** French *équiper*, to equip: EQUIP. [In Pok. *skĕi-* 919.]]

skot-. Dark, shade **1.** Suffixed form **skot-wo-* in Germanic **skadwaz* in Old English *sceadu*, shade: SHADE, SHADOW. **2.** Suffixed form **skot-o-* in Greek *skotos*, darkness: SCOTOMA. [Pok. *skot-* 957.]

skreu-. To cut; cutting tool. Extension of **sker-**[1]. **1.** Basic form **skreu-* in: **a.** Germanic **skraw-* in Old English *scrēawa*, shrew (having a pointed snout): SHREW, (SHREWD); **b.** Germanic **skraud-* in Old English *scrēade*, piece, fragment: SCREED, SHRED; **c.** Germanic **skrūd-* in *(i)* Old English *scrūd*, garment (< "piece of cloth"): SHROUD *(ii)* Old French *escro(u)e*, scroll: SCROLL *(iii)* Dutch *schrood*, a slice, shred: SCROD. **2.** Extended form **skreut-* in Latin *scrūta*, trash, frippery: SCRUTINY. **3.** Extended variant form **skraut-* in Latin *scrōtum*, scrotum (probably identified with *scrautum*, leather quiver for arrows): SCROTUM. [Pok. 4. *(s)ker-*, Section III. 947.]

skrībh-. To cut, separate, sift. Extension of **sker-**[1]. **1.** Latin *scrībere*, to scratch, incise, write: SCRIBBLE, SCRIBE, SCRIPT, SCRIPTORIUM, SCRIPTURE, SERIF, SHRIVE; ASCRIBE, CIRCUMSCRIBE, CONSCRIPT, DESCRIBE, INSCRIBE, MANUSCRIPT, POSTSCRIPT, PRESCRIBE, PROSCRIBE, RESCRIPT, SUBSCRIBE, SUPERSCRIBE, TRANSCRIBE. **2.** Greek *skariphos*, scratching, sketch, pencil: SCARIFY[1]. [Pok. 4. *sker-*, Section II. 945.]

skut-. To shake. Germanic **skŭd-* in Middle Low German *schöderen*, to tremble, be afraid, akin to the source of Middle English *shoddren*, to tremble: SHUDDER. [Pok. *(s)kŭt-* 957.]

(s)kʷal-o-. Big fish. **1.** Suffixed form **kʷal-o-* in Germanic **hwalaz*, whale, in: **a.** Old English *hwæl*, whale: WHALE[1]; **b.** Old Norse *hvalr*, whale: NARWAL, RORQUAL. **2.** Latin *squalus*, a sea fish: SQUALENE. [Pok. *(s)kʷalo-* 958.]

(s)lagʷ-. To seize. **1.** Suffixed form **lagʷ-yo-* in Germanic **lakjan* in Old English *læccan*, to seize, grasp: LATCH. **2.** Variant form **slagʷ-* becoming **lab-*, with nasalized form **la-m-b-* in Greek *lambanein* (verbal adjective *lēptos*), to take, seize: LEMMA[1], -LEPSY; ANALEPTIC, ASTROLABE, CATALEPSY, EPILEPSY, NYMPHOLEPT, ORGANOLEPTIC, PROLEPSIS, SYLLABLE, SYLLEPSIS. [Pok. *(s)lagʷ-* 958.]

slak-. To strike. **1.** Germanic **slahan* in Old English *slēan*, to strike, kill: SLAY. **2.** Germanic suffixed form **slag-jō-* in Old English *slecg*, hammer: SLEDGEHAMMER. **3.** Germanic suffixed form **slah-tram* in Old Norse *slātr*, butchery, "striking," probably akin to the Scandinavian source of Middle English *slaughter*, killing: SLAUGHTER. **4.** Germanic **slag-* in: **a.** Old High German *slag* (> German *Schlag*), a blow: SCHLOCK; **b.** Middle Dutch *slag*, a blow: ONSLAUGHT; **c.** probably Middle Low German *slagge*, metal dross (< "that which falls off in the process of striking"): SLAG. **5.** Germanic suffixed lengthened-grade form **slōgiz* in Old Norse *slœgr*, clever, cunning (< "able to strike"): SLEIGHT, SLY. [Pok. *slak-* 959.]

slēb-. To be weak, sleep. Possibly related to **slēg-** through a hypothetical base **slē-* (< **sleə-*). Germanic **slēpan*, **slēpaz* in Old English *slēpan*, to sleep, and *slēp*, sleep: SLEEP. [In Pok. 1. *leb-* 655.]

slēg-. To be slack, be languid. Possibly related to **slēb-** through a hypothetical base **slē-* (< **sleə-*). Zero-grade form **(s)lag-*, becoming **(s)laġ-*. **1.** Germanic **slak-* in Old English *slæc*, "loose," indolent, careless: SLACK[1]. **2.** Suffixed form **lag-so-* in Latin *laxus*, loose, slack: LAX; DELAY, RELAX, RELAY. **3.** Suffixed nasalized form **la-n-g-u-* in Latin *languēre*, to be languid: LANGUISH. **4.** Compound **lag-ous-*, "with drooping ears" (**ous-*, ear; see **ous-**), in Greek *lagōs*, *lagos*, hare: LAGOMORPH.

5. Suffixed form **lag-no-* in Greek *lagnos*, lustful, lascivious (> *lagneia*, lust, lasciviousness): ALGOLAGNIA. **6.** Variant form **lēg-* in Greek *lēgein*, to leave off: CATALECTIC. [Pok. *(s)lēg-* 959.]

sleidh-. To slip, slide. **1.** Germanic **slīdan*, to slip, slide, in Old English *slīdan*, to slide: SLIDE. **2.** Germanic **slid-* in: **a.** Middle Low German *sledde*, a sled, sledge: SLED; **b.** Middle Dutch *slēde*, a sled: SLEIGH; **c.** Middle Dutch *sleedse*, sleigh: SLEDGE.

slengʷh-. To slide, make slide, sling, throw. **1.** Germanic strong verb **slingwan* and derived suffixed noun form **slingw-ō-* in Old Frisian *slinge*, sling, akin to the possible source of Middle English *sling*, sling: SLING[1], (SLINGSHOT). **2.** Germanic variant strong verb **slinkan* in Old English *slincan*, to creep: SLINK. **3.** Suffixed o-grade form **slongʷh-rī-ko-* in Latin *lumbrīcus*, intestinal worm, earthworm: LUMBRICOID. [In Pok. *(s)leidh-* 960, *slenk-* 961.]

sleu-. Hypothetical base of a group of distantly related Germanic derivatives with various suffixes. **1.** Germanic **slū-m-* in Old English *slūma*, sleep: SLUMBER. **2.** Probably Germanic **slautjan-* in Old English **slēte*, sleet: SLEET. **3.** Germanic **slus-* in Norwegian *slusk*, sloppy weather, probably akin to the possible Scandinavian source of SLUSH. **4.** Germanic **sleura-* in Middle High German *slier*, mud, slime: SCHLIEREN. **5.** Extended form **sleug-* in Germanic **sluk-*, **slug-* in: **a.** Norwegian dialectal *slugg* and Swedish dialectal *slagga*, slow-moving animal or person, probably akin to the source of Middle English *slugge*, a sluggard, and *sluggen*, to be idle: SLUG[2], SLUGGARD; **b.** Dutch *log*, lazy, slack: LOGY. [Pok. *(s)leu-* 962.]

sleubh-. To slide, slip. **I.** Basic form **sleubh-*. **1.** Germanic **sleub-* in Old English *slēf*, *slīf*, *slīef*, sleeve (into which the arm slips): SLEEVE. **2.** Suffixed form **sleubh-ro-* in Latin *lūbricus*, slippery: LUBRICATE, LUBRICITY, LUBRICIOUS. **II.** Variant Germanic form **sleup-*. **1.** Germanic **slup-* in: **a.** Old English *slypa*, *slyppe*, *slipa*, slime, slimy substance: SLIP[3]; COWSLIP, OXLIP; **b.** Old English **sloppe*, liquid food (perhaps > Middle English *sloppe*, a muddy place): SLOP[1]; **c.** Old English *(ofer)slop*, surplice (perhaps > Middle English *sloppe*, a kind of garment): SLOP[2]. **2.** Germanic **slaup-* in Dutch *sloep*, sloop (< "gliding boat"): SLOOP. [Pok. *sleub(h)-* 963.]

slī-. Bluish. Contracted from **sliə-*. **1.** O-grade form **sloi-* in Germanic **slaihwōn* in Old English *slāh*, *slā*, sloe (< "bluish fruit"): SLOE. **2.** Suffixed form **slī-wo-* in Latin *līvēre*, to be bluish: LIVID. **3.** Suffixed form **slī-wā-* in Serbo-Croatian *šljiva*, plum: SLIVOVITZ. [Pok. *(s)lī-* 965.]

sloug-. Help, service. Celtic and Balto-Slavic. Suffixed form **sloug-o-* in Old Irish *slūag*, *slōg*, army, host, whence Gaelic *sluagh*, army, host: SLEW[1], SLOGAN. [Pok. *slougo-* 965.]

smē-. To smear. Contracted from **smeə-*. **1.** Extended root **smeid-* (< **smeə-id-*) in Germanic **smītan* in Old English *smītan*, to daub, smear, pollute: SMITE. **(2.** Attributed by some to this root, but more likely to be of unknown origin, is the Germanic root **mas-*, spot, speck, in: **a.** Middle Dutch *masel*, pustule, spot, akin to the source of Middle English *masel*, measles-spot: MEASLES; **b.** Old French *masere*, *mazre*, knot in wood: MAZER.) **3.** Attributed by some to this root, but perhaps distinct, is root **smīk-*, small, in: **a.** Latin *mīca*, crumb, small piece, grain: MICA; **b.** Greek *(s)mikros*, small: MICRO-, MICRON; CHYLOMICRON, OMICRON. [Pok. *smē-* 966.]

smeg-. To taste. Germanic **smak-* in: **a.** Old English *smæc*, flavor, taste: SMACK[2]; **b.** Middle Dutch and Middle Low German *smacken*, to taste, make a sound with the lips while tasting food, akin to the source of SMACK[1]. [Pok. *smeg(h)-* 967.]

smei-. To laugh, smile. **1.** Germanic reshaped forms **smer-*, **smar-* in Old English *smercian* (with *-k-* formative), to smile: SMIRK. **2.** Germanic extended form **smīl* in Swedish *smila*, to smile, probably akin to the Scandi-

navian source of Middle English *smilen,* to smile: SMILE.
3. Suffixed form **smei-ro-* in Latin *mīrus,* wonderful (>
mīrārī, to be amazed): MARVEL, (MI) MIRACLE, MIRAGE,
MIRROR; ADMIRE. **4.** Prefixed zero-grade form **ko(m)-
smi-,* smiling with (**ko-, *kom-,* together; see **kom**), in
Latin *cōmis* (< **cosmis*), courteous: COMITY. [Pok. 1.
(s)mei- 967.]

(s)meit(ə)-. To throw. Possibly Latin *mittere* (first person plural present indicative *mittimus,* to let go, send
off, throw): MASS, MESS, MESSAGE, MISSILE, MISSION,
MISSIVE, MITTIMUS; ADMIT, COMMIT, (COMPROMISE),
DEMIT, DISMISS, EMIT, INTERMIT, INTROMIT, OMIT, PERMIT, PREMISE, PRETERMIT, PROMISE, REMIT, SUBMIT,
SURMISE, TRANSMIT. [Pok. *smeit-* 968.]

(s)mer-¹. To remember. **1.** Suffixed zero-grade form
*mr̥-no- in Germanic **murnan,* to remember sorrowfully,
in Old English *murnan,* to mourn: MOURN. **2.** Reduplicated form **me-mor-* in: **a.** Germanic **mi-mer-* in Old
Norse *Mimir,* a giant who guards the well of wisdom:
MIMIR; **b.** Latin *memor,* mindful: MEMORABLE, (MEMORANDUM), MEMORY; COMMEMORATE, REMEMBER. [Pok.
(s)mer- 969.]

(s)mer-². To get a share of something. **1.** Suffixed (stative) form **mer-ē-* in Latin *merēre, merērī,* to receive a
share, deserve, serve: MERETRICIOUS, MERIT; EMERITUS.
2. Suffixed form **mer-o-* in Greek *meros* (feminine
meris), a part, division: -MERE, MERISTEM, MERO-, -MEROUS; (ALLOMERISM), (DIMER), (ISOMER), (MONOMER),
TRIMER. [In Pok. *(s)mer-* 969.]

(s)mer-³. Grease, fat. **1.** Suffixed form **smer-wo-* in
Germanic **smerwa-,* grease, fat, in Old High German
smero, fat (> German *Schmiere,* grease): SCHMEER.
2. Germanic denominative verb **smerwjan,* to spread
grease on, in: **a.** Old English *smierwan, smerian,* to
smear: SMEAR; **b.** Old High German *smirwen, smerian*
(> German *schmieren*), to apply salve, smear: SMEAR-CASE. **3.** Latin *medulla* (perhaps < **merulla,* influenced
by *medius,* middle), marrow: MEDULLA. [Pok. *smeru-*
970.]

smerd-. Pain. Extension of **mer-².** Germanic **smarta-* in
Old English *smeart,* causing pain, painful: SMART. [Pok.
smerd- 970.]

smeug-. To smoke; smoke. Germanic **smuk-* in Old
English *smoca,* smoke: SMOKE. [Pok. *(s)meukh-, (s)meug-,
(s)meugh-* 971.]

smī-. To cut, work with a sharp instrument. **1.** Germanic
*smithaz in Old English *smith,* smith: SMITH. **2.** Germanic **smith-ja-* in Old Norse *smidhja,* smithy: SMITHY.
[Pok. *smēi-* 968.]

snā-. To swim. Contracted from **snaə-.* **1.** Extended form
*snāgh- in Greek *nēkhein,* to swim: NEKTON. **2.** Suffixed
zero-grade form **(s)nə-to-* in Latin *natāre,* to swim:
NATANT, NATATION, NATATORIAL, NATATORIUM; SUPERNATANT. **3.** Attributed by some to this root (but more
likely obscure) is Greek *nēsos,* island: CHERSONESE. See
(s)nāu-. [Pok. *snā-* 971.]

(s)nāu-. To flow, let flow, whence suckle. Contracted
from **snaəu-;* extension of **snā-.** **1.** Suffixed basic form
*naw-yo- in Greek *naein,* to flow, whence probably
Naias, fountain nymph: NAIAD. **2.** Zero-grade form **nū-*
(< **nuə-*) in suffixed form **nū-trī-* (with feminine agent
suffix) in Latin *nūtrīx,* nurse, and *nūtrīre,* to suckle,
nourish: NOURISH, NURSE, NURTURE, NUTRIENT, NUTRIMENT, NUTRITION, NUTRITIOUS, NUTRITIVE. [In Pok.
snā- 971.]

(s)nē-. Also **nē-.** To spin, sew. Contracted from **(s)neə-.*
1. Suffixed form **nē-tlā* in Germanic **nēthlō* in Old
English *nǣdl,* needle: NEEDLE. **2.** Suffixed form **snē-mn̥*
in Greek *nēma,* thread: NEMATO-; CHROMONEMA, PROTONEMA, SYNAPTINEMAL COMPLEX, TREPONEME. [Pok.
(s)nē- 973.]

(s)neəu-. Tendon, sinew. Extension of **(s)nē-.** Suffixed
form **(s)neəw-r̥-,* further suffixed in: **a.** **neu-r-o-* in
Greek *neuron,* sinew: NEURO-, NEURON; APONEUROSIS;

b. metathesized form **nerwo-* in Latin *nervus,* sinew:
NERVE; ENERVATE. [Pok. *snēu-* 977.]

sneg-. To creep; creeping thing. **1.** Suffixed o-grade form
*snog-on- in Germanic **snak-ōn-* in Old English *snaca,*
snake: SNAKE. **2.** Variant Germanic root **sneg-* in suffixed o-grade form **snag-ila-* in Old English *snæg(e)l,
sneg(e)l,* snail: SNAIL. [Pok. ? *sneig-* 974.]

sneigʷh-. Snow; to snow. **1.** Suffixed o-grade form
*snoigʷh-o- in Germanic **snaiwaz* in Old English *snāw,*
snow: SNOW. **2.** Zero-grade form **snigʷh-* in Latin *nix*
(stem *niv-*), snow: NÉVÉ, NIVAL, NIVEOUS. [Pok. *sneigʷh-*
974.]

sneit-. To cut. **1.** Germanic **snīthan* in Dutch *snijden,* to
cut: SNICKERSNEE. **2.** Expressive Germanic **snitt-ja-* in
Middle High German *sniz* (> German *Schnitz*), slice:
SCHNITZEL. [Pok. *sneit-* 974.]

sner-. Expressive root of various verbs for making noises.
1. Germanic **sner-* in North Frisian *sneere,* scornful
remark, perhaps akin to the possible source of SNEER.
2. O-grade form **snor-* in Germanic **(s)nor-* in: **a.** Middle
High German *snurren,* to hum, whirr: SCHNORRER;
b. German *snarchen,* to snore: SNORKEL; **c.** Middle Low
German *snarren,* to snarl: SNARL¹; **d.** Middle English
snoren, to snort: SNORE; **e.** Middle English *snorten,* to
snort: SNORT; **f.** possibly Old Norse *Norn,* goddess of fate
(< "the whisperer"): NORN. Compare **snu-.** [Pok. 1.
(s)ner- 975.]

(s)ner-. To wind, twist. **1.** Suffixed extended zero-grade
form **snork-* in Germanic **snarh-ōn-* in: **a.** Old Norse
snara, cord, noose, trap: SNARE¹; **b.** Dutch *snaar,* string:
SNARE². **2.** Proposed by some as a derivative of this root
is Germanic **narwa-* in Old English *nearu,* narrow:
NARROW. **3.** Extended variant form **(s)nark-* in Greek
narkē, cramp, numbness: NARCO-, NARCOSIS, NARCOTIC.
[Pok. 2. *(s)ner-* 975.]

sneubh-. To marry. **1.** Latin *nūbere,* to marry, take a
husband: NUBILE, NUPTIAL; CONNUBIAL. **2.** Possibly
nasalized zero-grade form **nu-m-bh-* in Greek *numphē,*
nymph, bride: NYMPH. [Pok. *sneubh-* 977.]

sneudh-. Mist, cloud. Latin *nūbēs,* cloud: NUANCE. [Pok.
2. *sneudh-* 978.]

sneud(h)-. To be sleepy. Expressive root. Compare **snu-.**
Zero-grade form **snud-to-* giving **nusto-* in Greek *nustazein,* to be sleepy: NYSTAGMOUS. [Pok. 1. *sneud(h)-* 978.]

snu-. Imitative beginning of Germanic words connected
with the nose. **1.** Germanic **snūt-, *snut-* in: **a.** Old
English *gesnot(t),* nasal mucus (*ge-,* collective prefix; see
kom): SNOT; **b.** Middle Dutch *snut(e),* snout, akin to the
probable source of Middle English *snute,* snout: SNOUT;
c. German *Schnauze,* snout: SCHNAUZER, SCHNOZZLE.
2. Germanic **snuf-* in: **a.** Low German or Dutch *snuffelen,* to sniff at: SNUFFLE; **b.** Middle Dutch *snuffen,* to
snuffle: SNUFF¹; **c.** Old English **snyflan* (> Middle
English *snyvelen*), to run at the nose: SNIVEL; **d.** Middle
English *sniffen,* to sniff: SNIFF. **3.** Germanic **snup-* in
Dutch *snoepen,* to eat on the sly, pry: SNOOP. **4.** Germanic **snip-* in Low German and Dutch *snippen,* to snap
at: SNIP. **5.** Germanic **snap-* in Middle Low German and
Middle Dutch *snappen,* to snap at: SNAP. **6.** Germanic
*snub- in Old Norse *snubba,* "to snub, turn up one's nose
at," scold, rebuke: SNUB. **7.** Germanic **snak-* in Middle
Dutch *snakken,* to snap at, akin to the Low German
source of Middle English *snacchen,* to snatch: SNATCH.
[In Pok. *snā-* 971.]

so-. This, that (nominative). For other cases see **to-.**
1. Greek *ho* (nominative plural *hoi*), the: HOI POLLOI.
2. Feminine form **syā* in Germanic **sjō* in Old English
sēo, sīe, she: SHE. **3.** Compound variant form **sei-ke*
(**-ke,* "that"; see **ko-**) in Latin *sīc,* thus, so, in that
manner: SIC¹. [Pok. *so(s), sā, sī* 978.]

sol-. Also **sole-.** Whole. I. Basic form **sol-.* **1.** Suffixed
form **sol-ido-* in Latin *solidus,* solid: SOLID; CONSOLIDATE. **2.** Suffixed form **sol-wo-* in Greek *holos,* whole:
HOLO-; CATHOLIC. **3.** Dialectal geminated form **soll-o-*

in: **a.** Latin *sollus*, whole, entire, unbroken: SOLICITOUS; **b.** Latin *sollemnis* (second element obscure), celebrated at fixed dates (said of religious rites), established, religious, solemn: SOLEMN. **II.** Variant form *solə-*. **1.** Suffixed zero-grade form *slə-u-* giving *sal-u-* in Latin *salūs*, health, a whole or sound condition: SALUBRIOUS, SALUTARY, SALUTE. **2.** Suffixed zero-grade form *slə-wo-* giving *sala-wo-* in Latin *salvus*, whole, safe, healthy, uninjured: SAFE, SAGE², SALVAGE, SALVO¹, SAVE¹, SAVE². [Pok. solo- 979.]

spē-¹. To thrive, prosper. Contracted from *speə-*. **1.** Suffixed o-grade form *spō-ti-* in Germanic *spōdiz* in Old English *spēd*, success: SPEED. **2.** Suffixed form *spē-s-* in Latin *spēs* (plural *spērēs*), hope, with denominative *spērāre*, to hope: DESPAIR, ESPERANCE. **3.** Suffixed zero-grade form *spə-ro-* in Latin *prosperus*, favorable, prosperous (traditionally regarded as from *prō spērē*, according to one's hope; *pro-*, according to; see **per¹**): PROSPER. [Pok. 3. *sp(h)ēi-* 983.]

spē-². Long, flat piece of wood. Contracted from *speə-*. **I.** Basic form *spē-*. **1.** Germanic *spē-nu-* in: **a.** Old English *spōn*, chip of wood, splinter: SPOON; **b.** Old Norse *spānn*, shingle, chip: SPANNEW. **2.** Possibly Greek *sphēn*, wedge (formation unclear; earliest Greek form *sphān*): SPHENE, SPHENO-. **II.** Suffixed zero-grade form *spə-dh-*. **1.** Germanic *spadan* in: **a.** Old English *spadu*, digging tool: SPADE¹; **b.** Middle High German *spat* (> German *Spat*), spar: SPATHIC. **2.** Greek *spathē*, broad blade: SPADE², SPATHE, SPATULA, SPAY. [Pok. *sp(h)ē-* 980.]

spei-. Sharp point. **I.** Basic form *spei-*. **1.** Germanic *spituz* in Old English *spitu*, stake on which meat is roasted: SPIT². **2.** Germanic *spitja-* in German *spitz*, pointed: SPITZ. **3.** Germanic *spī-ra-* in: **a.** Old English *spīr*, slender stalk: SPIRE¹; ACROSPIRE; **b.** possibly Middle Dutch *spierlinc*, a small, slender fish, smelt, akin to the source of Old French *esperlinge*, smelt: SPARLING. **4.** Germanic *spīk-* in Old Norse *spīk*, nail, perhaps akin to the possible source of Middle English *spyk*, spike: SPIKE¹. **5.** Germanic *spīl-* in Middle Low German *spīle*, wooden peg: SPILE, SPILL². **6.** Suffixed form *spei-nā* in Latin *spīna* (> Old French *espin*), thorn, prickle, spine: SPINE, SPINEL, SPINNEY; PORCUPINE. **7.** *spei-kā* in Latin *spīca*, point, ear of grain: SPICA, SPICA, SPICULUM, SPIKE². **II.** Extended o-grade form *spoig-* in Germanic *spaikōn-* in Old English *spāca*, spoke: SPOKE¹. [Pok. 1. *sp(h)ēi-* 981.]

(s)peik-. Bird's name, woodpecker, magpie. **1.** Suffixed form *peik-o-* in Latin *pīcus*, woodpecker: PICARO, (PICKET), (PIKE¹), (PIQUE). **2.** Suffixed form *peik-ā-* in Latin *pīca*, magpie: PICA², PIE². [Pok. *(s)pīko-* 999.]

spek-. To observe. **I.** Basic form *spek-*. **1.** Germanic *spehōn* in: **a.** Old French *espier*, to watch: ESPY, SPY; **b.** Germanic derivative *speh-ōn-*, watcher, in Old Italian *spione*, spy: ESPIONAGE. **2.** Suffixed form *spek-yo-* in Latin *specere*, to look at: SPECIMEN, SPECIOUS, SPECTACLE, SPECTRUM, SPECULATE, SPECULUM; ASPECT, AUSPICE, CIRCUMSPECT, CONSPICUOUS, DESPISE, EXPECT, FRONTISPIECE, INSPECT, INTROSPECT, PERSPECTIVE, PROSPECT, RESPECT, (RESPITE), RETROSPECT, SUSPECT. **3.** Latin *speciēs*, a seeing, sight, form: SPECIES; ESPECIAL. **4.** Latin *-spex* (< *-spek-*), "he who sees," in: **a.** *haruspex*, diviner (see **ghera-**); **b.** *auspex*, augur (see **awi-**). **5.** Suffixed form *spek-ā-* in Latin (denominative) *dēspicāri*, to despise, look down on (*de-*, down; see **de-**): DESPICABLE. **6.** Suffixed metathetical form *skep-yo-* in Greek *skeptesthai*, to examine, consider: SKEPTIC. **II.** Extended o-grade form *spoko-* metathesized in Greek *skopos*, one who watches, also object of attention, goal, and its denominative *skopein* (< *skop-eyo-*), to see: SCOPE, -SCOPE, -SCOPY; BISHOP, EPISCOPAL, HOROSCOPE, TELESCOPE. [Pok. *spek-* 984.]

spel-¹. To split, break off. **1.** Extended form *speld-* in Germanic *spilt-* in Middle Dutch *spelte*, wheat (probably from the splitting of its husk at threshing), akin to the Germanic source of Late Latin *spelta*, spelt: SPELT¹. **2.** Extended form *spelt-* in Germanic *spilthjan* in Old English *spillan*, to spill, destroy: SPILL¹. **3.** Suffixed o-grade form *spol-yo-* perhaps in Latin *spolium*, hide torn from an animal, armor stripped from an enemy, booty: SPOIL; DESPOIL. [Pok. 1. *(s)p(h)el-* 985.]

spel-². To shine, glow. Extended form *splend-* in Latin *splendēre*, to shine: SPLENDID; RESPLENDENT. [Pok. 2. *(s)p(h)el-* 987.]

spel-³. To say aloud, recite. Suffixed form *spel-no-*. **1.** Germanic *spellam* in: **a.** Old English *spell*, discourse, story: SPELL²; **b.** Old English *spel*, news: GOSPEL. **2.** Germanic denominative *spellōn* in Old French *espeller*, *espelir*, to read out: SPELL¹. [Pok. *(s)pel-* 985.]

spelgh-. Spleen, milt. **1.** Deformation *(p)lihēn* in Latin *liēn*, milt, spleen: LIENAL. **2.** Uncertain preform in: **a.** Greek *splēn*, spleen: SPLEEN; **b.** Greek *splankhna*, inward parts: SPLANCHNIC. [Pok. *sp(h)elĝh(en)* 987.]

(s)pen-. To draw, stretch, spin. **I.** Basic form *spen-*. **1.** Suffixed form *spen-wo-* in Germanic *spinnan*, to spin, in: **a.** Old English *spinnan*, to spin, with derivative *spin-thrōn-*, "the spinner," contracted to *spīthra*, spider: SPIN, SPIDER; **b.** Germanic derivative *spin-ilōn* in Old English *spinel*, spindle: SPINDLE. **2.** Extended form *pend-* in Latin *pendēre*, to hang (intransitive), and *pendere*, to cause to hang, weigh, with its frequentative *pensāre*, to weigh: PAINTER², (PANSY), PENCHANT, PENDANT, PENDENTIVE, PENDULOUS, PENSILE, PENSION¹, PENSIVE, PESO, POISE¹; ANTEPENDIUM, APPEND, (APPENDIX), COMPENDIUM, COMPENSATE, DEPEND, DISPENSE, EXPEND, IMPEND, PENTHOUSE, PERPEND, PERPENDICULAR, PREPENSE, PROPEND, SUSPEND, VILIPEND. **3.** Perhaps suffixed form *pen-ya-* in Greek *penia*, lack, poverty (< "a strain, exhaustion"): -PENIA. **II.** O-grade forms *spon-*, *pon-*. **1.** Germanic *spannan* in: **a.** Middle Dutch *spannen*, to bind: SPAN²; **b.** Old High German *spannan* (> German *spannen*), to stretch: SPANNER. **2.** Germanic *spanno-* in Old English *span(n)*, distance: SPAN¹. **3.** Perhaps Germanic *spangō* in Middle Dutch *spange*, clasp: SPANGLE. **4.** Suffixed and extended form *pond-o-* in Latin *pondō*, by weight: POUND¹. **5.** Suffixed and extended form *pond-es-* in Latin *pondus* (stem *ponder-*), weight, and its denominative *ponderāre*, to weigh: PONDER, PONDEROUS; EQUIPONDERATE, PREPONDERATE. **6.** Perhaps suffixed form *spon-t-* in Latin *sponte*, of one's own accord, spontaneously: SPONTANEOUS. **7.** Greek *penesthai*, to toil, with o-grade derivatives *ponos*, toil, and *ponein*, to toil: GEOPONIC. [Pok. *(s)pen-(d)-* 988.]

spend-. To make an offering, perform a rite, hence to engage oneself by a ritual act. O-grade form *spond-*. **1.** Suffixed form *spond-eyo-* in Latin *spondēre*, to make a solemn promise, pledge, betroth: SPONSOR, SPOUSE; DESPOND, ESPOUSE, RESPOND. **2.** Suffixed form *spond-ā* in Greek *spondē*, libation, offering: SPONDEE. [Pok. *spend-* 989.]

sper-¹. Spear, pole. **1.** Germanic *speru-* in: **a.** Old English *spere*, spear: SPEAR; **b.** Middle Low German *spēr*, spit: SPARERIBS. **2.** Germanic *sparjōn-* in Old Norse *sperra*, rafter, beam: SPAR¹. [Pok. 1. *(s)per-* 990.]

sper-². To turn, twist. **1.** Suffixed form *sper-ya-* in Greek *speira*, a winding, coil, spire: SPIRE². **2.** Suffixed zero-grade form *spr-to-* in Greek *sparton*, rope, cable: ESPARTO. [Pok. 3. *sper-* 991.]

sper-³. Bird's name, sparrow. Suffixed o-grade form *spor-wo-* in Germanic *sparwan-* in Old English *spearwa*, *spearwe*, sparrow: SPARROW. [Pok. *sper-(g)-* 997.]

sper-⁴. To strew. **I.** Zero-grade form *spr-*. **1.** Germanic *spr-* in Old English *sprēawlian*, to sprawl: SPRAWL. **2.** Extended form *spreut-* in Germanic *sprūt-* in: **a.** Old English *sprūtan*, to sprout: SPROUT; **b.** Old English *spryttan*, to sprout, come forth: SPURT; **c.** Old English

sprēot, pole (< "sprout, stem"): SPRIT; **d.** Middle English *bouspret*, bowsprit: BOWSPRIT. **3.** Extended form **spreit-* in Germanic **spraidjan* in Old English *sprǣdan*, to spread: SPREAD. **II.** Basic form **sper-*. **1.** Suffixed form **sper-yo-* in Greek *speirein*, to scatter: DIASPORA. **2.** Suffixed form **sper-mn̥* in Greek *sperma*, sperm, seed (< "that which is scattered"): SPERM[1]. **III.** O-grade form **spor-*. **1.** Suffixed form **spor-ā-* in Greek *spora*, a sowing, seed: SPORE, SPORO-. **2.** Suffixed form **spor-n̥d-* in Greek *sporas* (stem *sporad-*), scattered, dispersed: SPORADIC. [Pok. 2. *(s)p(h)er-* 993.]

spera-. Ankle. Zero-grade form **spr̥(ə)-*. **1.** Germanic suffixed form **spur-ōn-* in Old English *spura, spora*, spur: SPUR. **2.** Nasalized form **spr̥-n-ə-* in Germanic **spurnōn* in Old English *spurnan, spornan*, to kick, strike against: SPURN. **3.** Germanic suffixed form **spuram* in Middle Dutch *spor, spoor*, track of an animal: SPOOR. [Pok. 1. *sp(h)er-* 992.]

spergh-. To move, hasten, spring. Nasalized root form **sprengh-*. **1.** Germanic **springan* in: **a.** Old English *springan*, to spring: SPRING; **b.** Middle Dutch *springen* (> Dutch *springen* and Afrikaans *spring*), to leap: KLIPSPRINGER, SPRINGBOK; **c.** Old High German *springan*, to jump: GELÄNDESPRUNG. **2.** Germanic causative **sprangjan* in: **a.** Old English *besprengan*, to sprinkle, scatter: BESPRENT; **b.** Old English **sprencg*, snare used to catch game: SPRINGE. [Pok. *spergh-* 998.]

(s)peud-. To push, repulse. **1.** Latin *pudēre*, to feel shame: PUDENCY, PUDENDUM; IMPUDENT. **2.** Latin *repudium*, a casting off, divorce (*re-*, off; see **re-**): REPUDIATE. [In Pok. *pēu-* 827.]

sping-. Also **ping-.** Bird's name, sparrow, finch. Germanic **finki-* in Old English *finc*, finch: FINCH. [Pok. *(s)pingo-* 999.]

[spīrāre. To breathe. Latin word of unknown origin, with its derivative *spīritus*, breath, breath of a god, inspiration: SPIRACLE, SPIRIT; ASPIRATE, CESSPOOL, CONSPIRE, EXPIRE, INSPIRE, PERSPIRE, RESPIRE, SUSPIRE, TRANSPIRE. [In Pok. *peis-, speis-* 796.]]

splei-. To splice, split. Extension of **spel-**[1]. **1.** Germanic **flī-* in: **a.** Old English *flint*, flint: FLINT; **b.** Norwegian *flindra*, splinter, akin to the Scandinavian source of Middle English *flendris*, bits, splinters: FLINDERS. **2.** Germanic **splī-* in: **a.** Middle Dutch *splinter*, splinter: SPLINTER; **b.** Middle Dutch *splitten*, to split: SPLIT; **c.** Middle Dutch *splissen*, to splice: SPLICE; **d.** Middle Low German and Middle Dutch *splente, splinte*, splint: SPLINT. [Pok. *(s)plei-* 1000.]

(s)poi-mo-. Foam. **1.** Variant form **poimo-* in Germanic **faimaz* in Old English *fām*, foam: FOAM. **2.** Variant form **spoimā* in Latin *spūma*, foam: SPUME. **3.** Suffixed reduced form **poim-ik-* in Latin *pūmex*, pumice (from its spongelike appearance): POUNCE[2], PUMICE. [Pok. *(s)poimno-* 1001.]

spreg-. To speak. Germanic **sprek-, *spek-* (with Germanic loss of *r*) in: **a.** Old English *specan*, to speak: SPEAK; **b.** Germanic compound **bisprekan* (**bi-*, about; see **ambhi**) in Old English *bisprecan, besprecan*, to speak about: BESPEAK; **c.** Old English *sprǣc, spēc*, speech: SPEECH. [In Pok. *(s)p(h)ereg-* 996.]

(s)preg-. To jerk, scatter. **1.** Germanic **sprek-, *frek-* in: **a.** Middle Dutch *sprenkelen*, to sprinkle, akin to the possible source of Middle English *sprenklen*, to sprinkle: SPRINKLE; **b.** Old Norse *freknur*, freckles (< "that which is scattered on the skin"): FRECKLE; **c.** Swedish dialectal *spragg*, twig (< "that which is jerked off a branch"), akin to the Scandinavian source of SPRAG; **d.** Swedish dialectal *sprygg*, brisk, active, akin to the Scandinavian source of SPRY. **2.** Zero-grade form **sprg-* in variant **sparg-* in Latin *spargere*, to strew, scatter: SPARGE, SPARSE, ASPERSE, DISPERSE, INTERSPERSE. [Pok. *(s)p(h)ereg-* 996.]

spyeu-. Also **speu.** To spew, spit. Expressive root. **1.** Germanic **spitjan* in Old English *spittan*, to spit:

SPIT[1]. **2.** Germanic **speiw-* in Old English *spīwan, spīowan*, to spew: SPEW. **3.** Germanic **spait-* in Old English *spātl*, spittle: SPITTLE. **4.** Germanic **spūt-* in: **a.** Middle English *spouten*, to spout forth: SPOUT; **b.** Dutch *sputteren*, to sputter, akin to the probable Low German source of SPUTTER. **5.** Zero-grade form **spu-* in Latin *spuere*, to spit: SPUTUM; CUSPIDOR. **6.** Zero-grade form **(s)pyu-* in Greek *ptuein*, to spit: HEMOPTYSIS, PTYALIN. [Pok. *(s)p(h)ieu-* 999.]

srebh-. To suck, absorb. Zero-grade form **srbh-* in: **a.** Germanic **surp-* in altered form in Dutch *slurpen*, to slurp, lap: SLURP; **b.** suffixed form **srbh-ē-* in Latin *sorbēre*, to suck: ABSORB, ADSORB, RESORB. [Pok. *srebh-* 1001.]

srenk-. To snore. O-grade form **sronk-* in: **a.** Greek *rhonkos, rhonkhos*, a snoring: RHONCHUS; **b.** Greek *rhunkhos*, snout, bill, beak: RHYNCHOCEPHALIAN. [Pok. *srenk-* 1002.]

sreu-. To flow. **1.** Suffixed o-grade form **srou-mo-* in Germanic **straumaz*, stream, in: **a.** Old English *strēam*, stream: STREAM; **b.** Dutch *stroom*, stream: MAELSTROM. **2.** Basic form **sreu-* in: **a.** Greek *rhein*, to flow: RHEO-, -RRHEA; CATARRH, DIARRHEA, HEMORRHOID, RHYOLITE; **b.** suffixed form **sreu-mn̥* in Greek *rheuma*, stream, humor of the body: RHEUM. **3.** Suffixed zero-grade form **sru-dhmo-* in Greek *rhuthmos*, measure, recurring motion, rhythm: RHYME, RHYTHM. [Pok. *sreu-* 1003.]

srīg-. Cold. Suffixed form **srīg-os-* in Latin *frīgus*, cool, cold: FRIGID; REFRIGERATE. [Pok. *srīg-* 1004.]

stā-. To stand; with derivatives meaning "place or thing that is standing." Contracted from **staə-*. **I.** Basic form **stā-*. **1.** Extended form **stādh-* in: **a.** Germanic **stōdjōn-* in Old English *stēda*, stallion, studhorse (< "place for breeding horses"): STEED; **b.** Germanic **stōdō* in Old English *stōd*, establishment for breeding horses: STUD[2]. **2.** Suffixed form **stā-lo-* in Germanic **stōlaz* in: **a.** Old English *stōl*, stool: STOOL; **b.** compound **faldistōlaz* (see **pel-**[3]). **3.** Latin *stāre* (third person singular present subjunctive *stet*), to stand, with its past participle *status* (< **stə-to-*) and derivatives *statūra*, height, stature, and *statuere*, to set up, erect, cause to stand: STAGE, STANCE, STANCH, (STANCHION), (STANZA), STATOR, (STATUE), STATURE, STATUTE, STAY[1], STET; ARREST, CIRCUMSTANCE, CONSTANT, CONSTITUTE, CONTRAST, (COST), DESTITUTE, DISTANT, ESTANCIA, EXTANT, INSTANT, INSTITUTE, OBSTACLE, OBSTETRIC, (OUST), PROSTITUTE, REST[2], RESTITUTE, RESTIVE, SUBSTANCE, SUBSTITUTE, SUPERSTITION. **4.** Suffixed form **stā-men-* in Latin *stāmen*, thread of the warp (a technical term): STAMEN, STAMMEL. **5.** Suffixed form **stā-mon-* in Greek *stēmōn*, thread: PENSTEMON. **6.** Suffixed form **stā-ro-* in Russian *staryĭ*, old ("long-standing"): STARETS. **II.** Zero-grade form **stə-* (before consonants). **1.** Nasalized extended form **stə-n-t-* in Germanic **standan* in: **a.** Old English *standan*, to stand: STAND; **b.** Old English *understandan*, to know, stand under (*under-*, under; see **ndher-**): UNDERSTAND; **c.** Old French *estandard*, rallying place: STANDARD; **d.** secondary zero-grade form in Germanic **stund-ō* in Old English *stund*, a fixed time, while: STOUND. **2.** Suffixed form **stə-tyo-* in Germanic **stathjōn-* in Old Norse *stedhi*, anvil: STITHY. **3.** Suffixed form **stə-tlo-* in Germanic **stathlaz* in Old English *stathol*, foundation: STADDLE, STARLING[2]. **4.** Suffixed form **stə-mno-* in Germanic **staminz* in Old English *stefn*, stem, tree trunk: STEM[1]. **5.** Suffixed form **stə-ti-* in: **a.** Germanic **stadiz* in (i) Old English *stede*, place: STEAD (ii) Dutch *stad*, place: STADHOLDER (iii) Old High German *stat*, place: SHTETL; **b.** Latin *statio*, a standing still: STATION; **c.** Latin *-stitium*, a stoppage (in *solstitium*, solstice; see **sāwel-**): ARMISTICE; **d.** Greek *stasis*, a standing, a standstill: STASIS; HYPOSTASIS, ICONOSTASIS, ISOSTASY. **6.** Suffixed form **stə-to-* in Greek *statos*, placed, standing: STATIC, STATICE, STATO-; ASTASIA, ASTATINE. **7.** Suffixed form **stə-no-* in: **a.** Latin *dēsti-*

nāre, to make firm, establish (*dē-*, thoroughly; see **de-**): DESTINE; **b.** Latin *obstināre*, to set one's mind on, persist (*ob-*, on; see **epi**): OBSTINATE. **8.** Suffixed form **stə-tu-* in Latin *status*, manner, position, condition, attitude: STATE, STATISTICS, STATUS. **9.** Suffixed form **stə-dhlo-* in Latin *stabulum*, standing place: STABLE². **10.** Suffixed form **stə-dhli-* in Latin *stabilis*, standing firm: ESTABLISH, STABLE¹. **11.** Suffixed form **stə-tā-* in Greek *-statēs*, one that causes to stand, a standing: -STAT; ENSTATITE. **III.** Zero-grade form **st-*, **st(ə)-* (before vowels). **1.** Reduplicated form **si-st(ə)-* in: **a.** Latin *sistere*, to set, place, stop, stand: ASSIST, CONSIST, DESIST, EXIST, INSIST, INTERSTICE, PERSIST, RESIST, SUBSIST; **b.** Greek *histanai* (aorist *stanai*), to set, place: APOSTASY, CATASTASIS, DIASTASIS, ECSTASY, EPISTASIS, EPISTEMOLOGY, METASTASIS, PROSTATE, SYSTEM; **c.** Greek *histos*, web, tissue (< "that which is set up"): HISTO-; HISTIOCYTE. **2.** Compound form **tri-st-i-*, "third person standing by" (see **trei-**). **3.** Compound form **por-st-i-*, "that which stands before" (**por-*, before, forth; see **per¹**), in Latin *postis*, post: POST¹. **4.** Suffixed form **st-o-* in compound **upo-st-o-*, "one who stands under" (see **upo**). **IV.** Extended root **stāu-* (< **staəu-*), becoming **stau-* before consonants, **stāw-* before vowels; basic meaning "stout-standing, strong." **1.** Suffixed extended form **stāw-ā* in Germanic **stōwō* in Old English *stōw*, place: STOW. **2.** Probable o-grade suffixed extended form **stōw-yā* in Greek *stoa*, porch: STOA, STOIC. **3.** Suffixed extended form **stau-ro-* in: **a.** (i) Latin *instaurāre*, to restore, set upright again (*in-*, on; see **en**): STORE, INSTAURATION (ii) Latin *restaurāre*, to restore, rebuild (*re-*, anew, again; see **re-**): RESTORE; **b.** Greek *stauros*, cross, post, stake: STAUROLITE. **4.** Variant **tau-ro-*, bull (see **tauro-**). **V.** Zero-grade extended root *stū-* (< **stuə-*). Suffixed form **stū-lo-* in Greek *stulos*, pillar: STYLITE; AMPHISTYLAR, ASTYLAR, EPISTYLE, HYPOSTYLE, PERISTYLE, PROSTYLE, STYLOBATE. **VI.** Secondary full-grade form **steuə-*. Suffixed form **steuə-ro-* in Sanskrit *sthavira-*, thick, stout, old: THERAVADA. **VII.** Variant zero-grade extended root **stu-*. Suffixed form **stu-t-* in Old English *stuthu, studu*, post, prop: STUD¹. **VIII.** Secondary full-grade form **steu-*. **1.** Suffixed form **steu-rā* in Germanic **steurō*, "a steering," in Old English *stēor*, a steering: STARBOARD. **2.** Germanic denominative **steurjan* in: **a.** Old English *stīeran*, to steer: STEER¹; **b.** Old Norse *stȳra*, to steer, with its derivative *stjōrn*, a rudder, a steering, akin to the possible source of Middle English *sterne*, stern of a boat: STERN². **3.** Suffixed form **steu-ro-*, a larger domestic animal, in Germanic **steuraz*, ox, in Old English *stēor*, steer: STEER². **4.** Probably Germanic diminutive **steur-ika-* in Old English *stīrc, stierc*, calf: STIRK. See **stāk-**. [Pok. *stā-* 1004.]

stag-. To seep, drip. Possible root. **1.** Latin *stagnum*, pond, swamp: STAGNANT. **2.** Suffixed form **stag-yo-* in Greek *stazein*, to ooze, drip: STACTE; EPISTAXIS. [Pok. *stag-* 1010.]

stāk-. To stand, place. Zero-grade form **stək-*; extension of **stā-**. **1.** Suffixed form **stək-o-* in Germanic **staga-* in: **a.** Old English *stæg*, rope used to support a mast: STAY³; **b.** Old French *estaie*, a support: STAY². **2.** Suffixed form **stək-lo-* in Germanic **stahla-* in Old English *stēli, stȳle*, steel (< "that which stands firm"): STEEL. [Pok. *stāk-* 1011.]

[stam-. To push, stutter, stammer. Germanic root. **1.** Old English *stamerian*, to stammer: STAMMER. **2.** Middle Dutch *stom*, mute: STUM. **3.** Old Norse *stemma*, to stop: STEM². **4.** Old Norse *stumla, stumra*, to stumble, the probable Scandinavian source of Middle English *stumblen*, to stumble: STUMBLE. [In Pok. *stem-* 1021.]]

[staup-. (Cooking) vessel. Germanic root. **1.** Old Norse *staup*, vessel: STOUP. **2.** Middle Low German *stove*, heated chamber: STOVE¹. [In Pok. 1. *steu-* 1032.]]

stebh-. Post, stem; to support, place firmly on, fasten. **I.** Basic form **stebh-*. **1.** Germanic **stab-* in Old English

stæf, stick, rod: STAFF¹. **2.** Greek *stephein*, to tie around, encircle, crown, wreathe: STEMMA, STEPHANOTIS. **II.** Unaspirated form **steb-*. **1.** Germanic **stap-* in: **a.** Old English *stapol*, post, pillar: STAPLE²; **b.** Old English *stæpe*, step (< "a treading firmly on, foothold"): STEP; **c.** Middle Dutch *stapel*, pillar, foundation: STAPLE¹; **d.** Middle Dutch *stoep*, stoop: STOOP²; **e.** Low German *stope*, a step: STOPE. **2.** Germanic nasalized form **stamp-* in: **a.** Middle English *stampen*, to pound, stamp: STAMP; **b.** Middle Low German *stump*, stump: STUMP; **c.** Old High German *stam*, base, stem, in German *Stammlager*, base camp: STALAG; **d.** Provençal *estampir*, to stamp: STAMPEDE. **III.** Variant **stabh-* in Greek *staphulē*, grapevine, bunch of grapes: STAPHYLO-. [Pok. *steb(h)* 1011.]

steg-. Pole, stick. O-grade form **stog-* in Germanic **stak-* in: **a.** Old English *staca*, stake: STAKE¹; **b.** Old Norse *stakkr*, haystack: STACK; **c.** Old Norse *staka*, to push, cause to stumble (as with a stick): STAGGER; **d.** Old Italian *attacare*, to attack: ATTACK; **e.** Old French *attachier*, to attack: ATTACH; **f.** Spanish *estaca*, stake: STOCKADE. [Pok. 2. *(s)teg-* 1014.]

(s)teg-. To cover. **I.** O-grade form **tog-*. **1.** Germanic **thakjan* in: **a.** Old English *theccan*, to cover: THATCH; **b.** Middle Dutch *dekken*, to cover: DECK²; Old High German *decchen*, to cover: DECKLE. **2.** Germanic **thakam* in Middle Dutch *dec, decke*, roof, covering: DECK¹. **3.** Suffixed form **tog-ā-*, covering, in Latin *toga*, toga: TOGA. **4.** Possibly Sanskrit *sthagayati*, he covers: THUG. **II.** Basic form **steg-* in Greek *stegein*, to cover: STEGODON. **III.** Basic form **teg-*. **1.** Latin *tegere*, to cover, and *tegula*, tile: TECTRIX, TECTUM, TEGMEN, TEGMENTUM, TEGULAR, TEGUMENT, TILE, TUILLE; DETECT, INTEGUMENT, OBTECT, PROTECT. **2.** Persian *tāj*, crown: TAJ. [Pok. 1. *(s)teg-* 1013.]

stegh-. To stick, prick; pointed. **1.** Nasalized form **stengh-* perhaps in Germanic **stingan* in Old English *stingan*, to sting: STING. **2.** O-grade form **stogh-* in: **a.** Germanic **stag-* in Old English *stagga*, stag: STAG; **b.** Greek *stokhos*, pointed stake or pillar (used as a target for archers), goal: STOCHASTIC. [Pok. *stegh-* 1014.]

stei-. Stone. Suffixed o-grade form **stoi-no-* in Germanic **stainaz* in: **a.** Old English *stān*, stone: STONE; **b.** Middle Dutch *steen*, stone: STEENBOK; **c.** Old Norse *steinn*, stone: TUNGSTEN; **d.** Old High German *stein*, stone, in German *Steingut*, stoneware: STEIN. [Pok. *stāi-* 1010.]

steig-. To stick; pointed. Partly blended with **stegh-**. **I.** Zero-grade form **stig-*. **1.** Germanic suffixed form **stik-ilaz* in Old English *sticel*, a prick, sting: STICKLEBACK. **2.** Suffixed form **stig-i-* in Germanic **stikiz* in Old English *stice*, a sting, prick: STITCH. **3.** Germanic expressive form **stikkōn-* in Old English *sticca*, stick: STICK. **4.** Germanic blended variant **stekan* in Middle Dutch *steken* (> Dutch *steken*), to stick, stab: (ETIQUETTE), TICKET; SNICKERSNEE. **5.** Nasalized form **sti-n-g-* in Latin *stinguere*, to quench, perhaps originally to prick, and its apparent derivative *distinguere*, to separate (semantic transitions obscure): DISTINGUISH, EXTINGUISH, INSTINCT. **6.** Suffixed form **stig-yo-* in Greek *stizein*, to prick, tattoo: STIGMA; ASTIGMATISM. **7.** Suffixed reduced form **tig-ro-* in Old Persian *tigra-*, sharp, pointed, and Avestan *tighri-*, arrow, in Greek *tigris*, tiger (from its stripes): TIGER. **II.** Basic form **steig-* in Latin *-stīgāre*, to spur on, prod, in *instīgāre*, to urge: INSTIGATE. **III.** Suffixed o-grade form **stoig-ā-* in Germanic **staikō* in Old Norse *steik*, roast, steak, and *steikja*, to roast (on a spit): STEAK. [Pok. *steig-* 1016.]

steigh-. To stride, step, rise. **I.** Basic form **steigh-*. **1.** Germanic **stīgan* in Old English *stīgan*, to go up, rise: STY². **2.** Germanic compound **stīg-raipaz*, "mount-rope" (**raipaz*, rope; see **rei-¹**), in Old English *stīgrāp*, stirrup: STIRRUP. **II.** Zero-grade form **stigh-*. **1.** Germanic **stigila-* in Old English *stigel*, series of steps: STILE¹. **2.** Suffixed form **stigh-to-* in Germanic **stihtan*, "to place on a step or base," in Old English *stiht(i)an*, to settle, arrange:

STICKLE. **3.** Suffixed form *stigh-o- in Greek stikhos, row, line, line of verse: STICH; ACROSTIC, CADASTER, DISTICH, HEMISTICH, ORTHOSTICHOUS, STICHOMETRY, STICHOMYTHIA. **III.** O-grade form *stoigh-. **1.** Suffixed form *stoigh-ri- in Germanic *staigrī in Old English stæger, stair, step: STAIR. **2.** Greek stoikheion, shadow line, element: STOICHIOMETRY. [Pok. steigh- 1017.]

steip-. To stick, compress. **1.** Germanic *stīfaz in: **a.** Old English stīf, rigid, stiff: STIFF; **b.** Dutch stip, tip, point: STIPPLE. **2.** Latin stīpes, post, tree trunk: STIPE, STIPES. **3.** Suffixed form *steip-ā- in Latin stīpāre, to compress, stuff, pack: STEEVE[1], STEVEDORE; CONSTIPATE. [Pok. stēib(h)- 1015.]

stel-. To put, stand; with derivatives referring to a standing object or place. **I.** Basic form *stel-. **1.** Suffixed form *stel-ni- in Germanic *stilli- in Old English stille, quiet, fixed: STILL[1]. **2.** Suffixed form *stel-yo- in Greek stellein, to put in order, prepare, send, make compact (with o-grade and zero-grade forms stol- and stal-): APOSTLE, DIASTOLE, EPISTLE, PERISTALSIS, SYSTALTIC. **II.** O-grade form *stol-. **1.** Suffixed form *stol-no- in Germanic *stalla- in: **a.** Old English steall, standing place, stable: STALL; FORESTALL; **b.** Old French estal, place: INSTALLMENT[1]; **c.** Old French estalon, stallion: STALLION; **d.** Old Italian stallo, stall: PEDESTAL; **e.** Medieval Latin stallum, stall: INSTALL; **f.** Germanic denominative *stalljan in Old High German stellen, to set, place: GESTALT. **2.** Suffixed form stol-ōn- in Latin stolō, branch, shoot: STOLON. **3.** Suffixed form *stol-ido- in Latin stolidus, "firm-standing," stupid: STOLID. **4.** Suffixed form *stol-ā- in Greek stolē, garment, array, equipment: STOLE[1]. **III.** Zero-grade form *stḷ-. **1.** Suffixed form *stḷ-to- in Latin stultus, foolish (< "unmovable, uneducated"): STULTIFY. **2.** Suffixed zero-grade form *stḷ-no- in Germanic *stullōn- in Old High German stollo, post, support (> German Stolle, Stollen, stollen): STOLLEN. **3.** Suffixed zero-grade form *stal-nā- in Greek stēlē, pillar: STELE. **IV.** Extended form *stelg- in Germanic *stalk- in Norwegian dialectal stalk, stalk, akin to the source of Middle English stalk(e), stalk: STALK[1]. **V.** Extended form *steld- in: **a.** Germanic *stiltjōn- in Low German and Flemish stilte, stick, akin to the source of Middle English stilte, crutch, stilt: STILT; **b.** zero-grade form *stld- in Germanic *stult-, "walking on stilts," strutting, in Old French estout, stout: STOUT. [Pok. 3. stel- 1019.]

stelə-. To extend. Zero-grade form *stḷə-. **1.** Suffixed form *stḷə-to- in Latin lātus, broad, wide: LATITUDE; DILATE. **2.** Attributed by some to this root (but more likely of obscure origin) is Latin lāmina, place, layer: LAMELLA, OMELET. [Pok. 2. stel- 1018.]

sten-. Narrow. Suffixed form *sten-wo- in Greek stenos, narrow: STENO-, STENOSIS. [Pok. 2. sten- 1021.]

(s)tene-. To thunder. **1.** Zero-grade form *stṇə- in Germanic *thunaraz in: **a.** Old English thunor (genitive thunres), thunder, Thor: THUNDER; THURSDAY; **b.** Middle Dutch doner, donder (> Dutch donder), thunder: BLUNDERBUSS, DUNDERHEAD; **c.** Old Norse Thórr (older form Thunarr), "thunder," thunder god: THOR. **2.** O-grade form *tonə- in Latin tonāre, to thunder: TORNADO; ASTONISH, DETONATE, STUN. [Pok. 1. (s)ten- 1021.]

ster-[1]. Stiff. **I.** O-grade form *stor-. **1.** Suffixed form *stor-ē- in Germanic *staren in Old English starian, to stare: STARE. **2.** Suffixed form *stor-g- in: **a.** Germanic *starkaz in Old English stearc, hard, severe: STARK; **b.** Germanic denominative *starkjan in Old English *stercan (> Middle English starchen), to stiffen: STARCH. **II.** Full-grade form *ster-. **1.** Germanic *sternjaz in Old English stierne, styrne, firm: STERN[1]. **2.** Suffixed form *ster-ewo- in Greek stereos, solid: STERE, STEREO-; CHOLESTEROL. **3.** Lengthened-grade form *stēr- in Greek stērizein, to support: STERIGMA. **III.** Zero-grade form *stṛ-. **1.** Extended form *stṛg- in Germanic *sturkaz in

Old English storc, stork (probably from the stiff movements of the bird): STORK. **2.** Germanic *strūt- in Old English strūtian, to stand out stiffly: STRUT. **IV.** Extended form *sterd-. **1.** Germanic *stertaz in Old English steort, tail: REDSTART. **2.** Germanic *stert- in: **a.** Old English *styrtan, to leap up (< "move briskly, move stiffly"): START; **b.** Old English steartlian, to kick, struggle: STARTLE. **V.** Extended form *sterbh- in Germanic *sterban in Old English steorfan, to die (< "become rigid"): STARVE. **VI.** Extended form *(s)terp- in suffixed (stative) zero-grade form *tṛp-ē- in Latin torpēre, to be stiff: TORPEDO, TORPID, TORPOR. [Pok. 1. (s)ter- 1022.]

ster-[2]. Also **sterə-.** To spread. **I.** Extended form *streu-. **1.** Germanic suffixed form *streu-nam in Old English strēon, something gained, offspring: STRAIN[2]. **2.** Latin struere, to pile up, construct: STRUCTURE; CONSTRUCT, DESTROY, INSTRUCT, OBSTRUCT, SUBSTRUCTION. **3.** Zero-grade form *stru- in Latin industria, diligence, activity (endo-, within; see en): INDUSTRY. **4.** Russian struga, deep place: SASTRUGA. **5.** Germanic *strēlō in Old High German strāla, arrow, lightning bolt (> German Strahl, ray): BREMSSTRAHLUNG. **II.** O-grade extended form *strou-. **1.** Suffixed form *strou-eyo- in Germanic *strawjan in: **a.** Old English strē(o)wian, to strew: STREW; **b.** Old High German strouwen, strouwen, to sprinkle, strew: STREUSEL. **2.** Suffixed form *strow-o- in Germanic *strawam, "that which is scattered," in Old English strēaw, straw: STRAW. **III.** Basic forms *ster-, *sterə-. **1.** Nasalized form *ster-n-ə in Latin sternere (past participle strātus from zero-grade *strə-to-), to stretch, extend: STRATUS, STREET; CONSTERNATE, SUBSTRATUM. **2.** Suffixed form *ster-no- in Greek sternon, breast, breastbone: STERNUM. **IV.** Zero-grade form *stṛ-, strə-. **1.** Suffixed form *stṛ-to- in Greek stratos, multitude, army, expedition: STRATAGEM; STRATOCRACY. **2.** Suffixed form *strə-to- becoming Celtic s(t)rato- in Scottish Gaelic srath, a wide river valley: STRATH. **3.** Suffixed extended form *strə-mṇ in Greek strōma, mattress, bed: STROMA; STROMATOLITE. [Pok. 5. ster- 1029.]

ster-[3]. Star. **1.** Suffixed form *ster-s- in Germanic *sterrōn- in Old English steorra, star: STAR. **2.** Suffixed form *stēr-lā- in Latin stēlla, star: STELLAR, STELLATE; CONSTELLATION. **3.** Oldest root form *əster- in Greek astēr, star, with its derivative astron, star, and possible compound astrapē, asteropē, lightning, twinkling (< "looking like a star"; ōps, stem op-, eye, appearance; see okw-): ASTER, ASTERIATED, ASTERISK, ASTERISM, ASTRAEA, ASTRAL, ASTRO-; ASTEROID, ASTRAPHOBIA, DISASTER, STEROPE. **4.** Iranian stem *stār- in Persian sitareh, star: ESTHER. [Pok. 2. ster- 1027.]

ster-[4]. To rob, steal. **1.** Possibly dissimilated form in Germanic *stelan in Old English stelan, to steal: STEAL. **2.** Germanic derivative noun *stēl-ithō (-ithō, abstract suffix) in Middle English stelth, stealth: STEALTH. **3.** Extended dissimilated form in Germanic frequentative *stalkōn in Old English *stealcian, to move stealthily: STALK[2]. [Pok. 3. ster- 1028.]

ster-[5]. Barren. Latin sterilis, unfruitful: STERILE. [Pok. 6. ster- 1031.]

(s)ter-n-. Name of thorny plants. Extension of ster-[1]. Suffixed zero-grade form *tṛ-n-u- in Germanic *thurnu-, thorn, in Old English thorn, thorn: THORN. [Pok. 7. (s)ter-n- 1031.]

(s)teu-. To push, stick, knock, beat; with derivatives referring to projecting objects, fragments, and certain related expressive notions and qualities. **I.** Extended forms *steup-, steub-. **1.** Germanic *staup- in Old English stēap, lofty, deep, projecting: STEEP[1]. **2.** Germanic *staupilaz in Old English stȳpel, stēpel, steeple: STEEPLE. **3.** Germanic *steup-, "bereft" (< "pushed out"), in Old English stēop-, step-: STEP. **4.** Germanic *stūp- in Old English stūpian, to stoop: STOOP[1]. **5.** Germanic expressive form *stubb- in Old English stubb, stybb, stump: STUB. **6.** Germanic *stuf-, "fragment," small coin, in

Middle Dutch *stuyver*, stiver: STIVER. **II.** Extended form *steud-*. **1.** Nasalized form *stu-n-t-* in Germanic *stunt-jan* in Old English *styntan*, to dull: STINT[1]. **2.** Germanic *staut-* in: **a.** Old High German *stōzan*, to push: STOSS; **b.** Middle Low German and Middle Dutch *stōten*, to force, akin to the source of Middle English *stutten*, to stutter: STUTTER. **III.** Extended form *steug-*. **1.** Germanic *stukkaz* in: **a.** Old English *stocc*, tree trunk: STOCK; **b.** Old High German *stoc* (> German *Stock*), staff: ALPENSTOCK; **c.** Old French *estoc*, rapier, sword point: TUCK[3]. **2.** Germanic *stukkjam* in: **a.** Old High German *stukki*, crust, fragment, covering: SHTICK; **b.** Italian *stucco*, stucco: STUCCO. **3.** Germanic *stok-* in Dutch *stoken*, to poke, thrust: STOKER. **IV.** Suffixed (stative) zero-grade extended form *stup-ē-* in Latin *stupēre*, to be stunned: STUPENDOUS, STUPID; STUPEFY. **V.** Suffixed (stative) extended zero-grade form *stud-ē-* in Latin *studēre*, to be diligent (< "to be pressing forward"): STUDENT, STUDY. **VI.** Extended zero-grade form *stug-* in Greek *Stux*, the river Styx (< "hatred"): STYX. **VII.** Variant zero-grade form *tud-*. **1.** Latin *tudes*, hammer: TOIL[1]. **2.** Suffixed form *tud-ti-* in Latin *tussis*, cough: TUSSIS. **3.** Nasalized form *tu-n-d-* in Latin *tundere*, to beat: CONTUSE, OBTUND, PIERCE, RETUSE. **VIII.** Variant zero-grade form *tup-*. **1.** Suffixed form *tup-o-* in Greek *tupos*, a blow, mold, die: TYPE; ANTITYPE, ARCHETYPE. **2.** Nasalized form *tu-m-p-* in Greek *tumpanon*, drum: TYMPANUM. [Pok. 1. *(s)teu-* 1032.]

steu(ə)-. To condense, cluster. Possible root. **1.** Extended form *stūp-* in: **a.** Greek *stuppē*, tuft, tow: STOP, STUPE; **b.** Sanskrit *stūpaḥ*, tuft of hair, crown of the head: STUPA. **2.** Extended form *stūbh-* in Greek *stuphein*, to contract: STYPTIC. [Pok. *steuə-* 1035.]

stə-men-. Denoting various body parts and orifices. Greek *stoma*, mouth: STOMA, STOMACH, STOMATO-, (STOMATOUS), -STOMY; ANASTOMOSIS, ANCYLOSTOMIASIS, PROSTOMIUM, SCYPHISTOMA. [Pok. *stomen-* 1035.]

storo-. Starling. Germanic *staraz* in Old English *stær*, starling: STARLING[1]. [Pok. *storos* 1036.]

streb(h)-. To wind, turn. **1.** Greek *strephein*, to wind, turn, twist (> *strophion*, headband): STREPTO-, STROP, STROPHE, STROPHOID, STROPHULUS; ANASTROPHE, APOSTROPHE[1], BOUSTROPHEDON, CATASTROPHE, DIASTROPHISM. **2.** Unaspirated o-grade form *strob-* in Greek *strobos*, a whirling, whirlwind (> *strobilos*, ball, pine cone): STROBILE; STROBOSCOPE. **3.** Unaspirated zero-grade form *strb-* in Greek *strabos*, a squinting: STRABISMUS; STRABOTOMY. [Pok. *strebh-* 1025.]

strei-. To hiss, buzz. Imitative root. **1.** Extended form *strīd-* in Latin *strīdēre*, to make a harsh sound: STRIDENT. **2.** Extended variant form *trig-* in Greek *trismos*, *trigmus*, a scream: TRISMUS. [Pok. 3. *streig-* 1036.]

streig-. To stroke, rub, press. **I.** Basic form *streig-*. **1.** Germanic *strīkan* in Old English *strīcan*, to stroke: STRIKE. **2.** Germanic diminutive *strik-ila-* in Old English *stricel*, implement for leveling grain: STRICKLE. **3.** Germanic *strikōn-* in Old English *strica*, stroke, line: STREAK. **II.** O-grade form *stroig-* in Germanic *straik-* in Middle English *stroke*, stroke: STROKE. **III.** Zero-grade form *strig-*. **1.** Suffixed form *strig-ā-* in Latin *striga*, row of grain, furrow drawn lengthwise over the field: STRIGOSE. **2.** Suffixed form *strig-yā-* in Latin *stria*, furrow, channel: STRIA. **3.** Nasalized form *stri-n-g-* in Latin *stringere*, to draw tight, press together: STRAIN[1], STRAIT, STRICT, STRIGIL, STRINGENDO, STRINGENT; ASTRINGE, CONSTRAIN, DISTRAIN, PRESTIGE, RESTRICT. [Pok. 1. *streig-* 1036; 4. *ster-* 1028.]

strenk-. Tight, narrow. Possible root. **1.** O-grade form *stronk-* in: **a.** Germanic *strangi-* in Old English *streng*, string: STRING; **b.** Germanic *strangaz* in Old English *strang*, strong, powerful, strict: STRONG; **c.** Germanic *strangithō* in Old English *strengthu*, strength, strictness: STRENGTH. **2.** Variant *strang-* in: **a.** Greek *strangalē*, halter: STRANGLE, (STRANGLES), (STRANGULATE);

b. Greek *stranx*, drop (< "that which is squeezed out"): STRANGURY. [Pok. *strenk-*, *streng-* 1036.]

strep-. To make a noise. Imitative root. Latin *strepere*, to make noise: OBSTREPEROUS. [Pok. *(s)trep-* 1037.]

su-. Well, good. **1.** Sanskrit *su-*, well-being, good luck: SWASTIKA. **2.** Compound *su-gʷiə-es-*, "living in good condition" (see gʷei-). [Pok. *su-* 1037.]

sū-. Pig. Contracted from *suə-*; probably a derivative of **seuə-**[1]. **1.** Suffixed form *suə-īno-* in Germanic *swīnam* in Old English *swīn*, swine: SWINE. **2.** Celtic expressive form *sukko-*, swine, snout of a swine, plowshare, in: **a.** British *hukk-* in Old English *hogg*, hog: HOG; **b.** perhaps Old French *soc*, plowshare: SOCKET. **3.** Germanic *sū-* in Old English *sugu*, sow: SOW[2]. **4.** Latin *sūs*, pig: SOIL[2]. **5.** Greek *hus*, swine: HYENA; HYOSCINE. [Pok. *su-s* 1038.]

sūro-. Sour, salty, bitter. Germanic *sūraz* in: **a.** Old English *sūr*, sour: SOUR; **b.** Old High German *sūr*, sour: SAUERBRATEN SAUERKRAUT; **c.** Old French *sur*, sour: SORREL[1]. [Pok. *sūr-o* 1039.]

swād-. Sweet, pleasant. **1.** Germanic *swōtja-* in Old English *swēte*, sweet: SWEET. **2.** Suffixed form *swād-ē-* in Latin *suādēre*, to advise, urge (< "recommend as good"): SUASION; (ASSUASIVE), DISSUADE, PERSUADE. **3.** Suffixed form *swād-w-i-* in Latin *suāvis*, delightful: SOAVE, SUAVE; ASSUAGE. **4.** Suffixed form *swād-es-* in Greek *hēdos*, pleasure: AEDES. **5.** Suffixed form *swādonā* in Greek *hēdonē*, pleasure: HEDONIC, HEDONISM. [Pok. *sṷād-* 1039.]

(s)wāgh-. To resound. **1.** Germanic *swōgan* in Old English *swōgan*, to resound: SOUGH. **2.** Suffixed form *wāgh-ā-* in Greek *ēkhē*, sound: CATECHIZE. **3.** Suffixed form *wāgh-ōi-* in Greek *ēkhō*, noise, echo: ECHO. [Pok. *ṷāgh-* 1110.]

sward-. To laugh. Greek *sardanios*, sneering, scornful: SARDONIC. [Pok. *sṷard-* 1040.]

s(w)e-. Pronoun of the third person and reflexive (referring back to the subject of the sentence); further appearing in various forms referring to the social group as an entity, "(we our-)selves." **1.** Suffixed extended form *sel-bho-* in Germanic *selbaz*, self, in Old English *self*, *sylf*, self, same: SELF. **2.** Suffixed form *s(w)e-bh(o)-* in Germanic *sibja-*, "one's own," blood relation, relative, in Old English *sibb*, relative: SIB; GOSSIP. **3.** Suffixed form *se-ge* in Germanic *sik*, self, in Old Norse *sik*, oneself (reflexive pronoun), whence -*sk*, reflexive suffix, as in *būask*, to make oneself ready: BUSK[2], (BUSTLE). **4.** Suffixed form *swoi-no-* in Germanic *swainaz*, "one's own (man)," attendant, servant, in Old Norse *sveinn*, herdsman, boy: SWAIN. **5.** Suffixed form *s(u)w-o-*, one's own, in: **a.** Latin *suī* (genitive), of oneself: SUICIDE; **b.** Sanskrit *sva-* (< *swo-*), one's own, whence *svāmin*, "one's own master," owner, prince: SWAMI. **6.** Extended form *sed* in: **a.** Latin *sēd*, *sē*, self, oneself (accusative): FELO-DE-SE, PER SE; **b.** Latin *sēd*, *sē*, without, apart (< "on one's own"): SECEDE, SECERN, SECLUDE, SECRET, SECURE, SEDITION, SEDUCE, SEGREGATE, SELECT, SEPARATE, (SURE); **c.** Latin compound *sōbrius*, not drunk (*ēbrius*, drunk; see egʷh-): SOBER. **7.** Possibly suffixed lengthened o-grade form *sō-lo-* in Latin *sōlus*, by oneself alone: SOLE[2], SOLITARY, SOLITUDE, SOLO, SULLEN; DESOLATE, SOLILOQUY, SOLIPSISM. **8.** Extended root *swēdh-*, "that which is one's own," peculiarity, custom, in: **a.** Latin *sodālis*, companion (< "one's own," "relative"): SODALITY; **b.** suffixed form *swēdh-sko-* in Latin *suēscere*, to get accustomed: (CONSUETUDE), CUSTOM, DESUETUDE, MANSUETUDE, MASTIFF; **c.** Greek *ēthos*, custom, disposition, trait: ETHIC, ETHOS; CACOETHES; **d.** suffixed form *swedh-no-* in Greek *ethnos*, band of people living together, nation, people (< "people of one's own kind"): ETHNIC, ETHNO-. **9.** Suffixed extended form *swet-aro-* in Greek *hetaros*, later *hetairos*, comrade, companion: HETAERA. **10.** Suffixed extended form *swed-yo-* in Greek *idios*, personal, private ("particular to oneself"):

IDIO-, IDIOM, IDIOT; IDIOMORPHIC, IDIOPATHY, IDIOSYN-CRASY. **11.** Variant form *swei- in Irish féin, self: SINN FEIN. [Pok. se- 882.]

swei-¹. To whistle, hiss. Imitative root. Latin sībilāre, to whistle at, hiss down: SIBILATE; CHUFA, PERSIFLAGE. [Pok. sµei- 1040.]

swei-². To bend, turn. **1.** Germanic o-grade form *swaip- in Old English swāpan, to sweep, drive, swing: SWOOP. **2.** Germanic zero-grade form *swip- in Old English swift, swift, quick (< "turning quickly"): SWIFT. **3.** Germanic full-grade form *swīf- in Middle English swyvel, a swivel: SWIVEL. **4.** Possibly Germanic *swīh- in Middle Dutch swijch, bough, twig: SWITCH. **5.** German schwappen, to flap, splash, akin to the source of Middle English swappen, to splash: SWAP. [Pok. sµei- 1041.]

sweid-¹. To shine. Possible suffixed form *sweid-es- in: **a.** Latin sīdus, constellation, star: SIDEREAL; **b.** Latin augury terms consīderāre, to examine, "observe the stars carefully" (con-, intensive prefix; see **kom**), and dēsīderāre, to long for, investigate (formed on analogy with consīderāre; dē-, from; see **de-**): CONSIDER, DESIRE. [Pok. 1. sµeid- 1042.]

sweid-². Sweat; to sweat. **I.** O-grade form *swoid-. **1.** Germanic *swaitaz, sweat, with its denominative *swaitjan, to sweat, in Old English swǣtan, to sweat: SWEAT. **2.** Suffixed form *swoid-os- in Latin sūdor, sweat: SUDORIFIC; SUDORIFEROUS. **3.** O-grade form *swoid-ā- in Latin sūdāre, to sweat: SUDATORIUM, SUINT; EXUDE, TRANSUDE. **II.** Suffixed zero-grade form *swid-r-os- in Greek hidrōs, sweat: HIDROSIS. [Pok. 2. sµeid- 1043.]

s(w)eks. Six. **I.** Form *seks. **1.** Germanic *seks in Old English s(i)ex, six, six: SIX. **2.** Latin sex (> Italian sei), six: SENARY, SEX-; SEICENTO, SEMESTER. **3.** Suffixed form *seks-to- in Latin sextus, sixth: SESTET, SESTINA, SEXT, SEXTAN, SEXTANT, SEXTILE; SEXTODECIMO. **II.** Form *sweks in Greek hex, six: HEXA-, HEXAD. [Pok. sµeks 1044.]

swel-¹. To eat, drink. **1.** Perhaps Germanic *swil- in Old English swilian, to wash out, gargle: SWILL. **2.** Extended form *swelk- in Germanic *swelgan, *swelhan in Old English swelgan, to swallow: SWALLOW¹; GROUNDSEL¹. **3.** Iranian *khvāra- (attested in Avestan), to eat, in the probable source of Greek mantikhōras, manticore (see **mer-²**). [Pok. 1. sµel(k)- 1045.]

swel-². To shine, burn. **1.** Extended form *sweld- in Germanic *swiltan in Old English sweltan, to die, perish (perhaps < "be overcome with heat"): (SULTRY), SWELTER. **2.** O-grade form *swol- in Germanic *swal- in Old Norse svalr, cool (< "lukewarm" < "hot"), akin to the Scandinavian source of Middle English swale, shade, shady place: SWALE. [Pok. 2. sµel 1045.]

swel-³. Post, board. Germanic *suljō- in Old English syll(e), doorsill, threshold: SILL. [Pok. sel-, sµel- 898.]

swem-. To move, stir, swim. Possibly an Indo-European root, but perhaps Germanic only. **1.** Germanic *swimjan in Old English swimman, to swim: SWIM. **2.** Suffixed zero-grade form *swum-to- in Germanic *sundam in: **a.** Old English sund, swimming, sea: SOUND³; **b.** Old French sonde, sounding line: SOUND⁴; RADIOSONDE, ROCKETSONDE. [Pok. sµem- 1046.]

swen-. To sound. **1.** Suffixed o-grade form *swon-o- in: **a.** Germanic *swanaz, *swanōn, "singer," in Old English swan, swan: SWAN; **b.** Latin sonus, a sound: SONE, SONIC, SONNET, SOUND¹; UNISON. **2.** Form *swen-ā- in Latin sonāre, to sound: SONANT, SONATA, SONOROUS; ASSONANCE, CONSONANT, DISSONANT, RESOUND. [Pok. sµen 1046.]

sweng(w)-. To swing, turn, toss. Germanic root. **1.** Germanic *swingan in Old English swingan, to whip, strike, swing: SWING. **2.** Germanic *swing- in Middle Dutch swinghel, instrument for beating hemp: SWINGLETREE. **3.** O-grade form *swong- in: **a.** suffixed form *swong-eyo- in Germanic *swangjan in Old English swengan, to

swing, shake: SWINGE; **b.** Germanic variant *swank- in Middle High German swanken, to turn, swing: SWANK. **4.** Uncertain preform in Norwegian swagga, to sway, akin to the Scandinavian source of SWAG. [Pok. sµeng-, sµenk- 1047.]

swento-. Healthy, strong. Zero-grade form *sunto- in Germanic *sunth- in Old English gesund, healthy (ge-, intensive prefix; see **kom**): SOUND². [Pok. sµento- 1048.]

swep-¹. To sleep. **1.** Suffixed form in Latin sopor, a deep sleep: SOPOR; (SOPORIFIC). **2.** Suffixed form *swep-no- in Latin somnus, sleep: SOMNI-, SOMNOLENT; INSOMNIA. **3.** Suffixed zero-grade form *sup-no- in Greek hupnos, sleep: HYPNO-, HYPNOS, (HYPNOSIS), HYPNOTIC. [Pok. 1. sµep- 1048.]

swep-². To throw, sling, cast. **1.** O-grade form *swop-, perhaps in Germanic variant expressive form *swabb- in Middle Dutch swabbe, mop, splash: SWAB. **2.** Suffixed zero-grade form *sup-ā- in Latin dissipāre, to disperse (dis-, apart): DISSIPATE. [Pok. 2. sµep- 1049.]

swer-¹. To speak, talk. O-grade form *swor-: **a.** Germanic *swarjan in Old English swerian, to swear, proclaim: SWEAR; **b.** Germanic *and-swarō, "a swearing against," "rebuttal" (*andi-, against; see **ant-**), in Old English andswaru, answer: ANSWER. [Pok. 1. sµer- 1049.]

swer-². To buzz, whisper. Imitative root. **I.** O-grade form *swor-. **1.** Suffixed form *swor-mo- in Germanic *swarmaz in Old English swearm, swarm: SWARM. **2.** Germanic *swar- in Dutch zwirrelen, to whirl, akin to the Low German source of Middle English swyrl, eddy: SWIRL. **II.** Zero-grade form *sur-. **1.** Suffixed form *sur-do- perhaps in: **a.** Latin surdus, deaf, mute: SORDINO, SOURDINE, SURD; **b.** Latin absurdus, discordant, away from the right sound, harsh (ab-, away; see **apo-**): ABSURD. **2.** Reduplicated expressive form *su-surr- in Latin susurrus, whisper: SUSURRATION. [Pok. 2. sµer- 1049.]

swer-³. Post, rod. Suffixed zero-grade form *sur-o- in Latin surus, branch: SURCULOSE. [Pok. 3. sµer- 1050.]

swer-⁴. To cut, pierce. Germanic *swerdam in Old English sweord, sword, sword: SWORD. [Pok. 4. sµer- 1050.]

swer-⁵. Also **ser-.** To lift, hang on the scale; heavy. Variant *ser- in suffixed lengthened-grade form *sēr-yo- in Latin sērius, serious, grave: SERIOUS.

swerbh-. To turn, wipe off. **1.** Germanic *swerb- in Old English sweorfan, to file away, scour, polish: SWERVE. **2.** O-grade form *sworbh- in Germanic *swarb- in Old Norse svarf, filings, akin to the Scandinavian source of SWARF. [Pok. sµerbh- 1050.]

swergh-. To worry, be sick. Germanic *sorg- in Old English sorh, sorg, anxiety, sorrow: SORROW. [Pok. sµergh- 1051.]

swesor-. Sister. **1.** Zero-grade form *swesr- in: **a.** Germanic *swestr- in Old English sweostor, sister: SISTER; **b.** suffixed form *swesr-īno- in Latin sōbrīnus, maternal cousin: COUSIN. **2.** Latin soror, sister: SORORAL, SORORITY. [Pok. sµesor 1051.]

swī-. To be silent. Expressive formation in Greek siōpē, silence: APOSIOPESIS. [Pok. sµī- 1052.]

swo-. Pronominal stem; so. Derivative of **s(w)e-**. **1.** Germanic *swa- in. **a.** Old English swā, so: SO¹; **b.** Germanic compound *swa-līk-, "so like," of the same kind (*līk-, same; see **līk-**), in Old English swylc, such: SUCH. **2.** Adverbial form *swai in Latin sī, if, in quasi (quam, as; see **kʷo-** + si, if): NISI, QUASI. [In Pok. 2. seu- 882.]

s(w)okʷo-. Resin, juice. Variant form *sokʷo- in Greek opos (< *hopos), juice: OPIUM. [Pok. s(µ)ekʷo-s 1044.]

swombho-. Spongy. Germanic *swamba- in: **a.** Middle Low German sump, swamp: SUMP; **b.** Low German zwamp, swamp, akin to the Low German source of SWAMP. [Pok. sµomb(h)o-s 1052.]

swordo-. Black, dirty. **1.** Germanic *swartaz in Old English sweart, swarthy: SWART. **2.** Zero-grade suffixed (stative) form *swrd-ē- in Latin sordēre, to be dirty: SORDID. [Pok. sµordo-s 1052.]

syū-. To bind, sew. **I.** Basic form *syū- in Germanic

siwjan in Old English *seowian, siowan,* to sew: SEW. **II.** Variant form **sū-.* **1.** Germanic **saumaz* in Old English *sēam,* seam: SEAM. **2.** Latin *suere* (past participle *sūtus*), to sew: SUTURE; COUTURE. **3.** Suffixed form **sū-dhlā-* in Latin *sūbula,* awl (< "sewing instrument"): SUBULATE. **4.** Suffixed form **sū-tro-* in Sanskrit *sūtram,* thread, string: SUTRA; KAMASUTRA. **5.** Suffixed shortened form **syu-men-* in Greek *humēn,* thin skin, membrane: HYMEN. [Pok. *si̯ū-* 915.]

tā-. To melt, dissolve. **1.** Extended form **tāw-* in Germanic **thāwōn* in Old English *thāwian,* to thaw: THAW. **2.** Extended form **tābh-* in Latin *tābēs,* a melting, wasting away, putrefaction: TABES. **3.** Extended form **tāk-* in Greek *tēkein,* to melt: EUTECTIC. [Pok. *tā-* 1053.]

tag-. To touch, handle. **1.** Nasalized form **ta-n-g-* in Latin *tangere,* to touch (> *taxāre,* to touch, assess, and *tactus,* touch): TACT, TANGENT, TANGIBLE, TASTE, TAX; ATTAIN, CONTACT, INTACT, TACTORECEPTOR, TANGORECEPTOR. **2.** Compound form **n̥-tag-ro-,* "untouched, intact" (**n̥-,* negative prefix; see **ne**), in Latin *integer,* intact, whole, complete, perfect, honest: ENTIRE, INTEGER. **3.** Suffixed form **tag-smen-* in Latin *contāmināre,* to corrupt by mixing or contact (< **con-tāmen-,* "bringing into contact with"; *con-, com-,* with; see **kom**): CONTAMINATE. [Pok. *tag-* 1054.]

tāg-. To set in order. Suffixed form **tag-yo-* in Greek *tassein, tattein,* to arrange, and *taxis* (< **tag-ti-*), arrangement: TACTICS, TAXIS, -TAXIS, TAXO-; ATAXIA, HYPOTAXIS, PARATAXIS, SYNTAX. [Pok. *tāg-* 1055.]

tak-¹. To be silent. Suffixed (stative) form **tak-ē-* in Latin *tacēre,* to be silent: TACET, TACIT; RETICENT. [Pok. *tak-* 1055.]

[tak-². To take. Germanic root. Old Norse *taka,* to take: TAKE; WAPENTAKE.]

[tap-. Germanic base of various loosely related derivatives; "plug, wad, small compact object, projecting part; to plug, strike lightly." Variants **tap-, *tapp-, *topp-, *tupp-.* **1.** Old English *tæppa,* spigot: TAP². **2.** Dutch *tap,* spigot: TATTOO¹. **3.** Old French *tampon,* plug: TAMPON. **4.** Old French *taper,* to strike lightly: TAP¹. **5.** Old English *top,* summit: TOP¹. **6.** Old English *top,* a child's plaything, perhaps a spinning top: TOP². **7.** Old French *toup,* top, tuft of hair: TOUPEE. **8.** Old Norse *typpi* (> Middle English *tip*), end: TIP¹. **9.** Old French *tof(f)e,* tuft: TUFT. **10.** Old English *tæppe,* strip of cloth: TAPE.]

tauro-. Bull. Derivative of **stā-,** but an independent word in Indo-European. Greek *tauros* (> Latin *taurus*), bull: TAURINE¹, TAURINE², TAURUS, TOREADOR, TORERO, TAUROCHOLIC ACID. [In Pok. *tēu-* 1083.]

[taw-. To make, manufacture. Germanic root. **1.** Germanic **taw-* in Old English *tow-,* spinning (only in compounds such as *tow-hūs,* spinning house or room): TOW². **2.** Germanic **tawjan, *tawōn,* to fashion, in Old English *tawian,* to prepare: TAW¹. **3.** Germanic **gatawja-* (**ga-,* collective prefix; see **kom**), equipment, in Old English *geatwa, geatwe,* equipment: HERIOT. **4.** Germanic variant **tō(w)lam,* implement, in Old English *tōl,* implement (possibly borrowed from the cognate Old Norse *tōl*): TOOL. [In Pok. 2. *deu-* 218.]]

tegu-. Thick. Germanic **thiku-* in Old English *thicce,* thick: THICK. [Pok. *tegu-* 1057.]

tek-. To beget, give birth to. **1.** Suffixed form **tek-no-,* child, in: **a.** Germanic **thegnaz,* boy, man, servant, warrior, in Old English *thegn,* freeman, nobleman, military vassal, warrior: THANE; **b.** possibly Germanic **thewernō,* girl, in Old High German *thirona, diorna* (> German *Dirne*), girl: DIRNDL. **2.** Reduplicated form **ti-tk-,* metathesized in Greek *tiktein,* to beget, and suffixed o-grade form **tok-o-* in Greek *tokos,* birth: OXYTOCIC, POLYTOCOUS, TOCOLOGY. [Pok. 1. *tek-* 1057.]

teks-. To weave; also to fabricate, especially with an ax; also to make wicker or wattle fabric for (mud-covered) house walls. **1.** Latin *texere,* to weave, fabricate: TEXT, TISSUE; CONTEXT, PRETEXT. **2.** Suffixed form **teks-lā* in:

a. Latin *tēla,* web, net, warp of a fabric, also weaver's beam (to which the warp threads are tied): TILLER², TOIL²; **b.** Latin *subtīlis,* thin, fine, precise, subtle (< **sub-tēla,* "thread passing under the warp," the finest thread; *sub,* under; see **upo**): SUBTLE. **3.** Suffixed form **teks-ōn,* weaver, maker of wattle for house walls, builder (possibly contaminated with **teks-tōr,* builder), in Greek *tektōn,* carpenter, builder: TECTONIC; ARCHITECT. **4.** Suffixed form **teks-nā-,* craft (of weaving or fabricating), in Greek *tekhnē,* art, craft, skill: TECHNICAL, POLYTECHNIC, TECHNOLOGY. **5.** Possibly Germanic **thahsu-,* badger ("the animal that builds," referring to its burrowing skill), in Old High German *dahs* (> German *Dachs*), badger but more likely borrowed from the same pre-Indo-European source as the Celtic totemic name *Tazgo-,* Gaelic *Tadhg,* "badger"): DACHSHUND. [Pok. *tekth-* 1058.]

tekʷ-. To run, flee. Suffixed o-grade form **tokʷ-so-* in Iranian **taxša-,* bow, borrowed into Greek *toxon,* bow, also (in the plural) bow and arrow (< "that which flies"): TOXIC. [Pok. *tekʷ-* 1059.]

tel-. Ground, floor, board. **1.** Germanic **thil-jō-* in Middle Low German and Middle Dutch *dele,* plank: DEAL². **2.** Suffixed form **tel-n-* in Latin *tellūs* (stem *tellūr-*), earth, the earth: (TELLURIAN), (TELLURIC), (TELLURION), (TELLURIUM), TELLURO-. **3.** Possibly reduplicated form **ti-tel-* in Latin *titulus,* placard, label, superscription, title: TITLE. [Pok. 2. *tel-* 1061.]

tele-. To lift, support, weigh; with derivatives referring to measured weights and thence to money and payment. **1.** Suffixed form **telə-mon-* in Greek *telamōn,* supporter, bearer: TELAMON. **2.** Suffixed form **tel(ə)-es-* in: **a.** Greek *telos,* tax, charge: TOLL¹; PHILATELY; **b.** Latin *tolerāre,* to bear, endure: TOLERATE. **3.** Suffixed zero-grade form **tlə-i-,* becoming **tali-* (influenced by *tālis,* such), in Latin *tāliō,* reciprocal punishment in kind, "something paid out": TALION; RETALIATE. **4.** Suffixed variant zero-grade form **tala-nt-* in Greek *talanton,* balance, weight, any of several specific weights of gold or silver, hence the sum of money represented by such a weight: TALENT. **5.** Perhaps intensive reduplicated form **tantal-* in Greek *Tantalos,* name of a legendary king, "the sufferer": (TANTALIZE), TANTALUS. **6.** Perhaps zero-grade form **tlə-* in Greek *Atlas* (stem *Atlant-*), name of the Titan supporting the world: ATLANTIC, ATLAS. **7.** Suffixed zero-grade form **tlə-ē-* in Germanic **thulēn* in Old English *tholian,* to suffer, endure: THOLE. **8.** Suffixed zero-grade form **tlə-to-* in Latin *lātus,* "carried, borne," used as the suppletive past participle of *ferre,* to bear (see **bher-¹**), with its compounds: ABLATION, COLLATE, DILATORY, ELATE, ILLATION, LEGISLATOR, OBLATE¹, PRELATE, PROLATE, RELATE, SUPERLATIVE, TRANSLATE. **9.** Suffixed zero-grade form **tlə-ā-* in Sanskrit *tulā,* scales, balance, weight: TAEL, TOLA. **10.** Nasalized zero-grade form **tl̥-n-ə-* in Latin *tollere,* to lift: EXTOL. [Pok. 1. *tel-* 1060.]

tem-. Also **temə-.** To cut. **I.** Form **temə-.* Nasalized form **t(e)m-n-ə-* in Greek *temnein,* to cut: TMESIS, TOME, -TOME, -TOMY; ANATOMY, ATOM, DIATOM, DICHOTOMY, ENTOMO-, EPITOME. **II.** Form **tem-.* Suffixed form **tem-lo-* in Latin *templum,* temple, shrine, open place for observation (augury term < "place reserved or cut out"), small piece of timber: TEMPLE¹, TEMPLE³; CONTEMPLATE. **2.** Extended root **tem-d-* becoming **tend-* in o-grade suffixed (iterative) form **tond-eyo-* in Latin *tondēre,* to shear, shave: TONSURE. [Pok. 1. *tem-, tend-* 1062.]

temə-. Dark. Suffixed form **temə-s-.* **1.** Latin *temere,* blindly, rashly: TEMERARIOUS, TEMERITY. **2.** Suffixed form **teməs-rā-* in Latin *tenebrae* (plural), darkness: TENEBRAE, TENEBRIONID. [Pok. *tem(ə)-* 1063.]

temp-. To stretch. Extension of **ten-. 1.** Possibly Latin *tempus,* temple of the head (? where the skin is stretched from behind the eye to the ear): TEMPLE². **2.** Zero-grade form **tmp-* perhaps in: **a.** Persian *tāftan,* to weave (the

warp threads are stretched on the loom): TAFFETA;
b. Iranian **tap-,* "carpet," in Greek *tapēs,* carpet: TAPES-
TRY. [Pok. *temp-* 1064.]

ten-. To stretch. **I.** Derivatives with the basic meaning.
1. Suffixed form **ten-do-* in: **a.** Latin *tendere,* to stretch,
extend: TEND¹, TENDER², TENDON, TENSE¹, TENT¹; AT-
TEND, CONTEND, DETENT, DISTEND, EXTEND, INTEND,
OSTENSIBLE, PRETEND, SUBTEND; **b.** Latin *portendere,*
"to stretch out before" (*por-,* variant of *pro-,* before; see
per¹), a technical term in augury, "to indicate, presage,
foretell": PORTEND. **2.** Suffixed form **ten-yo-* in Greek
teinein, to stretch: TENESMUS; BRONCHIECTASIS, EPITA-
SIS, HYPOTENUSE, PERITONEUM, PROTASIS, TELANGIEC-
TASIA. **3.** Suffixed zero-grade form **tn̥-nu-* in Sanskrit
tanōti, he stretches or weaves, with suffixed (instrumental) derivative **ten-tro-* in *tantam,* loom: TANTRA. **4.** Suffixed form **ten-tro-* in Persian *tār,* string: SITAR.
5. Basic form (with stative suffix) **ten-ē-* in Latin *tenēre,*
to hold, keep, maintain (< "to cause to endure or continue, hold on to"): TENABLE, TENACIOUS, TENACULUM,
TENANT, TENEMENT, TENET, TENON, TENOR, TENURE,
TENUTO; ABSTAIN, CONTAIN, CONTINUE, DETAIN, ENTER-
TAIN, LIEUTENANT, MAINTAIN, OBTAIN, PERTAIN, PERTI-
NACIOUS, RETAIN, (RETINACULUM), SUSTAIN.
II. Derivatives meaning "stretched," hence "thin."
1. Suffixed zero-grade form **tn̥-u-* in Germanic **thunw-,*
whence **thunniz* in Old English *thynne,* thin: THIN.
2. Suffixed full-grade form **ten-u-* in Latin *tenuis,* thin,
rare, fine: TENUOUS, ATTENUATE, EXTENUATE. **3.** Suffixed full-grade form **ten-ero-* in Latin *tener,* tender,
delicate: TENDER¹, TENDRIL. **III.** Derivatives meaning
"something stretched or capable of being stretched, a
string." **1.** Suffixed form **ten-ōn-* in Greek *tenōn,* tendon: TENO-. **2.** Suffixed o-grade form **ton-o-* in Greek
tonos, string, hence sound, pitch: TONE; TONOPLAST.
3. Suffixed zero-grade form **tn̥-ya-* in Greek *tainia,*
band, ribbon: TAENIA; POLYTENE. [Pok. 1. *ten-* 1065.]

teng-. To soak. **1.** Latin *tingere,* to moisten, soak, dye:
TAINT, TINCT, TINGE, TINT; INTINCTION, STAIN.
2. Zero-grade form **tng-* in Germanic **thunk-* in Old
High German *thunkōn, dunkōn,* to soak: DUNK. [Pok. 1.
teng- 1067.]

tenk-¹. To stretch. Extension of **ten-.** Perhaps Germanic
*thingam in: **a.** Old English *thing,* assembly, (legal) case,
thing: THING; **b.** Old Norse *thing,* assembly: HUSTINGS;
c. Old High German *thing, ding* (> German *Ding*), thing:
DINGUS. [Pok. 1. *tenk-* 1067.]

tenk-². To become firm, curdle, thicken. **1.** Suffixed form
*tenk-to-, thickened, in Germanic **thinhtaz* in Old Norse
thēttr, dense, watertight, akin to the Scandinavian source
of Middle English *thight,* dense: TIGHT. **2.** Possibly
suffixed o-grade form **tonk-lo-* in Germanic **thangul-* in
Old Norse *thöngull,* seaweed (? < "thick mass"), akin to
the source of TANGLE². [Pok. 2. *tenk-* 1068.]

tens-. To stretch, draw. Extension of **ten-.** Suffixed
zero-grade form **tn̥s-ero-* in Sanskrit *tasaram,* shuttle:
TUSSAH. [Pok. *tens-* 1068.]

tep-. To be warm. Suffixed (stative) form **tep-ē-* in Latin
tepēre, to be warm: TEPID. [Pok. *tep-* 1069.]

ter-. Base of derivatives meaning peg, post, boundary
marker, goal. **1.** Suffixed form **ter-men-,* boundary
marker, in Latin *terminus,* boundary, limit: TERM, TER-
MINATE, TERMINUS; DETERMINE, EXTERMINATE. **2.** Suffixed zero-grade form **tr̥-m-* in Germanic **thrum-* in Old
English *thrum,* broken-off end (attested only in *tungeth-
rum,* the ligament of the tongue): THRUM². [Pok. 4. *ter-*
1074.]

tere-¹. To rub, turn; with some derivatives referring to
twisting, boring, drilling, and piercing; and others referring to the rubbing of cereal grain to remove the husks,
and thence to the process of threshing either by the
trampling of oxen or by flailing with flails. Variant **trē-,*
contracted from **treə-.* **I.** Full-grade form **ter(ə)-.*
1. a. Latin *terere* (past participle *trītus*), to rub away,

thresh, tread, wear out: TRITE, TRITURATE; ATTRITION,
CONTRITE, DETRIMENT; **b.** Greek *terēdōn,* a kind of
biting worm: TEREDO. **2.** Suffixed form **ter-et-* in Latin
teres (stem *teret-*), rounded, smooth: TERETE. **3.** Suffixed
form **ter-sko-* in Germanic **therskan, *threskan,* to
thresh, tread, in: **a.** Old English *therscan,* to thresh:
(THRASH), THRESH; **b.** Old English *therscold, threscold,*
sill of a door (over which one treads; second element
obscure): THRESHOLD. **II.** O-grade form **tor(ə)-.* **1.** Greek
toreus, a boring tool: TOREUTICS. **2.** Suffixed form
*tor(ə)-mo-, hole, in Germanic **tharma* in Old High
German *darm,* gut: DERMA². **3.** Suffixed **tor(ə)-no-*
in Greek *tornos,* tool for drawing a circle, circle, lathe (>
Latin *tornus,* lathe): TURN; (ATTORN), CONTOUR, (DE-
TOUR), (RETURN). **III.** Zero-grade form **tr-* in Germanic
*thr- in Dutch *drillen,* to drill: DRILL¹. **IV.** Variant form
*trē-. **1.** Germanic **thrēw-* in Old English *thrāwan,* to
turn, twist: THROW. **2.** Greek *trēma,* perforation: MONO-
TREME, TREMATODE. **3.** Suffixed form **trē-tu-* in Germanic **thrēdu-,* twisted yarn, in Old English *thrǣd,*
thread: THREAD. **V.** Extended form *trī-* (< **triə-*). **1.** Suffixed form **trī-ōn-,* probably in Latin *triō,* plow ox:
SEPTENTRION. **2.** Suffixed form **trī-dhlo-* in Latin *tribu-
lum,* a threshing sledge: TRIBULATION. **VI.** Various extended forms. **1.** Forms **trō-, *trau-* in Greek *trauma,*
hurt, wound: TRAUMA. **2.** Form **tru-* in Greek *truma,
trumē,* hole: TRYMA. **3.** Form **trīb-* in Greek *tribein,* to
rub, thresh, pound, wear out (> *tripsis,* a rubbing):
DIATRIBE, TRIBOELECTRICITY, TRIBOLOGY, TRYPSIN.
4. Form **trōg-* in Greek *trōgein,* to gnaw: TROGON.
5. Form **trup-* in Greek *trupē,* hole (> *trupanon,* auger):
TREPAN¹; TRYPANOSOME. **6.** Form **trūg-* possibly in Old
French *truant,* beggar: TRUANT. [Pok. 3. *ter-* 1071.]

tere-². To cross over, pass through, overcome. Variant
*trā-, contracted from **traə.* **I.** Zero-grade form **tr̥(ə)-.*
1. Germanic suffixed form **thur-ila-* in Old English
thyr(e)l, thȳrel, a hole (< "a boring through"): THRILL;
NOSTRIL. **2.** Suffixed form **tr̥ə-kʷe* in Germanic **thurh* in
Old English *thurh, thuruh,* through: THOROUGH,
THROUGH. **3.** Greek *nek-tar,* overcoming death "(see
nek-¹). **4.** Zero-grade form **tr̥ə-* and full-grade form
*ter(ə)- in Sanskrit *tirati, tarati,* he crosses over: AVATAR.
II. Variant form **trā-.* **1.** Latin *trāns,* across, over, beyond, through (perhaps originally the present participle
of a verb **trāre,* to cross over): TRANS-, TRANSIENT,
(TRANSOM). **2.** Suffixed form **trā-yo-* in Iranian *thrāya-,*
to protect, in Middle Persian *srāyīdhan,* to protect, in
Persian *sarāī,* inn: CARAVANSARY. **III.** Extended form
*tru-. **1.** Suffixed form **tru-k-* in Latin *trux* (stem *truc-*),
savage, fierce, grim (< "overcoming," "powerful," "pene-
trating"): TRUCULENT. **2.** Suffixed nasalized form
*tru-n-k-o- in Latin *truncus,* deprived of branches or
limbs, mutilated, hence trunk (? < "overcome, maimed"):
TRENCH, TRUNCATE, TRUNK. [Pok. 5. *ter-* 1075.]

terkʷ-. To twist. Extension of **tere-¹.** **1.** Possible variant
form **t(w)erk-* in Germanic **thwerh-,* twisted, oblique, in
Old Norse *thverr,* transverse: THWART. **2.** Suffixed (causative) o-grade form **torkʷ-eyo-* in Latin *torquēre,* to
twist: TORCH, TORMENT, TORQUE¹, TORQUE², TORSADE,
TORT, TORTUOUS; CONTORT, DISTORT, EXTORT, NASTUR-
TIUM, RETORT¹, TORTICOLLIS. [Pok. *terk-* 1077.]

terp-. To satisfy oneself. Greek *terpein,* to delight, cheer:
TERPSICHORE. [Pok. *terp-* 1077.]

ters-. To dry. **1.** Suffixed zero-grade form **tr̥s-t-* in
Germanic **thurs-* in: **a.** suffixed form **thurs-tu-* in Old
English *thurst,* dryness, thirst: THIRST; **b.** Old Norse
thorskr, cod (< "dried fish"), whence Norwegian *torsk,
tosk,* cod, with dialectal variant *tusk,* cod, stockfish:
CUSK. **2.** Suffixed form **ters-ā-* in Latin *terra,* "dry
land," earth (> French and Old French *terre,* earth,
ground): TERRACE, (TERRAIN), TERRAN, TERRENE, TER-
RESTRIAL, TERRIER, TERRITORY, TUREEN; FUMITORY,
INTER, MEDITERRANEAN, PARTERRE, SUBTERRANEAN,
TERRAQUEOUS, TERREPLEIN, TERRE-VERTE, TERRICO-

LOUS, TERRIGENOUS, VERDITER. **3.** Suffixed o-grade form *tors-eyo-* in Latin *torrēre*, to dry, parch, burn: TOAST[1], TORRENT, TORRID. **4.** Suffixed zero-grade form *t$r̥$s-o-* in Greek *tarsos*, frame of wickerwork (originally for drying cheese), hence a flat surface, sole of the foot, ankle: TARSUS. [Pok. *ters-* 1078.]

teu-. To pay attention to, turn to. **1.** O-grade form *tou-* in Germanic *thau-* in Old English *thēaw*, usage, custom (< "observance"): THEW. **2.** Suffixed zero-grade form *tu-ē-* in Latin *tuērī*, to look at, watch, protect: TUITION, TUTOR; INTUITION. [Pok. 2. *teu-* 1079.]

teuə-. Also **teu-.** To swell. **1.** Extended form *teuk-* in Germanic *theuham*, "the swollen or fat part of the leg," thigh, in Old English *thēoh*, thigh: THIGH. **2.** Extended form *tūs-* in Germanic compound *thūs-hundi-*, "swollen hundred," thousand (*hundi-*, hundred; see **dek$m̥$**), in Old English *thūsend*, thousand: THOUSAND. **3.** Suffixed zero-grade form *tu-l-* probably in Germanic *thul-* in Old English *thol(l)*, oar pin, oarlock (< "a swelling"): THOLE PIN. **4.** Extended zero-grade form *tūm-* in: **a.** Germanic *thūmōn-* in Old English *thūma*, thumb (< "the thick finger"): THIMBLE, THUMB; **b.** suffixed (stative) form *tum-ē-* in Latin *tumēre*, to swell, be swollen, be proud: TUMESCENT, TUMID, TUMOR; DETUMESCENCE, INTUMESCE, TUMEFACIENT, TUMEFY; **c.** suffixed form *tum-olo-* in Latin *tumulus*, raised heap of earth, mound: TUMULUS. **5.** Extended lengthened zero-grade form *tūbh-* in Latin *tūber*, lump, swelling: TRUFFLE, TUBER; PROTUBERATE. **6.** Suffixed zero-grade form *tu-r-yo-* in Greek *turos*, cheese (< "a swelling," "coagulating"): BUTTER, TYROSINE, TYROTHRICIN. **7.** Suffixed variant form *twō-ro-* in Greek *sōros*, heap, pile: SORITES, SORUS. **8.** Suffixed variant form *twō-m$n̥$* in Greek *sōma*, body (< "a swelling," "stocky form"): SOMA, SOMATO-, -SOME[2]; PROSOMA. **9.** Suffixed zero-grade form *twə-wo-* in Greek *saos*, *sōs*, safe, healthy (< "swollen," "strong"), with derivative verb *sōzein*, to save, rescue: CREOSOTE, SOTERIOLOGY. **10.** Perhaps nasalized extended form *tu-m-b(h)-* (or extended zero-grade form *tum-*) in Greek *tumbos*, barrow, tomb: TOMB. [Pok. *tēu-* 1080.]

teutā-. Tribe. **1.** Germanic *theudā-*, people, with derivative *theudiskaz*, of the people, in Middle Dutch *duutsch*, German, of the Germans or Teutons: DUTCH; PLATTDEUTSCH. **2.** Suffixed form *teut-onos*, "they of the tribe," in Germanic tribal name *theudanōz*, borrowed via Celtic into Latin as *Teutōnī*, the Teutons: TEUTON. **3.** Possibly Latin *tōtus*, all, whole (? < "of the whole tribe"): TOTAL, TUTTI; FACTOTUM, TEETOTUM. [In Pok. *tēu-* 1080.]

[threph-. To cause to grow, develop. Greek root (stem form *treph-*). **1.** Greek *trephein*, to feed, nourish, and *trophē*, nourishment: (TROPHIC-), TROPHO-, -TROPHY; ATROPHY, CHEMOTROPHY, EUTROPHIC, PHOTOTROPH, (POLYTROPHIC). **2.** Suffixed form *threph-ma* in Greek *thremma*, creature (< "nursling"): THREMMATOLOGY. [In Pok. *dherebh-* 257.]]

[thrix. Hair. Greek word of unknown origin (stem form *trikh-*). TRICHINA, TRICHO-, TRICHOME, -TRICHOUS; PERITRICH, STREPTOTHRICIN, TYROTHRICIN, ULOTRICHOUS. [In Pok. *dhrigh-* 276.]]

tit-. Also **tik-, kit-.** To tickle. Expressive root. **1.** Germanic *kit-* in Old Norse *kitla*, to tickle, akin to the probable source of Middle English *kytyllen*, to tickle: KITTLE. **2.** Latin *titillāre*, to tickle, titillate: TITILLATE. [In Pok. *geid-* 356.]

tkē-. To gain control of, gain power over. **1.** Possibly in Indo-Iranian suffixed form *ksa-tram* in: **a.** Sanskrit *kṣatram*, rule, power, and *kṣayati*, he rules: KSHATRIYA; **b.** Old Persian *khshathra-*, kingdom, province, in compound *khshathra-pāvā*, protector of the province (see **pā-**): SATRAP. **2.** Possibly in Indo-Iranian *kṣayati*, has power over, rules, in Old Persian *khshāyathiya-*, king, whence Persian *shāh*, king: CHECK, SHAH; CHECKMATE. [Pok. *kthē(i)-* 626.]

tkei-. To settle, dwell, be home. **1.** Suffixed o-grade form *(t)koi-mo-* in Germanic *haimaz*, home, in: **a.** Old English *hām*, home: HOME; **b.** Old Norse *heimr*, home: NIFLHEIM; **c.** Middle Dutch *hame*, hame (< "covering"): HAME; **d.** Old French *ham*, village, home: HAMLET; **e.** Germanic *haimatjan*, to go or bring home, in Old French *hanter*, to frequent, haunt: HAUNT. **2.** Zero-grade form *tki-* in Greek *kti-* in *ktizein*, to found, settle: AMPHYCTYONY. **3.** Probable zero-grade form *tki-* in Latin *si-* in suffixed form *si-tu-* in *situs*, location: SITUATE, SITUS. [Pok. 1. *k̑ei-* 539, *k̑thei-* 539.]

to-. Demonstrative pronoun. For the nominative singular see **so-.** **1.** Germanic *thē-* in: **a.** Old English *thē*, *thȳ* (instrumental case), by the: THE[1], THE[2]; NATHELESS; **b.** Middle Dutch *de*, the: DECOY. **2.** Germanic *thauh*, "for all that," in Old Norse *thō*, though, akin to the Scandinavian source of Middle English *though*, though: THOUGH. **3.** Germanic *thasi-* in Old English *thes*, this, this: (THESE), THIS. **4.** Germanic *thana-* in Old English *thanne*, *thænne*, *thenne*, than, then: THAN, THEN. **5.** Germanic *thanana-* in Old English *thanon*, thence: THENCE. **6.** Germanic *thēr* in Old English *thær*, *thēr*, there: THERE. **7.** Germanic *thathro* in Old English *thæder*, *thider*, thither: THITHER. **8.** Germanic nominative plural *thai* in Old English *thā* and Old Norse *their*, they: THEY. **9.** Germanic genitive plural *thaira* in Old Norse *their(r)a*, theirs: THEIR. **10.** Germanic dative plural *thaimiz* in Old Norse *theim* and Old English *thǣm*, them: THEM. **11.** Extended neuter form *tod-* in: **a.** Germanic *that* in Old English *thæt*, that: THAT, (THOSE); **b.** Greek *to*, the: TAUTO-. **12.** Germanic *thus-* in Old English *thus*, thus: THUS. **13.** Adverbial (originally accusative) form *tam* in Latin *tandem*, at last, so much (> Anglo-Norman *tant*): TANDEM, TANTAMOUNT. **14.** Suffixed reduced form *t-āli-* in Latin *tālis* (plural *tālēs*), such: TALES. [Pok. 1. *to-* 1086.]

tolkʷ-. To speak. Metathesized form *tlokʷ-* in Latin *loquī*, to speak: LOCUTION, LOQUACIOUS; ALLOCUTION, CIRCUMLOCUTION, COLLOQUIUM, (COLLOQUY), ELOCUTION, GRANDILOQUENCE, INTERLOCUTION, MAGNILOQUENT, OBLOQUY, PROLOCUTOR, SOLILOQUY, VENTRILOQUISM. [Pok. *tolkʷ-* 1088.]

tong-. To think, feel. **1.** Germanic *thankōn* in: **a.** Old English *thancian*, to thank: THANK; **b.** Old English *thencan*, to think: THINK. **2.** Germanic *(ga)thauht-* (*ga-*, collective prefix; see **kom**) in Old English *(ge)thōht*, thought: THOUGHT. **3.** Germanic factitive *thunkjan* in Old English *thyncan* (third person singular present indicative *thyncth*), to seem: METHINKS. [Pok. 1. *tong-* 1088.]

tragh-. To draw, drag, move. Rhyming variant **dhragh-.** Latin *trahere*, to pull, draw: TRACT[1], TRACTABLE, TRACTION, TRAIL, TRAIN, (TRAIT), TREAT; ABSTRACT, ATTRACT, CONTRACT, DETRACT, DISTRACT, EXTRACT, PORTRAY, PROTRACT, RETRACT, SUBTRACT. [Pok. *tragh-* 1089.]

treb-. Dwelling. **1.** Zero-grade form *t$r̥$b-* in Germanic *thurp-* in Old English *thorp*, village, hamlet: THORP. **2.** Latin *trabs*, beam, timber: TRABEATED, TRABECULA, TRAVE; ARCHITRAVE. [Pok. *treb-* 1090.]

trei-. Three. **I.** Nominative plural form *treyes*. **1.** Germanic *thrijiz* in Old English *thrīe*, *thrēo*, *thrī*, three, with its derivatives *thrīga*, *thrīwa*, thrice, and *thrītig*, thirty, and *thrēotīne*, thirteen: THREE, THRICE, THIRTY, THIRTEEN. **2.** Latin *trēs* (> Italian *tre* and French *trois*), three: TREY, TRIO; TRAMMEL, TRECENTO, TREPHINE, TRIUMVIR, TROCAR. **II.** Zero-grade form *tri-*. **1.** Suffixed form *tri-tyo-* in: **a.** Germanic *thridjaz*, third, in *(i)* Old English *thrid(d)a*, *thirdda*, third: THIRD *(ii)* Old Norse *thrithi*, third: RIDING[2]; **b.** Latin *tertius* (neuter *tertium*), third: TERCEL, TERCET, TERTIAN, TERTIARY, TIERCE; SESTERCE. **2.** Latin *tri-*, three: TRI-, TRIPLE. **3.** Greek *tri-*, three: TRI-; TRICLINIUM, TRICROTIC, TRIDACTYL, TRIGLYPH, TRITONE. **4.** Sanskrit *tri*, three: TRIMURTI.

5. Greek *trias*, the number three: TRIAD. **6.** Greek *trikha*, in three parts: TRICHOTOMY. **7.** Greek compound *triērēs*, galley with three banks of oars, trireme (-*ērēs*, oar; see **erə-**[1]): TRIERARCH. **8.** Suffixed form *tri-to-* in Greek *tritos*, third: TRITIUM; TRITANOPIA. **9.** Compound form *tri-pl-*, "threefold" (*-pl-* < combining form *-plo-*; see **pel-**[3]), in Greek *triploos*, triple: TRIPLE. **10.** Compound form *tri-plek-*, "threefold" (*-plek-*, -fold; see **plek-**), in Latin *triplex*, triple: TRIPLEX. **11.** Compound form *tri-st-i*, "third person standing by" (see **stā-**), in Latin *testis*, a witness: TESTAMENT, (TESTIMONY); ATTEST, CONTEST, DETEST, OBTEST, PROTEST, TESTIFY. **12.** Persian *si*, three: SITAR. **III.** Extended zero-grade form *tris*, "thrice." **1.** Latin *ter*, thrice: TERN[2]; TERPOLYMER. **2.** Greek *tris*, thrice: TRISOCTAHEDRON. **3.** Suffixed form *tris-no-* in Latin *trīnī*, three each: TRINE, (TRINITY). **IV.** Suffixed o-grade form *troy-o-* in Russian *troje*, three: TROIKA. [Pok. *trei-* 1090.]

trem-. To tremble. Possibly related to **trep-**[1] and **tres-** through a hypothetical base *ter-*. Latin *tremere*, to shake, tremble: TREMENDOUS, TREMOR, TREMULOUS. [Pok. *trem-* 1092.]

trep-[1]. To tremble. Possibly related to **trem-** and **tres-** through a hypothetical base *ter-*. Latin *trepidus*, agitated, alarmed: TREPID; INTREPID. [Pok. 1. *trep-* 1094.]

trep-[2]. To turn. **1.** Greek *trepein*, to turn: -TROPOUS; APOTROPAIC, TREPONEME. **2.** O-grade form *trop-* in: **a.** suffixed form *trop-o-* in Greek *tropos*, a turn, way, manner: TROPE, TROPO-, TROVER; CONTRIVE, (RE-TRIEVE); **b.** suffixed form *trop-ā-* in Greek *tropē*, a turning, change: TROPHY, TROPIC; ENTROPY. [Pok. 2. *trep-* 1094.]

tres-. To tremble. Possibly related to **trem-** and **trep-**[1] through a hypothetical base *ter-*. Metathesized form *ters-* in o-grade suffixed (causative) form *tors-eyo-* in Latin *terrēre*, to frighten (< "to cause to tremble"), with vowel *e* from *terror* (< *ters-os-*), terror: TERRIBLE, TERROR; DETER, TERRIFIC. [Pok. *tres-* 1095.]

treud-. To squeeze. **1.** Suffixed o-grade form *troud-o-* in Germanic *thrautam* in Old English *thrēat*, oppression, use of force: THREAT. **2.** Variant form *trūd-* in Germanic *thrūstjan* in Old Norse *thrŷsta*, to squeeze, compress: THRUST. **3.** Latin *trūdere*, to thrust, push: ABSTRUSE, EXTRUDE, INTRUDE, OBTRUDE, PROTRUDE. [Pok. *tr-eu-d* 1095.]

trozdo-. Thrush. **1.** Germanic *thrust-* in Old English *throstle*, thrush: THROSTLE. **2.** Germanic *thruskjōn-* in Old English *thrysce*, thrush: THRUSH[1]. **3.** Zero-grade reduced form *trzdo-* in Latin *turdus*, thrush: STURDY. **4.** Perhaps altered in Greek *strouthos*, sparrow, ostrich: STRUTHIOUS; (OSTRICH). [Pok. *trozdos* 1096.]

tu-. Second person singular pronoun; you, thou. **1.** Lengthened-grade form *tū* (accusative *te*, *tege*) in Germanic *thū* (accusative *theke*) in Old English *thū* (accusative *thec*, *thē*), thou: (THEE), THOU[1]. **2.** Suffixed extended form *t(w)ei-no-* in Germanic *thīnaz* in Old English *thīn*, thine: THINE, THY. [Pok. *tu-* 1097.]

twei-. To agitate, shake, toss. **1.** Extended form *tweid-* in Germanic *thwīt-* in: **a.** Old English *thwītan*, to strike, whittle down: WHITTLE; **b.** Middle Dutch *duit*, a small coin (? < "piece cut or tossed off"): DOIT. **2.** Extended form *tweis-* in Greek *seiein*, to shake: SEISM, SISTRUM. [Pok. 2. *tuei-* 1099.]

twengh-. To press in on. Germanic *thwang-* in: **a.** Old English *thwong*, *thwang*, thong, band (< "constraint"): THONG; **b.** by-form *twangjan* in Old English *twengan*, to pinch: TWINGE. [Pok. *tuengh-* 1099.]

twer-[1]. To turn, whirl. Zero-grade *tur-*. **I.** Variant form *stur-*. **1.** Suffixed form *stur-mo-* in Germanic *sturmaz*, storm (< "whirlwind"), in Old English *storm*, storm: STORM. **2.** Germanic *sturjan* in Old English *styrian*, to move, agitate: STIR[1]. **II.** Suffixed form *tur-bā* in Greek *turbē*, tumult, disorder (> Latin *turba*, disorder, *turbō*, spinning top, and *turbāre*, to confuse, disorder): (TROU-

BLE), TURBID, TURBINE; DISTURB, PERTURB. [Pok. 1. *tuer-*, *tur-* 1100.]

twer-[2]. To grasp, hold; hard. **1.** Slavic *tvrd-* altered in West Slavic *kvardy*, quartz, perhaps akin to the source of Middle High German *quarz*, quartz: QUARTZ. **2.** Possible (but very unlikely) suffixed form *twer-y-ēn-*, she who grasps, binds, enthralls, in Greek *Seirēn*, Siren: SIREN. [Pok. 2. *tuer-* 1101.]

twerk-. To cut. Zero-grade form *twrk-* in Greek *sarx*, flesh (< "piece of meat"): SARCASM, SARCO-, (SARCOID), (SARCOMA), (SARCOUS); ANASARCA, ECTOSARC, PERISARC, (SARCOCARP), SARCOPHAGUS, (SARCOPTIC MANGE), SYS-SARCOSIS. [Pok. *tuerk-* 1102.]

[twik-. To pinch off. Germanic root. **1.** Old English *twiccian*, to pinch: TWEAK. **2.** Low German *twikken*, to twitch, akin to the Low German source of Middle English *twicchen*, to twitch: TWITCH.]

ud-. Also **ūd-.** Up, out. **1.** Germanic *ūt-*, out, in: **a.** Old English *ūt*, OUT; UTMOST; **b.** Old High German *ūz* (> German *aus*), out, in German *garaus*, "all out": CA-ROUSE; AUSLANDER; **c.** Old Norse *ūt*, out: OUTLAW; **d.** Middle Dutch *ute*, *uut*, out: UITLANDER; **e.** Middle Dutch *ūteren*, to drive away, speak out: UTTER[1]; **f.** Germanic suffixed (comparative) form *ūt-era-* in Old English *ūtera*, outer: UTTER[2]; **g.** Germanic compound *bi-ūtana* (*bi-*, by, at; see **ambhi**), "at the outside," in Old English *būtan*, *būte*, outside (adverb): BUT; ABOUT. **2.** Extended form *uds* in Germanic *uz*, out, and prefix *uz-*, out, in: **a.** Old High German *ir-*, out, in *irsezzan*, to replace: ERSATZ; **b.** Middle Dutch *oor-*, out: ORT; **c.** Germanic *uz-dailjam*, "a portioning out," judgment (see **dail-**). **3.** Suffixed (comparative) form *ud-tero-* in Greek *husteros*, later, second, after: HYSTERESIS, HYSTERON PROTERON. **4.** Greek *hu-* in compound *hubris*, violence, outrage, insolence (*bri-*, perhaps "heavy," "violent"; see **gwerə-**[2]): HUBRIS. [Pok. *ŭd-* 1103.]

udero-. Abdomen, womb, stomach; with distantly similar forms (perhaps taboo deformations) in various languages. **1.** Latin *uterus* (reshaped from *udero-*), womb: UTERUS. **2.** Perhaps taboo deformation *wen-tri-* in Latin *venter*, belly: VENTER; VENTRILOQUISM. **3.** Perhaps taboo deformation *wns-ti-* in Latin *vēsīca*, bladder: VESICA. **4.** Variant form *ud-tero-* in Greek *hustera*, womb: HYSTERIC, HYSTERO-. [Pok. *udero-* 1104.]

ul-. To howl. Imitative root. **1.** Possibly Germanic *uwwalōn*, owl, in Old English *ūle*, owl: OWL. **2.** Germanic by-form *uwwilōn*, owl, possibly in Middle English *houlen*, to howl (like an owl): HOWL. **3.** Latin *ululāre*, to howl: ULULATE. [Pok. 1. *u-* 1103; *ul-* 1105.]

uper. Over. **1.** Extended form *uperi* in Germanic *uberi* in: **a.** Old English *ofer*, over: OVER; **b.** Middle Dutch *over*, over: ORLOP. **2.** Variant form *(s)uper* in: **a.** Latin *super*, *super-*, above, over: SOUBRETTE, SOVEREIGN, SUPER-, SUPERABLE, SUPERIOR, SUPREME, (SUPREMO), SUR-; SIRLOIN; **b.** suffixed form *(s)uper-no-* in Latin *supernus*, above, upper, top: SUPERNAL; **c.** suffixed form *super-bhw-o-*, "being above" (*bhw-o-*, being; see **bheuə-**), in Latin *superbus*, superior, excellent, arrogant: SUPERB; **d.** suffixed (superlative) reduced form *sup-mo-* in Latin *summus*, highest, topmost: SUM, SUMMIT; **e.** variant form *(s)uprā* in Latin *suprā*, above, beyond: (SO-PRANINO), SOPRANO, SUPRA-; SOMERSAULT. **3.** Basic form *uper* in Greek *huper*, over: HYPER-. [Pok. *uper* 1105.]

upo. Under, up from under, over. **1.** Germanic *upp-*, up, in: **a.** Old English *up*, *uppe*, up: UP; **b.** Old English *up-*, *upp-*, up-: UP-; **c.** Middle Dutch *op*, up: UPROAR. **2.** Germanic *upanaz*, "put or set up," open, in Old English *open*, open: OPEN. **3.** Germanic *ufana*, "on, above," in Old English *būfan*, above, over: ABOVE. **4.** Possibly suffixed form *up-t-* in Germanic *ufta*, frequently, in Old English *oft*, oft: OFT, OFTEN. **5.** Extended form *upes-* in Germanic *ubaswō*, *ubizwō*, vestibule, porch, eaves (< "that which is above or in front"), in: **a.** Old English *efes*,

eaves: EAVES; **b.** Germanic *obisdrup-*, dripping water from the eaves (*drup-*, to drip, from *dhrub-*; see **dhreu-**), in Old English *yfesdrype*, *yfæs drypæ*, water from the eaves: EAVESDROP. **6.** Variant form *(s)up-* in: **a.** Latin *sub*, under: SOUTANE, SUB-; **b.** Latin *supīnus*, lying on the back (< "thrown backward or under"): SUPINE¹, SUPINE²; **c.** suffixed form *sup-ter* in Latin *subter*, secretly: SUBTERFUGE; **d.** Latin *supplex*, "with legs folded under one" (*-plex*, -fold; see **plek-**): SUPPLE. **7.** Basic form *upo* in Greek *hupo*, under: HYPO-. **8.** Suffixed variant form *ups-o-* in Greek *hupsos*, height, top: HYPSO-. **9.** Basic form *upo-* in Celtic *vo-*, under, in Latin *verēdus*, post horse (see **reidh-**). **10.** Compound *upo-st-o-* probably in Celtic *wasso-*, "one who stands under," servant, young man (*sto-*, standing; see **stā-**), in Medieval Latin *vassus*, vassal: VALET, (VARLET), VASSAL. **11.** Sanskrit *úpa*, near to, under (in *upaniṣad*, Upanishad): OPAL, UPANISHAD. [Pok. *upo* 1106.]

us-. Point, thorn. Proposed by some as the root for Germanic *uzda-* in Old Norse *oddi*, point, triangle, third, odd number: ODD.

[**vīnum.** Wine. Latin noun, related to Greek *oinos*, wine. Probably from a Mediterranean word *wīn-*, *woin-* meaning "wine." **1.** Latin *vīnum*: VINACEOUS, VINE, VINI-, WINE; VINEGAR. **2.** Greek *oinos* (earlier *woinos*): OENOLOGY, OENOMEL.]

[**virēre.** To be green. Latin verb of unknown origin (> French *verte*, green). (FARTHINGALE), VERDANT, VIREO, VIRESCENT, VIRID; (BILIVERDIN); TERRE-VERTE.]

[**Volcae.** Celtic tribal name. Latin noun akin to the unknown source of Germanic *walhaz*. Germanic *walhaz* in: **a.** Old English *wealh*, *Wealh*, foreigner, Welshman, Celt: WELSH; WALNUT; **b.** Medieval Latin *wallō*, a foreigner: WALLOON.]

wā-. To bend apart. A possible root. Latin *vārus*, bent, knock-kneed: VARA, VARUS; DIVARICATE. [Pok. 2. *u̯ā-* 1108.]

wāb-. To cry, scream. Suffixed form *wāb-eyo-* in Germanic *wōpjan*, to wail, in Old English *wēpan*, to weep: WEEP. [Pok. *u̯āb-* 1109.]

wadh-¹. A pledge; to pledge. **1.** Germanic *wadi-* in: **a.** Old English *wedd*, a pledge, marriage: WEDLOCK. **b.** Old English *weddian*, to pledge, bind in wedlock: WED; **c.** Old French *gage*, a pledge: GAGE¹; DÉGAGÉ, ENGAGE, (ENGAGÉ), MORTGAGE; **d.** Old North French *wage*, a pledge, payment, and *wagier*, to pledge: WAGE, WAGER. **2.** Latin *praes* (< *prai-vad-*), surety, pledge (< "that which is given before"; *prae-*, before; see **per¹**): PRAEDIAL. [Pok. *u̯adh-* 1109.]

wadh-². To go. **1.** Basic form *wadh-* in: **a.** Germanic *wadan*, to go, in Old English *wadan*, to go: WADE; **b.** Latin *vadum*, ford: VADOSE. **2.** Lengthened-grade form *wādh-* in Latin *vādere*, to go, step: VAMOOSE, EVADE, INVADE, PERVADE. [Pok. *u̯ādh-* 1109.]

wag-. Sheath, cover. Suffixed lengthened-grade form *wāg-īnā* in Latin *vāgīna*, sheath: VAGINA, VANILLA; EVAGINATE, INVAGINATE. [Pok. 1. *u̯ăg-* 1110.]

wai. Alas (interjection). **1.** Germanic *wai* in Old English *wā*, *wei*, woe (interjection), alas: WOE, WELLAWAY. **2.** Germanic *waiwalōn* in Old Norse *væla*, *væla*, *veila*, to lament, akin to the Scandinavian source of Middle English *wailen*, to wail: WAIL. [Pok. *u̯ai-* 1110.]

wak-. Cow (perhaps "who calves for the first time"). Expressive form *wakkā* in Latin *vacca*, cow: BUCKAROO, VACCINE, VAQUERO. [Pok. *u̯akā* 1111.]

wal-. To be strong. **1.** Suffixed (stative) form *wal-ē-* in Latin *valēre*, to be strong: VALENCE, VALETUDINARIAN, VALIANT, VALID, VALOR, VALUE; AVAIL, CONVALESCE, COUNTERVAIL, EQUIVALENT, INVALID¹, (INVALID²), PREVAIL. **2.** Extended o-grade form *wold(h)-* in: **a.** Germanic *waldan*, to rule, in Old English *wealdan*, to rule, and *wieldan*, to govern: WIELD; **b.** Germanic *wald-*, power, rule, in Germanic *harja-waldaz*, "army commander"

(see **koro-**). **3.** Suffixed extended o-grade form *wold-ti-* in Russian *oblast'*, oblast: OBLAST. [Pok. *u̯al-* 1111.]

walso-. A post. **1.** Latin *vallus*, post, stake, whence *vallum*, a palisade, wall: VALLATION, WALL; INTERVAL. **2.** Greek *hēlos* (< *hālos* < *walsos*), stud, nail, wart: MYCELIUM. [In Pok. 7. *u̯el-* 1140.]

we-. We. For oblique cases of the pronoun see **nes-²**. Suffixed variant form *wei-es* in Germanic *wīz* in Old English *wē*, *we*, we: WE. [Pok. *u̯ě-* 1114.]

wē-. To blow. Contracted from *weə-*; oldest basic form *əwē-* (< *əweə-*). **1.** Suffixed irregular shortened form *we-dhro-* in Germanic *wedram*, wind, weather, in Old English *weder*, weather, storm, wind: WEATHER. **2.** Suffixed (participial) form *wē-nt-o-*, blowing, in: **a.** Germanic *windaz* in (i) Old English *wind*, wind: WIND¹ (ii) Old Norse *vindr*, wind: WINDOW; **b.** Latin *ventus*, wind: VENT, VENTAIL, VENTILATE. **3.** Suffixed Germanic form *wē-ingjaz* in Old Norse *vængr*, wing, akin to the Scandinavian source of Middle English *wenge*, wing: WING. **4.** Basic form *wē-* in Sanskrit *vāti* (stem *vā-*), he blows: NIRVANA. [Pok. 10. *au̯(e)-* 81.]

webh-. To weave, also to move quickly. **1.** Germanic *weban* in Old English *wefan*, to weave: WEAVE, WOOF¹. **2.** Germanic *wefta-* in Old English *wefta*, weft, cross thread: WEFT. **3.** Suffixed o-grade form *wobh-yo-* in Germanic *wabjam*, fabric, web, in Old English *web(b)*, web: WEB, WEBSTER. **4.** Suffixed Germanic form *webila-* in Old English *wifel*, weevil (< "that which moves briskly"): WEEVIL. **5.** Suffixed Germanic form *wabila-*, web, honeycomb, in: **a.** Middle Low German *wāfel*, honeycomb, akin to the source of Old North French *waufre*, wafer: GOFFER, WAFER; **b.** obsolete Dutch *waefel*, honeycomb: WAFFLE¹. **6.** Possibly Germanic *wab-*, to move back and forth as in weaving, in: **a.** Old English *wafian*, to move (the hand) up and down: WAVE; **b.** Low German *wabbeln*, to move from side to side, sway: WOBBLE. **7.** Suffixed zero-grade form *ubh-ā-* in Greek *huphē*, web: HYPHA. [Pok. *u̯ebh-* 1114.]

wed-¹. Water; wet. **1.** Suffixed o-grade form *wod-ōr* in Germanic *watar* in Old English *wæter*, water: WATER. **2.** Suffixed lengthened-grade form *wēd-o-* in Germanic *wēd-* in Old English *wæt*, *wēt*, wet: WET. **3.** O-grade form *wod-* in Germanic suffixed form *wat-skan*, to wash, in Old English *wæscan*, *wacsan*, to wash: WASH. **4.** Nasalized form *we-n-d-* in Germanic *wintruz*, winter, "wet season," in Old English *winter*, winter: WINTER. **5.** Suffixed zero-grade form *ud-ōr* in Greek *hudōr*, water: (HYDRANT), HYDRO-, (HYDROUS); ANHYDROUS, CLEPSYDRA, DROPSY, HYDATHODE, HYDATID. **6.** Suffixed nasalized zero-grade form *u-n-d-ā-* in Latin *unda*, wave: UNDINE, UNDULATE; ABOUND, INUNDATE, (REDOUND), REDUNDANT, SURROUND. **7.** Suffixed zero-grade form *ud-ro-*, *ud-rā-*, water animal, in: **a.** Germanic *otraz*, otter, in Old English *otor*, otter: OTTER; **b.** Latin *lutra*, otter (with obscure *l-*): NUTRIA; **c.** Greek *hudros*, a water snake: HYDRUS; **d.** Greek *hudra*, a water serpent, Hydra: HYDRA. **8.** Suffixed zero-grade form *ud-skio-* in Scottish and Irish Gaelic *uisge*, water: USQUEBAUGH, (WHISKEY). **9.** Suffixed o-grade form *wod-ā-* in Russian *voda*, water: VODKA. [Pok. 9. *au̯(e)-* 78.]

wed-². To speak. **1.** Possibly oldest root form *əwed-* becoming *awed-* in reduplicated form *awe-ud-* dissimilated to *aweid-*, with suffixed o-grade form *awoid-o-* respectively in Greek *aeidein* (Attic *aidein*), to sing, and *aoidē* (Attic *ōidē*), song, ode (but more likely a separate root *əweid-* becoming Greek *aweid-*, to sing): ODE; COMEDY, EPODE, HYMNODY, MELODY, MONODY, PARODY, RHAPSODY, TRAGEDY. **2.** Sanskrit *vādaḥ*, sound, statement: THERAVADA. [Pok. 6. *au̯-* 76.]

wedh-. To push, strike. Suffixed lengthened o-grade form *wōdh-eyo-* in Greek *ōthein*, to push: OSMOSIS. [Pok. 1. *u̯edh-* 1115.]

weg-¹. To weave a web. Related to **wokso-**. Suffixed

form *weg-slo- in Latin vēlum, a sail, curtain, veil: VEIL, VELUM, VEXILLUM, VOILE; REVEAL. [Pok. ueg- 1117.]

weg-². To be strong, be lively. **1.** Suffixed o-grade form *wog-ē- in Germanic *wakēn in Old English *wacan, to wake up, arise, and wacian, to be aware: WAKE¹. **2.** Suffixed o-grade form *wog-no- in Germanic *waknan in Old English wæcnan, wæcnian, to awake: WAKEN. **3.** Germanic *wakjan in Old English wæccan, to be awake: WATCH. **4.** Germanic *wahtwō in Old High German wahta, watch, vigil, in dialectal German beiwacht, supplementary night watch: BIVOUAC. **5.** Germanic *waht- in: **a.** Old North French waitier, to watch: WAIT; **b.** Middle Low German wachten, to watch, guard: WAFT. **6.** Suffixed (causative) o-grade form *wog-eyo- in Latin vegēre, to be lively: VEGETABLE. **7.** Suffixed (stative) form *weg-ē- in Latin vigēre, to be lively: VIGOR. **8.** Suffixed form *weg-eli- in Latin vigil, watchful, awake (> vigilāre, to watch, be awake): VEDETTE, VIGIL, (VIGILANT), VIGILANTE; REVEILLE, SURVEILLANT. **9.** Suffixed form *weg-slo- in Latin vēlōx, fast, "lively": VELOCITY. [Pok. ueg- 1117.]

wegh-. To go, transport in a vehicle. **1.** Germanic *wegan in Old English wegan, to carry, balance in a scale: WEIGH¹. **2.** Germanic lengthened form *wēg-ō in Old English wǣg(e), weight, unit of weight: WEE. **3.** Suffixed form *wegh-ti- in Germanic *wihti- in Old English wiht, gewiht, weight: WEIGHT. **4.** Germanic *wegaz, course of travel, way, in Old English weg, way: WAY; ALWAYS, (AWAY). **5.** Suffixed form *wogh-no- in Germanic *wagnaz, vehicle, in: **a.** Old English wæ(g)n, wagon: WAIN; **b.** Middle Dutch wagen, wagon: WAGON. **6.** Suffixed o-grade form *wogh-lo- in: **a.** Germanic *waglaz in Old Norse vagl, chicken roost, perch, beam: WALLEYED; **b.** Greek okhlos, populace, mob (< "moving mass"): OCHLOCRACY, OCHLOPHOBIA. **7.** Distantly related to this root are: **a.** Germanic *wag-, "to move about," in (i) possibly Middle English waggen, to wag: WAG¹ (ii) Old High German waggo, wacko, boulder rolling on a riverbed (> German Wacke, boulder): GRAYWACKE; **b.** Germanic *wēga-, water in motion, in Old Italian vogare, to row: VOGUE; **c.** Germanic *wig- in (i) Old English wicga, insect (< "thing that moves quickly"): EARWIG (ii) Middle Dutch and Middle Low German wiggelen, to move back and forth, wag: WIGGLE. **8.** Basic form *wegh- in Latin vehere (past participle vectus), to carry: VECTOR, VEHICLE; ADVECTION, CONVECTION, EVECTION, INVEIGH. **9.** Suffixed basic form *wegh-yā in Latin via, way, road: FOY, VIA, VOYAGE; CONVEY, DEVIATE, DEVIOUS, (ENVOI), ENVOY¹, OBVIOUS, PERVIOUS, PREVIOUS, (TRIVIAL), TRIVIUM, (VIADUCT). **10.** Suffixed form *wegh-s- in Latin vexāre, to agitate (< "to set in motion"): VEX. **11.** Probably suffixed form *wegh-so- in Latin convexus, "carried or drawn together (to a point)," convex (com-, together; see kom): CONVEX. [Pok. uegh- 1118.]

wegʷ-. Wet. **1.** Germanic *wakw-ō in Old Norse vök, a crack in ice (< "wet spot"): WAKE². **2.** Suffixed zero-grade form *ugʷ-sm- in: **a.** Latin (h)ūmēre, to be wet: HUMECTANT, HUMID; **b.** Latin (h)ūmor, fluid: HUMOR. **3.** Suffixed zero-grade form *ugʷ-ro- in Greek hugros, wet, liquid: HYGRO-. **4.** Regarded by some as an extended form of this root (with the meaning "the impregnator"), but probably a distinct Indo-European word, is *ukʷs-en-, bull, ox, in Germanic *uhsōn- in: **a.** Old English oxa, ox: OX; **b.** Old High German ohso, ox, in German Aurochs, aurochs: AUROCHS. [Pok. uegʷ- 1118.]

wegʷh-. Also **eugʷh-.** To preach, speak solemnly. Suffixed o-grade form *wogʷh-eyo- in Latin vovēre, to pledge, vow: VOTARY, VOTE, (VOTIVE), VOW; DEVOTE, (DEVOUT). [Pok. euegʷh- 348.]

wei-¹. Also **weiə-.** To turn, twist; with derivatives referring to suppleness or binding. **I.** Form *wei-. **1.** Germanic suffixed form *wī-ra-, *wē-ra- in Old English wīr, wire: WIRE. **2.** Probably suffixed Germanic form *wai-ra- in

Old English wār, seaweed: SEAWARE. **3.** Suffixed zero-grade form *wi-ria- in Latin (of Celtic origin) viriae, bracelets: FERRULE. **4.** Suffixed form *wei-ti- in Germanic *wīth- willow, in Old English wīthig, wiry: WITHY. **5.** Suffixed zero-grade form *wi-t- in Germanic withjōn- in Old English withthe, supple twig: WITHE. **II.** Form *weiə-, zero-grade form *wī- (< *wiə-). **1.** Suffixed form *wī-ti- in Latin vītis, vine: VISE, VITICULTURE. **2.** Suffixed form *wī-tā- becoming *wittā in Latin vitta, headband: VITTA. **3.** Suffixed form *wī-ri- probably in Greek iris, rainbow, and Iris, rainbow goddess: (IRIDACEOUS), IRIDO-, IRIS, IRIS; (IRIDIUM), (IRISITIS). **4.** Suffixed form *wī-n- perhaps in Greek is (genitive inos), sinew: EXINE, INOSITOL, INOTROPIC. [Pok. 1. uei- 1120.]

wei-². To go after something. Suffixed o-grade form in Germanic *wai-thjō-, "pursuit," with denominative *waithanjan, to hunt, plunder, in Old French gaaignier, gaigner, to obtain: GAIN¹; ROWEN. [Pok. 3. uei- 1123.]

wei-³. To wither. Extended form *weis- in Germanic *wis- in suffixed form *wis-n-ōn in Old English wisnian, to wither, shrivel, shrink: WIZEN. [Pok. 2. uei- 1123.]

wei-⁴. Vice, fault, guilt. **1.** Suffixed zero-grade form *wi-tio- in Latin vitium, fault, vice: VICE¹, VICIOUS, VITIATE. **2.** Suffixed *wi-tu- in: **a.** Latin vitilīgō, tetter (< "blemish"): VITILIGO; **b.** Latin vituperāre, to abuse (perhaps formed after Latin recuperāre, to regain; see kap-): VITUPERATE. [Pok. 1. uǐ- 1175.]

weid-. To see. **I.** Full-grade form *weid-. **1.** Germanic *wītan, to look after, guard, ascribe to, reproach, in: **a.** Old English wītan, to reproach: TWIT; **b.** Old Provençal guida, a guide: GUIDE; **c.** Germanic derivative noun *wīti- in Old English wīte, fine, penalty: WITE¹. **2.** Suffixed form *weid-to- in Germanic *wīssaz in: **a.** Old English wīs, wise: WISE¹; **b.** Old English wīsdōm, learning, wisdom (-dōm, abstract suffix; see dhē-¹): WISDOM; **c.** Old High German wīssago, seer, prophet: WISEACRE; **d.** Germanic *wīssōn-, appearance, form, manner, in (i) Old English wīse, wīs, manner: WISE² (ii) Old French guise, manner: GUISE. **3.** Suffixed form *weid-es- in Greek eidos, form, shape: EIDETIC, EIDOLON, IDOL, IDYLL, -OID; IDOCRASE, KALEIDOSCOPE. **4.** Perhaps Greek Haidēs (also Aidēs), the underworld, perhaps "the invisible" (> French Hadès): HADAL, HADES. **II.** Zero-grade form *wid-. **1.** Germanic *wit- in: **a.** Old English wit, witt, knowledge, intelligence: WIT¹; **b.** Old English wita (genitive plural witena), wise man, councilor: WITENAGEMOT. **2.** Germanic *witan in Old English witan, to know: WIT²; UNWITTING. **3.** Suffixed form *wid-to- in Germanic *wissaz, known, in Old English gewis, gewiss, certain, sure: IWIS. **4.** Form *wid-ē- (with participial stem *weid-to-) in Latin vidēre (past participle vīsus), to see, look: VIDE, VIEW, VISA, VISAGE, VISION, VISTA, VOYEUR; ADVICE, (ADVISE), BELVEDERE, CLAIRVOYANCE, ENVY, EVIDENT, INTERVIEW, PREVISE, PROVIDE, REVISE, SUPERVISE, SURVEY. **5.** Suffixed form *wid-es-ya in Greek idea, appearance, form, idea: IDEA, IDEO-. **6.** Suffixed form *wid-tor- in Greek histōr, wise, learned, learned man: HISTORY, (STORY); POLYHISTOR. **7.** Suffixed nasalized form *wi-n-d-no- in: **a.** Irish fionn, white (< "clearly visible"): COLCANNON; **b.** Welsh gwyn, gwynn, white: PENGUIN. **8.** Celtic compound *dru-wid-, "knower of trees" (*dru-, tree; see deru-). **III.** Suffixed o-grade form *woid-o- in Sanskrit vedaḥ, knowledge: VEDA; RIG-VEDA. [Pok. 2. u(e)di- 1125.]

weidh-. To divide, separate. **1.** Suffixed zero-grade form *widh-ewo-, "bereft," feminine *widh-ewā-, "woman separated (from her husband by death)," in Germanic *widuwō in Old English widuwe, widow: WIDOW. **2.** Zero-grade form *widh- in Latin dīvidere, to separate (dis-, intensive prefix): DEVISE, DIVIDE, POINT-DEVICE. [Pok. ueidh- 1127.]

weiə-. Vital force. Perhaps related to wī-ro-. Zero-grade form *wī- (< *wiə-) in Latin vīs, force, with irregular

derivatives *violāre*, to treat with force, and *violentus*, vehement: VIM, VIOLATE, VIOLENT. [In Pok. 3. *u̯ei-* 1123.]

weik-¹. Clan (social unit above the household). **1.** Suffixed form **weik-slā* in Latin *vīlla*, country house, farm: VILLA, VILLAGE, VILLAIN, VILLANELLE, (VILLEIN); (BIDONVILLE). **2.** Suffixed o-grade form **woik-o-* in: **a.** Latin *vīcus*, quarter or district of a town, neighborhood: (VICINAGE), VICINITY; **b.** Greek *oikos*, house, and its derivative *oikia*, dwelling: ANDROECIUM, AUTOECIOUS, DIOCESE, DIOECIOUS, DIOICOUS, ECESIS, ECOLOGY, ECONOMY, ECUMENICAL, HETEROECIOUS, MONOECIOUS, PARISH, TRIOECIOUS. **3.** Zero-grade form **wik-* in Sanskrit *viś-*, dwelling, with derivative *vaiśyaḥ*, settler: VAISYA. [Pok. *u̯eik-* 1131.]

weik-². In words connected with magic and religious notions (in Germanic and Latin). **1.** Germanic suffixed form **wīh-l-* in Old English *wigle*, divination, sorcery, akin to the Germanic source of Old French *guile*, cunning, trickery: GUILE. **2.** Germanic expressive form **wikk-* in: **a.** Old English *wicca*, wizard, and *wicce*, witch: WITCH; **b.** Old English *wiccian*, to cast a spell: BEWITCH. **3.** Possible suffixed zero-grade form **wik-t-imā* in Latin *victima*, animal used as sacrifice, victim (although this may belong to another root **(ə)wek-* not otherwise represented in English): VICTIM. [Pok. 1. *u̯eik-* 1128.]

weik-³. To be like. **1.** Suffixed variant form **eik-on-* in Greek *eikōn*, likeness, image: ICON, (ICONIC), ICONO-; ANISEIKONIA. **2.** Prefixed and suffixed zero-grade form **n̥-wik-ēs*, not like (**n̥-*, not; see **ne**), in Greek *aikēs*, unseemly: AECIUM. [Pok. 3. *u̯eik-* 1129.]

weik-⁴. Also **weig-.** To bend, wind. **I.** Form *weig-.* **1.** Germanic **wīk-* in: **a.** Old English *wice*, wych elm (having pliant branches): WYCH ELM; **b.** Swedish *viker*, willow twig, wand, akin to the Scandinavian source of Middle English *wiker*, wicker: WICKER; **c.** Old Norse *vikja*, to bend, turn, probably akin to the Scandinavian source of Old North French *wiket*, wicket (< "door that turns"): WICKET. **2.** Germanic **waikwaz* in: **a.** Old Norse *veikr*, pliant: WEAK; **b.** Dutch *week*, weak, soft: WEAKFISH. **3.** Germanic **wikōn-*, "a turning," series, in Old English *wicu, wice*, week: WEEK. **II.** Form *weik-.* Zero-grade form **wik-* in: **a.** Latin *vix* (genitive *vicis*), turn, situation, change: VICAR, (VICARIOUS), VICE³; VICISSITUDE; **b.** Latin *vicia*, vetch (< "twining plant"): VETCH. [Pok. 4. *u̯eik-* 1130.]

weik-⁵. To fight, conquer. **1.** Germanic **wīk-* in Old Norse *vígr*, able in battle: WIGHT². **2.** Nasalized zero-grade form **wi-n-k-* in Latin *vincere* (past participle *victus*), to conquer: VANQUISH, VICTOR, VINCIBLE; CONVINCE, EVICT. [Pok. 2. *u̯eik-* 1128.]

weip-. To turn, vacillate, tremble ecstatically. **1.** O-grade form **woip-* in Germanic **waif-* in Old Norse *veif*, waving thing, flag, probably akin to the Scandinavian source of Anglo-Norman *waif*, ownerless property: WAIF¹, (WAIVE), (WAIVER). **2.** Variant form **weib-* in Germanic **wīpjan*, to move back and forth, in: **a.** Old English *wīpian*, to wipe: WIPE; **b.** Old French *guiper*, to cover with silk: GUIPURE; **c.** Middle Dutch and Middle Low German *wippen*, to swing: WHIP. **3.** Perhaps suffixed nasalized zero-grade form **wi-m-p-ila-* in: **a.** Old English *wimpel*, covering for the neck (< "something that winds around"): WIMPLE; **b.** perhaps Middle Dutch *wimmel*, auger (< "that which turns in boring"): WIMBLE. **4.** Suffixed zero-grade variant form **wib-ro-* in Latin *vibrāre*, to vibrate: VIBRATE. [Pok. *u̯eip-* 1131.]

weis-. To flow. **I. 1.** Germanic **wisōn-, waisōn-* in Old English *wāse*, mire, mud: OOZE². **2.** Taken by many as a derivative of this root, but probably an independent Indo-European word, is the suffixed form **wīs-o-* in Latin *vīrus*, slime, poison: VIRUS. **3.** Extended zero-grade form **wisk-* possibly in Latin *viscum*, mistletoe, birdlime: VISCID, VISCOUS. **II.** Attributed by some to this root, but more likely of obscure origin, are some Germanic words

for strong-smelling animals. **1.** Germanic **wisulōn-* in Old English *wesle, weosule*, weasel: WEASEL. **2.** Suffixed form **wis-onto-* in Germanic **wisand-, *wisunt-*, European bison (which emits a musky smell in the rutting season), in: **a.** Old High German *wisunt*, bison: WISENT; **b.** Latin *bisōn* (plural *bisontēs*), bison: BISON. [Pok. 3. *u̯eis-* 1134.]

weit(ə)-. To speak, adjudge. Extended o-grade form **woito-* in Russian *vĕtŭ*, council (see **sem-¹**).

wekti-. Thing, creature. Germanic **wihti-* in Old English *wiht*, person, thing: WIGHT¹; (AUGHT²), NAUGHT, NOT. [Pok. *u̯ek-ti-* 1136.]

wekʷ-. To speak. **1.** O-grade form **wŏkʷ-* in: **a.** Latin *vōx* (stem *vōc-*), voice: VOCAL, VOICE, VOWEL; EQUIVOCAL, UNIVOCAL; **b.** Greek *ops*, voice: CALLIOPE. **2.** Suffixed o-grade form **wokʷ-ā-* in Latin *vocāre*, to call: VOCABLE, VOCATION, VOUCH; ADVOCATE, AVOCATION, CONVOKE, EQUIVOCAL, EVOKE, INVOKE, PROVOKE, REVOKE. **3.** Suffixed form **wekʷ-es-* in Greek *epos*, song, word: EPIC, EPOS. [Pok. *u̯ekʷ-* 1135.]

wel-¹. To see. **1.** Suffixed zero-grade form **wl-id-* in Germanic **wlituz*, appearance, in Old Norse *litr*, appearance, color, dye, akin to the source of LITMUS. **2.** Suffixed form **wel-uno-* perhaps in Sanskrit *Varunaḥ*, "seer, wise one," sovereign god: VARUNA. [Pok. 1. *u̯el-* 1136.]

wel-². To wish, will. **1.** Germanic **wel-* in Old English *wel*, well (< "according to one's wish"): WELL². **2.** Germanic **welōn-* in Old English *wela, weola*, well-being, riches: WEAL¹, WEALTH. **3.** Germanic **wiljōn-* in Old English *willa*, desire, will power: WILL¹. **4.** Germanic **wil(l)jan* in Old English *wyllan, willan*, to desire: WILL²; NILL. **5.** Germanic compound **wil-kumōn-* (see **gʷā-**). **6.** O-grade form **wol-* in Germanic **wal-* in Old French *galoper* and Old North French *waloper*, to gallop: GALLOP, WALLOP. **7.** Basic form **wel-* in Latin *velle* (present stem *vol-*), to wish, will: VELLEITY, VOLITION, VOLUNTARY; BENEVOLENT, MALEVOLENT. **8.** Suffixed form **wel-up-* in Latin *voluptās*, pleasure: VOLUPTUARY, VOLUPTUOUS. [Pok. 2. *u̯el-* 1137.]

wel-³. To turn, roll; with derivatives referring to curved, enclosing objects. **1.** Germanic **walt-* in: **a.** Old High German *walzan*, to roll, waltz: WALTZ; **b.** Middle Dutch *welteren*, to roll: WELTER. **2.** Germanic **weluka-* in Old English *weoluc, weoloc*, mollusk (having a spiral shell), whelk: WHELK¹. **3.** Perhaps Germanic **wel-* in Old English *welig*, willow (with flexible twigs): WILLOW. **4.** Perhaps Germanic **welk-* in Old English *wealcan*, to roll, toss, and *wealcian*, to muffle up: WALK. **5.** O-grade form **wol-* in Germanic **wall-* in: **a.** Old English *wiella, wælla*, a well (< "rolling or bubbling water," "spring"): WELL¹; **b.** Old High German *wallōn*, to roam: GABERDINE. **6.** Perhaps suffixed o-grade form **wol-ā-* in Germanic **walō-* in: **a.** Old English *walu*, streak on the skin, weal, welt: WALE; **b.** Old High German **-walu*, a roll, round stem, in **wurzwalu*, rootstock (see **wrād-**). **7.** Extended form **welw-* in: **a.** Germanic **walwōn* in Old English *wealwian*, to roll (in mud): WALLOW; **b.** Latin *volvere*, to roll: VAULT¹, VAULT², (VOLT²), VOLUBLE, VOLUME, VOLUTE, VOLUTIN, VOLVOX, VOUSSOIR; CIRCUMVOLVE, CONVOLVE, DEVOLVE, EVOLVE, INVOLVE, OBVOLUTE, REVOLVE; **c.** suffixed o-grade form **wolw-ā-* in Latin *vulva, volva*, covering, womb: VOLVA, VULVA; **d.** suffixed zero-grade form **wl̥w-ā-* in Latin *valva*, leaf of a door (< "that which turns"): VALVE; **e.** suffixed form **welu-tro-* in Greek *elutron*, sheath, cover: ELYTRON. **8.** Suffixed form **wel-n-* in Greek *eilein* (< **welnein*), to turn: ILEUS; NEURILEMMA. **9.** Perhaps variant **wall-* in Latin *vallēs, vallis*, valley (< "that which is surrounded by hills"): VAIL¹, VALE¹, VALLEY. **10.** Suffixed form **wel-enā*, possibly identical with the Greek name *Helenē* (earliest form *Welenā*), Helen, in Greek *helenion*, elecampane: ELECAMPANE, INULIN. **11.** Suffixed form **wel-ik-* in Greek *helix*, spiral object: HELIX. **12.** Suffixed form **wel-mi-nth-* in Greek *helmis, helmins* (stem *helminth-*), parasitic worm:

HELMINTH; ANTHELMINTIC, PLATYHELMINTH. [Pok. 7. *u̯el-* 1140.]

wel-⁴. To tear, pull. **1.** Suffixed form **wel-do-* in Latin *vellere*, to tear, pull: AVULSE, CONVULSE, DIVULSION, EVULSION, REVULSION, SVELTE. **2.** Suffixed form **wel-no-* in Latin *vullis*, shaggy hair, wool: VELOURS, VELVET, VILLUS [Pok. 8. *u̯el-* 1144.]

wele-¹. Wool. Probably related to **wel-⁴**. **1.** Suffixed extended zero-grade form **wl̥ə-nā-* in: **a.** Germanic **wullō* in Old English *wul(l)*, wool: WOOL; **b.** Italic **wlānā* in Latin *lāna* (> French *laine*), wool, and its derivative *lānūgō*, down: LANATE; DELAINE, LANIFEROUS, LANOLIN, LANUGO; **c.** Celtic **wlanā* in Welsh *gwlan*, wool (> Middle English *flannel*, woolen cloth): FLANNEL. **2.** Possible suffixed o-grade form **wol(ə)-no-* in Greek *oulos*, wooly, curly: ULOTRICHOUS. [Pok. 4. *u̯el-* 1139.]

wele-². To strike, wound. **1.** Suffixed o-grade form **wol(ə)-o-* in Germanic **walaz* in Old Norse *valr*, the slain in battle in: **a.** Old Norse *Valhöll*, Valhalla: VALHALLA; **b.** Old Norse *Valkyrja*, "chooser of the slain," name of one of the twelve war goddesses (*-kyrja*, chooser; see **geus-**): VALKYRIE. **2.** Suffixed basic form **welə-nes-* in Latin *vulnus* (stem *vulner-*), a wound: VULNERABLE. [In Pok. 8. *u̯el-* 1144.]

welg-. Wet. Germanic **welk-* in: **a.** Old English *wolc(e)n*, cloud, sky: WELKIN; **b.** Middle English *welken*, to wilt: WILT¹. [Pok. 2. *u̯elk-*, *u̯elg-*, 1145.]

welt-. Woods; wild. **1.** Suffixed form **wolt-u-* in Germanic **walthuz* in: **a.** Old English *weald*, *wald*, a forest: WEALD, WOLD¹; **b.** Old Norse *völlr*, field: VOLE¹. **2.** Germanic **walthōn-* in Middle English *welde*, a plant yielding a yellow dye, weld: WELD². **3.** Germanic **wilthigaz* in: **a.** Old English *wilde*, wild: WILD; **b.** Old English *wildēor*, *wilddēor*, wild beast (*dēor*, animal; see **dheu-¹**): WILDERNESS; **c.** Dutch *wild*, wild: WILDEBEEST. [In Pok. 4. *u̯el-* 1139.]

weme-. To vomit. **1.** Germanic **wam-* in Old Norse *vamla*, qualm, and Danish *vamle*, to become sick, probably akin to the Scandinavian source of Middle English *wam(e)len*, to feel nausea, stagger: WAMBLE. **2.** Latin *vomere*, to vomit: NUX VOMICA, VOMIT. **3.** Greek *emein*, to vomit: EMESIS, EMETIC. [Pok. *u̯em-* 1146.]

wen-¹. To desire, strive for. **1.** Suffixed form **wen-w-* in Germanic **winn(w)an*, to seek to gain, in Old English *winnan*, to win: WIN¹. **2.** Suffixed zero-grade form **wn̥-yā* in Germanic **wunjō* in Old English *wynn*, *wen*, pleasure, joy: WEN²; WINSOME. **3.** Suffixed (stative) zero-grade form **wn̥-ē-*, to be contented, in Germanic **wunēn* in Old English *wunian*, to become accustomed to, dwell: WON¹, (WONT). **4.** Suffixed (causative) o-grade form **won-eyo-* in Germanic **wanjan* in Old English *wenian*, to accustom, train, wean: WEAN¹. **5.** Germanic **wēniz*, hope, with denominative **wēnjan*, to hope, in Old English *wēnan*, to expect, imagine, think: WEEN. **6.** Suffixed zero-grade form **wn̥-sko-* in Germanic **wunsk-* in Old English *wȳscan*, to desire, wish: WISH. **7.** O-grade form **won-* perhaps in Germanic **wani-* in: **a.** Old Norse *Vanir*, the Vanir: VANIR; **b.** Old Norse *vana-* in *Vanadís*, name of the goddess Freya: VANADIUM **8.** Suffixed form **wen-es-* in: **a.** Latin *venus*, love (> *venerārī*, to worship): VENERATE, VENEREAL, VENERY¹, VENUS; **b.** suffixed form **wen-es-no-* in Latin *venēnum*, love potion, poison: VENOM. **9.** Suffixed form **wen-eto-*, "beloved," possibly in Germanic **Weneda*, a Slavic people, in Old High German *Winida*, the Wends: WEND. **10.** Suffixed form **wen-yā* in Latin *venia*, favor, forgiveness: VENIAL. **11.** Lengthened-grade form **wēn-ā-* in Latin *vēnārī*, to hunt: VENATIC, VENERY², VENISON. **12.** Suffixed basic form **wen-o-* in Sanskrit *vanam*, forest: WANDEROO. **13.** Possibly zero-grade suffixed form **wn̥-ig-* in Sanskrit *vaṇik*, *vāṇijaḥ*, merchant (? < "seeking to gain"): BANIAN. [Pok. 1. *u̯en-* 1146.]

wen-². To beat, wound. **1.** Suffixed zero-grade form **wn̥-to-* in Germanic **wundaz* in Old English *wund*, a wound: WOUND¹. **2.** Suffixed o-grade form **won-yo-* in Germanic **wanja-*, a swelling, in Old English *wen(n)*, *wæn(n)*, wen: WEN¹. [In Pok. 1. *u̯ā-* 1108.]

wendh-. To turn, wind, weave. **1.** Germanic **windan*, to wind, in: **a.** Old English *windan*, to wind: WIND²; **b.** Old Norse *vinda*, to wind: WINDLASS. **2.** Germanic causative **wandjan* in: **a.** Old English *wendan*, to turn to: WEND; **b.** Dutch *wenden*, to turn: WENTLETRAP. **3.** Germanic **wandrōn*, to roam about, in: **a.** Old English *wandrian*, to wander: WANDER; **b.** German *wandern*, to wander: WANDERLUST. **4.** Germanic **wanduz* in Old Norse *vöndr*, a supple twig: WAND. **5.** Germanic **wandljaz*, "wanderer," perhaps in Latin *Vandalus*, a Vandal: VANDAL. [Pok. 1. *u̯endh-* 1148.]

weng-. To bend, curve. **1.** Germanic **wink-* in Old English *wincian*, to close the eyes (< "to bend down the eyelids"): WINK. **2.** Germanic **winkja* in Old English *wince*, a reel, roller: WINCH. **3.** Germanic **winkil-* in Old English *-wincel*, spiral shell: PERIWINKLE¹. **4.** Germanic **wankil-*, **wankul-* in: **a.** Old English *wancol*, youth, maid (< "inconstant one"): WENCH; **b.** Old English *wancol*, inconstant, unsteady: WONKY. **5.** Germanic **wankj-* in: **a.** Old French *gauchir*, to turn aside: GAUCHE; **b.** Anglo-Norman **wencir*, to turn aside, avoid (> Middle English *wincen*, to kick): WINCE. [Pok. *u̯e-n-g-* 1148.]

wep-. Bad, evil. From earlier **əwep-*. Suffixed zero-grade form **up-elo-* in Germanic **ubilaz*, evil, in Old English *yfel*, evil: EVIL.

[wēpnam. Weapon. Germanic root. **1.** Old English *wǣp(e)n*, weapon: WEAPON. **2.** Old Norse *vāpn* (plural *vāpn*), weapon: WAPENTAKE.]

wer-¹. High raised spot. **1.** Suffixed form **wer-d-* in Germanic **wartōn-* in Old English *wearte*, wart: WART. **2.** Possibly Germanic **war-* in obsolete Swedish *varbulde*, "pus swelling" (*bulde*, swelling; see **bhel-²**), akin to the source of WARBLE². **3.** Latin *varius* (genitive plural *variōrum*), spotty, speckled, changeable: (VAIR), VARIEGATE, (VARIETY), VARIOLA, VARIORUM, VARIOUS, VARY; (MINIVER). **4.** Latin *varix*, varicose vein: VARIX. **5.** Suffixed and extended zero-grade form **wr̥su-ko-* in Latin *verrūca*, a wart: VERRUCA. [Pok. 2. *u̯er-* 1151, 2. *u̯ā-* 1108.]

wer-². To raise, lift, hold suspended. Earlier form **əwer-*. **1.** Basic form **awer-* in Greek *aeirein*, to raise, and Greek *artēria*, windpipe, artery: AORTA, ARSIS, ARTERIO-, ARTERIOLE, ARTERY. **2.** Possibly referred to root (obscure basic form **āwer-*) is Greek *aēr* (> Latin *aer* > Italian *aria*), air: AERIAL AERO-, AIR, ARIA, MALARIA. **3.** Related to Greek *aēr*, air, is Greek *aura* (< zero-grade form **aur-*), breath, vapor: AURA. [Pok. 1. *u̯er-* 1151.]

wer-³. Conventional base of various Indo-European roots; to turn, bend. **I.** Root **wert-*, to turn, wind. **1.** Germanic **werth-* in: **a.** Germanic variant **warth-* in (i) Old English *-weard*, toward (< "turned toward"): -WARD (ii) Germanic **inwarth*, inward (**in*, in; see **en**) in Old English *inweard*, inward: INWARD; **b.** perhaps Germanic derivative **werthaz*, "toward, opposite," hence "equivalent, worth," in Old English *weorth*, worth, valuable, and derivative noun *weorth*, *wierth*, value: WORTH¹; STALWART. **2.** Germanic **werthan*, to become (< "to turn into"), in Old English *weorthan*, to befall: WORTH². **3.** Zero-grade form **wr̥t* in Germanic **wurth-* in Old English *wyrd*, fate, destiny (< "that which befalls one"): WEIRD. **4.** Latin *vertere*, to turn, with its frequentative *versāre*, to turn, and passive *versārī*, to stay, behave (< "to move around a place, frequent"): VERSATILE, VERSE¹, VERSION, VERSUS, VERTEBRA, VERTEX, VERTIGO, VORTEX; ADVERSE, ANNIVERSARY, AVERT, BOULEVERSEMENT, CONTROVERSY, (CONVERSE¹), CONVERT, DEXTRORSE, DIVERT, EVERT, (EXTROVERSION), EXTROVERT, INTRORSE, INTROVERT, INVERT, MALVERSATION, OBVERT, PERVERT, PROSE, RETRORSE, REVERT, SINIS-

TRORSE, SUBVERT, TERGIVERSATE, TRANSVERSE, UNI-VERSE. **5.** Balto-Slavic *wirstā-, a turn, bend, in Russian *versta,* line: VERST. **II.** Root *weit-, to turn. Germanic *wrīth-, *wraith- in: **a.** Old English *writha,* band (< "that which is wound around"): WREATH; **b.** Old English *wrīthan,* to twist, torture: WRITHE; **c.** Old English *wrāth,* angry (< "tormented, twisted"): WRATH, WROTH. **III.** Root *wergh-, to turn. **1.** Germanic *wurgjan in Old English *wyrgan,* to strangle: WORRY. **2.** Nasalized variant *wrengh- in: **a.** Germanic *wreng- in Old English *wringan,* to twist: WRING; **b.** Germanic *wrang- in *(i)* Old Norse *vrangr, rangr,* curved, crooked, wrong, akin to the Scandinavian source of Middle English *wrong,* wrong: WRONG *(ii)* Low German *wrangeln,* to wrestle, akin to the Low German source of Middle English *wranglen,* to wrangle: WRANGLE. **IV.** Root *werg-, to turn. Nasalized variant form *wreng- in Germanic *wrankjan in: **a.** Old English *wrencan,* to twist: WRENCH; **b.** Old English *gewrinclian,* to wind (*ge-,* collective prefix; see **kom**): WRINKLE. **2.** Latin *vergere,* to turn, tend toward: VERGE²; CONVERGE, DIVERGE. **V.** Root *wreik-, to turn. **1.** Germanic *wrīg- in: **a.** Old English *wrīgian,* to turn, bend, go: WRY; **b.** Middle Low German *wriggeln,* to wriggle: WRIGGLE. **2.** Germanic *wrihst- whence *wristiz in Old English *wrist,* wrist: WRIST. **3.** Secondary Germanic derivative *wraistjan in Old English *wrǣstan,* to twist, with its frequentative *wrǣstlian,* to wrestle: WREST, WRESTLE. **4.** Possibly o-grade form *wroik- in Gaulish *brūko, heather (> French *bruyère,* heath): BRIAR¹. **VI.** Germanic root *wrib- in Old French *riber,* to be wanton: RIBALD. **VII.** Root *werb-, also *werbh-, to turn, bend. **1.** Germanic *werp-, *warp-, "to fling by turning the arm," in Old English *weorpan,* to throw away: WARP. **2.** Latin *verber,* whip, rod: REVERBERATE. **3.** Latin *verbēna,* sacred foliage: VERBENA, (VERVAIN). **4.** Zero-grade form *wṛb- in Greek *rhabdos,* rod: RHABDOMANCY, RHABDOVIRUS. **5.** Nasalized variant form *wrembh- in Greek *rhombos,* magic wheel, rhombus: RHOMBUS. **VIII.** Root *werp-, to turn, wind. **1.** Metathesized form *wrep- in Germanic *wrap- in Danish dialectal *vravle,* to wind, akin to the source of Middle English *wrappen,* to wrap: WRAP. **2.** Zero-grade form *wṛp- in Greek *rhaptein,* to sew (> *rhaphē,* suture): RAPHE, RAPHIDE; RHAPSODY, STAPHYLORRHAPHY, TENORRHAPHY. **IX.** Root *wṛmi-, worm; rhyme word to **kʷṛmi-. 1.** Germanic *wurmiz in Old English *wyrm,* worm: WORM. **2.** Latin *vermis,* worm: VERMEIL, VERMI-, VERMICELLI, VERMICULAR, VERMIN. [Pok. 3. u̯er- 1152.]

wer-⁴. To perceive, watch out for. **I.** O-grade form *wor-. **1.** Suffixed form *wor-o- in Germanic *waraz in: **a.** Old English *wær,* watchful: WARY; **b.** Old English *gewær,* aware (*ge-,* collective and intensive prefix; see **kom**): AWARE; **c.** Old English *warian,* to beware: WARE². **2.** Suffixed form *wor-to- in Germanic *wardaz, guard, and *wardōn, to guard, in: **a.** *(i)* Old English *weard,* a watching, keeper: WARD; STEWARD *(ii)* Old English *weardian,* to ward, guard: WARDER²; **b.** Old North French *warder,* to guard: WARDEN; REWARD, WARDROBE; **c.** Old French *guarder,* to guard: GUARD; **d.** Anglo-Norman *warde,* guard: REARWARD². **3.** Germanic *warō in: **a.** Old English *waru,* goods, protection, guard: WARE¹; **b.** Old English *-ware* (probably plural of *waru,* "goods"), inhabitants (< "defenders"): FIELDFARE. **4.** Suffixed form *wor-wo- in Greek *ouros,* a guard: ARCTURUS. **5.** Variant *(s)wor-, s(w)or- probably in Greek *horan,* to see: EPHOR, PANORAMA. **II.** Suffixed (stative) form *wer-ē- in Latin *verērī,* to respect, feel awe for: REVERE¹. [Pok. 8. u̯er- 1164.]

wer-⁵. To cover. **I.** Basic form *wer-. **1.** Germanic *werjōn- in Old English *wer,* dam, fish trap: WEIR. **2.** Compound form *ap-wer-yo- (*ap-, off, away; see **apo-**) in Latin *aperīre,* to open, uncover: APERIENT, APERITIF, APERTURE; OVERT, OVERTURE, PERT. **3.** Compound form

*op-wer-yo- (*op-, over; see **epi**) in Latin *operīre,* to cover: COVER, OPERCULUM. **II.** O-grade form *wor-. **1.** Germanic *war-nōn in Old English *war(e)nian,* to take heed: WARN. **2.** Germanic *war- in: **a.** *(i)* Old French *garant,* warrant, authorization: GUARANTY *(ii)* Old North French *warant,* warrant, and *warantir,* to guarantee: WARRANT, (WARRANTEE), WARRANTY; **b.** Old French *garer,* to guard, protect: GARAGE; **c.** Old French *g(u)arir,* to defend, protect: GARRET, GARRISON; **d.** Old North French *warenne,* enclosure, game preserve: WARREN; **e.** Old French *g(u)arnir,* to equip: GARMENT, GARNISH. [Pok. 5. u̯er- 1160.]

wer-⁶. Also **were-**. To speak. Variant *wrē-, contracted from *wreə-. **1.** Suffixed zero-grade form *wṛ-dho- in Germanic *wurdam in Old English *word,* word: WORD. **2.** Suffixed form *wer-dho- in Latin *verbum,* word: VERB, VERVE; ADVERB, PROVERB. **3.** Suffixed form *wer-yo- in Greek *eirein,* to say, speak: IRONY. **4.** Variant form *wrē in suffixed form *wrē-tor- in Greek *rhētōr,* public speaker: RHETOR. [Pok. 6. u̯er- 1162.]

wer-⁷. To burn. Suffixed lengthened o-grade (causative) form *wōr-yo- in Russian *varit',* to boil: SAMOVAR. [Pok. 12. u̯er- 1166.]

wer-⁸. Squirrel. Reduplicated expressive form *wī-wer(r)- in Latin *vīverra,* a ferret: VIVERRINE. [Pok. 13. u̯er- 1166.]

wēr-. Water. Suffixed zero-grade form *ūr-īnā- in Latin *ūrīna,* urine: URINE. [In Pok. 9. au̯(e)- 78.]

werə-¹. Wide, broad. Suffixed form *wer(ə)-u- metathesized in Greek *eurus,* wide: EURY-; ANEURYSM, EURYDICE. [Pok. 8. u̯er- 1165.]

werə-². To find. Variant *wrē-, contracted from *wreə-. Reduplicated form *we-wrē- in Greek *heuriskein* (first person singular perfect indicative active *heurēka*), to find: EUREKA, HEURISTIC. [Pok. 4. u̯er- 1160.]

werg-. To do. **I.** Suffixed form *werg-o-. **1.** Germanic *werkam, work, in: **a.** Old English *weorc, werc,* work: WORK; **b.** Old High German *werc,* work: (BOULEVARD), BULWARK. **2.** Greek *ergon,* work, action: ERG, -URGY; ADRENERGIC, ALLERGY, ARGON, CHOLINERGIC, DEMIURGE, DRAMATURGE, ENDERGONIC, ENDOERGIC, ENERGY, ERGOGRAPH, EXERGONIC, EXERGUE, EXOERGIC, GEORGIC, LITURGY, METALLURGY, SURGERY, (SYNERGID), SYNERGISM, THAUMATURGE. **II.** Zero-grade form *wṛg-. **1.** Suffixed forms *wṛg-yo-, *wṛg-to- in Germanic *wurkjan, to work, participle *wurhta-, in Old English *wyrcan,* to work, participle *geworht,* wrought: WROUGHT. **2.** Suffixed form *wṛg-t- in Germanic *wurhtjō- in Old English *wryhta,* maker, wright: WRIGHT. **III.** O-grade form *worg- in: **a.** Greek *organon* (with suffix *-ano-*), tool: ORGAN, ORGANON; **b.** Greek *orgia,* secret rites, worship (< "service"): ORGY. [Pok. 2. u̯erg- 1168.]

wēro-. True. **1.** Germanic *wēra- in Old English *wǣr,* faith, pledge: WARLOCK. **2.** Latin *vērus* (> Old French *voir,* truth), true, with its derivative *vērax,* truth: VERACIOUS, VERISM, VERITY, VERY; AVER, VERDICT, VERIDICAL, VERIFY, VERISIMILAR, VOIR DIRE. **3.** Latin *sevērus,* grave, serious; regarded by some as a compound of *se-, sed,* without (see **s(w)e-**), and *vērus,* true, but the semantic difficulties make this explanation improbable: SEVERE; ASSEVERATE, PERSEVERE. [Pok. 11. u̯er- 1165.]

wers-¹. To confuse, mix up. Compare **ers-¹. I.** Suffixed basic form. **1.** Germanic *werz-a-, whence *werra- in: **a.** Old North French *werre,* war: WAR; **b.** Spanish *guerra,* war: GUERRILLA. **2.** Germanic comparative *wers-izōn- in Old English *wyrsa,* worse: WORSE. **3.** Germanic superlative *wers-istaz in Old English *wyrsta,* worst: WORST. **II.** Suffixed zero-grade form *wṛs-ti- in Germanic *wursti- in Old High German *wurst* (> German *Wurst*), sausage (< "mixture"): WURST; (LIVERWURST). [Pok. u̯ers- 1169.]

wers-². To be wet. Compare **ers-². Suffixed o-grade (causative) form *wors-eyo- in Greek *ourein,* "to make water," to urinate, whence *ouron,* urine: URETER, URE-

THRA, URETIC, -URIA, URO-¹, URONIC; DIURETIC, ENURE-
SIS. [In Pok. 9. *au̯(e)- 78.*]

wes-¹. To buy. **1.** Suffixed form *wes-no-* in Latin *vēnum,*
sale: VENAL, VEND. **2.** Suffixed o-grade form *wos-nā-* in
Greek *ōneisthai,* to buy: DUOPSONY. [Pok. 8. *u̯es- 1173.*]

wes-². Wet. Germanic *wōs-* in Old English *wōs,* juice:
OOZE¹. [Pok. 3. *u̯es- 1171.*]

wes-³. To stay, dwell, pass the night, with derivatives
meaning "to be." **1.** O-grade form *wos-* in Germanic
was- in Old English *wæs,* was: WAS. **2.** Lengthened-grade form *wēs-* in Germanic *wēz-* in Old English
wǣre (subjunctive), *wǣron* (plural), were: WERE. **3.** Germanic *wesan* in Old Norse *vesa, vera,* to be: WASSAIL.
4. Suffixed form *wes-tā-* perhaps in Latin *Vesta,* household goddess: VESTA. **5.** Suffixed variant form *was-tu-*
possibly in Greek *astu,* town (< "place where one
dwells"), whence Latin *astus,* skill, craft (practiced in a
town): ASTUTE. [Pok. 1. *u̯es- 1170.*]

wes-⁴. To clothe. Extension of **eu-¹.** **1.** Suffixed o-grade
form *wos-eyo-* in Germanic *wazjan* in Old English
werian, to wear, carry: WEAR¹. **2.** Suffixed form *wes-ti-*
in Latin *vestis,* garment: VEST; DEVEST, INVEST, REVEST,
TRAVESTY. **3.** Suffixed form *wes-nu-* in Greek *hennunai,*
to clothe: HIMATION. [Pok. 5. *u̯es- 1172.*]

wes-pero-. Evening, night. **I.** Reduced form *wes-.*
1. Suffixed form *wes-to-* in Germanic *west-* in: **a.** Old
English *west,* west: WEST; **b.** Old English *westerne,*
western: WESTERN; **c.** Old English *westra,* more west-
erly: WESTERLY. **2.** Possibly Germanic *wis-* in Late
Latin *Visigothi,* "West Goths" (*Gothi,* the Goths): VISI-
GOTH. **II.** Basic form *wespero-.* **1.** Latin *vesper,* evening:
VESPER, VESPERTILIONID. **2.** Greek *hesperos,* evening:
HESPERIAN. [Pok. *u̯esperos 1173.*]

wesr̥. Spring. Latin *vēr,* spring (phonologically irregular):
VERNAL; PRIMAVERA. [Pok. *u̯es-r̥ 1174.*]

wet-¹. To blow, inspire, spiritually arouse. Related to **wē-.**
1. Lengthened-grade form *wōt-* in Germanic suffixed
form *wōd-eno-, wōd-ono-,* "raging," "mad," "inspired,"
hence "spirit," name of the chief Teutonic god, in: **a.** Old
English *Wōden,* Woden: WODEN; **b.** Old English *Wōd-
nesdæg,* "Woden's day": WEDNESDAY; **c.** Old Norse
Ôdhinn, Odin: ODIN; **d.** Old High German *Wuotan* (>
German *Wotan*), Wotan: WOTAN. **2.** Lengthened variant
form *wāt-* in Latin *vātēs,* prophet, poet: VATIC. **3.** Suffixed variant form *wat-no-* in Latin *vannus,* a winnow-
ing fan: FAN¹, VAN³. **4.** Oldest basic form *awet-* becoming
awet- in suffixed form *awet-mo-* in Greek *atmos* (<
aetmos), breath, vapor: ATMOSPHERE. [Pok. *u̯āt- 1113.*]

wet-². Year. **1.** Suffixed form *wet-ru-* in Germanic *weth-
ruz,* perhaps "yearling," in Old English *wether,* wether:
WETHER. **2.** Suffixed form *wet-es-* in: **a.** Latin *vetus,* old
(< "having many years"): VETERAN; INVETERATE;
b. Latin *veterīnus,* of beasts of burden, of cattle (perhaps
chiefly old cattle): VETERINARY; **c.** Greek *etos,* year:
ETESIAN. **3.** Suffixed form *wet-olo-* in Latin *vitulus,* calf,
yearling: VEAL, VITELLUS. [Pok. *u̯et- 1175.*]

wi-. Apart, in half. **1.** Suffixed form *wi-itos* in Germanic
wīdaz in Old English *wīd,* wide (< "far apart"): WIDE.
2. Suffixed (comparative) form *wi-tero-* in Germanic
withrō, against, in: **a.** Old English *wither,* against, with
its derivative *with,* with, against: WITH, WITHERS; **b.** Old
High German *widar,* against: GUERDON; WITHERSHINS.
[Pok. 1. *u̯ī- 1175.*]

widhu-. Tree. Germanic *widu-* in Old English *wudu,*
wood: WOOD. [Pok. *u̯idhu- 1177.*]

wīkm̥tī. Twenty. Compound of **wi-,** in half, hence two,
and *(d)km̥t-ī* (nominative dual), decade, reduced
zero-grade form of **dekm̥.** **1.** Latin *vīgintī,* twenty: VICE-
NARY, VIGESIMAL. **2.** Greek *eikosi,* twenty: ICOSAHE-
DRON. **3.** Sanskrit *viṃśatiḥ,* twenty: PACHISI. [Pok.
u̯ī-km̥t-ī 1177.]

wī-ro-. Man. Derivative of **weie-².** **1.** Germanic shortened
from *wiraz* becoming *weraz* in: **a.** Old English *wer,*
man: WEREWOLF, WERGELD; **b.** Germanic compound

wer-ald-, "life or age of man" (*-ald-,* age; see **al-³**), in
Old English *weorold,* world: WORLD; **c.** Frankish *wer-
wulf,* "man-wolf" (*wulf,* wolf; see **wl̥kʷo-**), in French
garou, werewolf: LOUP-GAROU. **2.** Latin *vir,* man: VI-
RAGO, VIRILE, VIRTUE, (VIRTUOSA), (VIRTUOSO); DECEM-
VIR, DUUMVIR, TRIUMVIR. **3.** Possibly Latin *cūria,* curia,
court, if regarded as from *co-vir,* "men together" (*co-,*
together; see **kom**): CURIA. [Pok. *u̯īro-s 1177.*]

wleik-. To flow, run. Zero-grade form *wlik-.* **1.** Adjective
wlik-u-, wet, in: **a.** suffixed form *wlik-w-ā-* in Latin
liquāre, to dissolve: LIQUATE; **b.** suffixed form *wlik-w-ē-*
in Latin *liquēre,* to be liquid: LIQUESCENT, LIQUID,
LIQUOR; DELIQUESCE, LIQUEFY. **2.** Suffixed form *wlik-s-*
in: **a.** Latin *lixa,* lye: LIXIVIATE; **b.** Latin *prōlixus,*
poured forth, stretched out in front, extended (*prō-,*
forth; see **per¹**): PROLIX. [In Pok. *leiku̯- 669.*]

wl̥kʷo-. Wolf. **1.** Germanic *wulfaz* in: **a.** Old English
wulf, wolf: WOLF; **b.** Middle Dutch *wolf, wulf,* wolf:
AARDWOLF; **c.** Old High German *wolf,* wolf, in German
Wolfram, tungsten: WOLFRAM; **d.** Frankish *wulf,* wolf
(see **wī-ro-**). **2.** Taboo variant *lupo-* in Latin *lupus,* wolf:
LOBO, LUPINE¹, LUPINE²; LOUP-GAROU. **3.** Taboo variant
lukʷo- in: **a.** Greek *lukos,* wolf: LYCANTHROPE, LYCOPO-
DIUM; **b.** Suffixed form *lukʷ-ya* in Greek *lussa,* martial
rage, madness, rabies ("wolf-ness"): LYTTA; ALYSSUM.
[Pok. *u̯l̥kʷos 1178.*]

wl̥p-ē-. Fox. **1.** Latin *vulpēs,* fox: VULPINE. **2.** Taboo
variant *əlōpĕk-* in Greek *alōpēx,* fox: ALOPECIA. [Pok.
u̯l̥p-, lup- 1179.]

wogʷh-ni-. Plowshare, wedge. **1.** Probably Germanic
wagjaz in Old English *wecg,* wedge: WEDGE. **2.** Probably Latin *vōmer,* plowshare: VOMER. [Pok. *u̯ogʷhni-s
1179.*]

wokso-. Wax. Related to **weg-¹.** Germanic *wahsam* in
Old English *wæx, weax,* wax: WAX¹. [Pok. *u̯okso- 1180.*]

wopsā. Wasp. Metathesized form *wospā.* **1.** Germanic
wosp- in Old English *wæsp, wæps,* wasp: WASP. **2.** Latin
vespa, wasp: VESPIARY. [Pok. *u̯obhsā 1179.*]

wōs. You (plural). Latin *vōs* (> Old French *vous*), you:
RENDEZVOUS. [In Pok. 1. *iu- 513.*]

wrād-. Branch, root. **I.** Basic form *wrād-* in Germanic
wrōt- in Old Norse *rōt,* root: ROOT¹; RUTABAGA.
II. Zero-grade form *wrəd-.* **1.** Germanic *wurtiz* in:
a. Old English *wyrt,* plant, herb: WORT; **b.** German
Wurzel (< *wurzwala,* rootstock; *-wala,* a roll, round
stem; see **wel-³**), root: MANGELWURZEL. **2.** Latin *rādix,*
root: RACE³, RADICAL, RADICLE, RADISH, RADIX; DERACI-
NATE, ERADICATE. **3.** Suffixed form *wrəd-mo-* in Latin
rāmus, branch: RAMOSE, RAMUS; RAMIFY. **4.** Suffixed
reduced form *wr(ə)d-ya* perhaps in Greek *rhiza,* root:
RHIZO-, RHIZOME; COLEORHIZA, LICORICE, MYCORRHIZA.
[Pok. *u̯(e)rād- 1167.*]

wrāgh-. Thorn, tip. Greek *rhakhis,* ridge, spine: RACHIS.
[Pok. 1. *u̯rāgh- 1180.*]

wreg-. To push, shove, drive, track down. **I.** Basic form
wreg- in Germanic *wrekan* in: **a.** Old English *wrecan,*
to drive, expel: WREAK; **b.** Old Norse *rek* (older form
vrek), wreckage, akin to the Scandinavian source of
Anglo-Norman *wrec,* wreck: WRECK. **II.** O-grade form
wrog-. **1.** Germanic *wrakjōn-,* "pursuer, one pursued,"
in: **a.** Old English *wrecca,* exile: WRETCH; **b.** Frankish
wrakjō, "one pursued, an exile," perhaps in French
garce, a girl: GASKET. **2.** Germanic *wrakaz* in: **a.** Old
English *wræc,* exile, punishment, and Middle Dutch
wrak, wreckage: WRACK¹; **b.** Swedish *rak,* wreckage, akin
to the source of Middle English *rak,* mass of driven
clouds: RACK³. **III.** Zero-grade form *wr̥g-eyo-, *urg-eyo-*
in Latin *urgēre,* to urge, drive: URGE. [Pok. *u̯reg- 1181.*]

wrēg-. To break. Suffixed form *wrēg-nu-* in Greek
rhēgnunai, to burst forth: -RRHAGIA. [Pok. *u̯rēg- 1181.*]

[wrod-. Rose. A word (not common Indo-European) of
unknown origin. **1.** Suffixed form *wrod-o-* in Greek
rhodon, rose: RHODO-; (RHODIUM). **2.** Suffixed form
wrod-ya- (perhaps via Etruscan) in Latin *rosa,* rose:

ROSE¹. **3.** Zero-grade form *wṛd- in Iranian *wṛd in Persian *gul*, rose: JULEP.]

wrōd-. To root, gnaw. Germanic *wrōt- in Old English *wrōtan*, to dig up: ROOT². [Pok. 7. u̯er- 1163.]

wrōdh-. To grow straight, upright. Suffixed zero-grade form *wṛdh-wo- in Greek *orthos*, straight, correct, right: ORTHO-, ORTHOTICS; ANORTHITE. [In Pok. u̯erdh- 1167.]

wrōg-. To burgeon, swell with strength. Suffixed zero-grade form *wṛg-ā- in Greek *organ*, to swell: ORGASM. [Pok. 3. u̯erg- 1169.]

wrughyo-. Rye. Germanic *rugi- in Old English *ryge*, rye: RYE¹. [Pok. u̯rughi̯o- 1183.]

[**xenos.** Strange; stranger. Greek word (earlier form *xenwos) of uncertain origin and formation; the initial *x*- may be the zero-grade form *ghs- of *ghos- (see **ghos-ti-**): XENO-; EUXENITE, PYROXENE.]

yā-. To be aroused. Suffixed form *yā-lo- in Greek *zēlos*, zeal: JEALOUS, ZEAL. [Pok. i̯ā- 501.]

yag-. To worship; reverence. Suffixed form *yag-yo- perhaps in Greek *hagios*, holy: HAGIO-. [Pok. i̯ag- 501.]

yē-. To throw. Contracted from *yeə-. **1.** Extended zero-grade forms *yak-yo- in Latin *jacere*, to throw, lay, and *yak-ē- (stative) in *jacēre*, to lie down (< "to be thrown"), and *jaculum*, dart: JESS, JET², JOIST; ABJECT, ADJACENT, ADJECTIVE, AMICE, CONJECTURE, DEJECT, (EASE), EJACULATE, EJECT, GIST, INJECT, INTERJECT, OBJECT¹, PARGET, PROJECT, REJECT, SUBJACENT, SUBJECT, SUPERJACENT, TRAJECT. **2.** Basic form *yē- and zero-grade form *yə- in Greek *hienai*, to send, throw: CATHETER, DIESIS, ENEMA, PARESIS, SYNESIS. [Pok. i̯ē- 502.]

yeg-. Ice. Germanic *jakilaz, *jekilaz, in Old English *gicel*, icicle, ice: ICICLE. [Pok. i̯eg- 503.]

yēgʷā-. Power, youthful strength. Greek *hēbē*, youth, youthful vigor: HEBE; EPHEBE, HEBEPHRENIA. [Pok. i̯ēgʷā 503.]

yek-. To speak. Suffixed o-grade form *yok-o- in Latin *jocus*, joke: JEWEL, JOCOSE, JOCULAR, JOKE, JUGGLE, (JUGGLER); JEOPARDY. [Pok. i̯ek- 503.]

yēk-. To heal. Possible suffixed zero-grade form *yək-es- in Greek *akos*, cure: AUTACOID, PANACEA. [Pok. i̯ek- 504.]

yēkʷṛ. Liver. Greek *hēpar*, liver: HEPATIC, HEPATO-; HEPARIN, (HEPATITIS), (HEPATOGENIC). [Pok. i̯ekʷ-ṛt 504.]

yem-. To pair. Perhaps altered into Latin *geminus*, twin, paired: GEMINATE, GEMINI, GIMMAL; BIGEMINAL, TRIGEMINUS. [Pok. i̯em- 505.]

yēr-. Year, season. **1.** Suffixed basic form *yēr-o- in Germanic *jēram in Old English *gēar*, year: YEAR. **2.** Suffixed o-grade form *yōr-ā- in Greek *hōrā*, season: HOUR; HOROLOGE, HOROLOGY, HOROSCOPE. [In Pok. 1. ei- 293.]

yes-. To boil, foam, bubble. **1.** Germanic *jest- in Old English *gist*, yeast: YEAST. **2.** Greek *zeein, zein*, to boil: ECZEMA, ZEOLITE. [Pok. i̯es- 506.]

yeu-. Vital force, youthful vigor. Earliest form *əyeu-; variant of **aiw-.** Suffixed zero-grade form *yuwen- (< *yu-əen-), "possessing youthful vigor," young. **1.** Further suffixed form *yuwṇ-ti- in Germanic *jugunthi-, *jugunthā- in Old English *geoguth*, youth: YOUTH. **2.** Further suffixed form *yuwṇ-ko- in: **a.** Germanic *juwungaz becoming *jungaz in (i) Old English *geong*, young: YOUNG (ii) Old High German *jung*, young: JUNKER (iii) compound *jung-frōwō-, young lady (see **per¹**); **b.** Old Irish *ōac*, Irish Gaelic *ōg*, in *oglach*, soldier: GALLOWGLASS. **3.** Latin *iuvenis*, young: JUNIOR, JUVENILE; JUVENOCRACY, REJUVENATE. [Pok. 3. i̯eu- 510.]

yeudh-. To move violently, fight. Zero-grade form *yudh-ē- in Latin *jubēre*, to command (< "to set in motion"): JUSSIVE. [Pok. i̯eu-dh- 511.]

yeuə-. To blend, mix food. Zero-grade form *yū- (< *yuə-) in: **a.** Suffixed form *yū-s- in Latin *jūs*, juice, broth: JUICE; **b.** suffixed form *yūs-mā in Greek *zumē*, leaven: -ZYME, ZYMO-; ENZYME. [Pok. 1. i̯eu- 507.]

yeug-. To join. **I.** Zero-grade form *yug-. **1.** Suffixed form *yug-o- in: **a.** Germanic *yukam in Old English *geoc*, yoke: YOKE; **b.** Latin *jugum*, yoke: JUGATE, JUGULAR, JUGUM; CONJUGATE, SUBJUGATE; **c.** Greek *zugon*, yoke, and *zugoun*, to join: ZYGO-, ZYGOMA, -ZYGOUS; (AZYGOUS), SYZYGY; **d.** Sanskrit *yugam*, yoke: YUGA. **2.** Suffixed (superlative) form *yug-istos in Latin *jugistā (viā), "on a nearby (road)," contracted to *juxtā*, close by: JOUST; ADJUST, JUXTAPOSE, (JUXTAPOSITION). **3.** Nasalized form *yu-n-g- in Latin *jungere*, to join: JOIN, JUNCTION, JUNCTURE, JUNTA; ADJOIN, CONJOIN, (CONJUGAL), (CONJUNCT), ENJOIN, INJUNCTION, SUBJOIN. **II.** Suffixed form *yeug-mn̥ in Greek *zeugma*, a bond: ZEUGMA. **III.** Suffixed o-grade form *youg-o- in Sanskrit *yogah̥*, union: YOGA. [Pok. 2. i̯eu- 508.]

yewes-. Law. **1.** Latin *jūs*, law, and its derivative *jūrāre*, "to pronounce a ritual formula," swear: JURAL, JURIST, JURY¹; ABJURE, ADJURE, CONJURE, INJURY, JURIDICAL, JURISCONSULT, JURISDICTION, JURISPRUDENCE, (NONJUROR), OBJURGATE, PERJURE. **2.** Compound form *yewes-dik-, "one who shows or pronounces the law" (see **deik-**), in Latin *jūdex*, judge: JUDGE; ADJUDICATE, PREJUDICE. **3.** Suffixed form *yewes-to- in Latin *jūstus*, just: JUST¹. [Pok. i̯eu̯os 512.]

yewo-. Grain. Suffixed form *yew-ya in Greek *zeia*, one-seeded wheat: ZEIN. [Pok. i̯eu̯o- 512.]

yōs-. To gird. **1.** Suffixed form *yōs-ter- in Greek *zōstēr*, girdle: ZOSTER. **2.** Suffixed form *yōs-nā in Greek *zōnē*, girdle: ZONE; EVZONE. [Pok. i̯ō(u)s- 513.]

yu-¹. You. Second person (plural) pronoun. Germanic *jūz (nominative) and *iwwiz (oblique) in Old English *gē* and *ēow*, you: YE², YOU. [Pok. 1. i̯u- 513.]

yu-². Outcry (of exultation). **1.** Latin *jūbilāre*, to raise a shout of joy: JUBILATE. **2.** Greek *iuzein*, to cry, call: JINX. [Pok. 2. i̯u- 514.]

Index

A

AMATIVE **amma**	-ANDRY **ner-²**	ANTITYPE **(s)teu-**	ARCHON **arkhein**
AMATORY **amma**	ANECDOTE **dō-**	ANTLIA **an-²**	-ARCHY **arkhein**
AMAZON **magh-²**	ANELE **elaia**	ANTONOMASIA **nō-men-**	ARCIFORM **arku-**
AMBAGE **ag-**	ANEMO- **ane-**	ANURAN **ors-**	ARCTIC **r̥tko-**
AMBASSADOR **ag-**	ANEROID **newo-**	ANUS **āno-**	ARCTURUS **r̥tko-, wer-⁴**
AMBERGRIS **gher-³**	ANESTHESIA **au-⁵**	ANVIL **pel-⁶**	ARCUATE **arku-**
AMBI- **ambhi**	ANEURYSM **were-¹**	ANXIOUS **angh-**	ARDENT **as-**
AMBIDEXTROUS **deks-**	ANFRACTUOUS **bhreg-**	ANY **oi-no-**	ARDOR **as-**
AMBIENT **ei-¹**	ANGARY **angelos**	AORTA **wer-²**	ARDUOUS **ered-**
AMBIGUOUS **ag-**	ANGEL **angelos**	APERIENT **wer-⁵**	ARE¹ **er-¹**
AMBITION **ei-¹**	ANGELIC **angelos**	APERITIF **wer-⁵**	ARGAL² **reg-¹**
AMBLYGONITE **genu-¹, mel-¹**	ANGELICA **angelos**	APERTURE **wer-⁵**	ARGENT **arg-**
AMBLYOPIA **mel-¹**	ÁNGELUS **angelos**	APEX **ap-¹**	ARGIL **arg-**
AMBROSIA **mer-²**	ANGER **angh-**	APHELION **sāwel-**	ARGININE **arg-**
AMBSACE **ambhō**	ANGINA **angh-**	APHONIA **bhā-²**	ARGON **werg-**
AMBULATE **al-²**	ANGLE¹ **ank-**	APLANATIC **pele-²**	ARGONAUT **nāu-²**
AMBUSCADE **busk-**	ANGLE² **ank-**	APLOMB **plumbum**	ARGUE **arg-**
AMBUSH **busk-**	ÁNGLE **ank-**	APNEA **pneu-**	ARHAT **algʷh-**
AMELIORATE **mel-⁴**	ANGST **apo-**	APO- **apo-**	ARIA **wer-²**
AMENABLE **men-²**	ANGUILLIFORM **angʷhi-**	APOCALYPSE **kel-²**	ARID **as-**
AMEND **mend-**	ANGUINE **angʷhi-**	APOCOPE **skep-**	ARIES **er-³**
AMENORRHEA **mē-²**	ANGUISH **angh-**	APOCRINE **krei-**	ARISE **rīsan**
AMENT¹ **ap-¹**	ANHYDROUS **wed-¹**	APOCRYPHA **krāu-**	ARISTOCRACY **ar-**
AMENT² **men-¹**	ANIL **nei-**	APODAL **ped-¹**	ARITHMETIC **ar-**
AMETHYST **medhu-**	ANILE **an-¹**	APODICTIC **deik-**	ARK **arek-**
AMIANTHUS **mai-²**	ANILINGUS **āno-, leigh-**	APODOSIS **dō-**	ARM¹ **ar-**
AMICABLE **amma**	ANIMA **ane-**	APOGEE **gē**	ARM² **ar-**
AMICE **yē-**	ANIMADVERT **ane-**	APOLOGUE **leg-¹**	ARMADILLO **ar-**
AMID **medhyo-**	ANIMAL **ane-**	APOLOGY **leg-¹**	ARMATURE **ar-**
AMIGO **amma**	ANIMATE **ane-**	APOMIXIS **meik-**	ARMIGER **gerere**
AMISS **mei-¹**	ANIMATO **ane-**	APONEUROSIS **(s)neəu-**	ARMILLARY SPHERE **ar-**
AMITY **amma**	ANIMISM **ane-**	APOPHYGE **bheug-¹**	ARMISTICE **stā-**
AMMUNITION **mei-³**	ANIMOSITY **ane-**	APOPLEXY **plāk-²**	ARMOIRE **ar-**
AMNESIA **men-¹**	ANIMUS **ane-**	APOSIOPESIS **swī-**	ARMY **ar-**
AMNESTY **men-¹**	ANION **ei-¹**	APOSTASY **stā-**	ARPENT **per¹**
AMNIOCENTESIS **kent-**	ANISEIKONIA **weik-³**	APOSTLE **stel-**	ARRAIGN **ar-**
AMOEBA **mei-¹**	ANKLE **ank-**	APOSTROPHE¹ **streb(h)-**	ARRANGE **sker-³**
AMONG **mag-**	ANKYLOSIS **ank-**	APOTHECARY **dhē-¹**	ARRAY **reidh-**
AMORETTO **amma**	ANLAGE **an¹, legh-**	APOTHECIUM **dhē-¹**	ARREARS **re-**
AMORTIZE **mer-²**	ANNALS **at-**	APOTHEOSIS **dhēs-**	ARREST **stā-**
AMOUNT **ad-, men-²**	ANNEAL **aidh-**	APOTROPAIC **trep-²**	ARRIÈRE-BAN **koro-**
AMOUR **amma**	ANNEX **ned-**	APPALL **pel-²**	ARRIVE **rei-¹**
AMPHI- **ambhi**	ANNIHILATE **ne**	APPANAGE **pā-**	ARROGATE **reg-¹**
AMPHIBIOUS **gʷei-**	ANNIVERSARY **at-, wer-³**	APPARATUS **pere-¹**	ARROW **arku-**
AMPHIBOLE **gʷele-**	ANNOTATE **gnō-**	APPAREL **pere-¹**	ARSENIC **ghel-²**
AMPHIBRACH **mregh-u-**	ANNOUNCE **neu-¹**	APPEAL **pel-⁶**	ARSIS **wer-²**
AMPHIMACER **māk-**	ANNOY **od-²**	APPEASE **pag-**	ARSON **as-**
AMPHIMIXIS **meik-**	ANNUAL **at-**	APPEND **(s)pen-**	ART¹ **ar-**
AMPHIOXUS **ak-**	ANNUITY **at-**	APPENDIX **(s)pen-**	ART² **er-¹**
AMPHISBAENA **gʷā-**	ANNUL **ne**	APPETITE **pet-**	ARTEL **ar-**
AMPHISTYLAR **stā-**	ANNULAR **āno-**	APPLE **abel-**	ARTERIO- **wer-²**
AMPHITHECIUM **dhē-¹**	ANNULET **āno-**	APPLY **plek-**	ARTERIOLE **wer-²**
AMPHORA **bher-¹**	ANNULUS **āno-**	APPOGGIATURA **ped-¹**	ARTERY **wer-²**
AMPHOTERIC **ambhō**	ANODE **sed-²**	APPOSITE **apo-**	ARTHRO- **ar-**
AMPHYCTYONY **tkei-**	ANODYNE **ed-**	APPOSITION **apo-**	ÁRTHUR **r̥tko-**
AMPLEXICAUL **kaul-, plek-**	ANOINT **ongʷ-**	APPRAISE **per-⁶**	ARTICLE **ar-**
AMPLIFY **dhē-¹**	ANOMALOUS **sem-¹**	APPRECIATE **per-⁶**	ARTIFACT **dhē-¹**
AMPUTATE **peu-**	ANOMIE **nem-**	APPREHEND **ghend-**	ARTIFICE **dhē-¹**
AMRITA **mer-², ne**	ANON **oi-no-**	APPRENTICE **ghend-**	ARTIODACTYL **artsan**
AMYLUM **mele-**	ANONYMOUS **nō-men-**	APPRESSED **per-⁵**	ARTISAN **ar-**
AN¹ **oi-no-**	ANOPHELES **obhel-**	APPRISE **ghend-**	ARTIST **ar-**
AN- **ne**	ANORECTIC **reg-¹**	APPROACH **per¹**	ÁRYAN **aryo-**
ANA² **an¹**	ANOREXIA **reg-¹**	APPROPRIATE **per¹**	ASBESTOS **gʷes-**
ANA- **an¹**	ANORTHITE **wrōdh-**	APPROVE **per¹**	ASCEND **skand-**
ANABAENA **gʷā-**	ANOSMIA **od-¹**	APPROXIMATE **per¹**	ASCRIBE **skrībh-**
ÁNABAPTIST **gʷebh-¹**	ANSATE **ans-**	APRICOT **pekʷ-**	ASH¹ **as-**
ANABIOSIS **gʷei-**	ANSERINE **ghans-**	APRON **mappa**	ASH² **os-**
ANACOLUTHON **sem-¹**	ANSWER **swer-¹**	APT **ap-¹**	ASININE **asinus**
ANACRUSIS **kreue-²**	ANT **mai-¹**	APTERYX **pet-**	ASK **ais-**
ANADEM **dē-**	ANTA **anetā**	APTITUDE **ap-¹**	ASPECT **spek-**
ANADIPLOSIS **dwo-**	ANTAGONIZE **ag-**	ÁPUS **ped-¹**	ASPEN **apsā**
ANADROMOUS **der-²**	ANTE **ant-**	AQUA **akʷā-**	ASPERSE **(s)preg-**
ANAGLYPH **gleubh-**	ANTEBELLUM **duellum**	AQUANAUT **nāu-²**	ASPIRATE **spīrāre**
ANAGOGE **ag-**	ANTECEDE **ked-**	AQUARELLE **akʷā-**	ASS² **ors-**
ANALCIME **alek-**	ANTEFIX **dhigʷ-**	AQUARIUM **akʷā-**	ASSAI² **sā-**
ANALECTS **leg-¹**	ANTEPENDIUM **(s)pen-**	AQUATIC **akʷā-**	ASSAIL **sel-⁴**
ANALEPTIC **(s)lagʷ-**	ANTERIOR **ant-**	AQUI- **akʷā-**	ASSAY **ag-**
ANALOGOUS **leg-¹**	ANTHELION **sāwel-**	ÁRA **as-**	ASSEMBLE **sem-¹**
ANALYSIS **leu-¹**	ANTHELMINTIC **wel-³**	ARABLE **are-**	ASSENT **sent-**
ANAMNESIS **men-¹**	ANTHEM **bhā-²**	ARBALEST **arku-**	ASSERT **ser-³**
ANAPEST **peu-**	ANTHEMION **andh-**	ARC **arku-**	ASSESS **sed-¹**
ANAPHORA **bher-¹**	ANTHER **andh-**	ARCADE **arku-**	ASSET **sā-**
ANARTHROUS **ar-**	ANTHESIS **andh-**	ARCANE **arek-**	ASSEVERATE **wēro-**
ANASARCA **twerk-**	ANTHO- **andh-**	ARCH¹ **arku-**	ASSIDUOUS **sed-¹**
ANASTOMOSIS **ste-men-**	-ANTHOUS **andh-**	-ARCH **arkhein**	ASSIGN **sekʷ-¹**
ANASTROPHE **streb(h)-**	ANTHROPIC **ner-²**	ARCHAEO- **arkhein**	ASSIMILATE **sem-¹**
ANATHEMA **dhē-¹**	ANTHROPO- **ner-²**	ARCHAEOPTERYX **pet-**	ASSIST **stā-**
ANATOMY **tem-**	ANTHURIUM **ors-**	ARCHAIC **arkhein**	ASSOCIATE **sekʷ-¹**
ANCESTOR **ked-**	ANTI- **ant-**	ARCHANGEL **angelos**	ASSOIL **leu-¹**
ANCHOR **ank-**	ANTIC **ant-**	ARCHEGONIUM **gene-**	ASSONANCE **swen-**
ANCHORITE **ghē-**	ANTICIPATE **kap-**	ARCHER **arku-**	ASSORT **ser-³**
ANCIENT¹ **ant-**	ANTIDOTE **dō-**	ARCHETYPE **(s)teu-**	ASSUAGE **swād-**
ANCILLARY **kʷel-¹**	ANTINOMIAN **nem-**	ARCHI- **arkhein**	ASSUASIVE **swād-**
ANCON **ank-**	ANTINOMY **nem-**	ARCHIMAGE **magh-¹**	ASSUME **em-**
ANCYLOSTOMIASIS **ank-, ste-men-**	ANTIPASTO **pā-**	ARCHIPELAGO **plāk-¹**	ASSURE **cūra**
AND **en**	ANTIPHON **bhā-²**	ARCHITECT **teks-**	ASTASIA **stā-**
ANDRO- **ner-²**	ANTIPODES **ped-¹**	ARCHITRAVE **treb-**	ASTATINE **stā-**
ANDROECIUM **weik-¹**	ANTIQUE **ant-**	ARCHIVES **arkhein**	ASTER **ster-³**
-ANDROUS **ner-²**	ANTITHESIS **dhē-¹**	ARCHIVOLT **arku-**	

ASTERIATED ster-³
ASTERISK ster-³
ASTERISM ster-³
ASTEROID ster-³
ASTIGMATISM steig-
ASTONISH (s)tenə-
ASTRAEA ster-³
ASTRAGAL ost-
ASTRAGALUS ost-
ASTRAL ster-³
ASTRAPHOBIA ster-³
ASTRINGE streig-
ASTRO- ster-³
ASTROBLEME gwelə-
ASTROLABE (s)lagw-
ASTRONAUT nāu-²
ASTRONOMER nem-
ASTRONOMY nem-
ASTUTE wes-³
ASTYLAR stā-
ASUNDER sen-²
ASYNDETON dē-
AT ad-
ATARACTIC dher-¹
ATAVISM atto-, awo-
ATAXIA tāg-
ATHEISM dhēs-
ATHELING athal-
ATLANTIC tele-
ATLAS tele-
ATMAN ētmen-
ATMOSPHERE wet-¹
ATOM tem-
ATONE oi-no-
ATRABILIOUS āter-
ATRIUM āter-
ATROCIOUS āter-
ATROPHY threph-
ATTACH steg-
ATTACK steg-
ATTAIN tag-
ATTEND ten-
ATTENUATE ten-
ATTEST trei-
ATTITUDE ap-¹
ATTO- oktō(u)
ATTORN terə-¹
ATTRACT tragh-
ATTRITION terə-¹
AUBADE albho-
AUBURN albho-
AUCTION aug-¹
AUDIBLE au-⁵
AUDIENCE au-⁵
AUDIENT au-⁵
AUDILE au-⁵
AUDING au-⁵
AUDIO- au-⁵
AUDIT au-⁵
AUDITOR au-⁵
AUDITORIUM au-⁵
AUDITORY au-⁵
AUGEND aug-¹
AUGER nobh-
AUGHT¹ aiw-
AUGHT² wekti-
AUGITE aug-²
AUGMENT aug-¹
AUGUR aug-¹
AUGUST aug-¹
AUK el-²
AULIC au-¹
AUNT amma
AURA wer-²
AURAL¹ ous-
AUREATE aurum
AUREOLE aurum
AURIC aurum
AURICLE ous-
AURIFEROUS aurum
AURIFORM ous-
AURIGA ōs-
AUROCHS wegw-
AURORA aus-¹
AUSCULTATION ous-
AUSLANDER lendh-², ud-
AUSPICE awi-, spek-
AUSTERE saus-
AUTACOID yēk-
AUTARCHY arkhein
AUTARKY arek-
AUTHOR aug-¹
AUTHORIZE aug-¹
AUTOBAHN gwhen-¹
AUTOCHTHON dhghem-
AUTOECIOUS weik-¹
AUTOGIRO gēu-
AUTOMATIC men-¹
AUTONOMOUS nem-

AUTOPSY okw-
AUXESIS aug-¹
AUXILIARY aug-¹
AUXIN aug-¹
AVAIL wal-
AVAST kel-³, past-
AVATAR au-³, terə-²
AVENGE deik-
AVENUE gwā-
AVER wēro-
AVERT wer-³
AVIAN awi-
AVIARY awi-
AVIATION awi-
AVICULTURE awi-
AVIFAUNA awi-
AVOCATION wekw-
AVOID eu-²
AVULSE wel-⁴
AVUNCULAR awo-
AWARE wer-⁴
AWAY wegh-
AWE agh-¹
AWKWARD apo-
AWN ak-
AX agwesī
AXILLA aks-
AXIOLOGY ag-
AXIOM ag-
AXIS aks-
AXLE aks-
AXON aks-
AYAH awo-
AYE² aiw-
AZALEA as-
AZO- gwei-
AZYGOUS yeug-

B

BABA baba-
BABBLE baba-
BABE baba-
BABKA baba-
BABU baba-
BABUSHKA baba-
BABY baba-
BACILLUS bak-
BACTERIUM bak-
BACULIFORM bak-
BAGEL bheug-³
BAGUETTE bak-
BAIL³ bheug-³
BAIRN bher-¹
BAIT¹ bheid-
BAKE bhē-
BAKSHEESH bhag-¹
BALALAIKA baba-
BALCONY bhelg-
BALE¹ bhel-²
BALE² bhelu-
BALEEN bhel-²
BALK bhelg-
BALL¹ bhel-²
BALL² gwelə-¹
BALLAD gwelə-¹
BALLAST bhoso-, klā-
BALLET gwelə-¹
BALLISTA gwelə-¹
BALLOON bhel-²
BALLOT bhel-²
BALLOTTEMENT bhel-²
BAMBINO baba-
BAN¹ bhā-²
BANAL bhā-²
BAND¹ bhendh-
BANDANNA bhendh-
BANDIT bhā-²
BANDOLEER bhā-¹
BANDORE pandoura
BANE gwhen-¹
BANG¹ bheg-
BANIAN wen-¹
BANISH bhā-²
BANK¹ bheg-
BANK² bheg-
BANK³ bheg-
BANKRUPT bheg-, reup-
BANNER bhā-¹
BANNERET bhā-¹
BANNS bhā-²
BANQUET bheg-
BANQUETTE bheg-
BANSHEE gwen-
BANTLING bheg-
BAPTIST gwēbh-¹

BAPTIZE gwēbh-¹
BAR² gwerə-²
BARB¹ bhardhā
BARBARIAN baba-
BARBARISM baba-
BARBAROUS baba-
BARBEL bhardhā
BARBELLATE bhardhā
BARBER bhardhā
BARBETTE bhardhā
BARBICEL bhardhā
BARBULE bhardhā
BARD¹ gwerə-³
BARE¹ bhoso-
BARGAIN bhergh-¹
BARITE gwerə-²
BARITONE gwerə-²
BARIUM gwerə-²
BARK¹ bherg-
BARLEY bhares-
BARM¹ bhreu-²
BARMY bhreu-²
BARN bhares-
BARO- gwerə-²
BAROUCHE dwo-, ret-
BARROW¹ bher-¹
BARROW² bhergh-²
BARROW³ bher-¹
BARYON gwerə-²
BARYSPHERE gwerə-²
BARYTA gwerə-²
BASCULE (s)keu-
BASE¹ gwā-
BASE² bassus
BASIS gwā-
BAS-RELIEF bassus
BASS¹ bhar-
BASS² bassus
BASSET¹ bassus
BASSO bassus
BAT² bhlag-
BATE² battuere
BATEAU bheid-
BATH¹ bhē-
BATHE bhē-
BATHOS gwadh-
BATHY- gwadh-
BATHYSCAPH skep-
BATTEN¹ bhad-
BATTERY battuere
BATTER¹ battuere
BATTER³ battuere
BATTLE battuere
BAWD bhel-²
BAWL bhel-⁴
BAY² bat-
BAY³ badyo-
BAY⁴ bat-
BAYADERE gwelə-¹
BE bheuə-
BE- ambhi
BEACON bhā-¹
BEAD gwhedh-
BEADLE bheudh-
BEAM bheuə-
BEAN bha-bhā-
BEAR¹ bher-¹
BEAR² bher-³
BEARD bhardhā
BEAT bheid-
BEATIFIC deu-², dhē-¹
BEATIFY deu-²
BEATITUDE deu-²
BEAU deu-²
BEAUTY deu-²
BEAVER¹ bher-³
BÊCHE-DE-MER mori-
BECK² bhegw-
BECKON bhā-¹
BECOME gwā-
BED bhedh-
BEE¹ bhei-¹
BEE² bheug-³
BEECH bhāgo-
BEEF gwou-
BEETLE¹ bheid-
BEETLE² bheid-
BEETLE³ bhau-
BEFALL p(h)ol-
BEFORE per¹
BEGET ghend-
BEHEST kei-³
BEHIND ko-
BEHOOF kap-
BEHOOVE kap-
BELAY legh-
BELCH bhel-⁴
BELDAM deu-²
BELEAGUER legh-
BELEMNITE gwelə-¹

BELFRY bhergh-²
BELIE leugh-
BELIEF leubh-
BELIEVE leubh-
BELL¹ bhel-⁴
BELL² bhel-⁴
BELLADONNA deu-²
BELLE deu-²
BELLICOSE duellum
BELLIGERENT duellum, gerere
BELLONA duellum
BELLOW bhel-⁴
BELLOWS bhelgh-
BELLY bhelgh-
BELONEPHOBIA gwel-¹
BELUGA bhel-¹
BELVEDERE deu-², weid-
BEMA gwā-
BEMOAN mei-no-
BEN¹ en
BENCH bheg-
BEND¹ bhendh-
BEND² bhendh-
BENEATH ni
BENEDICTION deik-
BENEFACTION deu-², dhē-¹
BENEFACTOR deu-²
BENEFIC deu-²
BENEFICE dhē-¹
BENEFICENCE deu-², dhē-¹
BENEFIT deu-², dhē-¹
BENEVOLENT deu-², wel-²
BENIGN deu-², gene-
BENTHOS gwadh-
BENUMB nem-
BEQUEATH gwet-²
BEQUEST gwet-²
BEREAVE reup-
BERM bhrem-²
BERRY bhā-¹
BERSERKER bher-³
BESPEAK spreg-
BESPRENT spergh-
BEST bhad-
BETOKEN deik-
BETRAY dō-
BETROTH deru-
BETTER bhad-
BETWEEN dwo-
BETWIXT dwo-
BEVEL bat-
BEVERAGE pō(i)-
BEWITCH weik-²
BEZOAR gwhen-¹, pā-
BHAGAVAD-GITA gēi-²
BI- dwo-
BIB pō(i)-
BIBLIOPOLE pel-⁵
BIBLIOTHECA dhē-¹
BIBULOUS pō(i)-
BICAMERAL kamer-
BICEPS kaput
BICORN ker-¹
BICYCLE kwel-¹
BID bheudh-, gwhedh-
BIDE bheidh-
BIDENTATE dent-
BIDONVILLE weik-¹
BIENNIUM at-
BIER bher-¹
BIFORATE bher-²
BIGEMINAL yem-
BIGHT bheug-³
BILANDER ambhi, lendh-²
BILBERRY bhel-¹
BILINGUAL dnghū
BILIRUBIN reudh-²
BILIVERDIN virēre
BILL¹ beu-¹
BILL² bhei-²
BILL³ bhel-¹
BILLET¹ beu-¹
BILLET-DOUX dlk-u-
BILLOW bhelgh-
BILTONG bhel-², dnghū
BIMESTRIAL mē-²
BIN bhendh-
BINAL dwo-
BINARY dwo-
BIND bhendh-
BINNACLE ghabh-
BINOMIAL nem-
BIO- gwei-
BIONT es-
BIOTA gwei-
BIOTIC gwei-
BIPARTITE perə-²
BIRCH bherəg-
BIREME erə-¹

BIRR¹ bher-¹	BOOM² bheuə-	BREEKS brāk-	BUSTARD awi-
BIRTH bher-¹	BOON¹ bhā-²	BREEZE bhreu-²	BUSTLE s(w)e-
BIS dwo-	BOON² deu-²	BREGMA mregh-m(n)o-	BUT ud-
BISCUIT dwo-, pekʷ-	BOOR bheuə-	BREMSSTRAHLUNG ster-²	BUTCHER bhugo-
BISHOP spek-	BOOT² bhad-	BREW bhreu-²	BUTT¹ bhau-
BISHOPRIC reg-¹	BOOTH bheuə-	BREWIS bhreu-²	BUTTER gʷou-, teuə-
BISON weis-	BORDELLO bherdh-	BRIAR¹ wer-³	BUTTOCK bhau-
BIT¹ bheid-	BORDER bherdh-	BRIDE² bherək-	BUTTON bhau-
BIT² bheid-	BORE¹ bher-²	BRIDEGROOM dhghem-	BUTTRESS bhau-
BITE bheid-	BORE³ bher-¹	BRIDGE¹ bhrū-	BUTYRIC gʷou-
BITTER bheid-	BOREAS gʷerə-¹	BRIDLE bherək-	BUXOM bheug-³
BITTERN¹ beu-²	BOROUGH bhergh-²	BRIEF mregh-u-	BUZZARD beu-²
BITUMEN gʷet-	BORROW bhergh-¹	BRIGHT bherəg-	BY¹ ambhi
BIVOUAC ambhi, weg-²	BORSCHT bhar-	BRIM bhrem-²	BYRE bheuə-
BLACK bhel-¹	BOSCAGE busk-	BRIMSTONE gʷher-	
BLACKMAIL mōd-	BOSOM beu-¹	BRINDLED gʷher-	
BLADDER bhlē-²	BOTH ambhō	BRING bher-¹	**C**
BLADE bhel-³	BOTHRIUM bhedh-	BRIO gʷerə-²	
BLAIN bhlei-	BO TREE bheudh-	BRIOCHE bhreg-	
BLAME bhā-²	BOTTOM bhudh-	BRISANCE bhrēi-	CABARET kamer-
BLANCH mel-¹	BOTTOMRY bhudh-	BRISTLE bhar-	CABEZON kaput
BLANCMANGE bhel-¹	BOTULIN gʷet-³	BRITTLE bhreu-¹	CABLE kap-
BLAND mel-¹	BOTULINUM gʷet-³	BRONCHIECTASIS ten-	CABRILLA kapro-
BLANDISH mel-¹	BOTULISM gʷet-³	BRONCHO- gʷerə-⁴	CABRIOLET kapro-
BLANK bhel-¹	BOUCLE beu-¹	BRONCHUS gʷerə-⁴	CACHE ag-
BLANKET bhel-¹	BOUGH bhāghu-	BRONTOSAUR bhrem-¹	CACHEXIA segh-
BLARE bhlē-¹	BOUILLABAISSE beu-¹	BROOD bhreu-²	CACO- kakka-
BLASPHEME bhā-²	BOUILLON beu-¹	BROOK² bhrūg-	CACODYL kakka-
BLASPHEMOUS bhā-²	BOULDER bhel-¹	BROOM bhrem-²	CACOETHES kakka-, s(w)e-
BLAST bhlē-²	BOULE¹ gʷelə-¹	BROTH bhreu-²	CACOPHONOUS bhā-², kakka-
-BLAST melst-	BOULE² beu-¹	BROTHEL bhreu-¹	CACOPHONY kakka-
BLASTEMA melst-	BOULEVARD bhel-², werg-	BROTHER bhrāter-	CACUMINAL keu-²
BLASTO- melst-	BOULEVERSEMENT beu-¹, wer-³	BROW bhrū-	CADASTER steigh-
BLASTULA melst-	BOUND¹ bamb-	BROWN bher-³	CADAVER kad-
BLATHER bhlē-²	BOUND⁴ bheuə-	BROWSE bhreus-¹	CADELLE kat-¹
BLAZE¹ bhel-¹	BOUNTY deu-²	BRUIN bher-³	CADENCE kad-
BLEACH bhel-¹	BOUQUET busk-	BRUISE bhreus-²	CADENT kad-
BLEAK¹ bhel-¹	BOURG bhergh-²	BRUMAL mregh-u-	CADET kaput
BLEAK² bhel-¹	BOURGEOIS bhergh-²	BRUNET bher-³	CADRE kʷetwer-
BLEAT bhlē-¹	BOURN bhreu-²	BRUT gʷerə-²	CADUCEUS kar-²
BLEMISH bhel-¹	BOURSE bursa	BRUTE gʷerə-²	CADUCICORN kad-, ker-¹
BLENCH¹ bhel-¹	BOUSTROPHEDON gʷou-, streb(h)-	BUBO beu-¹	CADUCOUS kad-
BLEND bhel-¹	BOUTIQUE dhē-¹	BUCCAL beu-¹	CAECILIAN kaiko-
BLENDE bhel-¹	BOUTON bhau-	BUCEPHALUS gʷou-	CAECUM kaiko-
BLENNY mel-¹	BOVINE gʷou-	BUCK¹ bhugo-	CAELUM kaə-id-
BLESBOK bhel-¹, bhugo-	BOW² bheug-³	BUCKAROO wak-	CAESURA kaə-id-
BLIND bhel-¹	BOW³ bheug-³	BUCKBOARD beu-¹	CAGE keuə-²
BLINDFOLD bhel-¹	BOWEL gʷet-³	BUCKLE¹ beu-¹	CAHIER kʷetwer-
BLINI melə	BOWERY bheuə-	BUCKLE² beu-¹	CAINOTOPHOBIA ken-³
BLINTZ melə	BOWER¹ bheuə-	BUCKSHEE bhag-¹	CAIRD kerd-²
BLISTER bhlei-	BOWL¹ bhel-²	BUCKWHEAT bhāgo-	CAISSON kap-
BLITE melə	BOWL² beu-¹	BUCOLIC gʷou-, kʷel-¹	CAKE kak-²
BLITZKRIEG bhel-¹, gʷerə-²	BOWSPRIT sper-⁴	BUDDHA bheudh-	CALAMITE koləm-
BLOAT bhleu-	BOX¹ puxos	BUDGET bhelgh-	CALAMITY kel-¹
BLOND bhel-¹	BOX³ puxos	BUDGE¹ bhelgh-	CALAMUS koləm-
BLOOM¹ bhel-³	BRACE mregh-u-	BUGLE¹ gʷou-	CALANDO ghē-
BLOOM² bhel-³	BRACERO mregh-u-	BUGLOSS glōgh-	CALDRON kelə-¹
BLOSSOM bhel-³	BRACH bhrag-	BUILD bheuə-	CALENDAR kelə-²
BLOW¹ bhel-³	BRACHIUM mregh-u-	BULGE bhelgh-	CALENDER skel-³
BLOW³ bhel-³	BRACHY- mregh-u-	BULIMIA gʷou-, leiə-	CALENDS kelə-²
BLUE bhel-¹	BRACKEN bhreg-	BULK¹ bhel-²	CALENTURE kelə-¹
BLUNDERBUSS (s)tenə-	BRACKET brāk-	BULL¹ bhel-²	CALIBER ped-¹
BLUSH bhel-¹	BRAD bhar-	BULL² beu-¹	CALIX kal-¹
BOARD bherdh-	BRADYLEXIA leg-¹	BULLA beu-¹	CALL gal-²
BOAST¹ beu-¹	BRAE bherək-	BULLATE beu-¹	CALLIGRAPHY kal-²
BOAT bheid-	Brahma¹ bhlagh-men-	BULLET beu-¹	Calliope kal-², wekʷ-
BOATSWAIN bheid-	BRAHMAN bhlagh-men-	BULLETIN beu-¹	CALLIPYGIAN kal-²
BOCACCIO beu-¹	BRAHMIN bhlagh-men-	BULLION beu-¹	Callisto kal-²
BODE¹ bheudh-	BRAID bherək-	BULLY² beu-¹	CALLOSE kal-³
BODEGA dhē-¹	BRAIL brāk-	BULWARK bhel-², werg-	CALLOUS kal-³
BODHISATTVA bheudh-, es-	BRAIN mregh-m(n)o-	BUNCO bheg-	CALLOW gal-¹
BOER bheuə-	BRAISE bhreu-²	BUND¹ bhendh-	CALLUS kal-³
BOG bheug-³	BRAKE³ bhreg-	BUND² bhendh-	CALM kēu-
BOIL¹ beu-¹	BRAKE⁴ bhreg-	Bundesrat ar-	CALOMEL kal-²
BOIL² beu-¹	BRAMBLE bhrem-²	BUNDLE bhendh-	CALORECEPTOR kelə-¹
BOLA beu-¹	BRAND gʷher-	BUNG peuk-	CALORIC kelə-¹
BOLD bhel-²	BRANDISH gʷher-	BUNGLE bheg-	CALORIE kelə-¹
BOLE¹ bhel-²	BRANDY gʷher-	BUPRESTID gʷou-	CALORIFIC kelə-¹
BOLL bhel-³	BRASS ferrum	BUR¹ bhar-	CALORIMETER kelə-¹
BOLLIX bhel-²	BRASSARD mregh-u-	BURDEN¹ bher-¹	CALORIMETRY kelə-¹
BOLOMETER gʷelə-¹	BRASSIERE mregh-u-	BURG bhergh-²	CALOYER gerə-¹, kal-²
Bolshevik bel-	BRATWURST bhreu-²	BURGESS bhergh-²	CALUMET koləm-
BOLSTER bhelgh-	BRAWN bhreu-²	BURGHER bhergh-²	CALUMNY kel-⁸
BOLT¹ bheid-	BRAY² bhreg-	BURGLAR bhergh-²	CALVARIUM klewo-
BOMB bamb-	BRAZE² bhreu-²	BURGOMASTER bhergh-²	Calypso kel-²
BOMBARD bamb-	BRAZEN ferrum	BURIAL bhergh-¹	CALYPTRA kel-²
BONANZA deu-²	BRAZIER¹ ferrum	BURIN bher-²	CALYX kal-¹
BONBON deu-²	BRAZIER² bhreu-²	BURN¹ gʷher-	CAM gembh-
BOND bhendh-	BREACH bhreg-	BURN² bhreu-²	CAMARILLA kamer-
BONDAGE bheuə	BREAD bhreu-²	BURNET bher-³	CAMBIST skamb-
BONHOMIE deu-², dhghem-	BREAK bhreg-	BURNISH bher-³	CAMBIUM skamb-
BONITO deu-²	BREAKFAST past-	BURSA bursa	CAMERA kamer-
BONNE deu-²	BREAM¹ bherək-	BURSAR bursa	CAMPYLOTROPOUS kamp-
BONNYCLABBER band-	BREAST bhreus-¹	BURSE bursa	CAN¹ gnō-
BONTEBOK bhugo-	BREATH gʷhrē-	BURST bhres-	CANAILLE kwon-
BONUS deu-²	BREATHE gʷhrē-	BURY bhergh-¹	CANARY kwon-
BOOBY baba-	BRECCIA bhreg-	BUSHEL² bhau-	CANCEL carcer-
BOODLE bheuə-	BREECH brāk-	BUSK¹ busk-	CANCER kar-¹
BOOK bhāgo-	BREED bhreu-²	BUSK² s(w)e-	

CANDENT kand-
CANDID kand-
CANDIDA kand-
CANDIDATE kand-
CANDLE kand-
CANDOR kand-
CANESCENT kas-
CANICULA kwon-
CANINE kwon-
CANKER kar-[1]
CANNABIS kannabis
CANOROUS kan-
CANT[2] kan-
CANTABILE kan-
CANTEEN kanto-
CANTICLE kan-
CANTILLATE kan-
CANTO kan-
CANTON kanto-
CANTOR kan-
CANVAS kannabis
CANZONE kan-
CAPABLE kap-
CAPACIOUS kap-
CAPE[2] kaput
CAPELLA kapro-
CAPIAS kap-
CAPITAL[1] kaput
CAPITAL[2] kaput
CAPITATE kaput
CAPITATION kaput
CAPITELLUM kaput
CAPITULATE kaput
CAPITULUM kaput
CAPO[1] kaput
CAPON skep-
CAPRIC ACID kapro-
CAPRICE kaput
CAPRICORN kapro-, ker-[1]
CAPRIFIG kapro-
CAPRIOLE kapro-
CAPROIC ACID kapro-
CAPSICUM kap-
CAPSID kap-
CAPSTAN kap-
CAPSULE kap-
CAPTAIN kaput
CAPTION kap-
CAPTIOUS kap-
CAPTIVATE kap-
CAPTIVE kap-
CAPTOR kap-
CAPTURE kap-
CAR kers-[2]
CARAMEL kolem-
CARAT ker-[1]
CARAVANSARY tere-[2]
CARBON ker-[4]
CARBUNCLE ker-[4]
CARCINO- kar-[1]
CARCINOGEN kar-[1]
CARCINOMA kar-[1]
CARD[2] kars-
CARDIA kerd-[1]
CARDIAC kerd-[1]
CARDIO- kerd-[1]
CARDOON kars-
CARE gar-
CAREEN kar-[1]
CAREER kers-[2]
CARESS kā-
CARET kes-[2]
CARGO kers-[2]
CARICATURE kers-[2]
CARIES ker-[5]
CARILLON kwetwer-
CARINA kar-[1]
CARIOLE kers-[2]
CARL karlaz
CARLING karlaz
CARMINATIVE kars-
CARNAGE sker-[1]
CARNAL sker-[1]
CARNASSIAL sker-[1]
CARNATION sker-[1]
CARNET kwetwer-
CARNIVAL legwh-, sker-[1]
CARNIVOROUS sker-[1]
CAROCHE kers-[2]
CAROL aulo-
CAROTID ker-[1]
CAROUSE ud-
CARP[1] ger-[2]
-CARP kerp-
CARPAL kwerp-
CARPEL kerp-
CARPENTER kers-[2]
CARPET kerp-
CARPO- kerp-

-CARPOUS kerp-
CARPUS kwerp-
CARRION sker-[1]
CARROT ker-[1]
CARRY kers-[2]
CART ger-[2]
CARUNCLE sker-[1]
CARVACROL ak-
CARVE gerbh-
CASCADE kad-
CASCARA kwēt-
CASE[1] kad-
CASE[2] kap-
CASHIER kes-[2]
CASTE kes-[2]
CASTIGATE kes-[2]
CASTLE kes-[2]
CASTRATE kes-[2]
CATA- kat-[1]
CATABOLISM gwele-[1]
CATACHRESIS gher-[5]
CATACLYSM kleu-[2]
CATALECTIC slēg-
CATALEPSY (s)lagw-
CATALOGUE leg-[1]
CATALYSIS leu-[1]
CATAMENIA mē-[2]
CATAPLEXY plāk-[2]
CATAPULT pōl-
CATARRH sreu-
CATASTASIS stā-
CATASTROPHE streb(h)-
CATCH kap-
CATCHPOLE pau-
CATECHIZE (s)wāgh-
CATEGORY ger-[1]
CATER-CORNERED kwetwer-
CATERPILLAR pilo-
CATHEDRA sed-[1]
CATHEPSIN kat-[1]
CATHETER yē-
CATHODE sed-[2]
CATHOLIC sol-
CATION ei-[1]
CATOPTRIC okw-
CATTLE kaput
CAUDILLO kaput
CAUDLE kelə-
CAULESCENT kaul-
CAULICLE kaul-
CAULIFLOWER bhel-[3], kaul-
CAULINE kaul-
CAUSTIC kēu-
CAUTERY kēu-
CAUTION keuə-[1]
CAVE keuə-[2]
CAVEAT keuə-[1]
CAVERN keuə-[2]
CAVETTO keuə-[2]
CAVIL kel-[8]
CAY kagh-
CEASE ked-
CEDE ked-
CELANDINE ghel-[1]
-CELE[2] keuə-[2]
CELEBRATE kel-[3]
CELEBRITY kel-[3]
CELERITY kel-[3]
-CELIAC keuə-[2]
CELL kel-[2]
CELLA kel-[2]
CELLAR kel-[2]
CELLARER kel-[2]
CEMBALO keu-[2], kleu-[3]
CEMENT kaə-id-
CEMETERY kei-[1]
CENACLE sker-[1]
-CENE ken-[3]
CENOBITE gwei-, kom
CENOGENESIS ken-[3]
CENOTAPH dhembh-, ken-[4]
CENOZOIC ken-[3]
CENSOR kens-
CENSUS kens-
CENT dekm
CENTAL dekm
CENTAVO dekm
CENTENARIAN dekm
CENTENARY dekm
CENTENNIAL dekm
CENTER kent-
CENTESIMAL dekm
CENTESIS kent-
CENTI- dekm
CENTIGRADE ghredh-
CENTIME dekm
CENTNER dekm
CENTO kentho-
CENTRIFUGAL bheug-[1]

CENTROBARIC gwerə-[2]
CENTUM dekm
CENTURY dekm
CEPHALIC ghebh-el-
CEPHALO- ghebh-el-
-CEPHALOUS ghebh-el-
CERAMIC ker-[4]
CERASTES ker-[1]
CERATODUS dent-, ker-[1]
CERATOID ker-[1]
CEREAL ker-[3]
CEREBELLUM ker-[1]
CEREBRUM ker-[1]
CERES ker-[3]
CERTAIN krei-
CERVINE ker-[1]
CERVIX ker-[1]
CESSION ked-
CESSPOOL spīrāre
CESTUS[1] kent-
CESTUS[2] kaə-id-
CHAETA ghait-
CHAETOGNATH genu-[2], ghait-
CHAFE dhē-[1], kelə-
CHAFER gep(h)-
CHAFF[1] gep(h)-
CHAIR sed-[1]
CHALAZA gheləd-
CHALAZION gheləd-
CHALCID ghelegh-
CHALCOCITE ghelegh-
CHALCOPYRITE ghelegh-
CHALCOSIS ghelegh-
CHALICE kal-[1]
CHALLENGE kel-[8]
CHALONE ghē-
CHAMAEPHYTE dhghem-
CHAMBER kamer-
CHAMELEON dhghem-
CHAMFER bhreg-
CHAMFRON kaput
CHAMOMILE dhghem-, mēlon
CHANCE kad-
CHANCEL carcer
CHANCELLOR carcer
CHANCRE kar-[1]
CHANGE skamb-
CHANT kan-
CHAOS ghēu-
CHAP[2] caupō
CHAPITER kaput
CHAPMAN caupō
CHAPTER kaput
CHARACIN gher-[4]
CHARACTER gher-[4]
CHARD kars-
CHARGE kers-[2]
CHARIOT kers-[2]
CHARISMA gher-[5]
CHARITY kā-
CHARIVARI ker-[1]
CHARM[1] kan-
CHARNEL sker-[1]
CHARY gar-
CHASE[1] kap-
CHASE[2] kap-
CHASE[3] kap-
CHASM ghāi-
CHASSIS kap-
CHASTE kes-[2]
CHAUDFROID kelə-[1]
CHEAP caupō
CHECK tkē-
CHECKMATE tkē-
CHEER ker-[1]
CHEESE[3] kwo-
CHEETAH kwei-[2], skai-
CHEILOSIS ghel-unā
CHELICERA ker-[1]
CHELONIAN ghelū-
CHEMOTROPHY threph-
CHENILLE kwon-
CHENOPOD ghans-
CHERISH kā-
CHERNOZEM kers-[1]
CHERRY ker-[6]
CHERSONESE ghers-, snā-
CHESS[3] spek-
CHEST kistā
CHEVRON kapro-
CHEW gyeu-
CHIAROSCURO kelə-[2], (s)keu-
CHICKEN ku-
CHIEF kaput
CHIEFTAIN kaput
CHILIAD gheslo-
CHILL gel-[3]
CHILOPOD ghel-unā
CHIME[1] keu-[2]

CHIME[2] gembh-
CHIMERA ghei-[2]
CHIN genu-[2]
CHINE skei-
CHINK[1] gēi-[1]
CHINTZ skai-
CHIRO- ghesor-
CHIRURGEON ghesor-
CHISEL kaə-id-
CHITTERLINGS ku-
CHLOASMA ghel-[2]
CHLORITE[1] ghel-[2]
CHLORO- ghel-[2]
CHOANA gheu-
CHOANOCYTE gheu-
CHOICE geus-
CHOIR gher-[1]
CHOLE- ghel-[2]
CHOLER ghel-[2]
CHOLERA ghel-[2]
CHOLESTEROL ster-[1]
CHOLINERGIC werg-
CHOLLA g(e)u-lo-
CHONDRO- ghrendh-
CHONDROMALACIA mel-[1]
CHOOSE geus-
CHORAGUS ag-, gher-[1]
CHORAL gher-[1]
CHORALE gher-[1]
CHORD[2] gherə-
-CHORE ghē-
CHORIC gher-[1]
CHORION gherə-
CHORISTER gher-[1]
CHOROGRAPHY ghē-
CHORUS gher-[1]
CHOWDER kelə-[1]
CHRESARD gher-[5]
CHRESTOMATHY gher-[5], mendh-[1]
CHRISM ghrēi-
CHRIST ghrēi-
CHRISTEN ghrēi-
CHRISTIAN ghrēi-
CHRISTMAS ghrēi-
CHROMA ghrēu-
CHROMATIC ghrēu-
CHROMATO- ghrēu-
-CHROME ghrēu-
CHROMIUM ghrēu-
CHROMO- ghrēu-
CHROMONEMA (s)nē-
CHRONAXY ag-
CHRYSANTHEMUM andh-
CHTHONIC dhghem-
CHUFA swei-[1]
CHUKAR kau-
CHUKKER kwel-[1]
CHURCH keuə-[2]
CHURL karlaz
CHUTE kad-
CHYLE gheu-
CHYLOMICRON smē-
CHYME gheu-
CICHLID ghel-[1]
-CIDE kaə-id-
CILIUM kel-[2]
CINCH kenk-[1]
CINCTURE kenk-[1]
CINDER sendhro-
CINEMATOGRAPH kei-[3]
CINEMATORADIOGRAPHY kei-[3]
CINERARIUM keni-
CINEREOUS keni-
CINGULUM kenk-[1]
CINQUAIN penkwe
CINQUE penkwe
CINQUEFOIL bhel-[3], penkwe
CIRCA sker-[3]
CIRCADIAN deiw-
CIRCLE sker-[3]
CIRCUIT ei-[1]
CIRCUM- sker-[3]
CIRCUMCISE kaə-id-
CIRCUMDUCTION deuk-
CIRCUMFUSE gheu-
CIRCUMLOCUTION tolkw-
CIRCUMSCRIBE skrībh-
CIRCUMSPECT spek-
CIRCUMSTANCE stā-
CIRCUMVENT gwā-
CIRCUMVOLVE wel-[3]
CIS- ko-
CIST[1] kistā
CISTERN kistā
CITE kei-[3]
CITY kei-[1]
CIVIC kei-[1]
CIVIL kei-[1]
CLADOCERAN kel-[1], ker-[1]

CLADODE kel-1
CLADOGENESIS kel-1
CLADOPHYLL kel-1
CLAG gel-1
CLAIM kelə-2
CLAIRVOYANCE kelə-2, weid-
CLAMANT kelə-2
CLAMMY gel-1
CLAMOR kelə-2
CLAM1 gel-1
CLAM2 gel-1
CLAMP gel-1
CLAN plat-
CLANDESTINE kel-2
CLANG kleg-
CLASMATOCYTE kel-1
CLASS kelə-2
CLAST kel-1
CLASTIC kel-1
CLATHRATE kleu-3
CLATTER gal-2
CLAUSE kleu-3
CLAVATE kleu-3
CLAVICHORD kleu-3
CLAVICLE kleu-3
CLAVICORN ker-1, kleu-3
CLAVIER kleu-3
CLAVIFORM kleu-3
CLAW gel-1
CLAY gel-1
CLAYMORE kel-1, mē-3
CLEAN gel-1
CLEANSE gel-2
CLEAR kelə-2
CLEAT gel-1
CLEAVE1 gleubh-
CLEAVE2 gel-1
CLEAVERS gel-1
CLEF kleu-3
CLEISTOGAMOUS kleu-3
CLEISTOTHECIUM dhē-1, kleu-3
CLEMATIS kel-1
CLENCH gel-1
CLEPSYDRA klep-, wed-1
CLERK kel-1
CLEVER gleubh-
CLEVIS gleubh-
CLEW1 gel-1
CLIENT klei-
CLIMATE klei-
CLIMAX klei-
CLIMB gel-1
CLINAL klei-
CLINANDRIUM klei-
CLINCH gel-1
CLINE klei-
CLING gel-1
CLINIC klei-
CLINO- klei-
CLIO kleu-1
CLIP2 kleu-1
CLITELLUM klei-
CLOACA kleu-2
CLOD gel-1
CLOISONNE kleu-3
CLOISTER kleu-3
CLONE kel-1
CLONUS kel-1
CLOSE kleu-3
CLOSURE kleu-3
CLOT gel-1
CLOTH peiə-
CLOUD gel-1
CLOUT gel-1
CLOVE1 kleu-3
CLOVE2 gleubh-
CLOY kleu-3
CLOZE kleu-3
CLUB1 gel-1
CLUE gel-1
CLUMP gel-1
CLUTCH1 gel-1
CLUTTER gel-1
CLYSTER kleu-2
CO- kom
COADUNATE oi-no-
COAGULUM ag-
COAL g(e)u-lo-
COALESCE al-3
COARCTATE ar-
COAST kost-
COBALT ku-
COCCID kokkos
COCCUS kokkos
COCHINEAL kokkos
COCHLEA konk(h)o-
COCK2 ku-
COCKAIGNE kak-2
COCKCHAFER gep(h)-

COCKLE1 konk(h)o-
COCKNEY awi-
COCYTUS kau-1
COD2 ku-
CODEINE keuə-2
-COEL keuə-2
COELACANTH ak-
COELOM keuə-2
COENO- kom
COERCE arek-
COETANEOUS aiw-
COEVAL aiw-
COG1 ku-
COGENT ag-
COGNATE genə-
COGNITION gnō-
COGNIZANCE gnō-
COGNOMEN nō-men-
COHABIT ghabh-
COHERE ghais-
COHORT gher-1
COIL1 leg-1
COITUS ei-1
COL kwel-1
COLANDER kagh-
COLCANNON kaul-, weid-
COLD gel-3
COLE kaul-
COLEOPTERA kel-2, pet-
COLEOPTERAN kel-2
COLEOPTILE kel-2, pet-
COLEORHIZA kel-2, wrād-
COLESLAW kaul-
COLEUS kel-2
COLLABORATE leb-1
COLLAGE koli-
COLLAPSE leb-1
COLLAR kwel-1
COLLATE tele-
COLLEAGUE leg-1
COLLECT1 leg-1
COLLEGIALITY leg-1
COLLET kwel-1
COLLIE g(e)u-lo-
COLLIER g(e)u-lo-
COLLIGATE leig-1
COLLIGATIVE leig-1
COLLO- koli-
COLLODION koli-
COLLOQUIUM tolkw-
COLLOQUY tolkw-
COLLUDE leid-
COLLUVIUM leu(ə)-
COLOBOMA kel-1
COLON1 skel-3
COLONEL kel-6
COLONNADE kel-6
COLONY kwel-1
COLOPHON kel-6
COLOR kel-2
-COLOUS kwel-1
COLPITIS kwelp-
COLPOSCOPE kwelp-
COLPOSCOPY kwelp-
COLTER skel-1
COLUMBA kel-3
COLUMBARIUM kel-5
COLUMBINE kel-5
COLUMN kel-6
COLZA sē-1
COM- kom
COMA1 kemə-
COMB gembh-
COMBAT battuere
COMBINE dwo-
COMBUSTION eus-
COME gwā-
COMEDO ed-
COMEDY wed-2
COMESTIBLE ed-
COMFIT dhē-1
COMFORT bhergh-2
COMITIA ei-1
COMITY smei-
COMMA skep-
COMMAND man-2
COMMANDO man-2
COMMEMORATE (s)mer-1
COMMENCE ei-1
COMMEND man-2
COMMENSURATE mē-2
COMMENT men-1
COMMERCE merk-2
COMMINUTE mei-2
COMMISERATE miser
COMMIT (s)meit(ə)-
COMMIX meik-
COMMODE med-
COMMODIOUS med-

COMMODITY med-
COMMON mei-1
COMMOTION meuə-
COMMUNE mei-1
COMMUNICATE mei-1
COMMUNISM mei-1
COMMUTE mei-1
COMPACT1 pag-
COMPANION pā-
COMPANY pā-
COMPARE perə-2
COMPART perə-2
COMPASSION pē(i)-
COMPEL pel-6
COMPELLATION pel-6
COMPENDIUM (s)pen-
COMPENSATE (s)pen-
COMPETE pet-
COMPLACENT plāk-1
COMPLAIN plāk-2
COMPLECT plek-
COMPLETE pelə-1
COMPLEX plek-
COMPLICATE plek-
COMPLICE plek-
COMPLIMENT pelə-1
COMPLY pelə-1
COMPONENT apo-
COMPORT per-2
COMPOSE apo-, paus-
COMPOSITE apo-
COMPOSITION apo-
COMPOUND apo-
COMPRADOR perə-1
COMPREHEND ghend-
COMPRESS per-5
COMPRISE ghend-
COMPROMISE (s)meit(ə)-
COMPUNCTION peuk-
COMPURGATION peuə-
COMPUTE peu-
COMRADE kamer-
CON1 kom
CON2 gnō-
CON3 deuk-
CONATION ken-1
CONCAVE keuə-2
CONCEAL kel-2
CONCEDE ked-
CONCEIVE kap-
CONCERN krei-
CONCESSION ked-
CONCH konk(h)o-
CONCHA konk(h)o-
CONCHO- konk(h)o-
CONCIERGE servus
CONCILIATE kelə-2
CONCISE kae-id-
CONCLAVE kleu-3
CONCLUDE kleu-3
CONCOCT pekw-
CONCOMITANT ei-1
CONCORD kerd-1
CONCOURSE kers-2
CONCRESCENCE ker-3
CONCRETE ker-3
CONCUBINE keu-2
CONCUPISCENCE kwēp-
CONCUR kers-2
CONCUSS kwēt-
CONDEMN dap-
CONDENSE dens-2
CONDESCEND skand-
CONDIGN dek-1
CONDIMENT dhē-1
CONDITION deik-
CONDOLE del-3
CONDONE dō-
CONDOTTIERE deuk-
CONDUCE deuk-
CONDUCT deuk-
CONDUPLICATE dwo-
CONE kō-
CONFECT dhē-1
CONFEDERATE bheidh-
CONFER bher-1
CONFESS bhā-2
CONFETTI dhē-1
CONFIDANT bheidh-
CONFIDE bheidh-
CONFIDENT bheidh-
CONFIGURATION dheigh-
CONFIRM dher-2
CONFLAGRANT bhel-1
CONFLAGRATION bhel-1
CONFLATE bhlē-1
CONFLICT bhlīg-
CONFLUENT bhleu-
CONFORM merph-

CONFOUND gheu-
CONFRERE bhrāter-
CONFUSE gheu-
CONFUTE bhau-
CONGE mei-1
CONGEAL gel-3
CONGENER genə-
CONGENIAL genə-
CONGENITAL genə-
CONGERIES gerere
CONGEST gerere
CONGLOBATE gel-1
CONGLOMERATE gel-1
CONGLUTINATE gel-1
CONGRATULATE gwerə-3
CONGREGATE ger-1
CONGRESS ghredh-
CONGRUENT ghrēu-
CONIDIUM keni-
CONIOSIS keni-
CONJECTURE yē-
CONJOIN yeug-
CONJUGAL yeug-
CONJUGATE yeug-
CONJUNCT yeug-
CONJURE yewes-
CONNATE genə-
CONNECT ned-
CONNIVE kneigwh-
CONNOISSEUR gnō-
CONNOTE gnō-
CONNUBIAL sneubh-
CONQUER quaerere
CONQUIAN kom, kwo-
CONSCIENCE skei-
CONSCIOUS skei-
CONSCRIPT skrībh-
CONSECRATE sak-
CONSENT sent-
CONSEQUENT sekw-1
CONSERVE ser-1
CONSIDER sweid-1
CONSIGN sekw-1
CONSIST stā-
CONSOCIATE sekw-1
CONSOLE1 sel-2
CONSOLIDATE sol-
CONSOLUTE leu-1
CONSONANT swen-
CONSORT ser-3
CONSPICUOUS spek-
CONSPIRE spīrāre
CONSTABLE ei-1
CONSTANT stā-
CONSTELLATION ster-3
CONSTERNATE ster-2
CONSTIPATE steip-
CONSTITUTE stā-
CONSTRAIN streig-
CONSTRUCT ster-2
CONSUETUDE s(w)e-
CONSUME em-
CONTACT tag-
CONTAIN ten-
CONTAMINATE tag-
CONTEMPLATE tem-
CONTEND ten-
CONTEST trei-
CONTEXT teks-
CONTINUE ten-
CONTORT terkw-
CONTOUR terə-1
CONTRA- kom
CONTRABAND bhā-2
CONTRACT tragh-
CONTRADICT deik-
CONTRARY kom
CONTRAST stā-
CONTRAVENE gwā-
CONTRITE terə-1
CONTRIVE trep-2
CONTROL ret-
CONTROVERSY wer-3
CONTUSE (s)teu-
CONVALESCE wal-
CONVECTION wegh-
CONVENE gwā-
CONVENIENT gwā-
CONVENT gwā-
CONVENTICLE gwā-
CONVENTION gwā-
CONVERGE wer-3
CONVERSE1 wer-3
CONVERT wer-3
CONVEX wegh-
CONVEY wegh-
CONVINCE weik-5
CONVIVIAL gwei-
CONVOKE wekw-

CONVOLVE wel-³
CONVULSE wel-⁴
COOK pekʷ-
COOKY kak-²
COOL gel-³
COOPER ku-
COOPERATE op-¹
CO-OPT op-²
COORDINATION ar-
COPE¹ kel-²
COPEPOD kap-
COPIOUS op-¹
COPRO- kekʷ-
COPULA ap-¹
COPULATE ap-¹
COPY op-¹
CORACIIFORM ker-², merph-
CORACOID ker-²
CORBEL ker-²
CORBINA ker-²
CORD ghere-
CORDATE kerd-¹
CORDIAL kerd-¹
CORDIFORM kerd-¹
CORDON ghere-
COREOPSIS sker-¹
CORGI kwon-
CORIACEOUS sker-¹
CORIUM sker-¹
CORM sker-¹
CORMORANT ker-²
CORN¹ gre-no-
CORN² ker-¹
CORNEA ker-¹
CORNEL ker-¹
CORNEOUS ker-¹
CORNER ker-¹
CORNET ker-¹
CORNICULATE ker-¹
CORNIFICATION ker-¹
CORNU ker-¹
CORNUCOPIA op-¹
CORONA sker-³
CORONOID sker-³
CORPORAL¹ kʷrep-
CORPORAL³ kʷrep-
CORPORATE kʷrep-
CORPOREAL kʷrep-
CORPOSANT kʷrep-, sak-
CORPS kʷrep-
CORPSE kʷrep-
CORPULENCE kʷrep-
CORPUS kʷrep-
CORPUSCLE kʷrep-
CORRADE rēd-
CORRECT reg-¹
CORRIDOR kers-²
CORRIE kʷer-²
CORROBORATE reudh-¹
CORRODE rēd-
CORRUGATE ruk-²
CORRUPT reup-
CORSAGE kʷrep-
CORSAIR kers-²
CORSE kʷrep-
CORSET kʷrep-
CORTEGE gher-¹
CORTEX sker-¹
CORUSCATE sker-²
CORVÉE reg-¹
CORVINE ker-²
CORVUS ker-²
CORYDALIS ker-²
CORYMB ker-¹
CORYNEBACTERIUM bak-, ker-¹
CORYPHAEUS ker-¹
COSMONAUT nāu-²
COSMOPOLITE pele-³
COSMOS kes-³
COST stā-
COSTA kost-
COSTARD kost-
COSTREL kost-
COT² ku-
COTE¹ ku-
COTTAGE ku-
COUCH GRASS gwei-
COULEE kagh-
COULOIR kagh-
COUNCIL kele-²
COUNT¹ peu-
COUNT² ei-¹
COUNTER¹ kom
COUNTER- kom
COUNTERFEIT dhē-¹
COUNTERMAND man-²
COUNTERVAIL wal-
COUNTRY kom
COUP kel-¹

COUPLE ap-¹
COURAGE kerd-¹
COURANTE kers-²
COURIER kers-²
COURSE kers-²
COURT gher-¹
COURTEOUS gher-¹
COURTESAN gher-¹
COURTESY gher-¹
COURTIER gher-¹
COUSIN swesor-
COUTH gnō-
COUTURE syū-
COUVADE keu-²
COVE¹ ku-
COVEN gwā-
COVENANT gwā-
COVER wer-⁵
COVET kwep-
COVEY keu-²
COW¹ gwou-
COW² ku-
COWER ku-
COWSLIP gwou-, sleubh-
COXA koksā
COY kwele-²
CRAB¹ gerbh-
CRACK gere-²
CRACKNEL gere-²
-CRACY kar-¹
CRADLE gere-²
CRAKE gere-²
CRAM gere-²
CRAMBO skerbh-
CRAMP¹ ger-²
CRAMP² ger-²
CRANBERRY gere-²
CRANE gere-²
CRANIUM ker-¹
CRANK¹ ger-²
CRASH² ker-⁴
CRATE kert-
CRATER kere-
CRAW gwere-⁴
CRAWL¹ gerbh-
CRAYFISH gerbh-
CREATE ker-³
CREATINE kreue-¹
CRÈCHE gere-²
CREDENCE kerd-¹
CREDIBLE kerd-¹
CREDIT kerd-¹
CREDO kerd-¹
CREDULOUS kerd-¹
CREEK ger-²
CREEP ger-²
CREMATE ker-⁴
CREODONT kreue-¹
CREOLE ker-³
CREOSOTE kreue-¹, teue-
CREPE sker-³
CREPITATE ker-²
CRESCENDO ker-³
CRESCENT ker-³
CRESS gras-
CREST sker-³
CREVICE ker-²
CREW¹ ker-³
CRIB ger-²
CRIBRIFORM krei-
CRICKET¹ ker-²
CRICOID sker-³
CRIME krei-
CRIMP¹ ger-²
CRIMSON kʷrmi-
CRINGE ger-²
CRINGLE ger-²
CRINITE sker-³
CRINKLE ger-²
CRINOLINE līno-, sker-³
CRIOSPHINX ker-¹
CRIPPLE ger-²
CRISIS krei-
CRISP sker-³
CRISPATE sker-³
CRISSUM sker-³
CRISTA sker-³
CRISTATE sker-³
CRITERION krei-
CRITIC krei-
CROCHET ger-²
CROCIDOLITE krek-¹
CROCK¹ ger-²
CROCK³ ger-²
CROCKET ger-²
CROFT ger-²
CROMLECH lēu-¹, skerbh-
CRONE sker-¹
CROOK ger-²

CROON gere-²
CROP ger-²
CROQUET ger-²
CROSIER ger-²
CROUCH ger-²
CROUP² ger-²
CROUPIER ger-²
CROUTON kreus-
CROW¹ gere-²
CROW² gere-²
CROWD¹ greut-
CROWD² krut-
CROWN sker-³
CRUCIFY dhīgw-
CRUD greut-
CRUDE kreue-¹
CRUEL kreue-¹
CRULLER ger-²
CRUMB ger-²
CRUMMIE ger-²
CRUMPET ger-²
CRUMPLE ger-²
CRUPPER ger-²
CRUSE ger-²
CRUST kreus-
CRUSTACEAN kreus-
CRUSTACEOUS kreus-
CRUSTOSE kreus-
CRUTCH ger-²
CRYO- kreus-
CRYPT krāu-.
CRYPTIC krāu-
CRYPTO- krāu-
CRYSTAL kreus-
CRYSTALLINE kreus-
CRYSTALLO- kreus-
CTENIDIUM pek-²
CTENOID pek-²
CTENOPHORE pek-²
CUBBY ku-
CUBE keu-²
CUBICLE keu-²
CUBIT keu-²
CUCKING STOOL kakka-
CUD gwet-¹
CUDGEL ku-
CUESTA kost-
CUIRASS koru-
CUISINE pekʷ-
CUISSE koksā
CULET (s)keu-
CULINARY pekʷ-
CULLET kʷel-¹
CULLIS kagh-
CULM¹ koləm-
CULMINATE kel-⁶
CULOTTES (s)keu-
CULT kʷel-¹
CULTIVATE kʷel-¹
CULTRATE skel-¹
CULTURE kʷel-¹
CULVER kel-⁵
CUM kom
CUMMERBUND bhendh-, kamer-
CUMULATE keue-²
CUMULUS keue-²
CUNCTATION konk-
CUNNILINGUS leigh-, (s)keu-
CUNNING gnō-
CUNT ku-
CUP keu-²
CUPID kwep-
CUPIDITY kwep-
CUPOLA keu-²
CUPULE keu-²
CUR gere-²
CURATE cūra
CURATOR cūra
CURB sker-³
CURD greut-
CURE cūra
CURETTE cūra
CURIA wī-ro-
CURIO cūra
CURIOUS cūra
CURL ger-²
CURRENT kers-²
CURRIER sker-¹.
CURSIVE kers-²
CURSOR kers-²
CURT sker-¹
CURTAL sker-¹
CURTILAGE gher-¹
CURTSY gher-¹
CURULE gher-¹
CURVATURE sker-³
CURVE sker-³
CURVET sker-³
CUSHION koksā

CUSK ters-
CUSPIDOR spyeu-
CUSTOM s(w)e-
CUTANEOUS (s)keu-
CUTICLE (s)keu-
CUTIN (s)keu-
CUTIS (s)keu-
CUTLASS skel-¹
CUTLET kost-
CUTTLE ku-
CYCLE kʷel-¹
CYCLO- kʷel-¹
CYCLOID kʷel-¹
CYCLONE kʷel-¹
CYCLOSIS kʷel-¹
CYGNET keuk-
CYGNUS keuk-
CYLINDER skel-³
CYMA keue-²
CYMBAL keu-²
CYMBIDIUM keu-²
CYNIC kwon-
CYNOSURE kwon-, ors-
CYPRIPEDIUM ped-¹
CYPSELA keu-²
CYST kwes-
CYSTO- kwes-
-CYTE (s)keu-
CYTO- (s)keu-

D

DACHA dō-
DACHSHUND kwon-, teks-
DADO dō-
DAFT dhabh-
DAINTY dek-¹
DAIRY dheigh-
DAISY agh-², okw-
DALE dhel-
DALLES dhel-
DAMAGE dap-
DAME deme-¹
DAMN dap-
DAMNIFY dap-
DAN² deme-¹
DANDELION dent-
DANE dan-
DANEGELD gheldh-
DANELAW dan-, legh-
DANGER deme-¹
DANISH dan-
DAPPER dheb-
DARE dhers-
DARK dher-¹
DASTARD dhē-²
DASYURE dens-²
DATE dō-
DATIVE dō-
DATUM dō-
DAUB albho-
DAUGHTER dhugheter-
DAUNT deme-¹
DAWN agh-²
DAY agh-²
DAZE dhē-²
DE- de-
DEACON ken-¹
DEAD dheu-³
DEAF dheu-¹
DEAL¹ dail-
DEAL² tel-
DEAN dekm
DEATH dheu-³
DEBACLE bak-
DEBASE bassus
DEBATE battuere
DEBAUCH bhelg-
DEBENTURE ghabh-
DEBILITATE bel-
DEBILITY bel-
DEBIT ghabh-
DEBONAIR deu-²
DEBOUCH beu-¹
DEBRIS bhrēi-
DEBT ghabh-
DECA- dekm
DECADE dekm
DECAGON dekm
DECALESCENCE kele-
DECALOGUE leg-¹
DECANAL dekm
DECANT kanto-
DECAPITATE kaput
DECAY kad-
DECEASE ked-

DECEIVE kap-
DECEMBER dekm̥
DECEMVIR dekm̥, wī-ro-
DECENARY dekm̥
DECENNIUM at-, dekm̥
DECENT dek-¹
DECI- dekm̥
DECIDE kaə-id-
DECIDUOUS kad-
DECIMAL dekm̥
DECIMATE dekm̥
DECK¹ (s)teg-
DECK² (s)teg-
DECKLE (s)teg-
DECLAIM kelə-¹
DECLARE kelə-²
DECLINE klei-
DECLIVITY klei-
DECOCT pekʷ-
DÉCOLLATE¹ kʷel-¹
DÉCOLLETÉ kʷel-¹
DÉCOR dek-¹
DECORATE dek-¹
DECOROUS dek-¹
DECORTICATE sker-¹
DECOY keuə-, to-
DECREASE ker-³
DECREE krei-
DECREPIT ker-²
DECREPITATE ker-²
DECUMBENT keu-²
DECUPLE dekm̥, pel-³
DECURRENT kers-²
DECUSSATE dekm̥
DEDANS en
DEDICATE deik-
DEDUCE deuk-
DEDUCT deuk-
DEED dhē-¹
DEEM dhē-¹
DEEP dheub-
DEER dheu-¹
DEFACE dhē-¹
DEFAME bhā-²
DEFEASANCE dhē-¹
DEFEAT dhē-¹
DEFECT dhē-¹
DEFEND gʷhen-¹
DEFENSE gʷhen-¹
DEFER¹ bher-¹
DEFER² bher-¹
DEFERVESCENCE bhreu-²
DEFIANCE bheidh-
DEFICIENT dhē-¹
DEFILE¹ pū-²
DEFILE² gʷhī-
DEFLAGRATE bhel-¹
DEFLATE bhlē-²
DEFLOWER bhel-³
DEFOLIATE bhel-³
DEFORCE bhergh-²
DEFORM merph-
DEFUNCT bheug-²
DEFY bheidh-
DEGAGE wadh-
DEGENERATE genə-
DEGLUTINATE gel-¹
DEGLUTITION gʷel-³
DEGRADE ghredh-
DEGREE ghredh-
DEGRESSION ghredh-
DEGUST geus-
DEHISCE ghāi-
DEICIDE deiw-
DEICTIC deik-
DEIFIC deiw-
DEIGN dek-¹
DEISM deiw-
DEITY deiw-
DEJECT yē-
DELAINE welə-¹
DELAY slēg-
DELEGATE leg-¹
DELIBERATE līthrā
DELINQUENT leikʷ-
DELIQUESCE wleik-
DELIRIUM leis-
DELIVER leudh-²
DELL dhel-
DELPHINIUM gʷelbh-
DELUDE leid-
DELUGE leu(ə)-
DELVE dhelbh-
DEMAGOGUE ag-, dā-
DEMAND man-²
DEMARCATION merg-
DEME dā-
DEMEAN¹ men-²
DEMEAN² mei-¹

DEMENT men-¹
DEMETER māter-
DEMILUNE leuk-
DEMIT (s)melt(ə)-
DEMIURGE dā-, werg-
DEMOCRACY dā-
DEMOLISH mō-
DEMON dā-
DEMONSTRATE men-¹
DEMOPHOBIA dā-
DEMOS dā-
DEMOTIC dā-
DEMUR merə-
DEN dan-
DENARIUS dekm̥
DENARY dekm̥
DENDRO- deru
DENDRON deru
DENIER² dekm̥
DENIGRATE negʷ-ro-
DENOMINATE nō-men-
DÉNOUEMENT ned-
DENOUNCE neu-¹
DENSE dens-²
DENTAL dent-
DENTATE dent-
DENTI- dent-
DENTICLE dent-
DENTIFRICE bhrēi-
DENUDE nogʷ-
DENY ne
DEODAR deiw-, deru
DEONTOLOGY deu-¹
DEPEND (s)pen-
DEPICT peig-¹
DEPILATE pilo-
DEPLOY plek-
DEPLUME pleus-
DEPONE apo-
DEPOPULATE populus
DEPORT per-²
DEPOSIT apo-
DEPRECATE prek-
DEPRECIATE per-⁶
DEPREDATE ghend-
DEPRESS per-⁵
DEPRIVE per¹
DEPTH dheub-
DEPURATE peuə-
DEPUTE peuə-
DERACINATE wrād-
DERANGE sker-³
DERELICT leikʷ-
DERIVE rei-³
-DERM der-²
DERMA¹ der-²
DERMA² terə-¹
-DERMA der-²
DERMATO- der-²
DEROGATE reg-¹
DERRIS der-²
DESCANT kan-
DESCEND skand-
DESCRIBE skrībh-
DESERT³ ser-³
DESERVE servus
DESICCATE seikʷ-
DESIGNATE sekʷ-¹
DESIRE sweid-¹
DESIST stā-
DESMID dē-
DESOLATE s(w)e-
DESPAIR spē-¹
DESPICABLE spek-
DESPISE spek-
DESPOIL spel-¹
DESPOND spend-
DESPOT deme-¹
DESTINE stā-
DESTITUTE stā-
DESTRIER deks-
DESTROY ster-²
DESUETUDE s(w)e-
DESULTORY sel-⁴
DETAIN ten-
DETECT (s)teg-
DETENT ten-
DETER tres-
DETERIORATE de-
DETERMINE ter-
DETEST trei-
DETONATE (s)tenə-
DETOUR terə-¹
DETRACT tragh-
DETRIMENT terə-¹
DETUMESCENCE teuə-
DEUCE¹ dwo-
DEUTERAGONIST deu-¹
DEUTERIUM deu-¹

DEUTERO- deu-¹
DEUTERONOMY deu-¹, nem-
DEVANAGARI deiw-
DEVASTATE eu-¹
DEVEST wes-⁴
DEVI deiw-
DEVIATE wegh-
DEVIL gʷele-¹
DEVIOUS wegh-
DEVISE weidh-
DEVOID eu-²
DEVOIR ghabh-
DEVOLVE wel-³
DEVOTE wegʷh-
DEVOUR gʷerə-⁴
DEVOUT wegʷh-
DEW dheu-²
DEXTER deks-
DEXTERITY deks-
DEXTRO- deks-
DEXTRORSE wer-³
DHARMA dher-²
DI-¹ dwo-
DIABASE gʷā-
DIABETES gʷā-
DIABOLIC gʷele-¹
DIACRITICAL krei-
DIADEM dē-
DIAGNOSIS gnō-
DIAGONAL genu-²
DIAGRAM gerbh-
DIAL deiw-
DIALECT leg-¹
DIALOGUE leg-¹
DIALYSIS leu-¹
DIAMETER mē-²
DIAMOND demə-²
DIANTHUS andh-
DIAPASON pant-
DIAPAUSE paus-
DIAPEDESIS ped-¹
DIAPHANOUS bhā-¹
DIAPHORESIS bher-¹
DIAPHRAGM bhrekʷ-
DIAPHYSIS bheuə-
DIARRHEA sreu-
DIARTHROSIS ar-
DIARY deiw-
DIASPORA sper-⁴
DIASTASIS stā-
DIASTOLE stel-
DIASTROPHISM streb(h)-
DIATESSARON kʷetwer-
DIATHESIS dhē-¹
DIATOM tem-
DIATRIBE terə-¹
DIAZO gʷei-
DICAST deik-
DICENTRA kent-
DICHASIUM dwo-
DICHO- dwo-
DICHOTOMY tem-
DICKER dekm̥
DICLINOUS klei-
DICROTISM kret-²
DICTATE deik-
DICTION deik-
DICTUM deik-
DIDACTIC dens-¹
DIDAPPER dub-
DIDYMIUM dwo-
DIDYMOUS dwo-
DIE¹ dheu-³
DIE² dō-
DIESIS yē-
DIET¹ ai-¹
DIET² deiw-
DIFFER bher-¹
DIFFICULTY dhē-¹
DIFFIDENT bheidh-
DIFFRACTION bhreg-
DIFFUSE gheu-
DIG dhigʷ-
DIGEST gerere
DIGIT deik-
DIGNIFY dek-¹
DIGNITY dek-¹
DIGRESS ghredh-
DIKE dhīgʷ-
DILATE stel-
DILATORY telə-
DILIGENT leg-¹
DILUTE leu(ə)-
DIME dekm̥
DIMENSION mē-²
DIMER (s)mer-²
DIMINISH mei-²
DIMITY mei-⁴

DIMPLE dub-
DIN dhwen-
DINGUS tenk-¹
DINOSAUR dwei-
DINOTHERE dwei-
DIOCESE weik-¹
DIOECIOUS weik-¹
DIOICOUS weik-¹
DIOPTER okʷ-
DIOSCURI deiw-, ker-³
DIP dheub-
DIPHTHERIA deph-
DIPHYODONT bheus-
DIPLO- dwo-
DIPLOCARDIAC kerd-¹
DIPLODOCUS dek-¹
DIPLOE dwo-
DIPLOID pel-³
DIPLOMA dwo-
DIPNOAN pneu-
DIRE dwei-
DIRECT reg-¹
DIRNDL tek-
DISARM ar-
DISASTER ster-³
DISBURSE bursa
DISCERN krei-
DISCIPLE dek-¹
DISCIPLINE dek-¹
DISCOMFIT dhē-¹
DISCORD kerd-¹
DISCOURSE kers-²
DISCRIMINATE krei-
DISCUSS kʷēt-
DISDAIN dek-¹
DISEMBOGUE beu-¹
DISFIGURE dheigh-
DISGUST geus-
DISK deik-
DISMAL deiw-, mel-⁵
DISMAY magh-¹
DISMISS (s)meit(ə)-
DISPARATE perə-¹
DISPATCH ped-¹
DISPEL pel-⁶
DISPENSE (s)pen-
DISPERSE (s)preg-
DISPLAY plek-
DISPOSE apo-
DISPUTE peuə-
DISQUISITION quaerere
DISRUPT reup-
DISSECT sek-
DISSEMINATE sē-¹
DISSENT sent-
DISSERTATE ser-³
DISSIDENT sed-¹
DISSILIENT sel-⁴
DISSIPATE swep-²
DISSOCIATE sekʷ-¹
DISSOLVE leu-¹
DISSONANT swen-
DISSUADE swād-
DISTANT stā-
DISTEND ten-
DISTICH steigh-
DISTINGUISH steig-
DISTORT terkʷ-
DISTRACT tragh-
DISTRAIN streig-
DISTURB twer-¹
DITCH dhigʷ-
DITTO deik-
DITTY deik-
DIURETIC wers-²
DIURNAL deiw-
DIVA deiw-
DIVARICATE wā-
DIVE dheub-
DIVERGE wer-³
DIVERT wer-³
DIVES deiw-
DIVIDE weidh-
DIVINE¹ deiw-
DIVINE² deiw-
DIVULSION wel-⁴
DIZZY dheu-¹
DO¹ dhē-¹
DOCENT dek-¹
DOCETISM dek-¹
DOCILE dek-¹
DOCK¹ deuk-
DOCK⁴ dheu-¹
DOCTOR dek-¹
DOCTRINE dek-¹
DOCUMENT dek-¹
DODDER¹ dud-
DODDER² dud-
DODECAGON dekm̥, dwo-

DOGE deuk-	DRONE1 dher-3	EASTER aus-1	ELDER2 el-2
DOGMA dek-1	DROOP dhreu-	EASTERN aus-1	ELDEST al-3
DOGMATIC dek-1	DROP dhreu-	EAT ed-	ELECAMPANE wel-3
DOIT twei-	DROPSY wed-1	EAVES upo	ELECT leg-1
DOLABRIFORM del-3	DROSHKY dhragh-	EAVESDROP upo	ELECTUARY leigh-
DOLCE dĺk-u-	DROSS dher-1	EBB apo-	ELEVATE legwh-
DOLDRUMS dheu-1	DROUGHT dreug-	EBLIS gwele-1	ELEVEN oi-no-
DOLE1 dail-	DROVE2 dhreibh-	EBULLIENCE beu-	ELF albho-
DOLE2 del-3	DROWN dhreg-	ECBOLIC gwele-1	ELIXIR ksero-
DOLERITE del-2	DROWSE dhreu-	ECCENTRIC kent-	ELK el-2
DOLICHOCEPHALIC del-1	DRUID deru	ECCHYMOSIS gheu-	ELL2 el-1
DOLICHOCRANIAL del-1	DRUPE deru, pekw-	ECCLESIA kele-2	ELLIPSIS leikw-
DOLOR del-3	DRY dreug-	ECCRINE krei-	ELM el-1
DOLPHIN gwelbh-	DUAD dwo-	ECESIS weik-1	ELOCUTION tolkw-
DOLT dheu-1	DUAL dwo-	ECHARD segh-	ELODEA sel-es-
DOM deme-1, dhē-1	DUB1 dheubh-	ECHELON skand-	ELOIGN del-1
DOMAIN deme-1	DUB2 dheubh-	ECHIDNA angwhi-	ELONGATE del-1
DOME deme-1	DUBIOUS dwo-	ECHINO- angwhi-	ELOPE klou-
DOMESTIC deme-1	DUCAL deuk-	ECHINUS angwhi-	ELSE al-1
DOMICILE deme-1	DUCAT deuk-	ECHO (s)wāgh-	ELUANT leu(e)-
DOMINATE deme-1	DUCHESS deuk-	ECHOLALIA lā-	ELUCIDATE leuk-
DOMINICAL deme-1	DUCHY deuk-	ÉCLAIR kele-2	ELUDE leid-
DOMINIE deme-1	DUCT deuk-	ÉCLAIRISSEMENT kele-2	ELUTE leu(e)-
DOMINION deme-1	DUCTILE deuk-	ECLAMPSIA lāp-	ELUVIUM leu(e)-
DOMINO1 deme-1	DUDEEN dheu-1	ECLECTIC leg-1	ELYTRON wel-3
DOMINO2 deme-1	DUE ghabh-	ECLIPSE leikw-	EMACIATE māk-
DONATION dō-	DUEL duellum	ECLOSION kleu-3	EMANATE mā-3
DONATIVE dō-	DUENNA deme-1	ECOLOGY weik-1	EMANCIPATE man-2
DONOR dō-1	DUET dwo-	ECONOMY weik-1	EMASCULATE mas
DOOM dhē-1	DUKE deuk-	ECRU kreue-1	EMBASSAGE ag-
DOOR dhwer-	DUKHOBOR bher-2, dheu-1	ECSTASY stā-	EMBASSY ag-
DOPE dub-	DULCET dĺk-u-	ECTO- eghs	EMBELLISH deu-2
DORMANT drem-	DULCIFY dĺk-u-	ECTOSARC twerk-	EMBER eus-
DORMER drem-	DULL dheu-1	ECU skei-	EMBER DAY ambhi, rei-3
DORMITORY drem-	DUMA dhē-1	ECUMENICAL weik-1	EMBLEM gwele-1
DORSAL dorsum	DUMB dheu-1	ECZEMA yes-	EMBLEMENTS bhel-3
DORSO- dorsum	DUMP dub-	EDACIOUS ed-	EMBOUCHURE beu-1
DORY2 aurum	DUN2 dheu-1	EDAPHIC sed-1	EMBRACE mregh-u-
DOSE dō-	DUNDERHEAD (s)tene-	EDDY eti	EMBROCATE mergh-
DOSS dorsum	DUNE dhūno-	EDELWEISS athal-, kweit-	EMEND mend-
DOSSAL dorsum	DUNGEON deme-1	EDEMA oid-	EMERGE mezg-1
DOSSER dorsum	DUNK teng-	EDENTATE dent-	EMERITUS (s)mer-2
DOSSIER dorsum	DUO- dwo-	EDGE ak-	EMESIS weme-
DOT2 dō-	DUODECIMAL dekm̥, dwo-	EDIBLE ed-	EMETIC weme-
DOTE dud-	DUOPSONY wes-1	EDICT deik-	EMIGRATE mei-1
DOUBLE dwo-	DUPLE dwo-	EDIFICE aidh-, dhē-1	EMINENT men-2
DOUBLET dwo-	DUPLEX dwo-	EDIFY aidh-, dhē-1	EMIT (s)meit(e)-
DOUBLOON dwo-	DUPLICATE dwo-	EDITION dō-	EMMET mai-1
DOUBLURE dwo-	DUPLICITY dwo-	EDUCATE deuk-	EMOLLIENT mel-1
DOUBT dwo-	DURABLE deue-	EDUCE deuk-	EMOTION meue-
DOUCEUR dĺk-u-	DURAMEN deru	EFFACE dhē-1	EMPEROR pere-1
DOUCHE deuk-	DURA MATER deru	EFFECT dhē-1	EMPHASIS bhā-1
DOUGH dheigh-	DURANCE deue-	EFFEMINATE dhē(i)-	EMPHYSEMA pū-1
DOUGHTY dheugh-	DURATION deue-	EFFERENT bher-1	EMPIRIC per-4
DOUR deru.	DURBAR dhwer-	EFFERVESCE bhreu-2	EMPLOY plek-
DOVE1 dheu-1	DURESS deru	EFFETE dhē(i)-	EMPORIUM per-2
DOWAGER dō-	DURING deue-	EFFICACIOUS dhē-1	EMPRISE ghend-
DOWEL dheubh-	DURST dhers-	EFFICIENT dhē-1	EMPTY med-
DOWER dō-	DURUM deru	EFFIGY dheigh-	EMPYEMA pū-2
DOWN1 dhūno-	DUSK dheu-1	EFFLORESCE bhel-3	EMPYREAL pūr-
DOWN2 dheu-1	DUST dheu-1	EFFLUENT bhleu-	EMULSION melg-
DOWN3 dhūno-	DUTCH teutā-	EFFLUVIUM bhleu-	EMUNCTORY meug-2
DOWRY dō-	DUTY ghabh-	EFFLUX bhleu-	EN-1 en
DOXOLOGY dek-1	DUUMVIR wī-ro-	EFFORT bhergh-2	EN-2 en
DOYEN dekm̥	DUVETYN dheu-1	EFFULGENT bhel-1	ENAMEL mel-1
DOZE dheu-1	DWELL dheu-1	EFFUSE gheu-	ENAMOR amma
DOZEN dekm̥, dwo-	DWINDLE dheu-3	EFTSOONS apo-	ENANTIOMER ant-
DRAB1 der-2	DYAD dwo-	EGEST gerere	ENANTIOMORPH ant-
DRAB2 der-1	DYNAMIC deu-2	EGG1 awi-	ENARTHROSIS ar-
DRABBLE dher-1	DYNAMITE deu-2	EGG2 ak-	ENATE gene-
DRACHMA dergh-	DYNAST deu-2	EGLANTINE ak-	ENCAUSTIC kēu-
DRAFT dhragh-	DYNASTY deu-2	EGO eg	ENCEINTE2 kenk-1
DRAG dhragh-	DYS- dus-	EGOIST eg	ENCEPHALO- ghebh-el-
DRAGON derk-	DYSENTERY en	EGOTISM eg	ENCHANT kan-
DRAGOON derk-	DYSLEXIA leg-1	EGREGIOUS ger-1	ENCHASE kap-
DRAIN dreug-	DYSMENORRHEA mē-2	EGRESS ghredh-	ENCHIRIDION ghesor-
DRAKE2 derk-	DYSPEPSIA pekw-	EIDER ēti-	ENCLAVE kleu-1
DRAMA dere-	DYSPLASIA pele-2	EIDERDOWN dheu-1	ENCLITIC klei-
DRAMATURGE werg-	DYSPNEA pneu-	EIDETIC weid-	ENCOUNTER kom
DRAPE dere-	DYSPROSIUM ei-1	EIDOLON weid-	ENCROACH ger-2
DRASTIC dere-		EIGHT oktō(u)	ENCYCLICAL kwel-1
DRAW dhragh-		EINKORN gre-no-, oi-no-	ENCYCLOPEDIA pau-
DRAY dhragh-		EISTEDDFOD bheue-, sed-1	END ant-
DREAM dhreugh-		EITHER kwo-	ENDEAVOR ghabh-
DREARY dhreu-	**E**	EJACULATE yē-	ENDEMIC dā-
DRECK sker-4		EJECT yē-	ENDERGONIC werg-
DREGS dher-1		EKE1 aug-1	ENDOCARDIUM kerd-1
DRENCH dhreg-		EKE2 au-2	ENDOCRINE krei-
DRIFT dhreibh-	EACH līk-	ELABORATE leb-1	ENDOERGIC werg-
DRILL1 tere-1	EAGER1 ak-	ELAND el-2	ENDORSE dorsum
DRINK dhreg-	EAR1 ous-	ELAPID lep-1	ENDOSTEUM ost-
DRIP dhreu-	EAR2 ak-	ELAPSE leb-1	ENDOTHECIUM dhē-1
DRIVE dhreibh-	EARLY ayer-	ELASMOBRANCH el-3	ENDOTHELIUM dhē(i)-
DRIVEL dher-1	EARN1 esen-	ELASTIC el-3	ENDOW dō-
DRIZZLE dhreu-	EARNEST1 er-1	ELATE tele-	ENDUE deuk-, eu-1
-DROME der-1	EARTH er-2	ELATER el-3	ENDURE deru
DROMEDARY der-1	EARWIG wegh-	ELATERITE el-3	ENEMA yē-
DROMOND der-1	EASE yē-	ELBOW el-1	ENEMY amma
-DROMOUS der-1	EASEL asinus	ELDER1 al-3	ENERGY werg-
	EAST aus-1		

ENERVATE (s)neǝu-
ENFILADE gʷhi-
ENFLEURAGE bhel-³
ENFORCE bhergh-²
ENGAGE wadh-¹
ENGAGE wadh-¹
ENGENDER gene-
ENGINE gene-
ENGRAVE ghrebh-²
ENGROSS gʷres-
ENHANCE al-³
ENIGMA ai-²
ENJOIN yeug-
ENJOY gāu-
ENKEPHALIN en, ghebh-el-
ENNEAD newṇ
ENNUI od-²
ENORMOUS gnō-
ENOUGH kom, nek-²
ENSEMBLE sem-¹
ENSIFORM ṇsi-
ENSTATITE stā-
ENSUE sekʷ-¹
ENSURE cūra
ENTELECHY kʷei-¹, segh-
ENTER en
ENTERIC en
ENTERO- en
ENTERON en
ENTERPRISE ghend-
ENTERTAIN ten-
ENTHUSIASM dhēs-
ENTHYMEME dheu-¹
ENTIRE tag-
ENTITY es-
ENTO- en
ENTOMO- tem-
ENTRAILS en
ENTRAP der-¹
ENTREPRENEUR ghend-
ENTRESOL sel-¹
ENTROPY trep-²
ENUMERATE nem-
ENUNCIATE neu-¹
ENURESIS wers-²
ENVOI wegh-
ENVOY¹ wegh-
ENVY weid-
ENZYME yeuǝ-
EO- aus-¹
EOHIPPUS ekwo-
EON aiw-
Eos aus-¹
EOSIN aus-¹
EPACT ag-
EPEIROGENY āpero-
EPENTHESIS dhē-¹
EPHEBE yēgʷā-
EPHEDRINE sed-¹
EPHEMERAL āmer-
EPHOR wer-⁴
EPI- epi
EPIBOLY gʷelǝ-¹
EPIC wekʷ-
EPICARDIUM kerd-¹
EPICENE kom
EPICRITIC krei-
EPIDEMIC dā-
EPIDERMIS der-²
EPIDIDYMIS dwo-
EPIDOTE dō-
EPIGASTRIUM gras-
EPIGEAL gē
EPIGENE gene-
EPIGONE gene-
EPIGRAM gerbh-
EPIGRAPH gerbh-
EPILEPSY (s)lagʷ-
EPILOGUE leg-¹
EPIMYSIUM mūs-
EPIPHANY bhā-¹
EPIPHYSIS bheuǝ-
EPISCOPAL spek-
EPISODE en, sed-²
EPISTASIS stā-
EPISTAXIS stag-
EPISTEMOLOGY stā-
EPISTLE stel-
EPISTYLE stā-
EPITAPH dhembh-
EPITASIS ten-
EPITHELIUM dhē(i)-
EPITHET dhē-¹
EPITOME tem-
EPOCH segh-
EPODE wed-²
EPONYM nō-men-
EPONYMOUS nō-men-
EPOS wekʷ-

EPSILON bhes-¹
EQUANIMITY anǝ-
EQUESTRIAN ekwo-
EQUILIBRIUM līthrā
EQUINE ekwo-
EQUINOX nekʷ-t-
EQUIP skipam
EQUIPONDERATE (s)pen-
EQUISETUM ekwo-
EQUITANT ekwo-
EQUITATION ekwo-
EQUIVALENT wal-
EQUIVOCAL wekʷ-
ERA ayes-
ERADICATE wrād-
ERASE rēd-
ERE ayer-
EREBUS regʷ-es-
ERECT reg-¹
EREMITE erǝ-²
EREMURUS erǝ-², ors-
EREPSIN rep-
ERG werg-
ERGO reg-¹
ERGOGRAPH werg-
ERNE or-
ERODE rēd-
ERR ers-¹
ERRANT ei-¹
ERRATIC ers-¹
ERRATUM ers-¹
ERRONEOUS ers-¹
ERROR ers-¹
ERSATZ sed-¹, ud-
ERSE peiǝ-
ERST ayer-
ERUBESCENCE reudh-¹
ERUCT reug-
ERUPT reup-
ERYSIPELAS pel-⁴, reudh-¹
ERYTHEMA reudh-¹
ERYTHRO- reudh-¹
ESCALADE skand-
ESCAROLE ed-
ESCHATOLOGY eghs
ESCHEAT kad-
ESCUDO skei-
ESCULENT ed-
ESCUTCHEON skei-
ESOTERIC en
ESPARTO sper-²
ESPECIAL spek-
ESPERANCE spē-¹
ESPIONAGE spek-
ESPOUSE spend-
ESPY spek-
ESQUIRE skei-
ESSAY ag-
ESSENCE es-
ESSONITE sēk-
ESTABLISH stā-
ESTANCIA stā-
ESTER ak-
ESTHER ster-³
ESTRONE eis-¹
ESTRUS eis-¹
ESTUARY aidh-
ESURIENT ar-
ET CETERA eti, ko-
ETCH ed-
ETERNAL aiw-
ETESIAN wet-²
ETHER aidh-
ETHIC s(w)e-
ETHMOID sē-³
ETHNIC s(w)e-
ETHNO- s(w)e-
ETHOS s(w)e-
ETIOLOGY ai-¹
ETIQUETTE steig-
EU- esu-
EUCALYPTUS kel-²
EUCARYOTE kar-¹
EUCHARIST gher-⁵
EUGLENA gel-²
EUMENIDES men-¹
EUNUCH segh-
EUONYMUS nō-men-
EUPATRID pǝter-
EUPEPTIC pekʷ-
EUPHEMISM bhā-²
EUPHONY bhā-²
EUPHORIA bher-¹
EUPHROSYNE gʷhren-
EUPNEA pneu-
EUREKA werǝ-²
EURUS eus-
EURY- werǝ-¹
EURYDICE deik-, werǝ-¹

EUTECTIC tā-
EUTHANASIA dhwenǝ-
EUTHENICS gʷhen-²
EUTROPHIC threph-
EUXENITE xenos
EVACUATE eu-²
EVADE wadh-²
EVAGINATE wag-
EVANESCE eu-²
EVANGEL angelos
EVAPORATE kwēp-
EVECTION wegh-
EVENT gʷā-
EVENTIDE dā-
EVER aiw-
EVERT wer-³
EVERY aiw-
EVICT weik-⁵
EVIDENT weid-
EVIL wep-
EVOKE wekʷ-
EVOLVE wel-³
EVULSION wel-⁴
EVZONE yōs-
EWE owi-
EWER akʷā-
EX¹ eghs
EX- eghs
EXACERBATE ak-
EXACT ag-
EXALT al-³
EXAMINE ag-
EXAMPLE em-
EXANTHEMA andh-
EXARCH arkhein
EXCALIBUR kal-³
EXCAVATE keuǝ-²
EXCEED ked-
EXCEL kel-⁶
EXCEPT kap-
EXCERPT kerp-
EXCISE² kaǝ-id-
EXCITE kei-³
EXCLAIM kelǝ-²
EXCLUDE kleu-³
EXCORIATE sker-¹
EXCREMENT krei-
EXCRESCENCE ker-³
EXCURSION kers-²
EXECRATE sak-
EXECUTE sekʷ-¹
EXEDRA sed-¹
EXEGESIS sāg-
EXEMPLARY em-
EXEMPLIFY em-
EXEMPLUM em-
EXEMPT em-
EXERCISE arek-
EXERGONIC werg-
EXERGUE werg-
EXERT ser-³
EXFOLIATE bhel-³
EXHAUST aus-²
EXHIBIT ghabh-
EXHILARATE sel-²
EXHORT gher-⁵
EXHUME dhghem-
EXIGENT ag-
EXILE al-²
EXINE wei-¹
EXIST stā-
EXIT¹ ei-¹
EXIT² ei-¹
EXO- eghs
EXOCRINE krei-
EXODUS sed-²
EXOERGIC werg-
EXONERATE en-es-
EXOPHTHALMOS okʷ-
EXORDIUM ar-
EXOSTOSIS ost-
EXOTERIC eghs
EXOTIC eghs
EXPAND petǝ-
EXPATRIATE pǝter-
EXPECT spek-
EXPECTORATE peg-
EXPEDITE ped-¹
EXPEL pel-⁶
EXPEND (s)pen-
EXPERIENCE per-⁴
EXPERIMENT per-⁴
EXPERT per-⁴
EXPIATE pius
EXPIRE spīrāre
EXPLAIN pelǝ-²
EXPLETIVE pelǝ-¹
EXPLICATE plek-
EXPLICIT plek-
EXPORT per-²

EXPOSTULATE prek-
EXPOUND apo-
EXPRESS per-⁵
EXPUNGE peuk-
EXPURGATE peuǝ-
EXQUISITE quaerere
EXSCIND skei-
EXSECT sek-
EXSICCATE seikʷ-
EXTANT stā-
EXTEND ten-
EXTENUATE ten-
EXTERIOR eghs
EXTERMINATE ter-
EXTERNAL eghs
EXTINGUISH steig-
EXTOL tele-
EXTORT terkʷ-
EXTRA- eghs
EXTRACT tragh-
EXTREME eghs
EXTROVERSION wer-³
EXTROVERT wer-³
EXTRUDE treud-
EXUBERANT euǝdh-
EXUBERATE euǝdh-
EXUDE sweid-²
EXULT sel-⁴
EXUVIAE eu-¹
EYAS nizdo-
EYE okʷ-
EYELET okʷ-
EYRE ei-¹
EYRIR aurum

F

FABRIC dhabh-
FABRICATE dhabh-
FAÇADE dhē-¹
FACE dhē-¹
FACET dhē-¹
FACIAL dhē-¹
FACIAS skei-
-FACIENT dhē-¹
FACIES dhē-¹
FACILE dhē-¹
FACILITY dhē-¹
FACSIMILE dhē-¹
FACT dhē-¹
FACTION dhē-¹
FACTITIOUS dhē-¹
FACTOR dhē-¹
FACTOTUM dhē-¹, teutā-
FACULTY dhē-¹
FAIN pek-¹
FAINT dheigh-
FAIR¹ pek-¹
FAIR² dhēs-
FAITH bheidh-
FALCON pel-²
FALDSTOOL pel-³
FALL p(h)ol-
FALLOW DEER pel-²
FALTBOAT pel-³
FAME bhā-²
FAMOUS bhā-²
FAN¹ wet-²
FANATIC dhēs-
FANG pag-
FANTASY bhā-¹
FANTOCCINI bhā-²
FAR per¹
FARCE bhrekʷ-
FARCI bhrekʷ-
FARCY bhrekʷ-
FARE per-²
FARINA bhares-
FARINACEOUS bhares-
FARM dher-²
FARRAGINOUS bhares-
FARRAGO bhares-
FARRIER ferrum
FARROW¹ porko-
FART perd-
FARTHING kʷetwer-
FARTHINGALE virēre
FASCES bhasko-
FASCIA bhasko-
FASCICLE bhasko-
FASCINATE bhasko-
FASCINE bhasko-
FASCISM bhasko-
FASHION dhē-¹
FAST¹ past-
FAST² past-

FASTEN past-
FASTIDIOUS bhar-
FASTIGIATE bhar-
FASTIGIUM bhar-
FAT peiə-
FATE bhā-[2]
FATHER pəter-
FATHOM petə-
FATIDIC deik-
FAUBOURG bhergh-[2], dhwer-
FAVA BEAN bha-bhā-
FAVOR ghow-ē-
FAVORITE ghow-ē-
FAWN[1] pek-[1]
FAWN[2] dhē(i)-
FAY[1] pag-
FEALTY bheidh-
FEAR per-[4]
FEASIBLE dhē-[1]
FEAST dhēs-
FEAT[1] dhē-[1]
FEATHER pet-
FEATURE dhē-[1]
FEBRIFUGE bheug-[1]
FECUND dhē(i)-
FEDERAL bheidh-
FEDERATE bheidh-
FEE peku-
FEEBLE bhlē-[1]
FEED pā-
FEEL pōl-
FEIGN dheigh-
FEINT dheigh-
FEIST pezd-
FELDSPAR pelə-[2]
FELICIFIC dhē(i)-
FELICITATE dhē(i)-
FELICITY dhē(i)-
FELL[1] p(h)ol-
FELL[3] pel-[4]
FELLATIO dhē(i)-
FELLOW legh-, peku-
FELO-DE-SE s(w)e-
FELON[2] ghel-[2]
FELT[1] pel-[6]
FEMALE dhē(i)-
FEMININE dhē(i)-
FEMTO- penkʷe
FEN pen-
FENCE gʷhen-[1]
FENNEL dhē(i)-
FENUGREEK dhē(i)-
-FER bher-[1]
FERAL ghwer-
FER-DE-LANCE ferrum
FERE per-[2]
FERIA dhēs-
FERMATA dher-[2]
FERMENT bhreu-[2]
FERN per-[2]
FEROCIOUS ghwer-
FERRET[1] bher-[1]
FERRET[2] bhel-[3]
FERRI- ferrum
FERRO- ferrum
FERROUS ferrum
FERRUGINOUS ferrum
FERRULE wei-[1]
FERRY per-[2]
FERTILE bher-[1]
FERVENT bhreu-[2]
FERVID bhreu-[2]
FERVOR bhreu-[2]
FESS bhasko-
-FEST dhēs-
FESTAL dhēs-
FESTINATE bhers-
FESTIVAL dhēs-
FESTIVE dhēs-
FESTOON dhēs-
FETAL dhē(i)-
FETCH[1] ped-[1]
FETE dhēs-
FETICIDE dhē(i)-
FETISH dhē-[1]
FETLOCK ped-[1]
FETTER ped-[1]
FETTLE ped-[2]
FETUS dhē(i)-
FEUD[1] peig-[2]
FEUD[2] peku-
FEUILLETON bhel-[3]
FEVERFEW bheug-[1]
FEW pau-
FEY peig-[2]
FIANCE bheidh-
FIAT bheuə-
FIBULA dhīgʷ-
-FIC dhē-[1]
FICHU dhīgʷ-
FICKLE peig-[2]
FICTILE dheigh-
FICTION dheigh-
-FID bheid-
FIDELITY bheidh-
FIDUCIAL bheidh-
FIDUCIARY bheidh-
FIELD pelə-[2]
FIELDFARE wer-[4]
FIEND pē(i)-
FIERCE ghwer-
FIESTA dhēs-
FIFE pipp-
FIFTEEN penkʷe
FIFTH penkʷe
FIGHT pek-[2]
FIGMENT dheigh-
FIGURE dheigh-
FILAMENT gʷhī-
FILAR gʷhī-
FILARIA gʷhī-
FILE[1] gʷhī-
FILE[2] peig-[1]
FILE[3] pū̆-[2]
FILIAL dhē(i)-
FILIATE dhē(i)-
FILIBUSTER prī-
FILIFORM gʷhī-
FILIGREE gr̥ə-no-, gʷhī-
FILL pelə-[1]
FILLET gʷhī-
FILLY pau-
FILM pel-[4]
FILOPLUME gʷhī-
FILOSE gʷhī-
FILTER pel-[6]
FILTH pū̆-[2]
FILUM gʷhī-
FIN[2] penkʷe
FINCH sping-
FIND pent-
FINGER penkʷe
FINOCHIO dhē(i)-
FIR perkʷu-
FIRE pūr-
FIRKIN kʷetwer-
FIRM dher-[2]
FIRMAMENT dher-[2]
FIRN per[1]
FIRST per[1]
FIRTH per-[2]
FISH peisk-
FISSI- bheid-
FISSILE bheid-
FISSION bheid-
FISSURE bheid-
FIST penkʷe
FIVE penkʷe
FIX dhīgʷ-
FIXATE dhīgʷ-
FIXITY dhīgʷ-
FIXTURE dhīgʷ-
FIZGIG peis-[2]
FIZZLE pezd-
FJELD pelis-
FJORD per-[2]
FLABELLUM bhlē-[2]
FLAG[4] plāk-[1]
FLAGELLATE bhlag-
FLAGELLUM bhlag-
FLAGITIOUS bhlag-
FLAGRANT bhel-[1]
FLAIL bhlag-
FLAIR bhrag-
FLAKE[1] plāk-[1]
FLAKE[2] plāk-[1]
FLAMBÉ bhel-[1]
FLAMBEAU bhel-[1]
FLAMBOYANT bhel-[1]
FLAME bhel-[1]
FLAMEN bhlād-
FLAMINGO bhel-[1]
FLAMMABLE bhel-[1]
FLAN plat-
FLÂNEUR pelə-[2]
FLANK kleng-
FLANNEL welə-[1]
FLAP plab-
FLAT[1] plat-
FLAT[2] plat-
FLATTER[1] plat-
FLATUS bhlē-[2]
FLAVESCENT bhel-[1]
FLAVIN bhel-[1]
FLAVO- bhel-[1]
FLAVONE bhel-[1]
FLAVOPROTEIN bhel-[1]
FLAVOR bhlē-[2]
FLAW[1] plāk-[1]
FLAX plek-
FLAY plēk-
FLEA plou-
FLÈCHE pleu-
FLECK plēk-
FLEDGE pleu-
FLEE pleu-
FLEECE pleus-
FLEET[1] pleu-
FLEET[2] pleu-
FLESH plēk-
FLETCHER pleu-
FLEY pleu-
FLIGHT[1] pleu-
FLIGHT[2] pleu-
FLINCH kleng-
FLINDERS splei-
FLING plāk-[2]
FLINT splei-
FLIT pleu-
FLITCH plēk-
FLOAT pleu-
FLOE plāk-[1]
FLOG bhlag-
FLOOD pleu-
FLOOR pelə-[2]
FLORA bhel-[3]
Flora bhel-[3]
FLORAL bhel-[3]
FLORIATED bhel-[3]
FLORID bhel-[3]
FLORIGEN bhel-[3]
FLORIN bhel-[3]
FLORIST bhel-[3]
-FLOROUS bhel-[3]
FLOSCULUS bhel-[3]
FLOTILLA pleu-
FLOTSAM pleu-
FLOUNCE[1] sker-[3]
FLOUNDER[2] plat-
FLOUR bhel-[3]
FLOURISH bhel-[3]
FLOW pleu-
FLOWER bhel-[3]
FLUCTUATE bhleu-
FLUENT bhleu-
FLUERIC bhleu-
FLUE[2] pleu-
FLÜGELHORN ker-[1], pleu-
FLUID bhleu-
FLUKE[1] plāk-[1]
FLUME bhleu-
FLUOR bhleu-
FLUORIDE bhleu-
FLUORO- bhleu-
FLUSH[2] bhleu-
FLUSTER pleu-
FLUTTER pleu-
FLUVIAL bhleu-
FLUVIOMARINE bhleu-
FLUX bhleu-
FLY[1] pleu-
FLY[2] pleu-
FOAL pau-
FOAM (s)poi-mo-
FODDER pā-
FOE peig-[2]
FOG[2] pū̆-[2]
FOIL[2] bhel-[3]
FOISON gheu-
FOIST penkʷe
-FOLD pel-[3]
FOLD[1] pel-[3]
FOLIAGE bhel-[3]
FOLICOLOUS bhel-[3]
FOLIO bhel-[3]
FOLIUM bhel-[3]
FOLKMOTE mōd-
FOLLICLE bhel-[2]
FOLLICULITIS bhel-[2]
FOMENT dhegʷh-
FOMITE dhegʷh-
FOND[2] bhudh-
FONDANT gheu-
FONDUE gheu-
FONT[1] dhen-[1]
FONT[2] gheu-
FOOD pā-
FOOL[1] bhel-[2]
FOOT ped-[1]
FOOTPAD pent-
FOR per[1]
FOR- per[1]
FORAGE pā-
FORAMEN bher-[2]
FORBEAR bher-[1]
FORBID bheudh-
FORCE bhergh-[2]
FORCEPS gʷher-
FORCIPATE gʷher-
FORD per-[2]
FORDO dhē-[1]
FORE per[1]
FORE- per[1]
FORECLOSE dhwer-
FOREFATHER per[1], pəter-
FOREGO[1] ghē-
FOREIGN dhwer-
FOREMOST per[1]
FORENSIC dhwer-
FOREST dhwer-
FORESTALL stel-
FORFEIT dhē-[1], dhwer-
FORFICATE bherdh-
FORGE[1] dhabh-
FORGET ghend-
FORGIVE ghabh-
FORGO ghē-
FORLORN leu-[1]
FORLORN HOPE keu-[2], leu-[1]
FORM merph-
FORMAL merph-
FORMER[2] per[1]
FORMIC morwi-
FORMICARY morwi-
FORMICIVOROUS morwi-
FORMULA merph-
Fornax gʷher-
FORNICATE gʷher-
FORSAKE sāg-
FORT bhergh-[2]
FORTALICE bhergh-[2]
FORTE[1] bhergh-[2]
FORTE[2] bhergh-[2]
FORTH per[1]
FORTIFY bhergh-[2]
FORTIS bhergh-[2]
FORTISSIMO bhergh-[2]
FORTITUDE bhergh-[2]
FORTRESS bhergh-[2]
FORTY kʷetwer-
FORUM dhwer-
FOSSA bhedh-
FOSSE bhedh-
FOSSIL bhedh-
FOSSORIAL bhedh-
FOSTER pā-
FOUDROYANT bhel-[1]
FOUL pū̆-[2]
FOUND[1] bhudh-
FOUND[2] gheu-
FOUNDER bhudh-
FOUNTAIN dhen-[1]
FOUR kʷetwer-
FOURTEEN kʷetwer-
FOURTH kʷetwer-
FOWL pleu-
FOX puk-[2]
FOY wegh-
Fra bhrāter-
FRACTED bhreg-
FRACTION bhreg-
FRACTIOUS bhreg-
FRACTURE bhreg-
FRAGILE bhreg-
FRAGMENT bhreg-
FRAGRANT bhrag-
FRAIL[1] bhreg-
FRANGIBLE bhreg-
FRANK[1] Frankon-
Frank Frankon-
FRANTIC gʷhren-
FRATERNAL bhrāter-
FRATRICIDE bhrāter-
Frau per[1]
FRAUGHT ēik-
Fräulein per[1]
FRAXINELLA bherəg-
FRAY[2] bhrēi-
FRECKLE (s)preg-
FREE prī-
FREEZE preus-
FREIGHT ēik-
FREMITUS bhrem-[1]
French Frankon-
FRENETIC gʷhren-
FRENULUM ghrendh-
FRENUM ghrendh-
FRENZY gʷhren-
FREQUENT bhrekʷ-
FRET[1] ed-
FRIABLE bhrēi-
FRIAR bhrāter-
FRICATIVE bhrēi-
FRICTION bhrēi-
Friday prī-
FRIEND prī-

FRIGG prī-
FRIGID srīg-
FRITTER[1] ped-[2]
FRO per[1]
FROG preu-
FROLIC līk-, preu-
FROM per[1]
FRONTISPIECE spek-
FROST preus-
FROTTAGE bhrēi-
FROWARD per[1]
FRUCTIFY bhrūg-
FRUGAL bhrūg-
FRUGIVOROUS bhrūg-
FRUIT bhrūg-
FRUITION bhrūg-
FRUMENTACEOUS bhrūg-
FRUMENTY bhrūg-
FRUSTULE bhreus-[2]
FRUSTUM bhreus-[2]
FRY[1] bher-[4]
FUGACIOUS bheug-[1]
-FUGE bheug-[1]
FUGITIVE bheug-[1]
FUGLEMAN man-[1], pleu-
FUGUE bheug-[1]
FÜHRER per-[2]
FULCRUM bhelg-
FULGENT bhel-[1]
FULGURATE bhel-[1]
FULIGINOUS dheu-[1]
FULL[1] pelə-[1]
FULMAR pū-[2]
FULMINATE bhel-[1]
FUMARIC ACID dheu-[1]
FUMAROLE dheu-[1]
FUMATORIUM dheu-[1]
FUMATORY dheu-[1]
FUME dheu-[1]
FUMIGATE ag-, dheu-[1]
FUMITORY dheu-[1], ters-
FUNAMBULIST al-[2]
FUNCTION bheug-[2]
FUND bhudh-
FUNDAMENT bhudh-
FUNDUS bhudh-
FUNGIBLE bheug-[2]
FUNNEL gheu-
FUR pā-
FURBISH prep-
FURL leig-[1]
FURLOUGH leubh-
FURNACE gwher-
FURNISH per[1]
FURROW perk-[2]
FURTHER per[1]
FURTIVE bher-[1]
FURUNCLE bher-[1]
FURUNCULOSIS bher-[1]
FURZE pūro-
FUSE[2] gheu-
FUSILE gheu-
FUSION gheu-
FUTILE gheu-
FUTURE bheuə-
FUZZY pū-[2]
-FY dhē-[1]

G

GABERDINE per-[2], wel-[3]
GABFEST dhēs-
GABION keuə-[2]
GABLE ghebh-el-
GABRO gladh-
GAD[2] ghasto-
GAEA gē
GAGE[1] wadh-[1]
GAIN[1] wei-[2]
GAINLY gagina
GAINSAY gagina
GAIT ghē-
GALACTIC melg-
GALACTO- melg-
GALAXY melg-
GALL[1] ghel-[2]
GALLIARD gal-[3]
GALLINACEOUS gal-[2]
GALLINULE gal-[2]
GALLOP klou-, wel-[2]
GALLOWGLASS yeu-
GALLOWS ghalgh-
GALORE lau-
GAM[2] kamp-
GAMBADO[2] kamp-
GAMBIT kamp-

GAMBOL kamp-
GAMBREL kamp-
GAMETE gemə-
GAMMON[3] kamp-
GAMO- gemə-
GAMOSEPALOUS gemə-
-GAMOUS gemə-
-GAMY gemə-
GANDER ghans-
GANG[1] ghengh-
GANGLING ghengh-
GANGLION gel-[1]
GANGRENE gras-
GANGUE ghengh-
GANNET ghans-
GANOID gâu-
GAP ghāi-
GAPE ghāi-
GAR[2] garwian
GARAGE wer-[5]
GARB garwian
GARBLE krei-
GARBOIL beu-[1]
GARDEN gher-[1]
GARFISH ghaiso-
GARGET gwerə-[4]
GARLIC ghaiso-, leug-[1]
GARMENT wer-[5]
GARNER grə-no-
GARNISH wer-[5]
GARRET wer-[5]
GARRISON wer-[5]
GARRULOUS gar-
GARTH gher-[1]
GAS gheu-
GASH gher-[4]
GASKET wreg-
GASP ghāi-
GAST gheis-
GASTRIC gras-
GASTRO- gras-
GASTRULA gras-
GATHER ghedh-
GAUCHE weng-
GAUD gâu-
GAUDY[1] gâu-
GAUDY[2] gâu-
GAUGE ghalgh-
GAUNTLET[2] klou-
GAUR gwou-
GAVEL[2] ghabh-
GAWK ghow-ē-
GAYAL gwou-
GEANTICLINE gē
GEAR garwian
GEGENSCHEIN gagina, skeei-
GELÄNDESPRUNG lendh-[2], spergh-
GELATIN gel-[3]
GELATION gel-[3]
GELD[1] ghel-[3]
GELD[2] gheldh-
GELDING ghel-[3]
GELID gel-[3]
GELIGNITE egni-
GELT[1] gheldh-
GEM gembh-
GEMINATE yem-
GEMINI yem-
GEMMA gembh-
GEMMATE gembh-
GEMMULE gembh-
GEMOT mōd-
GEMSBOK bhugo-
GEMÜTLICH mē-[1]
GEMÜTLICHKEIT mē-[1]
-GEN genə-
GENDARME genə-
GENDER genə-
GENEALOGY genə-
GENERAL genə-
GENERATE genə-
GENERATION genə-
GENERIC genə-
GENEROUS genə-
GENESIS genə-
-GENESIS genə-
GENIAL[1] genə-
GENIAL[2] genu-[1]
GENICULATE genu-[1]
GENITAL genə-
GENITIVE genə-
GENITOR genə-
GENIUS genə-
GENOCIDE genə-
GENOTYPE genə-
GENRE genə-
GENS genə-
GENT[1] genə-

GENTILE genə-
GENTLE genə-
GENUFLECT genu-[1]
GENUS genə-
-GENY genə-
GEO- gē
GEODE gē
GEODESY dā-
GEOMETRY mē-[2]
GEOPONIC (s)pen-
GEORGIC gē, werg-
GERANIUM gerə-[2]
GERENT gerere
GERIATRICS gerə-[1]
GERM genə-
GERMAN[2] genə-
GERMANDER deru, dhghem-
GERMANE genə-
GERMINAL genə-
GERMINATE genə-
GERONTO- gerə-[1]
GERUND gerere
GEST gerere
GESTALT stel-
GESTATION gerere
GESTICULATE gerere
GESTURE gerere
GET ghend-
GEYSER gheu-
GHAT gher-[4]
GHOST gheis-
GIDDY gheu(ə)-
GIFT ghabh-
GILD[1] ghel-[2]
GILL[1] ghel-unā
GILL[3] ghāi-
GILLYFLOWER bhel-[3], kar-[1]
GILT[2] ghel-[3]
GIMMAL yem-
GINGERLY genə-
GIRASOL sāwel-
GIRD gher-[1]
GIRDLE gher-[1]
GIRTH gher-[1]
GIST yē-
GIVE ghabh-
GLABELLA gladh-
GLABROUS gladh-
GLACÉ gel-[3]
GLACIAL gel-[3]
GLACIATE gel-[3]
GLACIER gel-[3]
GLACIS gel-[3]
GLAD ghel-[2]
GLADIATE kel-[1]
GLADIATOR kel-[1]
GLAIR kelə-[1]
GLAIVE kel-[1]
GLANCE[2] ghel-[2]
GLAND gwelə-[2]
GLANDERS gwelə-[2]
GLANDULAR gwelə-[2]
GLANS gwelə-[2]
GLARE[1] ghel-[2]
GLASS ghel-[2]
GLAZE ghel-[2]
GLEAM ghel-[2]
GLEBE gel-[1]
GLEDE ghel-[2]
GLEE ghel-[2]
GLEED ghel-[2]
GLEET gel-[1]
GLEG ghel-[2]
GLEY gel-[1]
GLIADIN ghel-[1]
GLIB ghel-[2]
GLIDE ghel-[2]
GLIMMER ghel-[2]
GLIMPSE ghel-[2]
GLINT ghel-[2]
GLISSADE ghel-[2]
GLISTEN ghel-[2]
GLISTER ghel-[2]
GLITCH ghel-[2]
GLITTER ghel-[2]
GLOAMING ghel-[2]
GLOAT ghel-[2]
GLOBE gel-[1]
GLOBULE gel-[1]
GLOCHIDIUM glōgh-
GLOMERATE gel-[1]
GLOMERULE gel-[1]
GLOSS[1] glōgh-
GLOSS[2] glōgh-
GLOSSARY glōgh-
GLOSSOLALIA glōgh-, lā-
GLOTTIS glōgh-
GLOVE lep-[2]
GLOW ghel-[2]

GLOWER ghel-[2]
GLUCAGON ag-
GLUCOSE dlk-u-
GLUE gel-[1]
GLUME gleubh-
GLUT gwel-[3]
GLUTEN gel-[1]
GLUTEUS gel-[1]
GLUTINOUS gel-[1]
GLUTTON gwel-[3]
GLYCERIN dlk-u-
GLYPH gleubh-
GLYPTIC gleubh-
GNAT ghen-
GNATHIC genu-[2]
-GNATHOUS genu-[2]
GNAW ghen-
GNOCCHI gen-
GNOME[2] gnō-
GNOMON gnō-
GNOSIS gnō-
GO ghē-
GOAD ghei-[1]
GOAT ghaido-
GOD gheu(ə)-
GODSEND sent-
GOFFER webh-
GOLD ghel-[2]
GOLIARD gwel-[3]
GOMPHOSIS gembh-
-GON genu-[1]
GONAD genə-
GONFALON gwhen-[1]
GONIOMETER genu-[1]
GONIOMETRY genu-[1]
GONION genu-[1]
GONO- genə-
GOOD ghedh-
GOOSE[1] ghans-
GORE[1] ghaiso-
GORE[2] ghaiso-
GORGE gwerə-[4]
GORGET gwerə-[4]
GORSE ghers-
GOSHAWK ghans-
GOSLING ghans-
GOSPEL spel-[3]
GOSSIP s(w)e-
GOUACHE akwā-
GOWAN ghel-[2]
GRAB[1] ghrebh-[1]
GRABEN ghrebh-[2]
GRACE gwerə-[3]
GRACKLE gerə-[2]
GRADE ghredh-
GRAFFITO gerbh-
GRAIN grə-no-
GRAM[1] gerbh-
GRAM[2] grə-no-
-GRAM gerbh-
GRAMA gras-
GRAMINEOUS gras-
GRAMMAR gerbh-
GRAMPUS peisk-
GRANADILLA grə-no-
GRANARY grə-no-
GRANDILOQUENCE tolkw-
GRANGE grə-no-
GRANITE grə-no-
GRANT kerd-[1]
GRANULE grə-no-
GRAPE ger-[2]
GRAPH gerbh-
-GRAPH gerbh-
-GRAPHER gerbh-
GRAPHIC gerbh-
GRAPHITE gerbh-
-GRAPHY gerbh-
GRAPNEL ger-[2]
GRAPPA ger-[2]
GRAPPLE ger-[2]
GRASP ghrebh-[1]
GRASS ghrē-
GRATE[1] grat-
GRATE[2] kert-
GRATEFUL gwerə-[3]
GRATIFY gwerə-[3]
GRATIS gwerə-[3]
GRATITUDE gwerə-[3]
GRAUPEL kreup-
GRAVE[1] ghrebh-[2]
GRAVE[2] gwerə-[2]
GRAVE[3] ghrebh-[2]
GRAVEL ghrēu-
GRAVID gwerə-[2]
GRAVURE ghrebh-[2]
GRAY gher-[3]
GRAYWACKE wegh-

GREAT ghrēu-
GREAVES ghrebh-²
GREEDY gher-⁵
GREEN ghrē-
GREET gher-²
GREGARIOUS ger-¹
GRENADE grə-no-
GRESSORIAL ghredh-
GREYHOUND gher-³
GRID kert-
GRIDDLE kert-
GRIDIRON kert-
GRIEF gʷerə-²
GRIEVE gʷerə-²
GRIM ghrem-
GRIMACE ghrem-
GRIME ghrēi-
GRIND ghrendh-
GRIP¹ ghreib-
GRIPE ghreib-
GRIPPE ghreib-
GRISAILLE gher-³
GRISEOUS gher-³
GRISETTE gher-³
GRISLY ghrēi-
GRISON gher-³
GRIST ghrendh-
GRIT ghrēu-
GRIZZLE gher-³
GROAT ghrēu-
GROATS ghrēu-
GROCER gʷres-
GROOVE ghrebh-²
GROPE ghreib-
GROSCHEN gʷres-
GROSS gʷres-
GROSSULARITE ger-²
GROSZ gʷres-
GROUNDSEL¹ ghendh-, swel-¹
GROUP ger-²
GROUT ghrēu-
GROW ghrē-
GRUB ghrebh-²
GRUDGE gru-
GRUEL ghrēu-
GRUESOME ghrēu-
GRUFF kreup-
GRUMBLE ghrem-
GRUNION gru-
GRUNT gru-
GRUS gerə-²
GUARANTY wer-⁵
GUARD wer-⁴
GUERDON lau-, wi-
GUERRILLA wers-¹
GUESS ghend-
GUEST ghos-ti-
GUIDE weid-
GUILD gheldh-
GUILDER ghel-²
GUILE weik-²
GUIPURE weip-
GUISE weid-
GULAR gʷel-³
GULDEN ghel-²
GULES gʷel-³
GULF kwelp-
GULLET gʷel-³
GUM² ghēu-
GUN gʷhen-¹
GURGITATION gʷerə-⁴
GURU gʷerə-²
GUSH gheu-
GUST¹ gheu-
GUST² geus-
GUSTO geus-
GUT gheu-
GYMNASIUM nogʷ-
GYMNAST nogʷ-
GYMNOSOPHIST nogʷ-
GYMNOSPERM nogʷ-
GYNAECEUM gʷen-
GYNECOCRACY gʷen-
GYNECOLOGY gʷen-
GYNO- gʷen-
-GYNOUS gʷen-
-GYNY gʷen-
GYRE gēu-
GYRFALCON ghaiso-, pel-²
GYRO² gēu-
GYRO- gēu-

H

HABILE ghabh-
HABIT ghabh-
HABITABLE ghabh-

HABITANT ghabh-
HABITAT ghabh-
HACIENDA dhē-¹
HACK¹ keg-
HADAL weid-
HADES weid-
HADRON sā-
HAFT kap-
HAG² kau-²
HAGGARD kagh-
HAGGLE kau-²
HAGIO- yag-
HAIL¹ kaghlo-
HAIL² kailo-
HAKE keg-
HALBERD bhardhā, kelp-
HALE¹ kailo-
HALE² kelə-²
HALF skel-¹
HALIBUT bhau-
HALL kel-²
HALLOW kailo-
HALO- sal-¹
HALT¹ kel-³
HALT² kel-¹
HALTER¹ kelp-
HALTER² sel-⁴
HAM konəmo-
HAMADRYAD deru, sem-¹
HAME tkei-
HAMLET tkei-
HAMMER ak-
HANDIWORK kom
HANDSEL sel-³
HANG konk-
HANKER konk-
HANUMAN genu-²
HAP kob-
HAPLESS kob-
HAPLOID pel-³, sem-¹
HAPPEN kob-
HAPPY kob-
HARANGUE koro-
HARBINGER koro-
HARBOR koro-
HARD kar-¹
HARDS kes-¹
HARDY¹ kar-¹
HARE kas-
HARM kormo-
HARMONY ar-
HARNESS nes-¹
HARPOON serp-¹
HARPSICHORD gherə-
HARQUEBUS keg-
HARRY koro-
HART ker-¹
HARTEBEEST ker-¹
HARUSPEX gherə-
HARVEST kerp-
HASH¹ skep-
HASLET ghasto-
HASTATE ghasto-
HAT kādh-
HATCHET skep-
HATE kād-
HATRED ar-, kād-
HAUBERK kʷel-¹
HAUGH kel-²
HAUGHTY al-³
HAUL kelə-²
HAULM koləm-
HAUNT tkei-
HAUSTELLUM aus-²
HAUSTORIUM aus-²
HAUTBOY al-³, busk-
HAVE kap-
HAVEN kap-
HAW² kagh-
HAWK¹ kap-
HAWKER keu-²
HAWSE kʷel-¹
HAWSER kʷel-¹
HAY kau-²
HAZEL koselo-
HE¹ ko-
HEAD kaput
HEAL kailo-
HEALTH kailo-
HEAP keu-²
HEAR keu-²
HEARKEN keu-¹
HEART kerd-¹
HEARTH ker-⁴
HEAT kai-
HEATH kaito-
HEATHEN kaito-
HEAVE kap-

HEAVEN ak-
HEAVY kap-
HEBDOMAD septm̥
HEBE yēgʷā-
HEBEPHRENIA yēgʷā-
HECATOMB dekm̥, gʷou-
HECKLE keg-
HECTIC segh-
HECTO- dekm̥
HEDDLE kap-
HEDGE kagh-
HEDONIC swād-
HEDONISM swād-
-HEDRON sed-¹
HEED kādh-
HEEL¹ kenk-³
HEEL² kel-⁴
HEGEMONY sāg-
HEIFER per-³
HEIGHT keu-²
HEINOUS kād-
HEIR ghē-
HEL kel-²
HELIACAL sāwel-
HELIO- sāwel-
HELIOS sāwel-
HELIUM sāwel-
HELIX wel-³
HELL kel-²
HELLEBORE el-², gʷerə-⁴
HELM¹ kelp-
HELM² kel-²
HELMET kel-²
HELMINTH wel-³
HELP kelb-
HELVE kelp-
HEM¹ kem-²
HEMATOCRIT krei-
HEMERALOPIA āmer-
HEMI- sēmi-
HEMISTICH steigh-
HEMOPTYSIS spyeu-
HEMORRHOID sreu-
HEMP kannabis
HEN kan-
HENCE ko-
HENDECASYLLABIC sem-¹
HENDIADYS dwo-, sem-¹
HENOTHEISM sem-¹
HEPARIN yēkʷr̥
HEPATIC yēkʷr̥
HEPATITIS yēkʷr̥
HEPATO- yēkʷr̥
HEPATOGENIC yēkʷr̥
HEPTA- septm̥
HEPTAD septm̥
HEPTATEUCH dheugh-
HER ko-
HERALD koro-
HERB BENNET deu-²
HERD kerdh-
HERE ko-
HEREDITAMENT ghē-
HEREDITY ghē-
HERIOT koro-, taw-
HERITAGE ghē-
HERMIT erə-²
HERNIA ghere-
HERO ser-¹
HERPES serp-²
HERPETOLOGY serp-²
HESITATE ghais-
HESPERIAN wes-pero-
HEST kei-²
HETAERA s(w)e-
HETERO- sem-¹
HETERODOX dek-¹
HETEROECIOUS weik-¹
HETEROGENEOUS genə-
HETERONYMOUS nō-men-
HEURISTIC werə-²
HEW kau-²
HEXA- s(w)eks
HEXAD s(w)eks
HEXATEUCH dheugh-
HIATUS ghēi-
HIBERNACULUM ghei-²
HIBERNATE ghei-²
HIDALGO al-¹, dhē(i)-, kʷo-
HIDE¹ (s)keu-
HIDE² (s)keu-
HIDE³ kei-¹
HIDROSIS sweid-²
HIE kīgh-
HIEMAL ghei-²
HIERARCH eis-¹
HIERARCHY eis-¹
HIERATIC eis-¹
HIERO- eis-¹

HIEROGLYPHIC eis-¹, gleubh-
HIEROPHANT bhā-¹, eis-¹
HIGH keu-²
HILARITY sel-²
HILL kel-⁶
HILT kel-¹
HIM ko-
HIMATION wes-⁴
HINAYANA ei-¹
HIND¹ ko-
HIND² kem-¹
HIND³ kei-¹
HINDER¹ ko-
HINGE konk-
HINTERLAND ko-, lendh-²
HIP¹ keu-²
HIP³ keub-
HIPPOCAMPUS ekwo-
HIPPOGRIFF ekwo-
HIPPOPOTAMUS ekwo-, pet-
HIRSUTE ghers-
HIS ko-
HISPID ghers-
HISTIOCYTE stā-
HISTO- stā-
HISTORY weid-
HITHER ko-
HIVE kei-¹
HOAR kei-²
HOARD (s)keu-
HOARDING kert-
HOCK¹ kenk-³
HOE kau-²
HOG sū-
HOI POLLOI pelə-¹, so-
HOLD¹ kel-³
HOLE kel-²
HOLLOW kel-²
HOLLY kel-⁷
HOLM kel-⁶
HOLO- sol-
HOLOCAUST kēu-
HOLOPHRASTIC gʷhren-
HOLSTER kel-²
HOLT kel-¹
HOLY kailo-
HOMAGE dhghem-
HOMBRE dhghem-
HOME tkei-
HOMEO- sem-¹
HOMICIDE dhghem-
HOMILY sem-¹
HOMINID dhghem-
HOMO¹ dhghem-
HOMO- sem-¹
HOMOIOUSIAN es-
HOMOLOGOUS leg-¹
HOMOLOGRAPHIC sem-¹
HOMOLOSINE PROJECTION sem-¹
HOMONYMOUS nō-men-
HOMUNCULUS dhghem-
HONE¹ kō-
HONEY k(e)nəko-
HOOD¹ kādh-
-HOOD skai-
HOOF kap(h)o-
HOOK keg-
HOOKER¹ keg-
HOP¹ keu-²
HOP² skeup-
HOPE keu-²
HORN ker-¹
HORNBEAM ker-¹
HORNBLENDE ker-¹
HORNET ker-¹
HORNITO gʷher-
HOROLOGE yēr-
HOROLOGY yēr-
HOROSCOPE spek-, yēr-
HORROR ghers-
HORST kert-
HORTATIVE gher-⁵
HORTICULTURE gher-¹
HOSE (s)keu-
HOSPICE ghos-ti-
HOSPITAL ghos-ti-
HOSPITALITY ghos-ti-
HOST¹ ghos-ti-
HOST² ghos-ti-
HOSTAGE ghos-ti-, sed-¹
HOSTEL ghos-ti-
HOSTILE ghos-ti-
HOSTLER ghos-ti-
HOT kai-
HOUND kwon-
HOUR yēr-
HOUSEL kwen-
HOUSING² kel-²
HOW¹ kʷo-

HOWL ul-
HOYDEN kaito-
HUBRIS ud-
HUCKSTER keu-2
HUE[1] kei-2
HUGUENOT neud-, oito-
HULL kel-2
HUM kem-3
HUMAN dhghem-
HUMANE dhghem-
HUMBLE dhghem-
HUMECTANT wegw-
HUMERUS omeso-
HUMID wegw-
HUMILIATE dhghem-
HUMILITY dhghem-
HUMOR wegw-
HUMUS dhghem-
HUNDRED dekm
HUNGER kenk-2
HUNKER keu-2
HURDLE kert-
HUSBAND bheue-
HUSSAR kers-2
HUSTINGS tenk-1
HUT (s)keu-
HYATHODE sed-2
HYDATHODE wed-1
HYDATID wed-1
HYDRA wed-1
HYDRANT wed-1
HYDRANTH andh-
HYDRAULIC aulo-
HYDRO- wed-1
HYDROCEPHALUS ghebh-el-
HYDROMEL melit-
HYDROUS wed-1
HYDRUS wed-1
HYENA sū-
HYGEIA gwei-
HYGIENE gwei-
HYGRO- wegw-
HYLOZOISM hulē
HYMEN syū-
HYMNODY wed-2
HYOSCINE sū-
HYPER- uper
HYPERBOLA gwele-1
HYPERBOLE gwele-1
HYPERBOREAN gwere-1
HYPERKINESIA kei-3
HYPERPNEA pneu-
HYPHA webh-
HYPNAGOGIC ag-
HYPNO- swep-1
HYPNOS swep-1
HYPNOSIS swep-1
HYPNOTIC swep-1
HYPO- upo
HYPOCHONDRIA ghrendh-
HYPOCORISM ker-3
HYPOGEAL gē
HYPOPHYSIS bheue-
HYPOPNEA pneu-
HYPOSTASIS stā-
HYPOSTYLE stā-
HYPOTAXIS tāg-
HYPOTENUSE ten-
HYPOTHERMIA gwher-
HYPOTHESIS dhē-
HYPOCRISY krei-
HYPSO- upo
HYSTERESIS ud-
HYSTERIC udero-
HYSTERO- udero-
HYSTERON PROTERON per1, ud-

I

I eg
ICE eis-2
ICEBERG bhergh-2
ICH dhgwher-
ICHTHYO- dhghū-
ICHTHYORNIS or-
ICICLE eis-2, yeg-
ICON weik-3
ICONIC weik-3
ICONO- weik-3
ICONOGRAPHY gerbh-
ICONOSTASIS stā-
ICOSAHEDRON wikmti
ID i-
IDEA weid-
IDEM i-
IDENTICAL i-

IDENTIFY i-
IDENTITY i-
IDEO- weid-
IDIO- s(w)e-
IDIOM s(w)e-
IDIOMORPHIC s(w)e-
IDIOPATHY s(w)e-
IDIOSYNCRACY kere-
IDIOSYNCRASY s(w)e-
IDIOT s(w)e-
IDOCRASE weid-
IDOL weid-
IDOLATER lē-1
IDYLL weid-
IF i-
IGNEOUS egni-
IGNITE egni-
IGNITRON egni-
IGNOMINY nō-men-
IGNORANT gnō-
IGNORE gnō-
ILEUS wel-3
ILK i-
ILLATION tele-
ILLITERATE deph-
ILLUMINATE leuk-
ILLUSION leid-
ILLUSTRATE leuk-
IMBECILE bak-
IMBIBE pō(i)-
IMBRICATE ombh-ro-
IMBRUE bhreu-2
IMBUE ombh-ro-
IMMACULATE macula
IMMANENT men-3
IMMATURE mā-1
IMMENSE mē-2
IMMERSE mezg-1
IMMINENT men-2
IMMIX meik-
IMMODERATE med-
IMMODEST med-
IMMOLATE mele-
IMMORTAL mer-2
IMMUNE mei-1
IMMURE dhē-3
IMP bheue-
IMPAIR ped-1
IMPALE pag-
IMPARITY pere-2
IMPART pere-2
IMPEACH ped-1
IMPECCABLE ped-1
IMPECUNIOUS peku-
IMPEDE ped-1
IMPEL pel-6
IMPEND (s)pen-
IMPERATIVE pere-1
IMPERIAL pere-1
IMPETRATE peter-
IMPETUS pet-
IMPINGE pag-
IMPIOUS pius
IMPLEMENT pele-1
IMPLICATE plek-
IMPONE apo-
IMPORT per-2
IMPORTANT per-2
IMPORTUNE per-2
IMPOSE apo-
IMPOTENT poti-
IMPOUND bend-
IMPRECATE prek-
IMPRESS[1] per-5
IMPRIMIS per1
IMPRINT per-5
IMPROBITY per1
IMPROMPTU em-
IMPROVE es-, per1
IMPUDENT (s)peud-
IMPUGN peuk-
IMPUNITY kwei-1
IMPUTE peu-
IN-1 ne
IN-2 en
INAMORATA amma
INAUGURATE aug-1
INCANDESCE kand-
INCANTATION kan-
INCARCERATE carcer
INCARNATE sker-
INCENDIARY kand-
INCENSE kand-
INCENTIVE kan-
INCEPTION kap-
INCERTITUDE krei-
INCEST kes-2
INCH[1] oi-no-
INCHOATE kagh-

INCIDENT kad-
INCINERATE keni-
INCIPIENT kap-
INCISE kae-id-
INCITE kei-3
INCLINE klei-
INCLUDE kleu-3
INCONDITE dhē-1
INCREASE ker-3
INCUBATE keu-2
INCULT kwel-1
INCUMBENT keu-2
INCUNABULUM kei-1
INCUR kers-2
INCUS kau-2
INDEMNIFY dap-
INDEMNITY dap-
INDENT[1] dent-
INDENTURE dent-
INDEX deik-
INDICATE deik-
INDICT deik-
INDIGEN gene-
INDIGENOUS gene-
INDIGENT eg-
INDIGN dek-1
INDIGNANT dek-1
INDIGNATION dek-1
INDITE deik-
INDOLENT del-2
INDOMITABLE deme-2
INDUCE deuk-
INDURATE deru-
INDUSTRY en, ster-2
INEBRIATE ēgwh-
INEFFABLE bhā-2
INELUCTABLE leug-1
INEPT ap-1
INERT ar-
INERTIA ar-
INEXORABLE ōr-
INFAMOUS bhā-2
INFANT bhā-2
INFANTRY bhā-2
INFARCT bhrek-w-
INFECT dhē-1
INFELICITY dhē(i)-
INFER bher-1
INFERIOR ṇdher-
INFERNAL ṇdher-
INFERNO ṇdher-
INFEST dhers-
INFEUDATION peku-
INFIDEL bheidh-
INFIRM dher-1
INFIRMARY dher-2
INFIX dhigw-
INFLAME bhel-1
INFLATE bhlē-2
INFLICT bhlīg-
INFLUENCE bhleu-
INFLUENZA bhleu-
INFRA- ṇdher-
INFRACT bhreg-
INFRANGIBLE bhreg-
INFRINGE bhreg-
INFUSE gheu-
INGENIOUS gene-
INGENUOUS gene-
INGEST gerere
INGRATE gwere-3
INGRATIATE gwere-3
INGRESS ghredh-
INGUINAL engw-
INGURGITATE gwere-4
INHABIT ghabh-
INHERE ghais-
INHERIT ghē-
INHIBIT ghabh-
INHUME dhghem-
INIMICAL amma
INITIAL ei-1
INITIATE ei-1
INJECT yē-
INJUNCTION yeug-
INJURY yewes-
INK kēu-
INNATE gene-
INNER en
INNOCENT nek-1
INNOCUOUS nek-1
INNOVATE newo-
INNUENDO neu-2
INOCULATE okw-
INORDINATE ar-
INOSCULATE ōs-
INOSITOL kes-2
INOTROPIC wei-1
INQUILINE kwel-1

INQUIRE quaerere
INSCRIBE skrībh-
INSECT sek-
INSERT ser-3, sē-1
INSESSORIAL sed-1
INSIGNIA sekw-1
INSIST stā-
INSOLATE sāwel-
INSOMNIA swep-
INSPECT spek-
INSPIRE spirāre
INSTALL stel-
INSTALLMENT[1] stel-
INSTANT stā-
INSTAURATION stā-
INSTIGATE steig-
INSTINCT steig-
INSTITUTE stā-
INSTRUCT ster-2
INSULT sel-4
INSURE cūra
INTACT tag-
INTEGER tag-
INTEGUMENT (s)teg-
INTELLIGENT leg-1
INTEND ten-
INTER en, ters-
INTERCALATE kele-2
INTERCEDE ked-
INTERCEPT kap-
INTERCOSTAL kost-
INTERCOURSE kers-2
INTERDICT deik-
INTEREST es-
INTERIM en
INTERIOR en
INTERJECT yē-
INTERLOCUTION tolkw-
INTERLOPE klou-
INTERLUDE leid-
INTERMEDIATE medhyo-
INTERMIT (s)meit(e)-
INTERNAL en
INTERNECINE nek-1
INTERPELLATE pel-6
INTERPOSE apo-
INTERPRET per-6
INTERREX reg-1
INTERROGATE reg-1
INTERRUPT reup-
INTERSECT sek-
INTERSPERSE (s)preg-
INTERSTICE stā-
INTERVAL walso-
INTERVENE gwā-
INTERVIEW weid-
INTESTINE en
INTIMA en
INTIMATE[2] en
INTINCTION teng-
INTINE en
INTRA- en
INTRADOS dorsum, en
INTRANSIGENT ag-
INTREPID trep-1
INTRINSIC en, sekw-1
INTRO- en
INTRODUCE deuk-, en
INTROIT ei-1, en
INTROMIT en, (s)meit(e)-
INTRORSE en, wer-3
INTROSPECT en, spek-
INTROVERT wer-3
INTRUDE treud-
INTUITION teu-
INTUMESCE teue-
INTUSSUSCEPTION en, kap-
INULIN wel-3
INUNCTION ongw-
INUNDATE wed-1
INURE op-1
INVADE wadh-2
INVAGINATE wag-
INVALID[1] wal-
INVALID[2] wal-
INVEIGH wegh-
INVEIGLE okw-
INVENT gwā-
INVERT wer-3
INVEST wes-4
INVETERATE wet-2
INVOKE wekw-
INVOLVE wel-3
INWARD wer-3
IODOPSIN okw-
ION ei-1
IRASCIBLE eis-1
IRATE eis-1
IRE eis-1

IRIDACEOUS wei-[1]
IRIDIUM wei-[1]
IRIDO- wei-[1]
IRIS wei-[1]
IRIS peie-[1]
IRISITIS wei-[1]
IRON eis-[1]
IRONY wer-[6]
IRREMEABLE mei-[1]
IRRIGATE reg-[2]
IRRUPT reup-
IS es-
ISALLOBAR gʷerə-[2]
ISCHEMIA segh-
ISINGLASS bhlē-[2]
ISLAND akʷā-
ISOBAR gʷerə-[2]
ISOCLINE klei-
ISOGLOSS glōgh-
ISOHEL sāwel-
ISOHYET seuə-[2]
ISOMER (s)mer-[2]
ISOMETRIC mē-[2]
ISOPIESTIC sed-[1]
ISOPLETH pelə-[1]
ISOSCELES skel-[3]
ISOSTASY stā-
ISSUE ei-[1]
IT ko-
ITEM i-
ITERATE i-
ITHYPHALLIC bhel-[2]
ITINERANT ei-[1]
ITINERARY ei-[1]
IWIS weid-

J

JAIL keuə-[2]
JAIN gʷeie-
JAMB kamp-
JANITOR ei-[1]
JANUARY ei-[1]
JANUS ei-[1]
JAVELIN ghabholo-
JEALOUS yā-
JELLY gel-[3]
JEOPARDY yek-
JESS yē-
JEST gerere
JET[2] yē-
JEWEL yek-
JINX yu-[2]
JOCOSE yek-
JOCULAR yek-
JOIN yeug-
JOIST yē-
JOKE yek-
JOSS deiw-
JOURNAL deiw-
JOURNEY deiw-
JOUST yeug-
JOVE deiw-
JOVIAL deiw-
JOWL[1] gep(h)-
JOWL[2] gʷel-[3]
JOY gāu-
JUBILATE yu-[2]
JUDGE deik-, yewes-
JUDICIAL deik-
JUGATE yeug-
JUGGERNAUT gʷā-
JUGGLE yek-
JUGGLER yek-
JUGULAR yeug-
JUGUM yeug-
JUICE yeuə-
JULEP ap-[2], wrod-
JULY deiw-
JUNCTION yeug-
JUNCTURE yeug-
JUNIOR yeu-
JUNKER kei-[2], yeu-
JUNTA yeug-
JUPITER deiw-
JURAL yewes-
JURIDICAL deik-, yewes-
JURISCONSULT yewes-
JURISDICTION deik-, yewes-
JURISPRUDENCE yewes-
JURIST yewes-
JURY[1] yewes-
JUSSIVE yeudh-
JUST[1] yewes-
JUSTIFY dhē-[1]

JUVENILE yeu-
JUVENOCRACY yeu-
JUXTAPOSE yeug-
JUXTAPOSITION yeug-

K

KAILYARD SCHOOL kaul-
KAINITE ken-[3]
KALE kaul-
KALEIDOSCOPE kal-[2], weid-
KAMA kā-
KAMASUTRA kā-, syū-
KAME gembh-
KARMA kʷer-[1]
KARYO- kar-[1]
KEEL[1] gʷel-[3]
KEEL[2] ku-
KEEL[3] gel-[3]
KEELHAUL kelə-[2]
KEELSON ku-
KEESHOND kwon-
KEN gnō-
KENNEL[1] kwon-
KENNING gnō-
KENO penkʷe
KENOSIS ken-[4]
KERATIN ker-[1]
KERATO- ker-[1]
KERCHIEF kaput
KERF gerbh-
KERMES kʷrmi-
KERN[1] kat-[2]
KERNEL grə-no-
KEVEL kleu-[3]
KEY[2] kagh-
KILL[1] gʷel-[1]
KILN pekʷ-
KILO- gheslo-
KIN genə-
KIND[1] genə-
KIND[2] genə-
KINDERGARTEN genə-, gher-[1]
KINDRED ar-, genə-
KINE gʷou-
KINEMATICS kei-[3]
KINESIOLOGY kei-[3]
-KINESIS kei-[3]
KINESTHESIA kei-[3]
KINETIC kei-[3]
KING genə-
KININ kei-[3]
KIRK keuə-[2]
KIRTLE sker-[1]
KISHKE (s)keu-
KISS kus-
KITCHEN pekʷ-
KITH gnō-
KITTLE tit-
KLEPTOMANIA klep-
KLIPSPRINGER spergh-
KLOOF gleubh-
KLUTZ gel-[1]
KNACKER ken-[5]
KNACKWURST gen-
KNAP[1] gep(h)-
KNAP[2] gen-
KNAPSACK gen-
KNAR gen-
KNEAD gen-
KNEE genu-[1]
KNEEL genu-[1]
KNELL gen-
KNIFE gen-
KNIT gen-
KNOB gen-
KNOBKERRIE gen-
KNOCK gen-
KNOLL[1] gen-
KNOLL[2] gen-
KNOP gen-
KNOT[1] gen-
KNOUT gen-
KNOW gnō-
KNUCKLE gen-
KNUR gen-
KOBOLD ku-
KOHLRABI kaul-, rāp-
KOINE kom
KOPECK skep-
KRISHNA kers-[1]-
KRISS KRINGLE genə-
KRYPTON krāu-
KSHATRIYA tkē-
KUCHEN kak-[2]
KUDOS keuə-[1]

KURTOSIS sker-[3]
KVASS kwat-
KVETCH kwēt-
KYLIX kal-[1]
KYPHOSIS keu-[2]
KYRIE keuə-[2]

L

LAAGER legh-
LABEL leb-[1]
LABELLUM leb-[2]
LABIAL leb-[2]
LABILE leb-[1]
LABIUM leb-[2]
LABOR leb-[1]
LABRET leb-[2]
LABRUM leb-[2]
LAC[1] reg-[3]
LACCOLITH laku-
LACERATE lēk-
LACHRYMAL dakru-
LACINIATE lēk-
LACK leg-[2]
LACROSSE ger-[2]
LACTATE melg-
LACTEAL melg-
LACTESCENT melg-
LACTO- melg-
LADDER klei-
LADE klā-
LADY dheigh-
LAG[2] leu-[1]
LAGER legh-
LAGOMORPH slēg-
LAIR legh-
LAKE[1] laku-
LAM[1] lem-[1]
LAMBENT lab-
LAME[1] lem-[1]
LAMELLA stele-
LAMELLICORN ker-[1]
LAMENT lā-
LAMIA lem-[2]
LAMMERGEIER ghāi-
LAMP lāp-
LAMPOON lab-
LANATE welə-[1]
LAND lendh-
LANDSCAPE lendh-[2], skep-
LANDSMAN[2] lendh-[2], man-[1]
LANGLAUF del-[1], klou-
LANGUAGE dn̥ghū
LANGUET dn̥ghū
LANGUISH slēg-
LANIFEROUS welə-[1]
LANK kleng-
LANOLIN welə-[1]
LANTERN lāp-
LANTHANUM lādh-
LANUGO welə-[1]
LAP[1] leb-[1]
LAP[3] lab-
LAPAROTOMY lep-[1]
LAPSE leb-[1]
LAPWING klou-
LARCENY lē-[1]
LARK[3] leig-[3]
LASCIVIOUS las-
LASSITUDE lē-[2]
LAST[1] lē-[2]
LAST[2] lēi-
LAST[3] leis-[1]
LAST[4] klā-
LATCH (s)lagʷ-
LATE lē-[2]
LATENT lādh-
LATEX lat-
LATHER leu(ə)-
LATIFUNDIUM bhudh-
LATITUDE stelə-
LATRINE leu(ə)-
-LATRY leu(ə)-
LATTER lē-[2]
LAUD lēu-[2]
LAUGH kleg-
LAUGHTER kleg-
LAVE leu(ə)-
LAW legh-
LAWN[1] lendh-[2]
LAX slēg-
LAY[1] legh-
LEA leuk-
LEAD[1] leit-[2]
LEAF leup-
LEAGUE[1] leig-[1]

LEAGUER[1] legh-
LEAK leg-[2]
LEAN[1] klei-
LEAP klou-
LEARN leis-[1]
LEASING leu-[1]
LEAST leis-[2]
LEATHER letro-
LEAVE[1] leip-
LEAVE[2] leubh-
LEAVEN legʷh-
LECHER leig-[1]
LECTERN leg-[1]
LECTION leg-[1]
LECTURE leg-[1]
LEDGE legh-
LEDGER legh-
LEE kelə-[1]
LEECH[1] leg-[1]
LEECH[2] leig-[1]
LEEK leug-[1]
LEER kleu-[1]
LEES legh-
LEGACY leg-[1]
LEGAL leg-[1]
LEGATE leig-[1]
LEGATO leig-[1]
LEGEND leg-[1]
LEGERDEMAIN legʷh-
LEGIBLE leg-[1]
LEGION leg-[1]
LEGISLATOR leg-[1], telə-
LEGIST leg-[1]
LEGITIMATE leg-[1]
LEITMOTIF leit-[2]
LEMAN leubh-
LEMMA[1] (s)lagʷ-
LEMMA[2] lep-[1]
LEMURES lem-[2]
LEND leikʷ-
LENGTH del-[1]
LENIENT lē-[1]
LENIS lē-[2]
LENITIVE lē-[2]
LENITY lē-[2]
LENT del-[1]
LENTO lento-, lep-[1]
LEPIDO- lep-[1]
LEPIDOTE lep-[1]
LEPRECHAUN kʷrep-, legʷh-
-LEPSY (s)lagʷ-
LEPTO- lep-[1]
LEPTON[1] lep-[1]
LESS leis-[2]
-LESS leu-[1]
LESSON leg-[1]
LET[1] lē-[2]
LET[2] lē-[2]
LETHAL ol-
LETHARGY lādh-
LETHE lādh-
LETTER deph-
LETTUCE melg-
LEVEL līthrā
LEVER legʷh-
LEVIGATE ag-, legʷh-
LEVIRATE daiwer-
LEVITY legʷh-
LEVO- laiwo-
LEVOROTATION laiwo-
LEVOROTATORY laiwo-
LEX leg-[1]
LEXICON leg-[1]
LIABLE leig-[1]
LIBATION lēi-
LIBERAL leudh-[2]
LIBERATE leudh-[2]
LIBERTINE leudh-[2]
LIBERTY leudh-[2]
LIBIDO leubh-
LIBRA līthrā
LICH GATE līk-
LICK leigh-
LICORICE dl̥k-u-, wrād-
LID klei-
LIE[1] legh-
LIE[2] leugh-
LIED lēu-[2]
LIEF leubh-
LIEGE lē-[2]
LIEN leig-[1]
LIENAL spelgh-
LIEUTENANT ten-
LIFE leip-
LIFT leup-
LIGASE leig-[1]
LIGATE leig-[1]
LIGHT[1] leuk-
LIGHT[2] legʷh-

LIGHTER² leg⁰ʰ-
LIGNEOUS leg-¹
LIGNI- leg-¹
LIGNUM VITAE gʷei-
LIGULE dṇghū
LIKE¹ līk-
LIKE² līk-
LIKELY līk-
LILAC nei-
LIMACINE lei-
LIME³ lei-
LIMICOLINE lei-
LIMN leuk-
LIMP kel-¹, leb-¹
LINDEN lento-
LINE¹ līno-
LINE² līno-
LINEN līno-
LING¹ del-¹
LING² lenk-
LINGER del-¹
LINGERIE līno-
LINGO dṇghū
LINGUA dṇghū
LINGUIST dṇghū
LINIMENT lei-
LININ līno-
LINK¹ kleng-
LINK² leuk-
LINKS kleng-
LINNET līno-
LINOLEIC ACID līno-
LINSEED līno-
LINT līno-
LIP leb-²
LIPO- leip-
LIQUATE wleik-
LIQUEFY wleik-
LIQUESCENT wleik-
LIQUID wleik-
LIQUOR wleik-
LIRA līthrā
LIST¹ leizd-
LIST² leizd-
LIST⁴ kleu-¹
LIST⁶ las-
LISTEN kleu-¹
LITER līthrā
LITERAL deph-
LITERARY deph-
LITERATE deph-
LITERATIM deph-
LITHARGE arg-
LITHE lento-
LITHOTRITY dhreu-
LITIGATE ag-
LITMUS meu-, wel-¹
LITOTES lei-
LITTER legh-
LITTLE leud-
LITTORAL lēi-
LITURGY werg-
LIVE¹ leip-
LIVELIHOOD leit-²
LIVELONG leubh-
LIVELY leip-
LIVER¹ leip-
LIVERWURST wers-¹
LIVERY leudh-²
LIVID slī-
LIVRE līthrā
LIXIVIATE wleik-
LLANO pelə-²
LOAD leit-²
LOAM lei-
LOAN leikʷ-
LOATH leit-¹
LOATHE leit-¹
LOBBY leup-
LOBE leup-
LOBO wḷkʷo-
LOBSTER lek-¹
LOCH laku-
LOCHIA legh-
LOCK¹ leug-¹
LOCK² leug-¹
LOCKET leug-¹
LOCUST lek-
LOCUTION tolkʷ-
LODE leit-²
LODGE leup-
LOESS leu-¹
LOFT leup-
LOGARITHM ar-, leg-¹
LOGE leup-
LOGIC leg-¹
LOGISTIC leg-¹
LOGO- leg-¹
Logos leg-¹

-LOGY leg-¹, sleu-
LOIN lendh-¹
LOITER leud-
LOLL lā-
LOMBARD del-¹
LOMENT leu(ə)-
LONE oi-no-
LONELY oi-no-
LONG¹ del-¹
LONG² del-¹
LONGANIMITY anə-
LONGERON del-¹
LONGEVITY aiw-, del-¹
LONGICORN ker-¹
LONGITUDE del-¹
LOON¹ lā-
LOOSE leu-¹
LOOT reup-
LOPE klou-
LOQUACIOUS tolkʷ-
LORDOSIS lerd-
LORE¹ leis-²
LORN leu-¹
LOSE leu-¹
LOSEL leu-¹
LOSS leu-¹
LOT kleu-³
LOTION leu(ə)-
LOTTERY kleu-³
LOTTO kleu-³
LOUD kleu-¹
LOUGH laku-
LOUP-GAROU wi-ro-, wḷkʷo-
LOUSE lūs-
LOUT¹ leud-
LOUT² leud-
LOVE leubh-
LOW¹ legh-
LOW² kelə-²
LOX¹ laks-
LOXODROMIC der-¹
LOYAL leg-¹
LUBRICATE sleubh-
LUBRICIOUS sleubh-
LUBRICITY sleubh-
LUCARNE leug-¹
LUCENT leuk-
LUCID leuk-
LUCIFER leuk-
LUCIFERIN leuk-
LUCINA leuk-
LUCRATIVE lau-
LUCRE lau-
LUCUBRATE leuk-
LUCULENT leuk-
LUDICROUS leid-
LUES leu-¹
LUFF lep-²
LUGUBRIOUS leug-²
LULL lā-
LUMBAGO lendh-¹
LUMBAR lendh-¹
LUMBER² lem-¹
LUMBRICOID slengʷh-
LUMEN leuk-
LUMINARY leuk-
LUMINOUS leuk-
LUMP¹ leb-¹
LUMPEN leb-¹
LUMPFISH leb-¹
LUNA leuk-
LUNAR leuk-
LUNATE leuk-
LUNATIC leuk-
LUNE leuk-
LUNG legʷh-
LUNGE del-¹
LUNULA leuk-
LUPINE¹ wḷkʷo-
LUPINE² wḷkʷo-
LUST las-
LUSTER leuk-
LUSTRUM leuk-
LUTE² leu-²
LUX leuk-
LUXATE leug-¹
LUXURY leug-¹
LYASE leu-¹
LYCANTHROPE ner-², wḷkʷo-
LYCHNIS leuk-
LYCOPODIUM ped-¹, wḷkʷo-
LYE leu(ə)-
LYMPHADENITIS engʷ-
LYNX leuk-
LYSIS leu-¹
LYSO- leu-¹
-LYTE leu-¹
-LYTIC leu-¹

LYTTA wḷkʷo-
-LY¹ līk-
-LY² līk-

M

MACERATE mag-
MACHICOLATE kʷel-¹
MACHICOLATION kʷel-¹
MACHINE magh-¹
MACHO mas
MACKLE macula
MACLE macula
MACRO- māk-
MACROCOSM kes-³
MACRON māk-
MACULA macula
MACULATE macula
MACULE macula
MAD mei-¹
MADAM demə-¹
MADAME demə-¹
MADDER¹ modhro-
Mademoiselle demə-¹
MADONNA demə-¹
MADREPORE māter-
MADURO mā-¹
MAELSTROM melə-, sreu-
MAENAD men-¹
MAESTOSO meg-
MAESTRO meg-
MAGI magh-¹
MAGIC magh-¹
MAGISTERIAL meg-
MAGISTRAL meg-
MAGISTRATE meg-
MAGMA mag-
MAGNANIMOUS anə-, meg-
MAGNATE meg-
MAGNIFIC meg-
MAGNIFICENT meg-
MAGNIFICO meg-
MAGNIFY meg-
MAGNILOQUENT meg-, tolkʷ-
MAGNITUDE meg-
MAGNUM meg-
MAGUS magh-¹
MAHARAJAH meg-, reg-¹
MAHARANI meg-, reg-¹
MAHARISHI meg-
MAHATMA ētmen-, meg-
Mahayana ei-¹, meg-
MAHOUT meg-, mē-²
Maia mā-²
MAID maghu-
MAIDEN maghu-
MAIEUTIC mā-²
MAIGRE māk-
MAIL¹ molko-
MAIL² macula
MAIL³ mōd-
MAILLOT macula
MAIM mai-¹
MAIN¹ magh-¹
MAINTAIN man-², ten-
MAJESTY meg-
MAJOR meg-
MAJOR-DOMO demə-¹, meg-
MAJORITY meg-
MAJUSCULE meg-
MAKE mag-
MAL- mel-⁵
MALACHITE malakhē
MALACOLOGY mel-¹
MALADY mel-⁵
MALARIA wer-²
MALE mas
MALEDICT deik-, mel-⁵
MALEFACTOR dhē-¹, mel-⁵
MALEVOLENT mel-⁵, wel-¹
MALFEASANCE dhē-¹
MALIC ACID mēlon
MALICE mel-⁵
MALIGN genə-, mel-⁵
MALLEABLE melə-
MALLEMUCK mel-⁷
MALLET melə-
MALLEUS melə-
MALLOW malakhē
MALM melə-
MALT mel-¹
MALTHA mel-¹
MALVERSATION mel-⁵, wer-³
MAMA mā-²
MAMMA² mā-²
MAMMALIA mā-²
MAMMILLA mā-²

MAN man-¹
MANACLE man-²
MANAGE man-²
MAÑANA mā-¹
-MANCY men-¹
MANDAMUS man-²
MANDARIN men-¹
MANDATE man-²
MANDIBLE mendh-²
MANDOLIN pandoura
MANE mon-
MANEGE man-²
MANES mā-¹
MANEUVER man-², op-¹
MANGE mendh-²
MANGELWURZEL wrād-
MANGER mendh-²
MANGLE¹ mai-¹
MANGONEL meng-
MANIA men-¹
MANIAC men-¹
MANICOTTI man-²
MANICURE cūra, man-²
MANIFEST dhers-, man-²
MANIKIN man-¹
MANIPLE man-²
MANIPULATION man-²
MANNEQUIN man-¹
MANNER man-²
MANOMETER men-⁴
MANOR men-³
MANQUE man-²
MANSE men-³
MANSION men-³
MANSUETUDE man-², s(w)e-
MANTIC men-¹
MANTICORE mer-²
MANTIS men-¹
MANTRA men-¹
MANUAL man-²
MANUBRIUM man-²
MANUFACTURE dhē-¹, man-²
MANUMIT man-²
MANURE man-², op-¹
MANUS man-²
MANUSCRIPT man-², skrībh-
MANY menegh-
MAP mappa
MAQUIS macula
MAR mers-
MARASCA om-
MARASCHINO om-
MARASMUS mer-²
MARC merg-
MARCESCENT merk-¹
MARCH¹ merg-
MARCH² merg-
March Māwort-
MARCHIONESS merg-
MARE¹ marko-
MARE² mori-
MARGARIC margaritēs
MARGARIC ACID margaritēs
MARGARINE margaritēs
MARGARITE¹ margaritēs
MARGARITE² margaritēs
MARGIN merg-
MARGRAVE gravo-, merg-
MARICOLOUS mori-
MARICULTURE mori-
MARINARA mori-
MARINE mori-
MARITAL mari-
MARITIME mori-
MARK¹ merg-
MARK² merg-
MARKET merk-²
MARKKA merg-
MARLINE mer-²
MARMALADE melit-, mēlon
MARQUEE merg-
MARQUETRY merg-
MARQUIS merg-
MARQUISE merg-
MARRAM mori-
MARROW mozgo-
MARRY¹ mari-
Mars Māwort-
MARSH mori-
MARSHAL marko-
MART merk-²
MARTIAL Māwort-
MARTIAN Māwort-
MARVEL smei-
MASCULINE mas
MASH meik-
MASON mag-.
MASS mag-¹
Mass (s)meit(ə)-

MASSETER mendh-[2]	MELON mēlon	MICROPYLE pulē	MITOCHONDRION ghrendh-, mei-[4]
MAST[1] mazdo-	MELT mel-[1]	MICTURATE meigh-	MITOSIS mei-[4]
MAST[2] mad-	MEMBER mēms-	MID[1] medhyo-	MITTEN medhyo-
MASTER meg-	MEMBRANE mēms-	MIDDLE medhyo-	MITTIMUS (s)meit(ə)-
MASTICATE mendh-[2]	MEMENTO men-[1]	MIDGARD medhyo-	MIX meik-
MASTIFF man-[2], s(w)e-	MEMORABLE (s)mer-[1]	MIDGE mu-[2]	MIXTURE meik-
MATADOR meg-	MEMORANDUM (s)mer-[1]	MIDRIFF kʷrep-	MIZZEN medhyo-
MATCH[1] mag-	MEMORY (s)mer-[1]	MIDWIFE me-[2]	MIZZLE meigh-
MATCH[2] meug-[2]	MENACE men-[2]	MIGHT[1] magh-[1]	MNEMONIC men-[1]
MATE[1] neud-	MENAGE mad-[3]	MIGRAINE ker-[1]	MNEMOSYNE men-[1]
MATELOTE neud-	MENARCHE arkhein, mē-[2]	MIGRATE mei-[1]	MOAN mei-no-
MATER māter-	MEND mend-	MIL[1] gheslo-	MOB meuə-
MATERIAL māter-	MENDACIOUS mend-	MIL[2] gheslo-	MOBILE meuə-
MATERNAL māter-	MENDICANT mend-	MILCH melg-	MODAL med-
MATERNITY māter-	MENHIR sē-[2]	MILCHIG melg-	MODE med-
MATHEMATICAL mendh-[1]	MENINX mēms-	MILD mel-[1]	MODEL med-
MATHEMATICS mendh-[1]	MENISCUS mē-[2]	MILDEW melit-	MODERATE med-
MATINEE mā-[1]	MENOPAUSE mē-[2]	MILE gheslo-	MODERN med-
MATINS mā-[1]	MENSCH man-[1]	MILFOIL bhel-[3], gheslo-	MODEST med-
MATRICLINOUS klei-	MENSES mē-[2]	MILIEU medhyo-	MODICUM med-
MATRICULATE māter-	Menshevik mei-[2]	MILIUM mele-	MODIFY dhē-[1], med-
MATRIMONY māter-	MENSTRUAL mē-[2]	MILK melg-	MODIOLUS med-
MATRIX māter-	MENSTRUATE mē-[2]	MILL[1] mele-	MODULATE med-
MATRON māter-	MENSURAL mē-[2]	MILLENARY gheslo-	MODULE med-
MATTER māter-	MENTAL men-[1]	MILLENNIUM at-, gheslo-	MODULUS med-
MATTOCK mat-	MENTION men-[1]	MILLEPORE gheslo-	MOGUL[1] mūk-
MATURE mā-[1]	Mentor men-[1]	MILLESIMAL gheslo-	MOIETY medhyo-
MATUTINAL mā-[1]	MENU mei-[2]	MILLET mele-	MOIL mel-[1]
MAUL mele-	MERCENARY merk-[2]	MILLI- gheslo-	MOIST meug-[2]
MAULSTICK mel-[2]	MERCER merk-[2]	MILLIARY gheslo-	MOLAR mel-[1]
MAUVE malakhē	MERCHANT merk-[2]	MILLIEME gheslo-	MOLASSES melit-
MAW mak-[2]	Mercury merk-[2]	MILLION gheslo-	MOLD[1] med-
MAXIM meg-	MERCY merk-[2]	MILLIPEDE gheslo-, ped-[1]	MOLD[2] meug-[2]
MAXIMUM meg-	MERE[1] mer-[1]	MILT mel-[1]	MOLD[3] mele-
May magh-[1], meg-	MERE[2] mori-	MIME mimos	MOLDER mele-, mai-[2]
MAYHEM mai-[1]	MERE[3] mei-[3]	MIMESIS mimos	MOLE[1] mai-[2]
MAYOR meg-	-MERE (s)mer-[2]	MIMIC mimos	MOLE[3] mō-
MAZAEDIUM aidh-, mag-.	MERETRICIOUS (s)mer-[2]	Mimir (s)mer-[1]	MOLE[4] mele-
MAZER smē-	MERGANSER ghans-, mezg-[1]	MINACIOUS men-[2]	MOLECULE mō-
ME me-[1]	MERGE mezg-[1]	MINCE mei-[2]	MOLEST mō-
MEAD[1] medhu-	MERIDIAN deiw-, medhyo-	MIND men-[1]	MOLLIFY dhē-[1], mel-[1]
MEAD[2] mē-[4]	MERISTEM (s)mer-[2]	MINE[2] me-[1]	MOLLUSK mel-[1]
MEADOW mē-[4]	MERIT (s)mer-[2]	Minerva men-[1]	MOLT mei-[1]
MEAGER māk-	MERLE ames-	MINESTRONE mei-[2]	MOLTO mel-[4]
MEAL[1] mele-.	MERLON ames-	MINGLE mag-	MOLY mō(u)lo-
MEAL[2] mē-[2]	MERMAID mori-	MINIKIN mei-[2]	MOLYBDENUM plumbum
MEALIE mele-.	MERO- (s)mer-[2]	MINIMUM mei-[2]	MOMENT meuə-
MEAN[1] mei-no-	-MEROUS (s)mer-[2]	MINISTER mei-[2]	MOMENTOUS meuə-
MEAN[2] mei-[1]	MERRY mregh-u-	MINISTRY mei-[2]	MOMENTUM meuə-
MEAN[3] medhyo-	MESENTERY en	MINIVER wer-[1]	MONAD men-[4]
MEASLES smē-	MESH mezg-[2]	MINNESINGER men-[1], sengwh-	MONANTHOUS andh-
MEASURE mē-[2]	MESO- medhyo-	MINNOW men-[4]	MONASTERY men-[4]
MEAT mad-	MESOGLEA gel-[1]	MINOR mei-[2]	MONAXON aks-
MEATUS mei-[1]	MESONEPHROS negʷh-ro-	MINT[1] men-[1]	Monday mē-[2]
MECHANIC magh-[1]	MESOTHELIUM dhē(i)-	MINUEND mei-[2]	MONEY men-[1]
MECHANISM magh-[1]	MESS (s)meit(ə)-	MINUS mei-[2]	MONGER meng-
MECHANO- magh-[1]	MESSAGE (s)meit(ə)-	MINUSCULE mei-[2]	MONGREL mag-
MECONIUM mak-[1]	MESTIZO meik-	MINUTE[2] mei-[2]	MONILIFORM mon-
MECOPTERAN māk-, pet-	META- me-[2]	MIOCENE mei-[2]	MONISH men-[1]
MEDDLE meik-	METABOLISM gʷelə-[1]	MIOSIS mu[1]-	MONITION men-[1]
MEDIAL medhyo-	METALLURGY werg-	MIR men-[4]	MONITOR men-[1]
MEDIAN medhyo-	METANEPHROS negʷh-ro-	MIRACLE smei-	MONK men-[4]
MEDIASTINUM medhyo-	METAPHOR bher-[1]	MIRAGE smei-	MONO- men-[4]
MEDIATE medhyo-	METAPHRASE gʷhren-	MIRE meu-	MONOCLE okʷ-
MEDICAL med-	METAPLASM pele-[2]	MIRROR smei-	MONOCLINIC klei-
MEDICATE med-	METASTASIS stā-	MIRTH mregh-u-	MONOCLINOUS klei-
MEDICINE med-	METATHESIS dhē-[1]	MIS-[1] mei-[1], mei-[2]	MONOCOQUE kokkos
MEDICO med-	METE[1] med-	MISADVENTURE gʷā-	MONODY wed-[2]
MEDIEVAL aiw-, medhyo-	METE[2] mei-[3]	MISANTHROPE ner-[2]	MONOECIOUS weik-[1]
MEDIOCRE medhyo-	METEMPSYCHOSIS bhes-[2]	MISCEGENATION gene-, meik-	MONOMER (s)mer-[2]
MEDITATE med-	METER[1] mē-[2]	MISCELLANEOUS meik-	Monophysite bheuə-
MEDITERRANEAN medhyo-, ters-	METER[2] mē-[2]	MISCHIEF kaput	MONOPODIUM ped-[1]
MEDIUM medhyo-	METER[3] mē-[2]	MISCIBLE meik-	MONOPOLY pel-[5]
MEDLEY meik-	-METER mē-[2]	MISCREANT kerd-[1]	MONOTREME terə-[1]
MEDULLA (s)mer-[3]	METHEGLIN med-	MISER miser	MONS men-[2]
MEED mizdho-	METHINKS tong-	MISERABLE miser	MONSTER men-[1]
MEEK meug-[2]	METHOD sed-[2]	MISERICORD kerd-[1]	Montagnard men-[2]
MEERSCHAUM mori-, (s)keu-	METHYLENE hulē, medhu-	MISERY miser	MONTANE men-[2]
MEET[1] mōd-	METONYMY nō-men-	MISFEASANCE dhē-[1]	MONTE men-[2]
MEET[2] med-	METOPE okʷ-	MISHAP kob-	MONTH mē-[2]
MEGA- meg-	METOPIC okʷ-	MISNOMER nō-men-	MONTICULE men-[2]
MEGALO- meg-	METRICAL mē-[2]	MISONEISM newo-	MONUMENT men-[1]
MEGALOCARDIA kerd-[1]	METRO- māter-	MISPRISION ghend-, mei-[1]	MOOCH meug-[1]
MEGALOPOLIS pele-[3]	METROLOGY mē-[2]	MISS[1] mei-[1]	MOOD[1] mō-
MEIOSIS mei-[2]	METRONOME mē-[2], nem-	MISSEL THRUSH meigh-	MOOD[2] med-
Meistersinger sengwh-	METRONYMIC nō-men-	MISSILE (s)meit(ə)-	MOON mē-[2]
MELANCHOLY ghel-[2], mel-[2]	METROPOLIS māter-, pele-[3]	MISSION (s)meit(ə)-	MOOR[1] mer-[3]
MÉLANGE meik-	-METRY mē-[2]	MISSIVE (s)meit(ə)-	MOOR[2] mā-[3]
MELANO- mel-[2]	MEW[1] mei-[1]	MIST meigh-	MOOT mōd-
MELD[1] meldh-	MEZZO-RELIEVO legʷh-	MISTAKE mel-[1]	MOP mappa
MELILOT melit-	MI smei-	MISTER meg-	MORA merə-
MELINITE mēlon	MIASMA mai-[2]	MISTLETOE meigh-	MORAL mē-[2]
MELIORATE mel-[4]	MICA smē-	MISTRAL men-[2]	MORALE mē-[2]
MELIORISM mel-[4]	MICKLE meg-	MISTRESS meg-	MORASS mori-
MELISMA mel-[3]	MICRO- smē-	MITE[1] mai-[1]	MORATORIUM merə-
MELLIFEROUS melit-	MICROBE gʷei-	MITE[2] mai-[1]	MORATORY merə-
MELLIFLUOUS bhleu-, melit-	MICROCOSM kes-[3]	MITER mei-[1]	MORBID mer-[2]
MELODRAMA mel-[3]	MICROFICHE dhīgʷ-	Mithras mei-[4]	MORDACIOUS mer-[2]
MELODY mel-[3], wed-[2]	MICRON smē-	MITIGATE mēi-	MORDANT mer-[2]

MORDENT mer-² | MUSTARD meu- | NEAT¹ nei- | NIPPLE nabja-
MORE mē-³ | MUSTELINE mūs- | NEAT² neud- | NIRVANA wē-
MORELLO om- | MUSTER men-² | NEB nabja- | NISI ne, swo-
MORES mē-¹ | MUSTY meug-¹ | NEBULA nebh- | NISUS kneigwh-
MORGANATIC mer-¹ | MUTATE mei-¹ | NEBULOUS nebh- | NIT knid-
MORGEN mer-¹ | MUTCHKIN med- | NECESSARY ked- | NIVAL sneigwh-
MORIBUND mer-² | MUTE mu¹- | NECK ken-⁵ | NIVEOUS sneigwh-
MORN mer-¹ | MUTILATE mut- | NECRO- nek-¹ | NIX¹ neigw-
MORNING mer-¹ | MUTTER mu¹- | NECRO- nek-¹ | NIX² ne
MORON mō(u)ro- | MUTTON mel-¹ | NECROMANCY negw-ro-, nek-¹ | NO¹ aiw-, ne
MOROSE mē-¹ | MUTUAL mei-¹ | NECROPOLIS pelə-³ | NO² ne
-MORPH merph- | MUZHIK man-¹ | NECROSIS nek-¹ | NOBLE gnō-
MORPHALLAXIS al-¹ | MUZZLE mūsum | NECTAR nek-¹ | NOCENT nek-¹
MORPHEME merph- | MY me-¹ | NECTARINE nek-¹ | NOCK ken-⁵
MORPHO- merph- | MYCELIUM walso- | NEE genə- | NOCTI- nekw-t-
MORPHOSIS merph- | -MYCETE meug-² | NEED nāu-¹ | NOCTILUCA leuk-
MORROW mer-¹ | MYCO- meug-² | NEEDLE (s)nē- | NOCTUID nekw-t-
MORSEL mer-² | MYCORRHIZA wrād- | NEFARIOUS dhē-¹, ne | NOCTULE nekw-t-
MORTAL mer-² | MYELO- mūs- | NEGATE ne | NOCTURN nekw-t-
MORTAR mer-² | MYIASIS mu-² | NEGLECT leg-¹, ne | NOCTURNAL nekw-t-
MORTGAGE mer-², wadh-¹ | MYLONITE melə- | NEGLIGEE ne | NOCUOUS nek-¹
MORTIFY mer-² | MYNA mad- | NEGOTIATE ne | NOD ken-²
MORTMAIN man-², mer-² | MYNHEER me-¹ | NEGRO negw-ro- | NODE ned-
MORTUARY mer-² | MYO- mūs- | NEIGHBOR bheuə-, nēhw-iz | NODULE ned-
MORT¹ mer-² | MYOCARDIUM kerd-¹ | NEITHER kwo-, ne | NODUS ned-
MORULA moro- | MYOPIA mu¹-, okw- | NEKTON snā- | NOËL genə-
MOSAIC men-¹ | MYOSOTIS mūs-, ous- | NEMATO- (s)nē- | NOESIS nous
MOSQUITO mu-² | MYRIAD meu- | NEMESIS nems- | NOISE nāu-²
MOSS meu- | MYRMECO- morwi- | NEO- newo- | NOISOME od-²
MOSSO meuə- | MYROBALAN gwelə-² | NEOGAEA gē- | NOMA nem-
MOST mē-³ | MYSELF me-¹ | NEON newo- | NOMAD nem-
MOSTACCIOLI mendh-² | MYSOPHILIA meu- | NEONATE genə- | NOMBRIL nobh-
MOT mu¹- | MYSOPHOBIA newo- | NEOPHYTE bheuə- | NOME nem-
MOTE² med- | MYSTAGOGUE ag- | NEOTERIC newo- | NOMENCLATOR kelə-², nō-men-
MOTH math- | MYSTERY¹ mu¹- | NEPENTHE kwent(h)-, ne | NOMINAL nō-men-
MOTHER¹ mater- | MYSTERY² mei-² | NEPHELINE nebh- | NOMINATE nō-men-
MOTIF meuə- | MYSTIC mu¹- | NEPHELOMETER nebh- | NOMOGRAM nem-
MOTION meuə- | MYSTICETE mūs- | NEPHEW nepōt- | NOMOGRAPH nem-
MOTIVE meuə- | MYTHOPOEIC kwei-² | NEPHOLOGY nebh- | -NOMY nem-
MOTOR meuə- | MYXO- meug-² | NEPHRO- negwh-ro- | NON- ne
MOTTO mu¹- | | NEPOTISM nepōt- | NONA- newn̥
MOUILLÉ mel-¹ | | NEREID nerə- | NONAGENARIAN dekm̥, newn̥
MOULAGE med- | | NEREIS nerə- | NONAGON newn̥
MOULIN melə- | # N | NEREUS nerə- | NONANOIC ACID newn̥
MOUNT¹ men-² | | NERITIC nerə- | NONCHALANT kelə-¹
MOUNT² men-² | | NERVE (s)neəu- | NONE ne, oi-no-
MOUNTAIN men-² | NACELLE nāu-² | NESCIENCE ne, skei- | NONES newn̥
MOURN (s)mer-¹ | NAG¹ ghen- | NESS nas- | NONJUROR yewes-
MOUSE mūs- | NAIAD (s)nāu- | NEST nizdo- | NONPAREIL perə-²
MOUTH men-² | NAIL nogh- | NESTLE nizdo- | NONPLUS pelə-¹
MOVE meuə- | NAINSOOK neiə- | NET² ned- | NOOK ken-⁵
MOVEMENT meuə- | NAIVE genə- | NET² nei- | NOON newn̥
MOW¹ mūk- | NAKED nogw- | NETHER ni | NOR¹ ne
MOW² mē-⁴ | NAME nō-men- | NETTLE ned- | NORDIC ner-¹
MUCH meg- | NANA nana | NEURILEMMA wel-³ | NORM gnō-
MUCILAGE meug-² | NANNY nana | NEURO- (s)neəu- | NORMA gnō-
MUCO- meug-² | NANO- nana | NEUROGLIA gel-¹ | NORMAL gnō-
MUCUS meug-² | NAP¹ ken-² | NEURON (s)neəu- | NORMAN man-¹, ner-¹
MUGGY meug-² | NAP² ken-² | NEUTER kwo-, ne | NORN sner-
MULBERRY moro- | NAPERY mappa | NEVÉ sneigwh- | NORSE ner-¹
MULCH mel-¹ | NAPKIN mappa | NEVER aiw-, ne | NORTH ner-¹
MULE² mel-² | NAPPE mappa | NEW newo- | NORTHERN ner-¹
MULEY mai-¹ | NARCO- (s)ner- | NEWEL ken-⁵ | NOSE nas-
MULL² melə- | NARCOSIS (s)ner- | NEXT nēhw-iz | NOSH ghen-
MULLET mel-² | NARCOTIC (s)ner- | NEXUS ned- | NOSTALGIA nes-¹
MULLION medhyo- | NARES nas- | NIB nabja- | NOSTRIL nas-, terə-²
MULTI- mel-⁴ | NARK² nas- | NIBBLE ken-² | NOSTRUM nes-²
MULTIFARIOUS dhē-¹ | NARRATE gnō- | NICE ne, skei- | NOT ne, wekti-
MULTIPLE pel-³ | NARROW (s)ner- | NICHE nizdo- | NOTCH sek-
MULTIPLEX plek- | NARWAL (s)kwal-o- | NICKNAME aug-¹ | NOTE gnō-
MULTITUDE mel-⁴ | NARWHAL nāu-¹ | NICTITATE kneigwh- | NOTHING ne
MUM¹ mu¹- | NASAL nas- | NIDDERING nei- | NOTICE gnō-
MUM² mu¹- | NASCENT nas- | NIDE nizdo- | NOTIFY dhē-¹, gnō-
MUMPS mu¹- | NASO- nas- | NIDIFY dhē-¹, nizdo- | NOTION gnō-
MUNDANE mundus | NASTURTIUM nas-, terkw- | NIDUS nizdo- | NOTOCHORD nepōt-
MUNICIPAL kap-, mei-¹ | NATAL genə- | NIECE nepōt- | NOTORIOUS gnō-
MUNIFICENT mei-¹ | NATANT snā- | NIELLO negw-ro- | NOTORNIS or-
MUNITION mei-³ | NATATION snā- | NIFLHEIM nebh-, tkei- | NOTTURNO nekw-t-
MURAL mei-³ | NATATORIAL snā- | NIGGARD ken-² | NOUGAT ken-⁵
MURAMIC ACID mei-³ | NATATORIUM snā- | NIGH nēhw-iz | NOUMENON nous
MURDER mer-² | NATES nōt- | NIGHT nekw-t- | NOUN nō-men-
MURE mei-³ | NATHELESS to- | NIGHTINGALE ghel-¹ | NOURISH (s)nāu-
MURINE mūs- | NATION genə- | NIGHTMARE mer-² | NOUS nous
MURK ner-¹ | NATIVE genə- | NIGRESCENCE negw-ro- | NOVA newo-
MURMUR mormor- | NATURE genə- | NIGRITUDE negw-ro- | NOVACULITE kes-¹
MURRAIN mer-² | NAUGHT ne, wekti- | NIGROSINE negw-ro- | NOVATION newo-
MURREY moro- | NAUGHTY ne | NIHILISM ne | NOVEL¹ newo-
MUSCA mu-² | NAUSEA nāu-² | NIHILITY ne | NOVEL² newo-
MUSCARINE mu-² | NAUTCH ner-² | NIKE nike | NOVELTY newo-
MUSCLE mūs- | NAUTICAL nāu-² | NIL ne | NOVEMBER newn̥
MUSE mūsum | NAUTILUS nāu-² | NILL ne, wel-² | NOVENA newn̥
MUSE men-¹ | NAVAL nāu-² | NIM nem- | NOVERCAL newo-
MUSEUM men-¹ | NAVE² nobh- | NIMBLE nem- | NOVICE newo-
MUSH² mu-² | NAVEL nobh-, nāu-² | NIMBUS nebh- | NOW nu-
MUSIC men-¹ | NAVIGATE ag-, nāu-² | NIMIETY ne | NOXIOUS nek-¹
MUSKET mu-² | NAVY nāu-² | NINE newn̥ | NUANCE sneudh-
MUST¹ med- | NAY aiw-, ne | NINETEEN newn̥ | NUB gen-
MUST³ meu- | NEAP TIDE ken-² | NINETY newn̥ | NUBILE sneubh-
MUSTACHE mendh-² | NEAR nēhw-iz | NINTH newn̥ | NUCELLUS ken-⁵
 | | NIP¹ ken-² |

NUCLEUS ken-5
NUDE nogw-
NUDGE2 nāu-1
NUDI- nogw-
NUDNIK nāu-1
NUISANCE nek-1
NULL ne
NULLIFY dhē-1, ne
NULLIPARA ne
NUMB nem-
NUMBER nem-
NUMEN neu-2
NUMISMATICS nem-
NUMMULAR nem-
NUMMULATE nem-
NUN1 nana
NUNCIO neu-1
NUNCUPATIVE kap-, nō-men-
NUPTIAL sneubh-
NURSE (s)nāu-
NURTURE (s)nāu-
NUT ken-5
NUTATION neu-2
NUTHATCH skep-
NUTRIA wed-1
NUTRIENT (s)nāu-
NUTRIMENT (s)nāu-
NUTRITION (s)nāu-
NUTRITIOUS (s)nāu-
NUTRITIVE (s)nāu-
NUX VOMICA weme-
NUZZLE nas-
NYCTALOPIA nekw-t-, okw-
NYCTITROPISM nekw-t-
NYMPH sneubh-
NYMPHOLEPT (s)lagw-
NYSTAGMOUS sneud(h)-

O

OAF albho-
OAKUM ē, gembh-
OAST aidh-
OAT oid-
OATH oito-
OB- epi
OBDURATE deru
OBERON albho-
OBESE ed-
OBEY au-5
OBFUSCATE dheu-1
OBITUARY ei-1
OBJECT1 yē-
OBJURGATE ag-, yewes-
OBLAST epi, wal-
OBLATE1 tele-
OBLIGE leig-1
OBLITERATE deph-
OBLIVION lei-
OBLONG del-1
OBLOQUY tolkw-
OBNOXIOUS nek-1
OBOE busk-
OBSCURE (s)keu-
OBSEQUIOUS sekw-1
OBSERVE ser-1
OBSESS sed-1
OBSTACLE stā-
OBSTETRIC stā-
OBSTINATE stā-
OBSTREPEROUS strep-
OBSTRUCT ster-2
OBTAIN ten-
OBTECT (s)teg-
OBTEST trei-
OBTRUDE treud-
OBTUND (s)teu-
OBVERT wer-3
OBVIOUS wegh-
OBVOLUTE wel-3
OCARINA awi-
OCCASION kad-
OCCIPUT kaput
OCCLUDE kleu-3
OCCULT kel-2
OCCUPY kap-
OCCUR kers-2
OCELLUS okw-
OCHLOCRACY wegh-
OCHLOPHOBIA wegh-
OCTAD oktō(u)
OCTANS oktō(u)
OCTANT oktō(u)
OCTAVE oktō(u)
OCTAVO oktō(u)
OCTENNIAL at-

OCTET oktō(u)
OCTO- oktō(u)
OCTOBER oktō(u)
OCTODECIMO dekm̥, oktō(u)
OCTOGENARIAN dekm̥, oktō(u)
OCTONARY oktō(u)
OCTOPUS oktō(u), ped-1
OCTROI aug-1
OCTUPLE pel-3
OCULAR okw-
OCULIST okw-
OCULOMETER okw-
OCULOMOTOR okw-
ODD us-
ODE wed-2
-ODE sed-2
ODIN wet-1
ODIUM od-2
ODOGRAPH sed-2
ODOMETER sed-2
-ODON dent-
-ODONT dent-
ODONTO- dent-
ODOR od-1
OENOLOGY vīnum
OENOMEL melit-, vīnum
OF apo-
OFF apo-
OFFAL apo-
OFFEND gwhen-1
OFFENSE gwhen-1
OFFER bher-1
OFFICE dhē-1
OFFICIAL dhē-1, op-1
OFT upo
OFTEN upo
OGLE okw-
-OID weid-
OIL elaia
OINTMENT ongw-
OKTOBERFEST dhēs-
OLD al-3
-OLE elaia
OLEAGINOUS elaia
OLEASTER elaia
OLECRANON el-1, ker-1
OLEO- elaia
OLFACTORY od-1
OLIGO- leig-2
OLIVE elaia
OLLA aukw-
OLLA PODRIDA pū-2
OMBRE dhghem-
OMBUDSMAN ambhi, bheudh-, man-1
OMEGA meg-
OMELET stele-
OMEN ō-
OMICRON smē-
OMIT (s)meit(ə)-
OMMATIDIUM okw-
OMMATOPHORE okw-
OMNI- op-1
OMNIBUS op-1
OMNIFARIOUS dhē-1
OMNISCIENT skei-
OMNIUM-GATHERUM op-1
OMPHALOS nobh-
ON an1
ONAGER agro-, asinus
ONCE oi-no-
ONCOGENESIS nek-2
ONCOLOGY nek-2
ONE oi-no-
ONEIROMANCY oner-
ONEROUS en-es-
ONOMASTIC nō-men-
ONOMATOPOEIA kwei-2, nō-men-
ONSLAUGHT an1, slak-
-ONT es-
ONTO- es-
ONUS en-es-
-ONYM nō-men-
-ONYMY nō-men-
ONYX nogh-
OO- awi-
OOZE1 wes-2
OOZE2 weis-
OPAL upo
OPEN upo
OPERA1 op-1
OPERATE op-1
OPERCULUM wer-5
OPEROSE op-1
OPHIDIAN angwhi-
OPHIOLOGY angwhi-
OPHITE angwhi-
OPHIUCHUS angwhi-, segh-
OPHTHALMO- okw-
OPINE op-2

OPINION op-2
OPISTHOBRANCH epi
OPISTHOGNATHOUS epi
OPIUM s(w)okwo-
OPPORTUNE per-2
OPPOSE apo-
OPPRESS per-5
OPPROBRIUM bher-1
OPPUGN peuk-
OPSIN okw-
-OPSIS okw-
-OPSY okw-
OPT op-2
OPTATIVE op-2
OPTIC okw-
OPTIMUM op-1
OPTION op-2
OPTOMETRY okw-
OPULENT op-1
OPUS op-1
OR2 ayer-
OR3 aurum
ORACLE ōr-
ORAL ōs-
ORATION ōr-
ORATOR ōr-
ORATORY1 ōr-
ORATORY2 ōr-
ORCHARD gher-1
ORCHESTRA ergh-
ORCHID ergh-
ORDAIN ar-
ORDEAL dail-
ORDER ar-
ORDINAL ar-
ORDINANCE ar-
ORDINARY ar-
ORDINATE ar-
ORDO ar-
ORDURE ghers-
ORE aurum
ORGAN werg-
ORGANOLEPTIC (s)lagw-
ORGANON werg-
ORGASM wrōg-
ORGEAT ghers-
ORGY werg-
ORIENT er-1
ORIFICE ōs-
ORIFLAMME aurum
ORIGIN er-1
ORIGINAL er-1
ORINASAL ōs-
ORIOLE aurum
ORLOP klou-, uper
ORMAZD ansu-, men-1
ORMER mori-, ous-
ORMOLU aurum, mela-
ORNAMENT ar-
ORNATE ar-
ORNITHO- or-
OROIDE aurum
OROTUND ōs-
ORPHAN orbh-
ORPHREY aurum
ORPIMENT aurum
ORT ed-, ud-
ORTHO- wrōdh-
ORTHODOX dek-1
ORTHOGONAL genu-1
ORTHOPEDICS pau-
ORTHOSTICHOUS steigh-
ORTHOTICS wrōdh-
ORTOLAN gher-1
OS1 ōs-
OS2 ost-
OS3 omeso-
OSCINE kan-
OSCITANCY kei-3, ōs-
OSCULATE ōs-
OSCULUM ōs-
OSMATIC od-1
OSMIUM od-1
OSMOSIS wedh-
OSPREY awi-, ghend-
OSSEOUS ost-
OSSICLE ost-
OSSIFRAGE bhreg-, ost-
OSSIFY ost-
OSSUARY ost-
OSTENSIBLE ten-
OSTEO- ost-
OSTEOCLAST kel-1
OSTEOMALACIA mel-1
OSTIARY ōs-
OSTIUM ōs-
OSTMARK aus-1
OSTRACIZE ost-
OSTRACOD ost-

OSTRICH awi-, trozdo-
OSTROGOTH aus-1
OTHER an2
OTIC ous-
OTO- ous-
OTTER wed-1
OUBLIETTE lei-
OUCH2 ned-
OUGHT1 ēik-
OUNCE1 oi-no-
OUNCE2 leuk-
OUR nes-2
OURS nes-2
OUST stā-
OUT ud-
OUTLAW legh-, ud-
OUTRE al-1
OUZEL ames-
OVAL awi-
OVARY awi-
OVATE awi-
OVEN aukw-
OVER uper
OVERT wer-5
OVERTURE wer-5
OVI- awi-
OVIBOS gwou-, owi-
OVINE owi-
OVOLO awi-
OVULE awi-
OVUM awi-
OWE ēik-
OWL ul-
OWN ēik-
OX wegw-
OXALIS ak-
OXLIP sleubh-
OXYGEN ak-
OXYMORON mō(u)ro-
OXYTOCIC tek-
OXYURIASIS ak-, ors-
OYEZ au-5
OYSTER ost-
OZONE od-1

P

PABULUM pā-
PACE1 petə-
PACE2 pag-
PACHISI penkwe, wīkm̥tī
PACHYDERM bhengh-
PACHYSANDRA bhengh-
PACIFIC pag-
PACIFY pag-
PACT pag-
PADISHAH poti-
PADRE petər-
PAELLA petə-
PAGAN pag-
PAGE2 pag-
PAGEANT pag-
PAILLASSE pel-1
PAIN kwei-1
PAINT peig-1
PAINTER2 (s)pen-
PAIR perə-2
PAISA ped-1
PAJAMAS ped-1
PAL bhrāter-
PALANQUIN ank-, per 1
PALAVER gwelə-1
PALE1 pag-
PALE2 pel-2
PALEA pel-1
PALEO- kwei-2
PALETTE pag-
PALFREY per1, reidh-
PALIMPSEST bhes-1, kwei-1
PALINDROME der-1, kwei-1
PALINGENESIS kwei-1
PALINODE kwei-1
PALISADE pag-
PALLID pel-2
PALL-MALL bhel-2, mela-
PALLOR pel-2
PALM1 pelə-2
PALM2 pelə-2
PALOMINO pel-2
PALP pōl-
PALPABLE pōl-
PALPATE1 pōl-
PALPEBRAL pōl-
PALPITATE pōl-
PALSGRAVE gravo-
PALUDAL pelə-1

PALUDISM pelə-[1]	PARTERRE ters-	PENAL kʷei-[1]	PERQUISITE quaerere
PALYNOLOGY pel-[1]	PARTICIPATE kap-	PENALTY kʷei-[1]	PER SE s(w)e-
PAM bhilo-	PARTRIDGE perd-	PENCHANT (s)pen-	PERSECUTE sekʷ-[1]
PAMPER pap-[2]	PARTURIENT perə-[1]	PENCIL pes-	PERSEVERE wēro-
PAN[1] petə-	PARURE perə-[1]	PENDANT (s)pen-	PERSIFLAGE swei-[1]
PAN[2] per-[2]	PARVENU gʷā-, per[1]	PENDENTIVE (s)pen-	PERSIST stā-
PAN pant-	PARVOVIRUS pau-	PENDULOUS (s)pen-	PERSPECTIVE spek-
PAN- pant-	PAS petə-	PENGUIN weid-	PERSPIRE spīrāre
PANACEA yēk-	PASS petə-	-PENIA (s)pen-	PERSUADE swād-
PANACHE pet-	PASSIBLE pē(i)-	PENICILLIUM pes-	PERT wer-[5]
PANADA pā-	PASSIM petə-	PENIS pes-	PERTAIN ten-
PANATELA pā-	PASSION pē(i)-	PENNA pet-	PERTINACIOUS ten-
PANCRATIUM pant-	PASSIVE pē(i)-	PENNATE pet-	PERTURB twer-[1]
PANCREAS kreuə-[1], pant-	PASTILLE pā-	PENNON pet-	PERVADE wadh-[2]
PANDECT dek-[1]	PASTOR pā-	PENOLOGY kʷei-[1]	PERVERT wer-[3]
PANDEMIC dā-	PASTURE pā-	PENSILE (s)pen-	PERVIOUS wegh-
PANDORE pandoura	PATEN petə-	PENSION[1] (s)pen-	PES ped-[1]
PANE pan-	PATENT petə-	PENSIVE (s)pen-	PESADE paus-
PANEGYRIC ger-[1]	PATER petər-	PENSTEMON stā-	PESO (s)pen-
PANEL pan-	PATERNAL petər-	PENTA- penkʷe	PESSIMISM ped-[1]
PANICLE pan-	PATERNOSTER nes-[2]	PENTACLE penkʷe	PESTER pā-
PANMICTIC meik-	PATH pent-	PENTAD penkʷe	PESTLE peis-[1]
PANMIXIS meik-	PATHETIC kʷent(h)-	PENTADACTYL penkʷe	PETAL petə-
PANNIER pā-	PATHO- kʷent(h)-	PENTAGON penkʷe	-PETAL petə-
PANOCHA pā-	PATHOGNOMIC gnō-	PENTAMETER penkʷe	PETARD pezd-
PANOPTIC okʷ-	PATHOGNOMONIC kʷent(h)-	PENTARCHY penkʷe	PETITION pet-
PANORAMA wer-[4]	PATHOS kʷent(h)-	PENTASTICH penkʷe	PETRIFY dhē-[1], petra
PANSY (s)pen-	-PATHY kʷent(h)-	PENTATEUCH dheugh-, penkʷe	PETRO- petra
PANT bhā-[1]	PATIENT pē(i)-	PENTATHLON penkʷe	PETROLEUM elaia
PANTHEON dhēs-	PATINA[1] petə-	PENTECOST dekm̥, penkʷe	PETROUS petra
PANTRY pā-	PATINA[2] petə-	PENTHOUSE (s)pen-	PETULANT pet-
PAP[2] pap-[2]	PATRI- petər-	PENUCHE pā-	PEW ped-[1]
PAPA papa	PATRIARCH petər-	PEON ped-[1]	-PHAGE bhag-[1]
PAPILLA pap-[1]	PATRICIAN petər-	PEOPLE populus	-PHAGIA bhag-[1]
PAPPUS papa	PATRICLINOUS klei-	PEPO pekʷ-	PHAGO- bhag-[1]
PAPULE pap-[1]	PATRIMONY petər-	PEPPER pippalī	-PHAGOUS bhag-[1]
PAR perə-[2]	PATRIOT petər-	PEPSIN pekʷ-	PHALANGE bhelg-
PARA-[1] per[1]	PATRON petər-	PEPTIC pekʷ-	PHALANX bhelg-
-PARA perə-[1]	PATRONYMIC nō̆-men-	PEPTONE pekʷ-	PHALAROPE bhel-[1], ped-[1]
PARABLE gʷelə-[1]	PATULOUS petə-	PER per[1]	PHALLUS bhel-[2]
PARABOLA gʷelə-[1]	PAUCITY pau-	PER- per[1]	PHANEROGAM bhā-[1]
PARACHUTE perə-[1]	PAUPER pau-	PERCEIVE kap-	PHANTASM bhā-[1]
PARACLETE kelə-[2]	PAUSE paus-	PER CENT dekm̥	PHANTASMAGORIA bhā-[1]
PARADE perə-[1]	PAVE peuə-	PERCH[2] perk-[1]	PHANTOM bhā-[1]
PARADIGM deik-	PAVE peuə-	PERCOLATE kagh-	PHARMACOPOEIA kʷei-[2]
PARADISE dheigh-, per[1]	PAVID peuə-	PERCURRENT kers-[2]	PHARYNX bher-[2]
PARADOX dek-[1]	PAWN[2] ped-[1]	PERCUSS kwēt-	PHASE bhā-[1]
PARAFFIN pau-	PAY[1] pag-	PERDITION dō-	-PHASIA bhā-[2]
PARAGRAPH gerbh-	PAY[2] pik-	PERDURABLE deuə-	PHELLEM bhel-[2]
PARALLAX al-[1]	PEACE pag-	PEREGRINE agro-	PHELLODERM bhel-[2]
PARALLEL al-[1]	PEARL[1] persnā	PEREMPTORY em-	PHELLOGEN bhel-[2]
PARALLELEPIPED ped-[1]	PEASANT pag-	PERENNIAL at-	PHENO- bhā-[1]
PARALOGISM leg-[1]	PECCABLE ped-[1]	PERFECT dhē-[1]	PHENOMENON bhā-[1]
PARALYSIS leu-[1]	PECCADILLO ped-[1]	PERFIDY bheidh-	PHEROMONE bher-[1]
PARAMECIUM māk-	PECCANT ped-[1]	PERFORATE bher-[2]	PHILANDER ner-[2]
PARAMOUNT ad-, per[1]	PECTEN pek-[2]	PERFUME dheu-[1]	PHILANTHROPY ner-[2]
PARAMOUR amma, per[1]	PECTIN pag-	PERFUNCTORY bheug-[2]	PHILATELY tele-
PARANOIA nous	PECTORAL peg-	PERFUSE gheu-	-PHILE bhilo-
PARAPET peg-	PECULATE peku-	PERGOLA perg-	-PHILIA bhilo-
PARAPHERNALIA bher-[1]	PECULIAR peku-	PERI- per[1]	PHILLUMENIST leuk-
PARAPHRASE gʷhren-	PECUNIARY peku-	PERICARDIUM kerd-[1]	PHILO- bhilo-
PARAPLEGIA plāk-[2]	-PED ped-[1]	PERICLINE klei-	PHILODENDRON deru
PARASOL perə-[1], sāwel-	PEDAGOGUE ag-	PERIGEE gē	-PHILOUS bhilo-
PARATAXIS tāg-	PEDAL ped-[1]	PERIHELION sāwel-	PHILTER bhilo-
PARBOIL beu-[1]	PEDATE ped-[1]	PERIL per-[4]	PHLEGETHON bhel-[1]
PARCAE per[1]	PEDESTAL stel-	PERIMYSIUM mūs-	PHLEGM bhel-[1]
PARCEL perə-[2]	PEDESTRIAN ped-[1]	PERINEPHRIUM negʷh-ro-	PHLEGMATIC bhel-[1]
PARCENER perə-[2]	PEDI- ped-[1]	PERIOD sed-[2]	PHLOEM bhleu-
PARDON dō-	PEDICEL ped-[1]	PERIONYCHIUM nogh-	PHLOGISTON bhel-[1]
PARE perə-[1]	PEDICULAR pezd-	PERIOSTEM ost-	PHLOGOPITE bhel-[1], okʷ-
PARENCHYMA en, gheu-	PEDICURE cūra	PERIPATETIC pent-	PHLOX bhel-[1]
PARENT perə-[1]	PEDIGREE gerə-[2]	PERIPETEIA pet-	PHLYCTENA bhleu-
PARENTHESIS dhē-[1], en	PEDO-[1] ped-[1]	PERIPHERY bher-[1]	-PHOBE bhegʷ-
PARESIS yē-	PEDO-[2] pau-	PERIPHRASIS gʷhren-	-PHOBIA bhegʷ-
PARGET per[1], yē-	PEDUNCLE ped-[1]	PERIPHYTON bheuə-	PHOEBE bheigʷ-
PARHELION sāwel-	PEEL[2] pag-	PERIPTERAL pet-	PHOEBUS bheigʷ-
PARI-MUTUEL perə-[2]	PEEL[3] pag-	PERISARC twerk-	PHONE[1] bhā-[2]
PARISH weik-[1]	PEEPUL pippalī	PERISH ei-[1]	-PHONE bhā-[2]
PARITY[2] perə-[2]	PEER[2] perə-[2]	PERISSODACTYL per[1]	PHONEME bhā-[2]
PARLAY perə-[2]	PEG bak-	PERISTALSIS stel-	PHONETIC bhā-[2]
PARLEY gʷelə-[1]	PEGMATITE pag-	PERISTYLE stā-	PHONO- bhā-[2]
PARLIAMENT gʷelə-[1]	PEJORATION ped-[1]	PERITHECIUM dhē-[1]	-PHONY bhā-[2]
PARLOR gʷelə-[1]	PELAGE pilo-	PERITONEUM ten-	-PHORE bher-[1]
PARLOUS per-[4]	PELAGIC plāk-[1]	PERITRICH thrix	-PHORESIS bher-[1]
PARODY wed-[2]	PELARGONIUM pel-[2]	PERIWINKLE[1] weng-	-PHOROUS bher-[1]
PAROL gʷelə-[1]	PELECYPOD yewes-	PERJURE yewes-	PHOS- bhā-[1]
PAROLE gʷelə-[1]	PELISSE pel-[4]	PERMANENT men-[3]	PHOSPHENE bhā-[1]
PARONOMASIA nō̆-men-	PELLAGRA ag-, pel-[4]	PERMEATE mei-[1]	PHOSPHORUS bhā-[1]
PARONYCHIA nogh-	PELLICLE pel-[4]	PERMIT (s)meit(ə)-	PHOT bhā-[1]
PARONYMOUS nō̆-men-	PELL-MELL meik-	PERMUTE mei-[1]	PHOTO- bhā-[1]
PAROTID GLAND ous-	PELLUCID leuk-	PERNICIOUS nek-[1]	PHOTOTROPH threph-
-PAROUS perə-[1]	PELOPS okʷ-, pel-[2]	PERONEAL per-[2]	PHRASE gʷhren-
PAROUSIA es-	PELORIA kʷer-[1]	PERORAL ōs-	PHRATRY bhrāter-
PAROXYSM ak-	PELT[1] pel-[4]	PERORATE ōr-	PHREATIC bhreu-[2]
PARRICIDE pāso-	PELTATE pel-[4]	PERPEND (s)pen-	-PHRENIA gʷhren-
PARRY perə-[1]	PELTRY pel-[4]	PERPENDICULAR (s)pen-	PHRENITIS gʷhren-
PARSE perə-[2]	PELVIS pel-[7]	PERPETRATE petər-	PHRENO- gʷhren-
PARSLEY petra	PEN[1] pet-	PERPETUAL pet-	PHTHIRIASIS dhgʷher-
PART perə-[2]	PEN[2] bend-	PERPLEX plek-	PHTHISIS dhgʷhei-

PHYLACTERY phulax	PIÙ pelə-1	PLUMBER plumbum	POOL2 pau-
PHYLAXIS phulax	PLACABLE plåk-1	PLUMBIFEROUS plumbum	POOR pau-
PHYLE bheuə-	PLACATE plåk-1	PLUMBISM plumbum	POORI pelə-1
PHYLETIC bheuə-	PLACE plat-	PLUME pleus-	POPE papa
-PHYLL bhel-3	PLACEBO plåk-1	PLUMMET plumbum	POPLAR p(y)el-
PHYLLO- bhel-3	PLACENTA plåk-1	PLUMOSE pleus-	POPPLE2 p(y)el-
PHYLLOCLADE kel-1	PLACID plåk-1	PLUMULE pleus-	POPPYCOCK kakka-, pap-2
-PHYLLOUS bhel-3	PLACOID plåk-1	PLUNGE plumbum	POPULACE populus
PHYLLOXERA ksero-	PLAGAL plåk-1	PLUPERFECT dhē-1, pelə-1	POPULAR populus
PHYLOGENY bheuə-	PLAGIARY plåk-1	PLURAL pelə-1	POPULATE populus
PHYLUM bheuə-	PLAGIO- plåk-1	PLUS pelə-1	PORCELAIN porko-
PHYSIC bheuə-	PLAGIOCLASE kel-1	PLUSH pilo-	PORCH per-2
PHYSIO- bheuə-	PLAGUE plåk-2	PLUTO pleu-	PORCINE porko-
PHYSIOGNOMY gnō-	PLAICE plat-	PLUTOCRACY pleu-	PORCUPINE porko-, spei-
PHYSIQUE bheuə-	PLAIN pelə-2	PLUVIAL pleu-	PORE2 per-2
PHYSOSTIGMINE pŭ-1	PLAINT plåk-2	PLUVIOUS pleu-	PORGY bhag-2
PHYSOSTOMOUS pŭ-1	PLAIT plek-2	PLY1 plek-	PORK porko-
-PHYTE bheuə-	PLAN plat-	PNEUMA pneu-	PORNOGRAPHY per-6
PHYTO- bheuə-	PLANARIAN pelə-2	PNEUMATIC pneu-	POROMERIC per-2
PHYTON bheuə-	PLANCHET plåk-1	PNEUMATO- pneu-	PORPOISE peisk-, porko-
PIACULAR pius	PLANE1 pelə-2	PNEUMO- pneu-	PORT1 per-2
PIANO2 pelə-2	PLANE2 pelə-2	PNEUMONIA pleu-	PORT3 per-2
PIANOFORTE bhergh-2	PLANE3 pelə-2	PNEUMONIC pleu-	PORT6 per-2
PIAZZA plat-	PLANE4 plat-	POACH1 beu-1	PORTABLE per-2
PIBROCH pipp-	PLANET pelə-2	POCK beu-1	PORTAGE per-2
PICA2 (s)peik-	PLANE TREE plat-	POCKET beu-1	PORTAL per-2
PICARO (s)peik-	PLANGENT plåk-2	POCO pau-	PORTAMENTO per-2
PICE ped-1	PLANISH pelə-2	POCOCURANTE cūra	PORTATIVE per-2
PICEOUS pik-	PLANK plåk-1	-POD ped-1	PORTCULLIS per-2
PICKET (s)peik-	PLANK-SHEER plåk-1	PODAGRA ag-, ped-1	PORTE-COCHERE per-2
PICOLINE pik-	PLANKTON plåk-1	PODESTA poti-	PORTEND ten-
PICRO- peig-1	PLANO- pelə-2	PODIATRY ped-1	PORTER1 per-2
PICTOGRAPH peig-1	PLANT plat-	PODITE ped-1	PORTER2 per-2
PICTURE peig-1	PLANTAIN1 plat-	PODIUM ped-1	PORTFOLIO bhel-3, per-2
PICTURESQUE peig-1, (s)peik-	PLANTAR plat-	PODOPHYLLIN bhel-3, ped-1	PORTICO per-2
PIE2 (s)peik-	PLANTIGRADE ghredh-, plat-	PODZOL ghel-2, ped-1	PORTIÈRE per-2
PIE3 ped-1	PLANULA pelə-2	POEM kʷei-2	PORTION perə-2
PIECEMEAL mē-2	-PLASIA pelə-2	POESY kʷei-2	PORTRAY tragh-
PIERCE (s)teu-	PLASMA pelə-2	POET kʷei-2	PORTULACA per-2
PIERIAN SPRING peiə-	PLASMODESMA dē-	POETIC kʷei-2	POSE1 paus-
PIETÀ pius	-PLAST pelə-2	POGROM apo-, ghrem-	POSITION apo-
PIETY pius	PLASTER pelə-2	-POIESIS kʷei-2	POSITIVE apo-
PIEZO- sed-1	PLASTIC pelə-2	-POIETIC kʷei-2	POSSESS poti-, sed-1
PIGEON pipp-	PLASTID pelə-2	POIGNANT peuk-	POSSIBLE poti-
PIGMENT peig-1	-PLASTY pelə-2	POIKILOTHERM peig-1	POST1 stā-
PIKE1 (s)peik-	PLATE plat-	POILU pilo-	POST2 apo-
PILAR pilo-	PLATEAU plat-	POINT peuk-	POST3 apo-
PILE2 peis-1	PLATITUDE plat-	POINT-DEVICE weidh-	POST- apo-
PILE3 pilo-	PLATY2 plat-	POINTILLISM peuk-	POSTBELLUM duellum
PILEUS pilo-	PLATY- plat-	POISE1 (s)pen-	POSTERIOR apo-
PILGRIM agro-	PLATYHELMINTH wel-3	POISON pō(i)-	POSTICHE apo-
PILLAGE pilo-	PLATYPUS ped-1	POKE3 beu-1	POSTMERIDIAN deiw-
PILLION pel-4	PLAY plegan	POLACK pelə-2	POST-MORTEM apo-, mer-2
PILOCARPINE pilo-	PLAYA plåk-1	POLE1 kʷel-1	POSTPARTUM perə-1
PILOSE pilo-	PLAZA plat-	POLE2 pag-	POSTSCRIPT skrībh-
PILOT ped-1	PLEA plåk-1	POLICE pelə-3	POSTULATE prek-
PILUS pilo-	PLEACH plek-	POLICLINIC pelə-3	POSTURE apo-
PIMENTO peig-1	PLEAD plåk-1	POLICY1 pelə-3	POTABLE pō(i)-
PIMPERNEL pippalī	PLEASANT plåk-1	POLICY2 deik-	POTATION pō(i)-
PIÑA peiə-	PLEASE plåk-1	POLIOMYELITIS pel-2	POTATORY pō(i)-
PINCE-NEZ nas-	PLEBE pelə-1	POLIS pelə-3	POTENT poti-
PINE1 peiə-	PLEBEIAN pelə-1	POLISH pel-6	POTION pō(i)-
PINE2 kʷei-1	PLEBISCITE pelə-1, skei-	POLITIC pelə-3	POTPOURRI pŭ-2
PINEAL peiə-	PLEBS pelə-1	POLITY pelə-3	POUCH beu-1
PINFOLD bend-	PLECOPTERAN pet-, plek-	POLKA pelə-2	POULARD pau-
PINNA pet-	PLECTOGNATH plek-	POLLEN pel-1	POULTICE pel-1
PINNACE peiə-	PLECTRUM plåk-2	POLLEX pol-	POUNCE1 peuk-
PINNACLE pet-	PLEDGE plegan	POLLUTE leu-2	POUNCE2 (s)poi-mo-
PINNATE pet-	-PLEGIA plāk-1	POLTERGEIST bhel-4, gheis-	POUNCE3 peuk-
PINNULE pet-	PLEIOTAXY pelə-1	POLTROON pau-	POUND1 (s)pen-
PINOCYTOSIS pō(i)-	PLEIOTROPISM pelə-1	POLY- pelə-1	POUND2 bend-
PIÑON peiə-	PLEISTOCENE pelə-1	POLYGALA melg-	POUSETTE pel-6
PINTLE bend-	PLENARY pelə-1	POLYGLOT glōgh-	POUT beu-1
PINTO peig-1	PLENIPOTENTIARY pelə-1	POLYGYNY gʷen-	POVERTY pau-
PIOLET skep-	PLENITUDE pelə-1	POLYHISTOR weid-	POWDER pel-1
PIONEER ped-1	PLENTY pelə-1	POLYMATH mendh-2	POWER poti-
PIOUS pius	PLENUM pelə-1	POLYNYA pelə-2	PRAAM per1
PIP5 peiə-	PLEO- pelə-1	POLYP ped-1	PRACTICAL prāk-
PIPE pipp-	PLEONASM pelə-1	POLYPNEA pneu-	PRACTICE prāk-
PIQUE (s)peik-	PLESIOSAURUS pel-6	POLYPOD ped-1	PRAEDIAL wadh-1
PIRATE per-4	PLETHORA pelə-1	POLYTECHNIC teks-	PRAEMUNIRE mei-3
PIROG pō(i)-	PLETHYSMOGRAPH pelə-1	POLYTENE ten-	PRAENOMEN nō-men-
PISCARY peisk-	PLEUSTON pleu-	POLYTHEISM dhēs-	PRAETOR ei-1
PISCATORIAL peisk-	PLEXOR plåk-2	POLYTOCOUS tek-	PRAGMATIC prāk-
PISCES peisk-	PLEXUS plek-	POLYTROPHIC threph-	PRAISE per-6
PISCI- peisk-	PLIANT plek-	POMACE pōmum	PRANDIAL ed-
PISCINA peisk-	PLICA plek-	POMADE pōmum	PRATINCOLE kʷel-1
PISCINE peisk-	PLICATE plek-	POME pōmum	PRAXIS prāk-
PISMIRE morwi-	PLIGHT1 plek-	POND bend-	PRAY prek-
PISTIL peis-1	PLIGHT2 plegan	PONDER (s)pen-	PRAYER2 prek-
PISTON peis-1	PLIOCENE pelə-1	PONDEROUS (s)pen-	PRE- per1
PIT1 peu-	PLISSÉ plek-	PONIARD peuk-	PREACH deik-
PITCH1 pik-	-PLOID pel-3	PONS pent-	PREAMBLE al-2
PITCHBLENDE pik-	PLOVER pleu-	PONTIFEX dhē-1, pent-	PREBEND ghabh-
PITTANCE pius	PLUCK pilo-	PONTIFF pent-	PRECARIOUS prek-
PITUITARY peiə-	PLUMATE pleus-	PONTIL peuk-	PRECAUTION keuə-
PITUITOUS peiə-	PLUMB plumbum	PONTINE pent-	PRECEDE ked-
PITY pius	PLUMBAGO plumbum	PONTOON pent-	PRECENTOR kan-
		PONY pau-	PRECEPT kap-

PRECINCT kenk-[1]	PRO[1] per[1]	PROSTYLE stā-	PURBLIND bhel-[1]
PRECIOUS per-[6]	PRO-[1] per[1]	PROTAGONIST ag-	PURCHASE per[1]
PRECIPITATE kaput	PRO-[2] per[1]	PROTASIS ten-	PURE peuə-
PRECISE kae-id-	PROBABLE per[1]	PROTECT (s)teg-	PURFLE gʷhī-
PRECLUDE kleu-[3]	PROBE per[1]	PROTEIN per[1]	PURGE peuə-
PRECOCIOUS pekʷ-	PROBITY per[1]	Proterozoic per[1]	PURITAN peuə-
PRECURSOR kers-[2]	PROBLEM gʷelə-[1]	PROTEST trei-	PURLOIN del-[1]
PREDATORY ghend-	PROBOSCIS gʷō-	PROTHALLUS dhal-	PURPORT per-[2]
PREDECESSOR ked-	PROCEED ked-	PROTHESIS dhē-	PURSE bursa
PREDICATE deik-	PROCLAIM kelə-[2]	PROTHONOTARY gnō-	PURSLANE porko-
PREDICT deik-	PROCLITIC klei-	PROTIST per[1]	PURSUE sekʷ-[1]
PREDOMINATE demə-[1]	PROCLIVITY klei-	PROTO- per[1]	PURULENT pū-[2]
PREEMPTION em-	PROCREATE ker-[3]	PROTOCOL koli-	PUS pū-[2]
PREFACE bhā-[2]	PROCTITIS prōkto-	PROTON per[1]	PUSH pel-[6]
PREFECT dhē-[1]	PROCTOLOGY prōkto-	PROTONEMA (s)nē-	PUSILLANIMOUS anə-, pau-
PREFER bher-[1]	PROCTOR cūra	PROTOPATHIC kʷent(h)-	PUSTULE pū-[1]
PREFIGURE dheigh-	PROCTOSCOPE prōkto-	PROTRACT tragh-	PUTAMEN peu-
PREFIX dhigʷ-	PROCUMBENT keu-[2]	PROTRUDE treud-	PUTATIVE peu-
PREGNABLE ghend-	PROCURATOR cūra	PROTUBERATE teuə-	PUTREFY dhē-[1], pū-[2]
PREGNANT[1] genə-	PROCURE cūra	PROUD es-	PUTRESCENT pū-[2]
PREGNANT[2] per-[5]	Procyon kwon-	PROVE per[1]	PUTRID pū-[2]
PREHENSILE ghend-	PRODIGAL ag-	PROVENANCE gʷā-	PYCNIDIUM puk-[1]
PREHENSION ghend-	PRODIGY ēg-	PROVENDER ghabh-	PYCNOMTER puk-[1]
PREJUDICE deik-, yewes-	PRODROME der-[1]	PROVENIENCE gʷā-	PYELITIS pleu-
PRELAPSARIAN leb-[1]	PRODUCE deuk-	PROVERB wer-[6]	PYGMAEAN peuk-
PRELATE tele-	PROFANE dhēs-	PROVIDE weid-	PYGMY peuk-
PRELECT leg-[1]	PROFESS bhā-[2]	PROVOKE wekʷ-	PYKNIC puk-[1]
PRELIBATION lēi-	PROFESSOR reg-[1]	PROVOST apo-	PYLON pulē
PRELUDE leid-	PROFFER bher-[1]	PROW per[1]	PYLORUS pulē
PREMATURE mā-[1]	PROFICIENT dhē-[1]	PROXIMATE per[1]	PYO- pū-[2]
PREMIER per[1]	PROFILE gʷhī-	PROXY cūra	PYRACANTHA ak-
PREMISE (s)meit(ə)-	PROFIT dhē-[1]	PRUINOSE preus-	PYRARGYRITE arg-
PREMIUM em-	PROFLIGATE bhlīg-	PRUNE[2] ret-	PYRE pūr-
PREMONITION men-[1]	PROFOUND bhudh-	PRURIENT preus-	PYRENE pūro-
PREMORSE mer-[2]	PROFUSE gheu-	PRURIGO preus-	PYRETIC pūr-
PREMUNITION mei-[3]	PROGENITOR genə-	PRURITUS preus-	PYRITES pūr-
PREPARE perə-[1]	PROGENY genə-	PRY[2] ghend-	PYRO- pūr-
PREPENSE (s)pen-	PROGLOTTID glōgh-	PSALM pōl-	PYROPE okʷ-
PREPONDERATE (s)pen-	PROGNOSIS gnō-	PSALTERY pōl-	PYROSIS pūr-
PREPOSITION apo-	PROGRAM gerbh-	PSEPHOLOGY bhes-[1]	PYROXENE xenos
PREPOSTEROUS apo-	PROGRESS ghredh-	PSEUDEPIGRAPHA gerbh-	PYRRHOTITE pūr-
PREPOTENT poti-	PROHIBIT ghabh-	PSEUDOMONAD men-[4]	PYRUVIC ACID ōg-
PREPUCE pū-[1]	PROJECT yē-	PSEUDONYM nō-men-	
PREROGATIVE reg-[1]	PROLAN al-[3]	PSILOMELANE bhes-[1], mel-[2]	
PRESAGE sāg-	PROLAPSE leb-[1]	PSYCHE bhes-[2]	**Q**
PRESBYOPIA per[1]	PROLATE tele-	PSYCHEDELIC deiw-	
PRESBYTER per[1]	PROLEGOMENON leg-[1]	PSYCHIC bhes-[2]	
PRESCIENT skei-	PROLEPSIS (s)lagʷ-	PSYCHO- bhes-[2]	
PRESCIND skei-	PROLETARIAN al-[3]	PSYLLA plou-	QUA kʷo-
PRESCRIBE skrībh-	PROLIFEROUS al-[3]	-PTER pet-	QUACKSALVER gʷēbh-[2], selp-
PRESENT[1] es-	PROLIFIC al-[3]	PTERIDOLOGY pet-	QUADRANT kʷetwer-
PRESENT[2] es-	PROLIX wleik-	PTEROCERCOID pet-	QUADRATE kʷetwer-
PRESENTIMENT sent-	PROLOCUTOR tolkʷ-	PTERYGOID pet-	QUADRENNIUM at-
PRESERVE ser-[1]	PROLOGUE leg-[1]	PTISAN peis-[1]	QUADRI- kʷetwer-
PRESIDE sed-[1]	PROLONG del-[1]	PTOMAINE pet-	QUADRILLE[1] kʷetwer-
PRESS[1] per-[5]	PROLUSION leid-	PTOSIS pet-	QUADRILLE[2] kʷetwer-
PRESSURE per-[5]	PROMENADE men-[2]	PTYALIN spyeu-	QUADROON kʷetwer-
PRESTIGE streig-	PROMINENT men-[2]	PUBERTY pūbēs	QUADRUMANOUS man-[2]
PRESUME em-	PROMISCUOUS meik-	PUBERULENT pūbēs	QUADRUPLE pel-[3]
PRETEND ten-	PROMISE (s)meit(ə)-	PUBESCENT pūbēs	QUAESTOR quaerere
PRETERIT ei-[1], per[1]	PROMOTE meuə-	PUBIC pūbēs	QUAGMIRE meu-
PRETERMIT (s)meit(ə)-	PROMPT em-	PUBIS pūbēs	QUAINT gnō-
PRETEXT teks-	PRONE per[1]	PUBLIC populus	QUALIFY dhē-[1]
PRETZEL mregh-u-	PRONEPHROS negʷh-ro-	PUCE plou-	QUALITY kʷo-
PREVAIL wal-	PRONOUN nō-men-	PUCKER beu-[1]	QUANTITY kʷo-
PREVENIENT gʷā-	PRONOUNCE neu-[1]	PUDENCY (s)peud-	QUARANTINE kʷetwer-
PREVENT gʷā-	PROOF per[1]	PUDENDUM (s)peud-	QUARREL[1] kwes-
PREVIOUS wegh-	PROPAGATE pag-	PUEBLO populus	QUARREL[2] kʷetwer-
PREVISE weid-	PROPEL pel-[6]	PUERILE pau-	QUARRY[1] kerd-[1]
PREY ghend-	PROPEND (s)pen-	PUERPERAL pau-	QUARRY[2] kʷetwer-
PRICE per-[6]	PROPER per[1]	PUFF beu-[1]	QUART kʷetwer-
PRIEST per[1]	PROPERTY per[1]	PUG[3] ped-[1]	QUARTAN kʷetwer-
PRIMA FACIE dhē-[1], per[1]	PROPHET bhā-[2]	PUGILISM peuk-	QUARTER kʷetwer-
PRIMAL per[1]	PROPHYLACTIC phulax	PUGIL STICK peuk-	QUARTO kʷetwer-
PRIMARY per[1]	PROPINQUITY per[1]	PUGNACIOUS peuk-	QUARTZ twer-[2]
PRIMATE per[1]	PROPIONIC ACID peiə-	PUISNE apo-, genə-	QUASH kes-[2]
PRIMAVERA per[1], wesṛ	PROPITIOUS pet-	PUKKA pekʷ-	QUASI kʷo-, swo-
PRIME per[1]	PROPOLIS pelə-[3]	PULICIDE plou-	QUATERNARY kʷetwer-
PRIMEVAL aiw-, per[1]	PROPORTION perə-[2]	PULLET pau-	QUATERNION kʷetwer-
PRIMIPARA per[1]	PROPOSE apo-	PULLEY kʷel-[1]	QUATRAIN kʷetwer-
PRIMITIVE per[1]	PROPRIOCEPTION per[1]	PULMONARY pleu-	QUATROCENTO dekṃ
PRIMO per[1]	PROPRIOCEPTOR per[1]	PULSATE pel-[6]	QUATTROCENTO kʷetwer-
PRIMOGENITOR per[1]	PROPTOSIS pet-	PULSE[1] pel-[6]	QUAVER gʷēbh-[2]
PRIMOGENITURE genə-, per[1]	PROPYLAEUM pulē	PULSE[2] pel-[6]	QUAY kagh-
PRIMORDIAL ar-, per[1]	PROPYLON pulē	PULVERIZE pel-[1]	QUEAN gʷen-
PRIMUS per[1]	PROROGUE reg-[1]	PUMICE (s)poi-mo-	QUEBRACHO ker-[2], skep-
PRINCE per[1]	PROS- per[1]	PUMPKIN pekʷ-	QUEEN gʷen-
PRINCIPAL per[1]	PROSCRIBE skrībh-	PUNCH[3] penkʷe	QUELL gʷel-[1]
PRINCIPLE per[1]	PROSE wer-[3]	PUNCHEON[1] peuk-	QUENELLE gen-
PRINT per-[5]	PROSECUTE sekʷ-[1]	PUNCTUATE peuk-	QUERCETIN perkʷu-
PRIOR[2] per[1]	PROSELYTE leudh-[1]	PUNCTURE peuk-	QUERCITRON perkʷu-
PRISON ghend-	PROSOMA teuə-	PUNGENT peuk-	QUERIST quaerere
PRISTINE per[1]	PROSOPOPEIA kʷei-[2], per[1]	PUNISH kʷei-[1]	QUERN gʷerə-[2]
PRIVATE per[1]	PROSPECT spek-	PUNITORY kʷei-[1]	QUERULOUS kwes-
PRIVILEGE leg-[1], per[1]	PROSPER spē-[2]	PUNKA pau-	QUERY quaerere
PRIVITY per[1]	PROSTATE stā-	PUNT[1] pent-	QUEST quaerere
PRIVY per[1]	PROSTHESIS dhē-[1]	PUNY apo-, genə-	QUESTION quaerere
PRIZE[2] ghend-	PROSTITUTE stā-	PUPA pap-[1]	QUIBBLE kʷo-
PRIZE[3] ghend-	PROSTOMIUM stə-men-	PUPIL[1] pap-[1]	QUICHE kak-[2]

QUICK gwei-
QUICKSILVER gwei-
QUID[1] gwet-
QUIDDITY kwo-
QUIDNUNC kwo-, nu-
QUIET kweie-[2]
QUILT kwelak-
QUINATE penkwe
QUINCUNX oi-no-, penkwe
QUINDECENNIAL at-, penkwe
QUINQUAGENARIAN penkwe
Quinquagesima penkwe
QUINQUE- penkwe
QUINQUENNIUM at-
QUINSY angh-, kwon-
QUINT[1] penkwe
QUINTAIN penkwe
QUINTESSENCE es-, penkwe
QUINTET penkwe
QUINTILE penkwe
QUINTILLION penkwe
QUINTUPLE penkwe, plek-
QUIP kwo-
QUIRE[1] kwetwer-
QUITCH GRASS gwei-
QUITTOR pekw-
QUODLIBET kwo-, leubh-
QUONDAM kwo-
QUORUM kwo-
QUOTE kwo-
QUOTH gwet-[2]
QUOTIDIAN deiw-, kwo-
QUOTIENT kwo-

R

RABBET battuere
RABBLE[2] reu-[2]
RABID rebh-[1]
RABIES rebh-[1]
RACE[2] ers-[1]
RACE[3] wrād-
RACHIS wrāgh-
RACK[1] reg-[1]
RACK[3] wreg-
RACLETTE rēd-
RADDLE[1] reidh-
RADICAL wrād-
RADICLE wrād-
RADIOSONDE swem-
RADISH wrād-
RADIX wrād-
RADULA rēd-
RAFT[1] rēp-[2]
RAFTER rēp-[2]
RAG[1] reu-[2]
RAGA reg-[3]
RAGE rebh-[1]
RAGOUT geus-
RAID reidh-
RAIL[1] reg-[1]
RAIN reg-[2]
RAINBOW reg-[2]
RAISE rīsan
RAJ reg-[1]
RAJAH reg-[1]
RAKE[1] reg-[1]
RALLENTANDO lento-
RALLY leig-[1]
RAMBUNCTIOUS reudh-[1]
RAMEKIN reugh-men-
RAMIFY wrād-
RAMOSE wrād-
RAMP[2] skerbh-
RAMPART pera-[1]
RAMPION rāp-
RAMSON krem-
RAMUS wrād-
RANCH sker-[3]
RANGE sker-[3]
RANI reg-[1]
RANK[1] sker-[3]
RANK[2] sker-[3]
RANKLE derk-
RANSACK sāg-
RANSOM em-
RAPACIOUS rep-
RAPE[1] rep-
RAPE[2] rāp-
RAPHE wer-[3]
RAPHIDE wer-[3]
RAPID rep-
RAPPORT per-[2]
RAPPROCHEMENT per[1]
RAPT rep-
RARE[1] era-[2]

RARE[2] kera-
RAREFY dhē-[1]
RASH[2] rēd-
RASORIAL rēd-
RATCHET ruk-[1]
RATE[1] ar-
RATHE kret-[1]
RATHER kret-[1]
RATHSKELLER ar-, kel-[2]
RATIO ar-
RATITE era-[2]
RAUCOUS reu-[1]
RAVEN[1] ker-[2]
RAVEN[2] rep-
RAVIN rep-
RAVIOLI rāp-
RAVISH rep-
RAW kreua-[1]
RE[2] rē-
RE- re-
REACH reig-[2]
READ ar-
READY reidh-
REAL[1] rē-
REAL[2] reg-[1]
REALM reg-[1]
REAP rei-[1]
REAR[2] rīsan
REAR GUARD re-
REARWARD[2] re-, wer-[4]
REASON ar-
REAVE[1] reup-
REBARBATIVE bhardhā
REBATE[1] battuere
REBATO battuere
REBEL duellum
REBUS rē-
REBUT bhau-
RECALESCENCE kela-[1]
RECANT kan-
RECAPITULATE kaput
RECEDE ked-
RECEIVE kap-
RECENSION kens-
RECENT ken-[3]
RECIDIVISM kad-
RECIPROCAL per[1]
RECISION kae-id-
RECK reg-[1]
RECKLESS reg-[1]
RECKON reg-[1]
RECLAIM kela-[2]
RECLINE klei-
RECLUSE kleu-[3]
RECOGNIZE gnō-
RECOIL (s)keu-
RECOMMEND man-[2]
RECONDITE dhē-[1]
RECORD kerd-[1]
RECOURSE kers-[2]
RECOVER kap-
RECREANT kerd-[1]
RECREMENT krei-
RECRIMINATE krei-
RECRUDESCE kreua-[1]
RECRUIT ker-[3]
RECTANGLE reg-[1]
RECTIFY dhē-[1], reg-[1]
RECTILINEAR reg-[1]
RECTITUDE reg-[1]
RECTO reg-[1]
RECTOR reg-[1]
RECTUM reg-[1]
RECUMBENT keu-[2]
RECUPERATE kap-
RECUR kers-[2]
RED reudh-[1]
REDE ar-
REDEEM em-
REDEMPTION em-
REDOLENT od-[1]
REDOUBT deuk-
REDOUBTABLE dwo-
REDOUND wed-[1]
REDSTART ster-[1]
REDUCE deuk-
REDUNDANT wed-[1]
REDUVIID eu-[1]
REED kreut-
REEF[1] rebh-[2]
REEF[2] rebh-[2]
REEK reug-
REEL[1] krek-[1]
REFECT dhē-[1]
REFECTORY dhē-[1]
REFER bher-[1]
REFLUX bhleu-
REFRACT bhreg-
REFRAIN[1] ghrendh-

REFRAIN[2] bhreg-
REFRIGERATE srīg-
REFRINGENT bhreg-
REFUGE bheug-
REFULGENT bhel-[1]
REFUND gheu-
REFUSE[1] gheu-
REFUSE[2] gheu-
REFUTE bhau-
REGAL reg-[1]
REGENT reg-[1]
REGICIDE reg-[1]
REGIME reg-[1]
REGIMEN reg-[1]
REGIMENT reg-[1]
REGION reg-[1]
REGISTER gerere
REGIUS reg-[1]
REGLET reg-[1]
REGOLITH reg-[3]
REGRATE grat-
REGRESS ghredh-
REGULAR reg-[1]
REGULATE reg-[1]
REGULUS reg-[1]
REGURGITATE gwera-[4]
REIFY rē-
REIGN reg-[1]
REIMBURSE bursa
REINDEER dheu-[1], ker-[1]
REINFORCE bhergh-[2]
REITERATE i-
REJECT yē-
REJOICE gāu-
REJUVENATE yeu-
RELAPSE leb-[1]
RELATE tela-
RELAX slēg-
RELAY slēg-
RELEGATE leg-[1]
RELENT lento-
RELIEVE legwh-
RELINQUISH leikw-
RELUCENT leuk-
RELUCT leuk-
RELY leig-[1]
REMAIN men-[3]
REMAND man-[2]
REMARK merg-
REMEDY med-
REMEMBER (s)mer-[1]
REMEX era-[2]
REMINISCENT men-[1]
REMIT (s)meit(a)-
REMORA mera-
REMORSE mer-[2]
REMOTE meua-
REMOVE meua-
REMUDA mei-[1]
REMUNERATE mei-[1]
RENAISSANCE gena-
REND rendh-
RENDER dō-
RENDEZVOUS wōs-
RENEGADE ne
RENEGE ne
RENITENT kneigwh-
RENOUNCE neu-[1]
RENOVATE newo-
RENOWN nō-men-
RENT[1] dō-
REPAIR[1] pera-[1]
REPAND peta-
REPARTEE pera-[2]
REPAST pā-
REPEAT pet-
REPEL pel-[6]
REPENT[2] rēp-[1]
REPERTORY pera-[1]
REPINE kwei-[1]
REPLENISH pela-[1]
REPLETE pela-[1]
REPLEVIN plegan
REPLICATE plek-
REPORT per-[2]
REPOSE[1] paus-
REPOSIT apo-
REPREHEND ghend-
REPRESENT es-
REPRESS per-[5]
REPRIMAND per-[5]
REPRISAL ghend-
REPRISE ghend-
REPROACH per-[1]
REPROVE per-[1]
REPTILE rēp-[1]
REPUBLIC rē-
REPUDIATE (s)peud-
REPUGN peuk-
REPUTE peu-

REQUIEM kweie-[2]
REQUIESCAT kweie-[2]
REQUIRE quaerere
REREDOS dorsum, re-
RESCIND skei-
RESCRIPT skrībh-
RESCUE kwēt-
RESEAU era-[2]
RESECT sek-
RESEMBLE sem-[1]
RESENT sent-
RESERVE ser-[1]
RESERVOIR ser-[1]
RESIDE sed-[1]
RESIGN sekw-[1]
RESILE sel-[4]
RESIST stā-
RESOLVE leu-[1]
RESORB srebh-
RESOUND swen-
RESPECT spek-
RESPIRE spīrāre
RESPITE spek-
RESPLENDENT spel-[2]
RESPOND spend-
REST[2] stā-
RESTITUTE stā-
RESTIVE stā-
RESTORE stā-
RESTRICT streig-
RESULT sel-[4]
RESUME em-
RESUSCITATE kei-[3]
RETAIN ten-
RETALIATE tela-
RETCH ker-[2]
RETE era-[2]
RETIARY era-[2]
RETICENT tak-[1]
RETICLE era-[2]
RETICULE era-[2]
RETIFORM era-[2]
RETINA era-[2]
RETINACULUM ten-
RETORT[1] terkw-
RETRACT tragh-
RETRAL re-
RETRIEVE trep-[2]
RETRO- re-
RETROACTIVE ag-
RETROCEDE ked-
RETROGRADE ghredh-
RETROGRESS ghredh-
RETRORSE wer-[3]
RETROSPECT spek-
RETURN tera-[1]
RETUSE (s)teu-
REVEAL weg-[1]
REVEILLE weg-[1]
REVEL duellum
REVENANT gwā-
REVENGE deik-
REVENUE gwā-
REVERBERATE wer-[3]
REVERE[1] wer-[4]
REVERT wer-[3]
REVEST wes-[4]
REVIEW weid-
REVILE gwei-
REVIVE gwei-
REVOKE wekw-
REVOLVE wel-[3]
REVULSION wel-[4]
REWARD wer-[4]
RHABDOMANCY wer-[3]
RHABDOVIRUS wer-[3]
RHAPSODY wed-[2], wer-[3]
RHEO- sreu-
RHETOR wer-[6]
RHEUM sreu-
RHINOCEROS ker-[1]
RHIZO- wrād-
RHIZOBIUM gwei-
RHIZOME wrād-
RHODIUM wrod-
RHODO- wrod-
RHODOCHROSITE ghrēu-
RHODODENDRON deru-
RHODOPSIN okw-
RHOMBUS wer-[3]
RHONCHUS srenk-
RHYME sreu-
RHYNCHOCEPHALIAN srenk-
RHYOLITE sreu-
RHYTHM sreu-
RIB rebh-[2]
RIBALD wer-[3]
RICH reg-[1]
RICOTTA pekw-
RID reudh-[2]

SEAR² ser-³
SEARCH sker-³
SEASON sē-¹
SEAT sed-¹
SEAWARE wei-¹
SECANT sek-
SECCO seikʷ-
SECEDE ked-, s(w)e-
SECERN krei-, s(w)e-
SECLUDE kleu-³, s(w)e-
SECOND² sekʷ-¹
SECONDO sekʷ-¹
SECRET krei-, s(w)e-
-SECT sek-, sekʷ-¹
SECTILE sek-
SECTION sek-
SECTOR sek-
SECUND sekʷ-¹
SECUNDINES sekʷ-¹
SECURE cūra, s(w)e-
SEDATE¹ sed-¹
SEDENTARY sed-¹
SEDERUNT sed-¹
SEDGE sek-
SEDILIA sed-¹
SEDIMENT sed-¹
SEDITION ei-¹, s(w)e-
SEDUCE deuk-, s(w)e-
SEE¹ sekʷ-¹
SEE² sed-¹
SEED sē-¹
SEEK sāg-
SEEL kel-²
SEEM sem-¹
SEEMLY sem-¹
SEEP seib-
SEETHE seut-
SEGMENT sek-
SEGNO sekʷ-¹
SEGREGATE ger-¹, s(w)e-
SEGUE sekʷ-¹
SEGUIDILLA sekʷ-¹
SEICENTO dekm̥, s(w)eks
SEIGNIOR sen-¹
SEISIN sāg-
SEISM twei-
SEIZE sāg-
SELECT leg-¹, s(w)e-
SELF s(w)e-
SELL sel-³
SEMANTIC dheiə-
SEMAPHORE dheiə-
SEMASIOLOGY dheiə-
SEMATIC dheiə-
SEME sē-¹
SEMEME dheiə-
SEMEN sē-¹
SEMESTER mē-², s(w)eks
SEMI- sēmi-
SEMINARY sē-¹
SEMINATION sē-¹
SEMIOLOGY dheiə-
SEMIOTIC dheiə-
SEMPITERNAL aiw-, sem-¹
SEMPLICE sem-¹
SEMPRE sem-¹
SEN¹ dekm̥
SEN² dekm̥
SENARY s(w)eks
SENATE sen-¹
SEND¹ sent-
SENECTITUDE sen-¹
SENESCENT sen-¹
SENESCHAL sen-¹
SENILE sen-¹
SENIOR sen-¹
SENITI dekm̥
SENOPIA sen-¹
SENSE sent-
SENSILLUM sent-
SENTENCE sent-
SENTIENT sent-
SENTIMENT sent-
SENTINEL sent-
SEPARATE perə-¹, s(w)e-
SEPTEMBER septm̥
SEPTENNIAL at-, septm̥
SEPTENTRION septm̥, terə-¹
SEPTET septm̥
SEPTI- septm̥
SEPTIFRAGAL bhreg-
SEPTUAGINT dekm̥, septm̥
SEPTUPLE pel-³, septm̥
SEPULCHER sep-²
SEPULTURE sep-²
SEQUACIOUS sekʷ-¹
SEQUEL sekʷ-¹
SEQUENCE sekʷ-¹
SEQUESTER sekʷ-¹

SEQUESTRUM sekʷ-¹
SERAC ser-²
SERE¹ saus-
SERENE ksero-
SERF servus
SERGEANT servus
SERIES ser-³
SERIF skrībh-
SERIOUS swer-⁵
SERMON ser-³
SEROTINOUS sē-²
SERPENT serp-²
SERPIGO serp-²
SERRIED ser-³
SERTULARIAN ser-³
SERUM ser-²
SERVAL ker-¹
SERVE servus
SERVICE servus
SERVILE servus
SERVITUDE servus
SESQUI- kʷe, sēmi-
SESQUIPEDALIAN ped-¹
SESSILE sed-¹
SESSION sed-¹
SESTERCE sēmi-, trei-
SESTET s(w)eks
SESTINA s(w)eks
SET¹ sed-¹
SETTLE sed-¹
SEVEN septm̥
SEVER perə-¹
SEVERAL perə-¹
SEVERE wēro-
SEW syū-
SEWER¹ akʷā-
SEWER² sed-¹
SEX- s(w)eks
SEXAGENARY dekm̥
SEXCENTENARY dekm̥
SEXENNIAL at-
SEXT s(w)eks
SEXTAN s(w)eks
SEXTANT s(w)eks
SEXTILE s(w)eks
SEXTODECIMO dekm̥, s(w)eks
SEXTUPLE pel-³
SHABBY skep-
SHADE skot-
SHADOW skot-
SHAFT¹ skep-
SHAH tkē-
SHAKO dek-²
SHAKTI kak-¹
SHALE skel-¹
SHALL skel-²
SHAMBLES skabh-
SHANK skeng-
SHAPE skep-
SHARD sker-¹
SHARE¹ sker-¹
SHARE² sker-¹
SHARP sker-¹
SHATTER sked-
SHAVE skep-
SHAWM koləm-
SHE so-
SHEAF skeup-
SHEAR sker-¹
SHEARS sker-¹
SHEATH skei-
SHEAVE² skei-
SHED¹ skei-
SHEEN keu-¹
SHEET¹ skeud-
SHEET² skeud-
SHELDRAKE sker-¹
SHELF skel-¹
SHELL skel-¹
SHIELD skel-¹
SHIMMER skeəi-
SHIN¹ skei-
SHINE skeəi-
SHINGLE sked-
SHINGLES kenk-¹
SHIP skipam
-SHIP skep-
SHIRT sker-¹
SHIT skei-
SHIVA kei-¹
SHIVER² sker-¹
SHOAL² skel-¹
SHOOT skeud-
SHORT sker-¹
SHOT¹ skeud-
SHOVE skeubh-
SHOVEL skeubh-
SHOW keu-¹
SHOWER¹ kēwero-

SHRED skreu-
SHREW skreu-
SHREWD skreu-
SHRIKE ker-²
SHRIMP skerbh-
SHRINK skers-³
SHRIVE skrībh-
SHROUD skreu-
SHRUB¹ sker-¹
SHTETL stā-
SHTICK (s)teu-
SHUDDER skut-
SHUFFLE skeubh-
SHUT skeud-
SHUTTLE skeud-
SIALADENITIS engʷ-
SIB s(w)e-
SIBILATE swei-¹
SIC¹ so-
SICCATIVE seikʷ-
SICKLE sek-
SIDE sē-²
SIDEREAL sweid-¹
SIEGE sed-¹
SIEGFRIED prī-, segh-
SIEROZEM dhghem-
SIEVE seib-
SIFT seib-
SIGHT sekʷ-²
SIGN sekʷ-¹
SIGNORY sen-¹
SIKH kak-¹
SILENT si-lo-
SILL swel-³
SILLY sēl-²
SILT sal-¹
SILURID ors-
SILVICOLOUS kʷel-¹
SIMILAR sem-¹
SIMPLE sem-¹
SIMPLEX sem-¹
SIMPLICITY sem-¹
SIMULTANEOUS sem-¹
SIN¹ es-
SINCE sē-²
SINCERE ker-³
SINCIPUT kaput
SINECURE cūra, sen-²
SINEW sē-⁴
SING sengʷh-
SINGE senk-
SINGLE sem-¹
SINGSPIEL sengʷh-
SINISTRORSE wer-³
SINK sengʷ-
SINN FEIN s(w)e-
SINTER sendhro-
SIP seuə-²
SIR sen-¹
SIRDAR dher-², ker-¹
SIRE sen-¹
SIREN twer-²
SIRLOIN lendh-¹, uper
SIRVENTE servus
SISTER swesor-
SISTRUM twei-
SIT sed-¹
SITAR ten-, trei-
SITH sē-²
SITUATE tkei-
SITUS tkei-
SITZ BATH sed-¹
SITZKRIEG gʷerə-², sed-¹
SITZMARK sed-¹
SIX s(w)eks
SKALD sekʷ-³
SKATOLE sker-⁴
SKEAN skei-
SKEET skeud-
SKELETON skelə-
SKEPTIC spek-
SKI skei-
SKIAGRAM skeəi-
SKIASCOPE skeəi-
SKIFF skipam
SKIJORING geuə-
SKILL skel-¹
SKIN skei-
SKIPPER¹ skipam
SKIRMISH sker-¹
SKIRT sker-¹
SKIVE skei-
SKOAL skel-¹
SKY (s)keu-
SLAB² skel-¹
SLACK¹ slēg-
SLAG slak-
SLAM¹ leb-¹
SLAP leb-¹

SLAUGHTER slak-
SLAVER¹ leb-¹
SLAY slak-
SLED sleidh-
SLEDGE sleidh-
SLEDGEHAMMER slak-
SLEEP slēb-
SLEET sleu-
SLEEVE sleubh-
SLEIGH sleidh-
SLEIGHT slak-
SLEW¹ sloug-
SLICK lei-
SLIDE sleidh-
SLIGHT lei-
SLIM leb-¹
SLIME lei-
SLING¹ slengwh-
SLINGSHOT slengwh-
SLINK slengwh-
SLIP¹ lei-
SLIP³ sleubh-
SLIPPERY lei-
SLIVOVITZ slī-
SLOB leb-¹
SLOE slī-
SLOGAN gar-, slougʱ
SLOOP sleubh-
SLOP¹ sleubh-
SLOP² sleubh-
SLUG² sleu-
SLUGGARD sleu-
SLUMBER sleu-
SLUMGULLION leb-¹
SLUMP leb-¹
SLURP srebh-
SLUSH sleu-
SLY slak-
SMACK¹ smeg-
SMACK² smeg-
SMALL mēlo-
SMALT mel-¹
SMART smerd-
SMEAR (s)mer-³
SMEARCASE (s)mer-³
SMELT¹ mel-¹
SMELT² mel-¹
SMILE smei-
SMIRK smei-
SMITE smē-
SMITH smī-
SMITHY smī-
SMOCK meug-²
SMOKE smeug-
SMORGASBORD bherdh-
SMUG meug-²
SMUGGLE meug-²
SNAIL sneg-
SNAKE sneg-
SNAP snu-
SNARE¹ (s)ner-
SNARE² (s)ner-
SNARL¹ sner-
SNATCH snu-
SNEER sner-
SNEEZE pneu-
SNICKERSNEE sneit-, steig-
SNIFF snu-
SNIP snu-
SNIVEL snu-
SNOOP snu-
SNORE sner-
SNORKEL sner-
SNORT sner-
SNOT snu-
SNOUT snu-
SNOW sneigwh-
SNUB snu-
SNUFF¹ snu-
SNUFFLE snu-
SNUG¹ kes-¹
SO swo-
SOAK seuə-²
SOAP seib-
SOAVE swād-
SOBER s(w)e-
SOCIABLE sekʷ-¹
SOCIAL sekʷ-¹
SOCIETY sekʷ-¹
SOCIO- sekʷ-¹
SOCKET sū-
SODALITY s(w)e-
SODDEN seut-
SOIL¹ sed-¹
SOIL² sū-
SOIREE sē-²
SOJOURN deiw-
SOKE sāg-
SOL³ sāwel-

SOL sāwel-
SOLACE sel-²
SOLANINE sāwel-
SOLAR sāwel-
SOLARIUM sāwel-
SOLE¹ sel-¹
SOLE² s(w)e-
SOLEMN sol-
SOLICITOUS kei-³, sol-
SOLID sol-
SOLILOQUY s(w)e-, tolkʷ-
SOLIPSISM s(w)e-
SOLITARY s(w)e-
SOLITUDE s(w)e-
SOLO s(w)e-
SOLSTICE sāwel-
SOLUBLE leu-¹
SOLUM sel-¹
SOLUTE leu-¹
SOLVE leu-¹
SOMA teuə-
SOMATO- teuə-
SOME sem-¹
-SOME¹ sem-¹
-SOME² teuə-
SOMERSAULT sel-⁴, uper
SOMNI swep-¹
SOMNOLENT swep-¹
SON seuə-¹
SONANT swen-
SONATA swen-
SONE swen-
SONG sengʷʰ-
SONIC swen-
SONNET swen-
SONOROUS swen-
SOOT sed-¹
SOOTH es-
SOOTHE es-
SOP seuə-²
SOPOR swep-¹
SOPORIFIC swep-¹
SOPRANINO uper
SOPRANO uper
SORCERER ser-³
SORDID swordo-
SORDINO swer-²
SORE sai-
SORITES teuə-
SORORAL swesor-
SORORITY swesor-
SORREL¹ sūro-
SORREL² saus-
SORROW swergh-
SORRY sai-
SORT ser-³
SORTILEGE leg-¹, ser-³
SORUS teuə-
SOTERIOLOGY teuə-
SOUBRETTE uper
SOUFFLE bhlē-²
SOUGH (s)wāgh-
SOUND¹ swen-
SOUND² swento-
SOUND³ swem-
SOUND⁴ swem-
SOUP seuə-²
SOUR sūro-
SOURDINE swer-²
SOUSE sal-¹
SOUTANE upo
SOUTH sāwel-
SOUTHERN sāwel-
SOUVENIR gʷā-
SOVEREIGN uper
SOVIET sem-¹
SOW¹ sē-¹
SOW² sū-
SPADE¹ spē-²
SPADE² spē-²
SPAN¹ (s)pen-
SPAN² (s)pen-
SPANGLE (s)pen-
SPANNER (s)pen-
SPAN-NEW newo-, spē-²
SPAR¹ sper-¹
SPARERIBS rebh-², sper-¹
SPARGE (s)preg-
SPARLING spei-
SPARROW sper-³
SPARSE (s)preg-
SPATHE spē-²
SPATHIC spē-²
SPATULA spē-²
SPAY spē-²
SPEAK spreg-
SPEAR sper-¹
SPECIES spek-
SPECIMEN spek-

SPECIOUS spek-
SPECTACLE spek-
SPECTRUM spek-
SPECULATE spek-
SPECULUM spek-
SPEECH spreg-
SPEED spē-¹
SPELL¹ spel-³
SPELL² spel-³
SPELT¹ spel-¹
SPERM sper-⁴
SPEW spyeu-
SPHENE spē-²
SPHENO- spē-²
SPICA spei-
SPICA spei-
SPICULUM spei-
SPIDER (s)pen-
SPIKE¹ spei-
SPIKE² spei-
SPILE spei-
SPILL¹ spel-¹
SPILL² spei-
SPIN (s)pen-
SPINDLE (s)pen-
SPINE spei-
SPINEL spei-
SPINIFEX dhē-¹
SPINNEY spei-
SPIRACLE spīrāre
SPIRE¹ spei-
SPIRE² sper-²
SPIRIT spīrāre
SPIT¹ spyeu-
SPIT² spei-
SPITTLE spyeu-
SPITZ spei-
SPLANCHNIC spelgh-
SPLEEN spelgh-
SPLENDID spel-²
SPLICE splei-
SPLINT splei-
SPLINTER splei-
SPLIT splei-
SPOIL spel-¹
SPOKE¹ spei-
SPONDEE spend-
SPONSOR spend-
SPONTANEOUS (s)pen-
SPONTOON peuk-
SPOON spē-²
SPOOR spere-
SPORADIC sper-⁴
SPORE sper-⁴
SPORO- sper-⁴
SPORRAN bursa
SPORT per-²
SPOUSE spend-
SPOUT spyeu-
SPRAG (s)preg-
SPRAWL sper-⁴
SPREAD sper-⁴
SPREE ghend-
SPRING spergh-
SPRINGE spergh-
SPRINKLE (s)preg-
SPRIT sper-⁴
SPROUT sper-⁴
SPRY (s)preg-
SPUME (s)poi-mo-
SPUR spere-
SPURGE peuə-
SPURN spere-
SPURRY (s)preg-
SPURT sper-⁴
SPUTNIK ksun, pent-
SPUTTER spyeu-
SPUTUM spyeu-
SPY spek-
SQUAD kʷetwer-
SQUALENE (s)kʷal-o-
SQUARE kʷetwer-
SQUASH² kʷēt-
SQUAT ag-
SQUIRE skei-
SQUIRREL ors-, skeəi-
STABLE¹ stā-
STABLE² stā-
STACK steg-
STACTE stag-
STADDLE stā-
STADHOLDER stā-
STAFF¹ stebh-
STAG stegh-
STAGE stā-
STAGGER steg-
STAGNANT stag-
STAIN teng-

STAIR steigh-
STAKE¹ steg-
STALAG legh-, stebh-
STALK¹ stel-
STALK² ster-⁴
STALL stel-
STALLION stel-
STALWART wer-³
STAMEN stā-
STAMMEL stā-
STAMMER stam-
STAMP stebh-
STAMPEDE stebh-
STANCE stā-
STANCH stā-
STANCHION stā-
STAND stā-
STANDARD kar-¹, stā-
STANZA stā-
STAPHYLO- stebh-
STAPHYLORRHAPHY wer-³
STAPLE¹ stebh-
STAPLE² stebh-
STAR ster-³
STARBOARD bherdh-, stā-
STARCH ster-¹
STARE ster-¹
STARETS stā-
STARK ster-¹
STARLING¹ storo-
STARLING² stā-
START ster-¹
STARTLE ster-¹
STARVE ster-¹
STASIS stā-
-STAT stā-
STATE stā-
STATIC stā-
STATICE stā-
STATION stā-
STATISTICS stā-
STATO- stā-
STATOR stā-
STATUE stā-
STATURE stā-
STATUS stā-
STATUTE stā-
STAUROLITE stā-
STAVESACRE agro-
STAY¹ stā-
STAY² stāk-
STAY³ stāk-
STEAD stā-
STEADFAST past-
STEAK stā-
STEAL ster-⁴
STEALTH ster-⁴
STEAROPTENE pet-
STEED stā-
STEEL stā-
STEENBOK bhugo-, stei-
STEEP¹ (s)teu-
STEEPLE (s)teu-
STEER¹ stā-
STEER² stā-
STEEVE¹ steip-
STEGODON (s)teg-
STEIN stei-
STELE stel-
STELLAR ster-³
STELLATE ster-³
STEM¹ stā-
STEM² stam-
STEMMA stebh-
STENCIL skeəi-
STENO- sten-
STENOSIS sten-
STEP stebh-
STEP- (s)teu-
STEPHANOTIS stebh-
STERCORACEOUS sker-⁴
STERE ster-¹
STEREO- ster-¹
STEREOBATE gʷā-
STERIGMA ster-¹
STERILE ster-⁵
STERN¹ ster-¹
STERN² stā-
STERNOCOSTAL kost-
STERNUM ster-²
STERNUTATION pster-
STEROPE ster-³
STERTOR pster-
STET stā-
STEVEDORE steip-
STEWARD wer-⁴
STICH steigh-
STICHOMETRY steigh-
STICHOMYTHIA steigh-

STICK steigh-
STICKLE steigh-
STICKLEBACK steig-
STIFF steip-
STIGMA steig-
STILE¹ steigh-
STILL¹ stel-
STILT stel-
STING stegh-
STINT¹ (s)teu-
STIPE steip-
STIPES steip-
STIPPLE steip-
STIR¹ twer-¹
STIRK stā-
STIRRUP steigh-
STITCH steig-
STITHY stā-
STIVER (s)teu-
STOA stā-
STOCHASTIC stegh-
STOCK (s)teu-
STOCKADE steg-
STOIC stā-
STOICHIOMETRY steigh-
STOKER (s)teu-
STOLE¹ stel-
STOLID stel-
STOLLEN stel-
STOLON stel-
STOMA stə-men-
STOMACH stə-men-
STOMATO- stə-men-
STOMATOUS stə-men-
STOMODEUM sed-²
-STOMY stə-men-
STONE stā-
STOOL stā-
STOOP¹ (s)teu-
STOOP² stebh-
STOP steu(ə)-
STOPE stebh-
STORE stā-
STORK ster-¹
STORM twer-¹
STORY¹ weid-
STOSS (s)teu-
STOUND stā-
STOUP staup-
STOUT stel-
STOVE¹ staup-
STOW stā-
STRABISMUS streb(h)-
STRABOTOMY streb(h)-
STRAIN¹ streig-
STRAIN² ster-²
STRAIT streig-
STRANGE eghs
STRANGLE strenk-
STRANGLES strenk-
STRANGULATE strenk-
STRANGURY strenk-
STRATAGEM ag-, ster-²
STRATH ster-²
STRATOCRACY ster-²
STRATUS ster-²
STRAW ster-²
STREAK streig-
STREAM sreu-
STREET ster-²
STRENGTH strenk-
STREPTO- streb(h)-
STREPTOMYCES meug-²
STREPTOMYCIN meug-²
STREPTOTHRICIN thrix
STREUSEL ster-²
STREW ster-²
STRIA streig-
STRICKLE streig-
STRICT streig-
STRIDENT strei-
STRIGIL streig-
STRIGOSE streig-
STRIKE streig-
STRING strenk-
STRINGENDO streig-
STRINGENT streig-
STROBILE streb(h)-
STROBOSCOPE streb(h)-
STROKE streig-
STROMA ster-²
STROMATOLITE ster-²
STRONG strenk-
STROP streb(h)-
STROPHANTHIN andh-
STROPHE streb(h)-
STROPHOID streb(h)-
STROPHULUS streb(h)-
STRUCTURE ster-²

STRUDEL ser-²	SUMMON men-¹	SWING sweng(w)-	TAR¹ deru-
STRUT ster-¹	SUMP swombho-	SWINGE sweng(w)-	TARGE dergh-
STRUTHIOUS trozdo-	SUMPTUARY em-	SWINGLETREE sweng(w)-	TARGET dergh-
STUB (s)teu-	SUMPTUOUS em-	SWIRL swer-	TARSUS ters-
STUCCO (s)teu-	SUN sāwel-	SWITCH swei-²	TART¹ der-²
STUD¹ sta-	SUNDAY sāwel-	SWIVEL swei-²	TASTE tag-
STUD² stā-	SUNDER sen-²	SWOOP swei-²	TATTOO¹ tap-
STUDENT (s)teu-	SUNDRY sen-²	SWORD swer-⁴	TAURINE¹ tauro-
STUDY (s)teu-	SUP¹ seue-¹	SYCAMORE moro-	TAURINE² tauro-
STULTIFY stel-	SUP² seue-²	SYCOPHANT bhā-¹	TAUROCHOLIC ACID tauro-
STUM stam-	SUPER- uper	SYLLABLE (s)lagw-	TAURUS tauro-
STUMBLE stam-	SUPERABLE uper	SYLLEPSIS (s)lagw-	TAUTO- to-
STUMP stebh-	SUPERANNUATED at-	SYLLOGISM leg-¹	TAW¹ taw-
STUN (s)tenə-	SUPERB uper	SYMBIOSIS gwei-	TAX tag-
STUPA steu(ə)-	SUPERCILIOUS kel-²	SYMBOL gwelə-	TAXIS tāg-
STUPE steu(ə)-	SUPERCILIUM kel-²	SYMPATHY kwent(h)-	TAXO- tāg-
STUPEFY steu-	SUPEREROGATE reg-¹	SYMPATRIC pəter-	TEACH deik-
STUPENDOUS (s)teu-	SUPERFETATE dhē(i)-	SYMPHONY bhā-²	TEAM deuk-
STUPID (s)teu-	SUPERFLUOUS bhleu-	SYMPHYSIS bheuə-	TEAPOY ped-¹
STURDY trozdo-	SUPERIOR uper	SYMPODIUM ped-¹	TEAR¹ der-²
STUTTER (s)teu-	SUPERJACENT yē-	SYMPOSIUM pō(i)-	TEAR² dakru-
STY² steigh-	SUPERLATIVE tele-	SYMPTOM pet-	TECHNICAL teks-
STYLITE stā-	SUPERNAL uper	SYN- ksun	TECHNOLOGY teks-
STYLOBATE gwā-, stā-	SUPERNATANT snā-	SYNAGOGUE ag-	TECTONIC teks-
STYPTIC steu(ə)-	SUPERNUMERARY nem-	SYNALEPHA leip-	TECTRIX (s)teg-
STYX (s)teu-	SUPERSCRIBE skrībh-	SYNAPTINEMAL COMPLEX (s)nē-	TECTUM (s)teg-
SUASION swād-	SUPERSEDE sed-¹	SYNARTHROSIS ar-	TEEM¹ deuk-
SUAVE swād-	SUPERSTITION stā-	SYNCLINAL klei-	TEEN² deu-³
SUB- upo	SUPERVENE gwā-	SYNCOPE skep-	TEETER der-¹
SUBALTERN al-¹	SUPERVISE weid-	SYNDESMOSIS dē-	TEETOTUM teutā-
SUBAUDITION au-⁵	SUPINE¹ upo	SYNDETIC dē-	TEGMEN (s)teg-
SUBDUCTION deuk-	SUPINE² upo	SYNDIC deik-	TEGMENTUM (s)teg-
SUBDUE deuk-	SUPPLANT plat-	SYNECDOCHE dek-¹, eghs	TEGULAR (s)teg-
SUBITO ei-¹	SUPPLE plek-, upo	SYNERGID werg-	TEGUMENT (s)teg-
SUBJACENT yē-	SUPPLICATE plek-	SYNERGISM werg-	TEIGLACH dheigh-
SUBJECT yē-	SUPPLY pelə-¹	SYNESIS yē-	TELAMON tele-
SUBJOIN yeug-	SUPPORT per-²	SYNIZESIS sed-¹	TELANGIECTASIA ten-
SUBJUGATE yeug-	SUPPOSE apo-	SYNKARYON kar-¹	TELE- kʷel-²
SUBLUNARY leuk-	SUPPRESS per-⁵	SYNOD sed-²	TELEKINESIS kei-³
SUBMERGE mezg-	SUPPURATE pū-²	SYNONYMOUS nō-men-	TELEOLOGY kʷel-¹
SUBMIT (s)meit(ə)-	SUPRA- uper	SYNOPSIS okʷ-	TELEOST kʷel-¹, ost-
SUBORDINATE ar-	SUPRALAPSARIAN leb-¹	SYNOSTOSIS ost-	TELESCOPE spek-
SUBORN ar-	SUPREME uper	SYNTAX tāg-	TELIC kʷel-¹
SUBPOENA kʷei-	SUPREMO uper	SYRINGOMYELIA mūs-	TELIUM kʷel-¹
SUBREPTION rēp-¹	SUR- uper	SYSSARCOSIS twerk-	TELL del-²
SUBROGATE reg-¹	SURCULOSE swer-³	SYSTALTIC stel-	TELLURIAN tel-
SUBSCRIBE skrībh-	SURD swer-²	SYSTEM stā-	TELLURIC tel-
SUBSEQUENT sekʷ-¹	SURE cūra, s(w)e-	SYZYGY yeug-	TELLURION tel-
SUBSIDE sed-¹	SURFACE dhē-¹		TELLURIUM tel-
SUBSIDY sed-¹	SURFEIT dhē-¹		TELLURO- tel-
SUBSIST stā-	SURGE reg-¹		TELO- kʷel-¹
SUBSTANCE stā-	SURGEON ghesor-		TELPHER bher-¹
SUBSTITUTE stā-	SURGERY ghesor-, werg-	**T**	TEMERARIOUS temə-
SUBSTRATUM ster-²	SURLY sen-¹		TEMERITY temə-
SUBSTRUCTION ster-²	SURMISE (s)meit(ə)-	TAAL del-²	TEMPLE¹ tem-
SUBSUME em-	SURMULLET mel-², saus-	TABES tā-	TEMPLE² temp-
SUBTEND ten-	SURPLICE pel-⁴	TACET tak-¹	TEMPLE³ tem-
SUBTERFUGE bheug-¹, upo	SURPLUS pelə-¹	TACHE dek-²	TEN dekm
SUBTERRANEAN ters-	SURPRISE ghend-	TACHISM deik-	TENABLE ten-
SUBTLE teks-	SURRENDER dō-	TACHYLYTE leu-¹	TENACIOUS ten-
SUBTRACT tragh-	SURREPTITIOUS rep-	TACHYPNEA pneu-	TENACULUM ten-
SUBULATE syū-	SURROUND wed-¹	TACIT tak-¹	TENANT ten-
SUBVENTION gwā-	SURVEILLANT weg-²	TACK¹ dek-²	TEND¹ ten-
SUBVERT wer-³	SURVEY weid-	TACT tag-	TENDER¹ ten-
SUCCEED ked-	SURVIVE gʷei-	TACTICS tāg-	TENDER² ten-
SUCCINCT kenk-¹	SUSCEPTIBLE kap-	TACTORECEPTOR tag-	TENDON ten-
SUCCOR kers-²	SUSPECT spek-	TAEL tele-	TENDRIL ten-
SUCCUBUS keu-²	SUSPEND (s)pen-	TAENIA tele-	TENEBRAE temə-
SUCCULENT seuə-²	SUSPIRE spīrāre	TAFFETA temp-	TENEBRIONID temə-
SUCCUMB keu-²	SUSTAIN ten-	TAG¹ dek-²	TENEMENT ten-
SUCCUSSION kwēt-	SUSURRATION swer-²	TAHSILDAR dher-²	TENESMUS ten-
SUCH swo-	SUTLER seut-	TAIL¹ dek-²	TENET ten-
SUCK seuə-²	SUTRA syū-	TAINT teng-	TENO- ten-
SUCTION seuə-²	SUTTEE es-	TAJ (s)teg-	TENON ten-
SUCTORIAL seuə-²	SUTURE syū-	TAKE tak-²	TENOR ten-
SUDATORIUM sweid-²	SVELTE wel-⁴	TALE del-²	TENORRHAPHY wer-³
SUDDEN ei-¹	SWAB swep-²	TALENT tele-	TENSE¹ ten-
SUDORIFEROUS sweid-²	SWAG sweng(w)-	TALES to-	TENT¹ ten-
SUDORIFIC sweid-²	SWAIN s(w)e-	TALION tele-	TENTH dekm
SUDS seut-	SWALE swel-²	TALISMAN kʷel-¹	TENUOUS ten-
SUE sekʷ-¹	SWALLOW¹ swel-¹	TALK del-²	TENURE ten-
SUFFER bher-¹	SWAMI s(w)e-	TALLOW del-⁴	TENUTO ten-
SUFFICE dhē-¹	SWAMP swombho-	TAME demə-²	TEPID tep-
SUFFICIENT dhē-¹	SWAN swen-	TAMPON temp-	TERATOCARCINOMA kwer-¹
SUFFIX dhīgw-	SWANK sweng(w)-	TANDEM to-	TERATOGEN kwer-¹
SUFFRAGAN bhreg-	SWAP swel-²	TANG¹ denk-	TERATOID kwer-¹
SUFFRAGE bhreg-	SWARF swerbh-	TANGENT tag-	TERATOMA kwer-¹
SUFFUSE gheu-	SWARM swer-²	TANGIBLE tag-	TERCEL trei-
SUGGEST gerere	SWART swordo-	TANGLE² tenk-²	TERCET trei-
SUICIDE s(w)e-	SWASTIKA es-, su-	TANGORECEPTOR tag-	TEREDO terə-¹
SUINT sweid-²	SWEAR swer-¹	TANSY dhwenə-	TERETE terə-¹
SUITOR sekʷ-¹	SWEAT sweid-²	TANTALIZE tele-	TERGIVERSATE wer-³
SULCATE selk-	SWEET swād-	TANTALUS tele-	TERM ter-
SULCUS selk-	SWELTER swel-²	TANTAMOUNT to-	TERMINATE ter-
SULLEN s(w)e-	SWERVE swerbh-	TANTRA ten-	TERMINUS ter-
SULTRY swel-²	SWIFT swei-²	TAP¹ tap-	TERN² trei-
SUM uper	SWILL swel-¹	TAP² tap-	TERPOLYMER trei-
SUMMER¹ sem-²	SWIM swem-	TAPE tap-	TERPSICHORE gher-¹, terp-
SUMMIT uper	SWINE sū-	TAPESTRY temp-	

TERRACE ters-	THRASH tera-[1]	TORQUE[1] terkw-	TRIAD trei-
TERRAIN ters-	THREAD tera-[1]	TORQUE[2] terkw-	TRIBOELECTRICITY tera-[1]
TERRAN ters-	THREAT treud-	TORRENT ters-	TRIBOLOGY tera-[1]
TERRAQUEOUS ters-	THREE trei-	TORRID ters-	TRIBRACH mregh-u-
TERRENE ters-	THREMMATOLOGY threph-	TORSADE terkw-	TRIBULATION tera-[1]
TERREPLEIN pele-[1], ters-	THRENODY dher-[3]	TORT terkw-	TRICEPS kaput
TERRESTRIAL ters-	THRESH tera-[1]	TORTICOLLIS kwel-[1], terkw-	TRICERATOPS ker-[1]
TERRE-VERTE ters-, virēre	THRESHOLD tera-[1]	TORTUOUS terkw-	TRICHINA thrix
TERRIBLE tres-	THRICE trei-	TORY ret-	TRICHO- thrix
TERRICOLOUS ters-	THRILL tera-[2]	TOTAL teutā-	TRICHOME thrix
TERRIER ters-	THRONE dher-[2]	TOUGH denk-	TRICHOTOMY trei-
TERRIFIC tres-	THROSTLE trozdo-	TOUPEE tap-	-TRICHOUS thrix
TERRIGENOUS ters-	THROUGH tera-[2]	TOW[1] deuk-	TRICHURIASIS ors-
TERRITORY ters-	THROW tera-[1]	TOW[2] taw-	TRICLINIUM klei-, trei-
TERROR ters-	THRUM[2] ter-	TOWN dhūno-	TRICORN ker-[1]
TERTIAN trei-	THRUSH[1] trozdo-	TOXIC tekw-	TRICROTIC kret-[2], trei-
TERTIARY trei-	THRUST treud-	TOXOPLASMA pele-[2]	TRIDACTYL trei-
TESSERA kwetwer-	THUG (s)teg-	TRABEATED treb-	TRIDENT dent-
TESTAMENT trei-	THUJA dheu-[1]	TRABECULA treb-	TRIENNIUM at-
TESTIFY trei-	THUMB teue-	TRACHEA dher-[1]	TRIERARCH era-[1], trei-
TESTIMONY trei-	THUNDER (s)tena-	TRACHEOPHYTE bheua-	TRIG[1] deru
TETCHY deik-	THURIBLE dheu-[1]	TRACHOMA dher-[1]	TRIGEMINUS yem-
TETRA- kwetwer-	THURIFER dheu-[1]	TRACHYTE dher-[1]	TRIGLYPH trei-
TETRACHORD ghere-	THURSDAY (s)tena-	TRACT[1] tragh-	TRIM deru
TETRAD kwetwer-	THUS to-	TRACTABLE tragh-	TRIMER (s)mer-[2]
TETRADYMITE dwo-	THWART terkw-	TRACTION tragh-	TRIMESTER mē-[2]
TETRAGRAMMATON gerbh-	THY tu-	TRADE der-[1]	TRIMURTI trei-
TETRAHEDRON sed-[1]	THYME dheu-[1]	TRADITION dō-	TRINE trei-
TETTER der-[2]	-THYMIA dheu-[1]	TRADUCE deuk-	TRINITY trei-
TEUTON teutā-	THYROID dhwer-	TRAGACANTH ak-	TRIO trei-
TEXT teks-	TICK[2] deigh-	TRAGEDY wed-[2]	TRIOECIOUS weik-[1]
THALIA dhal-	TICK[3] dhē-[1]	TRAIL tragh-	TRIP der-[1]
THALLUS dhal-	TICKET steig-	TRAIN tragh-	TRIPEDAL ped-[1]
THAN to-	TIDE[1] dā-	TRAIN OIL dakru-	TRIPLE pel-[3], trei-
THANATOS dhwena-	TIDE[2] dā-	TRAIT tragh-	TRIPLEX trei-
THANE tek-	TIDINGS dā-	TRAITOR dō-	TRIPLOBLASTIC pel-[3]
THANK tong-	TIE deuk-	TRAJECT yē-	TRIREME era-[1]
THAT to-	TIERCE trei-	TRAMMEL macula, trei-	TRISKELION skel-[3]
THATCH (s)teg-	TIFFANY bhā-[1]	TRAMP der-[1]	TRISMUS strei-
THAUMATURGE werg-	TIGER steig-	TRAMPOLINE der-[1]	TRISOCTAHEDRON trei-
THAW tā-	TIGHT tenk-[2]	TRANCE ei-[1]	TRITANOPIA trei-
THE[1] to-	TILE (s)teg-	TRANQUIL kweie-[2]	TRITE ter-
THE[2] to-	TILLER[2] teks-	TRANS- tera-[2]	TRITIUM trei-
THEANTHROPIC ner-[2]	TILLER[3] del-[3]	TRANSACT ag-	TRITONE trei-
THECA dhē-[1]	TILT[2] del-[3]	TRANSCEND skand-	TRITURATE tera-[1]
THEE tu-	TIMBER deme-	TRANSCRIBE skrībh-	TRIUMVIR trei-, wī-ro-
THEELIN dhē(i)-	TIME dā-	TRANSDUCER deuk-	TRIUNE oi-no-
THEIR to-	TIMOCRACY kweie-[1]	TRANSECT sek-	TRIVET ped-[1]
THEM to-	TINCT teng-	TRANSFER bher-[1]	TRIVIAL wegh-
THEMATIC dhē-[1]	TINGE teng-	TRANSFIGURE dheigh-	TRIVIUM wegh-
THEME dhē-[1]	TINSEL skeei-	TRANSFIX dhīgw-	TROCAR kwetwer-, trei-
THEN to-	TINT teng-	TRANSFUSE gheu-	TROCHAL dhregh-
THENAR dhen-[2]	TIP[1] tap-	TRANSGRESS ghredh-	TROCHANTER dhregh-
THENCE to-	TIRE[1] deu-[1]	TRANSHUMANCE dhghem-	TROCHE dhregh-
THEO- dhēs-	TISANE peis-[1]	TRANSIENT ei-[1], tera-[2]	TROCHEE dhregh-
THEOBROMINE gwere-[4]	TISSUE teks-	TRANSIT ei-[1]	TROCHLEA dhregh-
THEODICY deik-	TITHE dekm	TRANSITIVE ei-[1]	TROCHOPHORE dhregh-
THEOPHANY bhā-[1]	TITILLATE tit-	TRANSLATE tela-	TROGON tera-[1]
THERAVADA stā-, wed-[2]	TITLE tel-	TRANSLITERATE deph-	TROIKA trei-
THERE to-	TIU deiw-	TRANSLUCENT leuk-	TROPE trep-[2]
-THERM gwher-	TMESIS tem-	TRANSMIT (s)meit(e)-	TROPHALLAXIS al-[1]
THERMO- gwher-	TO de-	TRANSMUTE mei-[1]	TROPHIC- threph-
THERMODURIC deue-	TOAST[1] ters-	TRANSOM tera-[2]	TROPHO- threph-
-THERMY gwher-	TOCOLOGY tek-	TRANSPIRE spīrāre	-TROPHY threph-, trep-[2]
THEROPOD ghwer-	TOCOPHEROL bher-[1]	TRANSPONTINE pent-	TROPIC trep-[2]
THESE to-	TODAY agh-[2]	TRANSPORT per-[2]	TROPO- trep-[2]
THESIS dhē-[1]	TOE deik-	TRANSUDE sweid-[2]	-TROPOUS trep-[2]
THETIC dhē-[1]	TOFT deme-[1]	TRANSVERSE wer-[3]	TROT der-[1]
THEW teu-	TOGA (s)teg-	TRAP[1] der-[1]	TROTH deru
THEY to-	TOGETHER ghedh-	TRAP[2] der-[2]	TROUBLE twer-[1]
THICK tegu-	TOIL[1] (s)teu-	TRAP[3] deru	TROUGH deru
THIGH teue-	TOIL[2] teks-	TRAPEZIUM kwetwer-, ped-[1]	TROVER trep-[2]
THIGMOTAXIS dheigh-	TOKEN deik-	TRAPUNTO peuk-	TROW deru
THIMBLE teue-	TOLA tela-	TRAUMA tera-[1]	TRUANT tera-[1]
THIN ten-	TOLERATE tela-	TRAVAIL pag-	TRUCE deru
THINE tu-	TOLL[1] tela-	TRAVE treb-	TRUCK[1] dhregh-
THING tenk-[1]	TOMB teue-	TRAVEL pag-	TRUCKLE dhregh-
THINK tong-	TOME tem-	TRAVESTY wes-[4]	TRUCULENT tera-[2]
THIO- dheu-[1]	-TOMY tem-	TRAY deru	TRUE deru
THION- dheu-[1]	TONE ten-	TREACLE ghwer-	TRUFFLE teue-
THIRD trei-	TONGS denk-	TREAD der-[1]	TRUNCATE tera-[2]
THIRST ters-	TONGUE dnghū	TREADLE der-[1]	TRUNK tera-[2]
THIRTEEN trei-	TONOPLAST ten-	TREASON dō-	TRUST deru
THIRTY trei-	TONSURE tem-	TREAT tragh-	TRUTH deru
THIS to-	TOO de-	TREBUCHET beu-[1]	TRYMA tera-[1]
THITHER to-	TOOL taw-	TRECENTO dekm, trei-	TRYPANOSOME tera-[1]
THIXOTROPY dheigh-	TOOTH dent-	TREE deru	TRYPSIN tera-[1]
THOLE tela-	TOP[1] tap-	TREFOIL bhel-[3]	TRYST deru
THOLE PIN teue-	TOP[2] tap-	TREMATODE tera-[1]	TUBER deru
THONG twengh-	TOPOGRAPHY gerbh-	TREMENDOUS trem-	TUBIFEX dhē-[1]
THOR (s)tena-	TORCH terkw-	TREMOR trem-	TUCK[3] (s)teu-
THORN (s)ter-n-	TOREADOR tauro-	TREMULOUS trem-	TUESDAY deiw-
THOROUGH tera-[2]	TORERO tauro-	TRENCH tera-[1]	TUFT tap-
THORP treb-	TOREUTICS tera-[1]	TREPAN[1] tera-[1]	TUG deuk-
THOSE to-	TORMENT terkw-	TREPHINE trei-	TUILLE (s)teg-
THOU[1] tu-	TORNADO (s)tena-	TREPID trep-[1]	TUITION teu-
THOUGH to-	TORPEDO ster-[1]	TREPONEME (s)nē-, trep-[2]	TUMEFACIENT dhē-[1], teue-
THOUGHT tong-	TORPID ster-[1]	TREY trei-	TUMEFY teue-
THOUSAND teue-	TORPOR ster-[1]	TRI- trei-	TUMESCENT teue-

VOTIVE wegʷh-
VOUCH wekʷ-
VOUSSOIR wel-3
VOW wegʷh-
VOWEL wekʷ-
VOYAGE wegh-
VOYEUR weid-
VROUW per1
VULNERABLE wele-2
VULPINE wl̥p-ē-
VULTURE gʷl̥tur-
VULVA wel-3

W

WADE wadh-2
WAFER webh-
WAFFLE1 webh-
WAFT weg-2
WAG1 wegh-
WAGE wadh-1
WAGER wadh-1
WAGON wegh-
WAGON-LIT legh-
WAIF1 weip-
WAIL wai
WAIN wegh-
WAIT weg-2
WAIVE weip-
WAIVER weip-
WAKE1 weg-2
WAKE2 wegʷ-
WAKEN weg-2
WALE wel-3
WALK wel-3
WALL walso-
WALLEYED okʷ-, wegh-
WALLOON Volcae
WALLOP klou-, wel-2
WALLOW wel-3
WALNUT Volcae
WALTZ wel-3
WAMBLE weme-
WAND wendh-
WANDER wendh-
WANDERLUST las-, wendh-
WANDEROO wen-1
WANE eu-2
WANT eu-2
WANTON deuk-
WAPENTAKE tak-2, wēpnam
WAR wers-1
WARBLE1 kwerp-
WARBLE2 wer-4
WARD wer-3, wer-4
WARDEN wer-4
WARDER2 wer-4
WARDROBE wer-4
WARE1 wer-4
WARE2 wer-4
WARLOCK leugh-, wēro-
WARN wer-5
WARP wer-3
WARRANT wer-5
WARRANTEE wer-5
WARRANTY wer-5
WARREN wer-5
WART wer-1
WARY wer-4
WAS wes-3
WASH wed-1
WASP wopsā
WASSAIL kailo-, wes-3
WASTE eu-2
WATCH weg-2
WATER wed-1
WATTLE au-3
WAVE webh-
WAX1 wokso-
WAX2 aug-1
WAY wegh-
WAYFARER per-2
WAYFARING per-2
WE we-
WEAK weik-4

WEAKFISH peisk-, weik-4
WEAL1 wel-2
WEALD welt-
WEALTH wel-2
WEAN1 wen-1
WEAPON wēpnam
WEAR1 wes-4
WEASEL weis-
WEATHER wē-
WEAVE webh-
WEB webh-
WEBSTER webh-
WED wadh-1
WEDGE wogʷh-ni-
WEDLOCK leig-3, wadh-1
WEDNESDAY wet-1
WEE wegh-
WEED2 au-4
WEEK weik-4
WEEN wen-1
WEEP wāb-
WEEVIL webh-
WEFT webh-
WEIGH1 wegh-
WEIGHT wegh-
WEIR wer-5
WEIRD wer-3
WELCOME gʷā-
WELD2 welt-
WELFARE per-2
WELKIN welg-
WELL1 wel-3
WELL2 wel-2
WELLAWAY wai
WELSH Volcae
WELTER wel-3
WEN1 wen-2
WEN2 wen-1
WENCH weng-
WEND wendh-, wen-1
WENTLETRAP der-1, wendh-
WERE wes-3
WEREWOLF wī-ro-
WERGELD gheldh-, wī-ro-
WEST wes-pero-
WESTERLY wes-pero-
WESTERN wes-pero-
WET wed-1
WETHER wes-3
WHALE1 (s)kʷal-o-
WHARF kwerp-
WHAT kʷo-
WHEAT kweit-
WHEEL kʷel-1
WHEEZE kwes-
WHELK1 wel-3
WHELM kwelp-
WHEN kʷo-
WHENCE kʷo-
WHERE kʷo-
WHET kʷed-
WHETHER kʷo-
WHICH kʷo-
WHILE kʷeie-2
WHILOM kʷeie-2
WHINE kwei-
WHIP weip-
WHIR kwerp-
WHIRL kwerp-
WHISKEY wed-1
WHISPER kwei-
WHISTLE kwei-
WHITE kweit-
WHITHER kʷo-
WHITING2 kweit-
WHITTLE twei-
WHO kʷo-
WHOLE kailo-
WHOLESOME kailo-
WHOM kʷo-
WHORE kā-
WHOREDOM kā-
WHOSE kʷo-
WHY kʷo-
WICKER weik-4
WICKET weik-4
WIDE wi-

WIDOW weidh-
WIELD wal-
WIGGLE wegh-
WIGHT1 wekti-
WIGHT2 weik-5
WILD welt-
WILDEBEEST welt-
WILDERNESS welt-
WILL1 wel-2
WILL2 wel-2
WILLOW wel-3
WILT1 welg-
WIMBLE weip-
WIMPLE weip-
WIN1 wen-1
WINCE weng-
WINCH weng-
WIND1 wē-
WIND2 wendh-
WINDLASS wendh-
WINDOW okʷ-, wē-
WINE vīnum
WING wē-
WINK weng-
WINSOME wen-1
WINTER wed-1
WIPE weip-
WIRE wei-1
WISDOM weid-
WISE1 weid-
WISE2 weid-
WISEACRE weid-
WISENT weis-
WISH wen-1
WIT1 weid-
WIT2 weid-
WITCH weik-2
WITE1 weid-
WITENAGEMOT mōd-, weid-
WITH wi-
WITHE wei-1
WITHERS wi-
WITHERSHINS sent-, wi-
WITHY wei-1
WIZEN wei-3
WOBBLE webh-
WODEN wet-1
WOE wai
WOLD1 welt-
WOLF wl̥kʷo-
WOLFRAM wl̥kʷo-
WON1 wen-1
WONKY weng-
WONT wen-1
WOOD widhu-
WOODBINE bhendh-
WOOF1 webh-
WOOL wele-1
WORD werg-
WORK werg-
WORLD wī-ro-
WORM wer-3
WORRY wer-3
WORSE wers-1
WORST wers-1
WORT wrād-
WORTH1 wer-3
WORTH2 wer-3
WOTAN wet-1
WOUND1 wen-2
WRACK1 wreg-
WRANGLE wer-3
WRAP wer-3
WRATH wer-3
WREAK wreg-
WREATH wer-3
WRECK wreg-
WRENCH wer-3
WREST wer-3
WRESTLE wer-3
WRETCH wreg-
WRIGGLE wer-3
WRIGHT werg-
WRING wer-3
WRINKLE wer-3
WRIST wer-3
WRITHE wer-3
WRONG wer-3

WROTH wer-3
WROUGHT werg-
WRY wer-3
WURST wers-1
WYCH ELM weik-4

X

XENO- xenos
XERO- ksero-
XEROPHTHALMIA ksero-
XYSTER kes-1

Y

YARD1 ghasto-
YARD2 gher-1
YARE garwian
YARN ghere-
YAWN ghāi-
YCLEPT kom
YE2 yu-1
YEA i-
YEAN agʷh-no-
YEAR yēr-
YEARN gher-5
YEAST yes-
YELL ghel-1
YELLOW ghel-2
YELP ghel-1
YES es-, i-
YESTER- dhgh(y)es-
YESTERDAY dhgh(y)es-
YET i-
YEW ei-2
YIELD gheldh-
-YL hulē
YLEM hulē
YOGA yeug-
YOKE yeug-
YON i-
YOND i-
YONDER i-
YOU yu-1
YOUNG yeu-
YOUNKER kei-2
YOUTH yeu-
YUGA yeug-

Z

ZABAGLIONE sab-
ZAMIA as-
ZAMINDAR dher-2, dhghem-
ZEAL yā-
ZEIN yewo-
ZEMSTVO dhghem-
ZENANA gʷen-
ZEN BUDDHISM dheie-
ZEOLITE yes-
ZEUGMA yeug-
ZEUS deiw-
ZINC denk-
ZLOTY ghel-2
-ZOA gʷei-
-ZOIC gʷei-
ZONE yōs-
ZOO- gʷei-
ZOOGLOEA gel-1
ZOON gʷei-
ZOSTER yōs-
ZWIEBACK bhē-, dwo-
ZWITTERION dwo-
ZYGO- yeug-
ZYGOMA yeug-
-ZYGOUS yeug-
-ZYME yeue-
ZYMO- yeue-

Table of Indo-European Sound Correspondences

This table shows the correspondences between initial consonants in the principal older Indo-European languages. For example, in the first row, it can be seen that Latin initial *p* corresponds to Old English initial *f*: compare Latin *piscis*, "fish," and Old English *fisc*, "fish." An alternative way of describing this situation is to say that Indo-European initial *p* remained *p* in Latin but became *f* in Germanic and thus in Old English; Indo-European ***peisk**- or ***pisk**-, "fish," became Latin *piscis* and Germanic **fiska-*, Old English *fisc*. These correspondences are regular; they always occur as stated unless specific factors intervene. This table shows only the initial consonants, which are generally the simplest element involved in sound change. All other phonetic elements including stress and environment show equally regular correspondences, but often with considerable complexity.

INDO-EUROPEAN	Hittite	Tocharian	Sanskrit	Avestan	Old Persian	Old Church Slavonic	Lithuanian	Armenian	Greek	Latin	Old Irish	Common Germanic	Gothic	Old English	Old Norse	Old High German	Middle Dutch
Stops — unvoiced																	
p	p	p	p	p	p	p	p	h	p	p	*-	f	f	f	f	f	v
t	t	t	t	t	t	t	t	th	t	t	t	th	th	th	th	d	th/d
k	k	k	ś	s	th	s	s	s	k	c	c	h	h(j)	h	h	h	h
kʷ	ku	k	k/c	k/c	k	k/č/c	k	kh	p/t/k	qu	c	hw	hw/w	hw	hv	hw/w	w
Stops — voiced																	
b	p	p	b	b	b	b	b	p	b	b	b	p	p	p	p	p/pf	p
d	t	t(c)	d	d	d	d	d	t	d	d	d	t	t	t	t	z	t
g	k	k	j	z/g	g/d	z	z	c	g	g	g	k	k	k	k	k	k
gʷ	ku	k	g/j	g/j	g/j	g/ž/z g	k	b/d/g	v/gu	b		kw/k	qu	cw/k	kv	qu	qu
voiced aspirate																	
bh	p	p	bh	b	b	b	b	b	ph	f(b)	b	b	b	b	b	b	b
dh	t	t	dh	d	d	d	d	d	th	f(d)	d	d	d	d	d	t/d	d
gh	k	k	h	g/z	g/d	z	z	z(j)	kh	h	g	g	g	g	g	g	g
gʷh	ku	k	gh/h	g/j	g/j	g/ž/z g	g	ph th/kh	f	g		b/g	b/g	b/g	b/g	b/g	b/g
Continuant																	
s	s	s	s	h	h	s	s	h	h	s	s	s	s	s	s	s
Sonorants — nasals																	
m	m	m	m	m	m	m	m	m	m	m	m	m	m	m	m	m
n	n	n	n	n	n	n	n	n	n	n	n	n	n	n	n	n
liquids																	
r	r	r	r/l	r	r	r	r	r	r	r	r	r	r	r	r	r
l	l	l	l/r	r	r	l	l	l	l	l	l	l	l	l	l	l
glides																	
i/y	y	y	y	y	y	j	j	y	h/z	j	*-	j	j	g(y)	*-	j	g
w/u	w	w	v	v	v	v	v	g/v	*-	v	f	w	w	w	v	w	w

*- equals zero: w was lost in Greek.
    y was lost in Old Irish, Old Norse.

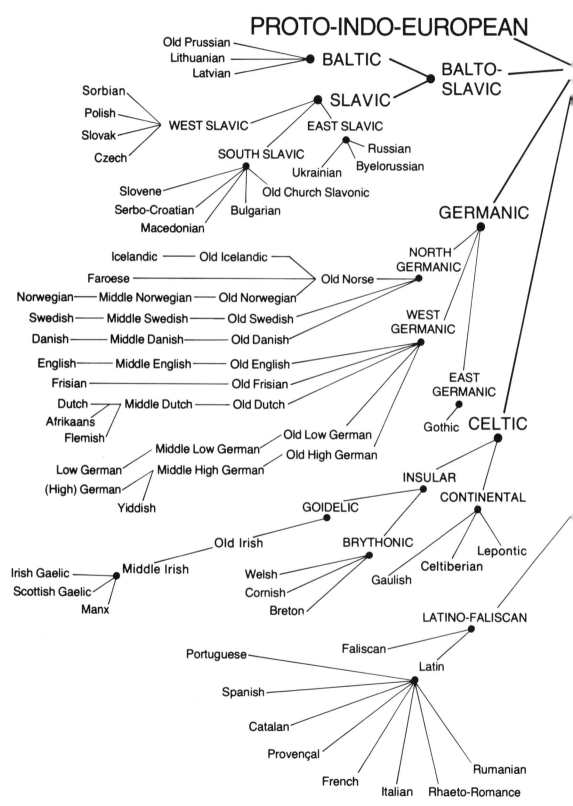

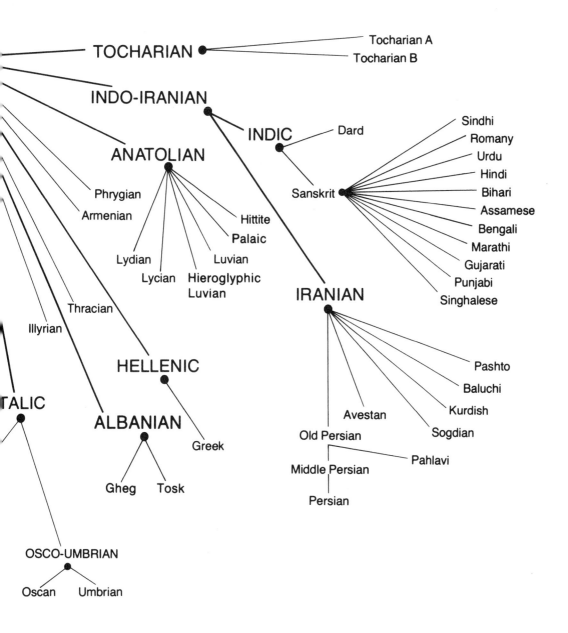

TOCHARIAN ● — Tocharian A
Tocharian B

INDO-IRANIAN

INDIC — Dard

ANATOLIAN

Phrygian

Armenian

Hittite

Palaic

Lydian Luvian

Lycian Hieroglyphic
Luvian

Thracian

Illyrian

HELLENIC

TALIC

ALBANIAN

Greek

Gheg Tosk

OSCO-UMBRIAN

Oscan Umbrian

Sanskrit

Sindhi
Romany
Urdu
Hindi
Bihari
Assamese
Bengali
Marathi
Gujarati
Punjabi
Singhalese

IRANIAN

Pashto
Baluchi
Kurdish
Avestan Sogdian
Old Persian
Pahlavi
Middle Persian
Persian

The Indo-European Family of Languages,

of which English is a member, is descended from a prehistoric language, Proto-Indo-European, spoken in a region that has not yet been identified, possibly in the fifth millennium B.C. The chart shows the principal languages of the family, arranged in a diagrammatic form that displays their genetic relationships and loosely suggests their geographic distribution. The European groups are shown in somewhat fuller detail than the Asian ones, and in the Germanic group, to which English belongs, the intermediate historical phases of the languages are also shown. A chart of the principal Indo-European sound correspondences appears on page 111.